C000240596

Oxford
Mini
School
FRENCH
DICTIONARY

Editorial Manager: Valerie Grundy
New Edition: Nicholas Rollin
with the assistance of Natalie Pomier

OXFORD
UNIVERSITY PRESS

OXFORD
UNIVERSITY PRESS

Great Clarendon Street, Oxford OX2 6DP

Oxford University Press is a department of the University of Oxford.
It furthers the University's objective of excellence in research,
scholarship, and education by publishing worldwide in

Oxford New York

Auckland Cape Town Dar es Salaam Hong Kong Karachi
Kuala Lumpur Madrid Melbourne Mexico City Nairobi
New Delhi Shanghai Taipei Toronto

With offices in

Argentina Austria Brazil Chile Czech Republic France Greece
Guatemala Hungary Italy Japan Poland Portugal Singapore
South Korea Switzerland Thailand Turkey Ukraine Vietnam

Oxford is a registered trade mark of Oxford University Press
in the UK and in certain other countries

British Library Cataloguing in Publication Data
Data available

ISBN: 978 0 19 275708 1

10 9 8 7 6 5

Printed in Italy by L.E.G.O. S.p.A., Lavis (TN)

Paper used in the production of this book is a natural, recyclable product
made from wood grown in sustainable forests. The manufacturing process
conforms to the environmental regulations of the country of origin.

INTRODUCTION

This dictionary has been specially written for students who are in their first years of learning French all the way through to preparing for exams. We have paid particular attention to making the dictionary user-friendly. With the help of colour headwords, alphabet tabs, easy-to-follow signposts and examples, the right translation can quickly be found. French verbs on both sides of the dictionary are numbered to direct the student to the appropriate verb table in the centre pages.

Throughout the writing of this dictionary we have worked in close consultation with students, teachers, inspectors, and examining boards. We gratefully acknowledge the examining boards AQA (formerly NEAB and SEG), OCR, and EDEXCEL, who have read and commented on the dictionary text.

Since the first edition of this dictionary there have been many changes in French life. Not least has been the introduction of the euro. This new edition takes full account of these changes and many new words and examples have been included in order to provide the best possible learner's dictionary of French.

HOW A BILINGUAL DICTIONARY WORKS

A bilingual dictionary has two languages in it. When you look up a word in one of the languages, it gives the translation for that word in the other language. This dictionary is divided into two halves separated by a section of blue-edged pages. In the first half you look up French words, which are in alphabetical order, to find out what they mean in English and in the second half you look up English words, also in alphabetical order, to find out how to say them in French. The blue-edged pages are verb tables and you can see how to use these further on in this section.

At the entry you will find **translations** but also other information that will help you get the right translation and use the word correctly. Here is a guide to the different things you will find in an entry:

headword	a word you look up in the dictionary
translation	translations are the only things that are in 'ordinary' type in the dictionary. They are always typed like this, and something which is typed in a different way can never be a translation
noun	word class (part of speech): tells you whether the word you are looking up is a noun, a verb, an adjective, or another part of speech. One headword can be more than one part of speech. For instance, book can be a noun (she was reading a book) or a verb (I've booked the seats)
(*signpost*)	helpful information: to guide you to the right translation, to show you how to use the translation, or to give you extra information about either the headword or the translation
example	a phrase or sentence using the word you have looked up. You should read through them carefully to see if they are close to what you want to understand or say
Masc.	gender: after a French noun, to tell you that it is masculine
Fem.	gender: after a French noun, to tell you that it is feminine
•	indicates a phrasal verb such as to carry on
★	shows an idiomatic expression such as over the moon
[27]	verb number – tells you which verb pattern to look at in the blue-edged of the dictionary

USING THE DICTIONARY

To find out what a French word means

Suppose you want to find out what the French word **bouton** means. You need to use the first half of the dictionary to find the French words that you are looking for. To help you do this, the guide words at the top of each page show the alphabetical range of words on the pages you have open. Notice that hyphens, spaces between words, and accents on letters in French words make no difference to the alphabetical order.

When you find the entry for **bouton** you will find the translation. But you will also see that **bouton** is a *noun* and because all nouns are either masculine or feminine in French, you are given the gender *Masc.* (*Masc.* = masculine gender, *Fem.* = feminine gender).

However, it often happens that a French word has more than one English translation so you will see that the translation for **bouton** is divided into sections numbered **1** and **2**.

bouton *noun Masc.* **1** button;
  2 spot, pimple.

The first translation is **button** and the second is **spot** or **pimple**. You will need to look at both translations to work out which one fits the French sentence you are trying to understand. So:

il y a quatre boutons sur ma veste *means* there are four buttons on my jacket

BUT

j'ai un bouton sur le nez *means* I've got a spot on my nose

The plurals of most French nouns are formed by adding an –s, as in **boutons** in the first sentence. Exceptional plural forms can be found after the headword:

animal *noun* animal *Masc.* (*plural*
  animaux).

French like English has certain words that you would use when chatting with friends but not in more formal situations. French words like this are marked *informal* in the dictionary, like **bouquin** here:

bouquin *noun Masc.* (*informal*)
  book.

Note that the usual word for **book** is **livre**.

To find an English word and how to say it in French

You can see that it is quite easy once you know how the dictionary works to look up a French word and find out what it means. Students usually find it harder to use the dictionary to find out how to say something in French. This dictionary is written specially to help you do this and to make it easy to find the right way of saying things in French.

Suppose you want to know how to say **garden** in French. Look up the word in the second part of the dictionary. If you follow the same method of going through the alphabetical order of the headwords as you did when you were looking up a French word, you will find **garden** on page 428.

garden noun jardin *Masc.*

Now you can see that the French word for **garden** is **jardin**. But if you want to make a sentence using a noun like **jardin** you need to know whether it is masculine or feminine. The *Masc.* after **jardin** tells you that it is masculine so *in the garden* is **dans le jardin**. It is not always as easy as this to know which French word you need. Sometimes there will be more than one French word for the English word you are looking up. When the dictionary entry gives you more than just one translation, it is very important to take the time to read through the whole entry. If you look up **plug** the entry looks like this:

plug noun **1** (*electrical*) prise *Fem.*;
2 (*in a bath or sink*) bonde *Fem.*; **to
pull out the plug** retirer la bonde.

You can see that **1** tells you that the French word for an electrical plug is **prise** and **2** tells you that the word for a bath plug or a sink plug is **bonde**.

Remember that information which is either in brackets or italics or both is there to help you, but it *will never be* the translation itself. Wherever there is more than one translation, depending on what meaning of the English word you are looking for, the dictionary will always help you to choose the right one. Often it is not enough to find the translation of one word. In the case of more common words the dictionary also gives you a selection of common phrases you will often want to use. In the entry for **hair** below you can find out how to use the translation in different expressions:

hair noun **1** cheveux *Masc. plural*; **to
have short hair** avoir les cheveux
courts; **to brush your hair** se
brosser les cheveux; **to wash your
hair** se laver les cheveux; **to have
your hair cut** se faire couper les
cheveux; **she's had her hair cut**
elle s'est fait couper les cheveux;
2 a hair (*from the head*) un cheveu;
(*from the body*) un poil.

HOW TO USE THE VERB TABLES NUMBERS

On the French side of the dictionary all the headwords which are verbs look like this: **faire** *verb* [10]. On the English side of the dictionary all the verbs given as translations of English verbs look like this: **frighten** *verb* effrayer [59].

If you look at the pages edged in blue in the centre of the dictionary, you will find tables showing you how to use the different types of French verbs.

The verb **faire** above has the number 10. If you look at number 10 in the verb tables, you will see that because **faire** is a very common and very irregular verb it has a whole page to itself giving you all the tenses you will need. The verb **effrayer** has number 59 after it. When you look up verb table number 59, you will see the verb **payer**. This means that the verb endings given for **payer** will also be the endings for **effrayer**. So **payer** is there to show you the pattern that other verbs like it, such as **effrayer**, will follow.

With practice you will soon be able to find your way easily around the dictionary and identify what you are looking for in an entry. Some entries may seem long and complicated at first glance. Reading carefully through the signposts and examples will lead you to the translation you need.

Aa

a *verb* SEE **avoir**.

à *preposition* (note that 'à + le' becomes 'au' and 'à + les' becomes 'aux') **1** at; **à la maison** at home; **à l'école** at school; **au bureau** at the office; **à deux heures** at two o'clock; **2** in; **à Londres** in London; **à la campagne** in the country; **au printemps** in the spring; **3** to; **aller à Londres** to go to London; **donner quelque chose à quelqu'un** to give something to somebody; **4** by; **à la main** by hand; **à vélo** by (or on a) bicycle; **5** with; **une petite fille aux yeux bleus** a little girl with blue eyes; **6** à **trois kilomètres d'ici** three kilometres from here; **7** ce **bracelet est à Natalie** this bracelet is Natalie's.

abandonner *verb* [1] **1** to give up; **elle a abandonné les maths** she has given up maths; **j'abandonne** I give up; **2** to abandon; **un enfant abandonné** an abandoned child.

abat-jour *noun Masc.* lampshade.

abats *plural noun Masc.* **les abats** offal (*liver, kidneys, heart, etc*).

abattoir *noun Masc.* slaughterhouse.

abattre *verb* [21] **1** to shoot down; **deux policiers ont été abattus par des gangsters hier** two policemen were shot down by gangsters yesterday; **2** to slaughter (*an animal*); **3** to demolish (*a building*).

abbaye *noun Fem.* abbey; **l'abbaye de Cluny** Cluny Abbey.

abbé *noun Masc.* priest.

abcès *noun Masc.* abscess.

abeille *noun Fem.* bee; **une piqûre d'abeille** a bee sting.

abîmer *verb* [1] **1** to damage; **la pluie avait abîmé la porte** the rain had damaged the door; **tu vas t'abîmer les yeux** you'll ruin your eyesight; **des fruits abîmés** fruit which is going bad; **2 s'abîmer** to get damaged; **les pommes vont s'abîmer** the apples are going to go bad; **la viande s'abîme vite** meat goes off quickly.

aboiement *noun Masc.* barking; **on entendait des aboiements** we could hear dogs barking.

abolir *verb* [2] to abolish.

abominable *adjective* abominable.

abondance *noun Fem.* **une abondance de** plenty of, lots of; **il y a des fruits en abondance** there's plenty of fruit.

abonné, abonnée *noun Masc., Fem.* **1** season ticket holder; **2** subscriber (*to a magazine, journal, etc*).

abonné *adjective* **être abonné to** have a subscription (*to a magazine, journal, etc*); to have a season ticket (*for the bus, train, theatre, etc*).

abonnement *noun Masc.* **1** subscription; **2** season ticket.

abonner *verb* [1] **s'abonner à** to subscribe to; **je me suis abonné pour un an** I have a year's subscription.

abord *noun Masc.* **1 d'abord** first; **tout d'abord** first of all; **je vais d'abord faire du thé** I'll make some tea first; **2 d'abord** at first;

j'ai d'abord cru qu'il était français I thought at first that he was French; **3 les abords** the surroundings.

abordable adjective **1 des prix abordables** affordable prices; **2 une personne abordable** an approachable person.

aborder verb [1] **1** to tackle (a problem, a piece of work, a subject, etc); **2** to approach.

aboutir verb [2] **1 aboutir à** to lead to; **la rue aboutit à une petite place** the street leads to a little square; **2 aboutir à** to end up in; **nous avons abouti à Paris** we ended up in Paris; **3** to succeed, to be successful (of discussions or negotiations).

aboyer verb [39] to bark.

abrégé noun Masc. summary.

abrégé adjective **la version abrégée** the abridged version.

abréger verb [15] to shorten.

abréviation noun Fem. abbreviation.

abri noun Masc. **1** shelter; **trouver un abri** to take shelter; **les sans-abri** the homeless; **2** shed; **3 à l'abri de** sheltered from; **à l'abri du vent** sheltered from the wind, out of the wind; **à l'abri de la lumière** in a dark place.

abricot noun Masc. apricot; **de la confiture d'abricots** apricot jam; **une tarte aux abricots** an apricot tart.

abricotier noun Masc. apricot tree.

abriter verb [1] **1** to shelter; **2 s'abriter** to take shelter.

abrupt adjective **1** steep; **une pente abrupte** a steep slope; **2** abrupt.

abrutir verb [2] **1** to deafen; **2** to stupefy.

absence noun Fem. **1** absence; **pendant mon absence** while I was out, while I was away; **2 l'absence de** the lack of.

absent adjective **1 être absent** to be out, to be away; **je serai absent pendant une heure** I'll be out for an hour; **elle a été absente tout le mois de mai** she was away for the whole of May; **2** absent; **3** absent-minded.

absenter verb [1] **s'absenter** to go out, to go away; **je m'absente quelques minutes** I'm just popping out for a few minutes.

absolu adjective absolute.

absolument adverb absolutely.

absorbant adjective **1** absorbing; **un livre absorbant** an absorbing book; **2** absorbent (material).

absorber verb [1] **1** to absorb; **2** to take (food or drink).

abstenir verb [81] **s'abstenir de** to refrain from.

abstrait adjective abstract.

absurde adjective absurd.

absurdité noun Fem. absurdity; **dire des absurdités** to talk nonsense.

abus noun Masc. abuse; **l'abus d'alcool** alcohol abuse.

abuser verb [1] **1 abuser de** to misuse; **abuser de l'alcool** to drink too much (regularly); **2 abuser de** to take advantage of, to exploit; **elle**

3

abuse de ta gentillesse she's taking advantage of your kindness.

abusif (Fem. **abusive**) adjective 1 excessive; 2 unfair.

acajou noun Masc. mahogany; **une table en acajou** a mahogany table.

accablant adjective overwhelming.

accabler verb [1] to overwhelm.

accéder verb [24] 1 **accéder à** to reach, to get to ; **pour accéder à la salle de bains, il faut passer par la chambre** to get to the bathroom you have to go through the bedroom; 2 **accéder au pouvoir** to come to power.

accélérateur noun Masc. accelerator; **appuyer sur l'accélérateur** to accelerate.

accélération noun Fem. acceleration.

accélérer verb [24] 1 to speed up (the rhythm, process, etc); 2 to accelerate (in a car).

accent noun Masc. 1 accent; **un accent étranger** a foreign accent; **parler français sans accent** to speak French without an accent; 2 accent (on a letter in written French) **un accent aigu** an acute accent; **un accent grave** a grave accent; **un accent circonflexe** a circumflex; 3 **mettre l'accent sur quelque chose** to put the emphasis on something.

accentuer verb [1] to emphasize.

acceptation noun Fem. acceptance.

accepter verb [1] 1 to accept; **accepter une invitation** to accept an invitation; 2 **accepter de faire**

to agree to do; **elle a accepté de m'aider** she agreed to help me.

accès noun Masc. 1 access; **accès interdit** no entry; 2 **un accès de colère** a fit of anger.

accessible adjective 1 accessible; **un livre accessible** a book which is easy to read; 2 **des prix accessibles** affordable prices.

accessoire noun Masc. accessory; **les accessoires** accessories (gloves, handbags, etc).

accessoire adjective incidental.

accident noun Masc. 1 accident; **avoir un accident** to have an accident; **un accident de la route** a road accident; 2 hitch; **il y a eu un petit accident** there's been a slight hitch.

accidenté adjective 1 injured; 2 damaged; 3 **'chaussée accidentée'** 'uneven road surface'.

acclamations plural noun Fem. cheering.

accommodant adjective easy-going.

accompagnateur, accompagnatrice noun Masc., Fem. 1 tourist guide; 2 courier (for a group on a package holiday); 3 accompanying adult (with a child); 4 accompanist (for example, a pianist accompanying a singer).

accompagner verb [1] 1 to accompany; **je t'accompagne** I'll go with you, I'll come with you; **je t'accompagne jusqu'à chez toi** I'll see you home; 2 **accompagné de** accompanied by; **elle est partie accompagnée de son frère** she left accompanied by her brother;

a b c d e f g h i j k l m n o p q r s t u v w x y z

4

a
b
c
d
e
f
g
h
i
j
k
l
m
n
o
p
q
r
s
t
u
v
w
x
y
z

3 to accompany (*on the piano, for example*).

accomplir verb [2] to carry out (*a task, project, mission, etc*).

accord noun Masc. **1** agreement; **2 d'accord** all right, OK; **je suis d'accord** I agree; **je suis d'accord avec Rosie** I agree with Rosie; **Paul est d'accord pour venir avec nous** Paul's agreed to come with us; **se mettre d'accord** to come to an agreement; **ils se sont mis d'accord sur le prix** they came to an agreement over the price; **3** chord (*in music*).

accordéon noun Masc. accordeon; **jouer de l'accordéon** to play the accordeon.

accorder verb [1] **1** to grant (*a favour, permission, etc*); **2** to tune (*a musical instrument*); **3 s'accorder** to agree.

accotement noun Masc. verge (*on the edge of the road*); hard shoulder (*on the motorway*); **'accotements non stabilisés' 'soft verges'** (*as road sign*).

accouchement noun Masc. childbirth, delivery.

accoucher verb [1] to give birth.

accoutumé adjective **1** usual; **2 accoutumé à** used to, accustomed to.

accoutumer verb [1] **s'accoutumer à** to become accustomed to.

accro noun Masc. (*informal*) addict.

accro adjective (*informal*) **être accro de quelque chose** to be hooked on something.

accroc noun Masc. **1** tear; **tu as un accroc à ta jupe** you've got a tear in your skirt; **2** hitch; **sans accroc(s)** without a hitch.

accrocher verb [1] **1** to hang; **accrocher un tableau au mur** to hang a picture on the wall; **accroché au mur** hanging on the wall; **2** to catch, to snag (*something on a nail or thorn, for example*).

accroupir verb [2] **s'accroupir** to crouch (down), to squat.

accueil noun Masc. **1** welcome; **un accueil chaleureux** a warm welcome; **ma famille d'accueil est très sympathique** my host family is very nice; **2** reception desk; **Madame Jones est priée de se présenter à l'accueil** would Ms Jones please go to the reception desk.

accueillant adjective **1** (*of a person*) hospitable, welcoming; **2** (*of a place*) inviting, friendly.

accueillir verb [35] **1** to welcome; **2** to receive, to greet.

accumuler verb [1] **1** to collect; **2 s'accumuler** to pile up.

accusation noun Fem. accusation.

accusé de réception noun Masc. **envoyer une lettre avec accusé de réception** to send a letter recorded delivery.

accuser verb [1] to accuse; **il m'a accusé d'avoir volé son stylo** he accused me of stealing his pen.

acharner verb [1] **s'acharner à faire** to persist in doing.

achat noun Masc. purchase; **je te montre mes achats** I'll show you what I've bought.

acheter verb [16] **1** to buy; **je vais acheter du pain** I'm going to buy some bread; **2** acheter quelque chose à quelqu'un to buy somebody something; **je t'achète un sandwich?** shall I buy you a sandwich?; **je lui ai acheté un cadeau** I bought him (or her) a present; **3** acheter quelque chose à quelqu'un to buy something from somebody; **j'ai vendu ma voiture – c'est Lisa qui me l'a achetée** I've sold my car – Lisa bought it from me.

acheteur, acheteuse noun Masc., Fem. buyer.

achever verb [50] **1** to finish (a piece of work); **2** to finish off (meaning 'kill').

acide noun Masc. acid.

acide adjective sharp, sour.

acier noun Masc. steel.

acné noun Fem. acne.

acoustique noun Fem. acoustics.

acquérir verb [17] to acquire.

âcre adjective pungent.

acrobate noun Masc. & Fem. acrobat.

acrobatie noun Fem. acrobatics.

acte noun Masc. act.

acte de naissance noun Masc. birth certificate.

acteur, actrice noun Masc., Fem. actor, actress.

actif (Fem. **active**) adjective active; **la vie active** working life.

action noun Fem. action, act; **une bonne action** a good deed.

activement adverb actively.

activer verb [1] **1** to speed up; **2** s'activer to hurry up.

activité noun Fem. activity.

activité professionnelle noun Fem. occupation.

actualité noun Fem. **1** current affairs; **2** les actualités the news.

actuel (Fem. **actuelle**) adjective present, current; **la situation actuelle** the present situation.

actuellement adverb at the moment; **elle est actuellement à Rome** she's in Rome at the moment.

adapté adjective **1** suitable; **adapté à** suitable for, suited to; **2** adapted.

adapter verb [1] **1** to adapt; **2** s'adapter à to adapt to, to get used to.

additif noun Masc. additive.

addition noun Fem. **1** addition; **2** bill (in a restaurant) l'addition, s'il vous plaît can I have the bill please.

additionner verb [1] to add up.

adhésif (Fem. **adhésive**) adjective adhesive; **ruban adhésif** sticky tape.

adieu (plural **adieux**) noun Masc. goodbye, farewell (the usual expression is 'au revoir' since 'adieu' is properly used to mean 'goodbye for ever').

adjectif noun Masc. adjective.

adjoint, adjointe noun Masc., Fem. **1** assistant; **2** deputy.

a

admettre *verb* [11] **1** to admit; j'admets qu'elle a raison I admit that she's right; **2 admettre dans** to admit to (*a restaurant, a club, etc*).

b

c

administratif (*Fem.* **administrative**) *adjective* administrative.

d

e

administration *noun Fem.* administration.

f

admiratif (*Fem.* **admirative**) *adjective* admiring; **des regards admiratifs** admiring glances.

g

h

admiration *noun Fem.* admiration.

i

admirer *verb* [1] to admire.

j

adolescence *noun Fem.* adolescence.

k

adolescent, adolescente *noun Masc., Fem.* teenager, adolescent.

l

m

adolescent *adjective* teenage, adolescent.

n

o

adopter *verb* [1] to adopt.

p

adoptif (*Fem.* **adoptive**) *adjective* **un enfant adoptif** an adopted child.

q

adoption *noun Fem.* adoption.

r

adorable *adjective* adorable.

s

adorer *verb* [1] to adore, to love.

t

adresse *noun Fem.* **1** address; **quelle est ton adresse?** what's your address?; **se tromper d'adresse** to get (*or* go to) the wrong address; **2** skill; **elle l'a fait avec beaucoup d'adresse** she did it very skilfully; **3** speech, address.

u

v

w

x

y

z

adresser *verb* [1] **1 adresser une lettre à quelqu'un** to send somebody a letter; **2 adresser la parole à quelqu'un** to speak to somebody; **3 s'adresser à** to enquire at; **adressez-vous à la réception** enquire at reception; **4 s'adresser à** to be aimed at; **le film s'adresse aux adolescents** the film is aimed at teenagers.

adroit *adjective* skilful.

adulte *noun Masc. & Fem., adjective* adult.

adverbe *noun Masc.* adverb.

adversaire *noun Masc. & Fem.* opponent.

adverse *adjective* opposing.

aération *noun Fem.* ventilation.

aérer *verb* [24] to air.

aérobic *noun Masc.* aerobics.

aéro-club *noun Masc.* flying club.

aérogare *noun Fem.* (flight) terminal (*in an airport*).

aéronautique *noun Fem.* aeronautics.

aéroport *noun Masc.* airport; **à l'aéroport** at (*or* to) the airport.

aérosol *noun Masc.* aerosol.

affaire *noun Fem.* **1** matter, business; **c'est une drôle d'affaire** it's a funny business; **c'est une autre affaire** that's another matter; **2** affair, political crisis.

affaires *plural noun Fem.* **1 les affaires** business; **un homme d'affaires** a businessman; **une femme d'affaires** a businesswoman; **un voyage d'affaires** a business trip; **2** business; **occupe-toi de tes affaires!** mind your own business!;

3 belongings, things; **tu peux laisser tes affaires dans la chambre** you can leave your things in the bedroom.

affamé *adjective* starving.

affamer *verb* [1] to starve.

affecter *verb* [1] **1** to affect; **2 affecter de faire** to pretend to do.

affection *noun Fem.* affection; **j'ai beaucoup d'affection pour lui** I'm very fond of him.

affectueusement *adverb* affectionately.

affectueux (*Fem.* **affectueuse**) *adjective* affectionate.

affiche *noun Fem.* **1** poster; **2** notice.

afficher *verb* [1] to put up (*a poster or a notice*).

affliger *verb* [52] **1** to distress, to grieve; **2 affliger de** to afflict with.

affluence *noun Fem.* crowds; **aux heures d'affluence** at peak times.

affolant *adjective* (*informal*) frightening.

affoler *verb* [1] **1 affoler quelqu'un** to throw somebody into a panic; **2 s'affoler** to panic; **ne t'affole pas** don't panic.

affreux (*Fem.* **affreuse**) *adjective* **1** awful, dreadful; **2** hideous.

afin *preposition* **1 afin de faire** in order to; **2 afin que** in order that.

africain *adjective* African.

Africain, Africaine *noun Masc.,* *Fem.* African.

Afrique *noun Fem.* Africa; **en Afrique** in (*or* to) Africa.

agaçant *adjective* annoying.

agacer *verb* [61] to annoy.

âge *noun Masc.* age; **quel âge as-tu?** how old are you?; **à l'âge de cinq ans** at the age of five; **je ne sais pas son âge** I don't know how old he (*or* she) is; **il a l'âge de mon père** he's the same age as my father.

âgé *adjective* **1** old; **les personnes âgées** old people; **2 âgé de** aged; **une femme âgée de trente ans** a woman aged thirty.

agence *noun Fem.* **1** agency; **2** branch (*of a bank*).

agence de voyages *noun Fem.* travel agent's.

agence immobilière *noun Fem.* estate agent's.

agenda *noun Masc.* diary.

agenouiller *verb* [1] **s'agenouiller** to kneel down.

agent *noun Masc.* **1** official; **2** agent.

agent commercial *noun Masc.* sales representative.

agent de police *noun Masc.* police officer; **une femme agent de police** a woman police officer.

aggraver *verb* [1] **1** to make worse; **aggraver la situation** to make things worse; **2 s'aggraver** to get worse; **la situation s'aggrave** the situation is deteriorating, things are getting worse.

agir *verb* [2] **1** to act; **2** to behave; **3 il s'agit de** it is about; **il s'agit de ton frère** it's about your brother; **de quoi s'agit-il?** what's it about?

agitation *noun Fem.* **1** hustle and bustle; **2** unrest; **3** restlessness.

a b c d e f g h i j k l m n o p q r s t u v w x y z

agité *adjective* **1** restless, agitated; **2** rough (*sea*); **3** bustling (*street*); **4 mener une vie agitée** to lead a hectic life.

agiter *verb* [1] to shake; **agiter la main** to wave your hand.

agneau (*plural* **agneaux**) *noun Masc.* lamb; **un gigot d'agneau** a leg of lamb.

agrafe *noun Fem.* **1** staple; **2** hook (*on a garment*).

agrafer *verb* [1] **1** to staple; **2** to fasten.

agrafeuse *noun Fem.* stapler.

agrandir *verb* [2] to enlarge.

agrandissement *noun Masc.* enlargement (*of a photo*).

agréable *adjective* pleasant, nice.

agréé *adjective* **1** registered; **2** authorized.

agréer *verb* [32] **1** to agree to; **2 veuillez agréer l'expression de mes sentiments distingués** Yours faithfully, Yours sincerely (*this is one of a number of fixed expressions used to end any formal or business letter*).

agresser *verb* [1] **1** to attack; **2** to mug.

agresseur *noun Masc.* attacker.

agressif (*Fem.* **agressive**) *adjective* aggressive.

agression *noun Fem.* **1** attack; **2** mugging.

agressivité *noun Fem.* aggressiveness.

agricole *adjective* agricultural.

agriculteur, agricultrice *noun Masc., Fem.* farmer.

ahuri *adjective* amazed, stunned.

ai *verb* SEE **avoir.**

aide[1] *noun Fem.* **1** help; **avec l'aide de Claire** with Claire's help; **venir à l'aide de quelqu'un** to help somebody; **2** aid (*financial aid given to a person or a country*).

aide[2] *noun Masc. & Fem.* **1** assistant; **2** helper.

aider *verb* [1] **1** to help; **il m'a aidé à mettre la table** he helped me set the table; **est-ce que je peux t'aider?** would you like some help?; **2** to give aid to (*financial aid to a person, group, or country*).

aigle *noun Masc. & Fem.* eagle.

aiglefin *noun Masc.* haddock.

aigre *adjective* **1** sour; **2** sharp.

aigu (*Fem.* **aiguë**) *adjective* **1** high-pitched; **2** acute.

aiguille *noun Fem.* **1** needle; **une aiguille à coudre** a sewing needle; **une aiguille à tricoter** a knitting needle; **2** hand (*of a clock or watch*); **dans le sens des aiguilles d'une montre** clockwise; **ça tourne dans le sens des aiguilles d'une montre** it turns clockwise.

aiguilleur du ciel *noun Masc.* air traffic controller.

aiguiser *verb* [1] to sharpen.

ail *noun Masc.* garlic.

aile *noun Fem.* wing; ★ **voler de ses propres ailes** to stand on your own two feet (*literally: to fly with your own wings*).

ailleurs *adverb* **1** elsewhere, somewhere else; **2 d'ailleurs** besides, moreover; **3 par ailleurs** also, in addition.

aimable *adjective* kind, nice; **vous êtes très aimable** that's very kind of you.

aimant *noun Masc.* magnet.

aimer *verb* [1] **1** to like; **est-ce que tu aimes les fraises?** do you like strawberries?; **aimer faire quelque chose** to like doing something; **elle aime aller au cinéma** she likes going to the cinema; **elle aimerait aller au cinéma** she'd like to go to the cinema; **2 aimer mieux** to prefer; **j'aime mieux les fraises que les framboises** I prefer strawberries to raspberries, I like strawberries better than raspberries; **j'aimerais mieux aller au cinéma** I'd prefer to go to the cinema, I'd rather go to the cinema; **3** to love; **je t'aime** I love you; **4 s'aimer** to like each other, to love each other.

aîné, aînée *noun Masc., Fem.* **l'aîné(e)** the eldest, the oldest (*child*).

aîné *adjective* elder, older (*of two*) eldest, oldest (*of more than two*); **leur fille aînée** their elder (or eldest) daughter.

ainsi *adverb* **1** thus; **2** in this way; **3 ainsi que** as well as, along with.

aïoli *noun Masc.* garlic mayonnaise.

air *noun Masc.* **1** air; **aller prendre l'air** to go out and get some fresh air; **2 un courant d'air** a draught; **3 avoir l'air (…)** to look (…); **avoir l'air bon** to look good; **avoir l'air fatigué** to look tired; **4 avoir l'air de** to look; **il a l'air d'un policier** he looks like a policeman; **5 avoir l'air d'être** to look as if you are; **elle a l'air d'être perdue** she

looks as if she's lost; **6 avoir l'air de faire** to look as if you are doing; **il a l'air de comprendre** he looks as if he understands; **7 sourire d'un air heureux** to smile happily; **8** tune.

air bag™ *noun Masc.* airbag (*in a car*).

aire de jeu *noun Fem.* playground.

aire de pique-nique *noun Fem.* picnic area.

aire de services *noun Fem.* motorway service station.

aise *noun Fem.* **être à l'aise** to be comfortable, to feel at ease; **être mal à l'aise** to feel uncomfortable.

aisselle *noun Fem.* armpit.

ajout *noun Masc.* addition.

ajouter *verb* [1] to add; **ajoutez un œuf** add an egg.

alarme *noun Fem.* alarm; **sonner l'alarme** to sound the alarm.

album *noun Masc.* album.

album de bandes dessinées *noun Masc.* comic book.

album de photos *noun Masc.* photograph album.

album de timbres *noun Masc.* stamp album.

alcool *noun Masc.* alcohol.

alcoolique *noun Masc. & Fem., adjective* alcoholic.

alcoolisé *adjective* **une boisson alcoolisée** an alcoholic drink; **une boisson non alcoolisée** a non-alcoholic drink.

alcootest *noun Masc.* Breathalyzer™.

alcôve *noun Fem.* alcove.

alentours *plural noun Masc.* **1** surroundings; **2 aux alentours**

a b c d e f g h i j k l m n o p q r s t u v w x y z

a de in the vicinity (or neighbourhood) of.

algèbre noun Fem. algebra.

Algérie noun Fem. Algeria.

algérien (Fem. **algérienne**) adjective Algerian.

algues plural noun Fem. seaweed.

alibi noun Masc. alibi.

aliment noun Masc. food.

alimentaire adjective **des produits alimentaires** food products; **l'industrie alimentaire** the food industry.

alimentation noun Fem. 1 groceries; 2 diet.

allée noun Fem. path, drive.

alléger verb [15] 1 to lighten; 2 to reduce.

Allemagne noun Fem. Germany.

allemand noun Masc. German (language).

allemand adjective German.

Allemand, Allemande noun Masc., Fem. German (person).

aller¹ verb [7] 1 to go; **aller à Paris** to go to Paris; **je vais à Paris** I'm going to Paris, I go to Paris; 2 (used with another verb in much the same way as 'going to' is used in English) **je vais écrire à ma mère** I'm going to write to my mother this evening; 3 (comment) **ça va?** how are you?; **ça va bien** I'm fine; **comment va ta mère?** how's your mother?; **elle va bien** she's fine; 4 to suit; **cette robe te va bien** that dress really suits you; **est-ce que jeudi te va?** does Thursday suit you?; 5 **s'en aller** to leave; **je m'en vais!** I'm off!

aller² noun Masc. 1 **faire des allers et retours** to go to and fro; 2 **un aller simple** a single ticket; **un aller-retour** a return ticket; **Avignon aller simple, s'il vous plaît** a single to Avignon please.

allergie noun Fem. allergy.

allergique adjective **être allergique à** to be allergic to; **elle est allergique aux chats** she's allergic to cats.

alliance noun Fem. 1 wedding ring; 2 alliance.

allié, alliée noun Masc., Fem. ally.

alligator noun Masc. alligator.

allô exclamation hello (only used on the telephone).

allocation noun Fem. benefit, allowance.

allocation chômage noun Fem. unemployment benefit.

allocations familiales plural noun Fem. family allowance.

allonger verb [52] 1 to lengthen; 2 to extend; 3 **s'allonger** to lie down.

allumer verb [1] 1 to light; **allumer le feu** to light the fire; 2 to switch on; **allumer la lampe** to switch on the lamp; 3 to switch on the lights.

allumette noun Fem. match; **une boîte d'allumettes** a box of matches.

allure noun Fem. 1 speed; **à toute allure** at top speed; 2 appearance (of a person).

alors adverb 1 then, at that time; **elle travaillait alors à Paris** she was working in Paris then; 2 so; **alors, comment ça va?** so how are you?; **3 alors que** while; **alors qu'elle faisait ses devoirs** while she was doing her homework.

alouette *noun Fem.* skylark.

Alpes *noun Fem.* **les Alpes** the Alps.

alphabet *noun Masc.* alphabet.

alphabétique *adjective* alphabetical; **dans l'ordre alphabétique, par ordre alphabétique** in alphabetical order.

alpin *adjective* alpine.

alpinisme *noun Masc.* mountaineering.

alsacien (*Fem.* **alsacienne**) *adjective* from Alsace, Alsatian.

Alsacien, Alsacienne *noun Masc., Fem.* Alsatian.

alternatif (*Fem.* **alternative**) *adjective* alternative.

altitude *noun Fem.* altitude.

alu *noun Masc.* (*informal*) aluminium; **du papier alu** kitchen foil.

aluminium *noun Masc.* aluminium.

amalgame *noun Masc.* mixture.

amande *noun Fem.* **1** almond; **2** kernel (*of a fruit stone*).

amant *noun Masc.* lover.

amateur *noun Masc.* enthusiast; **un amateur de musique** a music lover.

amateur *adjective* amateur; **un photographe amateur** an amateur photographer.

ambassade *noun Fem.* embassy; **l'ambassade de France** the French Embassy.

ambassadeur *noun Masc.* ambassador.

ambiance *noun Fem.* atmosphere; **une bonne ambiance** a good atmosphere.

ambigu (*Fem.* **ambiguë**) *adjective* ambiguous.

ambitieux (*Fem.* **ambitieuse**) *adjective* ambitious.

ambition *noun Fem.* ambition.

ambulance *noun Fem.* ambulance.

ambulancier, ambulancière *noun Masc., Fem.* ambulance driver.

âme *noun Fem.* soul.

amélioration *noun Fem.* improvement.

améliorer, s'améliorer *verb* [1] to improve.

aménagé *adjective* **1** equipped; **une cuisine aménagée** an equipped kitchen; **2** converted.

aménager *verb* [52] **1** to convert, to do up (*a building, a room, etc*); **2** to develop (*an area*); **3** to construct, to improve (*a road or road system*).

amende *noun Fem.* fine; **une amende de 500 euros** a 500-euro fine.

amener *verb* [50] **1** to bring; **elle a amené son cousin** she brought her cousin (with her); **2** to take; **amener un enfant à l'école** to take a child to school.

amer (*Fem.* **amère**) *adjective* bitter.

américain *adjective* American.

Américain, Américaine *noun Masc., Fem.* American.

Amérique *noun Fem.* America.

a b c d e f g h i j k l m n o p q r s t u v w x y z

a
b
c
d
e
f
g
h
i
j
k
l
m
n
o
p
q
r
s
t
u
v
w
x
y
z

ami, amie noun Masc., Fem. friend; **un ami à moi** a friend of mine; **un ami à Lisa** a friend of Lisa's.

ami adjective friendly.

amiante noun Masc. asbestos.

amical (Masc. plural **amicaux**) adjective friendly.

amicale noun Fem. association.

amicalement adverb **1** in a friendly way; **2** Best wishes (at the end of a letter).

amitié noun Fem. **1** friendship; **faire quelque chose par amitié** to do something out of friendship; **2 amitiés** love (at the end of a letter).

amortisseur noun Masc. shock absorber.

amour noun Masc. love.

amoureux (Fem. **amoureuse**) adjective in love; **être amoureux de** to be in love with.

amour-propre noun Masc. self-esteem.

amovible adjective detachable.

amphi noun Masc. (informal) lecture theatre (in a university).

amphithéâtre noun Masc. **1** amphitheatre; **2** lecture theatre.

ample adjective **1** loose-fitting (jacket, dress, etc); **2** ample (quantity).

ampleur noun Fem. size, scope.

ampli noun Masc. (informal) amplifier.

amplificateur noun Masc. amplifier.

ampoule noun Fem. **1** light bulb; **2** blister.

amusant adjective **1** funny; **une histoire amusante** a funny story; **2** entertaining.

amuse-gueule noun Masc. des amuse-gueule nibbles (crisps, nuts, etc).

amuser verb [1] **1** to amuse; **2** to entertain; **3 s'amuser** to play; **4 s'amuser** to enjoy oneself, to have a good time; **on s'est bien amusé** we really enjoyed ourselves, we had a really good time.

an noun Masc. year; **elle a dix ans** she's ten (years old); **le nouvel an, le jour de l'an** New Year's Day; **il va en Normandie tous les ans** he goes to Normandy every year; ★ **bon an, mal an** year in, year out (literally: good year, bad year).

analgésique noun Masc. analgesic, painkiller.

analphabète adjective illiterate.

analyse noun Fem. **1** analysis; **2 une analyse de sang** a blood test.

analyser verb [1] to analyse.

ananas noun Masc. pineapple.

anatomie noun Fem. anatomy.

ancêtre noun Masc. & Fem. ancestor.

anchois noun Masc. anchovy.

ancien (Fem. **ancienne**) adjective **1** (coming before a noun) former; **l'ancien président** the former president, the ex-president; **mon ancienne école** my old school; **un ancien élève** a former pupil; **2** (coming after a noun) old; **une maison ancienne** an old house;

---

une table ancienne an antique table.

ancien combattant noun Masc. war veteran.

ancre noun Fem. anchor.

âne noun Masc. donkey.

anémone noun Fem. anemone.

anesthésie noun Fem. anaesthesia; **une anesthésie** an anaesthetic.

anesthésiste noun Masc. & Fem. anaesthetist.

ange noun Masc. angel; ★ **être aux anges** to be over the moon, to be absolutely delighted (*literally: to be at the level of the angels*).

angine noun Fem. throat infection; **avoir une angine** to have a throat infection.

anglais noun Masc. English (*language*); **parler l'anglais** to speak English.

anglais adjective English.

Anglais, Anglaise noun Masc., Fem. Englishman, Englishwoman; **les Anglais** the English; **il y a une Anglaise dans notre classe** there's an English girl in our class.

angle noun Masc. 1 angle; **un angle droit** a right angle; 2 corner; **à l'angle de la rue** at the corner of the street; **le magasin qui fait l'angle** the shop on the corner.

Angleterre noun Fem. England; **en Angleterre** in (*or* to) England; **aller en Angleterre** to go to England.

Anglo-Normande adjective **les îles Anglo-Normandes** the Channel Islands.

anglophone noun Masc. & Fem. English speaker.

anglophone adjective English-speaking.

angoisse noun Fem. anxiety.

angoissé adjective anxious.

anguille noun Fem. eel.

anguleux (Fem. **anguleuse**) adjective bony.

animal (plural **animaux**) noun Masc. animal.

animateur, animatrice noun Masc., Fem. 1 group leader; 2 organizer; 3 presenter.

animation noun Fem. 1 liveliness, life; **il y a beaucoup d'animation dans le quartier le soir** there's a lot going on in the area at night; 2 organization (*of a group, a programme, etc.*).

animé adjective 1 lively (*person or discussion*); 2 busy (*place*).

animer verb [1] 1 to run (*a course*); 2 to lead (*a group*); 3 to present (*a programme or a show*); 4 to liven up (*an occasion*); 5 **s'animer** to liven up.

anis noun Masc. aniseed.

anneau (plural **anneaux**) noun Masc. ring.

année noun Fem. year; **l'année prochaine** next year; **l'année dernière** last year; **les années 70** the seventies; **Bonne année** Happy New Year.

annexe noun Fem. 1 appendix (*of book*); 2 annexe (*of building*).

anniversaire noun Masc. 1 birthday; **fêter son anniversaire** to celebrate one's birthday; **Bon**

a
b
c
d
e
f
g
h
i
j
k
l
m
n
o
p
q
r
s
t
u
v
w
x
y
z

anniversaire, Joyeux anniversaire Happy Birthday; **2** anniversary.

annonce noun Fem. **1** advertisement; **les petites annonces** the small ads (*in a newspaper*); **2** announcement; **3** sign.

annoncer verb [61] **1** to announce; **2** to forecast; **ils annoncent de la neige pour demain** snow is forecast for tomorrow.

annuaire noun Masc. directory; **l'annuaire téléphonique** the telephone directory.

annuel (*Fem.* **annuelle**) *adjective* annual, yearly; **un événement annuel** a yearly event.

annuler verb [1] to cancel; **le vol a été annulé** the flight has been cancelled.

anonyme *adjective* anonymous.

anorak noun Masc. anorak.

anorexie noun Fem. anorexia.

anormal (*Masc. plural* **anormaux**) *adjective* abnormal.

anse noun Fem. handle (*of a basket, cup, jug, or teapot*).

Antarctique noun Masc. **l'Antarctique** the Antarctic.

antenne noun Fem. **1** aerial (*for a radio or television*); **2** antenna (*of an insect, a radio mast, or a spacecraft*).

anthropologie noun Fem. anthropology.

antibiotique noun Masc. antibiotic; **prendre des antibiotiques** to be on antibiotics.

antichoc *adjective* shockproof; **un casque antichoc** a crash helmet.

anticiper verb [1] to foresee, to anticipate.

antidérapant *adjective* nonslip, nonskid.

antidote noun Masc. antidote.

antigel noun Masc. antifreeze.

antillais *adjective* West Indian.

Antillais, Antillaise noun Masc., Fem. West Indian.

Antilles plural noun Fem. **les Antilles** the West Indies.

antilope noun Fem. antelope.

antipathique *adjective* unpleasant.

antiquaire noun Masc. & Fem. antique dealer.

antiquité noun Fem. antique.

antiseptique noun Masc., *adjective* antiseptic.

antitabac *adjective* antismoking.

antiterroriste *adjective* antiterrorist.

antivol noun Masc. anti-theft device.

anxieux (*Fem.* **anxieuse**) *adjective* anxious.

août noun Masc. August; **en août, au mois d'août** in August.

apercevoir verb [66] **1** to catch sight of; **2 s'apercevoir de** to notice; **s'apercevoir que** to notice that.

aperçu noun Masc. **1** insight; **2** glimpse.

apéritif noun Masc. drink (*usually alcoholic, before a meal*).

aphte noun Masc. mouth ulcer.

aplatir verb [2] 1 to flatten; 2 to smooth out.

apostrophe noun Fem. apostrophe.

apparaître verb [57] 1 to appear; 2 to seem; **il apparaît que** it seems that.

appareil noun Masc. 1 device, appliance, piece of equipment; 2 telephone; **c'est Paul à l'appareil** it's Paul speaking; 3 **un appareil (dentaire)** a brace (for teeth).

appareil photo noun Masc. camera.

apparemment adverb apparently.

apparence noun Fem. appearance.

apparent adjective 1 visible, obvious; 2 apparent.

apparition noun Fem. appearance.

appartement noun Masc. flat; **'appartement à louer'** 'flat to let'.

appartenir verb [81] **appartenir à** to belong to; **est-ce que ce stylo t'appartient?** does this pen belong to you?, is this pen yours?; **à qui appartiennent ces chaussures?** who do these shoes belong to?

appel noun Masc. 1 call, appeal; **un appel d'aide** a call for help; 2 **un appel (téléphonique)** a telephone call; 3 **faire appel à** to appeal to; 4 **faire l'appel** to take the register (at school).

appeler verb [18] 1 to call; **ils l'ont appelé Roger** they called him Roger; 2 **s'appeler** to be called; **il s'appelle Frank** he's called Frank, his name is Frank; **je m'appelle Anne** my name is Anne; **comment t'appelles-tu?, tu t'appelles comment?** what's your name?; 3 to phone; 4 to call; **appeler un taxi** to call a taxi.

appendice noun Masc. appendix (organ).

appendicite noun Fem. appendicitis.

appétissant adjective appetizing.

appétit noun Masc. appetite; **'bon appétit'** 'enjoy your meal'.

applaudir verb [2] to applaud.

applaudissements plural noun Masc. applause.

application noun Fem. 1 care; 2 application.

appliquer verb [1] 1 to apply; 2 **s'appliquer** to take care; 3 **s'appliquer à** to apply to; **cela ne s'applique pas à vous** that doesn't apply to you.

apporter verb [1] to bring.

apprécier verb [1] to appreciate.

appréhender verb [1] 1 to arrest; 2 to dread.

apprenant, apprenante noun Masc., Fem. learner.

apprendre verb [64] 1 to learn; **apprendre à lire** to learn to read; 2 to hear; **j'ai appris que tu vas partir** I hear you're leaving; 3 to teach; **apprendre quelque chose à quelqu'un** to teach somebody something; **elle leur apprend le français** she's teaching them French; **elle leur apprend à parler français** she's teaching them to speak French.

approche noun Fem. approach.

approcher verb [1] **1** to move (something) closer; **approche ta chaise** move your chair closer; **approche ta chaise de la table** move your chair closer to the table; **2 approcher quelqu'un** to go up to somebody; **3 s'approcher de quelque chose** to go (*or* come) near to something.

approprié adjective appropriate.

approuver verb [1] **1** to approve of; **2** to approve (*a document, project, budget, etc*).

approximatif (Fem. **approximative**) adjective approximate, rough.

approximativement adverb approximately, roughly.

appui noun Masc. support.

appuyer verb [41] **1 appuyer sur quelque chose** to press something; **appuie sur le bouton** press the button; **2** to lean; **appuyer quelque chose contre le mur** to lean something against the wall.

après adverb afterwards, later; **une heure après** an hour later; **peu après** shortly afterwards; **longtemps après** a long time later.

après preposition **1** after; **après dix heures** after ten o'clock; **après l'école** after school; **2 après avoir fait** after doing; **3 après que** after.

après-demain adverb the day after tomorrow.

après-midi noun Masc. OR Fem. afternoon; **cet après-midi** this afternoon; **demain après-midi** tomorrow afternoon; **hier après-midi** yesterday afternoon; **tous les après-midi** every afternoon.

après-rasage noun Masc. aftershave.

aptitude noun Fem. aptitude; **son aptitude pour le dessin** his aptitude for drawing.

aquarelle noun Fem. watercolours; **une aquarelle** a watercolour (painting).

aquarium noun Masc. **1** fish tank; **2** aquarium.

arabe noun Masc. Arabic.

arabe adjective **1** Arab; **2** Arabic.

Arabe noun Masc. & Fem. Arab.

araignée noun Fem. spider; **une toile d'araignée** a spider's web.

arbitraire adjective arbitrary.

arbitre noun Masc. referee, umpire.

arbre noun Masc. tree.

arbre généalogique noun Masc. family tree.

arc noun Masc. **1** bow (*as in 'bow and arrow'*); **2** arch.

arc-en-ciel noun Masc. rainbow.

archéologie noun Fem. archeology.

archéologue noun Masc. & Fem. archeologist.

archet noun Masc. bow (*for a musical instrument such as a violin.*).

archevêque noun Masc. archbishop.

architecte noun Masc. & Fem. architect.

architecture noun Fem. architecture.

Arctique noun Masc. **l'Arctique** the Arctic.

ardoise noun Fem. slate.

arène noun Fem. **1** arena; **2** bullring.

arête noun Fem. fishbone; **ce poisson est plein d'arêtes** this fish is full of bones.

argent noun Masc. **1** money; **dépenser de l'argent** to spend money; **2** silver; **une cuillère en argent** a silver spoon.

argent de poche noun Masc. pocket money.

argile noun Fem. clay.

argot noun Masc. slang.

aristocrate noun Masc. & Fem. aristocrat.

aristocratie noun Fem. aristocracy.

arithmétique noun Fem. arithmetic.

arme noun Fem. weapon.

armé adjective **1** armed; **2 armé de** armed with, equipped with.

arme à feu noun Fem. firearm.

armée noun Fem. army.

armée de l'air noun Fem. Air Force.

armée de terre noun Fem. Army.

armoire noun Fem. **1** cupboard; **2** wardrobe.

arobase noun Masc. at, @ (in email addresses); **jean-point-dupont-arobase-mondecom-point-com** jean-dot-dupont-at-mondecom-dot-com.

aromates plural noun Masc. herbs and spices.

aromathérapie noun Fem. aromatherapy.

aromatisé adjective flavoured.

arôme noun Masc. **1** flavouring; **2** aroma.

arracher verb [1] **1** arracher quelque chose à quelqu'un to snatch something from somebody; **2** to rip out, to rip off (a page or pages); **3** to pull up (weeds or vegetables).

arrangement noun Masc. arrangement.

arranger verb [52] **1** to arrange; **arranger une réunion** to arrange a meeting; **2** to arrange (flowers, books, etc); **3** to sort out; **4** to fix; **5 s'arranger** to get better; **ça va s'arranger** it will sort itself out; **6 s'arranger avec quelqu'un** to sort it out with somebody; **tu t'arranges avec Paul** sort it out with Paul.

arrestation noun Fem. arrest.

arrêt noun Masc. **1** stop; **un arrêt de bus** a bus stop; **2 sans arrêt** non-stop.

arrêter verb [1] **1** to stop; **arrêter la voiture** to stop the car; **2** to switch off (an engine, a machine, etc); **3 arrêter de faire** to stop doing; **il a arrêté de fumer** he's stopped smoking; **elle n'arrête pas de travailler** she never stops working; **4 s'arrêter** to stop; **on va s'arrêter à la boulangerie** we'll stop at the baker's.

arrhes plural noun Fem. deposit; **verser des arrhes** to pay a deposit.

arrière noun Masc. back; **à l'arrière** in the back (of a car); **regarder en arrière** to look back.

arrière *adjective* back (*door, pocket, etc*).

arrière-goût *noun Masc.* aftertaste.

arrière-grand-mère *noun Fem.* great-grandmother.

arrière-grand-père *noun Masc.* great-grandfather.

arrière-grands-parents *plural noun Masc.* great-grandparents.

arrière-petits-enfants *plural noun Masc.* great-grandchildren.

arrivage *noun Masc.* **1** delivery (*of goods*); **2** batch (*of students*).

arrivée *noun Fem.* arrival.

arriver *verb* [1] **1** to arrive; **arriver à Londres** to arrive in London, to get to London; **je suis arrivé à cinq heures** I arrived at five o'clock, I got there (*or* here) at five o'clock; **j'arrive!** just coming!; **2** to happen; **un accident est arrivé** an accident has happened; **tu sais ce qui m'est arrivé?** do you know what happened to me?; **3 arriver à faire** to manage to do; **je n'arrive pas à tourner la clef** I can't manage to turn the key.

arrogant *adjective* arrogant.

arrondi *adjective* rounded.

arrondissement; *noun Masc.* arrondissement; **elle habite à Paris dans le neuvième arrondissement** she lives in Paris in the ninth arrondissement (*large French cities are divided into numbered administrative areas called 'arrondissements'*).

arroser *verb* [1] to water; **arroser les plantes** to water the plants; on va **arroser l'anniversaire de mon frère** we're going to have a few drinks to celebrate my brother's birthday.

arrosoir *noun Masc.* watering can.

art *noun Masc.* art; **une galerie d'art** an art gallery; **l'art de faire** the art of doing.

art dramatique *noun Masc.* drama.

artère *noun Fem.* **1** artery; **2** arterial road; **3** main road.

arthrite *noun Fem.* arthritis.

artichaut *noun Masc.* artichoke.

article *noun Masc.* **1** article (*in a newspaper, magazine, etc*); **2** item (*for sale*); **articles de sport** sports equipment; **articles de toilette** toiletries; **3** article (*in grammar*); **l'article défini** the definite article; **l'article indéfini** the indefinite article.

articulation *noun Fem.* joint; **articulation du coude/de la hanche** elbow/hip joint.

artificiel (*Fem.* **artificielle**) *adjective* artificial.

artisan *noun Masc.* craftsman.

artisanal (*Masc. plural* **artisanaux**) *adjective* **1** traditional; **2** hand-crafted.

artisanat *noun Masc.* arts and crafts.

artiste *noun Masc. & Fem.* **1** artist; **2** performer.

as¹ *verb* SEE **avoir**.

as² *noun Masc.* ace.

ascenseur *noun Masc.* lift; **prendre l'ascenseur** to take the lift.

asiatique *adjective* Asian.

Asie *noun Fem.* Asia.

asile *noun Masc.* **1** refuge; **2 le droit d'asile** political asylum.

aspect *noun Masc.* **1** aspect; **2** appearance; **d'un aspect bizarre** strange-looking; **3** side; **l'aspect positif** the positive side.

asperger *verb* [52] to sprinkle.

asperges *plural noun Fem.* asparagus.

asphyxier, s'asphyxier *verb* [1] to suffocate.

aspirateur *noun Masc.* vacuum cleaner.

aspirine *noun Fem.* aspirin.

assaisonnement *noun Masc.* **1** seasoning; **2** dressing.

assaisonner *verb* [1] **1** to season; **2** to put the dressing on (*a salad*).

assassin, assassine *noun Masc., Fem.* murderer.

assassinat *noun Masc.* murder.

assassiner *verb* [1] to murder.

assemblée *noun Fem.* meeting.

assembler *verb* [1] **1** to put together, to assemble (*a kit, a machine, etc*); **2** to gather together; **3 s'assembler** to gather (*of a group, crowd, demonstration, etc*); ★ **qui se ressemble s'assemble** birds of a feather flock together (*literally: those who are similar gather together*).

asseoir *verb* [20] **s'asseoir** to sit down; **s'asseoir sur une chaise** to sit down on a chair; **assieds-toi** take a seat; **asseyez-vous** do sit down SEE ALSO **assis.**

assez *adverb* **1 assez de** enough; **assez de pain** enough bread; **2** enough; **elle ne mange pas assez** she doesn't eat enough; **3** enough; **est-ce que l'eau est assez chaude?** is the water hot enough?; **4** quite; **leur maison est assez grande** their house is quite big; **assez souvent** quite often; **assez joli** quite pretty; **5 j'en ai assez (de)** (*informal*) I'm fed up (with).

assiette *noun Fem.* plate; **une assiette plate** a dinner plate; **une assiette creuse, une assiette à soupe** a soup plate; ★ **je ne suis pas dans mon assiette aujourd'hui** I'm not my usual self today.

assis *adjective* **être assis** to be sitting; **elle était assise dans un fauteuil** she was sitting in an armchair; **rester assis** to remain seated.

assistance *noun Fem.* **1** audience; **dans l'assistance** in the audience; **2** assistance.

assistant, assistante *noun Masc., Fem.* assistant.

assister *verb* [1] **1** to assist; **2** to aid (*a country, the poor, etc*); **3** assister à to be present at, to be at; **j'ai assisté à leur mariage** I was at their wedding.

association *noun Fem.* association.

associé, associée *noun Masc., Fem.* associate, partner.

associer *verb* [1] **1 associer quelqu'un à quelque chose** to include somebody in something;

a
b

2 **s'associer à un groupe** to join a group; 3 **s'associer pour faire** to get together to do.

c
d
e
f

assommer verb [1] 1 **assommer quelqu'un** to knock somebody senseless; 2 **assommer quelqu'un** (informal) to bore somebody stiff; 3 **être assommé par une nouvelle** to be stunned by a piece of news.

assorti adjective matching; **rideaux et coussins assortis** matching curtains and cushions; **une veste assortie à sa robe** a jacket to match her dress.

g
h
i

assortiment noun Masc. assortment, selection.

j
k

assortir verb [2] 1 to match; 2 **s'assortir à** to match.

l

assouplissant noun Masc. fabric softener.

m
n

assourdir verb [2] 1 to deafen; 2 to muffle.

o
p

assourdissant adjective deafening.

q
r
s

assumer verb [1] **assumer la responsabilité de quelque chose** to take responsibility for something; **assumer une fonction** to hold a position.

t
u

assurance noun Fem.
1 confidence; **avec assurance** confidently; 2 insurance.

assurance automobile noun Fem. car insurance.

v
w
x

assurance maladie noun Fem. health insurance; **est-ce que vous avez une assurance maladie?** do you have health insurance?

y
z

assurance voyage noun Fem. travel insurance.

assuré adjective 1 confident; 2 insured.

assurer verb [1] 1 to assure; **je vous assure que c'est vrai** I assure you it's true; 2 to insure; **assurer sa voiture** to insure one's car; 3 to provide (a service); 4 to carry out (a task or a responsibility); 5 **s'assurer** to make sure.

astérisque noun Masc. asterisk.

asthmatique adjective asthmatic.

asthme noun Masc. asthma.

asticot noun Masc. maggot.

astiquer verb [1] to polish.

astrologie noun Fem. astrology.

astrologue noun Masc. & Fem. astrologer.

astronome noun Masc. & Fem. astronomer.

astronomie noun Fem. astronomy.

astronomique adjective astronomical.

astuce noun Fem. 1 cleverness; 2 **une astuce** a trick (for managing to do something); **il doit y avoir une astuce** there must be a trick to it.

astucieux (Fem. **astucieuse**) adjective clever; **c'était très astucieux de sa part de faire ça** it was very crafty of her to do that.

atelier noun Masc. 1 workshop; 2 studio (of an artist, a sculptor, etc); 3 work group.

athée noun Masc. & Fem. atheist.

Athènes noun Athens.

athlète noun Masc. & Fem. athlete.

athlétique adjective athletic.

athlétisme noun Masc. athletics.

Atlantique noun Masc. l'Atlantique the Atlantic.

atlas noun Masc. atlas.

atmosphère noun Fem. atmosphere.

atome noun Masc. atom.

atomique adjective atomic.

atomiseur noun Masc. spray, atomizer.

atout noun Masc. **1** trump card; c'est atout pique spades are trumps; **2** asset, advantage.

atroce adjective dreadful, terrible.

atrocité noun Fem. **1** atrocity; **2** monstrosity.

attachant adjective lovable.

attache noun Fem. **1** tie, string, strap; **2** attaches familiales family ties.

attacher verb [1] **1** attacher ses cheveux to tie (or fix) your hair back; **2** s'attacher to stick (to the pan).

attaque noun Fem. attack.

attaquer verb [1] **1** to attack; **2** to tackle (a job).

attarder verb [1] s'attarder to linger.

atteindre verb [60] **1** to reach; **2** to achieve.

atteint adjective être atteint d'une maladie to be suffering from an illness.

attendant in phrase en attendant meanwhile, in the meantime.

attendre verb [3] **1** to wait; tu peux attendre deux minutes? can you wait two minutes?; **2** to wait for; j'attends le bus I'm waiting for the bus; je t'attends dehors I'll wait for you outside; **3** s'attendre à to expect.

attendrissant adjective touching.

attentat noun Masc. **1** un attentat (à la bombe) a bomb attack, a bombing; **2** assassination attempt.

attente noun Fem. wait; une attente de vingt minutes a twenty-minute wait.

attentif (Fem. **attentive**) adjective **1** attentive; **2** careful.

attention noun Fem. **1** attention; **2** faire attention à to be careful of; faites attention aux pickpockets! look out for pickpockets!; **3** attention! watch out!; attention au chien! beware of the dog!

atterrir verb [2] to land.

atterrissage noun Masc. landing.

attirant adjective attractive.

attirer verb [1] to attract; attirer l'attention de quelqu'un sur quelque chose to attract (or draw) somebody's attention to something.

attitude noun Fem. attitude.

attraction noun Fem. attraction.

attraper verb [1] **1** to catch; **2** attraper un rhume to catch a cold; **3** to catch hold of.

attrayant adjective attractive.

attrister verb [1] to sadden.

au see À.

aubaine noun Fem. godsend.

aube noun Fem. dawn; à l'aube at dawn.

aubépine noun Fem. hawthorn.

a

auberge noun Fem. inn; ★ **on n'est pas sorti de l'auberge** our problems are not over yet (*literally: we're not out of the inn*).

auberge de jeunesse noun Fem. youth hostel.

aubergine noun Fem. aubergine.

aucun adjective no; **en aucun cas** under no circumstances; **sans aucun doute** without any doubt.

aucun pronoun none; **aucun des deux** neither of them; **aucun d'entre eux** none of them.

aucunement adverb in no way.

audace noun Fem. daring.

audacieux (Fem. **audacieuse**) adjective daring.

au-delà de preposition beyond.

au-dessous adverb
1 underneath; 2 below; 3 **au-dessous de** underneath; **au-dessous de la table** underneath the table; 4 **au-dessous de** below; **au-dessous de la limite** below the limit.

au-dessus adverb 1 above; 2 **au-dessus de** above.

audience noun Fem. audience.

audiovisuel (Fem. **audiovisuelle**) adjective audiovisual.

auditeur, auditrice noun Masc., Fem. listener.

audition noun Fem. audition.

augmentation noun Fem. increase; **l'augmentation des prix** the increase in prices; **une augmentation de salaire** a pay rise.

augmenter verb [1] 1 to raise, to increase; **augmenter les prix** to

raise prices; 2 to rise, to go up; **le prix a augmenté** the price has gone up.

aujourd'hui adverb today; **nous sommes lundi aujourd'hui** today is Monday.

auparavant adverb before, beforehand.

auprès de preposition beside, next to.

auquel pronoun **le garçon auquel je parle** the boy I'm talking to.

aura, aurai, auras, aurez, aurons, auront verb SEE **avoir**.

au revoir exclamation goodbye.

aussi adverb 1 also, too; **moi aussi** me too; **j'ai aussi invité ton frère** I also invited your brother, I invited your brother as well; 2 **aussi ...que** as ...as; **mon panier est aussi lourd que le tien** my basket is as heavy as yours; 3 **aussi bien que** as well as; **les enfants aussi bien que les adultes** children as well as adults.

aussi conjunction so, therefore.

aussitôt adverb immediately.

Australie noun Fem. Australia.

australien (Fem. **australienne**) adjective Australian.

Australien, Australienne noun Masc., Fem. Australian.

autant adverb 1 as much, so much; **je n'ai jamais mangé autant** I've never eaten so much; 2 **autant que** as much as, as many as; **tu en as autant que moi** you have as much (or as many) as me; 3 **autant de ...que** as much ...as, as many ...as; **tu as autant de problèmes que**

moi you have as many problems as I do.

autel noun Masc. altar.

auteur noun Masc. author.

authentique adjective genuine.

auto noun Fem. car.

autobiographie noun Fem. autobiography.

autobus noun Masc. bus.

autocar noun Masc. coach.

autocollant noun Masc. sticker.

autocollant adjective self-adhesive.

autodéfense noun Fem. self-defence.

auto-école noun Fem. driving school.

automate noun Masc. robot.

automatique adjective automatic.

automatiquement adverb automatically.

automne noun Masc. autumn; **en automne** in autumn.

automobile noun Fem. car.

automobile adjective **l'industrie automobile** the car industry.

automobiliste noun Masc. & Fem. motorist.

autoradio noun Masc. car radio.

autorisation noun Fem. 1 permission; 2 permit.

autoriser verb [1] 1 to allow, to authorize; 2 **autoriser quelqu'un à faire** to allow somebody to do.

autoritaire adjective authoritarian, strict.

autorité noun Fem. authority.

autoroute noun Fem. motorway; **l'autoroute de l'information** the information super-highway.

auto-stop noun Masc. hitchhiking; **faire de l'auto-stop** to hitchhike.

auto-stoppeur, auto-stoppeuse noun Masc., Fem. hitchhiker.

autour adverb 1 around; 2 **autour de** round, around; **autour de la table** round the table.

autre adjective 1 other; **l'autre couteau** the other knife; **l'autre jour** the other day; 2 **un/une autre** another; **tu peux me passer un autre verre?** can you pass me another glass?; 3 **quelqu'un d'autre** somebody else; **personne d'autre** nobody else.

autre pronoun 1 **un/une autre** another one; **donne-moi un autre** give me another one; 2 **les autres** the others; **où sont les autres?** where are the others?

autrefois adverb in the past, in the old days.

autrement adverb 1 differently; **autrement dit** in other words; 2 otherwise.

autre part adverb somewhere else.

Autriche noun Fem. Austria.

autrichien (Fem. **autrichienne**) adjective Austrian.

Autrichien, Autrichienne noun Masc., Fem. Austrian.

autruche noun Fem. ostrich.

aux SEE **à**.

auxiliaire noun Masc. & Fem., adjective auxiliary.

b
c
d
e
f
g
h
i
j
k
l
m
n
o
p
q
r
s
t
u
v
w
x
y
z

auxquelles *pronoun* les filles auxquelles je parlais the girls I was talking to.

auxquels *pronoun* les garçons auxquels je parlais the boys I was talking to.

avalanche *noun Fem.* avalanche.

avaler *verb* [1] **1** to swallow; **2** to inhale.

avance *noun Fem.* **1** advance, progress; **2** je suis arrivé dix minutes en avance I arrived ten minutes early; **avoir dix minutes d'avance** to be ten minutes early; **3** être en avance to be early; **4** à l'avance in advance.

avancer *verb* [61] **1** to move forward, to advance; **2** avancer quelque chose to move something forward; **3** ma montre avance de cinq minutes my watch is five minutes fast.

avant *adverb* **1** before; longtemps avant a long time before; **2** forward; plus avant further forward.

avant *preposition* **1** before; avant Noël before Christmas; avant six heures before six o'clock; elle est arrivée avant moi she arrived before me; **2** avant de faire before doing; avant de partir je vais téléphoner à ma mère before leaving (or before I leave) I'll phone my mother; **3** avant que before.

avant *noun Masc.* front.

avant *adjective* front; la roue avant the front wheel.

avantage *noun Masc.* advantage.

avantageux (*Fem.* avantageuse) *adjective* **1** des prix avantageux

attractive prices; **2** des conditions avantageuses favourable conditions.

avant-bras *noun Masc.* forearm.

avant-dernier, avant-dernière *noun Masc., Fem.* l'avant-dernier the last but one.

avant-dernière *adjective* second last, last but one.

avant-hier *adverb* the day before yesterday.

avare *noun Masc. & Fem.* miser.

avare *adjective* mean, miserly.

avec *preposition* with; avec Marie with Marie; avec un couteau with a knife; avec ça? anything else? (*in a shop*).

avenir *noun Masc.* future; l'avenir the future; à l'avenir in the future.

aventure *noun Fem.* adventure.

avenue *noun Fem.* avenue.

averse *noun Fem.* shower.

avertir *verb* [2] **1** to inform; **2** to warn.

avertissement *noun Masc.* warning.

aveuglant *adjective* blinding.

aveugle *adjective* blind.

aveuglément *adverb* blindly.

aveugler *verb* [1] to blind.

avez *verb* SEE **avoir**.

aviation *noun Fem.* **1** aviation; **2** aircraft industry; **3** flying; **4** air force.

avion *noun Masc.* aeroplane; plane; aller à Paris en avion to go to Paris by plane, to fly to Paris; par avion by airmail.

aviron *noun Masc.* **1** rowing; faire de l'aviron to row; **2** oar.

avis noun Masc. **1** opinion; **à mon avis** in my opinion; **2 changer d'avis** to change one's mind; **3** notice.

avocat[1], **avocate** noun Masc., Fem. **1** solicitor; **2** barrister.

avocat[2] noun Masc. avocado (pear).

avoine noun Fem. oats; **des flocons d'avoine** porridge oats.

avoir verb [5] **1** have (got); **elle a trois frères** she has (or she's got) three brothers; **tu as beaucoup de livres** you have (or you've got) a lot of books; **2** (talking about age) **avoir dix ans** to be ten; **Claudie a dix ans** Claudie's ten; **quel âge a-t-il?** how old is he?; **3 avoir chaud** to be hot; **j'ai chaud** I'm hot; **j'ai froid** I'm cold; **4** (used with another verb, like 'have' in English, to form past tenses) **j'ai perdu mon stylo** I have lost my pen; **j'ai vu ta mère hier** I saw your mother yesterday; **5 j'en ai pour dix minutes** it'll take me ten minutes; **6 il y a** there is, there are; **il y a un livre sur la table** there's a book on the table; **il y a trois livres sur la table** there are three books on the table; **7 il y a** ago; **il y a trois ans** three years ago; **8 qu'est-ce qu'il y a?** what's the matter?

avons verb SEE **avoir**.

avortement noun Masc. abortion.

avouer verb [1] to confess, to admit.

avril noun Masc. April; **en avril, au mois d'avril** in April.

azalée noun Fem. azalea.

azote noun Masc. nitrogen.

Bb

babouin noun Masc. baboon.

baby-foot noun Masc. table football; **jouer au baby-foot** to play table football; **on va faire une partie de baby-foot** we're going to have a game of table football.

bac noun Masc. **1** (informal) SHORT FOR **baccalauréat**; **2** tub.

bac à glace noun Masc. ice tray.

bac à sable noun Masc. sandpit.

baccalauréat noun Masc. baccalaureate (school-leaving certificate sat at the age of 17-18 and giving access to higher education); **passer le baccalauréat** to sit the baccalaureate; **réussir au baccalauréat** to pass the baccalaureate.

bâche noun Fem. tarpaulin.

badaud, **badaude** noun Masc., Fem. passerby, onlooker.

baffe noun Fem. (informal) slap.

baffle noun Masc. speaker (on a music system).

bagage noun Masc. **un bagage** a piece of luggage; **des bagages** luggage; **où sont tes bagages?** where is your luggage?; **j'ai fait mes bagages** I've packed.

bagarre noun Fem. fight.

bagarrer verb [1] **se bagarrer** to fight.

bagnole noun Fem. (informal) car.

bague noun Fem. ring.

baguette noun Fem. **1** baguette, French bread stick; **2** stick; **3** drumstick; **4** chopstick.

a
b
c
d
e
f
g
h
i
j
k
l
m
n
o
p
q
r
s
t
u
v
w
x
y
z

baguette magique noun Fem.
magic wand.

Bahamas noun Fem. plural **les
îles Bahamas** the Bahamas.

baie noun **1** bay (on the sea);
2 berry; **3** une baie vitrée a
picture window.

baignade noun Fem. swimming;
'baignade interdite' 'no
swimming'.

baigner verb [1] **se baigner** to go
swimming.

baignoire noun Fem. bath.

bail (plural **baux**) noun Masc. lease;
un bail de trois ans a three-year
lease.

bâiller verb [1] to yawn.

bain noun Masc. bath; **prendre un
bain** to have a bath.

baiser noun Masc. kiss; **bons
baisers** love and kisses (at the end
of a letter).

baisse noun Fem. drop, fall; **être en
baisse** to be falling; **la
température est en baisse** the
temperature is falling.

baisser verb [1] **1** to lower; **baisser
le store** to lower (or pull down) the
blind; **baisser le volume** to turn
down the volume; **baisser la
lumière** to turn down the lights;
baisser les prix to cut prices; **2 se
baisser** to bend down.

bal noun Masc. dance; **un bal
populaire** a village dance (or
disco).

balade noun Fem. walk, drive; **faire
une balade (à pied)** to go for a
walk; **faire une balade (en
voiture)** to go for a drive; **faire une**

balade à la campagne to go for a
walk (or drive) in the country.

balader verb [1] **1 se balader** to go
for a walk (or drive); **se balader en
Écosse** to tour around Scotland;
2 balader quelque chose to carry
something around.

baladeur noun Masc. Walkman™,
personal stereo.

balai noun Masc. broom, (long-
handled) brush; **passer le balai** to
sweep the floor.

Balance noun Fem. Libra (sign of
the Zodiac).

balance noun Fem. scales; **une
balance de cuisine** kitchen scales.

balancer verb [61] **1** to sway; **2** to
swing; **3** (informal) to throw, to
chuck; **balance-moi les clés!**
chuck me the keys!; **4** (informal) to
chuck out; **je vais balancer tous
ces vieux bouquins** I'm going to
chuck out all these old books.

balançoire noun Fem. **1** swing;
2 seesaw.

balayer verb [59] **1** to sweep;
balayer la cuisine to sweep the
kitchen floor; **2** to sweep up;
balayer les miettes to sweep up
the crumbs.

balayeur, balayeuse noun
Masc., Fem. roadsweeper.

balbutier verb [1] to mumble.

balcon noun Masc. balcony.

baleine noun Fem. whale.

baliser verb [1] **1** to signpost; **2** to
mark out.

balle noun Fem. **1** ball; **2** bullet.

ballerine noun Fem. **1** ballerina;
2 ballerina shoe; **3** ballet shoe.

a
b
c
d
e
f
g
h
i
j
k
l
m
n
o
p
q
r
s
t
u
v
w
x
y
z

ballet noun Masc. ballet.

ballon noun Masc. **1** ball; **2** balloon; **3** (informal) Breathalyzer™; ★ **souffler dans le ballon** to be breathalyzed.

ball-trap noun Masc. clay pigeon shooting.

balnéaire adjective seaside; **une station balnéaire** a seaside resort.

bambou noun Masc. bamboo.

banal adjective ordinary; **peu banal** unusual.

banane noun Fem. **1** banana; **2** bumbag.

banc noun Masc. bench; **assis sur un banc** sitting on a bench.

bancaire adjective **1** banking; **2 une carte bancaire** a bank card.

bancal adjective **1** rickety; **2** wobbly.

bande noun Fem. **1** group; **une bande de jeunes** a group of young people; **2** gang; **une bande de criminels** a criminal gang; **3** strip (of fabric or paper); **4** tape (for recording); **5** bandage.

bande-annonce noun Fem. trailer (for a film).

bandeau (plural **bandeaux**) noun Masc. **1** headband; **2** blindfold.

bande d'arrêt d'urgence noun Fem. hard shoulder (on motorway).

bande de fréquence noun Fem. wavelength (on radio).

bande dessinée noun Fem. **1** comic strip; **2** comic book.

bande publique noun Fem. Citizen's Band, CB radio.

bande rugueuse noun Fem. rumble strip (on motorway).

bande sonore noun Fem. **1** soundtrack (of film); **2** rumble strip (on motorway).

bandit noun Masc. bandit.

banditisme noun Masc. crime.

banlieue noun Fem. **la banlieue** the suburbs; **une banlieue** a suburb; **une maison de banlieue** a house in the suburbs; **un train de banlieue** a commuter train.

banque noun Fem. **1** bank; **aller à la banque** to go to the bank; **2** banking; **travailler dans la banque** to work in banking.

banquet noun Masc. banquet.

banquette noun Fem. **1** wall seat (in a café or restaurant); **2** seat (in a car, bus, or train).

banquier noun Masc. banker.

baptême noun Masc. christening.

baptiser verb [1] **1** to christen; **2** to name; **3** to nickname.

baquet noun Masc. tub.

bar noun Masc. bar.

baraque noun Fem. (informal) house.

Barbade noun Fem. **la Barbade** Barbados.

barbadien (Fem. **barbadienne**) adjective Barbadian.

Barbadien, Barbadienne noun Masc., Fem. Barbadian.

barbant adjective (informal) boring.

barbe noun Fem. beard; ★ **c'est la barbe!** what a drag!; ★ **faire quelque chose à la barbe de quelqu'un** to do something behind somebody's back (literally: to do something in somebody's beard).

barbe à papa noun Fem. candyfloss.

barbecue noun Masc. barbecue.

barbelé noun Masc. barbed wire.

barbouiller verb [1] **1** to smear; **tu es tout barbouillé de confiture** you've got jam all over your face; **2** to daub; **barbouillé de slogans** daubed with slogans.

barbu noun Masc. **un barbu** a man with a beard.

barbu adjective bearded.

barème noun Masc. scale.

barmaid noun Fem. barmaid.

barman noun Masc. barman.

baromètre noun Masc. barometer.

barque noun Fem. rowing boat.

barquette noun Fem. tub, container; **une barquette de fraises** a punnet of strawberries.

barrage noun Masc. **1** dam; **2** roadblock.

barre noun Fem. bar; **une barre de fer** an iron bar; **une barre de chocolat** a chocolate bar.

barreau (plural **barreaux**) noun Masc. bar; **derrière les barreaux** behind bars (in prison).

barrer verb [1] **1** to block; **'route barrée'** 'road closed'; **2** to cross out; **barrer trois mots** to cross out three words; **3 se barrer** (informal) to clear off, to leave; **je me barre!** I'm off!; ★ **on est mal barré** (informal) we're in trouble.

barrette noun Fem. hairslide.

barrière noun Fem. **1** fence; **2** gate.

bar-tabac noun Masc. cafe (selling cigarettes, tobacco, and stamps as well as drinks and snacks).

bas noun Masc. **1** bottom, lower part; **en bas de la page** at the bottom of the page; **2** stocking.

bas adjective (Fem. **basse**) low.

bas adverb **1** low; **plus bas** further down; **parler plus bas** to lower one's voice; **2 en bas** at the bottom, down below, downstairs; **les voisins d'en bas** the neighbours in the flat below.

bas-côté noun Masc. verge (on the roadside).

basculant adjective **un camion à benne basculante** a dump truck.

bascule noun Fem. **1** rocker; **un fauteuil à bascule** a rocking chair; **un cheval à bascule** a rocking horse; **2** seesaw.

basculer verb [1] to topple over.

base noun Fem. **1** basis; **être à la base de quelque chose** to be at the root of something; **2** base; **à base de chocolat** chocolate-based; **3 de base** basic; **les ingrédients de base** the basic ingredients.

base-ball noun Masc. baseball.

base de données noun Fem. database.

baser verb [1] to base; **basé sur** based on.

basilic noun Masc. basil; **une sauce au basilic** a basil sauce.

basket noun Masc. **1** basketball; **2** sports shoe, trainer; ★ **lâche-moi les baskets!** (informal) get off my back!

basketteur, basketteuse noun Masc., Fem. basketball player.

basque noun Masc. Basque (language).

basque *adjective* Basque.

Basque *noun* Masc. & Fem. Basque (*person*).

basse *noun* Fem. bass (*in music.*).

basse *adjective* SEE **bas.**

bassin *noun* Masc. **1** pond; **2** pelvis.

bassine *noun* Fem. bowl.

bassiste *noun* Masc. & Fem. bassist.

bataille *noun* Fem. **1** battle; **la bataille de Trafalgar** the Battle of Trafalgar; **la bataille du pouvoir** the battle for power; **une bataille de boules de neige** a snowball fight; **2** a card game (*similar to beggar-my-neighbour*); ★ **avoir les sourcils en bataille** to have bushy eyebrows; ★ **elle avait les cheveux en bataille** her hair was all over the place.

bateau (*plural* **bateaux**) *noun* Masc. boat, ship; **faire du bateau** to go boating (*or* sailing).

bateau à moteur *noun* Masc. motorboat.

bateau de plaisance *noun* Masc. pleasure boat.

bateau-mouche *noun* Masc. pleasure boat (*a large river boat for sightseeing trips*).

bateau pneumatique *noun* Masc. rubber dinghy.

bâti *adjective* built; **bien bâti** well-built.

bâtiment *noun* Masc. **1** building; **les bâtiments de l'école** the school buildings; **2 le bâtiment** the building trade; **travailler dans le bâtiment** to work in the building trade; **3** ship.

bâtir *verb* [2] to build.

bâtisse *noun* Fem. building.

bâton *noun* Masc. stick.

bâton de ski *noun* Masc. ski stick.

bâtonnet *noun* Masc. stick.

bâtonnet de poisson *noun* Masc. fish finger.

bâtonnet ouaté *noun* Masc. cotton bud.

batte *noun* Fem. bat (*for cricket, baseball, etc*).

batterie *noun* Fem. **1** battery; **2** drum kit, drums.

batterie de cuisine *noun* Fem. pots and pans.

batteur *noun* Masc. **1** drummer; **2** whisk.

batteur électrique *noun* Masc. (electric) mixer.

battre *verb* [21] **1** to beat (*in a game*) **Nicole m'a battu au tennis** Nicole beat me at tennis; **2** to beat, to batter; **battre un chien** to beat a dog; **3** to beat (*a mixture*); **battre les œufs** to whisk the eggs; **battre la crème** to whip the cream; **4 se battre** to fight; **5 battre des mains** to clap your hands; **6 le cœur bat** the heart beats; **7 la porte bat** the door bangs.

bavard *adjective* talkative.

bavarder *verb* [1] to chat, to chatter.

baver *verb* [1] to dribble.

bavure *noun* Fem. **1** smudge; **2** blunder.

bazar *noun* Masc. **1** general store; **2** (*informal*) mess.

BCBG SHORT FOR **bon chic bon genre** chic and stylish (*in appearance*).

a
b
c
d
e
f
g
h
i
j
k
l
m
n
o
p
q
r
s
t
u
v
w
x
y
z

B.D. *noun Fem.* comic strip SHORT FOR **bande dessinée.**

beau, bel *(before a vowel or silent 'h') (Fem.* **belle***) (Masc. plural* **beaux***) adjective* **1** beautiful, lovely; **une belle maison** a beautiful house; **un bel homme** a handsome man; **fais de beaux rêves!** sweet dreams!; **2 il fait beau** it's a nice day; ★ **faire le beau** to sit up and beg *(of a dog).*

beaucoup *adverb* **1** a lot; **tu m'en as donné beaucoup** you've given me a lot; **tu ne m'en as pas donné beaucoup** you haven't given me much; **cinquante euros c'est beaucoup** fifty euros is a lot; **2** a lot; **il lit beaucoup** he reads a lot; **il ne lit pas beaucoup** he doesn't read much; **3** very much; **j'aime beaucoup ta robe** I like your dress very much, I really like your dress; **j'aime beaucoup aller au cinéma** I really like going to the cinema; **4 beaucoup de** a lot of money; **beaucoup d'argent** a lot of money; **elle a beaucoup d'argent** she has a lot of money; **elle n'a pas beaucoup d'argent** she doesn't have much money; **il a beaucoup d'amis** he has a lot of friends; **il n'a pas beaucoup d'amis** he doesn't have many friends; **5 beaucoup plus** much more; **beaucoup moins** much less; **beaucoup trop** far too much; **beaucoup trop court** far too short.

beau-fils *(plural* **beaux-fils***) noun Masc.* **1** son-in-law; **2** stepson.

beau-frère *(plural* **beaux-frères***) noun Masc.* brother-in-law.

beau-père *(plural* **beau-pères***) noun Masc.* **1** father-in-law; **2** stepfather.

beauté *noun Fem.* beauty.

beaux-arts *plural noun Masc.* fine arts; **école des beaux-arts** art school.

beaux-parents *plural noun Masc.* parents-in-law, in-laws.

bébé *noun Masc.* baby.

bec *noun Masc.* beak.

bêche *noun Fem.* spade.

bégayer *verb* [59] to stammer.

beige *adjective* beige.

beignet *noun Masc.* **1** fritter; **2** doughnut.

bel *adjective* SEE **beau.**

belette *noun Fem.* weasel.

belge *adjective* Belgian.

Belge *noun Masc. & Fem.* Belgian.

Belgique *noun Fem.* Belgium.

bélier *noun Masc.* ram.

Bélier *noun Masc.* Aries *(sign of the Zodiac).*

belle *noun Fem.* **1 ma belle** darling; **2 la Belle au bois dormant** Sleeping Beauty.

belle *adjective* SEE **beau.**

belle-famille *noun Fem.* in-laws.

belle-fille *(plural* **belles-filles***) noun Fem.* **1** daughter-in-law; **2** stepdaughter.

belle-mère *(plural* **belles-mères***) noun Fem.* **1** mother-in-law; **2** stepmother.

belle-sœur *(plural* **belles-sœurs***) noun Fem.* sister-in-law.

bénédiction *noun Fem.* blessing.

bénéfice noun Masc. profit; **faire un bénéfice de dix mille euros** to make a profit of ten thousand euros.

bénéfique adjective beneficial.

bénévole noun Masc. & Fem. voluntary worker.

bénévole adjective voluntary, unpaid.

bénir verb [2] to bless.

benne noun Fem. skip (for rubbish).

béquille noun Fem. crutch.

berceau (plural **berceaux**) noun Masc. cradle.

bercer verb [61] to rock (a baby).

berceuse noun Fem. **1** lullaby; **2** rocking chair.

béret noun Masc. beret.

berge noun Fem. bank (of a river or canal).

berger, bergère noun Masc., Fem. shepherd, shepherdess.

berger allemand noun Masc. Alsatian (dog).

besoin noun Masc. need; **avoir besoin de quelque chose** to need something; **j'ai besoin d'un marteau** I need a hammer; **avoir besoin de faire** to need to do; **j'ai vraiment besoin de me reposer** I really need to take a rest.

bestiole noun Fem. (informal) creepy-crawly.

bétail noun Masc. **1** livestock; **2** cattle.

bête noun Fem. animal.

bête adjective stupid.

bêtise noun Fem. stupidity; **faire une bêtise** to do something stupid.

béton noun Masc. concrete.

bétonnière noun Fem. cement mixer.

betterave (rouge) noun Fem. beetroot.

beurre noun Masc. butter; ★ **un œil au beurre noir** a black eye (literally: an eye with black butter).

beurrer verb [1] to butter.

bibelot noun Masc. ornament.

biberon noun Masc. (feeding) bottle.

bible noun Fem. bible; **la Bible** the Bible.

bibliothécaire noun Masc. & Fem. librarian.

bibliothèque noun Fem. **1** library; **2** bookcase.

bic™ noun Masc. **un stylo bic™** a Biro™.

biche noun Fem. doe.

bicyclette noun Fem. bicycle; **faire de la bicyclette** to cycle.

bidet noun Masc. bidet.

bidon noun Masc. can.

bidon adjective (informal) phoney.

bidonville noun Masc. shanty town.

bidule noun Masc. (informal) whatsit, thingamajig.

bien noun Masc. **1** good; **le bien et le mal** good and evil; **ça te fera du bien** that'll do you good; **2** possession; **tous leurs biens** all their possessions.

bien adjective **1** good, nice; **des gens bien** nice people; **ce sera bien de le revoir** it will be nice to see him again; **2** well; **je ne me sens pas bien** I don't feel well; **3** happy, comfortable; **on est bien**

a
b
c
d
e
f
g
h
i
j
k
l
m
n
o
p
q
r
s
t
u
v
w
x
y
z

a
b
c
d
e
f
g
h
i
j
k
l
m
n
o
p
q
r
s
t
u
v
w
x
y
z

ici it's nice here; **on est très bien dans ce fauteuil** this chair's really comfortable.

bien *adverb* **1** well; **elle chante bien** she sings well; **bien joué!** well done!; **tu vas bien?** are you well?; **2** well; **bien habillé** well dressed; **cette couleur te va bien** that colour suits you; **3** very, really; **bien triste** really sad; **bien chaud** really hot; **4** very much; **j'aime bien ta robe** I like your dress really much, I really like your dress; **j'aimerais bien savoir** I'd really like to know; **j'aimerais bien aller au cinéma** I'd really like to go to the cinema; **'veux-tu du thé?'** – **'oui, je veux bien'** 'would you like some tea?' – 'yes, I'd love some'; **'tu aimes le poisson?'** – **'oui, je l'aime bien'** 'do you like fish?' – 'yes, I do'; **je veux bien le faire** I'm quite happy to do it; **5** much; **bien mieux** much better; **bien plus chaud** much hotter; **6 bien de** many, a number of; **bien des gens** many people; ★ **c'est bien fait pour elle!** serves her right!

bien entendu *adverb* of course.

bien-être *noun Masc.* well-being.

bien que *conjunction* although.

bien sûr *adverb* of course.

bientôt *adverb* soon; **à bientôt** see you soon.

bienvenu, bienvenue¹ *noun Masc., Fem., adjective* welcome; **soyez le bienvenu** (*or* **la bienvenue)!** welcome!

bienvenue² *noun Fem.* welcome; **bienvenue!** welcome!; **bienvenue en France!** welcome to France!;

souhaiter la bienvenue à quelqu'un to welcome somebody.

bière *noun Fem.* beer; **boire de la bière** to drink beer; **trois bières, s'il vous plaît** three beers, please.

bière blonde *noun Fem.* lager.

bière brune *noun Fem.* brown ale.

bifteck *noun Masc.* steak.

bifurcation *noun Fem.* fork (*in the road*).

bigoudi *noun Masc.* hair curler.

bijou (*plural* **bijoux**) *noun Masc.* jewel, piece of jewellery.

bijouterie *noun Fem.* jeweller's (shop).

bijoutier, bijoutière *noun Masc., Fem.* jeweller.

bilan *noun Masc.* balance sheet; ★ **faire le bilan de quelque chose** to assess something.

bilingue *adjective* bilingual.

billard *noun Masc.* **1** billiards; **jouer au billard** to play billiards; **2** billiard table.

billard américain *noun Masc.* pool.

billard anglais *noun Masc.* snooker.

billard électrique *noun Masc.* pinball machine.

bille *noun Fem.* **1** marble; **jouer aux billes** to play marbles; **2** billiard ball.

billet *noun Masc.* **1** note, banknote; **un billet de cent euros** a hundred-euro note; **2** ticket; **un billet de train** a train ticket.

billion *noun Masc.* billion.

biochimie *noun Fem.* biochemistry.

biographie *noun Fem.* biography.

biologie *noun Fem.* biology.

biologique *adjective* **1** biological; **2** organically grown.

biologiste *noun Masc. & Fem.* biologist.

bip *noun Masc.* beep; **'après le bip sonore'** 'after the tone' (*on an answering machine*).

biscotte *noun Fem.* continental toast.

biscuit *noun Masc.* biscuit.

bise *noun Fem.* (*informal*) kiss; **faire la bise à quelqu'un** to kiss somebody on the cheek; **grosses bises** lots of love.

bissextile *adjective* **une année bissextile** a leap year.

bistro, bistrot *noun Masc.* bistro, cafe.

bizarre *adjective* odd, strange.

blague *noun Fem.* (*informal*) **1** joke; **sans blague!** no kidding!; **2** trick; **faire une blague à quelqu'un** to play a trick on somebody.

blaguer *verb* [1] (*informal*) to joke.

blaireau (*plural* **blaireaux**) *noun Masc.* **1** badger; **2** shaving brush.

blâmer *verb* [1] **1** to criticize; **2** to blame.

blanc *noun Masc.* **1** white; **peint en blanc** painted white; **2** white meat, breast; **3** white wine; **4** blank; **laisser un blanc** to leave a blank.

blanc *adjective* (Fem. **blanche**) **1** white; **2** blank; **une feuille blanche** a blank sheet of paper.

Blanc, Blanche *noun Masc., Fem.* white man, white woman.

blanche *adjective* SEE **blanc.**

blanchir *verb* [2] to whiten.

blanchisserie *noun Fem.* laundry.

blé *noun Masc.* wheat.

blessé, blessée *noun Masc., Fem.* injured person, casualty.

blessé *adjective* injured.

blesser *verb* [1] **1** to hurt, to injure; **2 se blesser** to hurt oneself; **tu t'es blessé?** did you hurt yourself?

blessure *noun Fem.* **1** injury; **2** wound.

bleu[1] *noun Masc., adjective* blue; **peint en bleu** painted blue; **bleu marine** navy blue.

bleu[2] *noun Masc.* bruise.

bleuet *noun Masc.* cornflower.

bloc *noun Masc.* **1** block; **un bloc de ciment** a block of cement; **2 un bloc de papier à lettres** a writing pad.

bloc-notes *noun Masc.* notepad.

blond *adjective* blonde, fair-haired.

bloqué *adjective* **1** blocked; **2** jammed; **3** stuck.

bloquer *verb* [1] **1** to block; **2** to jam.

blouse *noun Fem.* overall.

blouson *noun Masc.* jacket.

blue-jean *noun Masc.* jeans; **j'ai acheté un blue-jean** I bought a pair of jeans.

bobine *noun Fem.* reel.

bocal (*plural* **bocaux**) *noun Masc.* jar.

bœuf *noun Masc.* **1** bullock; **2** beef; **est-ce que tu aimes le bœuf?** do you like beef?

bof *exclamation* (*informal*) 'c'était bien hier soir?' – 'bof!' 'did you have a good time last night?' – 'nothing special'.

bohémien, bohémienne *noun Masc., Fem.* gipsy.

boire *verb* [22] to drink; **qu'est-ce que tu veux boire?** what would you like to drink?; **il n'y a rien à boire** there's nothing to drink.

bois *noun Masc.* wood; **une table en bois** a wooden table; ★ **avoir la gueule de bois** (*informal*) to have a hangover (*literally: to have a mouth made of wood*).

boisson *noun Fem.* drink; **une boisson fraîche** a cold drink.

boîte *noun Fem.* 1 tin; **une boîte de sardines** a tin of sardines; 2 box; **une boîte d'allumettes** a box of matches; 3 (*informal*) **une boîte de nuit** a nightclub; **aller dans une boîte** to go to a club; 4 (*informal*) firm, company.

boîte aux lettres *noun Fem.* post box.

boiter *verb* [1] to limp.

bol *noun Masc.* 1 bowl; **un bol de riz** a bowl of rice; 2 (*informal*) luck; **un coup de bol** a stroke of luck; ★ **en avoir ras le bol** (*informal*) to be fed up (*literally: to have a bowlful*); **j'en ai ras le bol d'attendre** I'm fed up with waiting.

bombarder *verb* [1] 1 to bombard; 2 to bomb, to shell.

bombe *noun Fem.* 1 bomb; 2 spray can (*containing hairspray, fly spray, etc*).

bôme *noun Fem.* boom (*of a sail*).

bon (*Fem.* **bonne**) *adjective* 1 good; **un bon repas** a good meal; **bon en français** good at French; 2 **un bon kilomètre** a good kilometre, at least a kilometre; 3 right; **le bon numéro** the right number; **la bonne adresse** the right address; **c'est bon** it's OK, it's fine.

bon *noun* 1 voucher; 2 **cela a du bon** that has its good points; **pour de bon** for good.

bon *adverb* **sentir bon** to smell good (*or nice*); **il fait bon aujourd'hui** it's a nice day today; **il fait bon dans mon appartement** it's lovely and warm in my flat.

bon anniversaire *greeting* happy birthday.

bon appétit *exclamation* enjoy your meal.

bonbon *noun Masc.* sweet.

bonbonne *noun Fem.* 1 **une bonbonne à gaz** a gas cylinder; 2 demijohn.

bond *noun Masc.* leap; **se lever d'un bond** to leap to your feet.

bondé *adjective* crowded, packed; **bondé d'étudiants** packed with students.

bondir *verb* [2] to leap; **bondir de joie** to jump for joy.

bonheur *noun Masc.* 1 happiness; 2 pleasure; **avoir le bonheur de faire** to have the pleasure of doing.

bonhomme (*plural* **bonshommes**) *noun Masc.* fellow, man.

bonhomme de neige *noun Masc.* snowman.

bonjour *greeting* hello, good morning, good afternoon; ★ **être**

simple comme bonjour to be really easy, to be as easy as pie (literally: to be as simple as hello).

bon marché adjective cheap.

bonne noun Fem. maid.

bonne adjective SEE **bon**.

bonne année greeting happy New Year.

bonne chance exclamation good luck.

bonne heure in phrase **de bonne heure** early.

bonne nuit greeting goodnight.

bonnet noun Masc. hat, bonnet.

bon retour exclamation safe journey back.

bon sens noun Masc. common sense.

bonsoir greeting good evening.

bonté noun Fem. kindness.

bon voyage exclamation have a good trip.

boom noun Masc. boom (time of prosperity).

bord noun Masc. **1** edge (of a table, cliff, etc); **2** rim (of a glass, cup, vase, etc); **3** side, edge (of a road, path, etc); **au bord de la route** on the edge of the road; **4** bank (of a stream or lake); **5** **au bord de la mer** at the seaside.

bordeaux adjective maroon.

border verb [1] **1** to line; **bordé d'arbres** tree-lined; **2** to edge, to trim.

bordure noun Fem. **1** border; **2** edge; **3** **en bordure de** on the edge of.

borne noun Fem. **1** kilometre marker (the equivalent of a milestone); **2** bollard.

Bosnie noun Fem. Bosnia.

bosse noun Fem. bump.

bosser verb [1] (informal) to work.

botanique noun Fem. botany.

botanique adjective **les jardins botaniques** the botanic gardens.

botte noun Fem. **1** boot; **des bottes de cuir** leather boots; **des bottes de caoutchouc** wellington boots; **2** **une botte de foin** a bale of hay.

bottine noun Fem. ankle boot.

bouc noun Masc. billy goat.

boucan noun Masc. (informal) din, racket.

bouc émissaire noun Masc. scapegoat.

bouche noun Fem. mouth.

bouche-à-bouche noun Masc. mouth-to-mouth resuscitation.

bouche d'égout noun Fem. manhole.

bouchée noun Fem. mouthful.

boucher[1] verb [1] **1** to cork (a bottle); **2** to block up, to fill (a hole, gap, or crack); **3** **se boucher** to get blocked up; **4** **se boucher le nez** to hold one's nose.

boucher[2] noun Masc., Fem. butcher.

boucherie noun Fem. butcher's (shop).

bouchon noun Masc. **1** cork; **2** screw-cap; **3** traffic jam.

boucle noun Fem. **1** buckle; **2** curl.

bouclé adjective curly.

boucle d'oreille noun Fem. earring.

a
b
c
d
e
f
g
h
i
j
k
l
m
n
o
p
q
r
s
t
u
v
w
x
y
z

a
b
c
d
e
f
g
h
i
j
k
l
m
n
o
p
q
r
s
t
u
v
w
x
y
z

Bouddha noun Masc. Buddha.

bouddhisme noun Masc. Buddhism.

bouder verb [1] **1** to sulk; **2 bouder quelque chose** to stay away from something.

boudin noun Masc. black pudding.

boudin blanc noun Masc. white pudding.

boue noun Fem. mud.

bouée noun Fem. **1** rubber ring; **2** buoy.

bouée de sauvetage noun Fem. lifebelt.

boueux (Fem. **boueuse**) adjective muddy.

bouffe noun Fem. (informal) food.

bouffée noun Fem. **une bouffée d'air frais** a breath of fresh air.

bouffer verb [1] (informal) to eat.

bougeoir noun Masc. candlestick.

bouger verb [52] to move.

bougie noun Fem. **1** candle; **2** spark plug.

bouillabaisse noun Fem. Mediterranean fish soup (made with several varieties of fish and vegetables).

bouillant adjective boiling; **faire cuire à l'eau bouillante** cook in boiling water.

bouillir verb [23] to boil; **faire bouillir le lait** to boil the milk; **le lait bout** the milk is boiling.

bouilloire noun Fem. kettle.

bouillon noun Masc. stock (made with meat, fish, or vegetables).

bouillon-cube noun Masc. stock cube.

bouillotte noun Fem. hot-water bottle.

boulanger, boulangère noun Masc., Fem. baker.

boulangerie noun Fem. bakery, baker's.

boule noun Fem. **1** bowl; **jouer aux boules** to play bowls; **2** scoop (of ice-cream); **vous voulez combien de boules?** how many scoops would you like?

bouleau (plural **bouleaux**) noun Masc. birch tree.

boule de neige noun Fem. snowball.

boulette noun Fem. pellet.

boulette de viande noun Fem. meatball.

boulevard noun Masc. boulevard.

boulevard périphérique noun Masc. ring road.

bouleverser verb [1] **1** to overwhelm, to shatter; **être bouleversé** to be overwhelmed (or shattered); **2** to disrupt (a schedule, plans, etc); **3** to turn upside down.

boulot noun Masc. (informal) **1** work; **j'ai trop de boulot** I've got too much work to do; **c'est un boulot immense** it's a huge amount of work; **2** job; **elle cherche du boulot** she's looking for a job.

boum noun Fem. (informal) party.

bouquet noun Masc. bunch, bouquet (of flowers or herbs).

bouquin noun Masc. (informal) book.

bouquiner verb [1] (informal) to read.

bouquiniste noun Masc. & Fem. secondhand bookseller.

bourdon noun Masc. bumblebee.

bourg noun Masc. market town.

bourgeois, bourgeoise noun Masc., Fem. middle-class person.

bourgeois adjective middle-class.

bourgeon noun Masc. bud.

Bourgogne noun Fem. Burgundy.

bourratif (Fem. **bourrative**) adjective very filling.

bourré adjective **1** bourré de crammed with, stuffed with; **2** drunk.

bourrer verb [1] to cram.

bourse noun Fem. grant.

Bourse noun Fem. stock exchange.

bousculer verb [1] to push, to jostle.

boussole noun Fem. compass.

bout noun Masc. **1** end; au bout de at the end of; **2** tip (of nose or finger); **3** un bout de papier a scrap of paper; un petit bout de fromage a little bit of cheese; **4** au bout de after; au bout d'une demi-heure after half an hour.

bouteille noun Fem. bottle.

boutique noun Fem. shop.

bouton noun Masc. **1** button; **2** spot, pimple.

bouton d'or noun Masc. buttercup.

boxe noun Fem. boxing.

boxeur noun Masc. boxer.

bracelet noun Masc. **1** bracelet; **2** bangle.

bracelet-montre noun Masc. wristwatch.

braise noun Fem. embers (of a fire).

brancard noun Masc. stretcher.

branche noun Fem. branch.

branché adjective (informal) trendy.

brancher verb [1] **1** to plug in (an iron, a television, etc); **2** to connect (electricity, gas, water, telephone).

bras noun Masc. sleeve; en bras de chemise in one's shirtsleeves.

bras de fer noun Masc. arm wrestling.

brasse noun Fem. breaststroke.

brasserie noun Fem. **1** brasserie, cafe-restaurant; **2** brewery.

brave adjective nice (person).

break noun Masc. estate car.

brebis noun Fem. ewe.

bref (Fem. **brève**) adjective short, brief.

Brésil noun Masc. Brazil.

brésilien noun Masc. Brazilian Portuguese (language).

brésilien, brésilienne adjective Brazilian.

Brésilien, Brésilienne noun Masc., Fem. Brazilian.

Bretagne noun Fem. Brittany.

bretelle noun Fem. **1** strap; **2** slip road; **3** des bretelles braces.

breton noun Masc. Breton (language).

Breton, Bretonne noun Masc., Fem. Breton.

breton (Fem. **bretonne**) adjective Breton.

brevet noun Masc. certificate.

bribes plural noun Fem. bits, fragments.

bricolage noun Masc. DIY, do-it-yourself.

bricoler verb [1] to do DIY.

bricoleur, bricoleuse noun Masc., Fem. DIY enthusiast.

brièvement adverb briefly.

brillamment adverb brilliantly.

brillant adjective 1 shiny; 2 brilliant.

briller verb [1] to shine.

brin noun Masc. sprig (of herb or plant); **un brin d'herbe** a blade of grass.

brindille noun Fem. twig.

brioche noun Fem. brioche, bun.

brique noun Fem. 1 brick; 2 carton (of fruit-juice, milk, etc).

briquet noun Masc. lighter.

brise noun Fem. breeze.

briser verb [1] to break.

britannique adjective British.

Britannique noun Masc. & Fem. British person; **les Britanniques** the British.

brocante noun Fem. 1 junk shop; 2 second-hand goods.

broche noun Fem. 1 brooch; 2 spit (for roasting).

brochet noun Masc. pike.

brochette noun Fem. 1 skewer; 2 kebab; **une brochette de viande** a meat kebab.

brochure noun Fem. 1 booklet; 2 brochure.

brocolis plural noun Masc. broccoli.

broder verb [1] to embroider.

broderie noun Fem. embroidery; **des broderies** embroidery.

bronchite noun Fem. bronchitis; **avoir une bronchite** to have bronchitis.

bronzage noun Masc. suntan.

bronzer verb [1] to tan.

brosse noun Fem. brush.

brosse à cheveux noun Fem. hairbrush.

brosse à dents noun Fem. toothbrush.

brosser verb [1] 1 to brush; 2 **se brosser les dents** to brush your teeth.

brouette noun Fem. wheelbarrow.

brouillard noun Masc. fog.

brouillon noun Masc. rough draft.

bru noun Fem. daughter-in-law.

brugnon noun Masc. nectarine.

bruit noun Masc. 1 noise; **entendre un bruit** to hear a noise; **entendre le bruit d'une voiture** to hear the sound of a car; 2 rumour.

brûlant adjective 1 boiling hot; 2 burning hot.

brûlé noun Masc. **un goût de brûlé** a burnt taste; **ça sent le brûlé** there's a smell of burning.

brûler verb [1] 1 to burn; 2 **se brûler** to burn yourself.

brûlure noun Fem. burn.

brume noun Fem. mist.

brun adjective 1 brown; 2 dark-haired.

brushing noun Masc. blow-dry; **se faire faire un brushing** to have a blow-dry.

brut adjective 1 raw (material); 2 crude (oil); 3 gross (income); 4 dry (champagne).

brutal (Masc. plural **brutaux**) adjective **1** violent, brutal; **2** sudden.

brutalement adverb **1** suddenly; **2** violently.

Bruxelles noun Brussels.

bruyant adjective noisy, loud.

bruyère noun Fem. heather.

bu verb SEE **boire**.

bûche noun Fem. log.

budget noun Masc. budget.

buffet noun Masc. **1** sideboard; **2** buffet.

buisson noun Masc. bush.

buissonnière adjective **faire l'école buissonnière** to play truant.

Bulgarie noun Fem. Bulgaria.

bulle noun Fem. bubble.

bulletin noun Masc. report, bulletin.

bulletin de salaire noun Masc. payslip.

bulletin scolaire noun Masc. school report.

bureau (plural **bureaux**) noun Masc. **1** desk; **elle est à son bureau** she is at her desk; **2** office; **au bureau** at (or to) the office.

bureaucratie noun Fem. bureaucracy.

bureau de poste noun Masc. post office.

bureau de tabac noun Masc. tobacconist's.

bureau de tourisme noun Masc. tourist information office.

burin noun Masc. chisel.

bus noun Masc. bus.

buse noun Fem. buzzard.

buste noun Masc. bust.

but noun Masc. **1** goal, aim, purpose; **2** goal (in football, hockey); **marquer un but** to score a goal; **3** target.

buté adjective stubborn.

buvable adjective drinkable.

buvard noun Masc. blotter; **du papier buvard** blotting paper.

buvette noun Fem. bar (at a dance, village fair, etc).

buvez, buvons verb SEE **boire**.

Cc

ça pronoun **1** that, this; **donne-moi ça** give me that; **ça c'est un moineau** that's a sparrow; **2 comment ça va?,ça va?** how are you?; **ça va bien merci** I'm fine thanks; **3 c'est ça** that's right; **ça ne fait rien** it doesn't matter.

çà adverb **çà et là** here and there.

cabane noun Fem. hut, shed.

cabas noun Masc. shopping bag.

cabillaud noun Masc. cod.

cabine noun Fem. **1** cubicle; **cabine de douche** shower cubicle; **cabine d'essayage** fitting room (in a clothes shop); **2** cabin (on a ship); **3** cab (on a lorry).

cabinet noun Masc. **1** office (of a solicitor); **2** surgery (of a doctor or dentist); **3** **cabinet de médecins** medical practice.

cabine téléphonique noun Fem. phone box.

a
b
c
d
e
f
g
h
i
j
k
l
m
n
o
p
q
r
s
t
u
v
w
x
y
z

cabinets plural noun Masc. toilet.

câble noun Masc. **1** cable; **2** rope.

câblé adjective être câblé to have cable television.

cabosser verb [1] to dent.

cacahuète noun Fem. peanut; des cacahuètes grillées roasted peanuts.

cacao noun Masc. cocoa.

cache noun Fem. hiding place.

caché adjective hidden.

cache-cache noun Masc. jouer à cache-cache to play hide and seek.

cachemire noun Masc. **1** cashmere; **2** motif cachemire paisley pattern.

cache-nez noun Masc. (thick) scarf.

cache-pot noun Masc. flowerpot holder.

cacher verb [1] **1** to hide; cacher quelque chose to hide something; elle a caché son portefeuille dans un tiroir she's hidden her wallet in a drawer; **2** se cacher to hide; il s'est caché derrière la porte he hid behind the door.

cachet noun Masc. **1** tablet; un cachet d'aspirine an aspirin; **2** official stamp (made with a rubber stamp); **3** le cachet de la poste the postmark.

cachette noun Fem. **1** hiding place; **2** en cachette secretly, on the sly.

cachot noun Masc. dungeon.

cactus noun Masc. cactus.

cadavre noun Masc. corpse, body.

caddie noun Masc. trolley (in the supermarket).

cadeau (plural cadeaux) noun Masc. present; faire un cadeau à quelqu'un to give somebody a present; du papier cadeau wrapping-paper; je vous fais un paquet-cadeau? shall I gift-wrap it for you?

cadenas noun Masc. padlock.

cadence noun Fem. rhythm.

cadet, cadette noun Masc., Fem. younger child, youngest child.

cadet (Fem. cadette) adjective younger, youngest.

cadran noun Masc. **1** face (of a watch or clock); **2** dial (on an instrument such as the speedometer in a car).

cadran solaire noun Masc. sundial.

cadre noun Masc. **1** frame (of a picture, mirror, or window); **2** surroundings, setting; **3** executive (a person with a management job in a company); **4** frame (of a bicycle).

cafard noun Masc. **1** cockroach; **2** depression; avoir le cafard to be down in the dumps.

café noun Masc. **1** coffee; café instantané, café soluble instant coffee; café moulu ground coffee; café en grains coffee beans; café au lait coffee with milk; prendre un café to have a coffee; **2** cafe.

café-crème noun Masc. white coffee.

caféine noun Fem. caffeine.

cafétéria noun Fem. cafeteria.

cafetière noun Fem. **1** coffee pot; **2** coffee maker.

cage noun Fem. cage.

cageot noun Masc. crate.

cagibi noun Masc. store cupboard.

cagnotte noun Fem. **1** kitty (of money); **2** jackpot.

cagoule noun Fem. hood.

cahier noun Masc. **1** exercise book; **2** notebook.

caille noun Fem. quail.

cailler verb [1] to curdle.

caillou (plural **cailloux**) noun Masc. pebble, stone.

caisse noun Fem. **1** till, cash register; **2** cash desk; **3** checkout (in a supermarket); **4** box, crate.

caisse à outils noun Fem. toolbox.

caisse d'épargne noun Fem. savings bank.

caissier, caissière noun Masc., Fem. **1** checkout assistant; **2** cashier.

cajou noun **une noix de cajou** a cashew nut.

cake noun Masc. fruit cake.

calamité noun Fem. disaster, calamity.

calcaire noun Masc. **1** limestone; **2** furring (the sediment which clogs up kettles, steam irons, etc).

calcaire adjective **eau calcaire** hard water; **l'eau ici est très calcaire** the water here is very hard.

calcium noun Masc. calcium.

calcul noun Masc. **1** calculation; **2** arithmetic.

calculatrice noun Fem. pocket calculator.

calculer verb [1] to calculate, to work out.

calculette noun Fem. pocket calculator.

caleçon noun Masc. **1** boxer shorts; **2** leggings.

calembour noun Masc. pun, play on words.

calendrier noun Masc. **1** calendar; **2** schedule.

calepin noun Masc. notebook.

caler verb [1] **1** to wedge; **2** to prop up; **3 ma voiture a calé** my car stalled.

calibre noun Masc. **1** size, grade (of eggs, fruit, or vegetables); **2** calibre, bore (of a gun).

câlin noun Masc. cuddle; **fais-moi un câlin** give me a cuddle (usually said to a child); **fais un câlin à ta grand-mère** give your gran a cuddle.

câlin adjective affectionate.

câliner verb [1] to cuddle.

calmant noun Masc. sedative.

calmant adjective soothing.

calmar noun Masc. squid.

calme noun Masc. peace and quiet.

calme adjective **1** calm; **2** quiet.

calmement adverb calmly.

calmer verb [1] **1 calmer quelqu'un** to calm somebody down; **2 se calmer** to calm down; **calme-toi** calm down; **3** to soothe; **l'aspirine a calmé la douleur** the aspirin soothed the pain.

calorie noun Fem. calorie.

calque *noun Masc.* **un calque** a tracing; **papier-calque** tracing paper.

calvados *noun Masc.* calvados *(apple brandy made in Normandy).*

camarade *noun Masc. & Fem.* friend; **camarade de classe** classmate.

cambriolage *noun Masc.* burglary.

cambrioler *verb* [1] **cambrioler une maison** to burgle a house; **ils ont été cambriolés** they were burgled.

cambrioleur, cambrioleuse *noun Masc., Fem.* burglar.

caméra *noun Fem.* cine-camera.

caméscope *noun Masc.* camcorder.

camion *noun Masc.* truck, lorry.

camion-citerne *noun Masc.* tanker lorry.

camionnette *noun Fem.* van.

camionneur *noun Masc.* lorry driver, truck driver.

camp *noun Masc.* camp.

campagnard, campagnarde *noun Masc., Fem.* country person.

campagnard *adjective* country; **la vie campagnarde** country life.

campagne *noun Fem.* **1** country, countryside; **à la campagne** in the country, in the countryside; **aller se promener à la campagne** to go for a country walk; **2** campaign.

camper *verb* [1] to camp.

campeur, campeuse *noun Masc., Fem.* camper.

camping *noun Masc.* **1** camping; **faire du camping** to go camping;

2 un camping, un terrain de camping a campsite.

camping-car *noun Masc.* camper van.

camping-gaz™ *noun Masc.* camping stove.

Canada *noun Masc.* Canada; **au Canada** in (*or* to) Canada.

canadien (*Fem.* **canadienne**) *adjective* Canadian.

Canadien, Canadienne *noun Masc., Fem.* Canadian.

canal (*plural* **canaux**) *noun Masc.* canal.

canapé *noun Masc.* sofa.

canapé-lit *noun Masc.* sofa bed.

canard *noun Masc.* duck.

canari *noun Masc.* canary.

cancer *noun Masc.* cancer; **avoir un cancer** to have cancer.

Cancer *noun Masc.* Cancer (*sign of the Zodiac*).

candidat, candidate *noun Masc., Fem.* **1** candidate; **2** applicant.

candidature *noun Fem.* **poser sa candidature à un poste** to apply for a job.

cane *noun Fem.* female duck.

caneton *noun Masc.* duckling.

canette *noun Fem.* **une canette de bière** a small bottle of beer.

canevas *noun Masc.* canvas.

caniche *noun Masc.* poodle.

canicule *noun Fem.* **1** scorching heat; **2** heat wave.

canif *noun Masc.* penknife.

caniveau (*plural* **caniveaux**) *noun Masc.* gutter.

canne *noun Fem.* walking stick.

canne à pêche *noun Fem.* fishing rod.

canne à sucre *noun Fem.* sugar cane.

cannelle *noun Fem.* cinnamon.

canoë *noun Masc.* 1 canoe; 2 **faire du canoë** to go canoeing.

canon *noun Masc.* 1 gun; 2 barrel (*of a gun*); 3 cannon.

canot *noun Masc.* small boat, dinghy; **un canot pneumatique** a rubber (*or* inflatable) dinghy.

canot de sauvetage *noun Masc.* lifeboat.

cantatrice *noun Fem.* opera singer.

cantine *noun Fem.* canteen; **manger à la cantine** to have school lunch.

caoutchouc *noun Masc.* 1 rubber; **des bottes en caoutchouc** wellington boots; 2 rubber band.

cap *noun Masc.* 1 cape, headland; 2 course (*of a ship*).

capable *adjective* capable; **être capable de faire** to be capable of doing.

capacité *noun Fem.* 1 ability; 2 capacity.

cape *noun Fem.* cape, cloak.

capitaine *noun Masc.* captain; **le capitaine des pompiers** the chief fire officer.

capital (*plural* **capitaux**) *noun Masc.* capital (*financial*).

capital *adjective* 1 **d'une importance capitale** of major importance; 2 **une question**

capitale a key question; 3 **la peine capitale** capital punishment.

capitale *noun Fem.* capital city; **la capitale française** the French capital.

capot *noun Masc.* bonnet (*of a car*).

câpre *noun Fem.* caper.

caprice *noun Masc.* 1 whim; 2 tantrum; **faire un caprice** to throw a tantrum.

Capricorne *noun Masc.* Capricorn (*sign of the Zodiac*).

capsule *noun Fem.* 1 cap, top (*of a bottle*); 2 capsule.

capter *verb* [1] 1 **capter une chaîne (de télévision)** to get a (television) channel; 2 **capter l'attention de quelqu'un** to catch somebody's attention.

captif, captive *noun Masc., Fem.* captive.

captivant *adjective* 1 fascinating; 2 gripping, riveting.

captivité *noun Fem.* captivity; **être gardé en captivité** to be kept in captivity.

capturer *verb* [1] to capture.

capuche *noun Fem.* hood.

capuchon *noun Masc.* 1 hood; 2 top, cap (*of a pen*).

capucine *noun Fem.* nasturtium.

car[1] *conjunction* because.

car[2] *noun Masc.* coach, bus; **voyager en car** to travel by coach; **un voyage en car** a coach journey.

carabine *noun Fem.* rifle.

caractère *noun Masc.* 1 character, nature; **avoir mauvais caractère** to be bad-tempered; 2 character; **leur maison a**

a b c d e f g h i j k l m n o p q r s t u v w x y z

beaucoup de caractère their house has a lot of character; **3** character, letter; **en gros caractères** in large print.

caractéristique *noun Fem., adjective* characteristic.

carafe *noun Fem.* carafe, jug (*for wine or water*).

Caraïbes *noun plural Fem.* **les îles Caraïbes** the Caribbean Islands; **aller aux Caraïbes** to go to the Caribbean.

caramel *noun Masc.* **1** caramel; **2** toffee.

caravane *noun Fem.* caravan.

carbone *noun Masc.* **1** carbon; **2** carbon paper.

carbonisé *adjective* burnt to a cinder.

carburant *noun Masc.* fuel.

carburateur *noun Masc.* carburettor.

carcasse *noun Fem.* carcass.

cardiaque *adjective* **une crise cardiaque** a heart attack.

cardinal (*plural* **cardinaux**) *noun Masc.* **1** cardinal; **2** cardinal number.

carême *noun Masc.* Lent.

caresser *verb* [1] to stroke, to caress.

cargaison *noun Fem.* cargo.

caricature *noun Fem.* caricature.

caricaturiste *noun Masc. & Fem.* caricaturist, cartoonist.

carie *noun Fem.* **la carie dentaire** tooth decay; **avoir une carie** to have a hole in your tooth.

carillon *noun Masc.* **1** church bells; **2** wind chimes.

caritatif (*Fem.* **caritative**) *adjective* charitable; **une association caritative** a charity.

carnaval *noun Masc.* carnival.

carnet *noun Masc.* **1** notebook; **2** book (*of tickets or stamps*).

carnet de chèques *noun Masc.* chequebook.

carotte *noun Fem.* carrot.

carpe *noun Fem.* carp.

carpette *noun Fem.* rug.

carré *noun Masc., adjective* square; **un mètre carré** a square metre.

carreau (*plural* **carreaux**) *noun Masc.* **1** floor tile; **2** wall tile; **3** windowpane; **4 du tissu à carreaux** checked fabric; **5 du papier à carreaux** squared paper; **6** diamonds (*suit of playing cards*); **le roi de carreau** the king of diamonds.

carrefour *noun Masc.* crossroads, junction.

carrelage *noun Masc.* **1** tiled floor; **2** tiling, tiles.

carrelet *noun Masc.* plaice.

carrément *adverb* downright, completely; **c'est carrément malhonnête** it's downright dishonest.

carrière *noun Fem.* **1** career; **2** quarry.

carrosserie *noun Fem.* **1** bodywork (*of car, etc*); **2** bodywork repairs.

cartable *noun Masc.* **1** satchel, schoolbag; **2** briefcase.

carte *noun Fem.* **1** card; **2** playing card; **jouer aux cartes** to play cards; **un jeu de cartes** a pack of cards, a card game; **3** map; **4** menu.

carte à jouer *noun Fem.* playing card.

carte à mémoire *noun Fem.* smart card.

carte à microprocesseur *noun Fem.* smart card.

carte à puce *noun Fem.* smart card.

carte bancaire *noun Fem.* bank card.

carte d'abonnement *noun Fem.* season ticket.

carte d'anniversaire *noun Fem.* birthday card.

carte de crédit *noun Fem.* credit card.

carte d'embarquement *noun Fem.* boarding card.

carte de fidelité *noun Fem.* loyalty card.

carte d'identité *noun Fem.* identity card.

carte de séjour *noun Fem.* resident's permit.

carte des vins *noun Fem.* wine list.

carte de téléphone *noun Fem.* telephone card.

carte de visite *noun Fem.* business card.

carte de vœux *noun Fem.* greetings card.

carte postale *noun Fem.* postcard.

carte routière *noun Fem.* road map.

carte SIM *noun Fem.* SIM card.

carte téléphonique *noun Fem.* phonecard.

carton *noun Masc.* **1** cardboard; **une chemise en carton** a cardboard folder; **carton ondulé** corrugated cardboard; **2** cardboard box.

cartouche *noun Fem.* cartridge.

cas *noun Masc.* **1** case; **au cas où tu oublierais** in case you forget; **en aucun cas** on no account; **en tout cas** in any case, at any rate; **2** case; **trois cas de rougeole** three cases of measles.

cascade *noun Fem.* **1** waterfall; **2** stunt.

cascadeur, cascadeuse *noun Masc., Fem.* stuntman, stuntwoman.

case *noun Fem.* **1** square (*on a board game*); **2** box (*on a form*); **3** hut.

casher *adjective* kosher.

casier *noun Masc.* **1** pigeonhole; **2** locker; **3** rack.

casino *noun Masc.* casino.

casque *noun Masc.* **1** crash helmet; **2** safety helmet, hard hat; **3** headphones, headset.

casquette *noun Fem.* cap; **une casquette de base-ball** a baseball cap.

casse-croûte *noun Masc.* snack.

casse-noisettes *noun Masc.* nutcrackers.

casse-pieds *adjective* (*informal*) **elle est casse-pieds!** she's a pain in the neck!

casser *verb* [1] **1** to break; **casser un verre** to break a glass; **2 se casser** to break; **le verre s'est**

a
b
c
d
e
f
g
h
i
j
k
l
m
n
o
p
q
r
s
t
u
v
w
x
y
z

cassé the glass broke; **3 se casser la jambe** to break your leg; ★ **se casser la tête** to go to a lot of trouble (*literally: to break your head*); **ne te casse pas la tête!** don't go to a lot of trouble!.

casserole noun Fem. saucepan.

casse-tête noun Masc. **1** puzzle; **2** problem.

cassette noun Fem. cassette, tape.

cassis noun Masc. blackcurrant; **sirop de cassis** blackcurrant cordial.

cassoulet noun Masc. oven-baked beans (*with meat and sausage*).

castor noun Masc. beaver.

catalogue noun Masc. catalogue.

catastrophe noun Fem. disaster, catastrophe.

catch noun Masc. wrestling.

catcheur, catcheuse noun Masc., Fem. wrestler.

catégorie noun Fem. category.

cathédrale noun Fem. cathedral.

catholicisme noun Masc. (Roman) Catholicism.

catholique noun Masc. & Fem., adjective (Roman) Catholic.

cauchemar noun Masc. nightmare; **faire un cauchemar** to have a nightmare.

cause noun Fem. **1** cause; **la cause du problème** the cause of the problem; **2 à cause de** because of; **3 la cause de quelque chose** the reason for something; **fermé pour cause de maladie** closed for reasons of illness; **4** cause; **une bonne cause** a good cause.

causer verb [1] **1** to cause; **2** to talk, to chat; **causer de quelque chose** to talk (*or* chat) about something; **causer avec quelqu'un** to talk (*or* chat) to somebody.

caution noun Fem. **1** deposit (*when renting a flat or house*); **2** bail.

cavalier, cavalière noun Masc., Fem. rider.

cave noun Fem. cellar.

caveau (plural **caveaux**) noun Masc. vault.

caverne noun Fem. cave.

ce[1], **cet** (*before a vowel or mute 'h'*) (Fem. **cette**) adjective **1** this, that; **ce stylo ne marche pas** this pen doesn't work; **cette semaine** this week; **ce couteau-ci** this knife; **2** that; **passe-moi cette assiette** pass me that plate; **cette chaise-là** that chair; **3 cette nuit** last night, tonight.

ce[2], **c'** (*before an 'e'*) pronoun **1** this, that, it; **qui est-ce?** who is it?; **c'est moi** it's me; **qu'est-ce que c'est?** what is it?; **c'est la première maison à gauche** it's the first house on the left; **2** he, she, they; **c'est un médecin** he's a doctor; **ce sont les enfants de Paul** they're Paul's children; **3 ce qui** what; **mange ce qui reste** eat what's left; **4 ce que** what; **prends ce que tu veux** take what you want; **5 c'est tout ce qui reste** that's all that's left; **prends tout ce que tu veux** take everything you want.

ceci pronoun this; **ceci n'est pas à moi** this is not mine.

cécité noun Fem. blindness.

céder verb [24] **1** to give in; **2** 'cédez le passage' 'give way' (at a road junction); **3** céder sa place to give up your seat; **4** céder à quelque chose to give in to something.

cédille noun Fem. cedilla.

cèdre noun Masc. cedar.

ceinture noun Fem. **1** belt; **2** waistband; **3** waist.

ceinture de sauvetage noun Fem. lifebelt.

ceinture de sécurité noun Fem. seatbelt.

cela pronoun this, that, it ('cela' is used in the same way as 'ça' but is more formal); **cela ne me concerne pas** that does not concern me; **cela ne fait rien** that doesn't matter.

célébration noun Fem. celebration.

célèbre adjective famous.

célébrer verb [24] to celebrate.

céleri noun Masc. celery.

célibataire noun Masc. & Fem. **1** bachelor; **2** single woman.

célibataire adjective single; **elle est célibataire** she's single.

celle pronoun SEE celui.

celle-ci pronoun SEE celui-ci.

celle-là pronoun SEE celui-là.

celles pronoun SEE ceux.

celles-ci pronoun SEE ceux-ci.

celles-là pronoun SEE ceux-là.

cellule noun Fem. **1** (prison) cell; **2** cell (in biology and medicine); **3** unit.

celui, celle pronoun the one; **'quel livre?'** – **'celui qui est sur la table'** 'which book?' – 'the one on the table'; **'quelle casserole?'** – **'celle qui est sur la cuisinière'** 'which saucepan?' – 'the one on the cooker'.

celui-ci, celle-ci pronoun this one.

celui-là, celle-là pronoun that one.

cendre noun Fem. ash; **les cendres** the ashes.

cendrier noun Masc. ashtray.

Cendrillon noun Cinderella.

censé adjective supposed; **être censé faire/être** to be supposed to do/be; **je suis censé être là à dix heures** I'm supposed to be there at ten o'clock.

cent[1] number a hundred, one hundred; **trois cents personnes** three hundred people; **deux cent cinquante personnes** two hundred and fifty people (note that there is no 's' on 'cent' when it is followed by another number).

cent[2] noun Masc. cent (one hundredth of a euro or dollar).

centaine noun Fem. **une centaine de personnes** a hundred people, a hundred or so people; **plusieurs centaines de personnes** several hundred people; **des centaines de lettres** hundreds of letters.

centenaire noun Masc. centenary.

centième number hundredth.

centime noun Masc. **1** cent (one hundredth of a euro); **2** centime (one hundredth of former French currency: the franc).

centimètre noun Masc. **1** centimetre; **un centimètre carré**

a
b
c
d
e
f
g
h
i
j
k
l
m
n
o
p
q
r
s
t
u
v
w
x
y
z

a square centimetre; **un centimètre cube** a cubic centimetre; **2** tape measure.

central noun Masc. **un central téléphonique** a telephone exchange.

central adjective (Masc. plural **centraux**) **1** central; **2** main.

centrale noun Fem. power station; **une centrale nucléaire** a nuclear power station.

centraliser verb [1] to centralize.

centre noun Masc. centre; **au centre de** in the centre of.

centre commercial noun Masc. shopping centre, mall.

centre de loisirs noun Masc. leisure centre.

centre sportif noun Masc. sports centre.

centre-ville noun Masc. town centre, city centre.

cependant adverb however.

cercle noun Masc. circle; **en cercle** in a circle.

cercueil noun Masc. coffin.

céréale noun Fem. cereal, grain.

cérémonie noun Fem. ceremony.

cerf noun Masc. stag.

cerf-volant noun Masc. kite.

cerise noun Fem. cherry.

cerisier noun Masc. cherry tree.

certain adjective **1** certain, sure; **être certain de** to be certain (*or* sure) of; **2** certain; **un certain nombre de** a certain number of; **3** some; **certaines personnes** some people.

certains pronoun some; **certains de mes amis** some of my friends.

certainement adverb **1** most probably; **2** certainly; **3** of course.

certes adverb admittedly.

certificat noun Masc. certificate.

certifier verb [1] to certify.

cerveau (plural **cerveaux**) noun Masc. **1** brain; **2** mind.

ces adjective **1** these; **c'est Sara qui m'a acheté ces fleurs** it was Sara who bought me these flowers; **2** those; **ces livres que je t'ai prêtés** those books I lent you; **ces arbres-là** those trees.

CES noun Masc. (*Collège d'enseignement secondaire*) secondary school (*from 11 to 15, when students can go on to a 'lycée' for a further 3 years*).

cesse noun Fem. **sans cesse** constantly.

cesser verb [1] to stop; **cesser de faire** to stop doing.

cessez-le-feu noun Masc. ceasefire.

c'est-à-dire phrase that is, that's to say.

cet, **cette** adjective SEE **ce**.

ceux, **celles** pronoun the ones; **'quels livres?' – 'ceux qui sont sur la table'** 'which books?' – 'the ones on the table'; **'quelles chaussettes?' – 'celles que tu m'as prêtées hier'** 'which socks?' – 'the ones you lent me yesterday' SEE **celui**.

ceux-ci, **celles-ci** pronoun these ones.

ceux-là, **celles-là** pronoun those ones.

chacal noun Masc. jackal.

chacun, chacune *pronoun*
1 each; **ils ont chacun un billet** they each have a ticket; **2** everyone; **comme chacun sait** as everyone knows.

chagrin *noun Masc.* grief.

chaîne *noun Fem.* **1** chain; **2** channel (*on TV*).

chaîne hi-fi *noun Fem.* hi-fi system.

chaîne laser *noun Fem.* CD player.

chaîne stéréo *noun Fem.* stereo system.

chair *noun Fem.* **1** flesh; **2** meat; **la chair à saucisse** sausage meat; ★ **avoir la chair de poule** to have goose pimples (*literally: to have hen's flesh*).

chaise *noun Fem.* chair.

châle *noun Masc.* shawl.

chalet *noun Masc.* chalet.

chaleur *noun Fem.* heat, warmth.

chaleureux (*Fem.* **chaleureuse**) *adjective* warm.

chambre *noun Fem.* **1** bedroom; **dans ma chambre** in my bedroom; **2** (hotel) room; **une chambre pour une personne** a single room; **une chambre pour deux personnes** a double room; **3** **la musique de chambre** chamber music.

chambre d'amis *noun Fem.* spare bedroom.

chambre de commerce *noun Fem.* chamber of commerce.

chambres d'hôte *plural noun Fem.* bed and breakfast.

chameau (*plural* **chameaux**) *noun Masc.* camel.

champ *noun Masc.* field.

champagne *noun Masc.* champagne.

champ de bataille *noun Masc.* battlefield.

champ de courses *noun Masc.* racetrack.

champignon *noun Masc.* **1** mushroom; **des champignons de Paris** button mushrooms; **2** fungus.

champion, championne *noun Masc., Fem.* champion.

championnat *noun Masc.* championship.

chance *noun Fem.* **1** luck; **un coup de chance** a stroke of luck; **Bonne chance!** Good luck!; **j'ai eu la chance de pouvoir passer un an en France** I was lucky enough to be able to spend a year in France; **avoir de la chance** to be lucky; **tu as de la chance d'avoir une sœur pareille!** you're lucky to have a sister like that!; **2** chance.

chancelier *noun Masc.* chancellor.

chandail *noun Masc.* jumper.

chandelier *noun Masc.* **1** candlestick; **2** candelabra.

change *noun Masc.* exchange rate; **bureau de change** bureau de change (*for changing money*).

changeant *adjective* changeable.

changement *noun Masc.* change.

changer *verb* [52] **1** to change; **tu n'as pas changé** you haven't changed; **2** **changer quelque chose** to change something; **changer les draps** to change the sheets; **changer une prise** to change a plug; **3 changer quelque chose** to exchange something (*in a shop*); **4 changer de** to change; **changer de train** to change trains; **changer d'avis** to change your mind; **j'ai changé d'avis** I've changed my mind; **5 se changer** to get changed, to change your clothes.

chanson *noun Fem.* song.

chant *noun Masc.* **1** singing; **2** song.

chantage *noun Masc.* blackmail.

chanter *verb* [1] to sing.

chanteur, chanteuse *noun Masc., Fem.* singer.

chantier *noun Masc.* **1** building site; **2** roadworks.

chantonner *verb* [1] to hum.

chaos *noun Masc.* chaos.

chaotique *adjective* chaotic.

chapeau (*plural* **chapeaux**) *noun Masc.* **1** hat; **2 chapeau!** well done!

chapeau melon *noun Masc.* bowler hat.

chapelle *noun Fem.* chapel.

chapelure *noun Fem.* breadcrumbs.

chapiteau (*plural* **chapiteaux**) *noun Masc.* **1** marquee; **2** big top (*circus tent*).

chapitre *noun Masc.* chapter.

chaque *adjective* each, every.

char *noun Masc.* **1** (*military*) tank; **2** carnival float.

charabia *noun Masc.* (*informal*) gobbledygook, rubbish.

charade *noun Fem.* riddle.

charbon *noun Masc.* coal.

charbon de bois *noun Masc.* charcoal.

charcuterie *noun Fem.* **1** pork butcher's (*selling salads and ready-prepared dishes as well as pork, bacon, ham, sausages, etc*); **2** pork products (*ham, salami, pâté, etc*).

charcutier, charcutière *noun Masc., Fem.* pork butcher.

chardon *noun Masc.* thistle.

charge *noun Fem.* **1** load; **2** responsibility; **avoir la charge de** to be responsible for; **3** charges costs, charges.

charger *verb* [52] **1** to load; **2** to charge (*a battery*).

chariot *noun Masc.* **1** trolley (*in a supermarket*); **1** waggon.

charité *noun Fem.* charity.

charmant *adjective* charming.

charme *noun Masc.* **1** charm; **2** spell.

charmer *verb* [1] to charm.

charnière *noun Fem.* hinge.

charpentier *noun Masc.* carpenter.

charrette *noun Fem.* cart.

charrue *noun Fem.* plough.

charte *noun Fem.* charter.

charter *adjective* **un vol charter** a charter flight.

chasse *noun Fem.* hunting, shooting.

chasse d'eau *noun Fem.* (toilet) flush; **tirer la chasse d'eau** to flush the toilet.

chasse-neige *noun Masc.* snowplough.

chasser *verb* [1] to chase off.

chasseur noun Masc. hunter.

chat noun Masc. cat.

châtaigne noun Fem. sweet chestnut.

châtaignier noun Masc. sweet chestnut tree.

châtain adjective **les cheveux châtains** brown hair.

château (plural **châteaux**) noun Masc. **1** castle; **2** large country house.

château d'eau noun Masc. water tower.

chatouiller verb [1] to tickle.

chatroom noun Masc. chatroom.

chatte noun Fem. (female) cat.

chaud adjective hot, warm; **du lait chaud** hot milk; **un pull chaud** a warm jumper; **j'ai chaud** I'm hot; **il fait chaud ici** it's hot here.

chaudière noun Fem. boiler; **une chaudière à gaz** a gas boiler.

chauffage noun Masc. heating.

chauffage central noun Masc. central heating.

chauffe-eau noun Masc. water heater.

chauffer verb [1] **1** to heat, to heat up; **2** to warm.

chauffeur noun Masc. **1** driver; **un chauffeur de taxi** a taxi driver; **2** chauffeur.

chaumière noun Fem. thatched cottage.

chaussée noun Fem. roadway.

chaussette noun Fem. sock.

chausson noun Masc. **1** slipper; **2** ballet shoe.

chaussure noun Fem. shoe.

chauve adjective bald.

chauve-souris noun Fem. bat.

chavirer verb [1] to capsize.

chef noun Masc. **1** leader; **2** head; **3** boss; **4** chef de cuisine chef.

chef-d'œuvre noun Masc. masterpiece.

chemin noun Masc. **1** country road; **2** track, path; **3** way; **perdre son chemin** to lose your way; **en chemin** on the way.

chemin de fer noun Masc. railway.

cheminée noun Fem. **1** chimney; **2** fireplace; **3** mantlepiece.

cheminot noun Masc. railway worker.

chemise noun Fem. shirt.

chemise de nuit noun Fem. nightdress.

chemisier noun Masc. blouse.

chêne noun Masc. **1** oak tree; **2** oak; **une table en chêne** an oak table.

chenil noun Masc. **1** dog kennel; **2** kennels.

chenille noun Fem. caterpillar.

chèque noun Masc. cheque; **un carnet de chèques** a cheque book.

chèque de voyage noun Masc. traveller's cheque.

chéquier noun Masc. cheque book.

cher (Fem. **chère**) adjective **1** dear; **Chère Anne** Dear Anne; **2** expensive, dear; **pas trop cher** reasonably priced.

cher adverb **coûter cher** to be expensive.

chercher verb [1] **1** to look for; **qu'est-ce que tu cherches?** what are you looking for?; **je cherche**

a
b
c
d
e
f
g
h
i
j
k
l
m
n
o
p
q
r
s
t
u
v
w
x
y
z

mes lunettes I'm looking for my glasses; **je cherche un emploi** I'm looking for a job; **2 chercher quelque chose** to look something up (in a dictionary, for example); **3 aller chercher** to go and get (or fetch) (somebody or something); **je vais chercher des verres** I'll go and get some glasses; **4** to pick up; **je viendrai te chercher à l'école** I'll come and pick you up from school; **5 chercher à faire** to try to do.

chercheur, chercheuse noun Masc., Fem. scientist.

chéri, chérie noun Masc., Fem. darling.

chérir verb [2] to cherish.

cheval (plural **chevaux**) noun Masc. **1** horse; **à cheval** on horseback; **monter à cheval** to ride a horse; **2 faire du cheval** to go horseriding.

cheval à bascule noun Masc. rocking horse.

chevalet noun Masc. easel.

chevet noun Masc. **1** bedhead; **au chevet de** at somebody's bedside; **un livre de chevet** a bedside book; **une lampe de chevet** a bedside lamp; **2** bedside table.

cheveu (plural **cheveux**) noun Masc. **1 un cheveu** a hair; **2 les cheveux** hair; **il a les cheveux blonds** he has blond hair; ★ **avoir un cheveu sur la langue** to have a lisp (literally: to have a hair on one's tongue); ★ **couper les cheveux en quatre** to split hairs (literally: to cut hairs in four).

cheville noun Fem. ankle.

chèvre[1] noun Fem. goat, nanny-goat.

chèvre[2] noun Masc. goat's cheese.

chèvrefeuille noun Masc. honeysuckle.

chevreuil noun Masc. **1** roe deer; **2** venison.

chez preposition **1 chez quelqu'un** at (or to) somebody's house; **je vais chez Paul ce soir** I'm going to Paul's this evening; **elle est chez les Brown** she's at the Browns'; **viens chez moi** come round to my place; **il est chez lui** he's at home; **je rentre chez moi maintenant** I'm going home now; **fais comme chez toi** make yourself at home; **2 chez le boucher** at (or to) the butcher's; **je l'ai rencontrée chez le coiffeur hier** I met her at the hairdresser's yesterday; **je vais chez le coiffeur demain** I'm going to the hairdresser's tomorrow.

chic adjective **1** chic, well-dressed; **2** nice; **c'était vachement chic de ta part** it was really nice of you; **3 Chic!** (informal) Cool!

chicorée noun Fem. **1** endive; **2** chicory powder (for adding to coffee).

chien noun Masc. dog; **'chien méchant'** beware of the dog'.

chien d'aveugle noun Masc. guide dog.

chien de berger noun Masc. sheepdog.

chien de garde noun Masc. guard dog.

chienne noun Fem. (female) dog, bitch.

chiffon *noun Masc.* **1** rag; **2** duster.

chiffre *noun Masc.* figure; **un numéro à cinq chiffres** a five-figure number.

chignon *noun Masc.* bun, chignon.

chimie *noun Fem.* chemistry.

chimique *adjective* chemical.

chimpanzé *noun Masc.* chimpanzee.

Chine *noun Fem.* China.

chinois *noun Masc.* Chinese (*language*).

chinois *adjective* Chinese.

Chinois, Chinoise *noun Masc., Fem.* Chinese man, Chinese woman; **les Chinois** the Chinese.

chiot *noun Masc.* puppy.

chips *noun Fem.* crisp; **un paquet de chips** a packet of crisps.

chirurgical (*Masc. plural* **chirurgicaux**) *adjective* surgical; **une intervention chirurgicale** an operation.

chirurgie *noun Fem.* surgery.

chirurgie au laser *noun Fem.* laser surgery.

chirurgien *noun Masc.* surgeon.

chirurgien-dentiste *noun Masc.* dental surgeon.

choc *noun Masc.* **1** shock; **ça m'a fait un choc** it gave me a shock; **2** crash.

chocolat *noun Masc.* chocolate; **chocolat au lait** milk chocolate; **chocolat blanc** white chocolate; **chocolat en poudre** drinking chocolate; **un gâteau au chocolat** a chocolate cake; **un chocolat chaud** a hot chocolate.

chœur *noun Masc.* **1** choir (*professional*); **2** chorus.

choisir *verb* [2] to choose.

choix *noun Masc.* **1** choice; **un bon choix** a good choice; **un grand choix** a wide choice (*or* variety).

chômage *noun Masc.* unemployment; **être au chômage** to be unemployed.

chômeur, chômeuse *noun Masc., Fem.* unemployed person.

chope *noun Fem.* beer mug.

choquer *verb* [1] to shock.

chorale *noun Fem.* choir (*amateur*).

choriste *noun Masc. & Fem.* **1** member of a choir; **2** member of a chorus; **3** backing singer.

chose *noun Fem.* thing; **les choses qui m'intéressent** the things that interest me; **j'ai plusieurs choses à te dire** I have several things to tell you; **je prends la même chose** I'll have the same.

chou (*plural* **choux**) *noun Masc.* cabbage.

chouchou¹, chouchoute *noun Masc., Fem.* teacher's pet.

chouchou² *noun Masc.* scrunchy (*for holding back your hair*).

choucroute *noun Fem.* sauerkraut (*pickled cabbage with different types of sausage, ham, and bacon*).

chou de Bruxelles *noun Masc.* Brussels sprout.

chouette *noun Fem.* owl.

chouette *adjective* (*informal*) great; **c'est chouette!** that's great!;

a
b
c
d
e
f
g
h
i
j
k
l
m
n
o
p
q
r
s
t
u
v
w
x
y
z

leur maison est très chouette their house is really lovely.

chou-fleur (*plural* **choux-fleurs**) *noun Masc.* cauliflower.

chrétien, chrétienne *noun Masc., Fem., adjective* Christian.

christianisme *noun Masc.* Christianity.

chrome *noun Masc.* chromium.

chronique *noun Fem.* **1** column, page (*devoted to a particular journalist in a newspaper*); **2** (*radio*) programme.

chronique *adjective* chronic.

chronomètre *noun Masc.* stopwatch.

chrysanthème *noun Masc.* chrysanthemum.

chuchoter *verb* [1] to whisper.

chut *exclamation* shh!

chute *noun Fem.* **1** fall; **faire une chute de 5 mètres** to fall 5 metres; **2** chutes de neige snowfall; **chutes de pluie** rainfall; **3** fall, drop (*in price, value, temperature*).

chuter *verb* [1] to fall, to drop.

Chypre *noun Fem.* Cyprus.

ci *adverb* **ce mois-ci** this month; **ces timbres-ci** these stamps; **ces jours-ci** these last few days.

cible *noun Fem.* target.

ciboulette *noun Fem.* de la ciboulette chives.

cicatrice *noun Fem.* scar.

ci-contre *adverb* opposite.

ci-dessous *adverb* below.

ci-dessus *adverb* above.

cidre *noun Masc.* cider.

ciel (*plural* **cieux**) *noun Masc.* **1** sky; **au ciel** in the sky; **2** heaven.

cigale *noun Fem.* cicada.

cigare *noun Masc.* cigar.

cigarette *noun Fem.* cigarette.

cigogne *noun Fem.* stork.

ci-inclus *adjective* enclosed; **la copie ci-incluse** the enclosed copy.

ci-inclus *adverb* enclosed.

ci-joint *adverb* **veuillez trouver ci-joint** please find enclosed (*in a letter*).

cil *noun Masc.* eyelash.

ciment *noun Masc.* cement.

cimetière *noun Masc.* **1** cemetery; **2** graveyard.

cinéaste *noun Masc. & Fem.* film director.

ciné-club *noun Masc.* film club.

cinéma *noun Masc.* **1** cinema; **aller au cinéma** to go to the cinema; **2** (*informal*) play-acting; **arrête ton cinéma!** stop that nonsense!

cinéphile *noun Masc. & Fem.* keen cinema-goer.

cinglé *adjective* (*informal*) crazy.

cinq *number* five; **Lucie a cinq ans** Lucie's five; **à cinq heures** at five o'clock; **le cinq avril** the fifth of April.

cinquantaine *noun Fem.* **une cinquantaine (de)** about fifty; **une cinquantaine de personnes** about fifty people; **avoir la cinquantaine** to be about fifty.

cinquante *number* fifty.

cinquantième *number* fiftieth.

cinquième *noun Fem.* (*in a French school*) the equivalent of Year 8.

cinquième *noun Masc.* **au cinquième** on the fifth floor.

cinquième *adjective* fifth.

cintre *noun Masc.* clothes hanger.

cirage *noun Masc.* shoe polish.

circonférence *noun Fem.* circumference.

circonflexe *noun Masc.* **un accent circonflexe** a circumflex.

circonstance *noun Fem.* circumstance.

circuit *noun Masc.* **1** circuit (*in an athletics stadium*); **2** tour; **3** (*electrical*) circuit.

circulaire *noun Fem., adjective* circular.

circulation *noun Fem.* **1** traffic; **il y a beaucoup de circulation ce soir** there's a lot of traffic this evening; **2** circulation.

circuler *verb* [1] **1** to run (*of a bus or train*); **ce train ne circule pas le dimanche** that train doesn't run on Sundays; **2** to circulate.

cire *noun Fem.* wax.

cirer *verb* [1] to polish.

cirque *noun Masc.* circus; **au cirque** at (*or* to) the circus.

ciseaux *plural noun Masc.* scissors; **une paire de ciseaux** a pair of scissors.

citadin, citadine *noun Masc., Fem.* city dweller.

citation *noun Fem.* quotation.

cité *noun Fem.* **1** city, town; **2** housing estate; **3 une cité universitaire** university halls of residence.

citer *verb* [1] to quote.

citerne *noun Fem.* tank.

citoyen, citoyenne *noun Masc., Fem.* citizen.

citron *noun Masc.* lemon; **une tarte au citron** a lemon tart.

citronnade *noun Fem.* still lemonade.

citronnier *noun Masc.* lemon tree.

citron vert *noun Masc.* lime.

citrouille *noun Fem.* pumpkin.

civet *noun Masc.* stew.

civil *noun Masc.* **1** civilian; **2 un policier en civil** a plain-clothes policeman.

civil *adjective* **1** civilian; **2 un mariage civil** a civil wedding (*as opposed to a church wedding*).

civilisation *noun Fem.* civilization.

civique *adjective* civic.

clair *adjective* **1** light; **bleu clair** light blue; **2 la chambre est très claire** the bedroom is very light; **3** clear.

clair *adverb* clearly; **voir clair** to see clearly.

clair de lune *noun Masc.* moonlight.

clairement *adverb* clearly.

clapier *noun Masc.* rabbit hutch.

claque *noun Fem.* slap.

claqué *adjective* (*informal*) exhausted, wiped out.

claquer *verb* [1] **claquer la porte** to slam the door.

clarifier *verb* [1] to clarify.

clarinette *noun Fem.* clarinet; **jouer de la clarinette** to play the clarinet.

clarté *noun Fem.* **1** light; **2** clarity.

a
b
c
d
e
f
g
h
i
j
k
l
m
n
o
p
q
r
s
t
u
v
w
x
y
z

a
b
c
d
e
f
g
h
i
j
k
l
m
n
o
p
q
r
s
t
u
v
w
x
y
z

classe noun Fem. **1** class; **elle est dans ma classe à l'école** she's in my class (or year) at school; **en classe** in class; **2** classroom; **3 première/deuxième classe** first/second class; **4** (social) class.

classement noun Masc. **1** classification; **2** placing; **3** grading; **4** filing.

classer verb [1] **1** to classify; **2** to grade; **3** to file.

classeur noun Masc. **1** ring binder, file; **2** filing cabinet.

classique adjective **1** classical; **2** classic; **3** usual; **c'est classique!** that's typical!

clavier noun Masc. keyboard.

clé noun Fem. **1** key; **fermer quelque chose à clé** to lock something; **2** spanner.

clef = clé.

clémentine noun Fem. clementine.

clic noun Masc. click (with mouse); **un clic sur le bouton droit de la souris** a right-click; **un clic sur le bouton gauche de la souris** a left-click.

client, cliente noun Masc., Fem. **1** customer; **2** client.

clientèle noun Fem. customers.

cligner verb [1] **cligner des yeux** to blink.

clignotant noun Masc. indicator (on a motor vehicle).

clignoter verb [1] to flash.

climat noun Masc. climate.

climatisation noun Fem. air-conditioning.

climatisé adjective air-conditioned.

clin d'œil noun Masc. wink; **faire un clin d'œil à quelqu'un** to wink at somebody; ★ **en un clin d'œil** in a flash.

clinique noun Fem. clinic, private hospital.

clip noun Masc. **1** video clip; **2** clip brooch; **3** clip-on earring.

cliquer verb [1] **cliquer sur quelque chose** to click on something (using a computer mouse); **cliquer en appuyant sur le bouton gauche de la souris** to left-click; **cliquer deux fois sur l'icône** to double-click the icon.

cliqueter verb [48] **1** to jingle; **2** to rattle.

clochard, clocharde noun Masc., Fem. tramp, down-and-out.

cloche noun Fem. bell.

clocher noun Masc. **1** steeple; **2** bell tower.

cloison noun Fem. **1** partition; **2** partition wall; **3** screen.

cloître noun Masc. cloister.

clos adjective closed.

clôture noun Fem. **1** fence; **2** close; **3** closing.

clou noun Masc. **1** nail; **2** stud.

clou de girofle noun Masc. clove.

clouer verb [1] **clouer quelque chose** to nail something down.

clown noun Masc. clown.

club noun Masc. club; **un club de foot** a football club.

cobaye noun Masc. guinea pig.

Coca™ noun Masc. Coke™.

cocaïne noun Fem. cocaine.

coccinelle noun Fem. ladybird.

cocher verb [1] to tick.

cochon noun Masc. pig.

cochon adjective (Fem. **cochonne**) (informal) dirty (joke, story).

cochon d'Inde noun Masc. guinea pig.

cocktail noun Masc. 1 cocktail; 2 cocktail party.

coco noun Masc. **une noix de coco** a coconut.

cocorico noun Masc. cock-a-doodle-do.

cocotte noun Fem. 1 casserole; 2 hen (in baby talk); 3 chocolate hen (traditionally sold at Easter).

cocotte-minute™ noun Fem. pressure cooker.

code noun Masc. 1 code; **le code de la route** the highway code; 2 **codes** dipped headlights.

code postal noun Masc. postcode.

cœur noun Masc. 1 heart; 2 hearts (suit of playing cards); **le roi de cœur** the king of hearts; **3 par cœur** by heart; **apprendre quelque chose par cœur** to learn something by heart; ★ **avoir mal au cœur** to feel sick.

coffre noun Masc. 1 chest; 2 safe; 3 boot (of a car).

coffre-fort noun Masc. safe.

cogner verb [1] to bump, to bang; **se cogner la tête** to bang your head.

coiffer verb [1] **se coiffer** to brush (or comb) your hair.

coiffeur, coiffeuse¹ noun Masc., Fem. hairdresser.

coiffeuse² noun Fem. dressing table.

coiffure noun 1 hairdressing; 2 hairstyle; **tu as changé de coiffure** you've changed your hairstyle.

coin noun Masc. 1 corner; **au coin** in the corner; **au coin de** in the corner of; 2 **le café du coin** the local cafe; **les gens du coin** the local people; ★ **au coin du feu** by the fireside (literally: in the corner of the fire).

coincé adjective stuck, jammed.

coincer verb [61] to jam.

coïncidence noun Fem. coincidence.

col noun Masc. 1 collar; 2 neck; 3 (mountain) pass.

colère noun Fem. anger; **être en colère** to be angry.

colin noun Masc. hake.

colique noun Fem. diarrhoea.

colis noun Masc. parcel.

collant noun Masc. **un collant** (a pair of) tights.

collant adjective sticky.

colle noun Fem. 1 glue; 2 detention; **une heure de colle** an hour's detention.

collecte noun Fem. collection (of money).

collection noun Fem. collection.

collectionner verb [1] to collect.

collectionneur, collectionneuse noun Masc., Fem. collector.

collège noun Masc. secondary school (from 11 to 15, when students can either leave school altogether or go on to a *'lycée' for a further 3 years*).

collégien, collégienne *noun Masc., Fem.* schoolboy, schoolgirl.

collègue *noun Masc. & Fem.* colleague.

coller *verb* [1] **1** to stick; **2** to stick down; **3** to glue; **4** to press.

collier *noun Masc.* **1** necklace; **2** collar (*for a dog, cat, etc*).

colline *noun Fem.* hill.

collision *noun Fem.* collision.

colombe *noun Fem.* dove.

colonel *noun Masc.* colonel.

colonie *noun Fem.* colony.

colonie de vacances *noun Fem.* holiday camp (*for children*).

colonne *noun Fem.* column.

colonne vertébrale *noun Fem.* spine.

colorant *noun Masc.* colouring.

coloré *adjective* **1** coloured; **2** colourful.

colorer *verb* [1] to colour.

colorier *verb* [1] to colour in.

coloris *noun Masc.* colour; **existe en plusieurs coloris** several colours available.

combat *noun Masc.* **1** fighting; **2 un combat de boxe** a boxing match.

combattant *noun Masc.* **un ancien combattant** a war veteran.

combattre *verb* [21] to fight.

combien *adverb* **1** how much; **tu en veux combien?** how much do you want?; **c'est combien?** how much is it?; **ça coûte combien?** how much does it cost?; **je vous dois combien?** how much do I owe you?, how much is that?; **2** how many; **tu en veux combien?** how many do you want?; **3 combien de** how much; **combien d'argent?** how much money?; **4 combien de** how many; **combien de tasses?** how many cups?; ★ **nous sommes le combien aujourd'hui?** what's the date today? (*literally: we are the the how many today?*).

combinaison *noun Fem.* **1** combination; **2** jumpsuit; **3** overalls; **4** slip, petticoat.

combiné *noun Masc.* receiver (*of a telephone*).

comble *noun Masc.* **1 le comble de** the height of; **le comble du luxe** the height of luxury; **2 ça c'est le comble!** that's the last straw!

comédie *noun Fem.* comedy.

comédien, comédienne *noun Masc., Fem.* actor, actress.

comestible *adjective* edible.

comique *noun Masc.* comic, comedian.

comique *adjective* funny.

comité *noun Masc.* committee.

commandant *noun Masc.* **1** major; **2** squadron leader; **3 commandant-en-chef** commander in chief.

commande *noun Fem.* order; **sur commande** to order.

commander *verb* [1] **1** to order; **avez-vous commandé?** have you ordered?; **2** to be in charge.

comme *preposition* **1** like; **une montre comme la tienne** a watch like yours; **2** like; **comme ça** like this; **3** as a; **travailler comme serveur dans un café** to work as a waiter in a cafe; **4 qu'est-ce que tu veux comme glace?** what kind of ice cream would you like?

comme *conjunction* **1** as; **comme tu veux** as you like; **2** as, since; **comme je suis malade** as (or since) I'm ill; **3** as; **comme je fermais la porte** as I was closing the door; **4 comme si** as if.

comme *adverb* **comme il est gentil!** he's so nice!; **comme c'est bon!** it's so good!; **comme il fait chaud!** it's so hot!; ★ **blanc comme la neige** as white as snow; ★ **fort comme un bœuf** as strong as an ox.

commencement *noun Masc.* beginning, start.

commencer *verb* [61] **1** to begin, to start; **le film a commencé** the film has started; **2** commencer de faire to start (or begin) to do; **elle a commencé à faire ses devoirs** she's started to do her homework; **je commence à comprendre** I'm beginning to understand; **il commence à pleuvoir** it's starting to rain.

comment *adverb* **1** how; **comment as-tu fait ce gâteau?** how did you make this cake?; **je ne sais pas comment le faire** I don't know how to do it; **2 comment vas-tu?** how are you?; **comment ça va?** how are you?; **comment va ta mère?** how's your mother?; **3 comment t'appelles-tu?** what's your name?; **il s'appelle comment, ton frère?** what's your brother's name?; **4 pardon?** **5 comment est**

leur maison?, **elle est comment, leur maison?** what's their house like?

commentaire *noun Masc.* **1** comment; **2** commentary.

commenter *verb* [1] **commenter quelque chose** to comment on something.

commerçant, commerçante *noun Masc., Fem.* shopkeeper.

commerce *noun Masc.* **1** shop; **2 le commerce** business; **je fais des études de commerce** I'm doing business studies; **3 le commerce** trade.

commercial (*Masc. plural* **commerciaux**) *adjective* **1** commercial; **2 un centre commercial** a shopping centre.

commettre *verb* [11] **1 commettre une erreur** to make a mistake; **2 commettre un crime** to commit a crime.

commissariat *noun Masc.* police station.

commission *noun Fem.* **1** committee; **2** commission; **3** message; **4** errand; **5 faire les commissions** to do the shopping.

commode *noun Fem.* chest of drawers.

commode *adjective* **1** convenient, handy; **2** easy.

commun *adjective* **1** common; **2** shared; **3** joint; **4 en commun** in common; **ils n'ont rien en commun** they have nothing in common; **5 en commun** jointly, together; **6 les transports en commun** public transport.

communauté noun Fem.
community.

communication noun Fem.
1 une communication
téléphonique a telephone call;
2 communication; se mettre en
communication avec quelqu'un
to get in touch with someone.

communion noun Fem.
communion.

communiquer verb [1] 1 to
communicate; 2 communiquer
quelque chose to pass something
on.

communisme noun Masc.
communism.

communiste noun Masc. & Fem.,
adjective communist.

compact adjective 1 dense;
2 compact; 3 un disque compact a
compact disc, a CD.

compagnie noun Fem.
1 company, firm; 2 company; elle
m'a tenu compagnie she kept me
company.

compagnie aérienne noun
Fem. airline.

compagnon noun Masc.
companion.

comparable adjective
comparable.

comparaison noun Fem.
comparison; en comparaison de
in comparison with.

comparatif (Fem. **comparative**)
adjective comparative.

comparé adjective comparé à
compared to (or with).

comparer verb [1] to compare.

compartiment noun Masc.
compartment.

compas noun Masc. compass.

compatir verb [2] to sympathize.

compensation noun Fem.
compensation.

compenser verb [1] compenser
quelque chose to compensate for
something.

compétence noun Fem. 1 ability;
2 skill; 3 competence.

compétent adjective competent.

compétitif (Fem. **compétitive**)
adjective competitive.

compétition noun Fem.
competition.

complémentaire adjective
further, supplementary.

complet noun Masc. suit.

complet adjective (Fem. **complète**)
1 complete; 2 total; 3 full (speaking
of a hotel or a train); 4 le pain
complet wholemeal bread.

complètement adverb
completely.

compléter verb [24] 1 to complete;
2 to fill in (a form).

complexe noun Masc., adjective
complex.

complication noun Fem.
complication.

complice noun Masc. & Fem.
accomplice.

compliment noun Masc.
compliment; faire des
compliments à quelqu'un to
compliment somebody.

compliqué adjective complicated.

compliquer verb [1] to
complicate.

complot noun Masc. plot.

comportement noun Masc. behaviour.

comporter verb [1] **1** to include; **2** to consist of; **3 se comporter** to behave.

composé adjective **1 composé de** made up of; **2 une salade composée** a mixed salad.

composer verb [1] **1** to make up; **2** to put together; **3** to compose (music); **4 composer un numéro (de téléphone)** to dial a (telephone) number; **composez le 00 44 pour le Royaume Uni** dial 00 44 for the United Kingdom.

compositeur, compositrice noun Masc., Fem. composer.

composition noun Fem. composition.

composter verb [1] to punch (a ticket); **'n'oubliez pas de composter votre billet'** remember to punch your ticket (in France it is an offence not to punch your ticket on trains and buses at the start of your journey in one of the machines provided for this).

compote noun Fem. stewed fruit; **la compote de pommes** apple puree.

compréhensible adjective understandable.

compréhensif (Fem. **compréhensive**) adjective understanding.

compréhension noun Fem. comprehension; **un test de compréhension** a comprehension test.

comprendre verb [64] **1** to understand; **je comprends** I understand; **j'ai compris** I understood; **j'ai mal compris** I misunderstood; **2** to include; **3 se comprendre** to understand each other; **4 ça se comprend** that's understandable.

comprimé noun Masc. tablet.

compris adjective **1** included; **service compris** service included; **non compris** not included; **2 y compris** including; **tout le monde y compris les enfants** everybody including the children.

compromis noun Masc. compromise.

comptabilité noun Fem. accounting, accountancy.

comptable noun Masc. & Fem. accountant.

compte noun Masc. **1** account; **un compte bancaire** a bank account; **un compte d'épargne** a savings account; **j'ai cent livres sur mon compte** I have a hundred pounds in my account; **2 le compte est bon** the amount is correct; **3 se rendre compte de quelque chose** to realize something; **se rendre compte que** to realize that; **je me suis rendu compte que j'avais oublié mes clés** I realized I had forgotten my keys; **4 tenir compte de quelque chose** to take something into account; **5 en fin de compte** all things considered.

compter verb [1] **1** to count; **compter les visiteurs** to count the visitors; **2 compter sur quelqu'un** to count on somebody; **3** to count

a
b
c
d
e
f
g
h
i
j
k
l
m
n
o
p
q
r
s
t
u
v
w
x
y
z

a

(to be valid); **ça ne compte pas que** that doesn't count.

b

compte rendu noun Masc. report.

c

compteur noun Masc. meter.

d

compteur de vitesse noun Masc. speedometer.

e

comptine noun Fem. nursery rhyme.

f

comptoir noun Masc. **1** counter; **2** bar.

g

concentré adjective concentrated.

h

concentré de tomate noun Masc. tomato puree.

i

concentrer verb [1] **se concentrer (sur)** to concentrate (on).

j

k

conception noun Fem. design.

l

concernant preposition concerning.

m

concerner verb [1] to concern; **en ce qui me concerne** as far as I'm concerned.

n

o

concert noun Masc. concert; **un concert de rock** a rock concert.

p

q

concessionnaire noun Masc. & Fem. dealer, agent.

r

concierge noun Masc. & Fem. caretaker.

s

t

conclure verb [25] to conclude.

conclusion noun Fem. conclusion.

u

concombre noun Masc. cucumber.

v

w

concours noun Masc. competition.

x

concret (Fem. **concrète**) adjective **1** concrete; **2** practical.

y

z

concurrence noun Fem. competition; **il y a beaucoup de**

concurrence there's a lot of competition.

concurrent, concurrente noun Masc., Fem. competitor.

condamner verb [1] to sentence (a criminal).

condition noun Fem. **1** condition; **en bonne condition** in good condition; **2 à condition de/que** provided that; **tu peux emprunter mon vélo à condition de me le rendre ce soir** you can borrow my bike provided you let me have it back this evening; **3 dans ces conditions** in that case.

conditionnel noun Masc. conditional tense.

conditionner verb [1] to package.

conducteur, conductrice noun Masc., Fem. driver.

conduire verb [26] **1** to drive; **apprendre à conduire** to learn to drive; **un permis de conduire** a driving licence; **je te conduis à la gare** I'll drive you to the station; **2** to take; **je vous conduis à votre chambre** I'll take you to your room; **3 se conduire** to behave.

conduite noun Fem. behaviour; **mauvaise conduite** bad behaviour.

conférence noun Fem. **1** lecture; **2** conference.

confesser verb [1] **se confesser** to go to confession.

confiance noun Fem. **1** trust; **avoir confiance en quelqu'un, faire confiance à quelqu'un** to trust somebody; **je te fais confiance** I'll leave it to you; **2** confidence.

confiant *adjective* confident.

confidence *noun Fem.* secret.

confier *verb* [1] **1 confier quelque chose à quelqu'un** to entrust something to somebody; **2 se confier à quelqu'un** to confide in somebody.

confirmation *noun Fem.* confirmation.

confirmer *verb* [1] to confirm.

confiserie *noun Fem.* **1** sweet shop; **1** confectionery.

confisquer *verb* [1] to confiscate.

confit *adjective* **les fruits confits** crystallized fruits.

confiture *noun Fem.* jam; **la confiture d'abricots** apricot jam.

conflit *noun Masc.* conflict.

confondre *verb* [69] to confuse, to mix up.

confort *noun Masc.* comfort; **tout confort** with all mod cons.

confortable *adjective* comfortable.

confrontation *noun Fem.* **1** confrontation; **2** clash.

confus *adjective* **1** confused; **2** embarrassed.

confusion *noun Fem.* **1** confusion; **2** embarrassment.

congé *noun Masc.* **1** holiday (*from work*); **Robert est en congé aujourd'hui** Robert's on holiday today; **quel est ton jour de congé?** when's your day off?; **je pars en congé le dix** I'm on holiday from the tenth; **prendre une semaine de congé** to take a week's holiday; **2** leave; **Sylvie est**

en congé de maladie Sylvie is on sick leave.

congélateur *noun Masc.* freezer.

congeler *verb* [45] to freeze.

congère *noun Fem.* snowdrift.

congestion *noun Fem.* congestion.

congrès *noun Masc.* conference.

conifère *noun Masc.* conifer.

conjoint, conjointe *noun Masc., Fem.* spouse (*husband or wife*).

conjonctivite *noun Fem.* conjunctivitis.

conjugaison *noun Fem.* conjugation.

connaissance *noun Fem.* **1** knowledge; **tes connaissances en français** your knowledge of French; **2** acquaintance; **3** consciousness; **perdre connaissance** to lose consciousness.

connaître *verb* [27] **1** to know; **est-ce que tu connais Gaby?** do you know Gaby?; **je ne connais pas Londres** I don't know London; **je la connais depuis trois ans** I've known her for three years; **2 se connaître** to know each other; **on se connaît** we know each other; **3 s'y connaître en quelque chose** to know about something; **je ne m'y connais pas du tout en informatique** I know absolutely nothing about computers.

connecter *verb* [1] to connect.

connexion *noun Fem.* connection.

connu *adjective* well-known; **elle est très connue en France** she's very well-known in France.

consacrer *verb* [1] to devote.

consciemment *adverb* consciously.

conscience *noun Fem.* conscience; **avoir mauvaise conscience** to have a guilty conscience.

consciencieux *(Fem. consciencieuse)* *adjective* conscientious.

conscient *adjective* 1 aware; **être conscient de quelque chose** to be aware of something; 2 conscious.

conseil *noun Masc.* 1 advice; **un conseil** a piece of advice; **donner un conseil à quelqu'un** to give someone a piece of advice; **des conseils** advice; **suivre les conseils de quelqu'un** to follow someone's advice; 2 council.

conseiller[1], **conseillère** *noun Masc., Fem.* adviser.

conseiller[2] *verb* [1] 1 to advise; **conseiller à quelqu'un de faire** to advise somebody to do; **je te conseille de voir un médecin** I advise you to see a doctor; 2 to recommend; **pouvez-vous me conseiller un dentiste?** Can you recommend me a dentist?

consentement *noun Masc.* consent.

consentir *verb* [58] **consentir à quelque chose** to agree to something.

conséquence *noun Fem.* 1 consequence; 2 **en conséquence** consequently.

conséquent *adjective* **par conséquent** consequently.

conservateur, conservatrice *noun Masc., Fem.* 1 conservative; 2 (museum) curator.

conservation *noun Fem.* 1 conservation; 2 **lait longue conservation** long-life milk.

conserve *noun Fem.* 1 **des conserves** canned food; 2 **en conserve** canned; **des légumes en conserve** canned vegetables.

conserver *verb* [1] 1 to keep; **je t'ai conservé une place** I've kept you a seat; **'à conserver au frais'** 'keep in a cool place'; 2 **se conserver** to keep; **ce fromage se conserve bien** this cheese keeps well.

considérable *adjective* considerable; **un pourcentage considérable des étudiants** a considerable percentage of the students.

considérablement *adverb* considerably.

considération *noun Fem.* consideration.

considérer *verb* [24] to consider.

consigne *noun Fem.* 1 left luggage office; 2 deposit *(on a returnable bottle)*; 3 instructions; **consignes à suivre en cas d'incendie** fire regulations.

consistant *adjective* substantial; **un repas consistant** a substantial meal.

consister *verb* [1] **consister en** to consist of, **to consist in**.

consommateur, consommatrice *noun Masc.,*

Fem. **1** consumer; **2** customer (*in a café*).

consommation *noun Fem.* **1** consumption (*of fuel, electricity, gas*); **2** drink.

consommer *verb* [1] **1** to use (*fuel*); **2** to have a drink (*in a café*).

consonne *noun Fem.* consonant.

conspiration *noun Fem.* conspiracy.

conspirer *verb* [1] to conspire, to plot.

constamment *adverb* constantly.

constant *adjective* constant.

constater *verb* [1] to notice.

constipé *adjective* constipated.

construction *noun Fem.* construction, building.

construire *verb* [26] to build; **construire une maison** to build a house; **faire construire une maison** to have a house built.

consul *noun Masc.* consul.

consulat *noun Masc.* consulate.

consultation *noun Fem.* **1** consultation; **2** (doctor's) surgery hours.

consulter *verb* [1] **1** to consult; **2** to hold surgery.

contact *noun Masc.* contact; **prendre contact avec quelqu'un** to contact somebody.

contacter *verb* [1] to contact.

contagieux (*Fem.* **contagieuse**) *adjective* infectious.

contamination *noun Fem.* contamination.

contaminer *verb* [1] to contaminate.

conte *noun Masc.* tale, story; **un conte de fées** a fairy tale.

contempler *verb* [1] to look at, to contemplate.

contemporain, contemporaine *noun Masc., Fem., adjective* contemporary.

contenant *noun Masc.* container.

conteneur *noun Masc.* container.

contenir *verb* [77] to contain; **'ne contient pas de sucre'** 'does not contain sugar'.

content *adjective* pleased, glad, happy; **être content de quelque chose** to be pleased with something; **elle est très contente de son nouveau travail** she's very pleased with her new job; **je suis content de te voir** I'm pleased to see you.

contenter *verb* [1] **1** to satisfy; **2 se contenter de faire** to content oneself with doing.

contenu *noun Masc.* contents.

contesté *adjective* controversial.

contester *verb* [1] to dispute, to challenge, to question.

contexte *noun Masc.* context.

continent *noun Masc.* continent.

continu *adjective* continuous.

continuation *noun Fem.* continuation.

continuer *verb* [1] to continue, to go on (with); **continue!** go on!; **elle a continué son histoire** she went on with her story; **continuer à faire, continuer de faire** to go on doing; **elle a continué à parler** she went on talking.

contour noun Masc. outline, contour.

contourner verb [1] to go round.

contraceptif noun Masc. contraceptive.

contraception noun Fem. contraception.

contractuel, contractuelle noun Masc., Fem. traffic warden.

contradiction noun Fem. contradiction.

contradictoire adjective contradictory.

contraindre verb [31] to force.

contraire noun Masc. **1** le contraire the opposite; **c'est le contraire de ce que je pensais** it's the opposite of what I thought; **2** au contraire on the contrary.

contraire adjective opposite.

contrairement adverb contrairement à contrary to, unlike; **contrairement à ce qu'il nous a dit** contrary to what he told us.

contrariant adjective annoying.

contrarier verb [1] **1** to upset; **2** to annoy.

contraste noun Masc. contrast.

contraster verb [1] to contrast.

contrat noun Masc. contract.

contravention noun Fem. **1** parking ticket; **2** speeding ticket.

contre preposition **1** against; **contre le mur** against the wall; **2** être contre quelque chose to be against something; **je suis plutôt contre** on the whole, I'm against it; **3** jouer contre quelqu'un to play against somebody; **4** versus;

5 échanger quelque chose **contre** to exchange something for (something else); **6** par contre on the other hand; ★ le pour et le contre the pros and cons.

contrebande noun Fem. **1** smuggling; **2** smuggled goods.

contrebasse noun Fem. double bass.

contredire verb [47] to contradict.

contrefaçon noun Fem. **1** forgery; **méfiez-vous des contrefaçons** beware of forgeries; **2** forged signature; **3** counterfeit banknote.

contremaître noun Masc. foreman.

contremaîtresse noun Fem. supervisor.

contreplaqué noun Masc. plywood.

contribuable noun Masc. & Fem. taxpayer.

contribuer verb [1] **contribuer à** to contribute to.

contribution noun Fem. contribution.

contrôle noun Masc. **1** control; **2** class test (at school); **j'ai un contrôle de français cet après-midi** I've got a French test this afternoon; **3** contrôle de police police check; **4** contrôle des passeports passport control; **contrôle des billets** ticket inspection.

contrôle continu noun Masc. continuous assessment.

contrôle des naissances noun Masc. birth control.

contrôler *verb* [1] **1** to check; **2** to control.

contrôleur, contrôleuse *noun Masc., Fem.* ticket inspector.

contrôleur aérien, contrôleuse aérienne *noun Masc., Fem.* air traffic controller.

controversé *adjective* controversial; **une décision controversée** a controversial decision.

convaincant *adjective* convincing.

convaincre *verb* [79] **1** to convince; **je ne suis pas convaincu** I'm not convinced; **2** to persuade; **je l'ai convaincu d'acheter un ordinateur** I persuaded him to buy a computer.

convenable *adjective* **1** suitable; **2** decent.

convenir *verb* [81] **1 convenir à** to suit, to be suitable for; **est-ce que dix heures te convient?** does ten o'clock suit you? **2 convenir de faire** to agree to do.

convention *noun Fem.* **1** agreement; **2** convention.

conversation *noun Fem.* conversation.

convertir *verb* [2] to convert.

conviction *noun Fem.* conviction.

convive *noun Masc. & Fem.* guest.

convivial *(Masc. plural* **conviviaux)** *adjective* **1** friendly; **une atmosphère conviviale** a friendly atmosphere; **2** user-friendly.

convoi *noun Masc.* **1** convoy; **2 'convoi exceptionnel'** 'dangerous load'.

convoquer *verb* [1] **1** to invite (*to a meeting*); **2** to summon.

coopératif *(Fem.* **coopérative)** *adjective* cooperative.

coopération *noun Fem.* cooperation.

coopérative *noun Fem.* cooperative.

coopérer *verb* [24] to cooperate.

coordonnées *plural noun Fem.* address and telephone number.

coordonner *verb* [1] to coordinate.

copain *noun Masc.* **1** friend, mate (*male*); **je sors avec les copains** I'm going out with my mates; **2** boyfriend; **elle est partie en vacances avec son copain** she's gone on holiday with her boyfriend.

copie *noun Fem.* **1** copy; **2** paper (*on which an exam or class exercise has been written*); **j'ai un tas de copies à corriger ce soir** I've got a pile of marking to do this evening.

copier *verb* [1] to copy.

copier-coller *verb* [1] to cut and paste; **copiez-collez le tableau** cut and paste the table.

copieux *(Fem.* **copieuse)** *adjective* hearty; **un petit déjeuner copieux** a hearty breakfast.

copine *noun Fem.* **1** friend, mate (*female*); **je sors avec les copines** I'm going out with my mates; **2** girlfriend; **il est parti en vacances avec sa copine** he's gone on holiday with his girlfriend.

a
b
c
d
e
f
g
h
i
j
k
l
m
n
o
p
q
r
s
t
u
v
w
x
y
z

coq noun Masc. cockerel.

coque noun Fem. 1 hull (of a boat); 2 shell (of a nut); 3 un œuf à la coque a soft-boiled egg.

coquelicot noun Masc. poppy.

coqueluche noun Fem. whooping-cough.

coquet (Fem. **coquette**) adjective 1 flirtatious; 2 pretty.

coquetier noun Masc. eggcup.

coquillage noun Masc. 1 shellfish; 2 seashell.

coquille noun Fem. 1 shell; 2 misprint.

coquille Saint-Jacques noun Fem. scallop.

coquin adjective cheeky, naughty.

cor noun Masc. horn (musical instrument).

corail (plural **coraux**) noun Masc. coral.

Coran noun Masc. le Coran the Koran.

corbeau noun Masc. crow.

corbeille noun Fem. basket; une corbeille à papier a wastepaper basket; une corbeille à linge a linen basket.

corbillard noun Masc. hearse.

corde noun Fem. 1 rope; 2 string (of a racket, a bow, or an instrument such as a guitar or violin);
★ pleuvoir des cordes to be pouring down (literally: to be raining ropes).

corde à linge noun Fem. clothes line.

corde à sauter noun Fem. skipping rope.

corde d'attache noun Fem. guy rope.

cordial (Masc. plural **cordiaux**) adjective warm, cordial.

cordialement adverb 1 warmly; 2 cordialement à vous Yours sincerely.

cordonnerie noun Fem. shoe repairer's.

cordonnier noun Masc. shoe repairer.

corne noun Fem. horn.

cornemuse noun Fem. bagpipes; jouer de la cornemuse to play the bagpipes.

cornet noun Masc. 1 un cornet de glace an ice cream cone; 2 un cornet de frites a bag of chips (in fact sold in a cardboard cornet).

corniche noun Fem. 1 ledge; 2 cornice; 3 (route de) corniche coastal road.

cornichon noun Masc. gherkin.

Cornouailles noun Fem. Cornwall.

corps noun Masc. body.

correct adjective 1 correct; 2 reasonable, fine; à un prix correct at a reasonable price; le repas était tout à fait correct the meal was absolutely fine.

correctement adverb 1 correctly; est-ce que vous avez rempli le formulaire correctement? have you filled in the form correctly?; 2 properly; 3 reasonably well.

correcteur orthographique noun Masc. spell checker.

correction noun Fem. correction.

correspondance noun Fem.
1 letters, correspondence;
2 **acheter quelque chose par correspondance** to buy something by mail order; 3 connection (a train or flight); **j'ai raté ma correspondance** I missed my connection; **un vol en correspondance** a connecting flight.

correspondant, correspondante noun Masc., Fem. pen friend.

correspondre verb [3] to correspond.

corrida noun Fem. bullfight.

corriger verb [52] 1 to correct; 2 to mark; **elle est en train de corriger ses copies** she's doing her marking.

corsage noun Masc. 1 blouse; 2 bodice.

corse adjective Corsican.

Corse[1] noun Fem. Corsica.

Corse[2] noun Masc. & Fem. Corsican (person).

corsé adjective full-bodied, strong.

corvée noun Fem. chore.

cosmétiques plural noun Masc. cosmetics.

costaud adjective strong, sturdy.

costume noun Masc. 1 suit;
2 costume.

côte noun Fem. 1 coast; 2 hill; 3 rib; 4 chop; **une côte d'agneau** a lamb chop.

côté noun Masc. 1 side; **de l'autre côté (de)** on the other side (of); **de l'autre côté de la rue** on the other side of the street; 2 **d'un autre côté**

on the other hand; 3 **à côté** nearby; **mon frère habite à côté** my brother lives nearby; 4 **à côté de** next to, beside; **elle était assise à côté de moi** she was sitting next to me.

Côte d'Azur noun Fem. French Riviera.

côtelette noun Fem. chop; **une côtelette de porc** a pork chop.

cotisation noun Fem.
1 subscription; 2 contribution.

coton noun Masc. 1 cotton; **un pull en coton** a cotton jumper;
2 sewing cotton; 3 cotton wool.

cou noun Masc. neck.

couchage noun Masc. **un sac de couchage** a sleeping bag.

couchant adjective **le soleil couchant** the setting sun; **au soleil couchant** at sunset.

couche noun Fem. 1 layer; 2 coat (of paint); 3 nappy.

couche d'ozone noun Fem. ozone layer.

coucher verb [1] 1 to sleep; **tu peux coucher chez Sophie** you can sleep at Sophie's house; 2 **se coucher** to go to bed; **elle se couche à dix heures** she goes to bed at ten o'clock; **se coucher avec quelqu'un** to sleep with someone; 3 **coucher un enfant** to put a child to bed.

coucher de soleil noun Masc. sunset; **un coucher de soleil magnifique** a magnificent sunset.

coucou noun Masc. 1 cuckoo;
2 cowslip.

coude noun Masc. elbow.

a
b
c
d
e
f
g
h
i
j
k
l
m
n
o
p
q
r
s
t
u
v
w
x
y
z

coudre verb [28] to sew; **coudre un bouton** to sew on a button.

couette noun Fem. duvet, continental quilt.

couler verb [1] **1** to flow; **2 avoir le nez qui coule** to have a runny nose; **3 faire couler un bain** to run a bath; **4** to sink.

couleur noun Fem. colour; **de quelle couleur est ta voiture?** what colour is your car?

couleuvre noun Fem. grass snake.

coulisses plural noun Fem. wings (in a theatre).

couloir noun Masc. corridor.

couloir d'autobus noun Masc. bus lane.

coup noun Masc. blow; **il a reçu un coup à l'estomac** he was hit in the stomach; ★ **boire un coup** (informal) to have a drink; ★ **donner un coup de balai** to sweep the floor; ★ **un coup de peinture** a lick of paint; ★ **sur le coup** at first; ★ **tenir le coup** to last out; ★ **tout d'un coup** all of a sudden.

coupable noun Masc. & Fem. culprit.

coupable adjective guilty.

coup d'œil noun Masc. glance; **jeter un coup d'œil à quelque chose** to have a quick look at something.

coup de chance noun Masc. stroke of luck.

coup de feu noun Masc. (gun)shot.

coup de main noun Masc. **donner un coup de main à quelqu'un** to give somebody a hand.

coup de pied noun Masc. kick.

coup de poing noun Masc. punch.

coup de soleil noun Masc. **attraper un coup de soleil** to get sunburnt.

coup de téléphone noun Masc. phone call.

coup de tonnerre noun Masc. clap of thunder.

coup de vent noun Masc. gust of wind.

coupe noun Fem. **1** cup (for sports); **la Coupe du Monde** the World Cup; **2** haircut; **3** fruit dish.

couper verb [1] **1** to cut; **se faire couper les cheveux** to have your hair cut; **2 se couper** to cut yourself; **se couper le doigt** to cut your finger; **3** to cut off, to turn off (gas, electricity); **4 excuse-moi, je t'ai coupé la parole** sorry, I interrupted you.

coup franc noun Masc. free kick.

couple noun Masc. couple.

couplet noun Masc. **1** verse (of song); **2** couplet.

coupon noun Masc. **1** remnant (of fabric); **2** coupon.

coupure noun Fem. cut; **une coupure de courant** a power cut.

cour noun Fem. **1** school playground; **2** inner courtyard (in an apartment block or hotel); **3** court (of a king or queen); **4** law court.

courage noun Masc. **1** courage, bravery; **2** energy; **avoir le courage de faire** to have the energy to do; **3 bon courage!** good luck!.

courageux (Fem. **courageuse**) *adjective* brave.

couramment *adverb* fluently.

courant *noun Masc.* **1** être au courant de quelque chose to know about something; est-ce que ta sœur est au courant? does your sister know?; je te tiens au courant I'll let you know what happens; **2** current; **3** electricity; couper le courant to cut off (or turn off) the electricity; une panne de courant a power cut.

courant *adjective* **1** common; **2** usual; **3** current.

courant d'air *noun Masc.* draught.

courbe *noun Fem.* curve.

courber *verb* [1] to bend.

coureur, coureuse *noun Masc., Fem.* runner.

courge *noun Fem.* (vegetable) marrow.

courgette *noun Fem.* courgette.

courir *verb* [29] **1** to run; traverser la rue en courant to run across the street; **2** courir un risque to run a risk.

couronne *noun Fem.* crown.

courrier *noun Masc.* mail, post.

courrier électronique *noun Masc.* electronic mail, email.

cours *noun Masc.* **1** class, lesson; le cours de français the French lesson; suivre des cours d'espagnol to go to Spanish classes; **2** course (of events); au cours de in the course of.

course *noun Fem.* **1** race; **2** running; **3** les courses

shopping; faire des courses to do some shopping; je fais mes courses à midi I do my shopping at lunchtime.

courses hippiques *plural noun Fem.* horse racing.

court *adjective* short.

court-circuit *noun Masc.* short-circuit.

court de tennis *noun Masc.* tennis court.

couru *verb* SEE **courir**.

cousin, cousine *noun Masc., Fem.* cousin; mon cousin germain my first cousin.

coussin *noun Masc.* cushion.

coût *noun Masc.* cost; le coût de la vie the cost of living.

couteau (*plural* **couteaux**) *noun Masc.* knife; un couteau à pain a bread knife.

coûter *verb* [1] to cost; ça coûte combien? how much is it?; ça coûte dix euros it's ten euros; coûter cher to be expensive; est-ce que ça t'a coûté cher? was it expensive?

coutume *noun Fem.* custom.

couture *noun Fem.* **1** sewing, dressmaking; faire de la couture to sew; **2** seam.

couturier *noun Masc.* fashion designer.

couturière *noun Fem.* dressmaker.

couvent *noun Masc.* convent.

couvercle *noun Masc.* **1** lid; **2** screwtop.

couvert noun Masc. place setting; **les couverts** the cutlery; **mettre les couverts** to set the table.

couvert adjective 1 covered; **un marché couvert** a covered market; 2 **couvert de** covered with; 3 overcast, cloudy.

couverture noun Fem. 1 blanket; 2 cover (of a book).

couvre-lit noun Masc. bedspread.

couvrir verb [30] 1 to cover; 2 **se couvrir** to cloud over; **ça s'est couvert dans l'après-midi** it clouded over in the afternoon.

crabe noun Masc. crab.

cracher verb [1] to spit.

crachin noun Masc. drizzle.

craie noun Fem. chalk.

craindre verb [31] to be afraid of.

crainte noun Fem. fear.

crampe noun Fem. cramp.

crâne noun Masc. skull; **avoir mal au crâne** (informal) to have a headache.

crâner verb [1] (informal) to show off.

crapaud noun Masc. toad.

craquement noun Masc. creak.

craquer verb [1] 1 to split; 2 to creak; 3 (informal) to crack up; ★ **j'ai craqué** I couldn't resist it!

crasse noun Fem. filth.

cravate noun Fem. tie.

crawl noun Masc. crawl (in swimming); **nager le crawl** to swim crawl.

crayon noun Masc. pencil.

créatif (Fem. **créative**) adjective creative.

création noun Fem. creation.

créativité noun Fem. creativity.

crèche noun Fem. 1 crèche, day nursery; 2 nativity scene (as a Christmas decoration).

crédit noun Masc. 1 credit; 2 funding.

crédit immobilier noun Masc. mortgage.

créer verb [32] to create.

crémaillère noun Fem. chimney hook (used in olden times to hang a pot for cooking over the fire); ★ **pendre la crémaillère** to have a house-warming party (literally: to hang the chimney hook).

crème noun Fem., adjective cream.

crème anglaise noun Fem. custard.

crème Chantilly noun Fem. whipped cream.

crémerie noun Fem. cheese shop.

crémeux (Fem. **crémeuse**) adjective creamy.

crêpe noun Fem. pancake.

crépon noun Masc. crepe paper.

crépuscule noun Masc. twilight.

cresson noun Masc. watercress.

creuser verb [1] 1 to dig; 2 to hollow out; **se creuser la cervelle** (informal) to rack your brains.

creux noun Masc. hollow.

creux adjective (Fem. **creuse**) 1 hollow; 2 **une assiette creuse** a soup plate.

crevaison noun Fem. puncture.

crevé adjective 1 burst; 2 (informal) knackered.

crever verb [50] **1** to burst; **un pneu crevé** a burst tyre, a puncture; **2** (informal) to die; **je crève de faim!** I'm starving!

crevette noun Fem. prawn.

cri noun Masc. cry, shout.

criard adjective garish.

cric noun Masc. (car) jack.

cricket noun Masc. cricket; **jouer au cricket** to play cricket.

crier verb [1] **1** to shout; **2** to scream.

crime noun Masc. crime.

criminel, criminelle noun Masc., Fem., adjective criminal.

crinière noun Fem. mane.

criquet noun Masc. grasshopper.

crise noun Fem. **1** crisis; **2** attack (of an illness).

crise cardiaque noun Fem. heart attack.

cristal (plural **cristaux**) noun Masc. crystal.

critère noun Masc. criterion.

critique[1] noun Masc. critic.

critique[2] noun Fem. **1** criticism; **les critiques** criticism; **2** review (of a film, book, etc).

critique[3] adjective critical.

critiquer verb [1] to criticize.

Croatie noun Fem. Croatia.

croche-pied noun Masc. **faire un croche-pied à quelqu'un** (informal) to trip somebody up.

crochet noun Masc. **1** hook; **2** detour; **3** crochet.

crocodile noun Masc. crocodile.

croire verb [33] **1** croire que to think that; **je crois qu'il est parti** I think he's left; **tu crois que c'est trop tard?** do you think it's too late?; **je ne crois pas** I don't think so; **2** to believe; **je n'arrive pas à le croire** I can't believe it; **3** croire à to believe in; **4** je n'en croyais pas mes yeux! I couldn't believe my eyes!

croiser verb [1] **1** to cross; **croiser les jambes** to cross your legs; **croiser les bras** to fold your arms; **2** croiser quelqu'un to bump into somebody (meet by chance); **j'ai croisé Odile devant la banque** I bumped into Odile outside the bank.

croisière noun Fem. cruise.

croissance noun Fem. growth.

croissant noun Masc. croissant.

croître verb [34] to grow.

croix noun Fem. cross.

Croix-Rouge noun Fem. Red Cross.

croquant adjective crunchy.

croque-monsieur noun Masc. toasted ham sandwich with cheese sauce on top.

croque-mort noun (informal) Masc. undertaker.

croquer verb [1] to munch.

croquis noun Masc. sketch.

crottes plural noun Fem. droppings; **des crottes de chien** dog dirt.

croustillant adjective crispy.

croûte noun Fem. **1** crust; **2** rind (of cheese); **3** scab.

croûton noun Masc. crouton.

croyance noun Fem. belief.

cru[1] verb SEE croire.

cru[2] adjective raw, uncooked.

cruauté noun Fem. cruelty; **ils ont été traités avec beaucoup de cruauté** they were treated with great cruelty.

cruche noun Fem. (large) jug.

crudités plural noun Fem. raw vegetables (served with dips as a starter).

cruel (Fem. **cruelle**) adjective cruel.

crustacé noun Masc. shellfish.

crypte noun Fem. crypt.

Cuba noun Fem. Cuba.

cubain adjective Fem. Cuban.

Cubain, Cubaine noun Masc., Fem. Cuban.

cube noun Masc. cube.

cube adjective cubic; **un mètre cube** a cubic metre.

cueillir verb [35] to pick (fruit or flowers).

cuiller noun Fem. **1** spoon; **2** spoonful.

cuillère noun Fem. = cuiller.

cuillerée noun Fem. spoonful.

cuir noun Masc. leather; **des chaussures en cuir** leather shoes.

cuir chevelu noun Masc. scalp.

cuire verb [36] to cook.

cuisine noun Fem. **1** kitchen; **2** cooking; **faire la cuisine** to cook, to do the cooking.

cuisiner verb [1] to cook.

cuisinier, cuisinière[1] noun Masc., Fem. cook.

cuisinière[2] noun Fem. cooker; **une cuisinière à gaz** a gas cooker; **une**

cuisinière à électrique an electric cooker.

cuisse noun Fem. thigh.

cuisse de poulet noun Fem. chicken leg, chicken thigh.

cuit adjective cooked; **bien cuit** well done (meat).

cuivre noun Masc. copper.

cuivre jaune noun Masc. brass; **un chandelier en cuivre jaune** a brass candlestick.

culot noun Masc. (informal) cheek; **quel culot!** what a cheek!, what a nerve!; **elle a du culot!** she's got a nerve!

culotte noun Fem. **une (petite) culotte** knickers, panties.

culpabilité noun Fem. guilt.

cultivateur, cultivatrice noun Masc., Fem. farmer.

cultiver verb [1] **1** to grow; **2** to cultivate.

culture noun Fem. **1** farming; **2** growing; **de culture biologique** organically produced; **3** crop; **4** culture.

culturel (Fem. **culturelle**) adjective cultural.

culturisme noun Masc. body-building.

cure noun Fem. course of treatment.

curé noun Masc. parish priest.

cure-dents noun Masc. toothpick.

curer verb [1] **se curer les ongles** to clean your nails; **se curer les dents** to pick your teeth.

curieux (Fem. **curieuse**) adjective **1** strange, odd; **2** curious, inquisitive.

curiosité noun Fem. curiosity.

curseur noun Masc. cursor (on a computer screen).

cuve noun Fem. vat, tank.

cuvette noun Fem. bowl; **la cuvette des wc** the lavatory bowl.

cybercafé noun Masc. Internet cafe; **où est-ce qu'il y a un cybercafé?** where is there an Internet cafe?

cybernaute noun Masc. & Fem. web surfer, cybernaut.

cyclable adjective **une piste cyclable** a cycle track.

cycle noun Masc. cycle.

cyclisme noun Masc. cycling.

cycliste noun Masc. & Fem. cyclist.

cyclone noun Masc. hurricane.

cygne noun Masc. swan.

cylindre noun Masc. **1** cylinder; **2** roller.

cynique adjective cynical.

cyprès noun Masc. cypress (tree).

Dd

d' preposition SEE de.

dactylo noun Masc. & Fem. typist.

dactylographie noun Fem. typing.

daigner verb [1] to deign.

daim noun Masc. **1** suede; **des chaussures en daim** suede shoes; **2** fallow deer.

dalle noun Fem. paving slab.

daltonien (Fem. **daltonienne**) adjective colour-blind.

dame noun Fem. **1** lady; **2** queen (in cards or chess).

dames plural noun Fem. draughts; **jouer aux dames** to play draughts.

dancing noun Masc. dance hall.

Danemark noun Masc. Denmark; **au Danemark** to (or in) Denmark.

danger noun Masc. danger.

dangereux (Fem. **dangereuse**) adjective dangerous.

danois noun Masc. Danish (language).

danois adjective Danish.

Danois, , Danoise noun Masc., Fem. Danish.

dans preposition **1** in; **elle est dans la cuisine** she's in the kitchen; **2** into; **va dans la cuisine** go into the kitchen; **3 dans trois mois** in three months' time; **4 boire dans un verre** to drink out of a glass.

danse noun Fem. **1** dance; **2** dancing; **faire de la danse** to go to dancing classes.

danse classique noun Fem. ballet.

danser verb [1] to dance.

danseur, danseuse noun Masc., Fem. dancer.

d'après preposition **1** according to; **d'après le ministre** according to the minister; **2** based on; **un film d'après le roman de** a film based on the novel by; **3** in the style of; **un tableau d'après Degas** a painting in the style of Degas.

date noun Fem. date.

date de naissance noun Fem. date of birth.

a
b
c
d
e
f
g
h
i
j
k
l
m
n
o
p
q
r
s
t
u
v
w
x
y
z

date limite noun Fem. closing date.

date limite de vente noun Fem. sell-by date.

datte noun Fem. date (fruit).

dauphin noun Masc. dolphin.

davantage adverb **1** more; **2** longer.

de, d' (before a vowel or a silent 'h') (note that 'de + le' becomes 'du' and 'de + les' becomes 'des').

de preposition **1** of; **une boîte d'allumettes** a box of matches; **le pied de la table** the leg of the table, the table leg; **2 le père de Marie** Marie's father; **la maison de tes parents** your parents' house; **3** from; **elle vient de Paris** she comes from Paris; **elle rentre du bureau à six heures** she comes home from the office at six o'clock; **4** made from; **une table de bois** a wooden table; **5** by; **le prix a augmenté de vingt euros** the price has gone up (by) twenty euros.

de determiner **du café** (some) coffee; **veux-tu du café?** would you like (some) coffee?; **je n'ai pas de café** I don't have any coffee; **nous avons des pommes et des oranges** we have apples and oranges; **veux-tu de l'eau?** would you like some water?

dé noun Masc. **1** dice; **2 un dé à coudre** a thimble.

dealer noun Masc. drug pusher.

déballer verb [1] to unpack.

débardeur noun Masc. camisole top, vest-style top.

débarquer verb [1] **1** to disembark; **2** to land; **3** (informal) to turn up; **elle a débarqué chez moi** she turned up at my place.

débarras noun Masc. junk room; ★ **bon débarras!** good riddance!

débarrasser verb [1] **1** to clear out (a room); **débarrasser la table** to clear the table; **2 se débarrasser de quelque chose** to get rid of something; **je me suis débarrassé de tous ces vieux bouquins** I got rid of all those old books.

débat noun Masc. debate.

débattre verb [21] to discuss, to negotiate; **'prix à débattre'** 'price negotiable'.

débile adjective (informal) stupid, crazy; **tu es débile ou quoi?** are you stupid or something?; **c'est complètement débile!** that's completely crazy!

déblayer verb [59] to clear.

débordé adjective **être débordé** to be up to your eyes in work.

débordement noun Masc. **1** overflowing; **2** flood.

déborder verb [1] to overflow.

débouché noun Masc. job prospect; **il y a peu de/beaucoup de débouchés pour les jeunes diplômés** there are few/many openings for recent graduates.

déboucher verb [1] **1** to uncork (a bottle); **2** to unblock (a drain or pipe); **3 déboucher sur** to lead into.

déboussoler verb [1] (informal) to confuse.

debout adverb **1** standing; **rester debout** to remain standing; **je suis resté debout toute la journée** I've been on my feet all day; **se mettre debout** to stand up; **tout le monde s'est mis debout** everybody stood up; **2** upright; **mettre quelque chose debout** to stand something upright; **3** up (*out of bed*); **je suis debout à six heures tous les jours** I'm up at six every day; ★ **ça ne tient pas debout** it doesn't make any sense (*literally: it doesn't stand upright*).

déboutonner *verb* [1] to unbutton.

débrancher *verb* [1] **1** to unplug (*an iron, a television set, etc*); **2** to disconnect (*the electricity, gas, water, telephone*).

débris *noun Masc.* **1** fragment; **2** piece of wreckage.

débrouiller *verb* [1] **se débrouiller** to manage; **je peux me débrouiller tout seul** I can manage by myself; **débrouille-toi!** get on with it!

début *noun Masc.* beginning, start; **le début de** the beginning of; **au début** at the beginning, to start with; **on commencera début mars** we'll start at the beginning of March; **en début d'après-midi** in the early afternoon.

débutant, débutante *noun Masc., Fem.* beginner.

débuter *verb* [1] to begin, to start.

décaféiné *adjective* decaffeinated.

décalage *noun Masc.* **1** gap; **2** discrepancy.

décalage horaire *noun Masc.* time difference (*between time zones*); **il y a une heure de**

décalage horaire entre la France et la Grande-Bretagne there's an hour's time difference between France and Britain.

décaler *verb* [1] to move (*forward or back*).

décapiter *verb* [1] to behead.

décapotable *adjective* **une voiture décapotable** a convertible (car).

décapsuleur *noun Masc.* (bottle) opener.

décéder *verb* [24] to die; **elle est décédée au mois de novembre** she died in November.

décembre *noun Masc.* December; **en décembre, au mois de décembre** in December.

décemment *adverb* decently.

décennie *noun Fem.* decade.

décent *adjective* decent.

déception *noun Fem.* disappointment.

décès *noun Masc.* death.

décevant *adjective* disappoir

décevoir *verb* [66] to disapp

décharge *noun Fem.* (pub' rubbish tip.

décharger *verb* [52] to

déchets *plural noun* '
1 waste; **les déchets**
nuclear waste; **2** ru'

déchiffrer *verb* ['

déchirant *adje*
rending.

déchirer *ver'*
déchiré mo
my trouser
une enve
envelop'

a
b
c
d
e
f
g
h
i
j
k
l
m
n
o

une feuille to tear off a sheet of paper; **4** to tear out; **déchirer une page** to tear out a page; **5 se déchirer** to tear, to rip.

décidé adjective determined.

décidément adverb really.

décider verb [1] **1** to decide; **décider de faire** to decide to do; **j'ai décidé de vendre mon vélo** I've decided to sell my bike; **2 se décider** to make up your mind; **il faut qu'on se décide une fois pour toutes** we must make up our minds once and for all; **3 se décider à faire** to decide to do.

décimal (Masc. plural **décimaux**) adjective decimal.

décimale noun Fem. decimal.

décision noun Fem. decision.

déclaration noun Fem. **1** statement; **2** declaration.

déclarer verb [1] to declare.

déclencher verb [1] **1** to cause; **2** to set off; **déclencher l'alarme** to set off the alarm.

déclic noun Masc. click.

décliner verb [1] to decline.

décollage noun Masc. takeoff (of a plane).

déco... ... **avoir les** ... to have ... **déverbally: to have** ... **pl...unstuck).** ... **to c...** ... **cake off (of a papi...e chose décoller** ... **off. ...le** ... **...ng**

décolleté adjective low-cut.

décolorer verb [1] **se décolorer** to fade; **se faire décolorer les cheveux** to have your hair lightened.

décombres plural noun Masc. rubble.

décongeler verb [45] to defrost.

déconseillé adjective not recommended; **'déconseillé pour les enfants'** 'not recommended for children'.

déconseiller verb [1] **déconseiller à quelqu'un de faire** to advise somebody not to do; **nous lui avons déconseillé de voyager toute seule** we advised her not to travel alone.

décontracté adjective relaxed, laid-back; **mon patron est très décontracté** my boss is very laid-back.

décontracter verb [1] **se décontracter** to relax.

décor noun Masc. **1** decor; **2** setting.

décorateur, décoratrice noun Masc., Fem. interior designer.

décoratif (Fem. **décorative**) adjective **1** ornamental; **2** decorative.

décoration noun Fem. **1** decorating; **2** interior design.

décorer verb [1] to decorate.

découper verb [1] **1** to cut out; **découper un article dans un journal** to cut an article out of a newspaper; **2** to carve (meat); **c'est Marie-Laure qui va découper le poulet** Marie-Laure's going to carve the chicken.

décourageant *adjective* discouraging.

décourager *verb* [52] to discourage.

découvert *noun Masc.* overdraft.

découverte *noun Fem.* discovery.

découvrir *verb* [30] to discover.

décrire *verb* [38] to describe.

décrocher *verb* [1] **1** to lift the receiver (*of a telephone*); '**décrochez**' 'lift the receiver'; **il faut décrocher avant de composer le numéro** you have to lift the receiver before dialling; **2** to take down (*a picture, curtains, etc*).

déçu *adjective* disappointed; **nous sommes tous très déçus** we're all very disappointed.

dedans *adverb* inside **1 elle a ouvert la boîte mais il n'y avait rien dedans** she opened the box but there was nothing in it; **2 là-dedans** in there.

dédommager *verb* [52] to compensate.

déduction *noun Fem.* deduction.

déduire *verb* [26] **1** to deduce; **2** to deduct.

déesse *noun Fem.* goddess.

défaire *verb* [10] **1** to undo, to untie; **2 se défaire** to come undone; **3 se défaire de** to get rid of.

défaite *noun Fem.* defeat.

défaut *noun Masc.* **1** flaw, defect; **2 à défaut de** for want of.

défavorisé *adjective* underprivileged; **les défavorisés** the underprivileged.

défectueux (*Fem.* **défectueuse**) *adjective* faulty; **une prise défectueuse** a faulty plug.

défendre *verb* [3] **1** to forbid; **2** to defend.

défendu *adjective* forbidden.

défense *noun* **1 défense de fumer** no smoking; **2** defence; **3** protection; **la défense de l'environnement** the protection of the environment; **4** tusk (*of an elephant*).

défi *noun Masc.* challenge.

déficit *noun Masc.* deficit.

défigurer *verb* [1] to disfigure.

défilé *noun Masc.* **1** parade; **2** procession; **3** march.

défiler *verb* [1] **1** to parade; **2** to march; **3** to come and go.

définir *verb* [2] to define.

définitif (*Fem.* **définitive**) *adjective* final, definitive.

définition *noun Fem.* definition.

définitivement *adverb* **1** for good; **2** definitely.

défoncer *verb* [61] to smash in (*a door*).

déformer *verb* [1] **1** to bend out of shape; **2** to distort; **3** to stretch (*a garment or shoes*).

défouler *verb* [1] **1 se défouler** to let off steam; **2** to unwind.

défunt *noun Masc.* **le défunt** the deceased.

dégagé *adjective* **1** clear; **2** casual.

dégager *verb* [52] **1** to clear; **2** to free (*a trapped person*).

dégâts *plural noun Masc.* damage.

dégel *noun Masc.* thaw.

a b c d e f g h i j k l m n o p q r s t u v w x y z

dégeler verb [45] to thaw.

dégénérer verb [24] 1 to degenerate; 2 to go from bad to worse.

dégivrer verb [1] 1 to defrost; 2 to de-ice.

dégonfler verb [1] to let down (a tyre, an airbed, etc).

dégouliner verb [1] to trickle.

dégourdi adjective smart, bright; **un gamin dégourdi** a bright kid.

dégoût noun Masc. disgust.

dégoûtant adjective 1 filthy; **tes mains sont dégoûtantes** your hands are filthy; 2 disgusting.

dégoûté adjective disgusted.

dégoûter verb [1] 1 to disgust; 2 **dégoûter quelqu'un de quelque chose** to put somebody off something; **ça m'a dégoûté du poisson** that put me off fish.

dégrader verb [1] 1 to damage; 2 **se dégrader** to deteriorate.

dégraisser verb [1] to dryclean.

degré noun Masc. degree.

dégringoler verb [1] (informal) to tumble down.

déguisé adjective 1 in fancy dress, in disguise; 2 **une soirée déguisée** a fancy-dress party; 3 disguised.

déguiser verb [1] 1 to disguise; 2 **se déguiser** to dress up in fancy dress.

dégustation noun Fem. tasting; **'dégustation de glaces'** 'a fine selection of ice creams'.

déguster verb [1] 1 to savour, to enjoy; 2 to taste (wine, cheese, etc).

dehors adverb 1 outside; **je t'attends dehors** I'll wait for you

outside; **j'ai passé toute la journée dehors** I've been outside all day; 2 **en dehors de** apart from; **en dehors de la salade, tout est prêt** everything's ready apart from the salad.

déjà adverb 1 already; **tu pars déjà?** are you leaving already?; **je t'ai déjà dit de ne pas faire ça!** I told you not to do that!; 2 before; **tu es déjà venu ici?** have you been here before?

déjeuner noun Masc. lunch; **petit déjeuner** breakfast.

déjeuner verb [1] 1 to have lunch; **nous déjeunons à une heure** we have lunch at one o'clock; 2 to have breakfast.

délabré adjective dilapidated.

délacer verb [61] to unlace.

délai noun Masc. period of time, waiting period.

délavé adjective 1 faded; 2 washed-out.

délecter verb [1] **se délecter à faire** to delight in doing.

délégué, déléguée noun Masc., Fem. 1 delegate; 2 representative.

délibéré adjective deliberate.

délibérer verb [24] to discuss.

délicat adjective 1 delicate; 2 tactful.

délice noun Masc. delight; **c'est un vrai délice!** it's absolutely delicious!

délicieux (Fem. **délicieuse**) adjective delicious.

délinquance noun Fem. 1 crime; 2 delinquency.

délinquant, délinquante noun Masc., Fem. offender.

délirant adjective (informal) crazy; **c'est complètement délirant!** it's completely crazy!

délire noun Masc. 1 (informal) madness; 2 frenzy.

délirer verb [1] (informal) to be crazy; **il délire!** he's crazy!

délit noun Masc. criminal offence.

délivrer verb [1] to free, to liberate.

déloyal (Masc. plural **déloyaux**) adjective disloyal.

deltaplane noun Masc. 1 hang-glider; 2 **faire du deltaplane** to go hang-gliding.

déluge noun Masc. 1 downpour; 2 **le Déluge** the Flood (in the Bible).

demain adverb tomorrow; **à demain!** see you tomorrow!; **après-demain** the day after tomorrow.

demande noun Fem. 1 request; 2 demand; 3 application; **faire une demande d'emploi** to apply for a job; **'demandes d'emplois'** 'situations wanted'; 4 claim; **faire une demande de remboursement auprès d'une compagnie d'assurance** to make a claim on insurance.

demandé adjective **très demandé** very much in demand, very popular.

demander verb [1] 1 **demander quelque chose** to ask for something; 2 **demander quelque chose à quelqu'un** to ask somebody (for) something; **demande à ton père!** ask your father!; **il m'a demandé ton adresse** he asked me for your address; 3 **demander à quelqu'un de faire** to ask somebody to do; **elle m'a demandé de téléphoner** she asked me to phone; 4 **se demander** to wonder; **je me demande ce qu'elle est en train de faire** I wonder what she's doing.

demandeur d'emploi noun Masc. job-seeker.

démangeaison noun Fem. itch.

démanger verb [52] **ça me démange** it itches.

démanteler verb [45] to dismantle.

démaquillant noun Masc. make-up remover.

démaquiller verb [1] **se démaquiller** to remove your make-up.

démarche noun Fem. 1 walk; 2 step.

démarrer verb [1] 1 to start (of engine or car); **la voiture ne veut pas démarrer** the car won't start; 2 to drive off; 3 to start up, to start off; **le projet va démarrer en juin** the project will start up in June.

démarreur noun Masc. starter (in a car).

démêler verb [1] to untangle.

déménagement noun Masc. (house) move, removal.

déménager verb [52] 1 to move (house); 2 to move out; **nous déménageons la semaine prochaine** we're moving out next week; 3 **déménager quelque chose** to move something.

déménageur noun Masc. removal man.

dément adjective crazy.

a
b
c
d
e
f
g
h
i
j
k
l
m
n
o
p
q
r
s
t
u
v
w
x
y
z

a

démentir verb [53] **1** to deny; **2** to refute.

b **démesuré** adjective excessive.

c **demeure** noun Fem. residence, mansion.

demeurer verb [1] to reside, to live.

e

demi[1] adjective **1** half; **trois et demi** three and a half; **elle a trois ans et demi** she's three and a half; **une heure et demie** an hour and a half; **2** **une demi-pomme** half an apple; **une demi-bouteille** half a bottle; **3** **à deux heures et demie** at half past two; **à trois heures et demie** at half past three.

g

h

i

j

k **demi**[2] noun Masc. half (of beer).

demi-cercle noun Masc. semicircle.

l

m **demi-douzaine** noun Fem. half a dozen.

demie noun Fem. half-hour; **à la demie** on the half-hour.

n

o **demi-écrémé** adjective semi-skimmed.

p **demi-finale** noun Fem. semifinal.

q **demi-frère** noun Masc. half brother.

r

demi-heure noun Fem. **une demi-heure** half an hour; **toutes les demi-heures** every half hour.

s

t **demi-journée** noun Fem. half a day.

u

v **demi-litre** noun Masc. half a litre.

w **demi-pension** noun Fem. half board.

x **demi-sel** adjective slightly salted.

demi-sœur noun Fem. half sister.

y **démission** noun Fem. resignation;

z **donner sa démission** to resign.

démissionner verb [1] to resign.

demi-tarif adjective half-price.

demi-tour noun Masc. **faire demi-tour** to turn back.

démocrate noun Masc. & Fem. democrat.

démocrate adjective democratic.

démocratie noun Fem. democracy.

démocratique adjective democratic.

démodé adjective old-fashioned.

demoiselle noun Fem. young lady.

demoiselle d'honneur noun Fem. bridesmaid.

démolir verb [2] to demolish, to wreck.

démolition noun Fem. demolition.

démon noun Masc. demon.

démonstrateur, **démonstratrice** noun Masc., Fem. demonstrator (for products).

démonstratif (Fem. **démonstrative**) adjective demonstrative.

démonstration noun Fem. **1** demonstration (of a product, appliance, etc); **2** display.

démonter verb [1] to dismantle, to take apart.

démontrer verb [1] to demonstrate, to prove.

démoraliser verb [1] to demoralize.

démouler verb [1] to turn out (a cake, mousse, etc, from a tin or mould).

démuni adjective **1** poverty stricken; **2** penniless.

dénoncer verb [61] to denounce.

dénouer verb [1] to undo.

denrée noun Fem. foodstuff.

dense adjective dense.

densité noun Fem. density.

dent noun Fem. tooth; **avoir mal aux dents** to have toothache.

dentaire adjective dental.

dent de sagesse noun Fem. wisdom tooth.

dentelé adjective 1 jagged; 2 serrated; 3 perforated.

dentelle noun Fem. lace.

dentier noun Masc. denture, false teeth.

dentifrice noun Masc. toothpaste.

dentiste noun Masc. & Fem. dentist.

déodorant noun Masc. deodorant.

dépannage noun Masc. repair; 'dépannages' 'emergency repairs'; **le service de dépannage** the breakdown service; **un véhicule de dépannage** a breakdown vehicle.

dépanner verb [1] **1** to fix, to repair; **2 dépanner quelqu'un** (informal) to help somebody out.

dépanneuse noun Fem. breakdown truck.

départ noun Masc. **1** departure; **je t'appellerai avant mon départ** I'll phone you before I leave; **elle m'a appelé avant son départ** she phoned me before she left; **2 au départ** at first, to start with.

département noun Masc. department (As well as other sorts of department, this is a French numbered administrative area, rather like a county in Britain. The two numbers on the end of vehicle registrations in France show the number of the department where the car is registered).

dépassé adjective outdated, old-fashioned.

dépasser verb [1] **1** to overtake; **2** to exceed; **3 ça me dépasse!** it's beyond me!

dépêcher verb [50] **se dépêcher** to hurry up; **dépêche-toi!** hurry up!

dépendance noun Fem. outbuilding.

dépendre verb [3] **1 dépendre de** to depend on; **ça dépend de l'heure** it depends on the time; **ça dépend** it depends; **2** to be dependent on.

dépenser verb [1] to spend.

dépenses plural noun Fem. **1** expenses; **2** spending.

dépensier (Fem. **dépensière**) adjective extravagant.

dépilatoire adjective **une crème dépilatoire** a hair-removing cream.

dépistage noun Masc. screening.

dépit noun Masc. **en dépit de** in spite of.

déplacé adjective out of place.

déplacement noun Masc. trip; **les frais de déplacement** travel expenses.

déplacer verb [61] **1** to move; **2 se déplacer** to travel.

déplaire verb [62] **déplaire à quelqu'un** to be displeasing to somebody; **cela me déplaît** I don't like that.

déplaisant adjective unpleasant.

dépliant noun Masc. leaflet.

déplier verb [1] to unfold.

déporter verb [1] to deport.

déposer verb [1] **1** to put down; **2** to drop off; **il m'a déposé à la gare** he dropped me off at the station; **3 déposer un chèque** to pay in a cheque.

dépôt noun Masc. **1** warehouse; **2** depot; **3** deposit.

dépôt d'ordures noun Masc. rubbish tip.

dépoussiérer verb [24] to dust.

dépressif (Fem. **dépressive**) adjective depressive.

dépression noun Fem. depression; **une dépression nerveuse** a nervous breakdown.

déprimant adjective depressing.

déprimer verb [1] **1** to depress; **2** to get depressed; **elle déprime en ce moment** she's depressed at the moment.

depuis preposition **1** since; **depuis vendredi** since Friday; **je suis à Paris depuis mardi** I've been in Paris since Tuesday; **j'habite à Londres depuis avril** I've been living in London since April; **2** for; **elle habite à Londres depuis cinq ans** she's lived in London for five years; **je le connais depuis longtemps** I've known him for a long time; **3 tu es là depuis combien de temps?** how long have you been here?; **tu le sais depuis combien de temps?** how long have you known?; **depuis quand es-tu à Paris?** how long have you been in Paris?; **4 depuis que** since; **depuis que ton frère**

est à Londres since your brother's been in London.

depuis adverb since; **je ne l'ai pas revu depuis** I haven't seen him since.

député noun Masc. deputy (the French equivalent of a member of Parliament).

déraciner verb [1] to uproot.

déranger verb [52] to disturb; **'ne pas déranger'** 'do not disturb'; **excusez-moi de vous déranger** sorry to bother you ; **est-ce que cela vous dérange si j'ouvre la fenêtre?** do you mind if I open the window?; **cela ne me dérange pas du tout** I don't mind at all; **ça vous dérange de venir me chercher?** do you mind coming to pick me up?

déraper verb [1] **1** to skid; **2** to get out of control.

dérisoire adjective pathetic, trivial; **je l'ai acheté pour une somme dérisoire** I bought it for next to nothing.

dériveur noun Masc. sailing dinghy.

dermatologue noun Masc. & Fem. dermatologist.

dernier (Fem. **dernière**) adjective **1** last; **le dernier train part à minuit** the last train leaves at midnight; **jeudi dernier** last Thursday; **la semaine dernière** last week; **l'année dernière** last year; **2** latest; **leur dernier album** their latest album; **3 en dernier** last; **il est arrivé en dernier** he arrived last.

dernier cri noun Masc. latest fashion; **le dernier cri en matière**

d'équipement hifi the latest in audio equipment.

dernièrement *adverb* recently.

dérouler *verb* [1] **1** to unroll, to unwind; **2 se dérouler** to take place; **ça s'est très bien déroulé** it went very well.

déroutant *adjective* puzzling.

derrière *noun Masc.* **1** back (*of an object or a house*); **2** bottom, backside.

derrière *preposition* behind; **derrière la porte** behind the door.

derrière *adverb* behind; **être derrière** to be in the back (*of the car*).

des *article* some, any SEE **de, un.**

dès *preposition* **1** from; **dès l'âge de cinq ans** from the age of five; **2 dès que** as soon as.

désagréable *adjective* unpleasant.

désarroi *noun Masc.* confusion.

désastre *noun Masc.* disaster.

désavantage *noun Masc.* disadvantage.

désavouer *verb* [1] **1** to deny; **2** to disown.

descendre *verb* [3] **1** to go down; **descendre les escaliers** to go down the stairs; **2** to come down; **je descends dans trois secondes!** I'll be down in a second!; **3** to get off (*a train or bus*); **je descends à Dijon** I'm getting off at Dijon; **4** to get down; **pouvez-vous descendre ma valise, s'il vous plaît?** could you get my case down for me, please?; **5** to take (*or bring*) downstairs; **je vais descendre mes bagages** I'm going to take my luggage downstairs; **est-ce que tu peux descendre une chaise de là-haut?** could you bring a chair down from upstairs?

descente *noun Fem.* descent.

descriptif (*Fem.* **descriptive**) *adjective* descriptive.

description *noun Fem.* description.

déséquilibrer *verb* [1] **déséquilibrer quelqu'un** to throw somebody off balance.

désert *noun Masc.* desert.

désert *adjective* deserted.

déserter *verb* [1] to desert.

désespéré *adjective* **1** desperate; **2** in despair; **3 une situation désespérée** a hopeless situation.

désespérer *verb* [24] to despair, to give up hope.

désespoir *noun Masc.* despair.

déshabiller *verb* [1] **1 se déshabiller** to undress, to get undressed; **2 déshabiller quelqu'un** to undress somebody.

désherbant *noun Masc.* weedkiller.

désherber *verb* [1] to weed.

déshérité *noun Masc.* **les déshérités** the underprivileged.

déshériter *verb* [1] to disinherit.

déshydraté *adjective* dehydrated.

désigner *verb* [1] **1** to point out; **2** to denote.

désinfectant *noun Masc.* disinfectant.

désinfecter *verb* [1] to disinfect.

désir *noun Masc.* **1** wish; **2** desire.

a

b **désirer** verb [1] to want; **que désirez-vous?** what would you like?

c **désobéir** verb [2] **1** to be disobedient; **2 désobéir à quelqu'un** to disobey somebody.

d

e **désobéissant** adjective disobedient.

f **désobligeant** adjective unpleasant.

g **désodorisant** noun Masc. air freshener.

h

i **désolé** adjective **être désolé** to be sorry; **je suis désolé** I'm sorry; **désolé de te déranger** sorry to disturb you.

j

k **désopilant** adjective hilarious.

l **désordonné** adjective untidy.

m **désordre** noun Masc. **1** untidiness, mess; **être en désordre** to be in a mess; **2** disorder.

n

o **désorganisé** adjective disorganized.

p **désorienté** adjective disorientated, confused.

q **désormais** adverb **1** from now on; **2** from then on.

r

s **desquels, desquelles** pronoun (= de lesquels, de lesquelles) of which, of whom.

t

u **dessécher** verb [24] **1** to dry out; **2 se dessécher** to dry out.

v **desserrer** verb [1] to loosen.

w **dessert** noun Masc. dessert, pudding.

x

y **desservir** verb [58] **le train dessert Vienne et Valence** the train calls at Vienne and Valence.

z

dessin noun Masc. **1** drawing; **un cours de dessin** a drawing class; **2 un dessin** a drawing; **3** design.

dessin animé noun Masc. (animated) cartoon.

dessiner verb [1] to draw.

dessin humoristique noun Masc. cartoon.

dessous noun Masc. **1** underside; **le dessous du pied** the sole of the foot; **2 les voisins du dessous** the neighbours below; **3 les dessous** underwear; **4 en dessous** underneath; **5 en dessous de** below.

dessous adverb underneath.

dessous-de-plat noun Masc. table mat (for dish).

dessus noun Masc. **1** top; **le dessus du carton** the top of the box; **un pantalon gris et un dessus rose** grey trousers and a pink top; **2 les voisins du dessus** the neighbours above; **3 en dessus** above; **4 au dessus de** above.

dessus adverb on top; **quelqu'un a écrit dessus** somebody's written on it.

dessus-de-lit noun Masc. bedspread.

destin noun Masc. **1** fate; **2** destiny.

destinataire noun Masc. & Fem. addressee.

destination noun Fem. destination; **le train à destination de Nice** the train for Nice; **les passagers à destination de Rome** passengers travelling to Rome.

destiner verb [1] **1 destiner quelque chose à** to design something for; **2 être destiné à** to be intended for; **3 être destiné à faire** to be intended to do.

détachable *adjective* detachable.

détachant *noun Masc.* stain remover.

détacher *verb* [1] **1** to untie; **2** to undo; **3** to tear off; **4** to remove; **5** to remove the stains from; **6 se détacher** to come off, to come undone.

détail *noun Masc.* **1** detail; **en détail** in detail; **2 regarder quelque chose dans le détail** to look closely at something; **3** retail.

détailler *verb* [1] to detail, to itemize; **une facture détaillée** an itemized bill.

détecter *verb* [1] to detect.

détective *noun Masc.* detective.

déteindre *verb* [60] **1** to fade; **2** to run (*in the wash*).

détendre *verb* [3] **1** to be relaxing; **2** to relax; **3 se détendre** to relax.

détendu *adjective* relaxed.

détenir *verb* [81] **1** to detain; **2** to keep.

détente *noun Fem.* relaxation.

détenu, détenue *noun Masc., Fem.* prisoner, detainee.

détergent *noun Masc.* detergent.

détériorer *verb* [1] **se détériorer** to deteriorate.

détermination *noun Fem.* determination.

déterminer *verb* [1] to fix.

détestable *adjective* appalling, revolting.

détester *verb* [1] to hate.

détour *noun Masc.* detour; ★ **ça vaut le détour** it's well worth

seeing (*literally: it's worth the detour*).

détournement *noun Masc.* **un détournement d'avion** a highjacking.

détourner *verb* [1] **1** to divert; **2 détourner un avion** to highjack a plane; **3 détourner les yeux** to look away.

détritus *plural noun Masc.* rubbish, refuse.

détruire *verb* [26] to destroy.

dette *noun Fem.* debt.

deuil *noun Masc.* **1** bereavement; **2** mourning.

deux *number* **1** two; **deux enfants** two children; **elle a deux ans** she's two; **il est deux heures** it's two o'clock; **2 deux fois** twice; **3** second (*in dates*); **le deux juin** the second of June; **4** both; **les deux frères** both brothers; **tous les deux, toutes les deux both; ils sont malades tous les deux, tous les deux sont malades** they're both ill, both of them are ill.

deuxième *noun* **au deuxième** on the second floor.

deuxième *adjective* **pour la deuxième fois** for the second time.

deuxièmement *adverb* secondly.

deux-points *noun Masc.* colon.

dévaliser *verb* [1] to rob.

dévaluer *verb* [1] to devalue.

devant *noun Masc.* front.

devant *preposition* **1** in front of; **elle était devant moi dans la queue** she was in front of me in the queue; **il l'a dit devant ses parents** he said it in front of his parents;

2 outside; **devant la boulangerie** outside the baker's.

développement *noun Masc.* development; **les pays en voie de développement** developing countries.

développer *verb* [1] **1** to develop; **2** to expand; **3 se développer** to expand; **la ville se développe** the town is expanding.

devenir *verb* [81] to become; **elle est devenue médecin/infirmière** she went into medicine/nursing.

déverser *verb* [1] **1** to pour out; **2** to tip out.

déviation *noun Fem.* diversion.

deviner *verb* [1] **1** to guess; **2** to foresee.

devinette *noun Fem.* riddle.

devis *noun Masc.* quote, estimate.

devises *plural noun Fem.* (foreign) currency.

dévisser *verb* [1] to unscrew.

devoir *noun Masc.* **1** exercise, test; **2 devoirs** homework; **faire ses devoirs** to do your homework; **3** duty.

devoir *verb* [8] **1** to owe; **elle me doit vingt euros** she owes me twenty euros; **je vous dois combien?** how much do I owe you?; **2** to have to; **je dois partir à dix heures** I have to (or I must) leave at ten o'clock; **3 tu dois être fatigué** you must be tired; **elle doit avoir quarante ans** she must be forty; **il a dû oublier** he must have forgotten; **4 tu devrais partir** you ought to leave, you should leave; **tu aurais dû partir** you should have left; **5 elle doit arriver à cinq**

heures she's supposed to arrive at five o'clock.

dévorer *verb* [1] to devour.

dévoué *adjective* devoted.

dévouement *noun Masc.* devotion.

dévouer *verb* [1] **se dévouer à** to devote oneself to.

diabète *noun Masc.* diabetes.

diabétique *noun Masc. & Fem.*, *adjective* diabetic.

diable *noun Masc.* devil.

diabolo *noun Masc.* fruit cordial and lemonade; **un diabolo menthe** a mint cordial and lemonade.

diagnostic *noun Masc.* diagnosis.

diagnostique *adjective* diagnostic.

diagnostiquer *verb* [1] to diagnose.

diagonal (*Masc. plural* **diagonaux**) *adjective* diagonal.

diagonale *noun Fem.* diagonal; **en diagonale** diagonally.

diagramme *noun Masc.* graph.

dialecte *noun Masc.* dialect.

dialogue *noun Masc.* dialogue.

dialyse *noun Fem.* dialysis.

diamant *noun Masc.* diamond.

diamètre *noun Masc.* diameter.

diapo *noun Fem.* (*informal*) slide SHORT FOR **diapositive**.

diapositive *noun Fem.* slide.

diarrhée *noun Fem.* diarrhoea.

dico *noun Masc.* (*informal*) dictionary SHORT FOR **dictionnaire**.

dictateur *noun Masc.* dictator.

dictature *noun Fem.* dictatorship.

dictée *noun Fem.* dictation.

dicter verb [1] to dictate.

dictionnaire noun Masc. dictionary.

dicton noun Masc. saying.

diesel noun Masc. diesel.

diététique noun Fem. **un magasin de diététique** a health-food shop.

diététique adjective dietary.

dieu (plural **dieux**) noun Masc. god.

Dieu noun Masc. God; **mon Dieu!** good heavens!

différemment adverb differently.

différence noun Fem.
1 difference; **quelle est la différence (entre)?** what's the difference (between)?; **2 à la différence de** unlike.

différend noun Masc. disagreement.

différent adjective 1 different; **différent de** different from; **2 various, different; différentes personnes** various people, different people.

difficile adjective 1 difficult, hard; **difficile à faire** difficult to do; **leur maison est difficile à trouver** their house is difficult to find; **c'est difficile à imaginer** it's hard to imagine; **2 hard to please, fussy.

difficilement adverb with difficulty.

difficulté noun Fem. difficulty; **avoir de la difficulté à faire** to have difficulty in doing; **j'ai eu de la difficulté à vous joindre** I had difficulty getting in touch with you.

difforme adjective deformed, misshapen.

difformité noun Fem. deformity.

diffuser verb [1] 1 to broadcast; **2 to distribute; 3 to spread.

digérer verb [24] to digest.

digestif noun Masc. (after-dinner) liqueur.

digestion noun Fem. digestion.

digital (Masc. plural **digitaux**) adjective digital.

digne adjective 1 worthy; **digne de** worthy of; **digne de foi** trustworthy; **2 dignified.

dignité noun Fem. dignity.

digue noun Fem. 1 sea wall; **2 dyke.

dilemme noun Masc. dilemma.

diligent adjective diligent.

diluant noun Masc. thinner.

diluer verb [1] 1 to dilute; **2 to thin (paint).

dimanche noun Masc. 1 Sunday; **nous sommes dimanche aujourd'hui** it's Sunday today; **dimanche dernier** last Sunday; **dimanche prochain** next Sunday; **2 on Sunday; je t'appellerai dimanche soir** I'll ring you on Sunday evening; **3 le dimanche** on Sundays; **fermé le dimanche** closed on Sundays; **4 tous les dimanches** every Sunday.

dimension noun Fem. size.

diminuer verb [1] 1 to reduce; **2 to come (or go) down; 3 to decrease; **4 to die down.

dinde noun Fem. turkey (as meat).

dindon noun Masc. turkey (when alive).

a
b
c
d
e
f
g
h
i
j
k
l
m
n
o
p
q
r
s
t
u
v
w
x
y
z

a b c **d** e f g h i j k l m n o p q r s t u v w x y z

dîner noun Masc. dinner, supper; **inviter quelqu'un à dîner** to invite somebody to dinner.

dîner verb [1] to have dinner; **viens dîner chez nous ce soir** come to dinner with us this evening.

dingue adjective (informal) crazy.

dinosaure noun Masc. dinosaur.

diplomate noun Masc. & Fem. diplomat.

diplomate adjective diplomatic.

diplomatie noun Fem. diplomacy.

diplomatique adjective diplomatic.

diplôme noun Masc. 1 diploma, certificate; 2 (university) degree.

diplômé adjective qualified.

dire verb [9] 1 to say; **elle dit qu'elle est malade** she says she's ill; 2 to tell; **dire quelque chose à quelqu'un** to tell somebody something; **j'ai dit à Anne que tu l'appellerais** I told Anne you'd ring her; **dire à quelqu'un de faire** to tell somebody to do; **je leur ai dit de venir à cinq heures** I told them to come at five o'clock; **on dirait qu'il va pleuvoir** it looks like rain; **dire la vérité** to tell the truth; **dire l'heure** to tell the time; **dire des mensonges** to tell lies.

direct adjective 1 direct; **un vol direct** a direct flight; 2 (in broadcasting) **en direct de** live from.

directement adverb 1 directly; 2 **aller directement à** to go straight to.

directeur, directrice noun Masc., Fem. 1 director; 2 manager; 3 head (of a school).

directeur général, directrice générale noun Masc.,Fem. managing director.

direction noun Fem. 1 direction; **en direction de** towards, in the direction of; 2 management; 3 steering (of a vehicle).

dirigeant, dirigeante noun Masc., Fem. leader.

diriger verb [52] 1 to direct; 2 to manage; 3 to conduct (an orchestra); 4 **se diriger vers** to make for; **elle s'est dirigée vers la porte** she made for the door.

discerner verb [1] 1 to make out; 2 to detect.

discipline noun Fem. 1 discipline; 2 subject (of study).

discipliner verb [1] 1 to discipline; 2 to control.

disco noun Masc. 1 disco; 2 disco music.

discothèque noun Fem. 1 disco, discotheque; 2 music library.

discours noun Masc. speech.

discret (Fem. **discrète**) adjective 1 discreet; 2 quiet; 3 subtle.

discrétion noun Fem. discretion.

discrimination noun Fem. discrimination.

discussion noun Fem. discussion.

discutable adjective questionable; **une décision discutable** a questionable decision.

discuter verb [1] 1 to talk; **on peut discuter tranquillement chez moi** we can talk in peace at my house; 2 to argue; **ça se discute** it's arguable; 3 **discuter de quelque**

chose to discuss something; **on va en discuter demain** we'll discuss it tomorrow.

disparaître verb [27] **1** to disappear; **2 faire disparaître quelque chose** to get rid of something; **3** to die; **4** to die out (traditions, customs).

disparition noun Fem. **1** disappearance; **2 une espèce en voie de disparition** an endangered species; **3** death.

disparu, disparue noun Masc., Fem. **1** missing person; **2 les disparus** the dead.

disparu adjective **1** missing; **2** lost; **3** dead; **4** extinct.

dispenser verb [1] **1** to hand out; **2** to give; **3 dispenser quelqu'un de** to exempt somebody from.

disperser verb [1] **1** to break up (a crowd or demonstration); **2 se disperser** to break up; **la foule s'est dispersée** the crowd broke up.

disponibilité noun Fem. availability.

disponible adjective available.

disposé adjective **1** arranged, laid out; **2 être disposé à faire** to be willing to do.

disposer verb [1] **1** to arrange, to lay out; **2 disposer de quelque chose** to have something (at your disposal).

dispositif noun Masc. **1** device; **2** system.

disposition noun Fem. **1** arrangement, layout; **2 à ta disposition** at your disposal; **3** measure.

dispute noun Fem. argument.

disputé adjective **1** contested; **2** controversial.

disputer verb [1] **1 se disputer** to argue; **ils se sont disputés** they had an argument; **2 se disputer quelque chose** to fight over something; **3 se faire disputer** (informal) to get told off; **je me suis fait disputer par mon patron** I got told off by my boss.

disqualifier verb [1] to disqualify.

disque noun Masc. **1** record; **passer un disque** to play a record (or CD); **2** disc; **3** (computer) disk.

disque compact noun Masc. compact disc, CD.

disque dur noun Masc. hard disk (of a computer).

disquette noun Fem. (computer) diskette.

disséquer verb [24] to dissect.

dissertation noun Fem. essay.

dissident, dissidente noun Masc., Fem. dissident.

dissimuler verb [1] to conceal.

dissocier verb [1] to separate.

dissolvant noun Masc. **1** nail polish remover; **2** solvent.

dissoudre verb [67] **1 dissoudre quelque chose** to dissolve something; **2 se dissoudre** to dissolve.

dissuader verb [1] **1 dissuader quelqu'un de faire** to persuade somebody not to do, to put somebody off doing; **il m'a dissuadé d'y aller** he persuaded me not to go; **2** to deter; **pour dissuader**

a
b
c
d
e
f
g
h
i
j
k
l
m
n
o
p
q
r
s
t
u
v
w
x
y
z

les voleurs in order to deter thieves.

distance noun Fem. **1** distance; **une distance de cinq kilomètres** a distance of five kilometres; **c'est à quelle distance d'ici?** how far is it from here?; **à distance** from a distance; **l'enseignement à distance** distance learning; **2** gap.

distant adjective distant; **distant de** far away from; **un village distant de trois kilomètres** a village three kilometres away.

distiller verb [1] to distil.

distillerie noun Fem. distillery.

distinct adjective distinct.

distinctif (Fem. **distinctive**) adjective distinctive.

distinction noun Fem. distinction.

distingué adjective distinguished.

distinguer verb [1] **1** to make out; **j'ai distingué un bateau à l'horizon** I made out a boat on the horizon; **2** distinguer entre to distinguish between.

distraction noun Fem. **1** entertainment; **on a besoin d'un peu de distraction** we need a bit of entertainment; **2** leisure; **3** leisure activity, form of entertainment; **4** absent-mindedness.

distraire verb [78] **1** to amuse, to entertain; **ça m'a distrait un peu** that cheered me up a bit; **2** to distract; **3 se distraire** to amuse yourself, to enjoy yourself.

distrait adjective absent-minded.

distribuer verb [1] **1** to hand out, to distribute; **2 distribuer les cartes** to deal (in a card game);

3 distribuer le courrier to deliver the mail.

distributeur noun Masc. **1** distributor; **2 un distributeur automatique** a vending machine; **3 un distributeur de tickets** a ticket machine; **4 un distributeur de billets** a cash dispenser.

distribution noun Fem. **1** distribution; **2** handing out; **3** delivery (of mail); **4** cast (of a play).

diverger verb [52] to diverge.

divers adjective various; **dans divers pays** in various countries.

divertir verb [2] **1** to amuse, to entertain; **2 se divertir** to amuse oneself.

divertissant adjective amusing, entertaining.

divin adjective divine.

diviser verb [1] to divide.

division noun Fem. division.

divorce noun Masc. divorce.

divorcé adjective divorced; **mes parents sont divorcés** my parents are divorced.

divorcer verb [61] to get divorced; **ils ont divorcé après dix ans de mariage** they got divorced after being married for ten years.

dix number ten; **elle a dix ans** she's ten; **il est dix heures** it's ten o'clock; **le dix juillet** the tenth of July.

dix-huit number eighteen; **il a dix-huit ans** he's eighteen; **à dix-huit heures** at six p.m.

dixième noun Masc. **au dixième** on the tenth floor.

dixième *adjective* tenth.

dix-neuf *number* nineteen; **elle a dix-neuf ans** she's nineteen; **à dix-neuf heures** at seven p.m.

dix-sept *number* seventeen; **elle a dix-sept ans** she's seventeen; **à dix-sept heures** at five p.m.

dizaine *noun Fem.* **1** ten; **2 une dizaine de personnes** about ten people.

docteur *noun Masc.* doctor.

document *noun Masc.* document.

documentaire *noun Masc., adjective* documentary.

documentaliste *noun Masc. & Fem.* librarian.

documentation *noun Fem.* **1** documentation; **2** material; **3** research.

documenter *verb* [1] **se documenter sur quelque chose** to gather information on something.

dodo *noun Masc.* **faire dodo** (*baby talk*) to sleep; **on va faire dodo** time to tuck up in bed.

dogmatique *adjective* dogmatic.

doigt *noun Masc.* finger; **se couper le doigt** to cut your finger; **avoir mal au doigt** to have a sore finger; ★ **être à deux doigts de** to be within an inch of (*literally: to be two fingers away from*).

doigt de pied *noun Masc.* toe.

domaine *noun Masc.* **1** estate; **2** field, domain.

dôme *noun Masc.* dome.

domestique *noun Masc. & Fem.* servant.

domestique *adjective* domestic.

domicile *noun Masc.* **1** place of residence; **2 à domicile** at home; **travailler à domicile** to work at home.

dominant *adjective* **1** dominant; **2** main.

dominer *verb* [1] **1** to dominate; **2** to control.

Dominicain, Dominicaine *noun Masc.,Fem.* Dominican.

dominicain *adjective* Dominican; **la République dominicaine** the Dominican Republic.

domino *noun Masc.* domino; **jouer aux dominos** to play dominoes.

dommage *noun Masc.* **1 c'est dommage** it's a pity; **c'est dommage qu'elle n'y soit pas allée** it's a pity she didn't go; **2 les dommages** damage.

dompter *verb* [1] to tame.

DOM-TOM SHORT FOR **départements et territoires d'outre-mer** (*French overseas departments and territories*).

don *noun Masc.* **1** gift; **faire don de** to give; **2** donation; **dons en argent** cash donations; **3** gift, talent; **elle a un don pour les langues** she has a gift for languages; **avoir le don de faire quelque chose** to have the gift of doing something.

donc *conjunction* so, therefore.

donne *noun Fem.* deal (*in card games*).

donné *adjective* given; **étant donné que** given that.

donnée *noun Fem.* **1** fact; **2 données** data.

donner *verb* [1] **1** to give; **donner quelque chose à quelqu'un** to give somebody something; **elle m'a donné dix euros** she gave me ten euros; **donne-moi ton adresse** give me your address; **2** to give away; **il a donné tous ses livres** he gave away all his books; **3 ma fenêtre donne sur la rue** my window looks onto the street; **4 se donner à quelque chose** to devote yourself to something.

dont *relative pronoun* whose, of which; **une personne dont j'ai oublié le nom** a person whose name I've forgotten; **la maison dont je parle** the house I'm talking about; **six verres dont l'un est cassé** six glasses, one of which is broken.

doré *adjective* **1** gold; **2** gilt; **3** golden.

dorénavant *adverb* from now on; **dorénavant je serai là tous les jours** from now on I'll be here every day.

dorer *verb* [1] **1** to gild; **2 faire dorer** to brown (*meat or vegetables*).

dormir *verb* [37] to sleep; **tu as bien dormi?** did you sleep well?; **elle va dormir chez moi** she's going to spend the night at my house; **il dort** he's asleep.

dortoir *noun Masc.* dormitory.

dos *noun Masc.* back; **avoir mal au dos** to have backache; **faire quelque chose dans le dos de quelqu'un** to do something behind somebody's back; **elle me tournait le dos** she had her back to me; **il m'a tourné le dos** he turned his back on me.

dosage *noun Masc.* **1** amount; **2** mixture.

dose *noun Fem.* **1** dose; **2** measure.

dossier *noun Masc.* **1** file; **2** application form; **remplir un dossier** to fill in an application form; **3 dossier médical** medical records; **4 le dossier d'une chaise** the back of a chair.

douane *noun Fem.* **la douane** customs; **passer la douane** to go through customs.

douanier *noun Masc.* customs officer.

double *noun Masc.* **1 le double (de)** twice as much, twice as many; **2** copy, duplicate; **3** double.

double *adjective* double.

doublé *adjective* **1** lined; **2** dubbed (*film*).

doublement *adverb* doubly.

doubler *verb* [1] **1** to double; **2** to overtake; **il m'a doublé dans un virage** he overtook me on a bend; **3** to line (*a garment*); **4** to dub (*a film*).

doublure *noun Fem.* lining.

douce *adjective* SEE **doux**.

doucement *adverb* **1** gently; **2** slowly; **3** softly.

douceur *noun Fem.* **1** softness; **2** gentleness; **3** mildness (*of weather*).

douche *noun Fem.* shower; **prendre une douche** to take a shower.

doucher *verb* [1] **se doucher** to have a shower.

doué adjective gifted; **être doué pour quelque chose** to have a gift for something.

douillet (Fem. **douillette**) adjective cosy.

douleur noun Fem. **1** pain; **2** grief.

douloureux (Fem. **douloureuse**) adjective painful.

doute noun Masc. **1** doubt; **2 sans doute** probably.

douter verb [1] **1** to doubt; **douter de** to have doubts about; **2 se douter de** to suspect; **je m'en doutais** I thought as much.

douteux (Fem. **douteuse**) adjective **1** doubtful; **2** dubious.

Douvres noun Dover.

doux (Fem. **douce**) adjective **1** soft; **2** gentle; **3** mild; **4** sweet.

douzaine noun Fem. **1** dozen; **2 une douzaine (de)** a dozen or so.

douze number twelve; **elle a douze ans** she's twelve; **le douze juillet** the twelfth of July.

douzième noun Masc. **au douzième** on the twelfth floor.

douzième adjective twelfth.

dragée noun Fem. sugared almond.

draguer verb [1] (informal) **draguer quelqu'un** to chat somebody up; **il est toujours en train de draguer les nanas** he's always chatting up the girls; **se faire draguer** to get chatted up; **Carole s'est fait draguer par ton copain** Carole got chatted up by your mate.

dramatique adjective **1** tragic; **2** dramatic; **l'art dramatique** drama.

drame noun Masc. **1** tragedy; **2** drama; **il en a fait tout un drame** he made a big scene about it.

drap noun Masc. sheet.

drapeau (plural **drapeaux**) noun Masc. flag.

drap-housse noun Masc. fitted sheet.

dresser verb [1] **1** to train (an animal); **2** to put up (a tent); **3** to draw up (a list); **4 se dresser** to stand up.

drogue noun Fem. drug; **la drogue** drugs; **les drogues douces** soft drugs; **les drogues dures** hard drugs.

droguer verb [1] **1** to drug, to give drugs to; **2 se droguer** to take drugs.

droguerie noun Fem. hardware shop.

droit noun Masc. **1** right; **les droits de l'homme** human rights; **2 avoir le droit de faire** to be allowed to do; **je n'ai pas le droit de sortir ce soir** I'm not allowed to go out tonight; **3 avoir le droit de faire** to have the right to do; **tu n'as pas le droit de me critiquer** you have no right to criticize me; **4 le droit** law; **un étudiant en droit** a law student; **5** fee; **les droits d'inscription** enrolment fees.

droit adjective **1** straight; **une ligne droite** a straight line; **cette ligne n'est pas droite** this line is crooked; **2** right; **ma main droite** my right hand; **3 un angle droit** a right angle.

droit adverb straight; **continuez tout droit** go straight ahead.

a

b

c

d

e

f

g

h

i

j

k

l

m

n

o

p

q

r

s

t

u

v

w

x

y

z

droite noun Fem. **1** right; **à droite** on the right; **tourner à droite** to turn right; **à la droite** on your right; **2 la droite** the right (in politics).

droitier (Fem. **droitière**) adjective right-handed.

drôle adjective **1** funny; **une histoire drôle** a funny story; **un film très drôle** a really funny film; **2** odd; **un drôle de film** an odd film.

drôlement adverb **1** (informal) really; **c'était drôlement bon!** it was really good!; **2** oddly, peculiarly.

dû, due, dus verb SEE **devoir**.

du article some, any SEE **de**.

duc noun Masc. duke.

duchesse noun Fem. duchess.

dune noun Fem. dune.

duo noun Masc. duet.

duplex noun Masc. maisonette.

duquel pronoun (= de lequel).

dur adjective **1** hard; **2** tough (meat); **3** difficult, hard.

dur adverb **travailler dur** to work hard.

durant preposition **1** for; **des années durant** for years; **2** during.

durcir verb [2] **1** to harden; **2 se durcir** to harden.

durée noun Fem. length.

durement adverb harshly.

durer verb [1] **1** to last; **2 durer pendant trois mois** to go on for three months.

dureté noun Fem. **1** hardness; **2** toughness; **3** difficulty.

duvet noun Masc. sleeping bag.

DVD noun Masc. DVD.

dynamique adjective dynamic, lively.

dyslexique noun Masc. & Fem. dyslexic.

Ee

eau noun Fem. water; **est-ce que tu veux de l'eau?** would you like some water?; **un verre d'eau** a glass of water; **eau gazeuse** sparkling mineral water; **eau plate** still mineral water; **'eau potable'** 'drinking water'; **'eau non potable'** 'not drinking water'; ★ **tomber à l'eau** to fall through (literally: to fall into the water); **nos projets sont tombés à l'eau** our plans have fallen through; ★ **mettre l'eau à la bouche de quelqu'un** to make somebody's mouth water; **ta sauce sent tellement bon que ça me met l'eau à la bouche** your sauce smells so good it's making my mouth water.

eau de Javel noun Fem. bleach.

eau de toilette noun Fem. toilet water.

eau minérale noun Fem. mineral water.

ébaucher verb [1] **1** to sketch; **2** to outline.

ébéniste noun Masc. & Fem. cabinet maker.

éblouir verb [2] to dazzle.

éblouissant adjective dazzling.

éboueur noun Masc. refuse collector.

ébouillanter verb [1] to scald.

ébranler verb [1] to shake.

ébullition noun Fem. boiling point; **porter à ébullition** to bring to the boil.

écaille noun Fem. **1** scale (of a fish or reptile); **2** tortoiseshell.

écailler verb [1] **s'écailler** to flake; **la peinture s'écaille** the paint's flaking.

écart noun Masc. **1** gap, distance; **faire un écart** to swerve; **la voiture a fait un écart pour éviter le chien** the car swerved to avoid the dog; **2** difference; **3** à l'écart de away from.

écarté adjective **1** un village écarté a remote village; **2** les jambes écartées with legs apart; **3** les bras écartés with arms outstretched.

écarter verb [1] **1** to move apart; **écarter les rideaux** to open the curtains; **2** to move back.

échafaudage noun Masc. scaffolding.

échalote noun Fem. shallot.

échange noun Masc. exchange; **en échange (de)** in exchange (for), in return (for).

échanger verb [52] to exchange, to swap; **nous avons échangé nos adresses** we exchanged addresses.

échangeur noun Masc. (motorway) interchange.

échantillon noun Masc. sample.

échapper verb [1] **1** échapper à to escape, to escape from, to get away from; **le week-end nous échappons à la ville** at weekends

we get away from the town; **2** s'échapper to escape.

écharde noun Fem. splinter.

écharpe noun Fem. scarf.

échasse noun Fem. stilt.

échec noun Masc. failure.

échecs plural noun Masc. chess; **jouer aux échecs** to play chess.

échelle noun Fem. **1** ladder; **2** scale.

échelon noun Masc. **1** rung; **2** grade.

échiquier noun Masc. chessboard.

écho noun Masc. **1** echo; **2** des échos rumours.

échographie noun Fem. (medical) scan; **passer une échographie** to have a scan.

échouer verb [1] to fail; **échouer à un examen** to fail an exam.

éclabousser verb [1] to splash.

éclair noun Masc. **1** flash of lightning; **2** un éclair au chocolat a chocolate eclair.

éclairage noun Masc. lighting.

éclairagiste noun Masc. & Fem. lighting engineer.

éclaircie noun Fem. sunny interval.

éclairer verb [1] to light (up).

éclat noun Masc. **1** splinter, fragment; **2** brightness; **3** splendour; **4** un éclat de rire a roar of laughter.

éclatant adjective brilliant; **des murs d'une blancheur éclatante** brilliant white walls.

éclater verb [1] **1** to burst; **un pneu a éclaté** a tyre has burst; **2** to shatter; **l'ampoule a éclaté** the bulb shattered; **3** to break out (*war or fighting*); **4 éclater de rire** to burst out laughing; **éclater en sanglots** to burst into tears.

éclipse noun Fem. eclipse.

écluse noun Fem. lock (*on a canal or river*).

écœurant adjective sickly.

écœurer verb [1] to make (somebody) feel sick.

école noun Fem. school; **aller à l'école** to go to school.

école de conduite noun Fem. driving school.

école de langue noun Fem. language, school.

école maternelle noun Fem. (state) nursery school (*age 2 – 6*).

école primaire noun Fem. primary school (*age 6 –11*).

écolier, écolière noun Masc., Fem. schoolchild.

écologie noun Fem. ecology.

écologique adjective **1** ecological; **2** environmentally friendly.

écologiste noun Masc. & Fem. ecologist.

économe noun Masc. potato peeler.

économe adjective economical.

économie noun Fem. **1** economy; **2** economics; **3 les économies** savings; **faire des économies** to save up.

économique adjective **1** economical; **2** economic.

économiser verb [1] to save.

économiste noun Masc. & Fem. economist.

écorce noun Fem. **1** bark (*of a tree*); **2** peel (*of an orange or a lemon*).

écorcher verb [1] **s'écorcher le genou** to graze your knee.

écorchure noun Fem. graze.

écossais noun Masc. tartan (cloth).

écossais adjective **1** Scottish; **2** tartan; **une jupe écossaise** a tartan skirt.

Écossais, Écossaise noun Masc., Fem. Scotsman, Scotswoman, Scot; **les Écossais** the Scots.

Écosse noun Fem. Scotland; **elle habite en Écosse** she lives in Scotland.

écourter verb [1] to shorten.

écouter verb [1] to listen to; **j'écoute beaucoup la radio** I listen to the radio a lot; **écoute-moi** listen to me.

écouteur noun Masc. **1** receiver (*on a telephone*); **2** headphones.

écran noun Masc. screen; **à l'écran** on the screen; **le petit écran** television; **la crème écran total** sun block.

écrasant adjective crushing, overwhelming; **une victoire/défaite écrasante** a crushing victory/defeat.

écraser verb [1] **1** to crush; **écrasez les noix** crush the walnuts; **2** to squash; **tu vas écraser les pêches!** you'll squash the peaches!; **3 écraser une cigarette** to stub out a cigarette; **4 se faire écraser** to get run over; **Attention! Tu vas te faire écraser!** Watch out! You'll get run over!; **5 s'écraser** to crash; **leur voiture s'est écrasée contre un mur** their car crashed into a wall.

écrémé *adjective* **le lait écrémé** skimmed milk; **le lait demi-écrémé** semi-skimmed milk.

écrevisse *noun Fem.* crayfish.

écrire *verb* [38] **1** to write; **elle m'a écrit une lettre** she wrote me a letter; **2 s'écrire** to write to each other; **ils s'écrivent tous les jours** they write to each other every day; **3 s'écrire** to be spelled; **comment ça s'écrit?** how do you spell it?

écrit *noun Masc.* **1** (*piece of an exam*) writing; **2** written paper (*of an exam*); **il a réussi à l'oral mais il a raté l'écrit** he passed the oral but failed the written paper; **3 à l'écrit** in writing.

écrit *adjective* written.

écriture *noun Fem.* handwriting.

écrivain *noun Masc.* writer.

écrou *noun Masc.* nut (*screwed onto a bolt*).

écrouler *verb* [1] **s'écrouler** to collapse.

écume *noun Fem.* **1** foam, froth; **2** scum.

écureuil *noun Masc.* squirrel.

écurie *noun Fem.* stable.

eczéma *noun Masc.* eczema.

EDF *SHORT FOR* **Électricité de France** French electricity company.

Édimbourg *noun* Edinburgh.

éditer *verb* [1] to publish.

éditeur *noun Masc.* publisher.

édition *noun Fem.* **1** publishing; **elle travaille dans l'édition** she works in publishing; **2** edition; **une**

édition de poche a paperback edition.

édredon *noun Masc.* eiderdown.

éducateur, éducatrice *noun Masc., Fem.* special needs teacher.

éducatif (*Fem.* **éducative**) *adjective* educational.

éducation *noun Fem.* education; **elle a reçu une bonne éducation** she had a good education.

éducation physique *noun Fem.* physical education, PE.

éduquer *verb* [1] to educate.

effacer *verb* [61] to rub out.

effaceur *noun Masc.* correction pen.

effarant *adjective* amazing.

effarer *verb* [1] to alarm.

effectivement *adverb* indeed (*used to show agreement with what someone has just said*); **il est effectivement extrêmement gentil** he is indeed extremely nice; **oui, elle m'a effectivement téléphoné hier** yes, that's right, she did phone me yesterday; **'Tu as oublié tes clés' – 'Ah oui, effectivement!'** 'You've left your keys behind' – 'Oh yes, so I have!'; **'Il est maintenant trop tard pour y aller' – 'Oui, effectivement'** 'It's too late to go now' – 'Yes, so it is.'

effectuer *verb* [1] to make, to carry out.

effet *noun Masc.* **1** effect; **2 en effet** indeed (*used to show agreement with what someone has just said*); **elle avait en effet raison** she was indeed right; **il fait très froid** – **'Oui, en effet'** 'It's very cold' – 'Yes,

a

it is, isn't it?'; 'Tu as laissé la porte ouverte' – 'Oui, en effet' 'You've left the door open' – 'Yes, so I have'.

b

c **efficace** *adjective* **1** efficient; **elle est très efficace** she's very efficient; **2** effective; **c'est un remède très efficace** it's a very effective remedy.

d

e **efficacité** *noun Fem.* **1** efficiency; **il est connu pour son efficacité** he's known for his efficiency; **2** effectiveness.

f **effondrer** *verb* [1] **s'effondrer** to collapse.

g **efforcer** *verb* [61] **s'efforcer de faire** to try hard to do; **elle s'efforce de rester calme** she tries hard to remain calm.

h

i **effort** *noun Masc.* effort; **faire un effort** to make an effort; **il n'a même pas fait l'effort de m'appeler** he couldn't even be bothered to phone me.

j

k

l **effrayant** *adjective* frightening.

effrayer *verb* [59] to frighten.

m **effroi** *noun Masc.* terror.

effronté *adjective* cheeky.

n **effroyable** *adjective* dreadful.

o **égal, égale** (*Masc. plural* **égaux**) *noun Masc., Fem.* equal.

p

égal *adjective* **1** equal; **une distance égale** an equal distance; **des quantités égales** equal quantities; **être égal à** to be equal to; **2 ça m'est égal** I don't mind; **'Tu veux aller au cinéma ou rester à la maison?' – 'Ça m'est égal'** 'Do you want to go to the cinema or stay at home?'– 'I don't mind'.

q

r

s

t

u

v

w

x

y

z

également *adverb* also; **elle est également prof d'allemand** she's also a German teacher.

égaler *verb* [1] to equal; **trois plus cinq égale huit** three plus five equals eight.

égaliser *verb* [1] to equalize; **ils ont égalisé dans la dernière minute** they equalized in the last minute.

égalité *noun Fem.* **1** equality; **2 les deux joueurs sont à égalité** the two players are level.

égard *noun Masc.* **1 à l'égard de** towards; **à mon égard** towards me; **2 à cet égard** in this respect.

égaré *adjective* stray; **un chien égaré** a stray dog.

égarer *verb* [1] **1** to mislay; **j'ai égaré mes lunettes** I've mislaid my glasses; **2 s'égarer** to get lost; **nous nous sommes égarés dans les petites rues** we got lost in the back streets.

égayer *verb* [59] **1** to brighten up; **j'ai acheté quelques fleurs pour égayer la pièce** I've bought some flowers to brighten up the room; **2** to cheer up; **un peu de musique va nous égayer un peu** a bit of music will cheer us up a bit.

églantine *noun Fem.* wild rose.

églefin *noun Masc.* haddock.

église *noun Fem.* church; **aller à l'église** to go to church.

égoïsme *noun Masc.* selfishness.

égoïste *adjective* selfish.

égout *noun Masc.* sewer.

égoutter *verb* [1] **1** to drain (*vegetables*); **2** to strain (*pasta*); **3** to drip.

égratignure noun Fem. scratch.

Égypte noun Fem. Egypt.

eh bien exclamation well; **eh bien, ça me fait plaisir de te revoir** well, it's nice to see you again.

élancer verb [61] **s'élancer** to dash.

élargir verb [2] to widen.

élastique noun Masc. **1** rubber band; **2** elastic.

élastique adjective **1** elastic; **2** elasticated.

électeur, électrice noun Masc., Fem. voter.

élection noun Fem. election; **une élection présidentielle** a presidential election; **se présenter aux élections** to be a candidate in the elections.

électricien, électricienne noun Masc., Fem. electrician.

électricité noun Fem. electricity.

électrique adjective **1** electric; **2** electrical.

électronique noun Fem. electronics.

électronique adjective electronic.

élégant adjective elegant.

élément noun Masc. **1** element; **2** part.

élémentaire adjective basic, elementary.

éléphant noun Masc. elephant.

élevage noun Masc. **1** farming (of livestock); **2** farm; **un élevage de porcs** a pig farm.

élevé adjective high; **une note élevée** a high mark.

élève noun Masc. & Fem. student, pupil.

élever verb [50] **1 élever un enfant** to bring up a child; **elle a été élevée en Écosse** she was brought up in Scotland; **2** to breed (animals); **3 élever la voix** to raise one's voice; **4 s'élever** to rise; **5 s'élever à** to amount to; **la facture s'élève à cinq cents euros** the bill amounts to five hundred euros.

éleveur, éleveuse noun Masc., Fem. breeder.

éliminer verb [1] **1** to eliminate; **2** to rule out; **nous ne pouvons pas éliminer cette possibilité** we cannot rule out that possibility.

élire verb [51] to elect.

elle pronoun **1** she; **où est Sylvie? — elle est dans la cuisine** where's Sylvie? — she's in the kitchen; **2** her; **Paul est avec elle** Paul's with her; **3** it (when referring to an object which is feminine in French); **où est ma tasse? — elle est sur la table** where's my cup? — it's on the table.

elle-même pronoun **1** herself; **elle me l'a dit elle-même** she told me herself; **2** itself (referring to an object which is feminine in French); **la pièce elle-même est jolie mais les meubles sont hideux** the room itself is pretty but the furniture is hideous.

elles pronoun they, them **1** they (referring to female people or feminine objects); **elles sont arrivées** they've arrived; **2** them; **avec elles** with them.

éloigné adjective distant; **la colline la plus éloignée** the most distant hill.

éloigner verb [1] **s'éloigner (de)** to move away (from).

Élysée noun Masc. the Élysée Palace (the official residence of the French President).

émail noun Masc. enamel.

emballage noun Masc. wrapping.

emballer verb [1] **1** to wrap, to pack; **2** (informal) to get enthusiastic; **elle s'est vraiment emballée pour son nouveau boulot** she's got really enthusiastic about her new job; **ça ne m'emballe pas vraiment** I'm not that keen.

embarquement noun Masc. boarding; **une carte d'embarquement** a boarding card.

embarquer verb [1] **1** (informal) to go off with; **elle a embarqué toutes mes chaises** she's gone off with all my chairs; **2 s'embarquer** to board.

embarras noun Masc. **1** embarrassment; **2** dilemma.

embarrassé adjective **1** embarrassed; **2** cluttered.

embarrasser verb [1] **1** to embarrass; **2** to clutter up.

embaucher verb [1] to take on (an employee); **ils embauchent en ce moment** they're taking people on at the moment.

embêtant adjective annoying; **c'est vraiment embêtant!** it's really annoying!

embêter verb [1] **1** to annoy; **arrête de m'embêter!** stop annoying me!; **2 s'embêter** to be bored; **on ne s'embête pas ici** there's plenty going on here; **on ne s'embête pas!** we're having a great time!

embouteillage noun Masc. traffic jam.

embrasser verb [1] to kiss; **je t'embrasse** lots of love (at the end of a letter or said on the phone to a friend).

embrayage noun Masc. clutch (in a vehicle).

émeraude noun Fem. emerald.

émerger verb [52] to emerge.

émeute noun Fem. riot.

émission noun Fem. programme (on television or radio).

emménager verb [52] to move in (to a flat or house); **nous avons emménagé la semaine dernière** we moved in last week.

emmener verb [50] to take; **c'est sa sœur qui l'emmène à l'école** it's his sister who takes him to school; **tu veux que je t'emmène?** would you like a lift?

émotif (Fem. **émotive**) adjective emotional.

émotion noun Fem. emotion.

émouvant adjective moving.

emparer verb [1] **s'emparer de** to seize.

empêcher verb [1] **1** to prevent, to stop; **rien ne t'empêche d'essayer** there's nothing to stop you trying; **2 elle n'a pas pu s'empêcher de rire** she couldn't help laughing.

empereur noun Masc. emperor.

empiler verb [1] to pile up.

empirer verb [1] to get worse.

emplacement noun Masc. site.

emploi noun Masc. **1** job; **2** use; **le mode d'emploi** instructions for use.

emploi du temps noun Masc. timetable (at school).

employé, employée noun Masc., Fem. employee.

employer verb [39] **1** to employ; **2** to use.

employeur, employeuse noun Masc., Fem. employer.

empoisonné adjective poisoned.

empoisonner verb [1] to poison.

emporter verb [1] to take (away); **'plats à emporter'** 'takeaway meals'.

empreinte noun Fem. footprint.

empreinte digitale noun Fem. fingerprint.

emprisonner verb [1] to imprison.

emprunt noun Masc. loan.

emprunter verb [1] to borrow.

emprunt-logement noun Masc. mortgage.

EMT noun (= éducation manuelle et technique) technology (at school).

ému adjective moved.

en preposition **1** in; **elle habite en Écosse** she lives in Scotland; **en été** in summer; **en avril** in April; **un livre en anglais** a book in English; **habillé en noir** dressed in black; **j'étais en pyjama** I was in my pyjamas; **2** into; **aller en ville** to go into town; **traduire en**

anglais to translate into English; **3** to; **aller en Italie** to go to Italy; **4** by; **en avion** by plane; **5** made of; **une table en bois** a table made of wood, a wooden table; **6** en **vacances** on holiday; **7** en **ami** as a friend; **8** en rentrant à la maison **j'ai rencontré Tom** as I was coming home I met Tom; **je me suis brûlé en repassant ma chemise** I burned myself (while) ironing my shirt.

en pronoun **1** j'en ai **I've got some;** **je n'en veux pas** I don't want any; **tu en as combien?** how many (of them) do you have?, how much (of it) do you have?; **elle en a quatre** she's got four; **'qui a un stylo?'** — **'j'en ai un'** 'who's got a pen?' — 'I've got one' (notice that in this sort of expression 'en' is often not translated at all); **2** elle m'en a **parlé** she told me about it; **3** j'ai **emprunté ton fer à repasser** — **est-ce que tu en as besoin?** I borrowed your iron — do you need it?

encadrement noun Masc. **1** frame; **2** framing; **3** door frame.

encadrer verb [1] to frame.

enceinte noun Fem. **1** surrounding wall; **2** enclosed space; **3** loudspeaker.

enceinte adjective pregnant.

encens noun Masc. incense.

encercler verb [1] to surround, to circle.

enchanté adjective **1** delighted; **2** (when meeting someone) **enchanté/enchantée** pleased to meet you.

a b c d e f g h i j k l m n o p q r s t u v w x y z

enchère noun Fem. bid; **une vente aux enchères** an auction sale.

encombrant adjective bulky.

encombrer verb [1] **1** to clutter; **2** to obstruct.

encore adverb **1** still; **elle est encore au bureau** she's still at the office; **il reste encore de la viande** there's still some meat left; **2 pas encore** not yet; **il n'est pas encore rentré** he hasn't come home yet, he's not home yet; **3** again; **je l'ai encore oublié** I've forgotten it again; **4** more; **encore un peu** a little more; **encore une fois** one more time; **attendre encore une semaine** to wait for another week; **5** even; **encore mieux** even better.

encourageant adjective encouraging.

encouragement noun Masc. encouragement.

encourager verb [52] **1** to encourage; **elle m'a encouragé à suivre des cours de dessin** she encouraged me to go to drawing classes; **2** to cheer on (a team).

encre noun Fem. ink.

encyclopédie noun Fem. encyclopedia.

endive noun Fem. chicory.

endommager verb [52] to damage.

endormi adjective asleep.

endormir verb [37] **1 endormir quelqu'un** to send somebody to sleep; **2 s'endormir** to fall asleep, to go to sleep.

endroit noun Masc. **1** place; **un bon endroit pour** a good place for; **2** the right side (of a garment); **3 à l'endroit** the right way up.

énergie noun Fem. energy.

énergique adjective energetic.

énervé adjective irritated, annoyed.

énerver verb [1] **1** to irritate, to annoy; **ça m'énerve!** this is getting on my nerves!; **2 s'énerver** to get annoyed.

enfance noun Fem. childhood.

enfant noun Masc. & Fem. child; **un enfant unique** an only child.

enfantin adjective **1** easy; **2** childish.

enfer noun Masc. hell.

enfermer verb [1] **1** to shut up; **2 s'enfermer** to shut yourself up; **elle s'est enfermée dans sa chambre** she shut herself up in her room.

enfiler verb [1] **1** to put on; **je vais juste enfiler mon pull** I'll just put my jumper on; **2 enfiler une aiguille** to thread a needle.

enfin adverb **1** at last; **je l'ai enfin fini** I've finished it at last; **2** finally; **elle a enfin réussi** she finally succeeded.

enflé adjective swollen; **il a le genou enflé** his knee is swollen.

enflure noun Fem. swelling.

enfoncer verb [61] **1** to push in; **2 s'enfoncer dans** to sink into.

enfreindre verb [2] to disobey; **elle a enfreint les règles** she disobeyed the rules.

engagement noun Masc. commitment.

engager verb [52] **1** to take on (an employee); **2** to commit; **3** s'engager à faire to promise to do; **je me suis engagé à organiser le repas** I promised to organize the meal.

engelure noun Fem. chilblain.

engin noun Masc. device.

engourdi adjective numb; **j'ai les doigts engourdis par le froid** my fingers are numb with cold.

engourdir verb [2] s'engourdir to go numb.

engrais noun Masc. fertilizer.

engueuler verb [1] (informal) to tell off; **elle m'a engueulé** she gave me a telling off; **se faire engueuler** to get a telling off.

énième adjective umpteenth; **pour la énième fois** for the umpteenth time.

énigme noun Fem. riddle.

enivrer verb [1] **1** enivrer quelqu'un to make somebody drunk; **2** s'enivrer to get drunk.

enjeu (plural enjeux) noun Masc. **1** stake (in a gambling game); **2** what is at stake.

enlèvement noun Masc. kidnapping.

enlever verb [50] **1** to take off (garment); **il a enlevé sa veste** he took off his jacket; **2** to remove; **enlever une tache** to remove a stain; **tu peux enlever les assiettes** you can clear the plates; **3** to kidnap.

enneigé adjective **1** snowy; **2** snow-covered.

ennemi, ennemie noun Masc., Fem. enemy.

ennui noun Masc. **1** boredom; **2** problem; **avoir des ennuis** to have problems.

ennuyé adjective **1** bored; **2** embarrassed.

ennuyer verb [41] **1** to bore; **son discours m'a ennuyé** I found his speech boring; **2** to bother; **je t'ennuie?** am I bothering you?; **3** s'ennuyer to be (or get) bored; **j'ai fini par m'ennuyer** I got bored in the end; **on s'ennuie ici** it's boring here.

ennuyeux (Fem. ennuyeuse) adjective **1** boring; **2** annoying; **ça c'est vraiment ennuyeux** that's really annoying.

énorme adjective huge.

énormément adverb **1** tremendously; **2** énormément de masses of; **j'ai énormément de choses à faire avant de partir** I've got masses of things to do before I leave.

enquête noun Fem. **1** investigation; **2** inquiry; **3** survey.

enregistrement noun Masc. **1** recording; **2** check-in (at airport).

enregistrer verb [1] **1** to record; **2** to register; **3** to check in (at airport).

enrhumer verb [1] s'enrhumer to catch a cold; **être enrhumé** to have a cold.

enrichir verb [2] **1** to make rich; **2** to enrich.

enrichissant adjective rewarding.

enrouler verb [1] to wind.

enseignant, enseignante noun Masc., Fem. teacher.

enseigne noun Fem. sign; **enseigne lumineuse** neon sign.

enseignement noun Masc. 1 teaching; 2 education.

enseigner verb [1] to teach.

ensemble noun Masc. 1 outfit; **j'ai acheté un joli ensemble pour le mariage** I've bought a lovely outfit for the wedding; 2 **l'ensemble de** the whole of; 3 **dans l'ensemble** on the whole.

ensemble adverb together; **on va y aller ensemble** we'll go together; **ils sont ensemble depuis trois ans** they've been together for three years.

ensoleillé adjective sunny.

ensommeillé adjective sleepy.

ensuite adverb then; **on va aller à la banque et ensuite chez Marianne** we'll go to the bank and then to Marianne's.

entamer verb [1] to start; **ce paquet n'a pas encore été entamé** this packet hasn't been started yet.

entasser verb [1] to pile up.

entendre verb [3] 1 to hear; **est-ce que tu l'entends?** can you hear it?; **se faire entendre** to make yourself heard; 2 **j'ai entendu dire que ...** I've heard that ...; 3 to mean; **qu'est-ce que tu entends par là?** what do you mean by that?; 4 **s'entendre bien** to get on well.

entendu exclamation 1 okay, fine; 2 **bien entendu** of course.

entente noun Fem. 1 understanding; 2 agreement.

enterrement noun Masc. funeral, burial.

enterrer verb [1] to bury.

entêté adjective stubborn.

entêter verb [1] **s'entêter à faire** to persist in doing.

enthousiasme noun Masc. enthusiasm.

enthousiasmer verb [1] **s'enthousiasmer** to get enthusiastic.

enthousiaste adjective enthusiastic.

entier (Fem. **entière**) adjective 1 whole; **une pomme entière** a whole apple; **le monde entier** the whole world; 2 **je n'ai pas lu sa lettre en entier** I haven't read his letter right through; 3 **le lait entier** full-fat milk.

entièrement adverb completely, entirely.

entorse noun Fem. sprain; **se faire une entorse à la cheville** to sprain your ankle.

entouré adjective **entouré de** surrounded by; **elle est entourée d'amis** she's surrounded by friends.

entourer verb [1] to surround; **entourer de** to surround with.

entracte noun Masc. interval (at the theatre).

entraînement noun Masc. 1 training; 2 practice.

entraîner verb [1] 1 to lead to; **entraîner des problèmes** to lead to problems; 2 to take; **il m'a entraîné chez sa copine** he took me off to his girlfriend's; 3 **entraîner une équipe** to train a team; 4 to drag;

5 s'entraîner to train; **elle s'entraîne tous les matins** she trains every morning.

entre *preposition* **1** between; **entre la porte et la fenêtre** between the door and the window; **on va le partager entre nous** we'll share it between us; **2** among; **entre eux** among themselves; **3 l'un d'entre eux** one of them.

entrée *noun Fem.* **1** entrance; **à l'entrée de** at the entrance to; **billets à l'entrée** tickets at the door; **2** hall(way); **3** admission; **4** starter, first course.

entremets *noun Masc.* dessert.

entrepôt *noun Masc.* warehouse.

entreprendre *verb* [64] **1** to undertake; **2** to start.

entreprise *noun Fem.* firm, business.

entrer *verb* [1] **1** to go in; **entrer dans un magasin** to go into a shop; **entrer à l'hôpital** to go into hospital; **2** to come in; **entrer dans** to come into; **Entrez!** Come in!

entre-temps *adverb* meanwhile.

entretenir *verb* [81] **1** to maintain (*a building, a road, etc*); **2** to support.

entretien *noun Masc.* **1** interview; **elle a été convoquée à un entretien** she's been invited for interview; **2** discussion; **j'ai eu un entretien avec mon patron** I had a discussion with my boss; **3** upkeep; **l'entretien de la maison** the upkeep of the house.

entrevue *noun Fem.* interview.

entrouvert *adjective* ajar, half-open.

envahir *verb* [2] to invade.

enveloppe *noun Fem.* envelope; **une enveloppe matelassée** a padded envelope.

envelopper *verb* [1] to wrap up.

envers *noun Masc.* **1** wrong side; **2 à l'envers** upside down, inside out, back to front.

envers *preposition* towards, to.

envie *noun Fem.* **1** urge; **avoir envie de faire** to want to do, to feel like doing; **j'ai envie de te voir** I want to see you; **j'ai envie d'aller au cinéma** I feel like going to the cinema; **2 avoir envie de quelque chose** to feel like something; **j'ai envie d'une glace** I feel like an ice cream; **3 ces frites me font envie** I fancy some of those chips.

envier *verb* [1] to envy.

envieux (*Fem.* **envieuse**) *adjective* envious.

environ *adverb* about; **environ trente personnes** about thirty people.

environnement *noun Masc.* environment.

environs *plural noun Masc.* surroundings; **aux environs de** near.

envisager *verb* [52] **envisager de faire** to plan to do; **qu'est-ce que vous envisagez de faire?** what are you planning to do?

envoi *noun Masc.* **1** dispatch; **faire un envoi de** to send; **2** consignment.

envoler *verb* [1] **s'envoler** to fly away.

a b c d e f g h i j k l m n o p q r s t u v w x y z

envoyer verb [40] to send; **envoyer quelque chose à quelqu'un** to send somebody something; **elle m'a envoyé une carte** she sent me a card; **elle m'a envoyé chercher les verres** she sent me to get the glasses.

épais (Fem. **épaisse**) adjective thick; **une tranche épaisse** a thick slice.

épaisseur noun Fem. thickness.

épargne noun Fem. savings; **une banque d'épargne** a savings bank; **un compte d'épargne** a savings account.

épatant adjective (informal) fantastic, great.

épaule noun Fem. shoulder.

épaulette noun Fem. **1** shoulder strap; **2** shoulder pad.

épave noun Fem. wreck.

épée noun Fem. sword.

épeler verb [18] to spell.

éphémère adjective fleeting.

épi noun Masc. ear (of corn); **un épi de maïs** a corn cob.

épice noun Fem. spice.

épicé adjective spicy, hot; **je n'aime pas les choses épicées** I don't like spicy food.

épicerie noun Fem. grocer's (shop); **à l'épicerie** at the grocer's.

épicier, épicière noun Masc., Fem. grocer.

épidémie noun Fem. epidemic.

épilepsie noun Fem. epilepsy.

épiler verb [1] **s'épiler les sourcils** to pluck your eyebrows; **une pince à épiler** eyebrow tweezers; **s'épiler**

les jambes to shave your legs (or use wax or cream to remove hair).

épinards plural noun Masc. spinach; **est-ce que tu aimes les épinards?** do you like spinach?

épine noun Fem. thorn.

épineux (Fem. **épineuse**) adjective prickly.

épingle noun Fem. pin; **une épingle de sûreté** a safety pin.

épingler verb [1] to pin.

éplucher verb [1] to peel.

épluchures plural noun Fem. peelings.

éponge noun Fem. **1** sponge; **2** towelling.

éponger verb [52] **1** to mop up; **2** to sponge.

époque noun Fem. time; **à cette époque-là** at that time.

épouse noun Fem. wife.

épouser verb [1] to marry.

épouvantable adjective dreadful.

épouvantail noun Masc. scarecrow.

épouvante noun Fem. terror; **un film d'épouvante** a horror film.

épouvanter verb [1] to terrify.

époux noun Masc. husband.

épreuve noun Fem. **1** test; **2** exam; **l'épreuve de français** the French exam; **3** event (sports); **4** ordeal.

éprouver verb [1] to feel, to experience.

éprouvette noun Fem. test tube.

EPS noun (éducation physique et sportive) PE.

épuisant *adjective* exhausting; **c'est un travail épuisant** it's exhausting work.

épuisé *adjective* **1** exhausted, worn out; **je suis épuisé** I'm worn out; **2** out of stock; **3** out of print.

épuiser *verb* [1] to wear out; **cette discussion m'a épuisé** that discussion's worn me out.

équateur *noun Masc.* equator.

équestre *adjective* **un centre équestre** a riding school.

équilibré *adjective* balanced.

équilibre *noun Masc.* balance.

équipage *noun Masc.* crew.

équipe *noun Fem.* team.

équipé *adjective* **1** equipped; **2 une cuisine équipée** a fitted kitchen.

équipement *noun Masc.* equipment.

équipements *plural noun Masc.* **les équipements sportifs** sports facilities.

équitation *noun Fem.* riding.

équivalent *adjective* equivalent.

érable *noun Masc.* maple tree; **le sirop d'érable** maple syrup.

errer *verb* [1] to wander.

erreur *noun Fem.* mistake; **par erreur** by mistake.

es *verb SEE* **être**[2].

escabeau *noun Masc.* stepladder.

escalade *noun Fem.* rock-climbing.

escalier *noun Masc.* **1** stairs; **dans l'escalier** on the stairs; **2** staircase; **3 un escalier mécanique, un escalier roulant** an escalator.

escargot *noun Masc.* snail.

escarpin *noun Masc.* court shoe.

esclavage *noun Masc.* slavery.

esclave *noun Masc. & Fem.* slave.

escompte *noun Masc.* discount; **un escompte de 10%** a 10% discount.

escorter *verb* [1] to escort.

escrime *noun Fem.* fencing (*the sport*).

escroc *noun Masc.* crook, swindler.

escroquer *verb* [1] to swindle.

escroquerie *noun Fem.* swindle; **quelle escroquerie!** what a swindle!

espace *noun Masc.* space.

espacer *verb* [61] to space out.

espadon *noun Masc.* swordfish.

espadrille *noun Fem.* espadrille.

Espagne *noun Fem.* Spain.

espagnol *noun Masc.* Spanish (*language*).

espagnol *adjective* Spanish.

Espagnol, Espagnole *noun Masc., Fem.* Spaniard; **les Espagnols** the Spanish.

espèce *noun Fem.* **1** sort; **une espèce de** a sort of; **on a mangé du poisson avec une espèce de sauce épicée** we had fish with a sort of spicy sauce; **2** species; **3 espèce d'idiot!** you idiot!; **4 en espèces** in cash.

espérer *verb* [24] to hope; **ils espèrent pouvoir venir** they're hoping to be able to come; **j'espère qu'elle n'a pas oublié** I hope she hasn't forgotten; **j'espère bien!** I certainly hope so.

espiègle *adjective* mischievous.

a
b
c
d
e
f
g
h
i
j
k
l
m
n
o
p
q
r
s
t
u
v
w
x
y
z

a
b
c
d
e
f
g
h
i
j
k
l
m
n
o
p
q
r
s
t
u
v
w
x
y
z

espion, espionne noun Masc., Fem. spy.

espionnage noun Masc. spying, espionage.

espionner verb [1] to spy on.

espoir noun Masc. hope.

esprit noun Masc. **1** mind; **ça ne m'est pas venu à l'esprit** it didn't cross my mind; **2** wit; **avoir de l'esprit** to be witty.

esquimau™ (plural **esquimaux**) noun Masc. ice lolly.

esquisse noun Fem. sketch.

esquisser verb [1] to sketch.

essai noun Masc. **1** trial; **2** test; **3** attempt, try.

essaim noun Masc. swarm.

essayer verb [59] **1** to try; **essayer de faire** to try to do; **j'ai essayé de t'appeler** I tried to phone you; **2** to try on; **essayer une robe** to try on a dress; **voulez-vous l'essayer?** would you like to try it on?; **3** to test.

essence noun Fem. **1** petrol; **essence sans plomb** unleaded petrol; **2** essential oil.

essentiel (Fem. **essentielle**) adjective essential; **c'est l'essentiel** that's the main thing.

essentiellement adverb **1** mainly; **2** essentially.

essorage noun Masc. spin-dry.

essorer verb [1] to spin-dry.

essoufflé adjective out of breath.

essuie-glace noun Masc. windscreen wiper.

essuie-tout noun Masc. (paper) kitchen towel.

essuyer verb [41] to wipe; **essuyer la vaisselle** to do the drying-up; **s'essuyer les mains** to dry your hands.

est¹ verb SEE **être²**.

est² noun Masc. east; **l'est de Paris** the east of Paris; **dans l'est de la France** in the east of France; **l'Europe de l'Est** Eastern Europe.

est adjective **1** east; **2** eastern.

est-ce que (used for asking questions) **est-ce qu'il pleut?** is it raining?; **est-ce que Julie est partie?** has Julie left?; **où est-ce qu'il habite?** where does he live?

esthéticienne noun Fem. beautician.

estime noun Fem. respect.

estimer verb [1] **1** to esteem; **2** to value; **3 j'estime que ...** I think that ....

estival (Masc. plural **estivaux**) adjective summer.

estivant, estivante noun Masc., Fem. summer visitor.

estomac noun Masc. stomach; **avoir mal à l'estomac** to have stomachache.

Estonie noun Fem. Estonia.

estrade noun Fem. platform.

estragon noun Masc. tarragon; **une sauce à l'estragon** a tarragon sauce.

et conjunction and.

établir verb [2] **1** to establish; **2 établir une liste** to draw up a list; **3 s'établir à son compte** to set up in business.

établissement *noun Masc.*
1 institution; **établissement
scolaire** school; **2** organization.

étage *noun Masc.* floor; **au premier
étage** on the first floor; **au dernier
étage** on the top floor; **à l'étage**
upstairs.

étagère *noun Fem.* **1** shelf; **2** set of
shelves.

étain *noun Masc.* **1** tin; **2** pewter.

étalage *noun Masc.* window
display.

étaler *verb* [1] **1** to spread; **2** to
spread out; **3** to roll out (*pastry*).

étanche *adjective* **1** watertight;
2 waterproof.

étang *noun Masc.* pond.

étape *noun Fem.* **1** stage;
2 stopping place.

état *noun Masc.* state, condition;
en mauvais état in a bad state;
en bon état in good condition;
en état de marche in working
order; **être dans tous ses états**
to be in a state.

État *noun Masc.* state, State.

États-Unis *plural noun Masc.* **les
États-Unis** the United States; **aux
États-Unis** in (*or* to) the United
States.

été[1] *verb* SEE **être**[2].

été[2] *noun Masc.* summer; **en été** in
summer; **l'été dernier** last
summer; **des vêtements d'été**
summer clothes.

éteindre *verb* [60] **1** to turn off, to
switch off; **éteindre la lumière** to
turn out the lights; **2** to put out (*a
fire or cigarette*); **3** s'éteindre to go
out.

éteint *adjective* extinct (*volcano*).

étendre *verb* [3] **1** to spread out;
2 to stretch out (*your arms or legs*);
3 **étendre le linge** to hang out the
washing; **4** s'étendre to stretch;
5 s'étendre to spread.

éternel (*Fem.* **éternelle**) *adjective*
eternal.

éternité *noun Fem.* eternity.

éternuement *noun Masc.* sneeze.

éternuer *verb* [1] to sneeze.

êtes *verb* SEE **être**[2].

ethnie *noun Fem.* ethnic group.

ethnique *adjective* ethnic.

étinceler *verb* [18] to sparkle, to
twinkle.

étincelle *noun Fem.* spark.

étiquette *noun Fem.* **1** label;
2 etiquette.

étirer *verb* [1] to stretch.

étoffe *noun Fem.* fabric.

étoile *noun Fem.* star; **une étoile
filante** a shooting star.

étonnant *adjective* **1** surprising;
2 astonishing.

étonnement *noun Masc.*
1 surprise; **2** astonishment.

étonner *verb* [1] **1** to surprise; **ça
m'a beaucoup étonné** that really
surprised me; **ça ne m'étonne pas
du tout** that doesn't surprise me at
all; **2** s'étonner to be surprised;
s'étonner de quelque chose to be
surprised at something.

étouffant *adjective* stifling.

étouffer *verb* [1] **1** to stifle; **2** to
suffocate; **3** s'étouffer to choke.

étourderie *noun Fem.* **1** absent-
mindedness; **2** **une étourderie** a
careless mistake.

étourdi, étourdie noun Masc., Fem. scatterbrain.

étourdi adjective scatterbrained.

étourdir verb [2] to daze, to stun.

étourneau noun Masc. starling.

étrange adjective strange.

étranger[1], **étrangère** noun Masc., Fem. 1 foreigner; 2 stranger.

étranger, étrangère adjective foreign; **un pays étranger** a foreign country.

étranger[2] noun Masc. **à l'étranger** abroad.

étrangler verb [1] 1 to strangle; 2 to choke.

être[1] noun Masc. being; **un être humain** a human being.

être[2] verb [6] 1 to be; **nous sommes dans la cuisine** we're in the kitchen; **elle est malade** she's ill; **c'est moi** it's me; 2 **elle est infirmière** she's a nurse; 3 **être à quelqu'un** to belong to somebody, to be somebody's; **ce livre est à Paul** this book is Paul's; **ce livre est à moi** this book is mine; 4 **il est 6 heures** it's 6 o'clock; 5 **nous sommes le 7 mars** it's the 7th of March (today); 6 (used with certain verbs to form past tenses: for a list of these, see the centre pages) **je suis allé à Paris** I went to Paris; 7 (used to form the passive of verbs) **ses robes sont faites par sa mère** her dresses are made by her mother.

étroit adjective 1 narrow; 2 close.

étroitement adverb closely.

étude noun Fem. 1 study; 2 **études** studies; **faire des études de médecine** to study medicine.

étudiant, étudiante noun Masc., Fem. student.

étudier verb [1] to study.

étui noun Masc. case.

eu verb SEE **avoir**.

euro noun Masc. euro; **l'euro est divisé en cents/centimes** the euro is divided into cents.

Europe noun Fem. Europe; **en Europe** in (or to) Europe.

européen (Fem. **européenne**) adjective European.

euthanasie noun Fem. euthanasia.

eux pronoun 1 them; **avec eux** with them; **des amis à eux** friends of theirs; 2 they.

eux-mêmes pronoun themselves.

évacuer verb [1] to evacuate; **la police a fait évacuer l'immeuble** the police evacuated the building.

évader verb [1] **s'évader** to escape.

évaluer verb [1] to assess.

évanouir verb [2] **s'évanouir** to faint.

évaporer verb [1] **s'évaporer** to evaporate.

évasion noun Fem. escape.

éveillé adjective awake.

éveiller verb [1] 1 to arouse; 2 to awaken.

événement noun Masc. event.

éventail noun Masc. fan.

éventualité noun Fem. possibility.

éventuel (Fem. **éventuelle**) adjective possible.

éventuellement adverb 1 possibly; 2 if necessary.

évêque noun Masc. bishop.

évidemment adverb of course.

évidence noun Fem. être en évidence to be clearly visible; de toute évidence clearly; de toute évidence il a oublié de venir he's clearly forgotten to come; mettre quelque chose en évidence to reveal something.

évident adjective obvious.

évier noun Masc. sink.

éviter verb [1] to avoid; éviter de faire to avoid doing; ça t'évitera de sortir that'll save you having to go out.

évolué adjective advanced.

évoluer verb [1] 1 to develop; nous ne savons pas comment la situation va évoluer we do not know how the situation will develop; 2 to progress; l'informatique a beaucoup évolué ces dernières années computer science has progressed a great deal in recent years; 3 to change; les choses ont évolué depuis things have changed since.

évolution noun Fem. 1 development; 2 progress; 3 evolution.

exact adjective 1 correct; c'est exact that's absolutely right; 2 exact, precise.

exactement adverb exactly.

exagéré adjective 1 exaggerated; 2 excessive.

exagérer verb [24] 1 to exaggerate; 2 to go too far.

examen noun Masc. 1 exam; passer un examen to sit an exam; réussir à un examen to pass an exam; un examen blanc a mock exam; 2 un examen médical a medical examination.

examinateur, examinatrice noun Masc., Fem. examiner.

examiner verb [1] to examine.

exaspérant adjective exasperating.

exaspérer verb [24] to exasperate.

excellence noun Fem. excellence.

excellent adjective excellent.

excentrique noun Masc. & Fem., adjective eccentric.

excepté preposition except.

exception noun Fem. exception; à l'exception de with the exception of.

exceptionnel (Fem. exceptionnelle) adjective 1 exceptional; 2 special.

exceptionnellement adverb exceptionally.

excès noun Masc. excess.

excès de vitesse noun Masc. speeding.

excessif (Fem. excessive) adjective excessive.

excessivement adverb excessively; il est excessivement timide he's incredibly shy.

excitant noun Masc. stimulant.

excitant adjective exciting.

excitation noun Fem. excitement.

excité adjective 1 frenzied; 2 over-excited; 3 thrilled;

a
b
c
d
e
f
g
h
i
j
k
l
m
n
o
p
q
r
s
t
u
v
w
x
y
z

exciter *verb* [1] **s'exciter** to get excited.

exclamation *noun Fem.* exclamation.

exclamer *verb* [1] **s'exclamer** to exclaim.

exclu *adjective* **il n'est pas exclu que** ... it's not impossible that ....

exclusif (*Fem.* **exclusive**) *adjective* exclusive.

excursion *noun Fem.* excursion, trip.

excuse *noun* **1** apology; **présenter ses excuses** to apologize; **2** excuse.

excuser *verb* [1] **1** to forgive; **excusez-moi!** sorry!; **excusez-moi de vous déranger** sorry to disturb you; **2 s'excuser** to apologize; **je m'excuse** I'm sorry; **je m'excuse d'être en retard** sorry I'm late.

exécuter *verb* [1] **1** to execute; **2** to carry out.

exemplaire *noun Masc.* copy; **six exemplaires du dictionnaire** six copies of the dictionary.

exemple *noun Masc.* example; **par exemple** for example; **donner l'exemple** to set an example.

exercer *verb* [61] **1** to exercise (*a right*); **2** to practise (*an art or a profession*); **3** to exert (*authority*); **4 s'exercer** to practise.

exercice *noun Masc.* exercise; **exercices de mise en forme** fitness exercises.

exhiber *verb* [1] **1** to show off; **2** to display.

exhibitionniste *noun Masc.* flasher.

exigeant *adjective* hard to please.

exiger *verb* [52] **1** to demand; **2** to require.

exil *noun Masc.* exile.

exilé, exilée *noun Masc., Fem.* exile.

existence *noun Fem.* existence.

exister *verb* [1] to exist.

exotique *adjective* exotic.

expansion *noun Fem.* **1** expansion; **2** growth.

expédier *verb* [1] to send (off); **expédier un paquet** to send off a package.

expéditeur, expéditrice *noun Masc., Fem.* sender.

expédition *noun Fem.* expedition.

expérience *noun Fem.* **1** experience; **avoir de l'expérience** to be experienced; **2** experiment; **faire une expérience** to carry out an experiment.

expérimenté *adjective* experienced.

expert *noun Masc.* expert.

explication *noun Fem.* explanation.

explicite *adjective* explicit.

expliquer *verb* [1] to explain.

exploit *noun Masc.* **1** achievement; **2** feat.

exploiter *verb* [1] **1** to exploit; **2** to use, to make use of.

explorer *verb* [1] to explore.

exploser *verb* [1] to explode, to blow up.

explosif (*Fem.* **explosive**) *adjective* explosive.

explosion noun Fem. 1 explosion; 2 boom.

export noun Masc. export.

exportateur, exportatrice noun Masc., Fem. exporter.

exportation noun Fem. export.

exporter verb [1] to export; **la Russie exporte beaucoup de pétrole** Russia exports a lot of oil.

exposé noun Masc. talk; **Gaby a fait un exposé sur le Japon** Gaby gave a talk about Japan.

exposé adjective 1 exposed; 2 on display.

exposer verb [1] 1 to exhibit; 2 to expose; 3 to explain.

exposition noun Fem. 1 exhibition; **une exposition d'art africain** an exhibition of African art; 2 exposure.

exprès adjective express.

exprès adverb 1 deliberately; **tu l'as fait exprès** you did it deliberately, you did it on purpose; **il a fait exprès de le casser** he broke it on purpose; **c'est fait exprès** it's meant to be like that; 2 specially; **je suis venu exprès pour te voir** I've come specially to see you.

express noun Masc. 1 fast train; 2 espresso coffee.

expression noun Fem. expression.

exprimer verb [1] 1 to express; 2 **s'exprimer** to express yourself; **je m'exprime mal** I'm expressing myself badly.

expulser verb [1] 1 to evict; 2 to expel.

exquis adjective exquisite, delightful.

extase noun Fem. ecstasy.

extensif (Fem. **extensive**) adjective extensive.

extension noun Fem. extension.

extérieur noun Masc. 1 outside; **à l'extérieur** outside; 2 exterior.

extérieur adjective 1 outside; 2 outer.

externat noun Masc. day school.

externe noun Masc. & Fem. day pupil.

extincteur noun Masc. fire extinguisher.

extinction noun Fem. extinction; **une espèce en voie d'extinction** an endangered species.

extra adjective (informal) great, fantastic; **ta sauce est vraiment extra!** your sauce is really fantastic!

extraction noun Fem. 1 extraction; 2 mining.

extraire verb [78] 1 to extract; 2 to mine.

extrait noun Masc. extract.

extraordinaire adjective extraordinary, amazing.

extra-terrestre noun Masc. & Fem. extra-terrestrial, alien (from outer space).

extravagant adjective 1 eccentric; **des vêtements extravagants** eccentric clothes; 2 extravagant.

extrême noun Masc., adjective extreme.

extrêmement adverb extremely.

a
b
c
d
e
f
g
h
i
j
k
l
m
n
o
p
q
r
s
t
u
v
w
x
y
z

a
b
c
d
e
f
g
h
i
j
k
l
m
n
o
p
q
r
s
t
u
v
w
x
y
z

Extrême-Orient noun Masc. the Far East.

extrémité noun Fem. 1 end; 2 tip; 3 edge; 4 extreme.

Ff

F SHORT FOR francs; 30 F 30 francs.

fabricant noun Masc. manufacturer.

fabrication noun Fem. manufacture.

fabriquer verb [1] to make; **fabriqué en France** made in France; **qu'est-ce que tu fabriques?** (informal) what are you up to?

fabuleux (Fem. **fabuleuse**) adjective fabulous.

fac noun Fem. (informal) university; **être en fac d'anglais** to be doing a degree in English.

face noun Fem. 1 face; **face à face** face to face; 2 **en face** opposite; **en face de l'école** opposite the school; **la maison d'en face** the house opposite; **le magasin en face de chez nous** the shop opposite our house; 3 **faire face à quelque chose** to face up to something; 4 **face à** facing; **face au mur** facing the wall; 5 **pile ou face?** heads or tails?

fâché adjective 1 angry; **elle est fâchée contre moi** she's angry with me; 2 **il est fâché avec son frère** he's fallen out with his brother.

fâcher verb [1] 1 **se fâcher** to get angry; **se fâcher contre quelqu'un** to get angry with somebody; **elle s'est fâchée contre moi** she got angry with me; 2 **se fâcher avec quelqu'un** to fall out with somebody.

facile adjective easy; **c'est facile** it's easy; **c'est facile à comprendre** it's easy to understand.

facilement adverb easily.

facilité noun Fem. easiness.

faciliter verb [1] to make (something) easier; **ça devrait nous faciliter les choses** that should make things easier for us.

façon noun Fem. 1 way; **il y a plusieurs façons de le faire** there are several ways of doing it; **d'une façon extraordinaire** in an extraordinary way; **de quelle façon?** in what way?; 2 **de toute façon** anyway.

façonner verb [1] 1 to make; 2 to shape.

facteur[1] noun Masc. factor.

facteur[2] noun Masc. postman; **est-ce que le facteur est passé?** has the postman been?

factrice noun Fem. postwoman.

facture noun Fem. bill; **la facture d'électricité** the electricity bill.

facultatif (Fem. **facultative**) adjective optional.

faculté noun Fem. faculty.

fade adjective tasteless; **la sauce est un peu fade** the sauce is a bit tasteless.

faible noun Masc. **avoir un faible pour** to have a soft spot for.

a
b
c
d
e
f
g
h
i
j
k
l
m
n
o
p
q
r
s
t
u
v
w
x
y
z

faible *adjective* **1** weak; **elle est encore très faible** she's still very weak; **2 elle est faible en chimie** she's not very good at chemistry; **3 un faible bruit** a faint noise.

faiblesse *noun Fem.* weakness.

faiblir *verb* [2] **1** to weaken; **2 le vent a faibli** the wind's died down a bit.

faïence *noun Fem.* earthenware; **des assiettes en faïence** earthenware plates.

faillir *verb* [42] **faillir faire** to nearly do; **j'ai failli tomber** I nearly fell; **j'ai failli rater le train** I nearly missed the train.

faillite *noun Fem.* bankruptcy; **faire faillite** to go bankrupt.

faim *noun Fem.* hunger; **avoir faim** to be hungry; **j'ai très faim** I'm really hungry; **je meurs de faim!** I'm starving!; **je n'ai plus faim** I've had enough to eat; **ces gâteaux me donnent faim** those cakes make me feel hungry.

fainéant *adjective* lazy.

faire *verb* [10] **1** to make; **faire un gâteau** to make a cake; **je vais me faire un café** I'm going to make myself a coffee; **faire du bruit** to make a noise; **2** to do; **qu'as-tu fait?** what are you doing?; **il est en train de faire ses devoirs** he's doing his homework; **faire du français** to do French; **fais comme tu veux** do as you like; **3 qu'as-tu fait du couteau?** what have you done with the knife?; **4 il fait froid** it's cold; **il fait chaud** it's hot; **5 quel temps fait-il?** what's the weather like?; **il fait beau** it's a nice

day; **il fait beau en été ici** the weather's nice here in summer; **6 ça ne fait rien** it doesn't matter; **7 faire faire quelque chose** to have (*or* get) something done; **elle a fait réparer son vélo** she got her bike repaired; **il s'est fait couper les cheveux** he's had his hair cut; **8 faire chauffer de l'eau** to heat some water; **faire cuire quelque chose** to cook something; **9 ne t'en fais pas** don't worry.

faire-part *noun Masc.* announcement (*of birth, marriage, or death*).

fais *verb* SEE **faire.**

faisan *noun Masc.* pheasant.

faisons *verb* SEE **faire.**

fait [1] *verb* SEE **faire.**

fait[2] *noun Masc.* **1** fact; **en fait** actually; **en fait je l'ai vu hier** in fact I saw him yesterday; **2 au fait** by the way; **au fait, est-ce que tu as fermé la porte?** by the way, did you shut the door?

fait d'actualité *noun Masc.* news item.

faites *verb* SEE **faire.**

falaise *noun Fem.* cliff.

fallait *verb* SEE **falloir.**

falloir *impersonal verb* [43] **1 il faut le faire** it has to be done, you must do it; **il ne faut pas faire ça** you mustn't do that; **il ne fallait pas faire ça** you shouldn't have done that; **il faudra partir à six heures** we'll have to leave at six o'clock; **2 il me faut un stylo** I need a pen; **il leur faut une voiture** they need a car; **qu'est-ce qu'il te faut?** what do you need?; **3 il faut que tu le**

fasses (*subjunctive*) you must do it; **il faut que tu prennes tes clés** you must take your keys; **4 comme il faut** properly; **tu ne l'as pas fait comme il faut** you haven't done it properly; **marche comme il faut!** walk properly.

famé *adjective* **un quartier mal famé** a rough area.

fameux (*Fem.* **fameuse**) *adjective* first-rate; **le repas n'était pas fameux** the meal wasn't great.

familial (*Masc. plural* **familiaux**) *adjective* family; **la vie familiale** family life; **les allocations familiales** child benefit.

familiariser *verb* [1] **se familiariser avec** to become familiar with.

familiarité *noun Fem.* familiarity.

familier (*Fem.* **familière**) *adjective* familiar; **un endroit familier** a familiar place.

famille *noun Fem.* **1** family; **un déjeuner en famille** a family lunch; **une famille nombreuse** a big family; **2** relatives; **j'ai de la famille à Londres** I have relatives in London.

famille monoparentale *noun Fem.* single-parent family.

fanatique *noun Masc. & Fem.* fanatic.

fané *adjective* withered; **les fleurs sont fanées** the flowers are withered.

fanfare *noun Fem.* brass band.

fantaisie *noun Fem.* **1** imagination; **2 des bijoux de fantaisie** costume jewellery.

fantaisiste *adjective* **1** unreliable; **il est un peu fantaisiste** he's rather unreliable; **2 une idée fantaisiste** a wild idea.

fantastique *adjective* fantastic.

fantôme *noun Masc.* ghost.

farce *noun Fem.* **1** practical joke; **un magasin de farces et attrapes** a joke shop; **2** stuffing (*for a chicken, for example*).

farci *adjective* stuffed; **des tomates farcies** stuffed tomatoes.

farcir *verb* [2] to stuff (*a chicken, for example*).

fard à paupières *noun Masc.* eye shadow.

fardeau (*plural* **fardeaux**) *noun Masc.* burden.

farfelu *adjective* bizarre; **c'est un type farfelu** he's a bizarre bloke; **elle a toujours des idées farfelues** she always has crazy ideas.

farine *noun Fem.* **1** flour; **2** baby cereal.

fascinant *adjective* fascinating; **son histoire était absolument fascinante** his story was absolutely fascinating.

fascination *noun Fem.* fascination.

fasciner *verb* [1] to fascinate; **ça me fascine** I find that fascinating.

fascisme *noun Masc.* fascism.

fast-food *noun Masc.* fast food.

fastidieux (*Fem.* **fastidieuse**) *adjective* tedious; **c'est un travail fastidieux** it's tedious work.

fatal *adjective* **1** inevitable; **c'était fatal** it was bound to happen; **2** fatal.

fatalité *noun Fem.* fate.

fatidique *adjective* fateful.

fatigant *adjective* tiring.

fatigue *noun Fem.* tiredness.

fatigué *adjective* tired; **je suis fatigué** I'm tired; **tu as l'air fatigué** you look tired.

fatiguer *verb* [1] **1** to tire (somebody) out; **la promenade m'a fatigué** the walk tired me out; **2 se fatiguer** to get tired.

faubourg *noun Masc.* suburb.

fauché *adjective* (*informal*) broke; **je suis fauché cette semaine** I'm broke this week.

faucher *verb* [1] **1** to mow, to scythe; **2** (*informal*) to nick; **quelqu'un m'a fauché mon vélo** somebody's nicked my bike.

faucon *noun Masc.* falcon, hawk.

faudra, faudrait *verb* SEE **falloir**.

faufiler *verb* [1] **se faufiler à travers la foule** to thread your way through the crowd.

faune *noun Fem.* wildlife.

fausse *adjective* SEE **faux**[1].

faussement *adverb* wrongly.

fausser *verb* [1] **1** to distort; **2** to bend.

faut *verb* SEE **falloir**.

faute *noun Fem.* **1** mistake, error; **faire une faute** to make a mistake; **une faute d'orthographe** a spelling mistake; **2** fault; **c'est de ma faute** it's my fault; **c'est la faute de Sophie** it's Sophie's fault; **3 faute de** for lack of; **faute de**

temps for lack of time; **faute de mieux** for want of anything better; **4 sans faute** without fail.

fauteuil *noun Masc.* armchair.

fauteuil roulant *noun Masc.* wheelchair.

fautif (*Fem.* **fautive**) *adjective* faulty.

fauve *noun Masc.* wild animal.

fauve *adjective* tawny.

faux[1] (*Fem.* **fausse**) *adjective* **1** wrong; **c'est faux** it's wrong; **2** untrue; **c'est totalement faux** it's totally untrue; **3** false; **une fausse barbe** a false beard; **4** imitation; **une table en faux marbre** an imitation marble table; **5 chanter faux** to sing out of tune.

faux[2] *noun Masc.* fake, forgery; **cette pièce est un faux** this coin's a forgery.

faux[3] *noun Fem.* scythe.

faux ami *noun Masc.* false friend (*a word in a foreign language which looks very like a word in your own language but does not mean the same thing at all*).

faux-filet *noun Masc.* sirloin.

faveur *noun Fem.* favour; **en faveur de** in favour of.

favorable *adjective* favourable.

favorablement *adverb* favourably.

favori (*Fem.* **favorite**) *adjective* favourite.

favoriser *verb* [1] to favour.

fax *noun Masc.* **1** fax; **envoyer un fax** to send a fax; **2** fax machine.

fédéral (**fédéraux**)

fédéral *adjective* federal.

fédération noun Fem. federation.

fée noun Fem. fairy; ★ **avoir des doigts de fée** to have nimble fingers (literally: to have the fingers of a fairy).

féerique adjective magical.

feignant adjective (informal) lazy.

fêler verb [1] **se fêler** to crack.

félicitations plural noun Fem. congratulations.

féliciter verb [1] to congratulate.

fêlure noun Fem. crack.

femelle noun Fem., adjective female (animal).

féminin noun Masc. **le féminin** the feminine (in French and other grammars); **au féminin** in the feminine.

féminin adjective **1** female; **le sexe féminin** the female sex; **2** feminine; **elle est très féminine** she's very feminine; **3** women's; **les vêtements féminins** women's clothing; **la presse féminine** women's magazines; **les questions féminines** women's issues.

féministe noun Masc. & Fem. feminist.

femme noun Fem. **1** woman; **c'est une femme très intéressante** she's a very interesting woman; **2** wife; **la femme de David** David's wife.

femme au foyer noun Fem. housewife.

femme d'affaires noun Fem. businesswoman.

femme de ménage noun Fem. cleaning lady.

fendre verb [3] **1** to split; **2** to crack.

fenêtre noun Fem. window; **regarder par la fenêtre** to look out the window; ★ **jeter l'argent par les fenêtres** to throw your money away (literally: to throw money out of the windows).

fenouil noun Masc. fennel.

fente noun Fem. **1** slit; **2** slot; **3** crack.

fer noun Masc. iron.

fer à cheval noun Masc. horseshoe.

fer à repasser noun Masc. iron (for ironing things with).

fer forgé noun Masc. wrought iron.

férié adjective **un jour férié** a public holiday.

ferme[1] noun Fem. **1** farm; **2** farmhouse.

ferme[2] adjective firm.

fermé adjective closed; **'fermé le dimanche'** closed on Sundays.

ferme d'éoliennes noun Fem. wind farm.

fermenter verb [1] to ferment.

fermer verb [1] **1** to close, to shut; **peux-tu fermer la porte, s'il te plaît** shut the door please; **il a fermé les yeux** he closed his eyes; **2** to turn off (the lights, the tap, the water, etc); **n'oublie pas de fermer les robinets** don't forget to turn off the taps; **3 se fermer** to close, to shut.

fermeture noun Fem. **1** closing; **heures de fermeture** closing times; **2** fastening (on a garment).

fermeture annuelle noun Fem. annual closure.

fermeture éclair noun Fem. zip.

fermier, fermière noun Masc., Fem. **1** farmer; **2 la fermière** the farmer's wife.

fermière adjective farm; **produits fermiers** farm produce; **un poulet fermier** a free-range chicken.

fermoir noun Masc. clasp.

féroce adjective **1** fierce; **2** ferocious.

ferraille noun Fem. scrap metal.

ferroviaire adjective rail; **le réseau ferroviaire** the rail network.

fertile adjective fertile.

fertilité noun Fem. fertility.

fesse noun Fem. buttock; **fesses** bottom.

festin noun Masc. feast.

festival noun Masc. festival.

fête noun Fem. **1** public holiday; **2** party; **faire la fête** to celebrate; **3 les fêtes de fin d'année** the festive season; **4** fête, fair; **5** saint's name day (in France each day of the year is associated with the name of a saint and many people still celebrate the day of the saint they are named after).

fête des Mères noun Fem. Mother's Day (in France on the last Sunday in May).

fête des Pères noun Fem. Father's Day.

fête foraine noun Fem. funfair.

Fête Nationale noun Fem. Bastille Day.

fêter verb [1] to celebrate.

feu noun Masc. **1** fire; **faire du feu** to light a fire; **prendre feu** to catch fire; **2** light; **as-tu du feu?** have you got a light?; **3 les feux de signalisation** the traffic lights; **un feu rouge** a red light; **4 faire cuire à feu doux** cook on a gentle heat; ★ **il n'y a pas le feu** there's no hurry (literally: there isn't a fire).

feu d'artifice noun Masc. **1** firework; **2** firework display.

feuillage noun Masc. leaves.

feuille noun Fem. **1** leaf; **2 une feuille de papier** a sheet of paper.

feuilleté noun Masc. savoury pasty.

feuilleté adjective **de la pâte feuilletée** puff pastry.

feuilleter verb [48] **feuilleter un livre** to leaf through a book.

feuilleton noun Masc. serial, soap (on television).

feutre noun Masc. **1** felt; **2 un feutre** a felt-tip pen.

fève noun Fem. broad bean.

février noun Masc. February; **en février, au mois de février** in February.

fiable adjective reliable.

fiançailles plural noun Fem. engagement (to be married).

fiancé, fiancée noun Masc., Fem. fiancé, fiancée.

fiancé adjective **être fiancé à quelqu'un** to be engaged to somebody.

fiancer verb [61] **se fiancer** to get engaged.

fibre noun Fem. fibre.

ficeler verb [18] to tie up.

a
b
c
d
e
f
g
h
i
j
k
l
m
n
o
p
q
r
s
t
u
v
w
x
y
z

ficelle noun Fem. **1** string; **2** thin baguette (of French bread).

fiche noun Fem. **1** form; **remplir une fiche** to fill in a form; **2** index card; **3** plug.

fiche d'inscription noun Fem. registration form.

ficher verb (informal) [1] **1** to do; **qu'est-ce que tu fiches?** what do you think you're doing?; **2 je m'en fiche!** I don't care!; **3 fiche-moi la paix!** leave me alone!

fichier noun Masc. file.

fichu adjective (informal) done for; **ma voiture est fichue** my car's had it.

fiction noun Fem. fiction.

fidèle adjective **1** faithful; **2** loyal.

fier¹ (Fem. **fière**) adjective proud.

fier² verb [1] **se fier à** to trust.

fierté noun Fem. pride.

fièvre noun Fem. fever; **avoir de la fièvre** to have a temperature.

figer verb [52] **1 se figer** to congeal; **2** to freeze to the spot.

figue noun Fem. fig.

figuier noun Masc. fig tree.

figure noun Fem. **1** face; **2** figure.

figurer verb [1] **1** to appear; **2 se figurer** to imagine.

fil noun Masc. **1** thread; **du fil à coudre** sewing thread; **2** wire, flex (of a telephone or electrical appliance); **3 un coup de fil** (informal) a phone call; **passer un coup de fil** to make a phone call; **passe-moi un coup de fil** give me a ring.

fil de fer noun Masc. wire; **fil de fer barbelé** barbed wire.

file noun Fem. **1 une file d'attente** a queue; **2 lane** (on a road).

filer verb [1] **1** to speed along; **2** (informal) to give; **elle m'a filé deux CD** she gave me two CDs (which she didn't want any more).

filet noun Masc. **1** net; **2** fillet; **un filet de poisson** a fish fillet.

fille noun Fem. **1** girl; **une petite fille** a little girl; **une jeune fille** a young woman; **2** daughter.

fillette noun Fem. little girl.

filleul, filleule noun Masc., Fem. godson, goddaughter.

film noun Masc. film.

film comique noun Masc. comedy (film).

film d'épouvante noun Masc. horror film.

filmer verb [1] to film.

film policier noun Masc. thriller.

fils noun Masc. son.

filtre noun Masc. filter.

filtrer verb [1] to filter.

fin¹ noun Fem. end; **à la fin** in the end; **à la fin du film** at the end of the film; **sans fin** endless.

fin² adjective **1** fine; **2** slender.

final (Masc. plural **finaux**) adjective final.

finale noun Fem. final, cup final.

finalement adverb **1** in the end, finally; **2** after all.

finance noun Fem. finance.

financer verb [61] to finance.

fines herbes plural noun Fem. mixed herbs.

finir verb [2] **1** to finish, to end; **le film finit à dix heures** the film finishes at ten o'clock; **2 finir de faire** to finish doing; **j'ai fini de faire la vaisselle** I've finished doing the washing-up; **3 finir quelque chose** to finish something; **as-tu fini tes devoirs?** have you finished your homework?; **j'ai fini le sucre** I've finished the sugar, I've used up all the sugar; **4 finir par faire** to end up doing; **il a fini par accepter** he accepted in the end.

finlandais noun Masc. Finnish (language).

finlandais adjective Finnish.

Finlande noun Fem. Finland.

firme noun Fem. firm.

fisc noun Masc. tax office.

fissure noun Fem. crack.

fixe adjective **1** fixed; **2 un emploi fixe** a steady job; **3 aux heures fixes** at set times.

fixer verb [1] **1** to fix (to attach); **2** to set (a date, a price); **fixer les élections législatives** to set the date for the general elections.

flacon noun Masc. (small) bottle.

flamand noun Masc. Flemish (language).

flamand adjective Flemish.

Flamand, Flamande noun Masc., Fem. Fleming (Dutch-speaking Belgian).

flamant noun Masc. flamingo.

flamber verb [1] to blaze.

flamme noun Fem. flame.

flan noun Masc. custard tart.

flanc noun Masc. side.

flâner verb [1] to stroll.

flaque noun Fem. **une flaque d'eau** a puddle.

flash noun Masc. **1** flash (on a camera); **2** newsflash.

flatter verb [1] to flatter.

flatteur (Fem. **flatteuse**) adjective flattering.

flèche noun Fem. **1** arrow; **2** spire.

fléchette noun Fem. dart; **jouer aux fléchettes** to play darts.

fléchir verb [2] **1** to bend; **2** to weaken.

fleur noun Fem. flower; **un tissu à fleurs** a flower-patterned fabric; **être en fleurs** to be in flower.

fleuri adjective **1** flowery; **du tissu fleuri** flowery material; **2 ton jardin est très fleuri** you've got lots of flowers in your garden.

fleurir verb [2] **1** to flower, to blossom; **2** to flourish.

fleuriste noun Masc. & Fem. florist.

fleuve noun Masc. river.

flexible adjective flexible.

flic noun Masc. (informal) policeman, cop.

flipper noun Masc. pinball machine.

flirter verb [1] to flirt.

flocon noun Masc. flake; **un flocon de neige** a snowflake.

flocons d'avoine plural noun Masc. porridge oats.

floral (Masc. plural **floraux**) adjective floral.

flotte noun Fem. fleet (of ships).

flotter verb [1] to float.

flou adjective **1** blurred; **une image floue** a blurred image; **2** vague; **ses**

projets sont un peu flous her plans are a bit vague.

fluide noun Masc., adjective fluid.

fluo adjective (informal) fluorescent; **vert fluo** fluorescent green.

fluor noun Masc. fluorine.

fluorescent adjective fluorescent.

flûte noun Fem. flute; **jouer de la flûte** to play the flute.

flûte à bec noun Fem. recorder.

focaliser verb [1] to focus.

foi noun Fem. faith.

foie noun Masc. liver; **une crise de foie** an upset stomach.

foin noun Masc. hay.

foire noun Fem. fair.

fois noun Fem. 1 time; **une fois** once; **deux fois** twice; **trois fois** three times; **trois fois dix** three times ten; **plusieurs fois** several times; **la première fois** the first time; **trois fois plus grand** three times as big; **2 à la fois** at the same time; **trois à la fois** three at a time; **3 une fois que** once; **une fois que j'aurai pris une douche** once I've had a shower; **4 j'ai vu une fois ...** I once saw ...; **il était une fois ...** once upon a time ...; **5 à chaque fois** whenever, each time; **à chaque fois que nous sortons, nous verrouillons la porte** whenever we go out, we lock the door.

folie noun Fem. madness; **c'est de la folie!** it's crazy!

folk noun Masc. folk music.

folle noun Fem., adjective SEE **fou**.

foncer verb [61] (informal) to rush; **tout le monde a foncé vers la**

porte everybody rushed for the door.

fonction noun Fem. 1 job; **une voiture de fonction** a company car; 2 function.

fonctionnaire noun Masc. & Fem. civil servant.

fonctionnel (Fem. **fonctionnelle**) adjective functional.

fonctionnement noun Masc. working; **comprendre le fonctionnement de quelque chose** to understand how something works.

fonctionner verb [1] to work.

fonction publique noun Fem. civil service.

fond noun Masc. 1 bottom; **au fond du lac** at the bottom of the lake; **au fond de la bouteille** in the bottom of the bottle; 2 back; **au fond du tiroir** at the back of the drawer; **au fond de la salle** at the back of the room; 3 end; **au fond du couloir** at the end of the corridor; 4 background; 5 **au fond** basically.

fondamental (Masc. plural **fondamentaux**) adjective basic, fundamental.

fondateur, fondatrice noun Masc., Fem. founder.

fondation noun Fem. foundation.

fond de teint noun Masc. make-up, foundation.

fonder verb [1] 1 to found; 2 to base.

fondre verb [3] to melt.

fondu adjective melted.

font verb SEE **faire**.

fontaine noun Fem. **1** fountain; **2** drinking fountain.

fonte noun Fem. **1** cast iron; **une poêle en fonte** a cast iron frying pan; **2** melting (of metal); **3** thawing (of ice).

foot noun (informal) **un match de foot** a football match; **jouer au foot** to play football.

football noun Masc. football.

footballeur noun Masc. footballer.

footing noun Masc. jogging; **faire du footing** to go jogging.

forain noun Masc. fairground worker.

forain adjective **une fête foraine** a funfair.

force noun Fem. **1** strength; **2** force; **de force** by force; **3** force; **force de vente** sales force; **4** à force de by; **à force de travailler toute la nuit, elle a fini sa dissertation** she finished her essay by working all night.

forcément adverb **1** inevitably; **il y a forcément une solution** there has to be a solution; **2 pas forcément** not necessarily.

forcer verb [61] **1** to force; **2 se forcer** to force yourself.

forêt noun Fem. forest.

forfait noun Masc. fixed price.

forgeron noun Masc. blacksmith.

formalité noun Fem. formality.

format noun Masc. format, size.

formation noun Fem. training; **elle a une formation d'infirmière** she's a trained nurse.

formation continue noun Fem. continuing education.

forme noun Fem. **1** shape, form; **2 être en forme** to be on form; **se mettre en forme** to get fit; **tu as l'air en forme** you're looking well.

formel (Fem. **formelle**) adjective **1** positive, categorical; **2** formal.

formellement adverb strictly; **formellement interdit** strictly forbidden.

former verb [1] **1** to form; **2** to train, to educate.

formidable adjective (informal) great, fantastic; **le film était formidable** the film was fantastic.

formulaire noun Masc. form; **remplir un formulaire** to fill in a form.

formule noun Fem. **1** formula; **Formule Un** Formula One (car racing); **2** form; **3** format.

fort adjective **1** strong; **il est très fort** he's very strong; **le café est très fort** the coffee's very strong; **2 être fort en quelque chose** to be good at something; **elle est très forte en maths** she's very good at maths; **3** stout.

fort adverb **1** extremely; **c'était fort bon** it was extremely good; **2** hard; **frapper fort** to knock (or hit) hard; **3** loudly; **chanter fort** to sing loudly; **parle plus fort** speak louder.

forteresse noun Fem. fortress.

fortifiant noun Masc. tonic.

fortifier verb [1] **1** to strengthen; **2** to fortify.

fortuit adjective accidental.

fortune noun Fem. **1** fortune; **faire fortune** to make a fortune; **2** de

a fortune makeshift; **un lit de fortune** a makeshift bed.

b fossé noun Masc. ditch.

c fossette noun Fem. dimple.

fou, folle noun Masc., Fem. madman, madwoman; **un fou m'a doublé dans un virage** a madman overtook me on a bend.

f fou (Fem. **folle**) adjective **1** mad; **devenir fou** to go mad; **2** crazy, amazing; **on a passé une soirée folle** we had an amazing evening; **il y avait un monde fou** there were masses of people; **3 être fou de** to be mad about; ★ **attraper un fou rire** to get the giggles.

foudre noun Fem. lightning; **être frappé par la foudre** to be struck by lightning.

fouet noun Masc. **1** whip; **2** whisk (for eggs, cream, etc).

fouetter verb [1] **1** to whip; **2** to whisk (eggs, cream, etc); ★ **avoir d'autres chats à fouetter** to have other fish to fry (literally: to have other cats to whip).

fougère noun Fem. **1** fern; **2** bracken.

fouille noun Fem. search.

fouiller verb [1] **1** to search; **fouiller quelqu'un** to search somebody; **la police a fouillé la chambre/la maison** the police searched the room/house; **2 fouiller dans quelque chose** to rummage through something.

fouillis noun Masc. mess.

foulard noun Masc. scarf.

foule noun Fem. **1** crowd; **2 une foule de** masses of.

four noun Masc. oven; **cuit au four** roasted, baked.

four à micro-ondes noun Masc. microwave oven.

fourche noun Fem. garden fork, pitchfork.

fourchette noun Fem. fork.

fourgon noun Masc. van.

fourgonnette noun Fem. (small) van.

fourmi noun Fem. ant; ★ **avoir des fourmis dans les jambes** to have pins and needles in your legs (literally: to have ants in your legs).

fourmiller verb [1] **fourmiller de** to be swarming with.

fourneau (plural **fourneaux**) noun Masc. stove.

fournée noun Fem. batch (of cakes, bread).

fournir verb [2] to supply.

fournisseur noun Masc. supplier.

fournitures plural noun Fem. stationery; **les fournitures de bureau** office stationery; **les fournitures scolaires** school equipment (stationery, school bags etc).

fourré adjective **1** filled; **fourré au chocolat** with a chocolate filling; **2** fur-lined.

fourrure noun Fem. **1** fur; **2** fur coat.

foyer noun Masc. **1** home; **rester au foyer** to stay at home (rather than going out to work); **une femme au foyer** a housewife; **2** hearth; **3** household; **4** hostel.

fracas noun Masc. crash.

fracasser verb [1] to smash.

fraction noun Fem. fraction.

fracture noun Fem. fracture.

fracturer verb [1] **1** to break open; **2** to fracture.

fragile adjective **1** fragile; **2** frail.

fragment noun Masc. fragment.

fraîche adjective SEE **frais**[2].

fraîcheur noun Fem. **1** coolness; **2** freshness.

frais[1] plural noun Masc. **1** expenses; **les frais de déplacement** travel expenses; **2** costs.

frais[2] (Fem. **fraîche**) adjective **1** cool, cold; **il fait frais ce matin** it's a chilly morning; **2** cool; **'boissons fraîches' 'cool drinks'**; **servir frais** serve chilled; **conserver au frais** keep in a cool place; **3** fresh; **des légumes frais** fresh vegetables; **'peinture fraîche' 'wet paint'**.

fraise noun Fem. strawberry; **une glace à la fraise** a strawberry ice cream.

framboise noun Fem. raspberry; **un yaourt à la framboise** a raspberry yoghurt.

franc[1] noun Masc. franc (the currency of Switzerland; name of the currencies used in France, Belgium and Luxembourg until replaced by the euro; 100 French francs = 15.24 euros).

franc[2] (Fem. **franche**) adjective frank.

français noun Masc. French; **j'apprends le français** I'm learning French; **Laura parle français** Laura speaks French.

français adjective French; **un film français** a French film.

Français, Française noun Masc., Fem. Frenchman, Frenchwoman; **les Français** the French.

France noun Fem. France; **aller en France** to go to France; **habiter en France** to live in France.

franche adjective SEE **franc**[2].

franchement adverb **1** frankly; **franchement, je ne le crois pas** frankly, I don't believe him; **2** really; **le film était franchement nul** the film was really awful.

franchir verb [2] to cross.

franchise noun Fem. **1** frankness, honesty; **2** franchise.

francophone adjective French-speaking.

frange noun Fem. fringe.

frangin noun Masc. (informal) brother.

frangine noun Fem. (informal) sister.

frangipane noun Fem. almond cream.

franglais noun Masc. Franglais (a mixture of French and English).

frapper verb [1] **1** to hit; **2 frapper à la porte** to knock on the door; **3** to strike; **être frappé par** to be struck by; **ça m'a beaucoup frappé** that made a big impression on me; **4 frappé par le chômage** hit by unemployment.

fraude noun Fem. **1** fraud; **2** cheating.

fredonner verb [1] to hum.

freezer noun Masc. freezer compartment (in a fridge).

frein noun Masc. brake; **les freins** the brakes; **le frein à main** the handbrake.

freiner verb [1] **1** to brake; **2** to slow down.

frêle adjective frail.

frelon noun Masc. hornet.

frémir verb [2] **1** to shudder; **2** to tremble.

frêne noun Masc. ash tree.

fréquemment adverb frequently.

fréquence noun Fem. frequency.

fréquenté adjective **1** busy; **un restaurant très fréquenté** a very busy restaurant; **2 un quartier mal fréquenté** a rough area.

fréquenter verb [1] **1** to go around with (people); **2** to go often to (a place).

frère noun Masc. brother.

fric noun Masc. (informal) money.

frictionner verb [1] to rub.

frigidaire™ noun Masc. fridge.

frigo noun Masc. (informal) fridge; **au frigo** in the fridge.

frileux (Fem. **frileuse**) adjective **être frileux** to feel the cold; **je ne suis pas frileuse** I don't feel the cold.

frime noun Fem. (informal) **c'est de la frime!** it's all show!

fringues plural noun Fem. (informal) clothes.

fripé adjective crumpled.

frire verb [74] **faire frire quelque chose** to fry something.

frisé adjective **1** curly; **2** curly-haired.

frisée noun Fem. curly endive, frisée (a sort of lettuce).

friser verb [1] to curl.

frisson noun Masc. shiver.

frissonner verb [1] **1** to shiver; **2** to shudder.

frit adjective fried.

frite noun Fem. chip, French fry; **steak frites** steak and chips.

friture noun Fem. **friture de poissons** fried fish.

froid noun Masc. **1 le froid** the cold; **2 avoir froid** to be cold; **j'ai froid** I'm cold; **3 il fait froid aujourd'hui** it's cold today; **4 prendre froid** to catch a chill.

froid adjective cold; **tes mains sont froides** your hands are cold.

froidement adverb coldly.

froideur noun Fem. coldness.

froisser verb [1] **1** to crease; **2 se froisser** to crease; **la soie se froisse facilement** silk crushes easily; **3 se froisser** to take offence; **4 se froisser** to strain (a muscle).

frôler verb [1] to brush against.

fromage noun Masc. cheese.

fromagerie noun Fem. cheese shop.

froment noun Masc. wheat.

froncer verb [61] **froncer les sourcils** to frown.

front noun Masc. **1** forehead; **2 faire front à** to face up to.

frontière noun Fem. border; **nous avons passé la frontière à Bâle** we crossed the border at Basle.

frotter verb [1] to rub; **se frotter les yeux** to rub your eyes.

fruit noun Masc. **les fruits** fruit; **acheter des fruits** to buy some fruit; **un fruit** a piece of fruit; **veux-tu un fruit?** would you like some fruit?

fruité adjective fruity.

fruits de mer plural noun Masc. seafood; **une omelette aux fruits de mer** a seafood omelette.

frustrant adjective frustrating.

frustrer verb [1] **1** to thwart; **2** to frustrate.

fugue noun Fem. **1** faire une fugue to run away; **2** fugue.

fuir verb [44] **1** to run away, to flee; **2 fuir quelque chose** to run away from something; **3** to leak; **la bouilloire fuit** the kettle's leaking.

fuite noun Fem. **1** flight; **2 prendre la fuite** to flee; **3** leak.

fulgurant adjective dazzling.

fumé adjective smoked; **du saumon fumé** smoked salmon.

fumée noun Fem. smoke; ★ **il n'y a pas de fumée sans feu** there's no smoke without fire.

fumer verb [1] **1** to smoke; **2 fumer une cigarette** to smoke a cigarette; **il fume la pipe** he smokes a pipe; ★ **fumer comme un pompier** to smoke like a chimney (literally: to smoke like a fireman).

fumeur, fumeuse noun Masc., Fem. smoker; **zone non-fumeur** no-smoking area.

fumier noun Masc. manure.

funambule noun Masc. & Fem. tightrope walker.

funèbre adjective **1** funeral; **pompes funèbres** undertaker's; **2** gloomy.

funérailles plural noun Fem. funeral.

funiculaire noun Masc. funicular.

fur noun Masc. **1 au fur et à mesure** as you go along; **je corrige les erreurs au fur et à mesure** I correct the mistakes as I go along; **2 au fur et à mesure que as**.

furet noun Masc. ferret.

fureur noun Fem. **1** rage, fury; **2** frenzy; ★ **faire fureur** to be all the rage; **ces boucles d'oreilles font fureur en ce moment** these earrings are all the rage at the moment.

furibond adjective furious.

furieusement adverb furiously.

furieux (Fem. **furieuse**) adjective furious; **elle est furieuse contre son copain** she's furious with her boyfriend.

furoncle noun Masc. boil.

fusain noun Masc. charcoal (for drawing).

fuseau noun Masc. ski pants.

fusée noun Fem. rocket.

fusible noun Masc. fuse.

fusil noun Masc. gun.

fusiller verb [1] to shoot.

fusionner verb [1] to merge.

fût noun Masc. cask, barrel.

futé adjective **1** crafty; **2** bright, clever.

futur noun Masc. future (tense).

futur adjective future; **son futur mari** her husband-to-be.

Gg

gâcher verb [1] **1** to waste; **gâcher la nourriture** to waste food; **2** to spoil; **ça m'a gâché la journée!** that's spoiled my day!

gâchis noun Masc. waste.

gadget noun Masc. gadget.

gaffe noun Fem. (informal) blunder; **j'ai fait une gaffe** I've done something stupid; ★ **fais gaffe!** watch out!.

gage noun Masc. forfeit (in a game).

gagnant, gagnante noun Masc., Fem. winner.

gagnant adjective winning.

gagner verb [1] **1** to win; **il a gagné** he's won; **gagner le match** to win the match; **2** to earn (money); **elle gagne bien sa vie** she makes a good living; **3 gagner du temps** to save time.

gai adjective cheerful.

gaieté noun Fem. cheerfulness.

gain noun Masc. **1** earnings; **2 c'est un gain de temps** it saves time.

galaxie noun Fem. galaxy.

galerie noun Fem. gallery.

galerie marchande noun Fem. shopping arcade.

galet noun Masc. pebble.

galette noun Fem. **1** biscuit; **2** round flat cake or loaf.

galette des Rois noun Fem. Twelfth Night cake (a cake eaten on Twelfth Night; it contains a 'fève', literally a bean, but usually a small ceramic figure; the person who gets this is the king or queen and is given a cardboard crown to wear).

galipette noun Fem. somersault (child's).

Galles noun **le pays de Galles** Wales.

Gallois, Galloise noun Masc., Fem. Welshman, Welshwoman; **les Gallois** the Welsh.

gallois noun Masc. Welsh (language).

gallois adjective Welsh.

galoper verb [1] to galop.

gamba noun Fem. king prawn.

gamin, gamine noun Masc., Fem. (informal) kid; **elle a trois gamins** she has three kids.

gamme noun Fem. **1** range; **la nouvelle gamme de produits de beauté** the new range of beauty products; **2** scale (in music).

gammé adjective **la croix gammée** the swastika.

gangster noun Masc. gangster.

gant noun Masc. glove.

gant de boxe noun Masc. boxing glove.

gant de ménage noun Masc. rubber glove.

gant de toilette noun Masc. facecloth.

garage noun Masc. garage.

garagiste noun Masc. & Fem. **1** garage owner; **2** motor mechanic.

garantie noun Fem. guarantee.

garantir verb [2] to guarantee.

garçon noun Masc. **1** boy; **2** young man; **un brave garçon** a nice chap; **3** waiter; **4 un vieux garçon** a bachelor.

garçon de café noun Masc. waiter (in a café).

garde noun Masc. & Fem. **1** guard; **2** nurse; **3 être de garde** to be on duty; **la pharmacie de garde** the duty chemist's; **mettre quelqu'un en garde** to warn somebody; ★ **prends garde!** watch out, be careful!

garder verb [1] **1** to keep; **est-ce que tu peux garder mon sac?** can you keep my bag for me?; **je t'ai gardé du gâteau** I've kept you some cake; **je t'ai gardé une place** I've kept you a seat; **elle a gardé son manteau** she kept her coat on; **3** to look after; **je garde mon petit-fils ce soir** I'm looking after my grandson this evening; **4 garder la maison** to guard the house.

garderie noun Fem. day nursery.

garde-robe noun Fem. wardrobe.

gardien, gardienne noun Masc., Fem. **1** security guard; **2** caretaker; **3** attendant (in a car park or museum).

gardien de but noun Masc. goalkeeper.

gardien de la paix noun Masc. policeman.

gare noun Fem. (railway) station.

garer verb [1] **1 garer une voiture** to park a car; **2 se garer** to park.

gare routière noun Fem. coach station.

garni adjective **bien garni** full, well-stocked.

garnir verb [2] **1** to decorate; **2** to stock (shelves, fridge).

garniture noun Fem. **1** side-dish; **2** filling (for sandwich); **3** topping (for pizza); **4** trimming, decoration.

gars noun Masc. (informal) guy.

Gascogne noun Fem. Gascony.

gasoil noun Masc. diesel (oil).

gaspiller verb [1] to waste.

gastronome noun Masc. & Fem. gourmet.

gastronomie noun Fem. gastronomy.

gâteau (plural **gâteaux**) noun Masc. cake; **un gâteau au chocolat** a chocolate cake.

gâter verb [1] **1** to spoil; **2 se gâter** to go bad; **la viande se gâte** the meat is going bad; **le temps se gâte** the weather's breaking.

gauche noun Fem. **1** left; **à gauche** on the left; **les Anglais conduisent à gauche** the English drive on the left; **tournez à gauche** turn left; **à ma gauche** on my left; **2 la gauche** the Left (in politics); **des idées de gauche** left-wing ideas.

gauche adjective left, left-hand; **sa main gauche** his left hand.

gaucher (Fem. **gauchère**) adjective left-handed.

gaufre noun Fem. waffle.

gaufrette noun Fem. wafer.

gaz noun Masc. gas; **le chauffage à gaz** gas central heating; **nous nous chauffons au gaz** we have gas heating.

gazeux (Fem. **gazeuse**) adjective fizzy; **eau gazeuse** fizzy mineral water.

gazole noun Masc. diesel (oil).

gazon noun Masc. grass, lawn.

a
b
c
d
e
f
g
h
i
j
k
l
m
n
o
p
q
r
s
t
u
v
w
x
y
z

géant, géante noun Masc., Fem. giant.

géant adjective huge.

gel noun Masc. **1** frost; **le gel des prix** the price freeze; **3** gel.

gelé adjective frozen.

gelée noun Fem. **1** jelly; **œuf en gelée** egg in aspic; **2** frost.

geler verb [45] to freeze; **il gèle dehors** it's freezing outside.

gélule noun Fem. capsule.

Gémeaux plural noun Masc. Gemini (sign of the Zodiac).

gémir verb [2] to moan.

gênant adjective **1** annoying; **ce bruit est très gênant** that noise is very annoying; **2** awkward; **c'est une situation gênante** it's an awkward situation.

gencive noun Fem. gum (part of your mouth).

gendarme noun Masc. policeman.

gendarmerie noun Fem. police station.

gendarmerie nationale noun Fem. (French) national police force.

gendre noun Masc. son-in-law.

gêne noun Fem. **1** embarrassment; **2** inconvenience; **3** discomfort.

gêné adjective embarrassed.

gêner verb [1] **1** to bother; **est-ce que mon sac vous gêne?** is my bag in your way?; **2** to embarrass; **3** to block (traffic); **ta voiture gêne** your car's in the way.

général (plural **généraux**) noun Masc. general; **le général Dubois** General Dubois.

général (Masc. plural **génèraux**) adjective general; **en général** in

general, generally; **de façon générale** generally.

généralement adverb generally.

génération noun Fem. generation.

généreux (Fem. **généreuse**) adjective generous.

générique noun Masc. (film) credits.

générosité noun Fem. generosity.

genêt noun Masc. broom (the bush).

génétique noun Fem. genetics.

Genève noun Geneva.

génial (Masc. plural **géniaux**) adjective **1** brilliant; **une idée géniale** a brilliant idea; **2** (informal) great; **c'était génial!** it was great!.

génie noun Masc. **1** genius; **2** engineering.

genou (plural **genoux**) noun Masc. knee; **avoir mal au genou** to have a sore knee; **être à genoux** to be kneeling; **se mettre à genoux** to kneel down; **sur mes genoux** on my lap.

genre noun Masc. kind; **un genre de sauce épicée** a kind of spicy sauce; **un peu dans le genre de** **ton pull** a bit like your sweater.

gens plural noun Masc. people; **beaucoup de gens** lots of people; **les gens disent que ...** people say that ....

gentil (Fem. **gentille**) adjective **1** kind, nice; **elle est très gentille** she's really nice; **2** kind; **c'est très gentil de ta part** it's very kind of you; **3** good; **sois gentil et mange ta viande** be a good boy and eat up your meat.

gentillesse noun Fem. kindness.

gentiment adverb **1** nicely; demande gentiment ask nicely; **2** kindly.

géographie noun Fem. geography.

géologie noun Fem. geology.

géométrie noun Fem. geometry.

gérant, gérante noun Masc., Fem. manager, manageress.

gérer verb [24] to manage, to run.

germain adjective un cousin germain a first cousin.

gésier noun Masc. gizzard.

geste noun Masc. gesture.

gestion noun Fem. management; gestion de fichiers file management (on a computer).

gibier noun Masc. game (for example, venison, pheasant).

gifle noun Fem. slap (in the face).

gifler verb [1] to slap (in the face).

gigantesque adjective huge, gigantic; un repas gigantesque a huge meal.

gigaoctet noun Masc. gigabyte; un disque dur de 20 gigaoctets a twenty gigabyte hard disk.

gigot noun Masc. leg of lamb.

gilet noun Masc. **1** cardigan; **2** waistcoat.

gilet de sauvetage noun Masc. life-jacket.

gingembre noun Masc. ginger.

girafe noun Fem. giraffe.

gitan, gitane noun Masc., Fem. gipsy.

gîte (rural) noun Masc. holiday house.

glaçage noun Masc. **1** glazing; **2** icing.

glace noun Fem. **1** ice cream; une glace au chocolat a chocolate ice cream; **2** ice; **3** mirror; se regarder dans la glace to look at yourself in the mirror; **4** window (in a car).

glacé adjective **1** icy cold; j'ai les mains glacées my hands are freezing; **2** un thé glacé an iced tea.

glacier noun Masc. glacier.

glacière noun Fem. cool-box.

glaçon noun Masc. ice cube.

glissant adjective slippery.

glisser verb [1] to slip, to slide; attention, ça glisse! be careful, it's slippery!

global (Masc. plural globaux) adjective total.

globalisation noun Fem. globalization.

gloire noun Fem. fame, glory.

glorieux (Fem. glorieuse) adjective glorious.

glossaire noun Masc. glossary.

gobelet noun Masc. cup, tumbler; un gobelet en carton a paper cup.

godasse noun Fem. (informal) shoe.

gogo (informal) à gogo as much as you like; pizza à gogo as much pizza as you can eat.

golden noun Fem. Golden Delicious (apple).

golf noun Masc. **1** golf; jouer au golf to play golf; **2** golf course.

golfe noun Masc. gulf.

golfeur, golfeuse noun Masc., Fem. golfer.

FRENCH-ENGLISH

gomme noun Fem. rubber.

gommer verb [1] to rub out.

gonfler verb [1] **1** to pump up (tyres); **2** to blow up (a balloon).

gorge noun Fem. **1** throat; **j'ai mal à la gorge** I've got a sore throat; **j'avais la gorge serrée** I had a lump in my throat; **il chantait à pleine gorge** he was singing at the top of his voice; **2** gorge.

gorgée noun Fem. sip; **une gorgée de thé** a sip of tea.

gorille noun Masc. gorilla.

gosse noun Masc. & Fem. kid.

goudron noun Masc. tar.

gourde noun Fem. water bottle.

gourmand adjective greedy.

gourmandise noun Fem. **1** greed; **2 elle aime les gourmandises** she likes sweet things.

gousse noun Fem. **une gousse d'ail** a clove of garlic.

goût noun Masc. taste; **ça a un goût bizarre** it has a strange taste; **de bon goût** in good taste; ★ **chacun ses goûts** it takes all sorts to make a world.

goûter noun Masc. **1** teatime snack; **2** children's party.

goûter verb [1] **1** to taste, to try; **est-ce que tu as goûté le gâteau?** have you tried the cake?; **2** to have a teatime snack.

goutte noun Fem. drop; **une goutte de** a drop of; **goutte à goutte** drop by drop.

gouvernement noun Masc. government.

gouverner verb [1] to govern, to rule.

grâce noun Fem. **grâce à** thanks to; **la soirée a été un grand succès grâce à toi** the evening was a great success thanks to you.

gracieux (Fem. **gracieuse**) adjective graceful.

grade noun Masc. rank; **monter en grade** to be promoted.

gradins plural noun Masc. terraces (in a stadium).

graduel (Fem. **graduelle**) adjective gradual.

graffiti plural noun Masc. graffiti.

grain noun Masc. **1** grain; **un grain de sable** a grain of sand; **2 du poivre en grains** peppercorns; **3 du café en grains** coffee beans; **4 un grain de beauté** a beauty spot; **5 un grain de raisin** a grape.

graine noun Fem. seed.

graisse noun Fem. fat, grease.

grammaire noun Fem. grammar.

gramme noun Masc. gramme.

grand adjective **1** big; **une grande maison** a big house; **c'est ma grande sœur** she's my big sister; **2** tall; **un grand arbre** a tall tree; **ton frère est très grand** your brother's very tall; **elle est plus grande que moi** she's taller than me; **3** great; **un grand artiste** a great artist; **un grand ami** a great friend; **4** main; **les grandes lignes** main (railway) lines.

grand adverb wide; **la porte était grande ouverte** the door was wide open.

grand bassin noun Masc. main pool (for experienced swimmers).

grand-chose pronoun much; **pas grand-chose** not much; **il ne reste**

pas grand-chose there's not much left.

Grande-Bretagne noun Fem. Great Britain.

grande personne noun Fem. grown-up.

grande surface noun Fem. hypermarket.

grandes vacances plural noun Fem. summer holidays.

grandeur noun Fem. size; **grandeur nature** life-size.

grandir verb [2] to grow, to grow up.

grand magasin noun Masc. department store.

grand-mère (plural **grands-mères**) noun Fem. grandmother.

grand-père (plural **grands-pères**) noun Masc. grandfather.

grands espaces plural noun Masc. open spaces.

grands-parents plural noun Masc. grandparents.

grange noun Fem. barn.

graphiste noun Masc. & Fem. graphic designer.

grappe noun Fem. **une grappe de raisin** a bunch of grapes.

gras (Fem. **grasse**) adjective **1** fatty, greasy; **40% matière grasse** 40% fat (on cheese or yoghurt label); **2 une peau grasse** oily skin; ★ **faire la grasse matinée** to have a lie-in.

gratitude noun Fem. gratitude.

gratte-ciel noun Masc. skyscraper.

gratter verb [1] **1 gratter quelque chose** to scratch something; **2 se**

gratter to scratch (yourself); **3** to itch; **ça gratte** it itches.

gratuit adjective free; **le concert est gratuit** the concert's free; **'entrée gratuite'** 'admission free'.

grave adjective **1** serious; **un grave accident** a serious accident; **2 ce n'est pas grave** it doesn't matter; **3** serious; **une expression grave** a serious expression; **4** deep; **une voix grave** a deep voice.

gravement adverb seriously; **elle est gravement malade** she's seriously ill.

gravure noun Fem. engraving, print.

gré noun Masc. **contre son gré** against his will.

grec noun Masc. Greek (language).

grec (Fem. **grecque**) adjective Greek.

Grec, Grecque noun Masc., Fem. Greek (person).

Grèce noun Fem. Greece.

grêle noun Fem. hail.

grelotter verb [1] to shiver.

grenade noun Fem. **1** grenade; **2** pomegranate.

grenadine noun Fem. grenadine (pomegranate cordial).

grenier noun Masc. attic, loft; **au grenier** in the attic.

grenouille noun Fem. frog; **les cuisses de grenouille** frogs' legs.

grève noun Fem. strike; **une grève des trains** a train strike; **le métro est en grève** the underground's on strike; **faire grève** to go (or be) on strike.

gréviste noun Masc. & Fem. striker.

grièvement adverb seriously; **grièvement blessé** seriously injured.

griffe noun Fem. claw.

griffonner verb [1] to scribble.

grillade noun Fem. grilled meat, meat for grilling; **une grillade de porc** a pork steak.

grillage noun Masc. wire netting.

grille noun Fem. 1 metal gate; 2 railings; 3 wire fence.

grillé adjective 1 grilled; 2 toasted; **du pain grillé** toast.

grille-pain noun Masc. toaster.

griller verb [1] 1 to grill; 2 to toast.

grillon noun Masc. cricket (the creature not the game).

grimace noun Fem. **faire des grimaces** to make faces.

grimper verb [1] to climb; **grimper dans un arbre** to climb a tree.

grincer verb [61] to creak, to squeak.

grincheux (Fem. **grincheuse**) adjective grumpy.

grippe noun Fem. flu; **avoir la grippe** to have flu; **une grippe intestinale** gastric flu.

gronder verb [1] 1 **gronder quelqu'un** to tell somebody off; **se faire gronder** to get a telling-off; 2 to rumble.

gros (Fem. **grosse**) adjective 1 big; **un gros morceau** a big piece; **un gros problème** a big problem;

2 fat; **un gros monsieur** a fat man; 3 **un gros rhume** a bad cold; 4 **un gros fumeur** a heavy smoker; 5 **un gros mot** a swear word; 6 **en gros** roughly.

groseille noun Fem. redcurrant.

groseille à maquereau noun Fem. gooseberry.

grosse adjective SEE **gros**.

grossesse noun Fem. pregnancy.

grosseur noun Fem. 1 lump; 2 size.

grossier (Fem. **grossière**) adjective 1 rude; 2 crude; **une idée grossière** a rough idea of; **une erreur grossière** a bad mistake.

grossir verb [2] to put on weight; **il a beaucoup grossi** he's put on a lot of weight.

grosso modo adverb roughly.

grotesque adjective ridiculous.

grotte noun Fem. cave.

groupe noun Fem. group; **travailler/voyager en groupe** to work/travel in a group.

grouper verb [1] 1 to group; 2 **se grouper** to gather, to form a group.

groupe sanguin noun Masc. blood group.

grue noun Fem. crane.

guépard noun Masc. cheetah.

guêpe noun Fem. wasp.

guère adverb **ne ...guère** hardly; **je ne l'ai guère vu depuis Noël** I've hardly seen him since Christmas.

guérir verb [2] 1 to cure; **le médecin l'a guéri** the doctor cured him; 2 to get better; **j'ai été malade mais je suis maintenant guéri** I've been ill but I'm better now.

guérison noun Fem. recovery (from an illness or injury).

guerre noun Fem. war; **le pays est actuellement en guerre** the country is at war at the moment; **la Seconde Guerre mondiale** World War II.

guetter verb [1] to watch out for.

gueule noun Fem. mouth (of an animal; considered rude if used of a person); **(ferme) ta gueule!** (rude) shut up!

gueule de bois noun Fem. (informal) **avoir la gueule de bois** to have a hangover.

gueuler verb [1] (informal) to yell.

gui noun Masc. mistletoe.

guichet noun Masc. **1** ticket office (in a station or museum); **2** box office (in a theatre or cinema); **3** counter, window (in a bank or post office).

guichet automatique noun Masc. cashpoint.

guide noun Masc. guide.

guider verb [1] to guide.

guidon noun Masc. handlebars.

guillemets plural noun Masc. inverted commas; **entre guillemets** in inverted commas.

guirlande noun Fem. **des guirlandes** tinsel; **des guirlandes en papier** paper chains.

guirlande électrique noun Fem. fairy lights, Christmas-tree lights.

guitare noun Fem. guitar; **jouer de la guitare** to play the guitar.

guitariste noun Masc. & Fem. guitarist.

gym noun Fem. (informal) PE, gymnastics.

gymnase noun Masc. gym; **je te verrai au gymnase** I'll see you in the gym.

gymnastique noun Fem. gymnastics, exercises.

Hh

habile adjective clever; **elle est habile de ses mains** she's clever with her hands; **de manière habile** cleverly.

habillé adjective **1** dressed; **je ne suis pas encore habillé** I'm not dressed yet; **2** smart (for example, a dress or suit).

habiller verb [1] **1** habiller quelqu'un to dress somebody; **2** s'habiller to get dressed; **habille-toi vite!** get dressed quick!; **3** s'habiller to dress up; **s'habiller en clown** to dress up as a clown.

habitant, habitante noun Masc., Fem. inhabitant.

habitation noun Fem. house.

habiter verb [1] to live; **ils habitent à Paris** they live in Paris.

habitude noun Fem. **1** habit; **c'est une mauvaise habitude** it's a bad habit; **2** d'habitude usually; **d'habitude il arrive à midi** he usually arrives at twelve; **3** comme d'habitude as usual; **j'ai pris le bus comme d'habitude** I took the bus as usual; **4** avoir l'habitude de faire to be used to doing; **j'ai l'habitude de travailler**

a b c d e f g h i j k l m n o p q r s t u v w x y z

a

le soir I'm used to working in the evening.

b

habitué, habituée noun Masc., Fem. regular (in a café, shop, etc).

c

habitué adjective **être habitué à quelque chose** to be accustomed to something.

d

habituel (Fem. **habituelle**) adjective usual.

e

f

habituer verb [1] **s'habituer à quelque chose** to get used to something; **je m'y suis habituée** I've got used to it.

g

h

hache noun Fem. axe.

i

haché adjective chopped; **du bœuf haché** mince.

j

hacher verb [1] **1** to chop (vegetables); **2** to mince (meat).

k

l

hachis Parmentier noun Masc. shepherd's pie.

m

haddock noun Masc. smoked haddock.

n

haie noun Fem. **1** hedge; **2 les haies** hurdles (sport).

o

haine noun Fem. hatred.

p

haïr verb [46] to hate.

q

Haïti noun Masc. Haiti.

r

haïtien Fem. **haïtienne** adjective Haitian.

s

Haïtien, Haïtienne noun Masc., Fem. Haitian.

t

u

haleine noun Fem. breath; **être hors d'haleine** to be out of breath.

v

hall noun Masc. **1** (entrance) hall; **2** concourse (in a station).

w

halles plural noun Fem. covered market.

x

y

halogène adjective halogen; **une lampe halogène** a halogen lamp.

z

halte noun Fem. stop; **halte!** stop!; **faire une halte** to stop somewhere.

halte-garderie noun Fem. playgroup.

haltérophilie noun Fem. weightlifting.

hamac noun Masc. hammock.

hameau (plural **hameaux**) noun Masc. group of houses.

hameçon noun Masc. fish hook.

hamster noun Masc. hamster.

hanche noun Fem. hip.

handball noun Masc. handball; **jouer au handball** to play handball.

handicap noun Masc. handicap.

handicapé, handicapée noun Masc., Fem. handicapped person.

handicapé adjective handicapped, disabled.

hanté adjective haunted.

harceler verb [45] **1** to pester; **2** to harass.

hareng noun Masc. herring.

haricot noun Masc. bean; **haricot vert** French bean; **haricot blanc** haricot bean.

harmonica noun Masc. mouth organ; **jouer de l'harmonica** to play the mouth organ.

harmonie noun Fem. harmony.

harmoniser verb [1] to coordinate, to harmonize.

harnais noun Masc. harness.

harpe noun Fem. harp.

hasard noun Masc. **1** chance; **par hasard** by chance; **je l'ai rencontré par hasard** I met him by chance; **2 au hasard** at random; **elle a choisi un livre au hasard** she chose a book at random; **3 à tout hasard** just in case; **prends un manteau à tout hasard** take a coat just in case; **4 à tout hasard** on the off chance.

hasardeux (*Fem.* **hasardeuse**) *adjective* risky.

hâte *noun Fem.* **à la hâte** hurriedly; **elle est partie à la hâte** she left in a rush.

hausse *noun Fem.* increase, rise; **une hausse des prix** a rise in prices; **les prix sont en hausse** prices are rising.

hausser *verb* [1] **1** to raise; **2 hausser les épaules** to shrug your shoulders.

haut *noun Masc.* **1** top; **le haut de l'échelle** the top of the ladder; **regarder quelqu'un de haut en bas** to look somebody up and down; **2 l'arbre fait 10 mètres de haut** the tree is 10 metres high; **3 en haut** upstairs; **elle est en haut** she's upstairs; **4 en haut de** at the top of; **en haut de l'escalier** at the top of the stairs.

haut *adjective* **1** high; **la branche la plus haute** the highest branch; **2 à haute voix** aloud; **lire à haute voix** to read aloud.

haut *adverb* high; **plus haut dans l'arbre** higher up the tree; **'voir plus haut'** 'see above' (*in a book*); **haut les mains!** hands up!

hautbois *noun Masc.* oboe.

hauteur *noun Fem.* height; **la hauteur de la pièce** the height of the room; **dans le sens de la hauteur** upright; **l'avion prend de la hauteur** the plane's gaining

height; **il n'est pas à la hauteur de son travail** he's not up to his job.

haut-parleur *noun Masc.* loudspeaker.

Haye *noun* **La Haye** The Hague.

hebdomadaire *noun Masc.* weekly magazine.

héberger *verb* [52] to put up; **Jess va nous héberger** Jess'll put us up.

hein *exclamation* (*informal*) what?, eh?

hélas *exclamation* unfortunately; **elle est déjà partie, hélas** she's already left, unfortunately; **hélas non** I'm afraid not.

hélicoptère *noun Masc.* helicopter.

hémorragie *noun Fem.* haemorrhage.

hennir *verb* [2] to neigh.

herbe *noun Fem.* **1** l'herbe grass; **2** herb; **les fines herbes** mixed herbs; **les herbes de Provence** mixed herbs; **3 une mauvaise herbe** a weed.

hérisson *noun Masc.* hedgehog.

héritage *noun Masc.* inheritance.

hériter *verb* [1] to inherit.

hermétique *adjective* airtight.

héroïne *noun Fem.* **1** heroine; **2** heroin.

héros *noun Masc.* hero.

hésitation *noun Fem.* hesitation.

hésiter *verb* [1] to hesitate; **à ta place, je n'hésiterais pas!** if I were you, I wouldn't hesitate!; **j'ai beaucoup hésité avant d'accepter** I thought about it for a long time before I agreed; **j'hésite entre le poulet et le poisson** I can't decide whether to have the chicken or the fish.

hêtre noun Masc. **1** beech tree; **2** beech wood.

heure noun Fem. **1** hour; **une heure plus tard** an hour later; **deux heures de train** two hours in the train; **une demi-heure** half an hour; **une heure et demie** an hour and a half; **Londres est à une heure d'avion de Paris** London is an hour from Paris by air; **toutes les quatre heures** every four hours; **toutes les heures** : **il y a des trains toutes les heures** there are trains every hour; **payé à l'heure** paid by the hour; **cent kilomètres à l'heure** a hundred kilometres an hour; **2** time; **quelle heure est-il?** what time is it?; **il est sept heures** it's seven o'clock; **à huit heures du matin** at eight o'clock in the morning; **tu te lèves à quelle heure demain?** what time are you getting up tomorrow?; **à neuf heures** at nine o'clock; **à six heures et demie** at half past six; **3 être à l'heure** to be on time; **4 à l'heure du déjeuner** at lunchtime; ★ **de bonne heure** early; **je me lève de bonne heure demain** I'm getting up early tomorrow.

heures d'affluence plural noun Fem. peak time, rush hour.

heureusement adverb fortunately.

heureux (Fem. **heureuse**) adjective **1** happy; **elle est heureuse d'être ici** she's happy to be here; **2** lucky, fortunate.

heurter verb [1] to hit, to bump into; **la voiture a heurté un**

camion the car collided with a lorry.

heurtoir noun Masc. (door) knocker.

hexagone noun Masc. **1** hexagon; **2 l'Hexagone** France (French journalists often refer to France as l'Hexagone as it has a six-sided shape on the map).

hibou (plural **hiboux**) noun Masc. owl.

hideux (Fem. **hideuse**) adjective hideous.

hier adverb yesterday; **je l'ai vue hier** I saw her yesterday; **hier matin** yesterday morning; **avant-hier** the day before yesterday.

hi-fi noun Fem. hi-fi; **une chaîne hi-fi** a stereo system.

hippique adjective equestrian; **un concours hippique** a horse show; **un club hippique** a riding school.

hippodrome noun Masc. racecourse.

hippopotame noun Masc. hippopotamus.

hirondelle noun Fem. swallow.

histoire noun Fem. **1** history; **l'histoire française** French history; **2** story; **l'histoire de ma vie** the story of my life; **3** matter; **c'est une histoire d'argent** it's a matter of money; ★ **faire des histoires** to kick up a fuss.

historique adjective **1** historic; **un monument historique** a historic monument; **2** historical.

hit-parade noun Masc. **le hit-parade** the charts (pop music).

hiver noun Masc. winter; **en hiver** in winter.

HLM noun Masc. or Fem. (= *habitation à loyer modéré*) council flat; **nous habitons dans un HLM à Valence** we live in a council flat in Valence; **les HLM** council housing.

hocher verb [1] **hocher la tête** to shake your head, to nod.

hockey noun Masc. hockey; **jouer au hockey** to play hockey; **le hockey sur glace** ice hockey.

hollandais noun Masc. Dutch (*language*).

hollandais adjective Dutch.

Hollandais, Hollandaise noun Masc., Fem. Dutchman, Dutchwoman; **les Hollandais** the Dutch.

Hollande noun Fem. Holland; **en Hollande** in (*or* to) Holland.

homard noun Masc. lobster.

homéopathique adjective homeopathic.

hommage noun Masc. tribute, homage; **rendre hommage à quelqu'un/quelque chose** to pay tribute to someone/something.

homme noun Masc. man; **l'homme de la rue** the man in the street; **l'homme moderne est plus grand que ses ancêtres** modern man is taller than his ancestors.

homme d'affaires noun Masc. businessman.

homme d'État noun Masc. statesman.

homogénéisé adjective homogenized.

homosexuel, homosexuelle noun, Masc., Fem.

homosexuelle adjective homosexual.

Hongrie noun Fem. Hungary.

hongrois noun Masc. Hungarian (*language*).

hongrois adjective Hungarian.

honnête adjective honest, respectable.

honnêtement adverb honestly, frankly; **honnêtement je ne sais pas ce que tu veux dire** I honestly don't know what you mean.

honnêteté noun Fem. honesty; **en toute honnêteté** in all honesty.

honneur noun Masc. honour.

honorer verb [1] to honour.

honte noun Fem. shame; **avoir honte de quelque chose** to be ashamed of something; **j'ai vraiment honte** I'm really ashamed of myself; **tu n'as pas honte!** what a thing to say (*or* do)!

honteux (Fem. **honteuse**) adjective disgraceful.

hôpital noun Masc. hospital; **être à l'hôpital** to be in hospital.

hoquet noun Masc. hiccup; **avoir le hoquet** to have hiccups.

horaire noun Masc. timetable, schedule; **les horaires de train** the train timetable.

horizon noun Masc. horizon; **à l'horizon** on the horizon.

horizontal (Masc. *plural* **horizontaux**) adjective horizontal.

horloge noun Fem. clock.

horodateur noun Masc. parking ticket machine.

horoscope noun Masc. horoscope.

horreur noun Fem. 1 horror; **quelle horreur!** how awful!; 2 **avoir horreur de quelque chose** to hate something; **j'ai horreur d'être en retard** I hate being late. **j'ai horreur des escargots!** I can't stand snails!

horrible adjective horrible.

horrifier verb [1] to horrify.

hors preposition **1 hors de** outside; **hors de France** outside France; **2 être hors jeu** to be offside; **3 les boutiques hors taxe** the duty-free shops; ★ **être hors de soi** to be beside yourself; **j'étais hors de moi** I was beside myself.

hors-d'œuvre noun Masc. starter (to a meal).

hortensia noun Masc. hydrangea.

hospitalier adjective **un centre hospitalier** a hospital.

hospitaliser verb [1] **elle a été hospitalisée** she's been taken into hospital.

hospitalité noun Fem. hospitality.

hostilité noun Fem. hostility.

hôte[1] noun Masc. host.

hôte[2] noun Masc., Fem. **1** guest; **hôte payant** paying guest; **2** host.

hôtel noun Masc. hotel; **un hôtel de luxe** a luxury hotel; **passer deux nuits à l'hôtel** to spend two nights in a hotel.

hôtel de ville noun Masc. town hall.

hôtesse noun Fem. **1** hostess; **2** receptionist.

hôtesse d'accueil noun Fem. receptionist.

hôtesse de l'air noun Fem. flight attendant.

housse noun Fem. cover (for a chair or a machine); **une housse de couette** a duvet cover.

houx noun Masc. holly.

hublot noun Masc. **1** window (in a plane); **2** porthole (in a boat).

huer verb [1] to boo; **la foule a hué l'arbitre** the crowd booed the referee.

huile noun Fem. oil; **huile de tournesol** sunflower oil; **huile d'olive** olive oil; **huile solaire** suntan oil.

huit number **1** eight; **Paul a huit ans** Paul's eight; **le huit juillet** the eighth of July; **2 huit jours** a week; **il y a huit jours** a week ago.

huitième noun Masc. **au huitième** on the eighth floor.

huitième adjective eighth.

huître noun Fem. oyster.

humain adjective human.

humanitaire adjective humanitarian.

humeur noun Fem. mood; **il est de bonne humeur** he's in a good mood; **elle est de mauvaise humeur** she's in a bad mood; **je ne suis pas d'humeur à faire ça** I'm not in the mood to do that.

humide adjective damp.

humidité noun Fem. damp.

humoristique adjective humorous; **un dessin humoristique** a cartoon.

humour noun Masc. humour; **avoir de l'humour** to have a sense of humour.

hurler verb [1] to yell, to howl.

hutte noun Fem. hut.

hydratant adjective moisturizing.

hygiène noun Fem. hygiene.

hygiénique adjective **1** hygienic; **2 une serviette hygiénique** a sanitary towel; **3 du papier hygiénique** toilet paper.

hymne noun Masc. hymn; **l'hymne national** the national anthem.

hypermarché noun Masc. hypermarket.

hypermétrope adjective long-sighted.

hypertension noun Fem. high blood pressure.

hypnotiser verb [1] to hypnotize.

hypocondriaque noun Masc. & Fem., adjective hypochondriac.

hypocrite noun Masc. & Fem. hypocrite.

hypothèse noun Fem. hypothesis.

hystérie noun Fem. hysteria.

Ii

iceberg noun Masc. iceberg.

ici adverb **1** here; **il y a trop de monde ici** there are too many people here; **les gens d'ici** the local people; **2 jusqu'ici** this far; **les bus ne viennent pas jusqu'ici** the buses don't come this far; **3 jusqu'ici** so far; **jusqu'ici il a fait beau** so far the weather's been good.

icône noun Fem. icon.

idéal (plural **idéaux**) noun Masc., adjective ideal; **l'idéal serait de louer une voiture** the ideal thing would be to hire a car.

idée noun Fem. idea; **quelle bonne idée!** what a good idea!; **je n'ai aucune idée** I've no idea; **se faire des idées** to imagine things.

identifier verb [1] to identify.

identique adjective identical.

identité noun Fem. identity; **une carte d'identité** an identity card.

idiot, idiote noun Masc., Fem. idiot; **ne fais pas l'idiot!** don't fool around!

idiot adjective stupid; **c'est vraiment idiot!** it's really stupid!

ignorance noun Fem. ignorance.

ignorant adjective ignorant.

ignorer verb [1] **1** not to know; **j'ignore leur adresse** I don't know their address; **j'ignore les détails** I don't know the details; **2** to ignore; **ils l'ont ignoré** they ignored him.

il pronoun **1** he; **il parle français** he speaks French; **2** it; **'où est mon sac?' – 'il est sur la chaise'** 'where's my bag?' – 'it's on the chair; **il pleut** it's raining.

île noun Fem. island.

illégal (Masc. plural **illégaux**) adjective illegal.

illimité adjective unlimited.

illisible adjective illegible.

illumination noun Fem. floodlighting; **les illuminations de Noël** the Christmas lights.

illuminer verb [1] to floodlight.

illusion noun Fem. illusion; **elle se fait des illusions** she's fooling herself.

a
b
c
d
e
f
g
h
i
j
k
l
m
n
o
p
q
r
s
t
u
v
w
x
y
z

illustration 144 FRENCH-ENGLISH

illustration noun Fem. illustration.

illustré noun Masc. comic.

illustré adjective illustrated.

illustrer verb [1] to illustrate.

ils pronoun they; **ils sont en vacances** they're on holiday.

il y a SEE avoir.

image noun Fem. picture; **il y a de belles images dans ton livre** there are some lovely pictures in your book.

imaginaire adjective imaginary.

imagination noun Fem. imagination.

imaginer verb [1] to imagine; **je n'arrive pas à l'imaginer** I can't imagine it; **elle va appeler, j'imagine** I suppose she'll phone.

imbattable adjective unbeatable.

imbécile noun Masc. & Fem. fool; **faire l'imbécile** to fool around.

imbécile adjective idiotic.

imitation noun Fem. imitation.

imiter verb [1] to imitate.

immangeable adjective inedible.

immanquablement adverb inevitably.

immatriculation noun Fem. registration (of a car); **une plaque d'immatriculation** a numberplate.

immédiat adjective immediate; **dans l'immédiat** for the time being; **je n'ai pas de projets dans l'immédiat** I don't have any plans for the time being.

immédiatement adverb immediately.

immense adjective huge.

immeuble noun Masc. **1** block of flats; **2** building; **un immeuble de six étages** a six-storey building; **3 un immeuble de bureaux** an office block.

immigration noun Fem. immigration.

immigré, immigrée noun Masc., Fem. immigrant.

immobile adjective motionless.

immobilier (Fem. **immobilière**) **une agence immobilière** an estate agent's.

immobiliser verb [1] to immobilize.

immodéré adjective excessive.

immoral (Masc. plural **immoraux**) adjective immoral.

immuniser verb [1] to immunize.

impact noun Masc. impact.

impair adjective odd; **un nombre impair** an odd number.

impardonnable adjective unforgivable.

imparfait noun Masc. imperfect (tense); **à l'imparfait** in the imperfect.

imparfait adjective imperfect.

impasse noun Fem. dead end.

impatience noun Fem. impatience.

impatient adjective impatient.

impeccable adjective **1** perfect; **un accent français impeccable** a perfect French accent; **2** spotless; **l'appartement est impeccable** the flat's spotless; **3** (informal) great; **'je viendrai te chercher chez toi à midi' – 'impeccable!'** I'll come and pick you up at your place at twelve' – 'great!'

impensable *adjective* unthinkable.

imper *noun Masc.* (*informal*) SHORT FOR **imperméable** raincoat.

impératif *noun Masc.* imperative; **à l'impératif** in the imperative.

impératrice *noun Fem.* empress.

imperfection *noun Fem.* imperfection.

imperméable *noun Masc.* raincoat.

impertinent *adjective* cheeky.

impitoyable *adjective* merciless.

impliquer *verb* [1] **1** to mean; **cela implique que nous n'aurons pas assez d'argent** this means that we won't have enough money; **2 être impliqué dans quelque chose** to be involved in something.

impoli *adjective* rude.

importance *noun Fem.* importance; **ça n'a pas d'importance** it doesn't matter.

important *adjective* **1** important; **il est important de savoir que ...** it's important to know that ...; **2** considerable; **une réduction importante** a considerable reduction; **il y aura des retards importants** there will be considerable delays.

importations *plural noun Fem.* imports.

importer *verb* [1] **1** to import (*goods*); **2** to matter; **'lequel veux-tu?' – 'n'importe!'** 'which one do you want?' – 'it doesn't matter!'; **n'importe où** anywhere; **viens n'importe quand** come any time;

n'importe qui sait faire ça anyone can do that; **il dit n'importe quoi** he's talking nonsense; **elle le fait n'importe comment** she does it any old how.

imposant *adjective* imposing.

imposer *verb* [1] **1** to impose; **imposer à quelqu'un de faire quelque chose** to make somebody do something; **la maman de Katy lui a imposé de rester à la maison** Katy's mum made her stay at home; **2 s'imposer** to establish oneself.

impossibilité *noun Fem.* impossibility.

impossible *adjective* impossible.

impossible *noun* **faire l'impossible** to do your utmost; **nous ferons l'impossible pour les contacter** we'll do our utmost to contact them.

impôt *noun Masc.* tax.

imprécis *adjective* vague.

impression *noun Fem.* impression; **sa première impression** his first impression; **elle a fait très bonne impression** she made a very good impression; **j'ai l'impression qu'il n'est pas heureux** I have a feeling he's not happy.

impressionnant *adjective* impressive.

impressionner *verb* [1] to impress.

imprévisible *adjective* unpredictable.

imprévu *adjective* unexpected.

a
b
c
d
e
f
g
h
i
j
k
l
m
n
o
p
q
r
s
t
u
v
w
x
y
z

a **imprimante** noun Fem. printer (for a computer).

b **imprimante laser** noun Fem. laser printer.

c **imprimé** noun Masc. form (to fill in).

d **imprimé** adjective printed.

e **imprimer** verb [1] to print.

f **improviser** verb [1] to improvise.

g **improviste** noun à l'improviste unexpectedly; **mon oncle est arrivé à l'improviste** my uncle arrived unexpectedly.

h **imprudent** adjective 1 careless; 2 rash.

i **impuissant** adjective helpless.

j **impulsif** (Fem. **impulsive**) adjective impulsive.

k **inabordable** adjective 1 inaccessible; 2 **des prix inabordables** prohibitive prices.

l **inacceptable** adjective unacceptable.

m **inaccessible** adjective inaccessible.

n **inachevé** adjective unfinished.

o **inadapté** adjective unsuitable.

p **inadmissible** adjective intolerable.

q **inaperçu** adjective passer inaperçu to go unnoticed; **son départ est passé inaperçu** her departure went unnoticed.

r **inattendu** adjective unexpected; **une visite inattendue** an unexpected visit.

s **inattention** noun Fem. lack of attention; **une faute d'inattention** a careless mistake.

t **inaudible** adjective inaudible.

inauguration noun Fem. inauguration, opening.

inaugurer verb [1] 1 to open (an exhibition, a new building); 2 to unveil (a monument).

incapable adjective 1 incapable; **je suis incapable de bouger!** I'm incapable of moving!; 2 incompetent; **il est complètement incapable** he's completely incompetent.

incassable adjective unbreakable.

incendiaire noun Masc. & Fem. arsonist.

incendiaire adjective **une bombe incendiaire** an incendiary bomb.

incendie noun Masc. fire; **l'incendie a détruit l'église** the fire destroyed the church.

incertain adjective 1 uncertain; **le résultat est toujours incertain** the result is still uncertain; 2 unsettled (weather).

incertitude noun Fem. uncertainty.

incident noun Masc. incident; **en cas d'incident** if anything should happen.

inciter verb [1] to encourage; **le père d'André l'a incité à apprendre la guitare** André's father encouraged him to learn to play the guitar.

inclure verb [25] 1 to include; 2 to enclose.

inclus adjective including; **il y aura trente invités, enfants inclus** there will be thirty guests, including children; **jusqu'à**

samedi inclus up to and including Saturday.

incollable *adjective* **le riz incollable** easy-cook rice.

incolore *adjective* colourless.

incommode *adjective* **1** awkward; **2** uncomfortable.

incomparable *adjective* incomparable.

incompétent *adjective* incompetent.

incompréhensible *adjective* incomprehensible.

inconditionnel, inconditionnelle *noun Masc., Fem.* devotee; **c'est un inconditionnel du jazz** he's a real jazz fan!

inconditionnel (*Fem.* **inconditionnelle**) *adjective* unconditional.

inconfortable *adjective* uncomfortable.

inconnu, inconnue *noun Masc., Fem.* stranger.

inconnu *adjective* unknown; **elle m'est inconnue** I don't know her.

inconsciemment *adverb* unconsciously.

inconscient *adjective* **1** unthinking; **2** unconscious (*in a faint*).

incontestable *adjective* unquestionable.

incontournable *adjective* unavoidable; **c'est un fait incontournable** it's an undeniable fact.

inconvénient *noun Masc.* **1** drawback; **il y a plusieurs**

inconvénients there are several drawbacks; **2 l'inconvénient, c'est que ...** the difficulty is that ...; **3 si vous n'y voyez pas d'inconvénient** if you have no objection.

incorporer *verb* [1] to blend in (*ingredients in cooking*); **incorporez l'huile une goutte à la fois** blend in the oil drop by drop.

incorrect *adjective* **1** incorrect; **2** rude.

incrédule *adjective* incredulous.

incroyable *adjective* incredible; **elle a des connaissances incroyables** her knowledge is incredible.

inculper *verb* [1] **inculper quelqu'un de** to charge somebody with (*a crime*); **elle a été inculpée de vol** she was charged with theft.

Inde *noun Fem.* India; **en Inde** in (*or* to) India.

indécis *adjective* **1** undecided; **elle est toujours indécise** she hasn't decided yet; **2** indecisive.

indemne *adjective* unharmed.

indemnisation *noun Fem.* compensation; **une demande d'indemnisation** a claim for compensation.

indemniser *verb* [1] to compensate; **demander à être indemnisé** to demand compensation.

indéniable *adjective* undeniable.

indépendamment *adverb* independently.

indépendance *noun Fem.* independence.

a

indépendant *adjective*
1 independent; 2 **cuisine indépendante** separate kitchen; 3 **une maison indépendante** a detached house.

index *noun Masc.* 1 index; 2 forefinger.

indicateur *noun Masc.* 1 timetable (*in a rail or coach station*); **l'indicateur des départs** the departures board; 2 street directory; 3 gauge (*for example, for oil levels*); 4 **un panneau indicateur** a road sign.

indicateur de pression *noun Masc.* pressure gauge.

indicatif *noun Masc.* 1 dialling code; **l'indicatif pour l'Espagne est 34** the dialling code for Spain is 34; 2 theme tune; 3 indicative (*of a verb*).

indications *plural noun Fem.* directions.

indice *noun Masc.* clue.

indien (*Fem.* **indienne**) *adjective* Indian.

indifférent *adjective* indifferent.

indigène *adjective* native; **les indigènes** the locals.

indigeste *adjective* indigestible.

indigestion *noun Fem.* indigestion; **avoir une indigestion** to have indigestion.

indignation *noun Fem.* indignation.

indigne *adjective* 1 unworthy; 2 disgraceful.

indigner *verb* [1] **s'indigner** to get indignant.

indiqué *adjective* recommended; **ce n'est pas très indiqué** it's not a very good idea.

indiquer *verb* [1] to point out, to show; **pouvez-vous m'indiquer la gare?** can you show me the way to the station?; **le nom est indiqué sur un grand panneau** the name is on a big sign; **cela indique que ...** this shows that ....

indirect *adjective* indirect.

indiscipliné *adjective* unruly.

indiscret (*Fem.* **indiscrète**) *adjective* 1 indiscreet; **ne le lui dis pas, elle est très indiscrète** don't tell her, she can't keep a secret; 2 **si ce n'est pas indiscret** if it's not being nosy.

indiscutable *adjective* unquestionable.

indispensable *adjective* essential; **les vêtements indispensables** essential clothing; **il est indispensable** it's essential.

indisposé *adjective* unwell.

individu *noun Masc.* individual; **c'est un drôle d'individu** he's a funny bloke.

individuel (*Fem.* **individuelle**) *adjective* 1 individual; 2 separate; **une chambre individuelle** a single room; **une maison individuelle** a detached house.

indolore *adjective* painless.

indulgent *adjective* indulgent; **notre prof de maths est trop indulgent avec nous** our maths teacher isn't strict enough with us.

industrialisé *adjective* **les pays industrialisés** the industrialized countries.

industrie *noun Fem.* industry.

industriel (*Fem.* **industrielle**) *adjective* industrial; **une ville industrielle** an industrial city.

inédit *adjective* **1** unpublished; **2** new.

inefficace *adjective* **1** inefficient; **en tant que patron il est très inefficace** as a boss he's very inefficient; **2** ineffective; **un remède inefficace** an ineffective remedy.

inégal (*Masc. plural* **inégaux**) *adjective* **1** uneven; **2** unequal.

inespéré *adjective* unhoped-for; **un succès inespéré** an unhoped-for success.

inévitable *adjective* **1** inevitable; **c'était inévitable** it was bound to happen; **2** unavoidable; **des problèmes inévitables** unavoidable problems.

inexact *adjective* **1** incorrect; **2** inaccurate.

inexpérimenté *adjective* inexperienced.

infarctus *noun Masc.* heart attack.

infect *adjective* foul; **le repas était infect!** the meal was foul!

infecter *verb* [1] **1** to infect; **2 s'infecter** to go septic.

infection *noun Fem.* infection.

inférieur *adjective* **1** lower; **sur une marche inférieure** on a lower step; **des prix inférieurs à la moyenne** lower than average prices; **2** smaller; **la taille inférieure** the smaller size;

3 inferior, worse; **de qualité inférieure** of a lower quality.

infernal (*Masc. plural* **infernaux**) *adjective* frightful, dreadful.

infini *adjective* infinite.

infinitif *noun Masc.* infinitive (*in grammar*); **à l'infinitif** in the infinitive.

infirme *noun* **les infirmes** the disabled.

infirme *adjective* disabled; **est-il infirme?** does he have a disability?

infirmerie *noun Fem.* medical room.

infirmier, infirmière *noun Masc., Fem.* nurse.

infirmité *noun Fem.* disability.

inflammable *adjective* flammable.

inflation *noun Fem.* inflation.

influence *noun Fem.* influence; **il a une bonne influence sur son frère** he's a good influence on his brother.

influencer *verb* [61] to influence.

informaticien, informaticienne *noun Masc., Fem.* computer scientist.

information *noun Fem.* **1** information; **une information très utile** a very useful piece of information; **2 les informations** the news (*on TV or radio*); **les informations sont à vingt heures** the news is at eight o'clock.

a
b
c
d
e
f
g
h
i
j
k
l
m
n
o
p
q
r
s
t
u
v
w
x
y
z

informatique noun Fem. computer science, IT.

informatique adjective computer; **un système informatique** a computer system.

informatiser verb [1] to computerize.

informer verb [1] **1** to inform; **2 s'informer** to find out; **je peux m'informer si tu veux** I can find out if you like.

infrarouge adjective infra-red.

infusion noun Fem. herbal tea.

ingénierie noun Fem. engineering.

ingénieur noun Masc. engineer; **faire des études d'ingénieur** to study engineering.

ingénieux (Fem. **ingénieuse**) adjective ingenious; **c'était très ingénieux de sa part** that was very ingenious of her.

ingrat adjective **1** ungrateful; **2 un travail ingrat** unrewarding work.

ingrédient noun Masc. ingredient.

inhabité adjective uninhabited.

inhabituel (Fem. **inhabituelle**) adjective unusual.

inhalateur noun Masc. inhaler.

inhumain adjective inhuman.

inimaginable adjective unimaginable, unthinkable.

ininterrompu adjective **1** uninterrupted; **2** continuous.

initial (Masc. plural **initiaux**) adjective initial.

initiale noun Fem. initial; **mes initiales sont là-dessus** my initials are on it.

initiation noun Fem. introduction (to a new place or skill); **une journée d'initiation** an introductory day (to a course, for example); **une initiation à l'anglais** an introduction to English.

initiative noun Fem. initiative.

initier verb [1] **1 initier quelqu'un à** to introduce somebody to (a skill); **2** to initiate (an idea or plan); **3 s'initier à quelque chose** to learn about something; **elle s'initie à la photo** she's starting to learn photography.

injecter verb [1] to inject.

injection noun Fem. injection.

injure noun Fem. insult.

injurier verb [1] to insult; **il m'a injurié** he swore at me.

injuste adjective unfair.

innocent adjective innocent.

innombrable adjective countless.

innovation noun Fem. innovation.

innover verb [1] to break new ground.

inoccupé adjective empty.

inondation noun Fem. flood; **des inondations** flooding.

inonder verb [1] to flood.

inoubliable adjective unforgettable.

inouï adjective incredible.

inox noun Masc. stainless steel; **une casserole en inox** a stainless steel pan.

inoxydable adjective **un évier en acier inoxydable** a stainless steel sink.

inquiet (Fem. **inquiète**) adjective anxious, worried.

inquiétant adjective worrying.

inquiéter verb [24] **1** to worry; **je ne veux pas t'inquiéter** I don't want to worry you; **ça m'inquiète un peu** I find that a bit worrying; **ce qui m'inquiète, c'est qu'elle n'a pas téléphoné** what I find worrying is the fact that she hasn't phoned; **2 s'inquiéter** to worry, to be worried; **elle va s'inquiéter si nous sommes en retard** she'll worry if we're late; **ne t'inquiète pas!** don't worry!

inquiétude noun Fem. anxiety.

insatisfait adjective dissatisfied.

inscription noun Fem. **1** enrolment (for a course or in a school); **2** registration.

inscrire verb [38] **1** to enrol, to register (someone for a course or school); **elle m'a inscrit pour l'examen** she's entered me for the exam; **2 s'inscrire** to enrol; **s'inscrire au club de foot** to join the football club.

insecte noun Masc. insect.

insérer verb [24] to, insert.

insertion noun Fem. **1** insertion (of an advertisement in a paper, for example); **2** integration (when somebody joins a new community); **l'insertion des jeunes dans la société** the integration of young people into society.

insignifiant adjective insignificant.

insister verb [1] to insist; **il faut insister** keep on trying; **la clé est un peu tordue, il faut insister un**

peu the key's a bit bent, you have to push it really hard.

insolation noun Fem. sunstroke; **attraper une insolation** to get sunstroke.

insolent adjective insolent.

insoutenable adjective unbearable.

inspecter verb [1] to inspect.

inspecteur, inspectrice noun Masc., Fem. inspector.

inspection noun Fem. **1** inspection; **2** inspectorate (an official department).

inspiration noun Fem. inspiration.

inspirer verb [1] **1** to inspire; **ça ne m'inspire pas** that doesn't appeal to me; **2** to breathe in; **inspire fort!** breathe in deep!; **3 s'inspirer** to be inspired by; **il s'est inspiré de Picasso** he was inspired by Picasso.

instable adjective unstable; **il fait un temps instable** the weather's unsettled.

installation noun Fem. **1** installation, putting in; **2** move (to a house or town); **avant son installation à Paris** before he moved to Paris; **3 des installations sportives** sports facilities.

installer verb [1] **1** to install, to put in (central heating or a dishwasher, for example); **2** to connect (gas, electricity, a phone); **3 s'installer** to settle, to settle in; **installez-vous** do sit down; **je me suis installée à mon bureau** I settled down at my desk.

a
b
c
d
e
f
g
h
i
j
k
l
m
n
o
p
q
r
s
t
u
v
w
x
y
z

a **instant** noun Masc. moment; **pour l'instant** for the moment; **à tout instant** all the time.

b

c **instantané** adjective instant; **du café instantané** instant coffee.

d **instinct** noun Masc. instinct.

e **institut** noun Masc. institute; **un institut de beauté** a beautician's.

f

g **instituteur, institutrice** noun Masc., Fem. primary school teacher.

h **institution** noun Fem.
1 institution; 2 private school.

i **institutrice** noun Fem. SEE **instituteur**.

j **instructeur, instructrice** noun Masc., Fem. instructor.

k

l **instruction** noun Fem.
1 education; **instruction civique** civics; 2 **instructions** instructions; **instructions de lavage** washing instructions.

m

n **instruire** verb [26] 1 to teach, to train; 2 **s'instruire** to learn.

o **instruit** adjective educated.

p **instrument** noun Masc.
1 instrument; **un instrument de mesure** a measuring instrument; **les instruments de bord** the controls; 2 **un instrument de musique** a musical instrument; **un instrument à cordes** a string instrument.

q

r

s

t **insu** noun **à mon insu** without my knowing.

u

v **insuffisance** noun Fem. shortage.

w **insuffisant** adjective
1 insufficient; 2 inadequate; **c'est insuffisant** it's not good enough.

x

y **insultant** adjective insulting.

z **insulte** noun Fem. insult.

insulter verb [1] to insult.

insupportable adjective unbearable; **je la trouve insupportable** I can't stand her.

intact adjective intact.

intégral (Masc. plural **intégraux**) adjective complete.

intégrale noun Fem. complete works (usually music); **l'intégrale des Beatles** the complete Beatles collection.

intellectuel, intellectuelle noun Masc., Fem., adjective intellectual.

intelligence noun Fem. intelligence.

intelligent adjective clever, intelligent.

intendance noun Fem. administration (in a school).

intense adjective intense.

intensif (Fem. **intensive**) adjective intensive.

intention noun Fem. intention; **avoir l'intention de faire** to mean to do; **j'avais l'intention d'y aller mais je n'ai pas pu** I meant to go but I wasn't able to.

interdiction noun Fem. ban; **'interdiction de fumer'** 'no smoking'.

interdire verb [47] to forbid; **je t'interdis de le faire** I forbid you to do it.

interdit adjective forbidden; **'entrée interdite'** 'no entry'; **il est interdit de fumer dans la salle** smoking is forbidden in the theatre.

intéressant adjective
1 interesting; **c'est un film très intéressant** it's a very interesting film; **2 à un prix intéressant** at a good price.

intéressé[1] adjective interested; **être intéressé par quelque chose** to be interested in something.

intéressé[2], **intéressée** noun Masc., Fem. person concerned.

intéresser verb [1] **1** to interest; **ça ne m'intéresse pas** that doesn't interest me; **2 s'intéresser à** to be interested in; **elle s'intéresse beaucoup à l'informatique** she's very interested in computing.

intérêt noun Masc. **1** interest; **ce livre est sans intérêt** this book is really boring; **2 tu as intérêt à faire** you'd better do; **tu as intérêt à le finir avant ce soir!** you'd better get it finished by this evening!

intérieur noun Masc. inside, interior; **l'intérieur du placard** the inside of the cupboard; **où est-elle? – à l'intérieur** where is she? – inside (in the house).

intérieur adjective inside, internal; **le côté intérieur** the inside.

intermédiaire noun Masc. & Fem. go-between.

intermédiaire adjective intermediate; **avez-vous la taille intermédiaire?** do you have the size in between?

internat noun Masc. boarding school.

international (Masc. plural **internationaux**) adjective international.

interne noun Masc. & Fem. boarder (in a school).

interne adjective internal.

Internet noun Masc. Internet; **sur Internet** on the Internet.

interpeller verb [1] **1** to call out to; **2 la police l'a interpellé** the police have taken him in for questioning.

interphone™ noun Masc. entry phone.

interprète noun Masc. & Fem. **1** (in the theatre) actor; (in music) performer, soloist; **2** interpreter.

interpréter verb [24] **1** to perform, to play (a role in the theatre or a piece of music), to sing (a song); **2** to interpret (a language or a remark).

interrogatif noun Masc. interrogative.

interrogation noun Fem. **1** test (at school); **2** questioning.

interroger verb [52] **1** to question, to ask; **il m'a interrogé sur mon séjour en France** he asked me about my stay in France; **2** to test (at school).

interrompre verb [69] to interrupt; **interrompre quelqu'un** to interrupt somebody; **il a interrompu son travail** he broke off his work.

interrupteur noun Masc. switch.

interruption noun Fem.
1 interruption; **2 sans interruption** without stopping.

intervalle noun Masc. **1** interval; **2 dans l'intervalle** in the meantime.

a
b
c
d
e
f
g
h
i
j
k
l
m
n
o
p
q
r
s
t
u
v
w
x
y
z

a **intervenir** verb [81] to intervene.

b **intervention** noun Fem. intervention.

c **interview** noun Fem. interview (on TV, radio, for a magazine).

d **intestin** noun Masc. intestine.

e **intime** adjective intimate; **un journal intime** a diary (kept by somebody).

f

g **intimider** verb [1] to intimidate.

intimité noun Fem. intimacy; **dans l'intimité** in private.

h **intolérable** adjective intolerable.

i **intolérant** adjective intolerant.

intoxication noun Fem. poisoning.

j

k **intoxiquer** verb [1] to poison.

l **intrigue** noun Fem. plot (of a novel, play, etc).

m **introduction** noun Fem. introduction.

n **introduire** verb [26] 1 to introduce (an idea, a measure, a new product); 2 **s'introduire** to get into; **un cambrioleur s'est introduit dans l'appartement** a burglar got into the flat.

o

p

q **intrus, intruse** noun Masc., Fem. intruder.

r **intuitif** (Fem. **intuitive**) adjective intuitive.

s **intuition** noun Fem. intuition.

t **inusable** adjective hard-wearing.

u **inutile** adjective pointless; **il est inutile de l'appeler** there's no point telephoning him; **inutile de dire que** ... needless to say ....

v

w

x **inutilement** adverb pointlessly; **je l'ai cherché inutilement** I looked for it in vain.

y

z

inutilisable adjective unusable.

invalide noun Masc. & Fem. disabled person.

invasion noun Fem. invasion.

inventer verb [1] to invent.

invention noun Fem. invention.

inverse noun Masc. **l'inverse** the opposite; **l'inverse est vrai** the opposite is true.

inverse adjective opposite; **en sens inverse** in the opposite direction; **dans l'ordre inverse** in reverse order.

investigation noun Fem. investigation.

investissement noun Masc. investment.

invisible adjective invisible.

invitation noun Fem. invitation.

invité, invitée noun Masc., Fem. guest; **nous avons des invités ce soir** we have people coming round this evening.

inviter verb [1] to invite; **ils m'ont invité à dîner** they invited me to dinner.

involontaire adjective unintentional.

invraisemblable adjective 1 unlikely; **une explication invraisemblable** an unlikely explanation; 2 (informal) amazing.

ira, irai, iraient, irais, irait, iras verb SEE **aller**.

iris noun Masc. iris.

irlandais noun Masc.,

irlandais adjective Irish.

Irlandais, Irlandaise noun Masc., Fem. Irishman, Irishwoman; **les Irlandais** the Irish.

Irlande noun Fem. Ireland; **la République d'Irlande** the Republic of Ireland.

Irlande du Nord noun Fem. Northern Ireland.

ironie noun Fem. irony.

ironique adjective ironic.

irons, iront verb SEE **aller**[1].

irradier verb [1] to irradiate.

irréel, irréelle adjective unreal.

irréfléchi adjective thoughtless.

irrégularité noun Fem. irregularity.

irrégulier (Fem. **irrégulière**) adjective irregular.

irrésistible adjective irresistible.

irresponsable adjective irresponsible.

irritable adjective irritable.

irritation noun Fem. irritation.

irriter verb [1] **1** to irritate; **cela m'irrite** that makes me cross; **2 s'irriter** to get irritated.

islamique adjective Islamic.

isolation noun Fem. insulation; **isolation acoustique** soundproofing.

isolé adjective **1** remote; **2** lonely.

isoler verb [1] **1** to insulate (a room or building); **2** to isolate (a sick person or a prisoner).

Israël noun Masc. Israel.

israélien (Fem. **israélienne**) adjective Israeli.

issue noun Fem. exit; **issue de secours** emergency exit; **une rue sans issue** a dead end.

Italie noun Fem. Italy; **en Italie** in (or to) Italy.

italien noun Masc. Italian (language).

italien adjective Italian.

Italien, Italienne noun Masc., Fem. Italian (person).

itinéraire noun Masc. route.

itinérant adjective travelling.

ivoire noun Masc., adjective ivory.

ivre adjective drunk.

ivresse noun Fem. drunkenness.

ivrogne noun Masc. & Fem. drunkard.

Jj

j' pronoun SEE **je**.

J.-C. noun Masc. short for Jésus-Christ; **200 avant J.-C.** 200 BC; **400 après J.-C.** 400 AD.

jacinthe noun Fem. hyacinth.

jalousie noun Fem. **1** jealousy; **2** blind.

jaloux (Fem. **jalouse**) adjective jealous; **elle est jalouse de mes résultats d'examen** she's jealous of my exam results.

jamaïquain adjective Jamaican.

Jamaïquain, Jamaïquaine noun Masc., Fem. Jamaican.

Jamaïque noun Fem. Jamaica.

jamais adverb **1** never; **elle ne fume jamais** she never smokes; **on ne sait jamais** you never know; **jamais plus!** never again!; **2** ever; **plus grand que jamais** bigger than ever; **si jamais il pleut** if by any chance it rains; **à jamais** forever.

a
b
c
d
e
f
g
h
i
j
k
l
m
n
o
p
q
r
s
t
u
v
w
x
y
z

jambe noun Fem. leg; **se casser la jambe** to break your leg.

jambon noun Masc. ham; **jambon blanc** cooked ham; **jambon de pays** cured raw ham.

janvier noun Masc. January; **en janvier, au mois de janvier** in January.

Japon noun Masc. Japan; **au Japon** in (or to) Japan.

japonais noun Masc. Japanese (language).

japonais adjective Japanese.

Japonais, Japonaise noun Masc., Fem. Japanese (person).

jardin noun Masc. garden; **Patrick est au jardin** Patrick's in the garden; **une chaise de jardin** a garden chair.

jardinage noun Masc. gardening.

jardinier, jardinière¹ noun Masc., Fem. gardener.

jardinière² noun Fem. (large) plant pot.

jardin public noun Masc. park (in a town).

jaune noun Masc. **1** yellow; **2 un jaune d'œuf** an egg-yolk.

jaune adjective yellow; **une robe jaune** a yellow dress.

jaunisse noun Fem. jaundice.

Javel noun eau de Javel bleach.

jazz noun Masc. jazz; **j'aime le jazz** I like jazz.

je, j' (before a vowel or silent 'h') pronoun I; **je sais où il habite** I know where he lives; **j'habite à Lyon** I live in Lyons.

jean noun Masc. **1** (pair of) jeans; **j'ai acheté un jean** I've bought some jeans; **2** denim; **une jupe en jean** a denim skirt.

jet noun Masc. **1** jet (of water or steam); **les jets d'eau de Versailles** the fountains at Versailles; **2** jet (plane).

jetée noun Fem. jetty.

jeter verb [48] **1** to throw; **jette-moi le ballon** throw me the ball; **2** to throw away; **j'ai jeté ces vieilles chaussures** I've thrown away those old shoes; **3 jeter un coup d'œil** to have a look; **est-ce que tu peux jeter un coup d'œil aux pommes de terre?** can you have a look at the potatoes?

jeton noun Masc. **1** counter (for a board game); **2** token (for a machine).

jeu (plural **jeux**) noun Masc. **1** game; **faire un jeu** to play a game; **gagner par trois jeux à deux** to win by three games to two; **2** gambling; **3** acting; ★ **ce n'est pas du jeu!** (informal) that's not fair!

jeu-concours noun Masc. competition.

jeu de cartes noun Masc. **1** pack of cards; **2** game of cards.

jeu de hasard noun Masc. game of chance.

jeu de mots noun Masc. pun.

jeu de société noun Masc. board game.

jeudi noun Masc. **1** Thursday; **nous sommes jeudi aujourd'hui** it's Thursday today; **jeudi prochain** next Thursday; **jeudi dernier** last Thursday; **2** on Thursday; **je l'ai vu jeudi soir** I saw him on Thursday evening; **3 le jeudi** on Thursdays; **fermé le jeudi** closed on Thursdays; **4 tous les jeudis** every Thursday.

jeune noun Masc. & Fem. young person; **une émission destinée aux jeunes** a programme aimed at young people.

jeune adjective young; **un jeune homme** a young man; **une jeune femme** a young woman; **une jeune fille** a girl.

jeunesse noun Fem. **1** young people; **la jeunesse d'aujourd'hui** young people today; **2** youth; **dans ma jeunesse** in my youth.

jeu-vidéo noun Masc. video game.

jogging noun Masc. **1 faire du jogging** to go jogging; **2 un jogging** a track-suit.

joie noun Fem. joy.

joindre verb [49] **1** to get hold of (often by telephone); **je n'ai pas pu la joindre** I wasn't able to get hold of her; **2** to enclose (in a letter or parcel); **3** to put together; **les pieds joints** feet together; ★ **joindre les deux bouts** to make ends meet (financially).

joli adjective pretty.

jongler verb [1] to juggle.

jongleur, jongleuse noun Masc., Fem. juggler.

jonquille noun Fem. daffodil.

joue noun Fem. cheek.

jouer verb [1] **1** to play; **elle joue avec le chien** she's playing with the dog; **à toi de jouer!** your go!; **bien joué!** well done!; **2 jouer à** to play (a sport); **on va jouer au foot** we're going to play football; **3 jouer**

de to play (an instrument); **Robert joue de la guitare** Robert plays the guitar; **4** to act; **il joue bien dans ce film** he's really good in this film.

jouet noun Masc. toy.

joueur, joueuse noun Masc., Fem. player.

jour noun Masc. **1** day; **les jours de la semaine** the days of the week; **trois jours plus tard** three days later; **le jour où** the day when; **un de ces jours** one of these days; **2 de nos jours** nowadays; **de nos jours, ils sont assez fréquents** nowadays they are quite common; **3 mettre quelque chose à jour** to bring something up to date; **4** daylight, light; **il fait jour** it's daylight; **en plein jour** in broad daylight; **jour et nuit** night and day.

jour de l'an noun Masc. New Year's Day.

jour férié noun Masc. public holiday.

journal (plural **journaux**) noun Masc. **1** newspaper, magazine; **le journal du soir** the evening paper; **du papier journal** newspaper (for wrapping); **2** news (on TV or radio); **le journal de vingt-deux heures** the ten o'clock news; **3 un journal intime** a diary.

journalisme noun Masc. journalism.

journaliste noun Masc. & Fem. journalist.

journée noun Fem. day; **toute la journée** all day, the whole day; **il est payé à la journée** he's paid by the day.

a
b
c
d
e
f
g
h
i
j
k
l
m
n
o
p
q
r
s
t
u
v
w
x
y
z

jour ouvrable noun Masc. working day.

joyeux (Fem. **joyeuse**) adjective happy; **Joyeux Anniversaire** Happy Birthday; **Joyeux Noël** Merry Christmas.

judaïsme noun Masc. Judaism.

judicieux (Fem. **judicieuse**) adjective sensible; **un choix judicieux** a wise choice.

judo noun Masc. judo.

juge noun Masc. judge.

juge d'instruction noun Masc. examining magistrate.

juge de ligne noun Masc. line judge (in tennis).

juge de touche noun Masc. linesman (in football, rugby).

jugement noun Masc. judgement.

juger verb [52] to judge.

juif, juive noun Masc., Fem. Jew.

juif, juive adjective Jewish.

juillet noun Masc. July; **en juillet, au mois de juillet** in July; **le quatorze juillet** Bastille Day (July 14, a national holiday to celebrate the taking of the Bastille prison in Paris by the people at the beginning of the French Revolution in 1789).

juin noun Masc. June; **en juin, au mois de juin** in June.

juive noun Fem., adjective SEE **juif**.

jumeau (plural **jumeaux**)

jumelle noun Masc., Fem. twin; **des vrais jumeaux** identical twins.

jumeler verb [18] to twin (towns); **Oxford est jumelé avec Grenoble** Oxford is twinned with Grenoble.

jumelles plural noun Fem.
1 binoculars; 2 SEE **jumeau**.

jument noun Fem. mare.

jungle noun Fem. jungle.

jupe noun Fem. skirt.

jupon noun Masc. petticoat.

jurer verb [1] to swear.

juridique adjective legal; **le système juridique** the legal system.

jury noun Masc. 1 jury; 2 board of examiners.

jus noun Masc. 1 juice; **un jus d'orange** an orange juice; 2 gravy.

jus de fruits noun Masc. fruit juice.

jusqu'à preposition 1 as far as (a place); **ce train va jusqu'à Paris** this train goes as far as Paris; **nous avons marché jusqu'à la mer** we walked as far as the sea; **il m'a accompagné jusqu'à chez moi** he took me all the way home; 2 until; **elle reste jusqu'à mardi** she's staying until Tuesday; **jusqu'à quand reste-t-il?** how long is he staying for?; **jusqu'à présent, jusqu'à maintenant** up to now; 3 **jusqu'à ce que** until.

juste adjective 1 right, correct; **le mot juste** the right word; **ce que tu dis est juste** what you say is right; 2 fair; **ce n'est pas juste!** it's not fair!; 3 in tune; **elle chante juste** she sings in tune; 4 **c'est un peu juste** it's a bit tight; **une heure est un peu juste** an hour's a bit tight.

juste adverb just; **juste à temps** just in time; **il vient tout juste d'arriver** he's only just arrived.

justement adverb 1 precisely; 2 just; **je parlais justement de toi**

I was just talking about you;
3 correctly; **comme elle a dit très justement** as she so rightly said.

justesse noun Fem. **1** correctness;
2 de justesse only just; **il a eu son avion, mais de justesse** he caught his plane, but only just.

justice noun Fem. justice.

justifier verb [1] to justify.

juteux (Fem. **juteuse**) adjective juicy.

juvénile adjective youthful.

Kk

K.O. adjective **1 mettre quelqu'un K.O.** to knock somebody out (in boxing); **2 je suis complètement K.O.** (informal) I'm completely knackered.

kaki noun Masc. persimmon.

kaki adjective khaki.

kangourou noun Masc. kangaroo.

karaté noun Masc. karate.

karting noun Masc. go-karting.

kascher adjective kosher.

kermesse noun Fem. (school) fête.

ketchup noun Masc. ketchup.

kidnapper verb [1] to kidnap.

kidnappeur, kidnappeuse noun Masc., Fem. kidnapper.

kilo noun Masc. kilo; **deux kilos de pommes** two kilos of apples; **j'ai pris trois kilos** I've put on three kilos.

kilogramme noun Masc. kilogramme.

kilométrage noun Masc. mileage.

kilomètre noun Masc. kilometre; **à dix kilomètres d'ici** ten kilometres from here; **Paris est à combien de kilomètres de Dijon?** how many kilometres is it from Paris to Dijon?; **elle a combien de kilomètres votre voiture?** what's the mileage on your car?

kinésithérapeute noun Masc. & Fem. physiotherapist.

kinésithérapie noun Fem. physiotherapy.

kiosque noun Masc. kiosk.

kiwi noun Masc. kiwi (the bird and the fruit).

klaxon™ noun Masc. horn (on a car).

klaxonner verb [1] to sound the horn (in a car).

km SHORT FOR **kilomètre; km/h** kph (kilometres per hour).

koala noun Masc. koala bear.

kraft noun Masc. **le papier kraft** brown paper.

K-way™ noun Masc. cagoule.

Ll

la, l' (before a vowel or silent 'h') definite article, pronoun SEE **le**.

là adverb **1** there; **est-ce que Paul est là?** is Paul there?; **c'est là qu'habite mon frère** that's where my brother lives; **2** here; **viens là** come here; **Danielle n'est pas là en ce moment** Danielle's not here at the moment; **3** then; **c'est là que j'ai pensé à toi** that's when I thought of you.

a
b
c
d
e
f
g
h
i
j
k
l
m
n
o
p
q
r
s
t
u
v
w
x
y
z

-là *adverb* **cette maison-là** that house; **ces gens-là** those people; **à ce moment-là** at that moment.

là-bas *adverb* **1** there; **qu'est-ce que vous avez fait là-bas?** what did you do there?; **2** over there; **notre maison est là-bas** our house is over there.

labo *noun Masc.* (*informal*) lab.

laboratoire *noun Masc.* laboratory.

laboratoire de langues *noun Masc.* language laboratory.

labourer *verb* [1] to plough.

labyrinthe *noun Masc.* maze, labyrinth.

lac *noun Masc.* lake; **le lac d'Annecy** Lake Annecy.

lacer *verb* [61] **lacer ses chaussures** to tie your shoelaces.

lacet *noun Masc.* lace (*for shoes*); **des chaussures à lacets** lace-up shoes.

lâche *adjective* **1** cowardly; **2** loose (*a belt or rope, for example*).

lâcher *verb* [1] **1** to drop (*an object*), to let go of (*a rope or branch*); **lâche-moi!** let go of me!; **ne lâche pas la corde!** don't let go of the rope!; **2** to drop; **elle a lâché son sac** she dropped her bag; **3** to give way; **la corde a lâché** the rope gave way.

lâcheté *noun Fem.* cowardice.

lacrymogène *adjective* **le gaz lacrymogène** teargas.

là-dedans *adverb* in there; **il y a un oiseau là-dedans** there's a bird in there; **il n'y a rien là-dedans** there's nothing inside.

là-dessous *adverb* under there; **les verres sont là-dessous** the glasses are under there.

là-dessus *adverb* **1** on there; **tu peux mettre les assiettes là-dessus** you can put the plates on there; **2** about it; **ils sont d'accord là-dessus** they agree about it; **a-t-il dit quelque chose là-dessus?** did he say anything about it?; **3** with that; **là-dessus il est sorti** with that, he went out.

là-haut *adverb* **1** up here, up there; **il est là-haut dans l'arbre** he's up there in the tree; **2** upstairs; **maman est là-haut** Mum's upstairs.

laid *adjective* ugly.

laideur *noun Fem.* ugliness.

laine *noun Fem.* wool; **un pull en laine** a woollen jumper.

laine vierge *noun Fem.* pure new wool.

laïque *adjective* **une école laïque** a state school.

laisse *noun Fem.* lead (*for a dog*).

laisser *verb* [1] **1** to leave; **j'ai laissé mes clés chez toi** I've left my keys at your house; **bon, je vous laisse** right, I must be off now; **2 laisser quelqu'un faire** to let somebody do; **laisse-le parler!** let him speak!; **laissez-la faire, elle reviendra** leave her alone, she'll come back; **3 il se laisse insulter** he puts up with being insulted; **elle s'est laissée aller** she's let herself go.

laisser-aller *noun Masc.* carelessness.

lait noun Masc. milk; **un thé au lait** a cup of tea with milk; **un café au lait** a white coffee.

lait demi-écrémé noun Masc. semi-skimmed milk.

lait écrémé noun Masc. skimmed milk.

laitier (Fem. **laitière**) adjective **les produits laitiers** milk products (such as yoghurt).

laiton noun Masc. brass.

laitue noun Fem. lettuce.

lame noun Fem. blade.

lamelle noun Fem. thin strip.

lamentable adjective awful.

lampadaire noun Masc. **1** standard lamp; **2** street lamp.

lampe noun Fem. lamp, light; **allumer la lampe** to turn on the lamp.

lampe de poche noun Fem. torch.

lampe électrique noun Fem. torch.

lance noun Fem. spear.

lancement noun Masc. launch.

lancer verb [61] **1** to throw; **il m'a lancé le ballon** he threw the ball to me; **2** to launch (a product, a spacecraft); **ils vont lancer leur nouveau produit en juin** they're going to launch their new product in June; **3 se lancer dans quelque chose** to embark on something.

landau noun Masc. pram.

lande noun Fem. moor.

langage noun Masc. language, type of language; **le langage administratif** official jargon.

langouste noun Fem. crayfish.

langue noun Fem. **1** tongue; **tirer la langue** to stick your tongue out; **2** language; **une langue étrangère** a foreign language; **ma langue maternelle** my mother tongue; ★ **je l'ai sur le bout de la langue** it's on the tip of my tongue.

lanière noun Fem. strap.

lapin noun Masc. rabbit; ★ **il m'a posé un lapin** (informal) he stood me up.

laque noun Fem. **1** hairspray; **2** lacquer, gloss paint.

laquelle pronoun SEE **lequel**.

lard noun Masc. streaky bacon.

lardons plural noun Masc. diced bacon; **salade aux lardons fumés** green salad with diced smoked bacon.

large noun Masc. open sea; **au large** offshore.

large adjective wide; **un large sourire** a broad smile; **être large de deux mètres** to be two metres wide.

largement adverb **c'est largement suffisant** that's more than enough; **j'ai largement le temps** I've got plenty of time.

largeur noun Fem. width.

larme noun Fem. tear; **en larmes** in tears; **rire aux larmes** to laugh till you cry.

laryngite noun Fem. laryngitis.

lasagnes plural noun Fem. lasagna; **manger des lasagnes** to eat lasagna.

laser noun Masc. laser; **une platine laser** a compact disc player.

lasser verb [1] **se lasser** to get tired.

a b c d e f g h i j k l m n o p q r s t u v w x y z

lassitude noun Fem. weariness.

latin noun Masc., adjective Latin.

lauréat, lauréate noun Masc., Fem. winner; **un lauréat du prix Nobel** a Nobel Prize winner.

laurier noun Masc. laurel; **un laurier commun** a bay tree; **une feuille de laurier** a bay leaf.

laurier-rose noun Masc. oleander.

lavable adjective washable; **lavable en machine** machine-washable.

lavabo noun Masc. washbasin.

lavage noun Masc. **1** washing; **2** wash (on a washing-machine programme); **3** car wash.

lavande noun Fem. lavender.

lave-linge noun Masc. washing machine.

laver verb [1] **1** to wash; **2 se laver** to wash; **se laver les mains** to wash your hands; **se laver les dents** to brush your teeth.

laverie noun Fem. launderette.

lave-vaisselle noun Masc. dish washer.

le, la, l', les definite article **1** the; **le chat** the cat; **la maison** the house; **les enfants** the children; **'quelle chemise?' – 'la verte'** 'which shirt?' – 'the green one'; **2** ('les' is often not translated) **je n'aime pas les chiens** I don't like dogs; **elle se lave les cheveux** she's washing her hair; **3 le père de mon ami** my friend's father; **4** a, an; **cinq euros le kilo** five euros a kilo.

le, la, l', les pronoun him, her, it, them; **je la vois tous les soirs** I see her every evening; **je le vois tous les soirs** I see him every evening;

où est-ce que tu les as mis? where did you put them?; **il l'a acheté chez Meyer** he bought it at Meyer's.

lécher verb [24] to lick.

lèche-vitrines noun Masc. **faire du lèche-vitrines** to go window-shopping.

leçon noun Fem. lesson; **une leçon de géographie** a geography lesson.

lecteur, lectrice noun Masc., Fem. **1** reader (of a book); **2** foreign language assistant (in a university).

lecteur de cassettes noun Masc. cassette player.

lecteur de disquettes noun Masc. floppy disk drive.

lecteur laser noun Masc. CD player.

lecture noun Fem. reading; **j'aime la lecture** I like reading; **le soir il fait de la lecture** he reads in the evenings.

légal (Masc. plural **légaux**) adjective legal.

légende noun Fem. **1** caption (to a picture); **2** key (to a map); **3** legend.

léger (Fem. **légère**) adjective **1** light; **une veste légère** a light jacket; **un repas léger** a light meal; **2** slight; **un léger retard** a slight delay; **3** weak; **un café léger** a weak coffee; ★ **faire quelque chose à la légère** to do something without thinking.

légèrement adverb **1** lightly; **légèrement parfumé** slightly perfumed; **2** slightly; **il est légèrement blessé** he's slightly hurt; **elle est légèrement plus**

grande que moi she's slightly taller than me.

légèreté *noun Fem.* lightness.

législatif (*Fem.* **législative**) *adjective* legislative; **les élections législatives** the general election.

légume *noun Masc.* vegetable; **des légumes verts** green vegetables.

lendemain *noun Masc.* **le lendemain** the next day; **Marc est arrivé le lendemain** Marc arrived the next day; **le lendemain matin** the next morning; **le lendemain de l'accident** the day after the accident.

lent *adjective* slow.

lentement *adverb* slowly.

lenteur *noun Fem.* slowness; **avec lenteur** slowly.

lentille *noun Fem.* **1** lentil; **soupe aux lentilles** lentil soup; **2** lens; **lentilles de contact** contact lenses; **elle met ses lentilles** she's putting in her contact lenses.

léopard *noun Masc.* leopard.

lequel, laquelle, lesquels, lesquelles *pronoun* **1** which one?, which?; '**passe-moi les verres**' – '**lesquels?**' 'pass me the glasses' – 'which ones?'; **2** which, who; **la voiture dans laquelle ils roulaient** the car they were driving in, the car in which they were driving; **le monsieur avec lequel je discutais** the man to whom I was talking (*often not translated*), the man I was talking to.

les *definite article,, pronoun* SEE **le**.

lesquelles, lesquelles SEE **lequel**.

lessive *noun Fem.* **1** washing; **faire la lessive** to do the washing; **2** washing powder, washing liquid.

lettre *noun Fem.* **1** letter; **écrire une lettre** to write a letter; **2** letter (*of the alphabet*); **une lettre minuscule** a small letter; **une lettre majuscule** a capital letter; ★ **il prend tout ce qu'on lui dit à la lettre** he takes everything you say literally.

lettres *plural noun Fem.* arts (*at university*).

leur *pronoun* them (*meaning 'to them'*); **je leur donne de l'argent** I give them money.

leur *adjective* (*plural* **leurs**) their; **leur voiture** their car; **leurs enfants** their children.

leur *pronoun* **le leur, la leur, les leurs** theirs; **ça, c'est notre maison, et ça, c'est la leur** that's our house and that's theirs; **nous avons appelé nos parents et ils ont appelé les leurs** we phoned our parents and they phoned theirs.

levant *adjective* **le soleil levant** the rising sun.

lever[1] *verb* [50] **1** to lift, to raise; **levons nos verres!** let's raise our glasses!; **levez la main!** put your hand up!; **il a levé les yeux** he looked up; **2 se lever** to get up (*out of bed or from a chair*); **je me lève à sept heures** I get up at seven o'clock; **nous nous sommes levés tôt** we got up early; **quand le soleil se lève** when the sun rises.

lever[2] *noun Masc.* **au lever du soleil** at sunrise.

a **lève-tard** noun Masc. late riser.

lève-tôt noun Masc. early riser.

b **levier** noun Masc. lever.

c **lèvre** noun Fem. lip.

d **lévrier** noun Masc. greyhound.

levure noun Fem. yeast.

e **lexique** noun Masc. word list.

f **lézard** noun Masc. lizard.

liaison noun Fem. 1 link,
connection; **une liaison routière** a
road link; **une liaison radio** radio
contact; **une liaison satellite** a
satellite link; 2 (love) affair.

liasse noun Fem. wad, bundle (of
papers or banknotes).

j **libellule** noun Fem. dragonfly.

k **libération** noun Fem. release,
liberation; **la libération des
femmes** women's liberation; **la
Libération (de 1944)** the end of the
Liberation (of 1944) (the end of the
German occupation of France).

n **libérer** verb [24] 1 to free, to release
(a prisoner or hostage); 2 to vacate
(a hotel room or flat).

p **liberté** noun Fem. freedom.

libraire noun Masc. & Fem.
bookseller.

r **librairie** noun Fem. bookshop.

s **librairie-papeterie** noun Fem.
bookseller's and stationer's.

t

u **libre** adjective 1 free; **vous êtes
libre de partir** you are free to go;
2 free (of a seat or telephone); **est-
ce que cette place est libre?** is
this seat free?

w **librement** adverb freely.

x **libre-service** noun Masc. self
service, self-service shop or

restaurant; **un libre-service
bancaire** a cash dispenser.

licence noun Fem. degree (at
university); **elle a une licence de
chimie** she has a chemistry degree.

licencier verb [1] **licencier
quelqu'un** to make somebody
redundant.

lien noun Masc. link; **mes liens
avec la famille** my links with my
family; **un lien d'amitié** a bond of
friendship.

lierre noun Masc. ivy.

lieu (plural **lieux**) noun Masc.
1 place; **un lieu public** a public
place; **date et lieu de naissance**
date and place of birth; **lieu de
travail** place of work; 2 **en premier
lieu** in the first place; 3 **avoir lieu**
to take place; **le mariage aura lieu
en juin** the marriage will take
place in June; 4 **au lieu de** instead
of; **au lieu de prendre le bus, il est
parti à pied** instead of taking the
bus, he went off on foot; 5 **les lieux**
the premises; **peut-on visiter les
lieux?** can one visit the premises?;
la police est arrivée sur les lieux
the police are now at the scene.

lieutenant noun Masc. lieutenant.

lièvre noun Masc. hare.

lifting noun Masc. face-lift.

ligne noun Fem. 1 line; **une ligne
droite** a straight line; **une ligne
blanche** a white line (on the road);
à la ligne! new paragraph! (in a
dictation); 2 line (of a bus or train);
la ligne Paris-Dijon the Paris-Dijon
line; **une ligne de chemin de fer** a
railway line; **les grandes lignes**
the main lines (sign at a railway

station); **3** cable; **ligne électrique** electric cable; **4** (telephone) line; **la ligne est mauvaise** it's a bad line; **restez en ligne, monsieur** hold the line, sir; **5** figure; **pour garder la ligne** to keep your figure, to stay slim; **6** fishing line.

ligne d'arrivée noun Fem. finishing line.

ligne de touche noun Fem. touch line.

lilas noun Masc. lilac.

limace noun Fem. slug.

lime noun Fem. file; **une lime à ongles** a nail file.

limite noun Fem. **1** limit; **une limite d'âge** an age limit; **2 la date limite** the closing date; **3 sans limites** endless; **une patience sans limites** endless patience; **4 à la limite** if it comes to it, at a pinch; **à la limite, je peux te prêter l'argent** if it comes to it, I can lend you the money; **5 dans la limite de** within the limits of; **dans la limite des places disponibles** subject to available seating space; **dans la limite du possible** as far as possible; **6** boundary; **les limites du village** the village boundaries; **7** maximum, last; **vitesse limite** maximum speed; **âge limite** maximum age; **date limite de vente** sell-by date.

limiter verb **1** to limit; **2 se limiter** to limit oneself; **je me limite à deux cafés par jour** I limit myself to two coffees a day.

limonade noun Fem. lemonade.

lin noun Masc. linen; **une jupe en lin** a linen skirt.

linge noun Masc. **1** linen (sheets, towels, etc); **linge de maison** household linen; **du linge sale** dirty linen; **2** washing; **as-tu du linge pour la machine?** have you any washing for the machine?; **une corde à linge** a washing line; ★ **elle était blanche comme un linge** she was white as a sheet.

lingerie noun Fem. lingerie.

Lion noun Masc. Leo (sign of the Zodiac).

lion noun Masc. lion.

liqueur noun Fem. liqueur.

liquidation noun Fem. clearance sale, closing-down sale; **'liquidation totale!'** 'everything must go!'

liquide noun Masc. **1** liquid; **2** cash; **payer quelque chose en liquide** to pay cash for something.

liquide adjective liquid.

lire verb [51] to read; **lire un roman** to read a novel; **elle sait lire maintenant** she can read now; **elle m'a lu une histoire** she read me a story; **un auteur qui est très lu** a popular author; **lire à haute voix** to read aloud; ★ **lire entre les lignes** to read between the lines.

lis verb SEE **lire**.

lisible adjective legible.

lisse adjective smooth.

liste noun Fem. list; **faire une liste** to make a list; **faire la liste de** to make a list of.

liste d'attente noun Fem. waiting list.

lit[1] verb SEE **lire**.

lit[2] noun Masc. bed; **aller au lit** to go to bed; **faire son lit** to make one's

bed; un lit à une place a single bed; **un lit à deux places** a double bed; **une chambre à deux lits** a twin-bedded room; **au lit!** bedtime!

literie noun Fem. bedding.

litière noun Fem. litter (for an animal's bed); **la litière pour chat** cat litter.

litre noun Masc. litre; **un litre d'eau** a litre of water.

littéralement adverb literally.

littérature noun Fem. literature; **la littérature française** French literature.

livraison noun Fem. delivery; **'livraisons à toute heure'** 'we deliver any time'; **'livraisons à domicile'** 'we deliver'.

livre[1] noun Masc. book; **un livre pour enfants** a children's book; **un livre de poche** a paperback.

livre[2] noun Fem. **1** pound (in money); **une livre sterling** a pound sterling; **2** pound (in France = 500 grammes); **une livre de tomates** a pound of tomatoes.

livrer verb [1] **1** to deliver; **2** to hand over; **3 se livrer** to surrender.

livret noun Masc. booklet.

livret de famille Masc.,

livret de famille noun Masc. family record book (with details of births, marriages, and deaths).

livret scolaire noun Masc. school report book.

local (plural **locaux**) noun Masc. place (usually a building); **locaux commerciaux** business premises; **dans les locaux du lycée** on school premises.

local (Masc. plural **locaux**) adjective local; **un journal local** a local paper; **dix heures heure locale** ten a.m. local time.

localement adverb locally.

locataire noun Masc. & Fem. tenant.

location noun Fem. **1** renting; **un appartement de location** a rented flat; **'locations'** 'to rent'; **2** hire, rental; **location de voitures** car hire; **location de vidéos** video rental; **3** reservation, booking (of theatre seats).

locomotive noun Fem. engine, locomotive.

loge noun Fem. **1** lodge (for the caretaker in a block of flats); **2** (in a theatre) dressing-room (for an actor), box (for a spectator).

logement noun Masc. **1** accommodation; **il a trouvé un logement tout près** he's found somewhere to live just nearby; **2** housing; **la crise du logement** the housing crisis.

loger verb [52] **1** to put up; **peux-tu me loger ce soir?** can you put me up tonight?; **2** to stay; **pour l'instant elle loge chez mes parents** for the moment she's staying with my parents.

logiciel noun Masc. **1** software; **2** program (for a computer); **un logiciel de jeux** a games program; **un logiciel antivirus** antivirus software.

logique noun Fem. logic.

logique adjective logical.

loi noun Fem. law.

loin adverb **1** (in distance) a long way, far off; **c'est loin** it's a long way; **c'est trop loin** it's too far; **c'est loin d'ici** it's a long way from here; **le cinéma est plus loin** the cinema is further on; **nous ne sommes pas allés plus loin** that's the farthest we went; **2** (in time) far off; **les vacances sont loin** the holidays are a long way off; **il n'est pas loin de midi** it's almost twelve; **3** de loin from a long way off; **on voit leur maison de loin** you can see their house from a long way off; **4** de loin by far; **c'est de loin le plus cher** it's by far the most expensive; **5** au loin in the distance.

lointain adjective distant.

loisirs plural noun Masc. **1** spare time; **je dessine pendant mes loisirs** I draw in my spare time; **2** spare-time activities.

Londonien, Londonienne noun Masc., Fem. Londoner.

Londres noun London; **à Londres** in (or to) London; **les rues de Londres** the streets of London.

long noun Masc. **1** une corde de cinq mètres de long a rope five metres long; **2 le long de** all along; **le long de la route** all along the road; **3 tout le long du film** all the way through the film.

long (Fem. **longue**) adjective long; **une longue vie** a long life; **un long silence** a long silence; **un long voyage** a long journey; **la rue la plus longue de Paris** the longest street in Paris; **une chemise à manches longues** a long-sleeved shirt; **la pièce est longue de**

quatre mètres, **la pièce fait quatre mètres de long** the room is four metres long; ★ **marcher de long en large** to walk up and down; ★ **à la longue** in the long run.

longtemps adverb (for) a long time; **elle est restée longtemps** she stayed for a long time; **longtemps après** a long time after; **elle est là depuis longtemps** she's been here for a long time; **j'y suis allé, mais il y a longtemps** I've been there, but a long time ago; **ça fait longtemps qu'on ne s'est pas vu!** it's ages since we've seen each other!; **je n'en ai pas pour longtemps** I won't be long.

longuement adverb for a long time.

longueur noun Fem. **1** length; **de quelle longueur est le couloir?** how long is the corridor?; **2 avoir des longueurs** to drag; **le film est intéressant mais il a des longueurs** it's an interesting film but it drags in places.

longueur d'onde noun Fem. wavelength.

lorsque, lorsqu' (before a vowel or silent 'h') conjunction when; **lorsque j'étais petite** when I was a little girl.

lot noun Masc. **1** batch; **un lot de trois boîtes** a pack of three cans; **2** prize (in a lottery); **elle a gagné le gros lot** she won the jackpot.

lot noun Masc. batch (in computing).

loterie noun Fem. **1** lottery; **2** raffle.

lotion noun Fem. lotion.

lotissement noun Masc. housing estate.

loto noun Masc. lottery.

lotte noun Fem. monkfish.

louche[1] noun Fem. ladle.

louche[2] adjective fishy; **il y a un type louche à la porte** there's a fishy-looking guy at the door.

louer verb [1] **1** to let (a house or flat); **pendant mon absence j'ai loué mon appartement** while I was away I let my flat; **'à louer'** 'to let'; **2** to rent; **nous avons loué un appartement à Lille** we've rented a flat in Lille; **3** to hire; **nous avons loué une voiture** we hired a car; **4** to praise.

loup noun Masc. wolf; ★ **j'ai une faim de loup** I'm absolutely starving (literally: I'm as hungry as a wolf); ★ **quand on parle du loup** (on en voit la queue) speak of the devil (literally: when you speak of the wolf (you see its tail)).

loupe noun Fem. magnifying glass.

louper verb [1] (informal) **1** to miss (a train); **on a loupé le train de dix heures** we missed the ten o'clock train; **2** to fail; **elle a loupé son permis** she failed her driving test.

loup-garou noun Masc. werewolf.

lourd adjective **1** heavy; **ta valise est très lourde** your case is very heavy; **le repas était un peu lourd** the meal was a bit heavy; **2** une **lourde erreur** a serious mistake.

loutre noun Fem. otter.

loyal (Masc. plural **loyaux**) adjective faithful.

loyauté noun Fem. loyalty.

loyer noun Masc. rent; **payer le loyer** to pay the rent.

lu verb SEE **lire**.

lucarne noun Fem. skylight.

luge noun Fem. sledge.

lugubre adjective gloomy.

lui pronoun **1** to him; **c'est lui** it's him; **Hélène travaille avec lui** Hélène works with him; **est-ce qu'il a aimé le bouquin que je lui ai prêté?** did he like the book I lent him?; **2** to him; **Pierre est en colère – qu'est-ce que tu lui as dit?** Pierre's angry – what did you say to him?; **3** to her; **Nadine est en colère – qu'est-ce que tu lui as dit?** Nadine's angry – what did you say to her?; **4** (for emphasis) **lui, il n'est jamais content!** he's never pleased!

lui-même pronoun **1** himself; **il l'a fait lui-même** he did it himself; **2** (on telephone) **'Monsieur Dubois?' – 'lui-même'** 'Monsieur Dubois?' – 'speaking'.

lumière noun Fem. light.

lumineux (Fem. **lumineuse**) adjective luminous; **un panneau lumineux** an electronic display board; **une enseigne lumineuse** a neon sign.

lunch noun Masc. buffet (lunch or supper).

lundi noun Masc. **1** Monday; **nous sommes lundi aujourd'hui** it's Monday today; **lundi prochain** next Monday; **lundi dernier** last Monday; **2** on Monday; **je l'ai vu lundi soir** I saw him on Monday evening; **3 le lundi** on Mondays;

fermé le lundi closed on Mondays; **4 tous les lundis** every Monday.

lune noun Fem. moon; ★ **il est dans la lune** he's got his head in the clouds; ★ **il m'a promis la lune** he promised me the earth.

lune de miel noun Fem. honeymoon.

lunettes plural noun Fem. glasses; **une paire de lunettes** a pair of glasses; **mets tes lunettes!** put on your glasses!; **je porte des lunettes pour lire** I wear glasses for reading.

lunettes de natation plural noun Fem. swimming goggles.

lunettes de soleil plural noun Fem. sun-glasses.

lutte noun Fem. fight, struggle; **la lutte contre la drogue** the fight against drugs.

lutter verb [1] to fight, to struggle; **ils luttaient pour la liberté et contre l'oppression** they were fighting for freedom and against oppression.

luxe noun Masc. luxury; **une voiture de luxe** a luxury car.

luxueux (Fem. **luxueuse**) adjective luxurious.

lycée noun Masc. secondary school (for ages 15-18).

lycéen, lycéenne noun Masc., Fem. secondary school student.

Mm

M. SHORT FOR **Monsieur**; **M. Dupont** Mr Dupont.

ma adjective my; SEE **mon.**

macaronis plural noun Masc. macaroni; **manger des macaronis** to have macaroni.

mâche noun Fem. lamb's lettuce.

mâcher verb [1] to chew.

machin noun Masc. (informal) whatsit, thingumajig; **tu n'as pas un machin pour ouvrir les enveloppes?** don't you have a whatsit for opening envelopes with?

machine noun Fem. **1** machine; **2 taper à la machine** to type.

machine à coudre noun Fem. sewing machine.

machine à écrire noun Fem. typewriter.

machine à laver noun Fem. washing machine.

machine à sous noun Fem. fruit machine.

mâchoire noun Fem. jaw.

mâchonner verb [1] to chew.

maçon noun Masc. **1** builder; **2** bricklayer.

Madame (plural **Mesdames**) noun Fem. **1 Madame Jones** Ms Jones, Mrs Jones; **2 Madame, ...** Dear Madam, ...; **3 bonsoir madame** good evening (when greeting a person you do not know well in French, it is polite to add 'Madame', 'Monsieur', or 'Mademoiselle' to the greeting).

Mademoiselle (plural **Mesdemoiselles**) noun Fem. **1** Miss, Ms; **2 bonsoir mademoiselle** good evening. SEE ALSO **Madame.**

a
b
c
d
e
f
g
h
i
j
k
l
m
n
o
p
q
r
s
t
u
v
w
x
y
z

magasin noun Masc. shop; **un grand magasin** a department store; **un magasin de vêtements** a clothes shop; **un magasin de sport** a sports shop; **faire les magasins** to go round the shops.

magazine noun Masc. magazine.

maghrébin adjective North African.

Maghrébin, Maghrébine noun Masc., Fem. North African.

magicien, magicienne noun Masc., Fem. magician.

magie noun Fem. magic.

magique adjective **1** magic; **2** magical.

magistral (Masc. plural **magistraux**) adjective **un cours magistral** a lecture (at university).

magnétique adjective magnetic.

magnétiser verb [1] **1** to magnetize; **2** to hypnotize.

magnétophone noun Masc. tape recorder.

magnétoscope noun Masc. video recorder.

magnifique adjective splendid.

magouille noun Fem. (informal) fiddling.

magret de canard noun Masc. duck breast.

mai noun Masc. May; **en mai, au mois de mai** in May; **le premier mai** May Day.

maigre adjective thin, skinny; ★ **maigre comme un clou** as thin as a rake (literally: as thin as a nail).

maigrir verb [2] to lose weight; **il a beaucoup maigri** he's lost a lot of weight.

maille noun Fem. stitch (in knitting).

maillot noun Masc. **1** shirt, jersey (in sports such as football); **2 maillot (de corps)** vest.

maillot de bain noun Masc. **1** swimsuit; **2** swimming trunks.

main noun Fem. hand; **avoir quelque chose à la main** to have something in your hand; **serrer la main à quelqu'un** to shake hands with somebody; **se serrer la main** to shake hands; **nous nous sommes serré la main** we shook hands; **se donner la main** to hold hands; **haut les mains!** hands up!; **donner un coup de main à quelqu'un** to give somebody a hand; **tu veux un coup de main?** do you want a hand?; **fait à la main** handmade.

main-d'œuvre noun Fem. labour.

maintenant adverb **1** now; **il est maintenant trop tard pour sortir** it's too late to go out now; **2** nowadays; **maintenant presque tout le monde a le téléphone** nowadays nearly everybody has a phone.

maintenir verb [81] **1** to maintain; **2** to support.

maire noun Masc. mayor.

mairesse noun Fem. mayoress.

mairie noun Fem. **1** town hall; **2** town council.

mais conjunction **1** but; **j'ai essayé de t'appeler mais tu n'étais pas là** I tried to phone you but you weren't

a

there; **2 mais oui** yes of course;
mais non of course not.

maïs noun Masc. **1** maize;
2 sweetcorn; **3 des épis de maïs**
corn on the cob.

maison noun Fem. **1** house; **leur
maison est petite mais très
confortable** their house is small
but very comfortable; **2** home;
rester à la maison to stay at home;
rentrer à la maison to go home.

maison de la culture noun Fem.
cultural centre, arts centre.

maison de retraite noun Fem.
old people's home.

maître, maîtresse noun Masc.,
Fem. **1** master, mistress; **2** teacher.

maître-nageur noun Masc.
swimming instructor.

maîtresse noun Fem. **1** SEE **maître**;
2 lover.

maîtrise noun Fem. **1** mastery;
2 command; **la maîtrise de soi** self-
control; **3** master's degree.

maîtriser verb [1] **1** to control; **2** to
master.

majestueux (Fem. **majestueuse**)
adjective majestic.

majeur adjective **1** major; **2 être
majeur** to be over 18.

majeur noun middle finger.

majorité noun Fem. majority.

majuscule noun Fem. capital
(letter); **en majuscules** in block
capitals; **un R majuscule** a capital
R.

mal (plural **maux**) noun Masc.
1 pain, ache; **faire mal** to hurt; **se
faire mal** to hurt yourself; **avoir
mal à la gorge** to have a sore
throat; **j'ai mal au dos** my back

hurts; **ça fait mal** it hurts; **2 faire
mal à quelqu'un** to hurt
somebody; **aïe! tu me fais mal!**
ouch! you're hurting me!; **3 avoir
du mal à faire** to have difficulty in
doing; **j'ai du mal à comprendre
ce qu'il dit** I have difficulty in
understanding what he says; **se
donner du mal à faire** to go to a lot
of trouble to do; **elle s'est donné
beaucoup de mal pour contacter
tout le monde** she went to a lot of
trouble to contact everybody;
4 evil.

mal adjective **1 pas mal** not bad;
2 être mal to be uncomfortable.

mal adverb **1** badly; **écrire mal** to
write badly; **2 je t'entends mal** I
can't hear you very well; **3 j'ai mal
compris** I misunderstood; **4 être
mal à l'aise** to feel uncomfortable.

malade noun Masc. & Fem. patient.

malade adjective ill, sick; **tomber
malade** to fall ill.

maladie noun Fem. **1** illness;
2 disease.

maladresse noun Fem.
1 clumsiness; **2** blunder.

maladroit adjective clumsy.

malaise noun Masc. **1 avoir un
malaise** to feel faint, to pass out;
2 créer un malaise to make people
feel uncomfortable; **ça a créé un
malaise** it made everybody feel
uncomfortable.

malaxer verb [1] **1** to knead; **2** to
cream.

malchance noun Fem. bad luck.

mal de mer noun Masc. **avoir le
mal de mer** to be seasick.

b
c
d
e
f
g
h
i
j
k
l
m
n
o
p
q
r
s
t
u
v
w
x
y
z

mal du pays noun Masc. avoir le mal du pays to be homesick.

mâle noun Masc., adjective male.

malédiction noun Fem. curse.

malencontreux (Fem. malencontreuse) adjective unfortunate.

malentendu noun Masc. misunderstanding.

malfaiteur noun Masc. criminal.

mal famé adjective un quartier mal famé a rough area.

malgré preposition 1 in spite of; malgré le froid in spite of the cold; 2 malgré tout all the same; mais malgré tout nous avons décidé d'y aller but we decided to go all the same.

malheur noun Masc. misfortune; porter malheur to bring bad luck.

malheureusement adverb unfortunately; Vincent était déjà parti, malheureusement unfortunately, Vincent had already left.

malheureux, malheureuse noun Masc., Fem. poor thing; la malheureuse! poor woman!

malheureux (Fem. malheureuse) adjective 1 unhappy; avoir l'air malheureux to look unhappy; rendre quelqu'un malheureux to make somebody unhappy; 2 unfortunate; un choix malheureux an unfortunate choice.

malhonnête adjective dishonest.

malice noun Fem. mischief.

malicieux (Fem. malicieuse) adjective mischievous.

malin (Fem. maligne) adjective 1 clever; ce n'était pas très malin ça that wasn't very clever; elle se croit maligne she thinks she's clever; 2 malignant (tumour).

malle noun Fem. trunk.

malodorant adjective smelly.

malpoli adjective rude.

malpropre adjective dirty.

malsain adjective unhealthy.

maltraiter verb [1] to ill-treat; les enfants maltraités battered children.

malveillance noun Fem. malice.

malveillant adjective malicious.

maman noun Fem. mum, mummy.

mamie noun Fem. granny, gran, nan.

mammifère noun Masc. mammal.

manager verb [52] to manage.

manageur noun Masc. manager.

manche[1] noun Masc. handle (of a tool).

manche[2] noun Fem. 1 sleeve; une chemise à manches courtes a short-sleeved shirt; sans manches sleeveless; 2 leg (of a match).

Manche noun Fem. la Manche the Channel; le tunnel sous la Manche the Channel Tunnel.

mandarine noun Fem. mandarin orange.

mandat noun Masc. money order.

manège noun Masc. 1 merry-go-round; 2 riding school.

manette noun Fem. lever.

mangeable adjective edible.

manger noun Masc. food.

173 **manquer**

manger verb [52] to eat; **qu'est-ce qu'on va manger?** what shall we have to eat?; **manger au restaurant** to go out for a meal; **j'ai déjà mangé** I've already eaten; **j'ai assez mangé** I'm full, I've had enough; **donner à manger à** to feed; **ils mangent trois fois par jour** they have three meals a day; ★ **manger ses mots** to mumble (*literally: to eat your words*).

mangue noun Fem. mango.

maniaque noun Masc. & Fem. fusspot.

maniaque adjective extremely fussy.

manie noun Fem. **1** odd habit; **2** mania.

manier verb [1] to handle.

manière noun Fem. **1** way; **une manière plus facile** an easier way; **on ne peut pas le faire d'une manière plus facile?** isn't there an easier way of doing it?; **de cette manière** like this, like that; **d'une autre manière** in another way; **d'une manière ou d'une autre** one way or another; **d'une certaine manière** in a way; **2 de toute manière** in any case; **3 de manière à faire** so as to do; **de manière à éviter de dépenser de l'argent** so as to avoid spending money; **4 manières** manners; **ne fais pas de manières!** don't make a fuss!

manifestant, manifestante noun Masc., Fem. demonstrator.

manifestation noun Fem. demonstration; **une manifestation contre le racisme** a demonstration against racism.

manifester verb [1] **1** to demonstrate, to take part in a demonstration; **2 manifester quelque chose** to express something.

manipuler verb [1] **1** to handle; **2** to manipulate.

manivelle noun Fem. handle.

mannequin noun Masc. **1** fashion model; **2** dummy (*either in a shop window or as used by a dressmaker*).

manoir noun Masc. manor house.

manque noun Masc. **manque de** lack of, shortage of; **leur manque d'imagination** their lack of imagination; **être en manque d'affection** to be in need of affection.

manqué adjective **1** failed; **un acteur manqué** a failed actor; **2** missed; **une occasion manquée** a missed opportunity.

manquer verb [1] **1 manquer quelque chose** to miss something; **il a manqué son train** he missed his train; **2 manquer un examen** to fail an exam; **3 manquer à quelqu'un** to be missed by somebody; **tu me manques** I miss you; **Londres leur manque** they miss London; **4 il manque quelque chose** something's missing; **il manque trois fourchettes** there are three forks missing, we're three forks short; **5 manquer de** to lack; **nous ne manquons pas de verres** there's no shortage of glasses; **manquer de faire** to fail to do; **il a manqué de fermer la porte à clé** he failed to lock the door.

a

mansarde noun Fem. attic room.

b

manteau (plural **manteaux**) noun Masc. coat.

c

manuel noun Masc. 1 manual; 2 textbook; **un manuel scolaire** a school book.

d

manuel adjective (Fem. **manuelle**) manual.

e

f

manufacture noun Fem. 1 factory; 2 manufacture.

g

manuscrit noun Masc. manuscript.

h

manuscrit adjective handwritten; **un petit mot manuscrit** a handwritten note.

i

j

maquereau (plural **maquereaux**) noun Masc. mackerel.

k

maquette noun Fem. scale model.

l

maquillage noun Masc. make-up.

maquiller verb [1] **se maquiller** to put on your make-up.

m

n

marais noun Masc. marsh.

marathon noun Masc. marathon.

o

marbre noun Masc. marble; **une cheminée en marbre** a marble fireplace.

p

q

marc de café noun Masc. coffee grounds.

r

marchand, marchande noun Masc., Fem. 1 shopkeeper; **la marchande de fromage** the woman in the cheese shop; 2 stallholder (on a market).

s

t

u

marchand de journaux noun Masc. newsagent.

v

w

marchander verb [1] to haggle (over).

x

y

marchandise noun Fem. goods.

z

marche noun Fem. 1 walking; **faire de la marche** to go walking; 2 march; 3 step; **les marches d'escalier** the stairs; **attention à la marche** mind the step; 4 **mettre en marche** to start up (a machine); **être en état de marche** to be in working order.

marché noun Masc. 1 market; **aller au marché** to go to market; **le marché aux fleurs** the flower market; **un marché aux puces** a flea market; **le marché de l'emploi** the job market; 2 deal.

marche arrière noun Fem. reverse; **faire marche arrière** to reverse.

marchepied noun Masc. step (on a train).

marcher verb [1] 1 to walk; **on va marcher jusqu'à la gare** we'll walk as far as the station; 2 **marcher dans quelque chose** to tread in something; **marcher sur quelque chose** to tread on something; 3 to march; 4 to work; **ça a marché** it worked; **la machine à laver ne marche pas** the washing machine doesn't work; **les trains ne marchent pas aujourd'hui** the trains are not running today; 5 **et ton boulot, ça marche?** (informal) and is your job going all right?; ★ **faire marcher quelqu'un** to pull somebody's leg.

marcheur, marcheuse noun Masc., Fem. walker.

mardi noun Masc. 1 Tuesday; **nous sommes mardi aujourd'hui** it's Tuesday today; **mardi prochain** next Tuesday; **mardi dernier** last Tuesday; 2 on Tuesday; **je**

t'appellerai mardi soir I'll ring you on Tuesday evening; **3 le mardi** on Tuesdays; **c'est fermé le mardi** it's closed on Tuesdays; **4 tous les mardis** every Tuesday.

Mardi gras noun Masc. Shrove Tuesday.

mare noun Fem. pond.

marécage noun Masc. swamp.

marée noun Fem. tide; **la marée monte** the tide's coming in; **la marée descend** the tide's going out.

marée noire noun Fem. oil slick.

margarine noun Fem. margarine.

marge noun Fem. **1** margin; **2 en marge de** on the fringe of.

marguerite noun Fem. **1** marguerite; **2** oxeye daisy.

mari noun Masc. husband; **le mari de Claire** Claire's husband.

mariage noun Masc. **1** marriage; **2** wedding; **être invité à un mariage** to be invited to a wedding.

Marianne noun Fem. Marianne (a female figure representing the French Republic in statues and paintings).

marié, mariée noun Masc., Fem. bridegroom, bride; **les jeunes mariés** the newlyweds.

marié adjective married.

marier verb [1] **1 se marier** to get married; **ils se sont mariés à Londres** they got married in London; **elle s'est mariée avec Frank** she married Frank; **2 le prêtre qui les a mariés** the priest who married them.

marin noun Masc. sailor.

marin adjective sea.

marine adjective **bleu marine** navy blue.

mariner verb [1] to marinate.

marionnette noun Fem. puppet.

marjolaine noun Fem. marjoram.

marketing noun Masc. marketing.

marmelade noun Fem. **marmelade d'oranges amères** orange marmalade.

marmite noun Fem. cooking pot.

marmonner verb [1] to mutter, to mumble.

Maroc noun Masc. Morocco.

marocain adjective Moroccan.

Marocain, Marocaine noun Masc., Fem. Moroccan (person).

maroquinerie noun Fem. **1** leather shop; **2** leather goods.

marquant adjective outstanding.

marque noun Fem. **1** brand; **une marque de nourriture pour chats** a brand of cat food; **2** make; **c'est une marque de jean bien connue** it's a well-known make of jeans; **3** mark; **4** point.

marque déposée noun Fem. registered trademark.

marquer verb [1] **1** to mark; **2** to write down; **j'ai marqué ton nom** I've written down your name; **3** marquer un but to score a goal.

marqueur noun Masc. marker pen.

marraine noun Fem. godmother.

marrant adjective (informal) funny.

marre adverb (informal) **j'en ai marre** I'm fed up; **j'en ai marrre d'écrire** I'm fed up with writing.

a
b
c
d
e
f
g
h
i
j
k
l
m
n
o
p
q
r
s
t
u
v
w
x
y
z

a

marrer verb [1] **1 se marrer** to have a great time; **2 se marrer** to have a good laugh.

b

marron noun Masc. **1** (sweet) chestnut; **2** (horse) chestnut.

c

marron adjective brown; **des chaussures marron** brown shoes; **marron clair** light brown; **marron foncé** dark brown.

d

e

f

marronnier noun Masc. chestnut tree.

g

mars noun Masc. March; **en mars, au mois de mars** in March.

h

Marseillaise noun Fem. **la Marseillaise** the Marseillaise (the French national anthem).

i

j

Marseille noun Marseilles.

k

marteau (plural **marteaux**) noun Masc. **1** hammer; **2** doorknocker.

l

m

marteau piqueur noun Masc. pneumatic drill.

n

marteler verb [45] to hammer.

martinet noun Masc. swift.

o

martin-pêcheur noun Masc. kingfisher.

p

q

martyrisé adjective **un enfant martyrisé** a battered child.

r

mascotte noun Fem. mascot.

s

masculin noun Masc. masculine (in French and other grammars); **au masculin** in the masculine.

t

u

masculin adjective **1** male; **le sexe masculin** the male sex; **2** men's; **les vêtements masculins** men's clothing; **3** masculine.

v

w

masque noun Masc. mask.

x

masquer verb [1] to hide.

y

massacre noun Masc. massacre.

z

massacrer verb [1] to massacre.

massage noun Masc. massage; **faire un massage à quelqu'un** to give somebody a massage.

masse noun Fem. **1** mass; **2 une masse de** (informal) masses of; **j'ai une masse de boulot à faire avant lundi** I've got masses of work to do for Monday.

masser verb [1] **1** to massage; **2 se masser** to assemble.

massif (Fem. **massive**) adjective **1** solid; **une table en pin massif** a solid pine table; **2** massive.

mass media plural noun Masc. **les mass media** the mass media.

mastic noun Masc. **1** putty; **2** filler.

mastiquer verb [1] **1** to chew; **2** to putty (a window); **3** to fill (a crack).

mat adjective matt.

mât noun Masc. **1** mast; **2** pole.

match noun Masc. match; **un match de foot** a football match; **faire match nul** to draw.

matelas noun Masc. mattress.

matelassé adjective quilted.

matelot noun Masc. sailor.

matériaux plural noun Masc. materials; **les matériaux de construction** building materials.

matériel noun Masc. equipment; **matériel de sport** sports equipment.

maternel (Fem. **maternelle**) adjective **1** motherly; **2** maternal; **ma tante maternelle** my aunt on my mother's side of the family.

maternelle noun Fem. (state) nursery school (for ages 2 - 6); **aller en maternelle** to go to nursery school.

maternité noun Fem.
1 motherhood; 2 pregnancy; **être
en congé de maternité** to be on
maternity leave; 3 maternity unit.

mathématiques plural noun
Fem. mathematics.

matheux, matheuse noun
Masc., Fem. maths genius.

maths plural noun Fem. maths.

matière noun Fem. subject; **la
matière que j'aime le mieux c'est
l'histoire** the subject I like best is
history; **en matière de: la
politique du gouvernement en
matière de l'éducation** the
government's education policy.

matières grasses plural noun
Fem. fat (in food).

matin noun Masc. morning; **à
quelle heure est-ce que tu te
lèves le matin?** what time do you
get up in the morning?; **à six
heures du matin** at six o'clock in
the morning; **du matin au soir**
from morning till night; **de bon
matin** early in the morning.

matinal (Masc. plural **matinaux**)

matinal adjective 1 morning;
2 **être matinal** to be an early riser.

matinée noun Fem. 1 morning; **au
cours de la matinée** during the
morning; 2 matinée.

matou noun Masc. tomcat.

matraque noun Fem. truncheon,
club.

matrimonial (Masc. plural
matrimoniaux) adjective **une
agence matrimoniale** a marriage
bureau.

maturité noun Fem. maturity.

maudire verb to curse.

maussade adjective 1 sullen;
2 dull, dreary (weather).

mauvais adjective 1 bad; **une
mauvaise expérience** a bad
experience; **ça sent mauvais ici**
there's a nasty smell here; **ça a
mauvais goût** it tastes horrible;
c'est du mauvais goût it's bad
taste; 2 wrong; **le mauvais numéro**
the wrong number; **la mauvaise
adresse** the wrong address; 3 **il fait
mauvais** the weather's bad; 4 **elle a
mauvaise mine** she doesn't look
well.

mauvaise herbe noun Fem.
weed.

maux plural noun Masc. SEE **mal.**

maximum noun Masc., adjective
maximum; **au maximum** as much
as possible; **au maximum** at the
most; **faire le maximum** to do your
utmost.

mayonnaise noun Fem.
mayonnaise.

mazout noun Masc. fuel oil.

me, m' (before a vowel or silent 'h')
pronoun me 1 **elle me déteste** she
hates me; **il m'a vu** he saw me; 2 to
me; **elle ne me parle jamais** she
never speaks to me; **elle m'a donné
son adresse** she gave me her
address; **il me l'a donné** he gave it
to me; 3 myself; **je me fais une
salade** I'm making myself a salad;
je me suis blessé I hurt myself; **je
me lève à sept heures** I get up at
seven o'clock; **je me brosse les
dents** I brush my teeth (literally: I
brush to myself the teeth).

mec noun Masc. (informal) guy.

a
b
c
d
e
f
g
h
i
j
k
l
m
n
o
p
q
r
s
t
u
v
w
x
y
z

mécanicien, mécanicienne
noun Masc., Fem. **1** mechanic;
2 train driver.

mécanique noun Fem.
1 mechanics; **2** mechanism.

mécanique adjective
1 mechanical; **2** clockwork.

mécanisme noun Masc.
mechanism.

méchamment adverb spitefully,
nastily.

méchanceté noun Fem.
1 nastiness; **2** spite.

méchant adjective **1** nasty; **elle a
été vraiment méchante avec moi**
she was really nasty to me;
2 spiteful; **3** vicious; **'chien
méchant'** 'beware of the dog'.

mèche noun Fem. **1** lock (of hair);
2 wick.

méconnaissable adjective
unrecognizable.

mécontent adjective dissatisfied.

mécontentement noun Masc.
1 annoyance; **2** displeasure.

médaille noun Fem. medal.

médecin noun Masc. doctor; **aller
chez le médecin** to go to the
doctor's.

médecine noun Fem. medicine;
faire des études de médecine to
go to medical school.

médias plural noun Masc. **les
médias** the media.

médiathèque noun Fem.
multimedia library.

médical (Masc. plural **médicaux**)
adjective medical.

médicament noun Masc. drug.

médiéval (Masc. plural
médiévaux) adjective medieval.

médiocre adjective second-rate,
poor; **un travail médiocre** a
second-rate piece of work.

méditation noun Fem. meditation.

méditer verb [1] **1** to meditate;
2 méditer quelque chose to mull
something over.

Méditerranée noun Fem. **la
Méditerranée** the Mediterranean.

méditerranéen (Fem.
méditerranéenne) adjective
Mediterranean; **la cuisine
méditerranéenne** Mediterranean
cooking.

méduse noun Fem. jellyfish.

méfait noun Masc. **1** crime; **2 les
méfaits de la pollution** the
detrimental effects of pollution.

méfiance noun Fem. suspicion.

méfiant adjective suspicious.

méfier verb [1] **se méfier de
quelqu'un** not to trust somebody;
méfie-toi! watch out!

mégère noun Fem. shrew.

mégot noun Masc. cigarette end.

meilleur noun Masc. best; **c'est le
meilleur** it's the best one; **le
meilleur des deux** the better of the
two.

meilleur adjective **1** better; **le
climat est bien meilleur au sud**
the climate's much better in the
south; **meilleur que** better than;
**ton écriture est meilleure que la
mienne** your writing's better than
mine; **c'est meilleur que l'autre**
it's better than the other one;
2 best; **le meilleur** the best
moment; **c'est ma meilleure amie**

she's my best friend; **meilleurs voeux** best wishes.

mélange noun Masc. mixture.

mélanger verb [52] **1** to mix; **2** to mix up; **j'ai mélangé les dates** I got the dates mixed up.

mélasse noun Fem. black treacle.

mêlée noun Fem. scrum.

mêler verb [1] **1** se mêler à to mingle with; **2** se mêler de to meddle in; ★ **mêle-toi de ce qui te regarde!** mind your own business!.

mélodie noun Fem. melody, tune.

mélomane noun Masc. & Fem. music lover.

melon noun Masc. **1** melon; **2** un chapeau melon a bowler hat.

membre noun Masc. **1** member; **2** limb.

même adjective same; **j'ai le même anniversaire que toi** I have the same birthday as you; **ils avaient des chapeaux de la même couleur** they had the same colour hats; **2 en même temps** at the same time; **3 tout de même** all the same.

même adverb even; **il n'a même pas demandé** he didn't even ask.

mémé noun (informal) Fem. **1** granny; **2 une vieille mémé** an old lady.

mémoire noun Fem. memory.

mémoriser verb [1] to memorize.

menace noun Fem. threat.

menacer verb [61] to threaten.

ménage noun Masc. **1** housework; **faire le ménage** to do the cleaning; **une femme de ménage** a cleaning lady; **2** household.

ménager[1] verb [52] **ménager quelqu'un** to handle somebody tactfully.

ménager[2] (Fem. **ménagère**) adjective household; **les appareils ménagers** household appliances; **les travaux ménagers** housework.

mendiant, mendiante noun Masc., Fem. beggar.

mendier verb [1] to beg.

mener verb [50] **1** to lead; **mener à** to lead to; **le chemin qui mène à la ferme** the track which leads to the farm; **2 mener une société** to run a company; **3 mener une campagne** to conduct a campaign.

méningite noun Fem. meningitis.

menottes plural noun Fem. handcuffs.

mensonge noun Masc. lie; **dire des mensonges** to tell lies.

mensualité noun Fem. monthly payment.

mensuel (Fem. **mensuelle**) adjective monthly.

mental (Masc. plural **mentaux**) adjective mental.

mentalité noun Fem. mentality.

menteur, menteuse noun Masc., Fem. liar.

menteur (Fem. **menteuse**) adjective untruthful.

menthe noun Fem. mint; **le sirop de menthe** mint cordial.

mention noun Fem. **1** mention; **2** grade (in an exam or a degree); **elle a eu son bac avec mention bien** she got a grade B plus pass in her baccalaureate.

mentionner verb [1] to mention.

mentir *verb* [53] to lie, to tell lies.

menton *noun Masc.* chin.

menu[1] *noun Masc.* menu; **qu'est-ce qu'il y a au menu?** what's on the menu?; **le menu du jour** today's menu; **est-ce qu'il y un menu à prix fixe?** is there a set menu?

menu[2] *adjective* very small.

menuiserie *noun Fem.* woodwork.

menuisier *noun Masc.* joiner.

mépris *noun Masc.* contempt.

mépriser *verb* [1] to despise.

mer *noun Fem.* sea; **aller à la mer** to go to the seaside; **au bord de la mer** at the seaside; **la mer du Nord** the North Sea; **la mer des Antilles** the Caribbean (Sea).

mercerie *noun Fem.* haberdashery.

merci[1] *exclamation* thank you, thanks; **merci beaucoup, merci bien** thank you very much; **merci de m'avoir rappelé** thank you for calling me back.

merci[2] *noun Fem.* mercy.

mercredi *noun Masc.*
1 Wednesday; **nous sommes mercredi aujourd'hui** it's Wednesday today; **mercredi prochain** next Wednesday; **mercredi dernier** last Wednesday; 2 on Wednesday; **je t'appellerai mercredi soir** I'll ring you on Wednesday evening; **le mercredi** on Wednesdays; **c'est fermé le mercredi** it's closed on Wednesdays; **tous les mercredis** every Wednesday.

mercure *noun Masc.* mercury.

mère *noun Fem.* mother; **la mère de Sophie** Sophie's mother.

merguez *noun Fem.* spicy lamb sausage.

méridional (*Masc. plural* **méridionaux**) *adjective* southern.

meringue *noun Fem.* meringue.

mérite *noun Fem.* merit.

mériter *verb* [1] to deserve.

merlan *noun Masc.* whiting.

merle *noun Masc.* blackbird.

merveille *noun Fem.* 1 wonder; **ton gâteau est une vraie merveille** your cake's absolutely wonderful; 2 **à merveille** wonderfully.

merveilleux (*Fem.* **merveilleuse**) *adjective* marvellous.

mes *adjective* SEE **mon.**

Mesdames *noun* SEE **Madame.**

Mesdemoiselles *noun* SEE **Mademoiselle.**

mesquin *adjective* petty, mean.

message *noun Masc.* message.

messager, messagère *noun Masc., Fem.* messenger.

messe *noun Fem.* mass; **aller à la messe** to go to mass.

Messieurs *noun* SEE **Monsieur.**

mesure *noun Fem.*
1 measurement; **prendre les mesures de la pièce** to take the measurements of the room; 2 **sur mesure** tailor-made; 3 measure; **prendre des mesures pour faire** to take measures to do; **le conseil municipal va prendre des mesures pour contrôler la pollution** the town council is going to take measures to control

pollution; **4 être en mesure de faire** to be in a position to do; **nous ne sommes pas en mesure de vous aider** we are not in a position to help you.

mesurer verb [1] to measure.

met verb SEE **mettre**.

métal (plural **métaux**) noun Masc. metal.

métallique adjective metallic.

métallisé adjective metallic; **bleu métallisé** metallic blue.

météo noun Fem. weather forecast.

méthode noun Fem. **1** method; **une méthode de faire** a method of doing; **2** manual, tutor.

métier noun Masc. **1** job; **2 un métier à tisser** a weaving loom.

mètre noun Masc. **1** metre; **2** metre rule.

métrique adjective metric.

métro noun Masc. underground; **une station de métro** an underground station.

mets verb SEE **mettre**.

metteur en scène noun Masc. **1** director (of a film); **2** producer (of a play).

mettre verb [11] **1** to put; **où as-tu mis le sel?** where have you put the salt?; **2** to put on; **je vais mettre mon manteau** I'm going to put my coat on; **3** to wear; **mets ta jupe rose** wear your pink skirt; **4** to turn on (radio, television, heating); **mettre le réveil** to set the alarm clock; **5 mettre quelqu'un en colère** to make somebody angry; **6 j'ai mis trois heures pour le faire** it took me three hours to do it; **7 se mettre quelque part** to

stand (or sit) somewhere; **8 se mettre debout** to stand up; **9 se mettre à faire** to start to do; **elle s'est mise à chanter** she started to sing.

meublé adjective furnished.

meuble noun Masc. **1 des meubles** furniture; **2 un meuble** a piece of furniture.

meule noun Fem. **1** millstone; **2 une meule de foin** a haystack.

meurtre noun Masc. murder.

meurtrier, meurtrière noun Masc., Fem. murderer.

meurtrier (Fem. **meurtrière**) adjective **1** deadly; **2** fatal.

mexicain adjective Mexican.

Mexicain, Mexicaine noun Masc. & Fem. Mexican.

Mexico noun Mexico City.

Mexique noun Masc. Mexico; **aller au Mexique** to go to Mexico.

mi- prefix **1** half-; **mi-clos** half-shut; **2** mid-; **à la mi-février** in mid-February.

mi-bas noun Masc. knee sock.

mi-chemin noun **à mi-chemin** halfway.

micro noun Masc. microphone.

microbe noun Masc. germ.

micro-ondes noun Masc. microwave; **faire cuire quelque chose au micro-ondes** to cook something in the microwave.

micro-ordinateur noun Masc. microcomputer.

microscope noun Masc. microscope.

midi noun Masc. **1** midday, noon; **il est midi vingt** it's twenty past

a b c d e f g h i j k l m n o p q r s t u v w x y z

twelve; **je viendrai vers midi** I'll
come around twelve; **2** lunchtime;
je fais mes courses à midi I do my
shopping in my lunch hour.

Midi *noun Masc.* **le Midi** the South of
France.

miel *noun Masc.* honey.

**mien, mienne, miens,
miennes** *pronoun* **le mien, la
mienne, les miens, les miennes**
mine; **'à qui sont ces
chaussures?' – 'ce sont les
miennes'** 'whose shoes are these?'
– 'they're mine'; **puis-je
t'emprunter ton vélo? le mien est
chez moi**
can I borrow your bike? mine's at
home.

miette *noun Fem.* crumb.

mieux *adjective, adverb* **1** better; **tu
la connais mieux que moi** you
know her better than I do; **je me
sens mieux** I feel better; **mon
père va mieux maintenant** my
father's better now; **c'est mieux
comme ça** it's better like that; **2 il
vaut mieux que tu restes chez
toi** it would be better if you stayed
at home; **3** best; **c'est le rouge que
j'aime le mieux** I like the red one
best, I prefer the red one.
mieux *noun Masc.* **le mieux est de
revenir** the best thing is to come
back; **au mieux** at best, at least;
pour le mieux for the best.

mignon (*Fem.* **mignonne**) *adjective*
sweet.

migraine *noun Fem.* headache,
migraine.

mijoter *verb* [1] to simmer.

milieu *noun Masc.* **1** middle; **au
milieu de** in the middle of;
2 background; **il vient d'un milieu
pauvre** he comes from a poor
background; **3** environment.

militaire *noun Masc.* serviceman.

militaire *adjective* military; **le
service militaire** military service.

mille *number* a thousand; **mille
personnes** a thousand people;
deux mille personnes two
thousand people.

millefeuille *noun Masc.* vanilla
slice.

millénaire *noun Masc.*
millennium.

mille-pattes *noun Masc.*
centipede.

milliard *noun Masc.* thousand
million.

milliardaire *noun Masc. & Fem.*
multimillionaire.

millier *noun Masc.* thousand; **des
milliers de euros** thousands of
euros.

milligramme *noun Masc.*
milligramme.

millimètre *noun Masc.* millimetre.

million *noun Masc.* million; **deux
millions de euros** two million
euros.

millionnaire *noun Masc. & Fem.*
millionaire.

mime *noun Masc. & Fem.* mime
artist.

mimer *verb* [1] **1** to mime; **2** to
mimic.

minable *adjective* (*informal*)
1 pathetic; **ses plaisanteries sont
minables** her jokes are pathetic;

2 crummy; **un film minable** a crummy film.

mince *adjective* **1** thin; **une mince tranche de viande** a thin slice of meat; **2** slim; **3 mince alors!** (*informal*) oh bother!.

minceur *noun Fem.* **1** thinness; **2** slimness.

mine *noun Fem.* **1 avoir bonne mine** to look well; **tu as mauvaise mine** you don't look well; **2** expression; **3** mine; **une mine de charbon** a coal mine; **4** pencil lead.

minéral (*plural* **minéraux**) *noun Masc.* mineral.

minéral *adjective* mineral; **eau minérale** mineral water.

minet, **minette** *noun Masc., Fem.* pussycat.

mineur[1] *noun Masc.* miner.

mineur[2], **mineure** *noun Masc., Fem.* minor, person under 18.

mineure *adjective* **1** minor; **2** under 18.

minijupe *noun Fem.* mini-skirt.

minimal (*Masc. plural* **minimaux**) *adjective* minimal.

minimiser *verb* [1] **1** to minimize; **2** to play down.

minimum *noun Masc., adjective* minimum; **au minimum** at the very least.

ministère *noun Masc.* ministry.

ministre *noun Masc.* minister.

Minitel™ *noun Masc.* (*Minitel is France Telecom's online data service; subscribers have a small computer linked to the telephone and can use it to access a large number of services including the telephone directories*).

minorité *noun Fem.* minority.

minou *noun Masc.* pussycat.

minuit *noun Masc.* midnight; **à minuit** at midnight.

minuscule *noun Fem.* small letter (*as opposed to a capital letter*).

minuscule *adjective* tiny.

minute *noun Fem.* minute; **dans dix minutes** in ten minutes; **dix minutes plus tard** ten minutes later; **d'une minute à l'autre** any minute now.

minuterie *noun Fem.* time-switch.

minutieux (*Fem.* **minutieuse**) *adjective* thorough.

mirabelle *noun Fem.* small yellow plum.

miracle *noun Masc.* miracle; **par miracle** miraculously.

miracle *adjective* wonder.

miraculeux (*Fem.* **miraculeuse**) *adjective* miraculous.

miroir *noun Masc.* mirror; **au miroir** in the mirror.

mis *verb* SEE **mettre**.

miser *verb* [1] to bet.

misérable *adjective* poor.

misère *noun Fem.* destitution, extreme poverty.

missile *noun Masc.* missile.

missionnaire *noun Masc. & Fem.* missionary.

mistral *noun Masc.* mistral (*a strong cold north wind which blows down the Rhône valley to the Mediterranean*).

mite *noun Fem.* clothes moth.

mi-temps[1] *noun Masc.* part-time job; **travailler à mi-temps** to work part-time.

mi-temps[2] *noun Fem.* half-time (*in a match*).

miteux (*Fem.* **miteuse**) *adjective* seedy, shabby.

mitraillette *noun Fem.* submachine gun.

mixage *noun Masc.* sound mixing.

mixer *verb* [1] to mix.

mixte *adjective* **1** mixed; **2** coeducational.

Mlle SHORT FOR **Mademoiselle.**

Mme SHORT FOR **Madame.**

mobile *noun Masc.* **1** motive; **2** mobile.

mobile *adjective* **1** mobile; **2** **feuilles mobiles** loose sheets (*as opposed to a pad of paper*).

mobilier *noun Masc.* furniture.

mobylette *noun Fem.* moped.

mocassin *noun Masc.* **1** loafer; **2** moccasin.

moche *adjective* (*informal*) **1** awful; **2** ugly.

mode[1] *noun Fem.* fashion; **être à la mode** to be fashionable.

mode[2] *noun Masc.* way, mode.

mode d'emploi *noun Masc.* instructions for use.

mode de vie *noun Masc.* way of life.

modèle *noun Masc.* **1** model; **2** style; **ce modèle existe en plusieurs coloris** this style is available in several colours.

modéré *adjective* moderate.

moderne *adjective* modern.

moderniser *verb* [1] to modernize.

modernité *noun Fem.* modernity.

modeste *adjective* **1** modest; **2** humble.

modestie *noun Fem.* modesty.

modifier *verb* [1] to change.

modiste *noun Fem.* milliner.

module *noun Masc.* **1** module; **2** kitchen unit.

moelle *noun Fem.* marrow (*of bone*).

moelleux (*Fem.* **moelleuse**) *adjective* **1** soft; **2** mellow.

mœurs *plural noun Fem.* **1** customs; **2** morals.

moi *pronoun* **1** me; **c'est pour moi** it's for me; **pas moi** not me; **2 moi, je pense que ...** I think that ...; **3 à moi** mine; **ce n'est pas à moi** it's not mine; **un ami à moi** a friend of mine.

moi-même *pronoun* myself; **je l'ai fait moi-même** I did it myself.

moindre *adjective* slightest; **le moindre problème** the slightest problem; **je n'ai pas la moindre idée** I haven't the slightest idea.

moine *noun Masc.* monk.

moineau (*plural* **moineaux**) *noun Masc.* sparrow.

moins *preposition* **1** minus; **sept moins deux égale cinq** seven minus two equals five; **2 il est dix heures moins cinq** it's five to ten.

moins *adverb* **1** less; **tu en as moins que moi** you've got less than me; **de moins en moins** less and less; **il est moins grand que son frère** he's not as tall as his brother;

c'est moins loin it's not as far; j'aime moins le bleu I don't like the blue one as much; **2 le moins** the least; **le moins difficile** the least difficult; **le moins gros** the smallest; **3** moins de less, fewer; moins de beurre less butter; moins de voitures fewer cars; **4 au moins** at least; **5 du moins** at least; **6 à moins que** (+ *subjunctive*) unless; **à moins qu'elle soit malade** unless she's ill.

mois *noun Masc.* month; **au mois de mai** in May; **le mois dernier** last month; **le mois prochain** next month.

moisi *noun Masc.* mould.

moisi *adjective* mouldy.

moisir *verb* [2] to go mouldy.

moisson *noun Fem.* harvest.

moite *adjective* **1** damp; **2** muggy.

moitié *noun Fem.* **1** half; **la moitié d'une pomme** half an apple; **donne-moi la moitié** give me half; **la moitié du temps** half the time; **2 à moitié** half; **à moitié vide** half empty.

moitié-moitié *adverb* half-and-half; **partager moitié-moitié** to go halves.

molaire *noun Fem.* molar, back tooth.

molle *adjective* SEE **mou.**

mollet *noun Masc.* calf (*of the leg*).

mollet *adjective* **un œuf mollet** a soft-boiled egg.

molleton *noun Masc.* flannel, flannelette.

môme *noun Masc. & Fem.* (*informal*) kid.

moment *noun Masc.* moment; **un moment, s'il vous plaît** just a moment please; **en ce moment** at the moment; **par moments** at times; **pour le moment** for the moment; **au moment où** just when; **à ce moment-là** just at that moment, just then; **j'ai attendu un bon moment** I waited for a good while.

mon, ma, mes *adjective* my; **mon fils** my son; **ma fille** my daughter; **mes enfants** my children.

monarchie *noun Fem.* monarchy.

monastère *noun Masc.* monastery.

monde *noun Masc.* **1** world; **2** people; **il y a beaucoup de monde** there are a lot of people; **peu de monde** not many people; **tout le monde** everybody.

mondial (*Masc. plural* **mondiaux**) *adjective* **1** world; **la Seconde Guerre mondiale** the Second World War; **2** worldwide.

monétique *noun Fem.* electronic banking.

moniteur[1] *noun Masc.* monitor.

moniteur[2]**, monitrice** *noun Masc., Fem.* **1** instructor (*sports or driving*); **un moniteur de ski** a ski instructor; **2** camp leader.

monnaie *noun Fem.* **1** currency; **2 une pièce de monnaie** a coin; **3** change; **je n'ai pas de monnaie** I don't have any change.

monopoliser *verb* [1] to monopolize.

monotone *adjective* monotonous.

Monsieur (*plural* **Messieurs**) *noun Masc.* **1 Monsieur Lejay** Mr

a b c d e f g h i j k l m n o p q r s t u v w x y z

monstre 186 FRENCH-ENGLISH

Lejay; **bonsoir monsieur** good evening (when greeting somebody you do not know well in French it is polite to add 'Monsieur', 'Madame', or 'Mademoiselle' to the greeting); **2** man; **un grand monsieur** a tall man; **les deux messieurs assis à la table** the two men sitting at the table.

monstre noun Masc. monster.

monstre adjective huge; **un travail monstre** a huge amount of work.

monstrueux (Fem. **monstrueuse**) adjective monstrous.

mont noun Masc. mountain; **le mont Blanc** Mont Blanc.

montagne noun Fem. **1** mountain; **la montagne** the mountains; **2 une montagne de** a mountain of.

montagneux (Fem. **montagneuse**) adjective mountainous.

montant noun Masc. sum.

montant adjective rising.

montée noun Fem. **1** ascent, way up; **2** rise, increase; **3** slope; **en montée** uphill.

monter verb [1] **1** to go up, to come up; **monter l'escalier** to go (or come) up the stairs; **monter la colline** to go up the hill; **monter se coucher** to go up to bed; **2 monter dans** to get on (a bus, train, etc); **3 monter quelque chose** to bring (or take) something up; **je vais monter tes valises** I'll take your cases up; **4** to assemble (a kit); **5** to rise; **les prix ont monté** prices have risen; **6** to increase; **7 monter à cheval** to ride a horse.

montgolfière noun Fem. hot-air balloon.

montre noun Fem. watch.

montrer verb [1] **1** to show; **montrer quelque chose à quelqu'un** to show somebody something; **montre-moi ton cadeau** show me your present; **2** to point out; **montrer quelque chose du doigt** to point to something.

monture noun Fem. frames (of glasses).

monument noun Masc. **1** monument; **un monument aux morts** a war memorial; **2** historic building.

moquer verb [1] **1 se moquer de** to make fun of; **tout le monde s'est moqué de moi** everybody made fun of me; **2 se moquer de** not to care about; **je m'en moque** I couldn't care less.

moquette noun Fem. fitted carpet.

moqueur (Fem. **moqueuse**) adjective mocking.

moral (plural **moraux**) noun Masc. morale; **je n'ai pas le moral** I'm feeling really down.

moral (Masc. plural **moraux**) adjective **1** moral; **2** mental.

morale noun Fem. **1** moral; **2** morality.

morceau (plural **morceaux**) noun Masc. piece, bit; **un morceau de pain** a piece of bread; **un morceau de sucre** a sugar lump.

mordre verb [3] to bite.

mordu adjective **être mordu de quelque chose** (informal) to be mad about something.

morne *adjective* **1** gloomy;
2 dismal, dreary.

morsure *noun Fem.* bite.

mort[1] *noun Fem.* death; **trois mois
avant sa mort** three months before
he died.

mort[2], **morte** *noun Masc., Fem.*
dead man, dead woman.

mort *adjective* dead.

mort-aux-rats *noun Fem.* rat
poison.

mortel (*Fem.* **mortelle**) *adjective*
1 deadly; **2** fatal.

morue *noun Fem.* **1** cod; **2** salt cod.

mosaïque *noun Fem.* mosaic.

Moscou *noun* Moscow.

mosquée *noun Fem.* mosque.

mot *noun Masc.* **1** word; **mot à mot**
word for word; **2 un petit mot** a
note.

motard, motarde *noun Masc.,
Fem.* (*informal*) motorcyclist.

mot de passe *noun Masc.*
password.

moteur *noun Masc.* engine.

motif *noun Masc.* **1** motive;
2 pattern.

motiver *verb* [1] to motivate.

moto *noun Fem.* motorbike; **je suis
venu en moto** I came by
motorbike.

motocycliste *noun Masc. & Fem.*
motorcyclist.

mots croisés *plural noun Masc.*
crossword.

motte *noun Fem.* **1** lump; **2** slab.

mou, mol (*before a vowel*) (*Fem.*
molle) *adjective* **1** soft; **2** flabby.

mouche *noun Fem.* fly.

moucher *verb* [1] **se moucher** to
blow your nose.

moucheron *noun Masc.* midge.

mouchoir *noun Masc.*
1 handkerchief; **2** tissue.

moue *noun Fem.* pout; **faire la
moue** to pout.

mouette *noun Fem.* seagull.

mouiller *verb* [1] **1** to wet; **2 se
mouiller** to get wet.

moulant *adjective* tight-fitting.

moule[1] *noun Masc.* mould.

moule[2] *noun Fem.* mussel.

mouler *verb* [1] to mould.

moulin *noun Masc.* mill.

moulin à vent *noun Masc.*
windmill.

moulu *adjective* ground; **le café
moulu** ground coffee.

moulure *noun Fem.* moulding.

mourir *verb* [54] to die; **elle est
morte en février** she died in
February; **je meurs de faim!** I'm
starving!; **je meurs d'envie d'y
aller** I'm dying to go there.

mousquetaire *noun Masc.*
musketeer.

moussant *adjective* foaming.

mousse *noun Fem.* **1** foam;
mousse à raser shaving foam;
2 lather; **3** froth; **4 mousse au
chocolat** chocolate mousse;
5 moss.

mousser *verb* [1] to foam.

mousseux (*Fem.* **mousseuse**)
adjective **du vin mousseux**
sparkling wine.

moustache *noun Fem.*
moustache.

moustique *noun Masc.* mosquito.

a
b
c
d
e
f
g
h
i
j
k
l
m
n
o
p
q
r
s
t
u
v
w
x
y
z

a **moutarde** noun Fem. mustard.

b **mouton** noun Masc. **1** sheep; **2** mutton.

c **mouvement** noun Masc. **1** movement; **2** activity, bustle.

d **mouvementé** adjective hectic, eventful; **j'ai eu une semaine mouvementée** I've had a hectic week.

g **Moyen-Âge** noun Masc. Middle Ages.

h **moyen** noun Masc. **1** means; **un moyen de transport** a means of transport; **un moyen de faire** a means of doing; **je n'ai aucun moyen de le contacter** I have no means of contacting him; **2 les moyens** the means, the wherewithal; **je n'ai pas les moyens de m'acheter un ordinateur** I can't afford to buy a computer; **3** way.

moyen (Fem. **moyenne**) adjective **1** medium; **2** medium-sized; **3** average.**un équipe de niveau très moyen** a very average team.

moyenne noun Fem. **1** average; **en moyenne** on average; **2 avoir la moyenne** to pass (an exam).

Moyen-Orient noun Masc. Middle East.

muet (Fem. **muette**) adjective **1** speechless, dumb; **2** silent.

muguet noun Masc. lily of the valley.

mulet noun Masc. mule.

multifonction adjective multipurpose.

multiple adjective **1** multiple; **2** various.

multiplication noun Fem. **1** multiplication; **2 multiplication de** increase in the number of.

multiplier verb [1] **1** to multiply; **2** to increase.

municipal (Masc. plural **municipaux**) adjective **1** local, town; **2** municipal.

municipalité noun Fem. **1** town (or local) council; **2** municipality.

munition noun Fem. ammunition.

mûr adjective **1** ripe; **2** mature.

mur noun Masc. wall.

muraille noun Fem. (defensive) wall; **la Grande Muraille de Chine** the Great Wall of China.

mûre noun Fem. blackberry.

mûrir verb [2] **1** to ripen; **2** to mature; **3** to develop.

murmure noun Masc. murmur.

murmurer verb [1] to murmur.

musc noun Masc. musk.

muscade noun Fem. nutmeg; **une noix de muscade** a nutmeg.

muscle noun Masc. muscle.

musclé adjective muscular.

musculation noun Fem. bodybuilding.

museau (plural **museaux**) noun Masc. muzzle, snout.

musée noun Masc. museum.

musical (Masc. plural **musicaux**) adjective musical.

musicien, musicienne noun Masc., Fem. musician.

musique noun Fem. music; **mettre de la musique** to put on some music.

musulman, musulmane noun Masc., Fem., adjective Muslim.

mutuel (Fem. **mutuelle**) adjective mutual.

myope adjective short-sighted; ★ **être myope comme une taupe** to be as blind as a bat (literally: to be as short-sighted as a mole).

myopie noun Fem. short-sightedness.

myosotis noun Masc. forget-me-not.

myrtille noun Fem. bilberry.

mystère noun Masc. mystery.

mystérieux (Fem. **mystérieuse**) adjective mysterious.

mystifier verb [1] to fool.

mystique adjective mystical.

mythe noun Masc. myth.

mythologie noun Fem. mythology.

Nn

n' adverb SEE ne.

nacre noun Fem. mother-of-pearl.

nage noun Fem. swimming.

nager verb [52] to swim.

nageur, nageuse noun Masc., Fem. swimmer.

naïf (Fem. **naïve**) adjective naïve.

nain, naine noun Masc., Fem., adjective dwarf.

naissance noun Fem. birth; **date de naissance** date of birth.

naître verb [55] to be born; **elle est née en 1975** she was born in 1975.

nana noun Fem. (informal) girl.

naphtaline noun Fem. mothballs.

nappe noun Fem. tablecloth.

narcisse noun Masc. narcissus.

narine noun Fem. nostril.

natal adjective native; **mon pays natal** my native country.

natalité noun Fem. **le taux de natalité** the birthrate.

natation noun Fem. swimming; **faire de la natation** to go swimming.

natif (Fem. **native**) adjective native.

nation noun Fem. nation.

national (Masc. plural **nationaux**) adjective national.

nationaliser verb [1] to nationalize.

nationalité noun Fem. nationality.

nativité noun Fem. Nativity.

natte noun Fem. **1** plait; **2** mat.

nature noun Fem. nature.

nature adjective **yaourt nature** plain yoghurt; **un thé nature** a cup of tea without milk or sugar.

naturel noun Masc. **1** nature; **2** **au naturel** plain.

naturel (Fem. **naturelle**) adjective natural.

naturellement adverb of course.

nausée noun Fem. nausea; **avoir la nausée** to feel sick.

nautique adjective water; **faire du ski nautique** to go water-skiing.

navet noun Masc. turnip.

navette noun Fem. shuttle; **j'ai pris la navette de l'aéroport** I took the

a b c d e f g h i j k l m n o p q r s t u v w x y z

shuttle from the airport; **faire la navette** to travel back and forth.

naviguer verb [1] to sail.

navire noun Masc. ship.

navire-citerne noun Masc. oil tanker.

navire-école noun Masc. training ship.

navré adjective sorry; **je suis vraiment navré** I'm terribly sorry.

né, née verb SEE **naître**.

ne, n' (before a vowel or silent 'h') adverb **1** ne + pas not; **je n'aime pas le lait** I don't like milk; **2** ne + jamais never; **je ne vais jamais à Londres** I never go to London; **3** ne + que only; **je n'ai que dix euros** I only have ten euros; **4** ne + plus no longer; **elle n'habite plus à Londres** she no longer lives in London; **5** ne + rien nothing; **il ne mange rien** he eats nothing; **rien ne t'empêche d'y aller** there's nothing to stop you going; **6** ne + personne nobody; **il n'y a personne** there's nobody; **personne n'a compris** nobody understood.

néanmoins adverb nevertheless.

nécessaire noun Masc. **faire le nécessaire** to do the necessary.

nécessaire adjective necessary; **il est nécessaire de faire** it is necessary to do; **est-ce qu'il est nécessaire de réserver?** is it necessary to book?

nécessairement adverb necessarily.

nécessité noun Fem. necessity.

nécessiter verb [1] to require.

nectarine noun Fem. nectarine.

néerlandais noun Masc. Dutch (language).

néerlandais adjective Dutch.

nef noun Fem. nave (of a church).

négatif noun Masc. negative.

négatif (Fem. **négative**) adjective negative.

négligé adjective scruffy.

négligent adjective careless.

négliger verb [52] **1** to neglect; **2 il a négligé de le faire** he didn't bother to do it.

négociant noun Masc. merchant.

négocier verb [1] to negotiate.

neige noun Fem. snow; **un bonhomme de neige** a snowman.

neiger verb [52] to snow; **il neige** it's snowing.

neigeux (Fem. **neigeuse**) adjective snowy.

nénuphar noun Masc. waterlily.

néon noun Masc. neon.

néo-zélandais adjective New Zealand.

Néo-Zélandais, Néo-Zélandaise noun Masc., Fem. New Zealander.

nerf noun Masc. nerve.

nerveux (Fem. **nerveuse**) adjective nervous.

n'est-ce pas? adverb **il fait froid ce soir, n'est-ce pas?** it's cold this evening, isn't it?; **il habite à Paris, n'est ce pas?** he lives in Paris, doesn't he?; **tu as déjà mangé, n'est-ce pas?** you've already eaten, haven't you?

net (Fem. **nette**) adjective **1** clear; **c'est très net** it's quite clear; **2** distinct; **une nette différence** a distinct difference; **une nette amélioration** a distinct improvement.

net adverb **1 s'arrêter net** to stop dead; **2 refuser net** to refuse flatly.

nettement adverb far; **nettement meilleur** much better.

nettoyage noun Masc. cleaning; **le nettoyage à sec** dry cleaning.

nettoyer verb [39] to clean.

neuf¹ number nine; **il est neuf heures du matin** it's nine o'clock in the morning; **Julie a neuf ans** Julie's nine; **le neuf juillet** the ninth of July.

neuf² (Fem. **neuve**) adjective new; **une voiture toute neuve** a brand new car.

neutre adjective neutral.

neuvième noun Masc. **au neuvième** on the ninth floor.

neuvième adjective ninth.

neveu (plural **neveux**) noun Masc. nephew.

nez noun Masc. nose.

ni conjunction **ni ...ni ...** neither ...nor; **ni lui ni son frère** neither he nor his brother; **il n'y a ni pain ni lait** there's neither bread nor milk; **ni Frank ni Paul ne le sait** neither Frank nor Paul knows; **ni moi non plus** me neither.

niche noun Fem. **1** kennel; **2** niche.

nid noun Masc. nest.

nièce noun Fem. niece.

nier verb [1] to deny.

n'importe adverb **1** either, it doesn't matter; **'tu veux une aile ou une cuisse?' – 'n'importe'** 'do you want a wing or a leg?' – 'either,

it doesn't matter'; **2 n'importe qui** anybody; **n'importe qui peut le faire** anybody can do it; **3 n'importe quoi** anything; **je ferai n'importe quoi pour t'aider** I'll do absolutely anything to help you; **elle a fait n'importe quoi** she's made a real mess of it; **tu dis n'importe quoi** you're talking complete rubbish; **4 n'importe quand** any time; **tu peux m'appeler n'importe quand** you can ring me any time; **5 n'importe comment** any old how; **tu peux jeter tous ces papiers dans un tiroir n'importe comment** you can throw all these papers into a drawer any old how; **6 n'importe où** anywhere; **pose tes valises n'importe où** put your cases down anywhere you like; **je ne peux pas habiter n'importe où** I can't live just anywhere.

niveau (plural **niveaux**)

niveau noun Masc. level; **au même niveau** at the same level.

niveau de vie noun Masc. standard of living.

noble adjective noble.

noces plural noun Fem. wedding.

nocif (Fem. **nocive**) adjective harmful.

nocturne noun Fem. late-night opening.

nocturne adjective nocturnal.

Noël noun Masc. Christmas; **Joyeux Noël** Merry Christmas; **un cadeau de Noël** a Christmas present; **le sapin de Noël** the Christmas tree.

a b c d e f g h i j k l m n o p q r s t u v w x y z

nœud noun Masc. knot; **faire un nœud** to tie a knot.

noir noun Masc. **1** black; **2 le noir** the dark.

noir adjective **1** black; **2** dark; **il fait noir** it's dark.

Noir, Noire noun Masc., Fem. black man, black woman; **les Noirs** black people.

noirceur noun Fem. blackness.

noircir verb [2] to blacken.

noisette noun Fem. hazelnut.

noix noun Fem. **1** walnut; **2 une noix de beurre** a knob of butter.

noix de cajou noun Fem. cashew nut.

noix de coco noun Fem. coconut.

nom noun Masc. **1** name; **nom de famille** surname; **nom de jeune fille** maiden name; **2 au nom de: au nom de la famille Dupont** on behalf of the Dupont family; **3** noun.

nombre noun Masc. number; **bon nombre de** a good many; **le nombre de victimes s'élève à 25** the number of dead is 25.

nombreux (Fem. **nombreuse**) adjective many; **de nombreuses personnes** many people; **ils étaient nombreux** there were a lot of them; **ils étaient peu nombreux** there weren't many of them; **une famille nombreuse** a big family.

nombril noun Masc. navel.

nommer verb [1] **1** to appoint; **2** to name.

non adverb no; **elle a dit non** she said no; **2 non seulement** not only; **non loin de** not far from; **moi non plus** me neither.

non- combining form un **non-fumeur** a nonsmoker.

nord noun Masc. north; **le nord de l'Espagne** northern Spain; **le vent du nord** the north wind.

nord adjective north, northern; **le côté nord** the north side.

nord-américain adjective North American.

Nord-Américain, Nord-Américaine noun Masc., Fem. North American.

nord-est noun Masc. north-east.

nord-ouest noun Masc. north-west.

normal (Masc. plural **normaux**) adjective **1** normal; **2 c'est normal** it's natural; **3 ce n'est pas normal** it's not right.

normalement adverb **1** normally; **2** according to plan; **normalement, elle doit être à Rome actuellement** if things have gone according to plan, she should be in Rome at the moment.

normand adjective Norman; **la côte normande** the Normandy coast.

Normand, Normande noun Masc., Fem. Norman.

Normandie noun Fem. Normandy.

norme noun Fem. **1** norm; **2** standard; **selon les normes européennes** according to European standards.

Norvège noun Fem. Norway.

norvégien (Fem. **norvégienne**) adjective Norwegian.

nos adjective SEE **notre**.

notaire noun Masc. notary public.

notamment adverb in particular.

note noun Fem. **1** bill; **la note, s'il vous plaît** can I have the bill please; **2** mark; **j'ai eu une bonne note en allemand** I got a good mark in German; **3 prendre des notes** to take notes.

noter verb [1] **1** to write down; **2** to notice.

notice noun Fem. instructions.

notion noun Fem. **1** idea; **2 des notions** basic knowledge; **j'ai des notions d'espagnol** I have a basic knowledge of Spanish.

notre (plural **nos**) adjective our; **notre fille** our daughter; **nos enfants** our children.

nôtre pronoun **le nôtre, la nôtre, les nôtres** ours.

nouer verb [1] to tie, to knot.

nougat noun Masc. nougat.

nouilles plural noun Fem. noodles, pasta.

nounours noun Masc. (baby talk) teddy bear.

nourrice noun Fem. childminder.

nourrir verb [2] to feed.

nourrissant adjective nourishing.

nourrisson noun Masc. infant.

nourriture noun Fem. food.

nous pronoun **1** we; **nous apprenons le français** we are learning French; **2** us; **viens avec nous** come with us; **elle nous aide** she helps us; **elle nous a aidés** she helped us; **3** to us; **elle ne nous a pas parlé** she didn't speak to us; **elle nous a donné son adresse** she gave us her address;

4 ourselves; **nous nous ferons une salade** we'll make ourselves a salad; **5** (reflexive) **nous levons à sept heures** we get up at seven o'clock.

nous-mêmes pronoun ourselves.

nouveau, nouvel (before a vowel or silent 'h') (Fem. **nouvelle**) (Masc. plural **nouveaux**) adjective **1** new; **viens voir mon nouvel appartement** come and see my new flat; **2 à nouveau, de nouveau** again.

nouveauté noun Fem. **1** novelty; **2** new release.

Nouvel An noun Masc. New Year.

Nouvelle adjective SEE **nouveau**

nouvelle noun Fem. **1 une nouvelle** news; **j'ai une bonne nouvelle!** I've got good news!; **2** short story; **nous étudions une nouvelle de Camus** we're doing a Camus short story; **3 des nouvelles** news; **nous n'avons pas de nouvelles pour l'instant** we have no news for the moment; **as-tu des nouvelles de lui?** have you heard from him?

Nouvelle-Zélande noun Fem. New Zealand.

novembre noun Masc. November; **en novembre, au mois de novembre** in November.

noyau (plural **noyaux**) noun Masc. **1** stone (in fruit); **2** nucleus.

noyer[1] verb [39] **1** to drown; **2 se noyer** to drown, to drown oneself.

noyer[2] noun Masc. **1** walnut tree; **2** walnut; **une table en noyer** a walnut table.

nu adjective **1** naked; **2** bare.

a

nuage noun Masc. cloud.

b

nuageux (Fem. nuageuse) adjective cloudy.

c

nuance noun Fem. 1 shade (of a colour); 2 nuance.

d

nucléaire adjective nuclear; l'énergie nucléaire nuclear power.

e

f

nœud ferroviaire noun Masc. (railway) junction.

g

nuisible adjective harmful.

h

nuit noun Fem. 1 night; cette nuit last night, tonight; dans la nuit in the night; toute la nuit all night; travailler la nuit to work at night; 2 il fait nuit it's dark; avant la nuit before dark; la nuit tombe à sept heures it gets dark at seven o'clock.

i

j

k

l

m

nul (Fem. nulle) adjective 1 (informal) hopeless, awful; le film était nul the film was awful; je suis nul en histoire I'm hopeless at history; 2 un match nul a draw.

n

o

nulle part adverb nowhere; je ne trouve nulle part mon dictionnaire I can't find my dictionary anywhere.

p

q

r

numéro noun Masc. number; ils habitent au numéro vingt-cinq they live at number twenty-five.

s

t

numéro de téléphone noun Masc. telephone number.

u

nu-pied noun Masc. open sandal.

v

nurse noun Fem. nanny.

w

nutritif (Fem. nutritive) adjective nourishing, nutritious; valeur nutritive nutritional value.

x

nutrition noun Fem. nutrition.

y

nylon noun Masc. nylon.

z

Oo

oasis noun Fem. oasis.

obéir verb [2] obéir à to obey.

obéissance noun Fem. obedience.

obéissant adjective obedient.

objectif noun Masc. objective.

objectif (Fem. objective) adjective objective.

objection noun Fem. objection.

objet noun Masc. object.

objets trouvés plural noun Masc. lost property; aller aux objets trouvés to go to the lost property office.

obligatoire adjective compulsory.

obligé adjective être obligé de faire to have to do; je suis obligé de partir I have to go.

obliger verb [52] obliger quelqu'un à faire to force somebody to do.

obscène adjective obscene.

obscur adjective 1 dark; 2 obscure.

obscurité noun Fem. 1 darkness; dans l'obscurité in the dark; 2 obscurity.

obséder verb [24] to obsess; être obsédé par quelque chose to be obsessed by something.

obsèques plural noun Fem. funeral.

observateur, observatrice noun Masc., Fem. observer.

observateur (Fem. observatrice) adjective observant.

observation noun Fem. 1 comment; 2 remark.

observatoire noun Masc. observatory.

observer verb [1] **1** to watch; **elle nous observait de loin** she was watching us from a distance; **2** to observe (rules).

obsession noun Fem. obsession.

obstacle noun Masc. obstacle.

obstination noun Fem. obstinacy.

obstiné adjective stubborn.

obtenir verb [77] to get.

occasion noun Fem.
1 opportunity; **avoir l'occasion de faire** to have the opportunity to do; **2** acheter quelque chose **d'occasion** to buy something second hand; **une voiture d'occasion** a second-hand car; **3** bargain; **une bonne occasion** a good bargain; **4** occasion; **à l'occasion de** on the occasion of; **5 à l'occasion** some time.

occasionner verb [1] to cause.

Occident noun Masc. **l'Occident** the West.

occidental (Masc. plural occidentaux) adjective western.

occupation noun Fem. occupation; **trouver une occupation** to find something to do.

occupé adjective **1** busy; **je suis occupé en ce moment** I'm busy at the moment; **2** engaged (of a telephone line or toilet); **3** cette place est occupée this seat is taken.

occuper verb [1] **1** to occupy; **2** s'occuper to keep yourself busy; **3** s'occuper de to deal with, to see to; **je vais m'occuper du dîner** I'll

go and see to dinner; **je m'en occupe** I'll see to it; **4** s'occuper **de quelqu'un** to attend to somebody; **est-ce qu'on s'occupe de vous?** are you being attended to?

occurrence noun Fem. **1** case; **plusieurs occurrences de typhoïde** several cases of typhoid; **2** occurrence.

océan noun Masc. ocean.

octet noun Masc. byte (in computing).

octobre noun Masc. October; **en octobre, au mois d'octobre** in October.

odeur noun Fem. smell; **des odeurs de cuisine** cooking smells.

odorat noun Masc. sense of smell.

œil (plural **yeux**) noun Masc. eye; ★ **cela saute aux yeux** it's obvious (literally: it jumps into your eyes).

œillet noun Masc. carnation.

œuf noun Masc. egg; **un œuf à la coque** a boiled egg; **un œuf dur** a hard-boiled egg; **un œuf mollet** a soft-boiled egg; **un œuf sur le plat** a fried egg; **des œufs brouillés** scrambled eggs.

œuvre noun Fem. work (of art or literature); **une œuvre d'art** a work of art.

offenser verb [1] to offend.

office noun Masc. **1** office; **2** office **religieux** religious service.

officiel noun Masc. official.

officiel (Fem. **officielle**) adjective official.

officier noun Masc. officer.

a
b
c
d
e
f
g
h
i
j
k
l
m
n
o
p
q
r
s
t
u
v
w
x
y
z

a

offre noun Fem. **1** offer; **2 'offres d'emploi'** 'situations vacant'.

b

c

offrir verb [56] **1 offrir quelque chose à quelqu'un** to give something to somebody; **elle m'a offert une montre pour mon anniversaire** she gave me a watch for my birthday; **2 s'offrir quelque chose** to treat yourself to something; **je vais m'offrir un nouveau dictionnaire** I'm going to treat myself to a new dictionary; **3** to offer.

d

e

f

g

h

oie noun Fem. goose.

i

oignon noun Masc. onion.

j

oiseau (plural **oiseaux**) noun Masc. bird.

k

olive noun Fem. olive; **l'huile d'olive** olive oil.

l

olivier noun Masc. olive tree.

m

ombragé adjective shaded (from the sun).

n

o

ombre noun Fem. **1** shade; **à l'ombre** in the shade; **2** shadow.

p

ombre à paupières noun Fem. eyeshadow.

q

ombrelle noun Fem. sun umbrella.

r

omelette noun Fem. omelette; **une omelette aux champignons** a mushroom omelette.

s

t

omettre verb [11] to omit, to leave out; **omettre de faire quelque chose** to fail to do something.

u

omoplate noun Fem. shoulder blade.

v

w

on pronoun **1** we; **on va au cinéma** we're going to the cinema; **on a oublié de fermer la porte** we forgot to shut the door; **2** you; **de la terrasse on voit la mer** from the

x

y

z

terrace you can see the sea; **on ne devrait pas mentir** you shouldn't tell lies; **3 on leur a dit que ...** they were told that ...; **on a volé leur voiture** their car's been stolen.

oncle noun Masc. uncle.

onde noun Fem. wave (on radio).

ondée noun Fem. shower (of rain).

onéreux (Fem. **onéreuse**) adjective costly.

ongle noun Masc. nail; **se faire les ongles** to do your nails; **je me suis coupé les ongles** I've cut my nails.

ongle de pied noun Masc. toenail.

ONU noun Fem. SHORT FOR **Organisation des Nations unies** UN, United Nations.

onze number eleven; **onze personnes** eleven people; **Marie-Ange a onze ans** Marie-Ange is eleven; **le onze juillet** the eleventh of July.

onzième noun Masc. **au onzième** on the eleventh floor.

onzième adjective eleventh.

opéra noun Masc. **1** opera; **2** opera house.

opérateur, **opératrice** noun Masc., Fem. operator.

opération noun Fem. **1** operation; **2** calculation.

opérer verb [24] to operate; **opérer quelqu'un** to operate on somebody; **est-ce qu'il va falloir opérer?** will they have to operate; **se faire opérer** to have an operation.

opinion noun Fem. opinion.

opposant, **opposante** noun Masc., Fem. opponent.

opposé noun l'opposé the opposite.

opposé adjective 1 opposite; 2 être opposé à quelque chose to be opposed to something.

opposer verb [1] 1 le match de samedi prochain oppose les Anglais et les Français the English are playing the French in next Saturday's match; 2 s'opposer à quelque chose to oppose something; ils s'opposent à un changement des règles they are opposed to a change in the rules.

opposition noun Fem. opposition.

opter verb [1] to opt.

opticien, opticienne noun Masc., Fem. optician.

optimisme noun Masc. optimism.

optimiste noun Masc. & Fem. optimist.

optimiste adjective optimistic.

option noun Fem. option.

optionnel (Fem. **optionnelle**) adjective optional.

or[1] noun Masc. 1 gold; **une montre en or** a gold watch; 2 **une occasion en or** a golden opportunity.

or[2] conjunction now.

orage noun Masc. storm.

orageux (Fem. **orageuse**) adjective 1 stormy; 2 thundery.

oral (plural **oraux**) noun Masc. oral (exam); **l'oral de français** the French oral.

oral (Masc. plural **oraux**) adjective oral; **une épreuve orale** an oral exam.

orange noun Fem., adjective orange.

oranger noun Masc. orange tree.

orbite noun Fem. orbit.

orchestral (Masc. plural **orchestraux**) adjective orchestral.

orchestre noun Masc. 1 orchestra; 2 band.

orchidée noun Fem. orchid.

ordinaire noun Masc. 1 2-star petrol; 2 **sortir de l'ordinaire** to be out of the ordinary; **ça sort un peu de l'ordinaire** it's a bit out of the ordinary; 3 **à l'ordinaire, d'ordinaire** usually.

ordinaire adjective ordinary; **une journée ordinaire** an ordinary day.

ordinateur noun Masc. computer; **un ordinateur portable** a portable computer.

ordonnance noun Fem. prescription.

ordonné adjective tidy.

ordonner verb [1] to order.

ordre noun Masc. 1 order; **donner des ordres** to give orders; 2 order; **par ordre alphabétique** in alphabetical order; **mettre de l'ordre** to tidy up; **mettre en ordre** to tidy.

ordures plural noun Fem. rubbish.

oreille noun Fem. ear.

oreiller noun Masc. pillow.

oreillons plural noun Masc. mumps.

organe noun Masc. organ (of the body).

organique adjective organic.

organisateur, organisatrice noun Masc., Fem. organizer.

a

b **organisation** noun Fem.
organization.

c **organiser** verb [1] 1 to organize;
2 s'organiser to get organized.

d **organisme** noun Masc.
1 organization; 2 body;
3 organism.

e **organiste** noun Masc. & Fem.
organist.

f

g **orge** noun Fem. barley; le sucre
d'orge barley sugar.

h **orgeat** noun Masc. le sirop
d'orgeat barley water.

i **orgue** noun Fem. organ; jouer de
l'orgue to play the organ.

j **orgueil** noun Masc. pride.

k **orgueilleux** (Fem. orgueilleuse)
adjective proud.

l **Orient** noun Masc. l'Orient the East.

m **oriental** (Masc. plural orientaux)
adjective 1 eastern; 2 oriental.

n **orientation** noun Fem.
1 orientation; 2 l'orientation
o professionnelle careers advice;
3 avoir le sens de l'orientation to
have a good sense of direction.

p **orienter** verb [1] 1 to position; 2 to
direct; 3 s'orienter to get one's
bearings; 4 s'orienter vers to move
q towards; Bernard s'oriente vers
les langues Bernard's going in for
languages.

r

s **originaire** adjective être
originaire de to be a native of;
t Giselle est originaire de Dijon
Giselle comes from Dijon.

u **original** (plural originaux) noun
Masc. original.

v

w **original** (Masc. plural originaux)
adjective 1 original; le film est en
x version originale the film isn't
dubbed; 2 eccentric; c'est une
y vieille dame assez originale she's
rather an eccentric old lady.

z **originalité** noun Fem.
1 originality; 2 eccentricity.

origine noun Fem. 1 origin; 2 elle
est d'origine écossaise she's
Scottish; 3 à l'origine originally; à
l'origine la maison appartenait à
mon oncle the house originally
belonged to my uncle.

orme noun Masc. elm tree.

orné adjective orné de decorated
with.

ornemental (Masc. plural
ornementaux) adjective
ornamental.

orphelin, orpheline noun Masc.,
Fem. orphan.

orphelinat noun Masc. orphanage.

orteil noun Masc. toe; gros orteil
big toe.

orthographe noun Fem. spelling.

ortie noun Fem. nettle.

os noun Masc. bone.

osé adjective daring; c'était un peu
osé de dire ça it was a bit daring to
say that.

oseille noun Fem. sorrel.

oser verb [1] to dare.

osier noun Masc. wicker; un panier
en osier a wicker basket.

osseux (Fem. osseuse) adjective
bony (knees, arms).

otage noun Masc. hostage; être pris
en otage to be taken hostage.

OTAN noun Fem. SHORT FOR
Organisation du traité de
l'Atlantique Nord NATO.

ôter verb [1] **1** to take off; **je vais ôter ma veste** I'll take off my jacket; **2** to take away; **3** to remove.

otite noun Fem. earache; **avoir une otite** to have earache.

ou conjunction **1** or; **est-ce que vous voulez du fromage ou le dessert?** would you like cheese or dessert?; **2** ou ...ou either ...or; **c'est ou dans ma chambre ou dans le salon** it's either in my bedroom or in the sitting-room; **3** ou bien or else; **on peut se retrouver au cinéma ou bien chez moi, si tu veux** we can meet at the cinema or else at my place, if you like.

où adverb where; **où es-tu?** where are you?; **ton frère habite où?** where does your brother live?; **tu l'as trouvé où ton sac?** where did you find your bag?; **je sais où elle habite** I know where she lives.

où pronoun **1** where; **le village où elle habite** the village where she lives; **la ville d'où il vient** the town he comes from; **2** when; that; **le jour où je suis arrivé** the day I arrived.

ouate noun Fem. cotton wool.

oubli noun Masc. **1** forgetfulness; **2** l'oubli de quelque chose forgetting something; **3** oversight; **c'était un oubli** I (or you, etc.) forgot about it.

oublier verb [1] **1** to forget; **j'ai oublié leur adresse** I've forgotten their address; **2** to leave; **j'ai oublié mes clefs chez Jérôme** I've left my keys at Jérôme's.

ouest noun Masc. west; **à l'ouest de Paris** west of Paris; **dans l'ouest de la France** in the west of France; **l'Ouest** the West; **l'Europe de l'Ouest** Western Europe.

ouest adjective **1** west; **le côté ouest** the west coast; **2** western.

ouf exclamation phew!

oui adverb yes; **elle a dit oui** she said yes; **dire oui de la tête** to nod.

ouragan noun Masc. hurricane.

ourlet noun Masc. hem.

ours noun Masc. bear.

oursin noun Masc. sea urchin.

outil noun Masc. tool.

outré adjective outraged.

outre preposition in addition to.

outremer noun Masc., adjective ultramarine.

outre-mer adverb overseas.

ouvert adjective **1** open; **laisse la porte ouverte** leave the door open; **'ouvert le dimanche'** 'open on Sundays'; **2** laisser le robinet ouvert** to leave the tap on.

ouvertement adverb openly.

ouverture noun Fem. **1** opening; **les heures d'ouverture** opening hours; **2** openness; **ouverture d'esprit** open-mindedness.

ouvre-boîte noun Masc. tin-opener.

ouvre-bouteille noun Masc. bottle-opener.

ouvrier, ouvrière noun Masc., Fem. worker.

ouvrier (Fem. **ouvrière**) adjective worker; **la classe ouvrière** the working class.

ouvrir verb [30] **1** to open; **ouvrir la fenêtre** to open the window; **2** ouvrir le robinet** to turn on the

tap; **3 elle n'a pas ouvert la
bouche** she didn't say a word;
4 s'ouvrir to open; **ça s'ouvre
comment?** how do you open it?

ovale *adjective* oval.

overdose *noun Fem.* overdose; **une
overdose d'héroïne** an overdose of
heroine.

ovni *noun Masc.* SHORT FOR **objet volant
non identifié** UFO.

oxygène *noun Masc.* oxygen.

ozone *noun Fem.* ozone.

Pp

Pacifique *noun Masc.* **l'océan
Pacifique** the Pacific Ocean.

pagaille *noun Fem.* (*informal*)
mess; **quelle pagaille!** what a mess!

page *noun Fem.* page; **à la
première/dernière page** on the
first/last page; **les Pages Jaunes**
the Yellow Pages.

paie *noun Fem.* pay; **un bulletin de
paie, une fiche de paie** a payslip.

paiement *noun Masc.* payment.

paillasson *noun Masc.* doormat.

paille *noun Fem.* straw.

pain *noun Masc.* **1** bread; **une
tranche de pain** a slice of bread;
2 un pain a loaf of bread; **trois
pains** three loaves of bread; **un
petit pain** a roll; **★ ils se vendent
comme des petits pains** they're
selling like hot cakes (*literally: like
rolls*).

pain au chocolat *noun Masc.*
chocolate pastry.

pain complet *noun Masc.*
wholemeal bread.

pain d'épices *noun Masc.*
gingerbread.

pain de mie *noun Masc.* sandwich
loaf.

pain de seigle *noun Masc.* rye
bread.

pain grillé *noun Masc.* toast.

pair *adjective* **1** even (*number*); **2 au
pair** au pair; **une jeune fille au pair**
an au pair; **travailler au pair** to
work as an au pair.

paire *noun Fem.* pair; **une paire de
chaussures** a pair of shoes.

paix *noun Fem.* peace.

pakistanais *adjective* Pakistani.

Pakistanais, Pakistanaise
noun Masc., Fem. Pakistani.

palais *noun Masc.* **1** palace;
2 palate.

palais de justice *noun Masc.* law
courts.

pâle *adjective* pale; **bleu pâle** pale
blue.

Palestine *noun Fem.* Palestine.

palier *noun Masc.* landing (*on a
staircase*).

pâlir *verb* [2] **1** to turn pale; **2** to
fade.

palme *noun Fem.* flipper (*for
swimming*).

palmier *noun Masc.* palm tree.

palpitant *adjective* thrilling.

pamplemousse *noun Masc.*
grapefruit.

panaché *noun Masc.* shandy.

panaché *adjective* **une salade
panachée** a mixed salad.

pancarte noun Fem. notice, sign.

pané adjective coated in breadcrumbs.

panier noun Masc. basket.

panier à salade noun Masc. salad shaker.

panique noun Fem. panic.

paniquer verb [1] to panic.

panne noun Fem. breakdown (of a car or machine); **la voiture est en panne** the car's broken down; **la photocopieuse est en panne** the photocopier's not working; **tomber en panne** to break down; **nous sommes en panne d'essence** we've run out of petrol; **une panne de courant** a power cut.

panneau (plural **panneaux**) noun Masc. sign, notice board.

panneau indicateur noun Masc. signpost.

panneau publicitaire noun Masc. advertisement hoarding.

panorama noun Masc. **1** panorama; **2** viewpoint.

pansement noun Masc. **1** sticking plaster; **2** dressing.

panser verb [1] to put a dressing on (a wound).

pantalon noun Masc. trousers; **mon pantalon gris** my grey trousers; **un pantalon neuf** a new pair of trousers; **deux pantalons** two pairs of trousers.

panthère noun Fem. panther.

pantoufle noun Fem. slipper.

paon noun Masc. peacock.

papa noun Masc. Dad, Daddy, father.

pape noun Masc. pope.

paperasse noun Fem. (informal) paperwork, bumph.

papeterie noun Fem. **1** stationer's shop; **2** stationery.

papi noun Masc. (informal) granddad.

papier noun Masc. paper; **du papier blanc** white paper; **vos papiers, s'il vous plaît monsieur** your (identity) papers please, sir.

papier à lettres noun Masc. writing paper.

papier aluminium noun Masc. kitchen foil.

papier cadeau noun Masc. gift wrap.

papier-calque noun Masc. tracing paper.

papier hygiénique noun Masc. toilet paper.

papier peint noun Masc. wallpaper.

papiers d'identité plural noun Masc. identity papers.

papillon noun Masc. butterfly.

paquebot noun Masc. liner.

pâquerette noun Fem. daisy.

Pâques noun Masc. Easter; **à Pâques** at Easter; **un œuf de Pâques** an Easter egg; **les vacances de Pâques** the Easter holidays; **le lundi de Pâques** Easter Monday.

paquet noun Masc. **1** packet; **un paquet de sucre** a packet of sugar; **2** parcel; **il y a un paquet pour vous** there's a parcel for you; **3** bundle (of clothes or papers).

paquet-cadeau noun Masc. gift-wrapped parcel; **est-ce que je**

a
b
c
d
e
f
g
h
i
j
k
l
m
n
o
p
q
r
s
t
u
v
w
x
y
z

a
vous fais un paquet-cadeau?
shall I gift-wrap it for you?

b

c
par *preposition* **1** by; **par moi** by me;
par la poste by post; **payer par
chèque** to pay by cheque; **par
accident** by accident; **par hasard**
by chance; **deux par deux** two by
two; **jeter quelque chose par la
fenêtre** to throw something out of
the window; **aller par Paris** to go
via (or by) Paris; **par ennui** out of
boredom; **2** in; **par endroits** in
places; **par cette chaleur** in this
heat; **3** per; **50 euros par personne**
50 euros per person; **deux repas
par jour** two meals a day; **deux fois
par semaine** twice a week.

d

e

f

g

h

i

j

k
parachute *noun Masc.* parachute.

parachutiste *noun Masc. & Fem.*
parachutist.

l

m
paradis *noun Masc.* heaven.

paragraphe *noun Masc.*
paragraph.

n

o

p
paraître *verb* [57] **1** to seem; **ça me
paraît étrange** that seems strange
to me; **il paraît qu'il est mort** it
seems he's dead; **2 paraît-il**
apparently; **elle est à Nice, paraît-
il** she's in Nice, apparently; **3** to
appear; **paraître en public** to
appear in public; **4** (*of a book*) to
come out, to be published; **le
roman va paraître en juin** the
novel will come out in June.

q

r

s

t

u

v
parallèle *adjective* parallel.

w
paralysé *adjective* paralysed.

x
parapente *noun Masc.*
1 paraglider; **2** paragliding.

y

z
parapluie *noun Masc.* umbrella.

parasite *noun Masc.* **1** parasite;
2 des parasites interference (*on
TV or radio*).

parasol *noun Masc.* parasol.

parc *noun Masc.* **1** park; **aller au
parc** to go to the park; **2** grounds (*of
a large house*); **3** fleet (*of vehicles*).

parc d'attractions *noun Masc.*
amusement park.

parce que *conjunction* because;
parce qu'elle est malade because
she's ill; **c'est parce que je t'aime**
it's because I love you.

par-ci *adverb* **par-ci par-là** here
and there.

parcmètre *noun Masc.* parking
meter.

parc naturel *noun Masc.* nature
park.

parcourir *verb* [29] to go all over,
to travel all over; **j'ai parcouru
l'Europe** I travelled all over
Europe.

parcours *noun Masc.* **1** route (*for a
bus or a traveller*); **2** course (*for a
race*).

par-derrière *adverb* from the
back, behind; **elle est passée par-
derrière** she went round the back.

par-dessous *adverb* underneath.

par-dessus *adverb* **1** on top;
2 over it; **il a sauté par-dessus** he
jumped over it.

par-dessus *preposition* over; **elle
a sauté par-dessus le ruisseau**
she jumped over the stream;
j'aime ça par-dessus tout! I like
that best of all!

pardessus *noun Masc.* overcoat.

par-devant *adverb* by the front.

pardon noun Masc. **1** pardon, forgiveness; **je te demande pardon** I'm sorry; **2** excuse me, sorry.

pardonner verb [1] to forgive; **je ne lui pardonnerai jamais** I'll never forgive him.

pare-balles adjective bullet-proof; **un gilet pare-balles** a bullet-proof vest.

pare-brise noun Masc. windscreen.

pare-chocs noun Masc. bumper (on a car).

pareil (Fem. **pareille**) adjective **1** the same; **les deux voitures sont presque pareilles** the two cars are almost the same; **c'est toujours pareil** it's always the same; **mais ce n'est pas du tout pareil!** but it's not the same at all!; **2** such; **je n'ai jamais dit une chose pareille** I never said any such thing; **tu ne peux pas sortir par un temps pareil** you can't go out in weather like this.

parent noun Masc. **1** parent; **mes parents** my parents; **2** relation; **parents et amis** friends and relations.

parenthèse noun Fem. bracket; **entre parenthèses** in brackets.

paresse noun Fem. laziness.

paresseux (Fem. **paresseuse**) adjective lazy.

parfait adjective perfect.

parfaitement adverb **1** perfectly; **tu le sais parfaitement!** you know perfectly well!; **parfaitement faux** totally wrong; **2 parfaitement!** absolutely!

parfois adverb sometimes.

parfum noun Masc. **1** perfume; **2** flavour; **tu veux quel parfum de yaourt?** what flavour yoghurt would you like?

parfumé adjective **1** perfumed, fragrant; **parfumé à la lavande** lavender-scented; **2** flavoured; **une glace parfumée au chocolat** a chocolate ice cream.

parfumerie noun Fem. perfume shop.

pari noun Masc. bet; **faire un pari** to make a bet.

parier verb [1] to bet.

Paris noun Paris; **à Paris** in (or to) Paris.

parisien (Fem. **parisienne**) adjective **1** Parisian; **2** Paris; **un restaurant parisien** a Paris restaurant.

Parisien, Parisienne noun Masc., Fem. Parisian.

parking noun Masc. car park; **dans le parking** in the car park.

Parlement noun Masc. parliament.

parler verb [1] **1** to speak; **parler (le) français** to speak French; **parler en italien** to speak in Italian; **parler fort/doucement** to speak loudly/softly; **parler à quelqu'un** to speak to someone; **2** to talk; **il parle très vite** he talks very fast; **parler cinéma** to talk (about) films; **3** parler de** to talk about, to mention; **tout le monde en parle** everyone's talking about it; **non, il n'en a pas parlé** no, he didn't mention it; **n'en parlons plus!** let's say no more about it!;

a
b
c
d
e
f
g
h
i
j
k
l
m
n
o
p
q
r
s
t
u
v
w
x
y
z

4 se parler to talk to each other; ★ **tu parles!** (*informal*) you must be joking!.

parmi *preposition* among; **parmi les invités** among the guests.

parole *noun Fem.* **1** **les paroles** the lyrics; **les paroles de la chanson** the lyrics of the song; **2 elle m'a donné sa parole** she gave me her word; **3** speech; **perdre la parole** to lose the power of speech.

parquet *noun Masc.* **1** wooden floor; **2** parquet.

parrain *noun Masc.* godfather.

parrainer *verb* [1] to sponsor.

parsemer *verb* [50] to sprinkle.

part *noun Fem.* **1** portion, helping; **une part de pizza** a portion of pizza; **2** share; **il a payé sa part** he paid his share; **elle a fait sa part du travail** she did her share of the work; **3** side; **de toutes parts** from all sides; **4 pour ma part, je pense que ...** for my part, I think that ...; **5 à part** separate, separately; **une chambre à part** a separate bedroom; **j'ai mis l'argent à part** I put the money aside; **à part ça, qu'est-ce qu'il t'a dit?** apart from that, what did he tell you?; **6 de la part de quelqu'un** on behalf of somebody, for somebody; **c'est de la part de qui?** who's calling?; **dis-lui bonjour de ma part** say hello to him from me.

partager *verb* [52] **1** to share (*possessions or food*); **2** to divide; **je partage mon temps entre mon travail et les enfants** I divide my time between my job and the children.

partenaire *noun Masc. & Fem.* partner.

parterre *noun Masc.* **1** flower bed; **2** stalls (*in a theatre*).

parti *noun Masc.* **1** party, group; **le parti communiste** the communist party; **2** side.

participation *noun Fem.* participation.

participe *noun Masc.* participle; **participe passé** past participle.

participer *verb* [1] **participer à quelque chose** to take part in something.

particulier *noun Masc.* private individual.

particulier (*Fem.* **particulière**) *adjective* **1** special; **rien de particulier** nothing special; **2** private; **une voiture particulière** a private car; **3 en particulier** in particular; **rien en particulier** nothing in particular; **4 en particulier** in private.

particulièrement *adverb* particularly.

partie *noun Fem.* **1** part; **une partie de ma vie** part of my life; **la première partie** the first part; **2 en partie** partly; **3 faire partie de quelque chose** to be part of something; **ce bâtiment fait partie du musée** this building is part of the museum; **elle fait partie de la famille** she's one of the family; **4** game; **faire une partie de tennis** to have a game of tennis; **gagner la partie** to win the game.

partir *verb* [58] **1** to leave, to go; **partir à pied** to go on foot; **tu pars**

déjà? are you leaving already?;
elle est partie en Italie she's gone
to Italy; **il est parti à Londres** he's
gone to London; **elle est partie au
travail** she's left for work; **partir
en vacances** to go away on
holiday; **elle est partie pour huit
jours** she's gone away for a week;
ils sont partis en courant they
ran off; **2 à partir de** from; **à partir
de lundi** from Monday (onwards).

partition noun Fem. score (in
music).

partout adverb **1** everywhere; **j'ai
cherché partout** I've looked
everywhere; **2 un peu partout:** ça
se trouve un peu partout you can
find it/them almost anywhere;
3 trois buts partout three goals
all.

parvenir verb [81] **1 parvenir à** to
reach; **2 parvenir à faire** to
manage to do; **il est parvenu à
ouvrir la porte** he managed to
open the door.

pas[1] adverb **1** (used with 'ne' to put
verbs into the negative) **je ne suis
pas** I am not; **je n'ai pas de stylo** I
don't have a pen; **je ne pense pas** I
don't think so; **ils n'ont pas le
téléphone** they're not on the
phone; **2** not; **c'est lui qui paie,
pas moi** he's paying, not me; **pas
du tout** not at all; **pas vraiment** not
really; **une radio pas chère** a
cheap radio; **pas de chance!** bad
luck!; **pas possible!** I don't believe
it!

pas[2] noun Masc. **1** step; **faire un
grand/petit pas** to take a big/small
step; **j'habite à deux pas d'ici** I live
very near here; **2** pace; **ralentir le**

pas to slow down; **'roulez au pas!'**
'dead slow' (road sign).

passage noun Masc. **1** traffic; **une
rue où il y a beaucoup de
passage** a street where there's a lot
of traffic; **passage interdit** no
through traffic; **2** visit; **je peux te
prendre au passage** I can pick you
up on my way.

passage à niveau noun Masc.
level crossing.

passage pour piétons noun
Masc. pedestrian crossing.

passager, passagère noun
Masc., Fem. passenger.

passager (Fem. **passagère**)
adjective passing, temporary.

passage souterrain noun Masc.
subway (under a road).

passant, passante noun Masc.,
Fem. passer-by.

passé noun Masc. **1** past; **c'est
dans le passé** it's in the past now;
2 past tense; **le passé composé**
the present perfect.

passé adjective **1 l'année passée**
last year; **2** past; **il est dix heures
passées** it's past ten o'clock.

passeport noun Masc. passport.

passer verb [1] **1** to pass; **le temps
passe vite** time passes quickly;
2 to spend (time); **j'ai passé deux
jours à Paris** I spent two days in
Paris; **3 en passant** in passing;
**4 passer quelque chose à
quelqu'un** to pass somebody
something; **passe-moi le sel** pass
me the salt; **5** to cross; **passer le
pont** to cross the bridge; **6** to drop
in; **Pierre est passé ce matin**
Pierre dropped in this morning;

passerelle

206

FRENCH-ENGLISH

est-ce que le facteur est passé? has the postman been?; **je passerai te prendre à huit heures** I'll pick you up at eight; **7** to get through; **laissez passer l'ambulance!** let the ambulance through!; **8** to be on, to be showing (*films*); **le film est passé à la télé lundi** the film was on telly on Monday; **9** to go; **passer à la caisse** to go to the checkout; **passons au salon** let's go through to the sitting room; **10** to give; **il m'a passé son vélo** he gave me his bike; **11** to put through, to hand over to (*on the telephone*); **je vous passe le responsable** I'll put you through to the manager; **12** to put (on) (*a garment*); **13** passer l'aspirateur to vacuum; **14** to take, to sit (*a test or an exam*); **15** passer par to go through; **nous sommes passés par Paris** we went through (or via) Paris; **16** se passer to happen; **qu'est-ce qui se passe?** what's happening?; **ça s'est passé en Chine** it happened in China; **17** se passer de to do without; **se passer d'un manteau** to do without a coat.

passerelle *noun Fem.* **1** footbridge; **2** gangway.

passe-temps *noun Masc.* hobby.

passif *noun Masc.* passive (*in grammar*).

passif (Fem. **passive**) *adjective* passive.

passion *noun Fem.* passion.

passionnant *adjective* exciting.

passionné, passionnée *noun Masc., Fem.* enthusiast; **c'est un passionné de tennis** he's a tennis enthusiast.

passionné *adjective* keen; **c'est une musicienne passionnée** she's a keen musician.

passionner *verb* [1] **l'histoire me passionne** history fascinates me.

passoire *noun Fem.* strainer.

patate *noun Fem.* (*informal*) potato.

pâte *noun Fem.* **1** pastry; **pâte feuilletée** puff pastry; **2** dough; **3** batter; **pâte à crêpes** pancake batter; **4** paste; **5 les pâtes** pasta; **on va manger des pâtes ce soir** we're having pasta tonight.

pâte à modeler *noun Fem.* Plasticine™.

patience *noun Fem.* patience.

patient, patiente *noun Masc., Fem., adjective* patient.

patienter *verb* [1] to wait; **patientez, s'il vous plaît** please hold the line?

patin *noun Masc.* skate.

patinage *noun Masc.* skating; **patinage artistique** figure skating.

patin à glace *noun Masc.* **1** ice skate; **2** ice skating.

patin à roulettes *noun Masc.* roller skate.

patiner *verb* [1] to skate.

patineur, patineuse *noun Masc., Fem.* skater.

patinoire *noun Fem.* ice rink.

pâtisserie *noun Fem.* **1** cake shop; **2** cake.

patois *noun Masc.* dialect.

patrie *noun Fem.* homeland, country.

patron[1] *noun Masc.* pattern (*for dressmaking*).

patron[2], **patronne** noun Masc., Fem. boss.

patronner verb [1] to sponsor.

patrouille noun Fem. patrol.

patte noun Fem. **1** paw; **2** leg (of an animal); ★ **à quatre pattes** on all fours.

paume noun Fem. palm (of the hand).

paumer verb [1] (informal) **1** to lose; **2 se paumer** to get lost.

paupière noun Fem. eyelid; **le fard à paupières** eyeshadow.

pause noun Fem. **1** break; **faire une pause** to take a break; **la pause café** the coffee break; **2** pause.

pauvre noun Masc. & Fem. poor man, poor woman; **les pauvres** the poor; **le pauvre!** poor thing!

pauvre adjective poor.

pauvreté noun Fem. poverty.

pavé noun Masc. cobblestone.

pavillon noun Masc. **1** detached house; **un pavillon de banlieue** a house in the suburbs; **2** wing (in a hospital).

payant adjective **1** (of a show or event) not free; **c'est payant?** do you have to pay to get in?; **un parking payant** a pay-and-display car park; **2 un hôte payant** a paying guest.

paye noun Fem. wages.

payer verb [59] **1** to pay (a bill or a person); **c'est moi qui paie** I'm paying; **être mal payé** to be badly paid; **être payé à l'heure** to be paid by the hour; **2** to pay for; **il a payé le repas** he paid for the meal; **3** (informal) **je te paie à boire** I'll

buy you a drink; **4 je me suis payé une semaine à Paris** I treated myself to a week in Paris.

pays noun Masc. **1** country; **la France est un beau pays** France is a beautiful country; **2** region; **des fruits du pays** locally grown fruit.

paysage noun Masc. landscape.

paysan, paysanne noun Masc., Fem. farmer.

Pays-Bas plural noun Masc. **les Pays-Bas** the Netherlands.

pays de Galles noun Masc. Wales; **au pays de Galles** in (or to) Wales.

PC noun Masc. PC, personal computer.

péage noun Masc. **1** toll; **autoroute à péage** toll motorway (motorists have to pay to travel on motorways in France); **2** tollbooth.

peau (plural **peaux**) noun Fem. **1** skin; **avoir la peau sèche** to have dry skin; **2** peel (of fruit); **peau d'orange** orange peel.

pêche noun Fem. **1** peach; **2** fishing; **aller à la pêche** to go fishing.

péché noun Masc. sin.

pêcher[1] verb [1] **1** to fish for (trout, salmon, etc); **2** to catch; **Denise a pêché trois truites** Denise caught three trout.

pêcher[2] noun Masc. peach tree.

pêcheur noun Masc. fisherman.

pédagogique adjective educational; **méthode pédagogique** teaching method.

pédale noun Fem. pedal; ★ perdre les pédales (informal) to lose your grip.

pédaler verb [1] to pedal.

pédalo™ noun Masc. pedalo, pedal boat.

pédestre adjective faire une randonnée pédestre to go walking (on a long-distance public footpath).

peigne noun Masc. comb.

peigner verb [1] 1 to comb; 2 se peigner to comb your hair.

peindre verb [60] to paint.

peine noun Fem. 1 effort, trouble; se donner de la peine to go to a lot of trouble; il n'a même pas pris la peine d'appeler he didn't even take the trouble to ring; 2 ce n'est pas la peine it's not worth it; 3 difficulty; elle a eu beaucoup de peine à trouver un logement she had a lot of difficulty finding somewhere to live; 4 faire de la peine à quelqu'un to upset somebody; 5 penalty (in law); sous peine d'amende offenders will be fined; 6 à peine hardly, scarcely; je le connais à peine I hardly know him; il était à peine cinq heures it was barely five o'clock.

peine de mort noun Fem. death penalty.

peintre noun Masc. painter.

peintre-décorateur noun Masc. decorator.

peinture noun Fem. 1 paint; 'peinture fraîche' 'wet paint'; 2 painting; faire de la peinture to paint; 3 une peinture a painting.

pèlerin noun Masc. pilgrim.

pèlerinage noun Masc. pilgrimage; faire un pèlerinage to go on a pilgrimage.

pelle noun Fem. 1 spade; 2 shovel.

pelle à poussière noun Fem. dustpan.

pelle mécanique noun Fem. mechanical digger.

pellicule noun Fem. 1 film (for a camera); une pellicule couleur a colour film; 2 les pellicules dandruff.

pelouse noun Fem. lawn; 'pelouse interdite' 'keep off the grass'.

peluche noun Fem. soft toy.

pencher verb [1] 1 to tilt; 2 to lean; 3 se pencher to bend down; 4 se pencher par la fenêtre to lean out of the window.

pendant preposition 1 for; je t'ai attendu pendant deux heures I waited for you for two hours; 2 during; pendant l'hiver during the winter; 3 pendant que while; pendant que les enfants sont à l'école while the children are at school; 4 pendant ce temps là meanwhile; pendant ce temps là elle attendait à la gare meanwhile she was waiting at the station.

pendentif noun Masc. pendant.

penderie noun Fem. wardrobe, hanging cupboard.

pendre verb [3] 1 to hang; 2 pendre quelque chose to hang something up; 3 to hang down.

pendule noun Fem. clock.

pénétrer verb [24] 1 pénétrer dans to enter; un voleur a pénétré dans le bureau a thief got into the office; 2 to penetrate.

pénible *adjective* **1** difficult, hard; **2 il est pénible** he's a pain.

péniche *noun Fem.* barge.

pénis *noun Masc.* penis.

pensée *noun Fem.* **1** thought; **2** pansy.

penser *verb* [1] **1** to think; **je pense que tu as raison** I think you're right; **oui, je pense** yes, I think so; **je ne pense pas** I don't think so; **2** to intend; **il pense arriver mardi** he's intending to arrive on Tuesday; **3 penser de** to think of; **qu'est-ce que tu penses de mon idée?** what do you think of my idea?; **4 penser à** to think about; **à quoi penses-tu?** what are you thinking about?; **5 cette chanson me fait penser à ta mère** this song reminds me of your mother; **6** to remember; **pendant que j'y pense** while I remember; **fais-moi penser à acheter des citrons** remind me to buy lemons.

pension *noun Fem.* **1** boarding school; **2** boarding house; **3** pension; **4 pension complète** full board; **demi-pension** half board, dinner, bed and breakfast.

pension de famille *noun Fem.* family hotel.

pensionnaire *noun Masc. & Fem.* boarder.

pensionnat *noun Masc.* boarding school.

pente *noun Fem.* slope; **en pente** sloping.

Pentecôte *noun Fem.* Whitsun; **à la Pentecôte** at Whitsun.

pépin *noun Masc.* **1** (grape) pip; **2** (*informal*) slight problem.

perçant *adjective* **1** piercing; **2** sharp.

perce-neige *noun Masc. OR Fem.* snowdrop.

percer *verb* [61] to pierce; **avoir les oreilles percées** to have pierced ears; **se faire percer les oreilles** to have your ears pierced; **percer un trou** to make a hole.

perceuse *noun Fem.* drill.

perdant, perdante *noun Masc., Fem.* loser.

perdre *verb* [3] **1** to lose; **notre équipe a perdu** our team lost; **2 perdre quelque chose** to lose something; **j'ai perdu mes clefs** I've lost my keys; **j'ai perdu mon chemin** I've lost my way; **3 être perdu** to be lost; **4 se perdre** to get lost; **je me suis perdu dans les petites rues** I got lost in the back streets; **5 perdre du temps** to waste time.

perdrix *noun Fem.* (*invariable*) partridge.

perdu *adjective* **1** lost; **un enfant perdu** a lost child; **je suis perdu** I'm lost; **vous êtes perdu?** are you lost?; **2** stray; **un chien perdu** a stray dog; **3 c'est du temps perdu** it's a waste of time.

père *noun Masc.* father; **le père Noël** Father Christmas.

perfectionner *verb* [1] to perfect.

performant *adjective* **1** efficient; **2** high-performance.

périmé *adjective* out-of-date.

période *noun Fem.* period.

périphérique *noun Masc.* ring road.

a b c d e f g h i j k l m n o **p** q r s t u v w x y z

perle noun Fem. **1** pearl; **2** bead.

permanence noun Fem.
1 service; 'permanence de 8h à 19h' 'open from 8 a.m. to 7 p.m.'; **2** en permanence permanently, all the time.

permanent adjective
1 permanent; **2** continuous.

permettre verb [11] permettre à quelqu'un de faire to allow someone to do; elle leur a permis de partir she allowed them to leave; permettez-moi de vous aider let me help you.

permis noun Masc. permit, licence.

permis de conduire noun Masc. driving licence; passer son permis to sit your driving test.

permission noun Fem.
1 permission; **2** leave (from the army).

perroquet noun Masc. parrot.

perruche noun Fem. budgie.

perruque noun Fem. wig.

persécution noun Fem. persecution.

persévérer verb [24] to persevere.

persil noun Masc. parsley.

persister verb [1] to persist.

personnage noun Masc.
1 character (in a book, film, or play); **2** figure, person; un personnage célèbre a famous person.

personnalité noun Fem. personality.

personne[1] pronoun **1** nobody; personne ne sait nobody knows; **2** anybody; je ne vois personne I can't see anybody; je n'ai parlé à

personne I didn't speak to anybody.

personne[2] noun Fem. person; vingt personnes twenty people; les personnes âgées the elderly; en personne in person.

personnel noun Masc. **1** staff; **2** le service du personnel the personnel department.

personnel (Fem. personnelle) adjective personal.

personnellement adverb personally.

perspective noun Fem.
1 perspective; **2** view; **3** prospect.

persuader verb [1] **1** to persuade; persuader quelqu'un de faire to persuade somebody to do; **2** être persuadé to be sure.

perte noun Fem. **1** loss; **2** waste; une perte de temps a waste of time.

perturber verb [1] to disrupt.

pesanteur noun Fem. gravity.

pèse-personne noun Masc. bathroom scales.

peser verb [50] **1** peser quelque chose to weigh something; **2** to weigh; je pèse 60 kilos I weigh 60 kilos.

pessimiste noun Masc. & Fem. pessimist.

pessimiste adjective pessimistic.

pétale noun Masc. petal.

pétanque noun Fem. bowls (the French version, played outdoors with metal bowls; also called 'boules').

pétard noun Masc. firecracker, banger.

pétillant *adjective* sparkling (*wine or mineral water*).

petit[1] *adjective* **1** little, small; **une petite fille** a little girl; **une toute petite maison** a tiny house; **2** short; **une petite distance** a short distance; ★ **petit à petit** little by little.

petit[2] *noun Masc.* little boy; **les petits** the children.

petite *noun Fem.* little girl; **les petites** the little girls.

petit ami *noun Masc.* boyfriend.

petit bassin *noun Masc.* shallow pool (*for non-swimmers*).

petit déjeuner *noun Masc.* breakfast.

petite amie *noun Fem.* girlfriend.

petite annonce *noun Fem.* small ad.

petite-fille *noun Fem.* granddaughter.

petit-fils *noun Masc.* grandson.

petit mot *noun Masc.* note.

petit pois *noun Masc.* garden pea.

petits-enfants *plural noun Masc.* grandchildren.

pétrole *noun Masc.* **1** oil, petroleum; **2** paraffin.

pétrolier *noun Masc.* **1** oil tanker, ship; **2** petroleum engineer.

peu *adverb* **1** not much; **il dort peu** he doesn't sleep much; **elle gagne très peu** she earns very little; **2** not very; **peu intéressant** not very interesting; **peu réaliste** unrealistic; **3** peu de not much, not many; **il reste peu de temps** there's not much time left; **peu de voitures** not many cars; **4** un peu

de a little, a bit; **il reste un peu de café** there's a bit of coffee left; **un tout petit peu de sel** a tiny amount of salt; **5** parle un peu plus fort speak a little louder; **juste un petit peu** just a little; **6** à peu près about; **il y avait à peu près vingt personnes** there were about twenty people.

peuple *noun Masc.* people, nation.

peuplier *noun Masc.* poplar.

peur *noun Fem.* fear; **avoir peur de** to be afraid of; **Nadine a peur des souris** Nadine's afraid of mice; **n'ayez pas peur!** don't be afraid!; **faire peur à quelqu'un** to frighten somebody; **tu m'as fait peur!** you gave me a fright!

peut *verb* SEE **pouvoir**[1].

peut-être *adverb* perhaps.

peuvent, peux *verb* SEE **pouvoir**[1].

phare *noun Masc.* **1** headlight; **allumer les phares** to turn the headlights on; **2** lighthouse.

pharmacie *noun Fem.* chemist's.

pharmacien, pharmacienne *noun Masc., Fem.* chemist, pharmacist.

phénomène *noun Masc.* phenomenon.

philo *noun Fem.* (*informal*) SHORT FOR **philosophie**.

philosophie *noun Fem.* philosophy.

phoque *noun Masc.* seal.

photo *noun Fem.* **1** photo, photograph; **une photo d'identité** a passport photo; **2** photography.

photocopie *noun Fem.* photocopy.

a b c d e f g h i j k l m n o p q r s t u v w x y z

a

photocopier verb [1] to photocopy.

photocopieuse noun Fem. photocopier.

b

c

photographe noun Masc. & Fem. photographer; **Sean est photographe** Sean's a photographer.

d

e

f

photographie noun Fem. 1 photography; 2 photograph.

g

photographier verb [1] to photograph.

h

photomaton™ noun Masc. photo booth.

i

j

phrase noun Fem. sentence.

physique[1] noun Fem. physics.

k

physique[2] adjective physical.

pianiste noun Masc. & Fem. pianist.

l

m

piano noun Masc. piano; **jouer du piano** to play the piano.

piano à queue noun Masc. grand piano.

n

o

pichet noun Masc. jug.

p

pièce noun Fem. 1 room; **notre maison a quatre pièces** our house has four rooms; 2 coin; **une pièce de deux euros** a two-euro coin; 3 play; **une pièce de Molière** a play by Molière; 4 bit, piece; **les pièces d'un puzzle** the pieces of a jigsaw; 5 item; **dix euros (la) pièce** ten euros each; 6 patch (for repairs).

q

r

s

t

u

pièce détachée noun Fem. spare part.

v

w

pièce de théâtre noun Fem. play.

x

pièce d'identité noun Fem. identification (such as a passport or identity card).

y

z

pièce jointe noun Fem. attachment.

pied noun Masc. 1 foot; **être pieds nus** to be barefoot; **aller à pied** to go on foot; **un coup de pied** a kick; **donner un coup de pied à quelqu'un** to kick someone; 2 bottom, foot; **au pied du lit** at the foot of the bed; 3 **le pied de la table** the table leg; 4 (in swimming) **j'ai pied** I can touch the bottom; **je n'ai plus pied** I'm out of my depth.

piège noun Masc. trap.

piéger verb [15] to trap; **une voiture piégée** a car bomb.

pierre noun Fem. stone.

pierre précieuse noun Fem. precious stone.

piéton, piétonne noun Masc., Fem. pedestrian; **un passage pour piétons** a pedestrian crossing.

piétonnier (Fem. **piétonnière**) adjective pedestrian; **une rue piétonnière** a pedestrian street.

pieuvre noun Fem. octopus.

pigeon noun Masc. pigeon.

pile[1] noun Fem. 1 battery; 2 pile; **une pile de vêtements** a pile of clothes; 3 tails (when tossing a coin); **pile ou face?** heads or tails?

pile[2] adverb (informal) 1 exactly; **à dix heures pile** at ten o'clock on the dot; 2 **s'arrêter pile** to stop dead.

pilône noun Masc. pylon.

pilote noun Masc. 1 pilot; 2 **un pilote de course** a racing driver.

piloter verb [1] to fly (a plane).

pilule noun Fem. pill.

piment noun Masc. chilli.

pin noun Masc. pine tree; **une pomme de pin** a pine cone.

pince noun Fem. **1 une pince** a pair of pliers; **2** dart (*in a garment*); **3** pincer (*of a crab*).

pince à épiler noun Fem. tweezers.

pince à linge noun Fem. clothes peg.

pinceau (*plural* **pinceaux**) noun Masc. paintbrush.

pincée noun Fem. pinch (*of salt, for example*).

pincer verb [61] to pinch.

pingouin noun Masc. penguin.

ping-pong noun Masc. ping-pong.

pintade noun Fem. guinea fowl.

pion[1] noun Masc. **1** counter (*in a board game*); **2** pawn (*in chess*); **3** piece (*in draughts*).

pion[2] noun Masc. & Fem. student supervisor of school pupils (*colloquial*) SEE **surveillant**.

pipe noun Fem. pipe; **fumer la pipe** to smoke a pipe.

pipi noun Masc. (*informal*) wee; **faire pipi** to have a wee.

piquant adjective **1** prickly; **2** spicy.

pique noun Masc. spades (*in a pack of cards*); **le trois de pique** the three of spades.

pique-nique noun Masc. picnic.

pique-niquer verb [1] to have a picnic.

piquer verb [1] **1** to sting; **j'ai été piqué par une guêpe** I've been stung by a wasp; **2** to bite; **piqué par des moustiques** bitten by mosquitoes; **3 se piquer** to prick

yourself; **je me suis piqué le doigt** I've pricked my finger; **4** (*informal*) to pinch; **quelqu'un a piqué mon stylo** somebody's pinched my pen; ★ **piquer une crise (de nerfs)** (*informal*) to throw a fit.

piquet noun Masc. **1** post; **2** peg.

piqûre noun Fem. **1** injection; **faire une piqûre à quelqu'un** to give somebody an injection; **2** bite, sting (*of an insect*).

pirate noun Masc. pirate.

pirate de l'air noun Masc. hijacker (*of plane*).

pirate de la route noun Masc. hijacker (*of lorry*).

pirate informatique noun Masc. computer hacker.

pire adjective **1** worse; **pire que** worse than; **c'est pire que ça!** it's worse than that!; **c'est encore pire** it's even worse; **2** worst; **le pire** the worst; **au pire** if the worst comes to the worst.

pis in phrase **tant pis** too bad; **tant pis pour lui!** that's his bad luck!

piscine noun Fem. swimming-pool; **est-ce que la piscine est surveillée?** is there a lifeguard at the swimming pool?

pissenlit noun Masc. dandelion.

pistache noun Fem. pistachio.

piste noun Fem. **1** trail (*left by an animal or fugitive*); **la police est sur sa piste** the police are on his trail; **2** track (*for racing or sport*); **faire un tour de piste** to do a lap; **3** piste, trail (*in skiing*); **4** runway (*at an airport*).

piste cyclable noun Fem. cycle lane.

a b c d e f g h i j k l m n o p q r s t u v w x y z

pistolet noun Masc. pistol.

pitié noun Fem. pity; **avoir pitié de quelqu'un** to feel sorry for someone.

pittoresque adjective picturesque.

pizza noun Fem. pizza; **vous voulez une pizza à quoi?** what kind of pizza would you like?

placard noun Masc. cupboard.

place noun Fem. **1** space, room; **il y a assez de place pour deux** there's enough room for two; **2** seat (in a theatre, cinema, train, or bus); **trois places pour ce soir** three seats for this evening's performance; **3** place; **remettez tous les livres à leur place!** put all the books back in their places!; **si j'étais à ta place** if I were you; **4** place; **en troisième place** in third place; **5** square; **la place Rouge** the Red Square; **la place du village** the village square; **6 à la place de** instead of; **il y est allé à ma place** he went instead of me; **7 être sur place** to be on the spot.

placer verb [61] **1** to place; **2** to seat (a person); **elle m'a placé à côté de Louis** she put me next to Louis.

plafond noun Masc. ceiling.

plage noun Fem. beach; **on va à la plage** we're going to the beach.

plaie noun Fem. wound.

plaindre verb [31] **1** to feel sorry for; **je te plains** I feel sorry for you; **2 se plaindre** to complain; **je ne me plains pas** I'm not complaining; **elle s'est plainte de la qualité du service auprès du responsable** she complained to the manager about the standard of service.

plaine noun Fem. plain.

plainte noun Fem. complaint; **porter plainte** to complain.

plaire verb [62] **1 s'il te plaît, s'il vous plaît** please; **deux billets, s'il vous plaît** two tickets, please; **2 le tissu me plaît** I like the material; **la chambre vous plaît?** do you like your room?; **le film a beaucoup plu à mon père** my father liked the film very much.

plaisanter verb [1] to joke.

plaisanterie noun Fem. joke.

plaisir noun Masc. pleasure; **le plaisir de lire** the pleasure of reading; **'vous venez avec nous?' — 'oui, avec plaisir'** 'will you come too?' — 'yes, with pleasure'; **faire plaisir à quelqu'un** to please someone; **j'y suis allé pour faire plaisir à ma mère** I went to please my mother.

plan noun Masc. **1** map (of a town or underground system); **le plan du métro** the underground map; **2** plan; **le plan du bâtiment** the plan of the building; **3 au premier plan** in the foreground, in the forefront.

planche noun Fem. plank.

planche à repasser noun Fem. ironing board.

planche à roulettes noun Fem. skateboard.

planche à voile noun Fem. **1** windsurfing board; **2** windsurfing; **faire de la planche à voile** to go windsurfing.

plancher noun Masc. floor.

plan d'eau noun Masc. artificial lake (often for swimming and other water sports).

planer verb [1] **1** to glide; **2** (informal) to have your head in the clouds.

planète noun Fem. planet.

plante noun Fem. plant; **une plante verte** a house-plant.

planter verb [1] **1** to plant (a tree, shrub, or plant); **2** to hammer in (a nail); **3 se planter** (informal) to make a blunder.

plaquage noun Masc. **1** tackle; **2** tackling.

plaqué adjective plaqué or gold-plated; **plaqué argent** silver-plated.

plaque noun Fem. **1** patch (of damp or ice); **2** plate, sheet (of metal or glass).

plaque d'immatriculation noun Fem. number plate (on a car).

plastique noun Masc. plastic; **un sac en plastique** a plastic bag.

plat noun Masc. **1** dish; **un plat chaud/froid** a hot/cold dish; **le plat du jour** the dish of the day; **2** course (of a meal); **le plat principal** the main course; ★ **faire tout un plat de quelque chose** (informal) to make a big deal of something.

plat adjective **1** flat; **à plat ventre** flat on your stomach; **2 l'eau plate** still water.

platane noun Masc. plane tree.

plateau (plural **plateaux**) noun Masc. **1** tray; **2** plateau.

plate-bande noun Fem. flower bed.

plâtre noun Masc. plaster; **il a une jambe dans le plâtre** he has a leg in plaster.

plein adjective **1** full; **le panier est plein** the basket's full; **elle est pleine d'idées** she's full of ideas; **2 en pleine nuit** in the middle of the night; **en plein été** at the height of summer; **en plein centre-ville** right in the middle of town; **en pleine mer** on the open sea.

plein noun Masc. **faire le plein** to fill up (a car with petrol); **le plein, s'il vous plaît** a full tank, please.

plein adverb **plein de** (informal) loads of; **elle a plein d'amis** she's got loads of friends.

pleurer verb [1] to cry.

pleut verb SEE pleuvoir.

pleuvoir verb [63] to rain; **il pleut** it's raining; **il va pleuvoir** it's going to rain; **il a plu cette nuit** it rained last night.

pli noun Masc. **1** fold; **2** pleat; **3** crease (in trousers).

plier verb [1] **1** to fold; **2** to bend (your arm or leg, or a stem); ★ **être plié en deux/en quatre** (informal) to be doubled up (with laughter or pain).

plomb noun Masc. **1** lead; **de l'essence sans plomb** unleaded petrol; **2** fuse; **faire sauter les plombs** to blow the fuses.

plombage noun Masc. filling (in a tooth).

plombier noun Masc. plumber.

plongée noun Fem. diving; **faire de la plongée** to go diving.

plongeoir noun Masc. diving board.

plonger verb [52] **1** to dive; **2** to plunge.

plongeur, plongeuse noun Masc., Fem. **1** diver; **2** washer-up.

plu verb SEE **plaire**; **pleuvoir**.

pluie noun Fem. rain; **un jour de pluie** a rainy day; **sous la pluie** in the rain.

plume noun Fem. **1** feather; **2** ink pen.

plupart noun Fem. **la plupart de** most; **la plupart des gens** most people; **la plupart du temps** most of the time.

pluriel noun Masc. plural; **au pluriel** in the plural.

plus adverb **1** plus de more; **voulez-vous un peu plus de fromage**? would you like a little more cheese?; **2** plus de more than; **il y avait plus de cent personnes** there were more than a hundred people; **3** plus que more than; **il mange plus que moi** he eats more than I do; **le film est plus intéressant que le livre** the film's more interesting than the book; **leur maison est plus grande que la nôtre** their house is bigger than ours; **4** le plus rapide the fastest; **le plus joli** the prettiest; **5** plus ...plus the more ...the more; **plus je gagne, plus je dépense** the more I earn the more I spend; **6** en plus more; **il nous faut trois côtelettes en plus** we need three more chops; **7** de plus more; **trois chaises de plus** three more chairs; **une fois de plus** one more time; **8** de plus en plus more and more; **elle fume de plus en plus** she smokes more and more; **je deviens de plus en plus fatigué** I'm getting more and more tired; **il fait de plus en plus chaud** it's getting hotter and hotter; **9** plus ou moins more or less; **la cuisine est plus ou moins propre** the kitchen's more or less clean; **10** le plus the most; **c'est lui qui gagne le plus** he earns the most; **au plus** at the most; **11** ne ... plus no longer; **elle n'habite plus ici** she no longer lives here; **12** je ne veux plus y aller I don't want to go there any more; **14** il n'y a plus de lait there's no milk left; **15** plus; **deux plus trois égalent cinq** two plus three is five.

plusieurs adjective several; **plusieurs personnes** several people; **plusieurs fois** several times.

plutôt adverb **1** rather; **prends le jaune plutôt que le vert** take the yellow one rather than the green one; **2** instead; **demande plutôt à Anne** ask Anne instead; **3** pretty; **le repas était plutôt bon** the meal was pretty good; **plutôt bien** pretty good; **4** rather; **elle est plutôt maigre** she's rather thin.

pluvieux (Fem. pluvieuse) adjective rainy.

pneu noun Masc. tyre.

pneumopathie atypique noun Fem. SARS (the disease).

poche noun Fem. pocket; **un livre de poche** a paperback; **l'argent de poche** pocket money; ★ **c'est dans la poche** (informal) it's in the bag; ★ **je connais Paris comme ma poche** (informal) I know Paris like the back of my hand.

poêle[1] *noun* Masc. stove (*for heating*); **un poêle à bois** a wood-burning stove.

poêle[2] *noun* Fem. frying pan.

poème *noun* Masc. poem.

poésie *noun* Fem. poetry.

poète *noun* Masc. poet.

poids *noun* Masc. weight; **prendre du poids** to put on weight; **perdre du poids** to lose weight.

poids lourd *noun* Masc. lorry.

poignée *noun* Fem. **1** handful; **une poignée de cailloux** a handful of pebbles; **2** handle; **3 une poignée de main** a handshake.

poignet *noun* Masc. wrist.

poil *noun* Masc. hair; **un poil** a hair; **le chat perd ses poils** the cat's moulting; ★ **être de bon/mauvais poil** to be in a good/bad mood.

poilu *adjective* hairy.

poing *noun* Masc. fist; **un coup de poing** a punch.

point *noun* Masc. **1** point; **et mon dernier point** and my last point; **un point de détail** a minor point; **un point faible** a weak point; **2 un point de rencontre** a meeting-place; **3 être sur le point de faire** to be just about to do; **j'étais sur le point de t'appeler** I was on the point of phoning you; **4** dot; **un petit point sur la carte** a tiny dot on the map; **5** full stop; **6** point (*when scoring*); **six points contre sept** six points to seven; **marquer/perdre des points** to win/lose points; **7** mark (*in a test*); **8 à point** just in time; **tu es arrivé à point** you arrived just in time; **un steak cuit à point** a medium-rare steak.

point chaud *noun* Masc. trouble spot.

point de départ *noun* Masc. starting point.

point d'exclamation *noun* Masc. exclamation mark.

point de vue *noun* Masc. point of view; **d'un point de vue politique** from a political point of view.

point d'interrogation *noun* Masc. question mark.

pointe *noun* Fem. **1** point; **la pointe d'un couteau** the point of a knife; **sur la pointe des pieds** on tip-toe; **être en pointe** to be pointed; **2 les heures de pointe** the rush hour, peak time; **3 une pointe de** a touch of; **une pointe d'ail** a touch of garlic; ★ **être à la pointe du progrès** to be in the forefront of progress.

pointillé *noun* Masc. dotted line.

point mort *noun* Masc. neutral (*gear*); **tu es au point mort** you're in neutral.

pointu *adjective* pointed.

pointure *noun* Fem. size (*of shoes*); **quelle est votre pointure?** what size do you take?

point-virgule *noun* Masc. semi-colon.

poire *noun* Fem. pear.

poireau (*plural* **poireaux**) *noun* Masc. leek.

poirier *noun* Masc. pear tree; **faire le poirier** to stand on your head.

pois *noun* Masc. **1** pea; **des petits pois** (garden) peas; **2 à pois** spotted; **un tissu à pois** a spotted fabric.

a b c d e f g h i j k l m n o p q r s t u v w x y z

pois chiche noun Masc. chick pea.

pois de senteur noun Masc. sweet pea.

poison noun Masc. poison.

poisson noun Masc. fish; **j'aime le poisson** I like fish.

poisson d'avril noun Masc. April fool; **il m'a fait un poisson d'avril** he played an April fool trick on me.

poissonnerie noun Fem. fishmonger's.

poissonnier, poissonnière noun Masc., Fem. fishmonger.

poisson rouge noun Masc. goldfish.

Poissons plural noun Masc. Pisces (sign of the Zodiac).

poitrine noun Fem. **1** chest; **2** bust; **quel est votre tour de poitrine?** what is your bust size?

poivre noun Masc. pepper; **poivre noir en grains** whole black peppercorns.

poivrier noun Masc. pepper pot.

poivron noun Masc. pepper (red, green, or yellow).

poker noun Masc. poker.

polar noun Masc. (informal) detective story.

pôle noun Masc. pole; **le pôle Nord/Sud** the North/South Pole.

poli adjective polite; **être poli avec quelqu'un** to be polite to somebody.

police noun Fem. **1** police; **appeler la police** to call the police; **2** (insurance) policy.

policier noun Masc. police officer; **une femme policier** a woman police officer.

policier adjective **un roman policier** a detective story.

poliment adverb politely.

politesse noun Fem. politeness; **par politesse** out of politeness.

politicien, politicienne noun Masc., Fem. politician.

politique noun Fem. **1** politics; **2** policy; **la politique sociale/étrangère** social/foreign policy.

politique adjective **1** political; **2** un homme politique a politician.

polluer verb [1] to pollute.

pollution noun Fem. pollution.

polo noun Masc. polo shirt.

Pologne noun Fem. Poland; **en Pologne** in (or to) Poland.

polonais (noun), Masc. Polish (language).

polonais adjective Polish.

Polonais, Polonaise noun Masc., Fem. Pole.

pommade noun Fem. ointment.

pomme noun Fem. **1** apple; **une tarte aux pommes** an apple tart; **2** potato; **pommes frites** chips; ★ **tomber dans les pommes** (informal) to faint (literally: to fall into the apples).

pomme de terre noun Fem. potato.

pommier noun Masc. apple tree.

pompe noun Fem. pump.

pompe à essence noun Fem. petrol pump.

pompes funèbres plural noun Fem. undertaker's.

pompier noun Masc. fire fighter; **appeler les pompiers** to call the fire brigade.

pompiste noun Masc. & Fem. petrol pump attendant.

poncer verb [61] to sand (wood).

ponctuation noun Fem. punctuation.

poney noun Masc. pony.

pont noun Masc. 1 bridge; 2 deck (of a ship); ★ faire le pont to take a long weekend (usually when the Thursday before or the Tuesday after is a public holiday).

populaire adjective 1 working-class (family, housing, or area); 2 popular (art or writing); 3 folk; la culture populaire folk culture; 4 popular.

population noun Fem. population.

porc noun Masc. 1 pig; un élevage de porcs a pig farm; 2 pork; manger un rôti de porc to have roast pork.

porcelaine noun Fem. china, porcelain.

porcherie noun Fem. pigsty; ta chambre est une vraie porcherie your room is a real pigsty.

port noun Masc. 1 port; 2 harbour.

portable adjective portable; un ordinateur portable a laptop computer.

portail noun Masc. gate.

portatif (Fem. portative) adjective portable.

porte noun Fem. 1 door; la porte d'entrée the front door; 2 gate (in an airport); la porte numéro douze gate number twelve; 3 l'entreprise a fermé ses portes the business has closed down;

mettre quelqu'un à la porte to sack somebody.

porte-bagages noun Masc. luggage rack.

porte-clés noun Masc. key-ring.

portée noun Fem. à portée de main within reach.

porte-fenêtre noun Fem. French window.

portefeuille noun Masc. wallet; une jupe en portefeuille a wrapover skirt.

porte-jarretelles noun Masc. suspender belt.

portemanteau (plural portemanteaux) noun Masc. coat rack.

portemine noun Masc. propelling pencil.

porte-monnaie noun Masc. purse.

porte-parole noun Masc. spokesperson.

porter verb [1] 1 to carry; porter une valise to carry a suitcase; 2 to take; porter un paquet à la poste to take a parcel to the post office; 3 to wear; elle portait une robe bleue she was wearing a blue dress; 4 se porter bien to be well; se porter mal to be in a bad way; ★ porter bonheur/malheur to bring good/bad luck.

portière noun Fem. door (of a car).

portion noun Fem. portion, helping.

porto noun Masc. port (wine).

portoricain adjective Puerto Rican.

Portoricain, Portoricaine noun Masc., Fem. Puerto Rican (person).

Porto Rico noun Fem. Puerto Rico.

portrait noun Masc. portrait.

portugais noun Masc. Portuguese (language).

portugais adjective Portuguese.

Portugais, Portugaise noun Masc., Fem. Portuguese (person).

Portugal noun Masc. Portugal; **au Portugal** in (or to) Portugal.

poser verb [1] **1** to put down; **il a posé sa tasse sur la table** he put his cup down on the table; **pose ta valise** put your case down; **2** **cela nous pose un problème** that's a problem for us; **3** **poser une question** to ask a question.

positif (Fem. **positive**) adjective positive.

position noun Fem. position.

posséder verb [24] to own.

possessif (Fem. **possessive**) adjective possessive.

possibilité noun Fem. **1** possibility; **c'est une possibilité** it's a possibility; **2** opportunity; **la possibilité de voyager** the opportunity to travel.

possible adjective possible; **aussi grand que possible** as big as possible; **le moins possible** as little as possible; **dès que possible** as soon as possible; **ce n'est pas possible!** I don't believe it!; ★ **faire tout son possible** to do your best.

poste[1] noun Masc. **1** job, post; **un poste de secrétaire** a job as a secretary; **2** **un poste de radio/**

télévision a radio/television set; **3** extension (on a telephone system); **le poste 578, s'il vous plaît** extension 578, please.

poste[2] noun Fem. post office; **il travaille pour la poste** he works for the post office; **mettre quelque chose à la poste** to post something.

poste de police noun Masc. police station.

pot noun Masc. **1** jar; **un pot de confiture** a jar of jam; **2** carton; **un pot de crème** a carton of cream; **3** **un pot de peinture** a tin of paint; ★ **prendre un pot** to have a drink.

potable adjective **eau (non) potable** (not) drinking water.

potage noun Masc. soup; **potage aux légumes** vegetable soup.

potager noun Masc. vegetable garden.

pot-au-feu noun Masc. boiled beef with vegetables.

pot d'échappement noun Masc. exhaust, silencer (for a car).

poteau (plural **poteaux**) noun Masc. post.

poteau télégraphique noun Masc. telegraph pole.

potelé adjective chubby.

poterie noun Fem. **1** pottery; **2** piece of pottery.

pou (plural **poux**) noun Masc. louse; ★ **chercher des poux** (informal) to nitpick.

poubelle noun Fem. dustbin; **mettre quelque chose à la poubelle** to throw something in the dustbin.

pouce noun Masc. **1** thumb; **2** inch; ★ **se tourner les pouces** (informal) to twiddle your thumbs.

poudre noun Fem. powder.

pouffer verb [1] **pouffer de rire** to burst out laughing.

poulain noun Masc. foal.

poule noun Fem. hen; ★ **quand les poules auront des dents** (informal) when pigs can fly (literally: when hens have teeth).

poulet noun Masc. chicken; **une cuisse de poulet** a chicken leg; **du poulet rôti** roast chicken.

poulet fermier noun Masc. free-range chicken.

pouls noun Masc. pulse; **le médecin a pris mon pouls** the doctor took my pulse.

poumon noun Masc. lung; **crier à pleins poumons** to shout at the top of your voice.

poupée noun Fem. doll.

pour preposition **1** for; **un cadeau pour Marie-Laure** a present for Marie-Laure; **un billet pour Calais** a ticket for Calais; **le train pour Londres** the train for London; **ce sera prêt pour samedi?** will it be ready for Saturday?; **être pour** to be in favour; **je n'y suis pour rien** I had nothing to do with it; **je n'en ai pas pour longtemps** it won't take long; **2 pour faire cela** in order to do that; **je suis allé au marché pour acheter des légumes** I went to the market to buy some vegetables; **je suis là pour t'aider** I'm here to help you; **c'était juste pour rire!** it was only meant as a joke!; **pour ainsi dire** so to speak;

★ **le pour et le contre** the pros and cons.

pourboire noun Masc. tip.

pour cent noun Masc. per cent; **dix pour cent** ten per cent.

pourcentage noun Masc. percentage.

pourquoi adverb why; **pourquoi ont-ils refusé?** why did they refuse?; **je veux savoir pourquoi** I want to know why; **pourquoi pas?** why not?

pourri adjective rotten.

pourrir verb [2] to go bad.

poursuivre verb [75] **1** to chase; **2** to continue.

pourtant adverb **1** though; **et pourtant c'est vrai** it's true though; **2** yet; **et pourtant ça aurait pu être bien** and yet it could have been good.

pourvu que conjunction (followed by subjunctive) **1** providing, as long as; **pourvu que tu reviennes samedi** providing you come back on Saturday; **2** let's hope that; **pourvu que ça dure!** let's hope it lasts!

pousser verb [1] **1** to push; **elle a poussé la porte** she pushed the door shut (or open); **2 pousser un cri** to let out a cry, to cry out; **3** to grow (of a child, hair, or a plant); **mes tomates poussent bien** my tomatoes are growing well; **4 se pousser** to move over; **pousse-toi!** move over!

poussette noun Fem. pushchair.

poussière noun Fem. dust; ★ **dix euros et des poussières** ten euros something, just over 10 euros.

poutre noun Fem. beam.

pouvez verb SEE **pouvoir**[1].

pouvoir[1] verb [12] can; **je peux être là à dix heures** I can be there at ten; **peux-tu m'aider?** can you help me?; **je ne peux pas l'ouvrir** I can't open it; **ils ne pouvaient pas téléphoner avant** they couldn't phone before; **je n'ai pas pu réserver** I wasn't able to book; **elle aurait pu nous le dire** she could have told us; **puis-je parler à Cécile, s'il vous plaît** may I speak to Cécile, please; **tu peux toujours essayer** there's no harm in trying.

pouvoir[2] noun Masc. power; **après dix ans au pouvoir** after ten years in power.

pouvons verb SEE **pouvoir**[1].

prairie noun Fem. meadow.

pratique noun Fem. practice; **mettre quelque chose en pratique** to put something into practice; **il manque de pratique** he lacks practical experience.

pratique adjective practical, convenient; **cet ouvre-boîte n'est pas très pratique** this can opener isn't very practical; **le nouvel appartement est très pratique pour les magasins** the new flat's very handy for the shops.

pratiquement adverb practically; **c'est pratiquement fini** it's practically finished.

pratiquer verb [1] **1** to play, to do (a sport or hobby); **je pratique le yoga** I do yoga; **2** to practise; **pendant mon séjour à Lille j'aurai la possibilité de pratiquer mon**

français during my stay in Lille I'll be able to practise my French.

pré noun Masc. meadow.

préalable adjective prior; **une condition préalable** a prior condition.

précaution noun Fem. precaution; **par précaution** as a precaution; **prendre ses précautions** to take precautions.

précédent adjective previous; **l'année précédente** the previous year, the year before.

précieux (Fem. **précieuse**) adjective precious, valuable; **une pierre précieuse** a precious stone; **des renseignements précieux** extremely useful information.

précipice noun Masc. precipice.

précipitation noun Fem. **1** haste; **2 précipitations** rainfall.

précipiter verb [1] **se précipiter** to rush; **ils se sont précipités vers la porte** they rushed for the door.

précis adjective **1** precise; **2** accurate; **3** specific.

précisément adverb precisely.

préciser verb [1] **1** to specify (details or one's intentions); **2** to explain; **pouvez-vous préciser comment?** could you explain exactly how?

précision noun Fem. **1** precision; **2** detail; **voici quelques précisions sur le voyage** here are some details about the journey.

précuit adjective precooked.

préfecture noun Fem. prefecture (France is divided into 96 'départements', which are roughly equivalent to British counties. The administration of each of these is done at the local level from the prefecture).

préfecture de police noun Fem. (local) police headquarters.

préférable adjective preferable.

préféré adjective favourite; **mon plat préféré** my favourite dish.

préférence noun Fem.
1 preference; **2 de préférence** preferably; **de préférence avant le dix mai** preferably before the tenth of May.

préférer verb [24] to prefer; **elle préfère le poisson à la viande** she prefers fish to meat.

préfet noun Masc. prefect (official with overall responsibility for running a French territorial department); **le préfet de police** the chief of police; SEE ALSO **préfecture**.

préjugé noun Masc. prejudice.

prélavage noun Masc. prewash.

prématuré adjective premature.

premier (Fem. **première**) adjective
1 first; **la première fois** the first time; **c'est la première fois que je le fais** it's the first time I've done it; **Michel, tu passes le premier** Michel, you go first; **le premier juin** the first of June; **2 top; de première qualité** top quality; **3 au premier étage** on the first floor; **4 en premier** first; **arriver en premier** to arrive first.

première noun Fem. 1 première (of a film or play); **2 une première mondiale** a world first (an important event or achievement);

3 **voyager en première** to travel first-class; **4** (in a French school) the equivalent of Year 12.

premièrement adverb firstly.

premier ministre noun Masc. prime minister.

prendre verb [64] **1** to take; **prends celui-ci!** take this one!; **prendre un taxi** to take a taxi; **2 prendre quelque chose à quelqu'un** to take something from somebody; **qui m'a pris mon vélo?** who's taken my bike?; **3** to have (something to eat or drink); **je prends une bière** I'll have a beer; **qu'est-ce que tu prends?** what would you like?; **4** to bring; **est-ce que tu as pris ton parapluie?** did you bring your umbrella?; **5** passer prendre quelqu'un to pick somebody up; **je passerai te prendre à dix heures** I'll pick you up at ten; ★ **c'est à prendre ou à laisser** take it or leave it.

prénom noun Masc. first name.

préparatifs plural noun Masc. preparations; **les préparatifs du voyage** the preparations for the journey.

préparation noun Fem. preparation, training.

préparer verb [1] **1** to prepare; **je vais préparer les légumes** I'll go and prepare the vegetables; **Françoise est en train de préparer le dîner** Françoise is busy making dinner; **as-tu préparé tes affaires pour le matin?** have you got your things ready for the morning?; **on a préparé une petite surprise pour**

a
b
c
d
e
f
g
h
i
j
k
l
m
n
o
p
q
r
s
t
u
v
w
x
y
z

a b c d e f g h i j k l m n o p q r s t u v w x y z

elle we've got a little surprise ready for her; **des plats préparés** ready-to-eat meals; **2 se préparer** to get ready; **je vais me préparer pour partir** I'll go and get ready to leave.

préposition noun Fem. preposition.

près adverb **1** nearby; **il y a un village tout près** there's a village nearby; **2 près de** near; **près de la gare** near the station; **près de toi** near you; **près de chez nous** near our house, near where we live; **3 près de** nearly, almost; **près de mille euros** nearly a thousand euros; **4 de près** closely; **regarder quelque chose de près** to look closely at something; **5 à peu près** more or less; **à peu près deux heures** two hours, more or less; **j'ai à peu près fini** I've more or less finished.

prescrire verb [38] **1** to prescribe; **2** to stipulate.

présence noun Fem. presence.

présent noun Masc. **1** present (tense); **au présent** in the present; **2 à présent** now; **à présent je n'ai pas le temps** I haven't got time just now.

présent adjective present (at an event); **toute la famille était présente** the whole family was there.

présentateur, présentatrice noun Masc., Fem. **1** presenter (of a broadcast or programme); **2** newsreader.

présentation noun Fem. **1** presentation; **2** introduction (to someone you haven't met before).

présenter verb [1] **1** to introduce; **je vous présente mon père?** may I introduce my father?; **Alain, je te présente Raphaël** Alain, this is Raphaël; **2** to present (a ticket, pass, or document); **il faut présenter votre passeport** you must show your passport; **3** présenter ses excuses to apologize; **4 se présenter** to go, to come; **en arrivant, présentez-vous à la réception** when you get there (or here), go (or come) to reception; **5 se présenter à quelqu'un** to introduce yourself to somebody.

préservatif noun Masc. condom.

préservation noun Fem. **1** preservation; **2** conservation.

préserver verb [1] to protect, to preserve.

président noun Masc. **1** president; **2** chairman.

présidente noun Fem. **1** president; **2** chairwoman.

présidentielles plural noun Fem. **les présidentielles** the presidential elections.

presque adverb **1** nearly; **j'ai presque fini** I've nearly finished; **2 presque rien** hardly anything; **il ne reste presque rien** there's hardly anything left; **3 presque pas de** hardly any; **il ne reste presque pas de lait** there's hardly any milk left.

presqu'île noun Fem. peninsula.

pressant adjective urgent.

presse noun Fem. **la presse** the press, the newspapers; **que dit la presse?** what do the papers say?

pressé adjective **1 être pressé** to be in a hurry; **2** urgent; **ce n'est pas pressé** it's not urgent; **3 un citron pressé** a fresh lemon juice (*served with water and sugar*).

presser verb [1] **1** to urge (*someone to do something*); **2** to squeeze; **presser une orange** to squeeze an orange; **3 ça ne presse pas** there's no hurry; **presser le pas** to hurry (on); **4 se presser** to hurry.

pressing noun Masc. dry cleaner's.

pression noun Fem. **1** pressure; **sous pression** pressurized; **2** press stud; **3** (*informal*) draught beer; **un demi pression** a half of draught beer.

prestidigitateur, prestidigitatrice noun Masc., Fem. conjurer.

prestige noun Masc. prestige.

prestigieux (*Fem.* **prestigieuse**) adjective prestigious.

présumer verb [1] to assume, to presume.

prêt noun Masc. loan.

prêt adjective ready; **le dîner est prêt!** dinner's ready!; **être prêt à partir** to be ready to leave.

prêt-à-porter noun Masc. ready-to-wear (clothes).

prétendre verb [3] to claim; **elle prétend que ce n'est pas sa faute** she claims it's not her fault.

prêter verb [1] **1** to lend; **prêter quelque chose à quelqu'un** to lend somebody something; **je te prêterai mon vélo** I'll lend you my

bike; **2 prêter attention** to pay attention; **3 prêter l'oreille** to listen.

prétexte noun Masc. excuse.

prêtre noun Masc. priest.

preuve noun Fem. **1** proof; **la preuve, c'est que ...** the proof is that ...; **2 faire preuve de** show; **ils ont fait preuve de beaucoup d'intelligence** they showed considerable intelligence.

prévenir verb [81] **1** to tell (*in advance*); **préviens-moi de ta visite** tell me when you're coming; **ils arrivent toujours sans nous prévenir** they always arrive without letting us know; **2** to call (*the police or a doctor*); **3** to warn; **je te préviens** I warn you.

prévention noun Fem. prevention.

prévision noun Fem. forecast, forecasting; **les prévisions météorologiques** the weather forecast.

prévoir verb [65] **1** to predict (*an event or change*); **2** to plan (*a journey or an arrangement*); **3 tout a été prévu** everything's been taken care of; **4 le départ est prévu pour huit heures** departure is scheduled for eight o'clock; **5** to allow (*time or money*); **prévoyez 10 euros pour le taxi** allow 10 euros for the taxi.

prier verb [1] **1 prier quelqu'un de faire** to ask someone to do; **il m'a prié d'excuser son retard** he asked me to forgive him for being late; **les clients sont priés de ne pas fumer** customers are kindly requested not to smoke; **2 je vous**

a
b
c
d
e
f
g
h
i
j
k
l
m
n
o
p
q
r
s
t
u
v
w
x
y
z

en prie you're welcome, it's nothing; **'merci beaucoup' – 'je vous en prie'** 'thank you very much' – 'you're welcome'; **3** to pray.

prière noun Fem. **1** prayer; **2** request; **'prière de fermer la porte'** 'please close the door'.

primaire adjective primary; **l'école primaire** primary school.

prime noun Fem. **1** bonus; **2** free gift.

primevère noun Fem. primrose.

prince noun Masc. prince; **le prince Charles** Prince Charles.

princesse noun Fem. princess.

principal (Masc. plural **principaux**) adjective principal, chief.

principe noun Masc. **1** principle; **2 en principe** as a rule; **en principe je rentre à six heures** as a rule I get back at six; **3 en principe** in theory; **en principe tout le monde a été informé** in theory, everybody's been informed.

printanier (Fem. **printanière**) adjective spring-like (weather).

printemps noun Masc. spring; **au printemps** in (the) spring.

priorité noun Fem. **1** priority; **2** right of way; **'vous n'avez pas la priorité'** 'you do not have right of way' (sign at a roundabout).

pris verb SEE **prendre**

pris adjective **1** busy; **je suis très prise ce matin** I'm very busy this morning; **2** taken; **toutes les places sont prises** all the seats are taken; **3** overcome (with an emotion

or a feeling); **être pris de panique** to be panic-stricken.

prise noun Fem. **1** socket, plug (for an electric appliance); **2** capture; **la prise de la Bastille** the storming of the Bastille.

prise de courant noun Fem. power point.

prise de sang noun Fem. blood test.

prise multiple noun Fem. adaptor plug.

prison noun Fem. prison.

prisonnier, prisonnière noun Masc., Fem. prisoner.

privé noun Masc. **1** private sector (of business or the school system); **2 en privé** in private, off the record.

privé adjective **1** private; **'propriété privée'** 'private property'; **2** without; **nous sommes privés d'électricité** we are without electricity; **privé de sens** senseless.

priver verb [1] **1 priver quelqu'un de quelque chose** to deprive someone of something; **2 se priver de quelque chose** to do without something.

privilège noun Masc. privilege.

privilégié adjective privileged, special, fortunate.

privilégier verb [1] **1** to favour; **2** to give priority to.

prix noun Masc. **1** price; **quel est le prix des places?** what price are the seats?; **le prix a augmenté** the price has gone up; **2 à tout prix** at all costs; **3** prize; **le premier prix** first prize.

probable adjective likely; **c'est peu probable** it's unlikely.

probablement adverb probably.

problème noun Masc. problem; **sans problème!** no problem!

procédé noun Masc. process.

procès noun Masc. **1** trial; **2** lawsuit.

procession noun Fem. procession.

prochain adjective next; **la prochaine fois** the next time; **le mois prochain** next month; **jeudi prochain** next Thursday; **à la prochaine!** see you soon!

prochainement adverb soon.

proche adjective **1** near; **la ville la plus proche est Valence** the nearest town is Valence; **2** close; **c'est une amie très proche de Julie** she' a very close friend of Julie's; **3** proche de near; **ils ont acheté une maison proche de Nice** they've bought a house near Nice.

Proche-Orient noun Masc. **le Proche-Orient** the Middle East.

proches plural noun Masc. close family and friends.

procurer verb [1] **se procurer quelque chose** to get something.

producteur, productrice noun Masc., Fem. producer.

production noun Fem. production.

produire verb [26] **1** to produce; **2 se produire** to happen; **ça s'est produit au mois de mai** that happened in May.

produit noun Masc. product; **les produits de beauté** beauty products; **les produits d'entretien** household products; **les produits laitiers** dairy products; **les produits congelés** frozen foods; **les produits d'exportation** export products.

prof noun Masc. (informal) SHORT FOR professeur teacher; **notre prof de français** our French teacher.

professeur noun Masc. **1** teacher; **ma sœur est professeur de physique** my sister's a physics teacher; **2** university lecturer; **3** university professor.

profession noun Fem. profession, occupation.

professionnel (Fem. **professionnelle**) adjective professional.

profil noun Masc. profile.

profit noun Masc. **1** profit; **les profits de la société** the company's profits; **au profit de** in aid of; **au profit des sans-abri** in aid of the homeless.

profiter verb [1] **1** profiter de to take advantage of (an opportunity); **j'ai profité des soldes pour m'acheter un manteau** I took advantage of the sales to buy myself a coat; **2** to make the most of; **profite bien de tes vacances!** make the most of your holiday!; **3** profiter à to benefit.

profond adjective deep; **un trou profond de 3 mètres** a hole three metres deep; **la France profonde** provincial France.

a b c d e f g h i j k l m n o p q r s t u v w x y z

a

b

c

d

e

f

g

h

i

j

k

l

m

n

o

p

q

r

s

t

u

v

w

x

y

z

profondément adverb deeply, profoundly.

profondeur noun Fem. depth; **la piscine a une profondeur de 3 mètres** the swimming pool is 3 metres deep; **étudier quelque chose en profondeur** to study something in depth.

programmateur[1] noun Masc. **1** timer; **2** programme selector (on appliance).

programmateur[2], **programmatrice** noun Masc., Fem. programmer (on radio, tv).

programme noun Masc. **1** programme; **ce n'est pas au programme** it's not on the programme; **2** program (for a computer); **3** syllabus; **le programme de maths** the maths syllabus.

programmer verb [1] **1** to schedule; **2** to program (on a computer).

programmeur, programmeuse noun Masc., Fem. (computer) programmer.

progrès noun Masc. progress; **les progrès de l'informatique** advances in computer science; **faire des progrès** to make progress.

progresser verb [1] **1** to progress; **2** to make progress.

projecteur noun Masc. **1** floodlight; **2** spotlight; **3** projector.

projet noun Masc. **1** plan; **mes projets pour l'été** my plans for the summer; **2** project; **3** rough draft.

projeter verb [48] **1** to throw, to hurl; **le choc l'a projeté de sa voiture** the impact hurled him out of his car; **2** to show (a film); **3** to cast (a shadow); **4** projeter de faire to plan to do.

prolongation noun Fem. **1** continuation; **2** extension; **3** extra time; **jouer les prolongations** to go into extra time.

prolongé adjective lengthy; **une discussion prolongée** a lengthy discussion.

prolonger verb [52] **1** to extend; **elle a prolongé son congé de maladie** she's extended her sick leave; **2 se prolonger** to go on; **les discussions se sont prolongées jusqu'à 23 h** discussions went on till 11 p.m.

promenade noun Fem. **1** walk; **faire une promenade** to go for a walk; **une promenade en voiture** a drive; **une promenade à vélo** a bike ride; **une promenade en bateau** a boat trip; **2** promenade (by the sea).

promener verb [50] **1** promener un enfant to take a child for a walk; **promener le chien** to walk the dog; **2** promener quelque chose to carry something around; **3 se promener** to go for a walk; **se promener en voiture** to go for a drive; **se promener à vélo** to go for a bike ride.

promesse noun Fem. promise; **il m'a fait une promesse** he made me a promise; **tenir sa promesse** to keep your promise.

prometteur (Fem. **prometteuse**) adjective promising.

promettre verb [11] to promise; **promettre de faire** to promise to do; **il a promis de téléphoner ce soir** he promised to ring this evening; **j'ai promis à ma mère de lui écrire une fois par semaine** I promised my mother I would write to her once a week.

promotion noun Fem. **1** special offer; **les fraises sont en promotion cette semaine** strawberries are on special offer this week; **2** promotion (to a higher job); **avoir une promotion** to be promoted.

pronom noun Masc. pronoun.

prononcer verb [61] **1** to pronounce (a word); **2** to mention (a name); to say (a word or phrase); **3** to make (a speech); **4** se **prononcer pour/contre quelque chose** to declare oneself for/against something.

prononciation noun Fem. pronunciation.

propagande noun Fem. propaganda.

proportion noun Fem. proportion; **en proportion de** in proportion to.

propos noun Masc. **1** à propos by the way; **à propos, as-tu appelé maman?** by the way, did you ring Mum?; **2** à propos de about; **il n'a rien dit à propos de son père** he said nothing about his father; **3** des propos remarks.

proposer verb [1] **1** proposer **quelque chose à quelqu'un** to suggest something to somebody; **je**

leur ai proposé une petite promenade I suggested we went for a little walk; **2** proposer **quelque chose à quelqu'un** to offer somebody something; **on lui a proposé un poste de technicien** she (or he) has been offered a job as a technician.

proposition noun Fem. offer.

propre adjective **1** (when it comes after the noun) clean; **une chemise propre** a clean shirt; **2** (when it comes before the noun) own; **ma propre voiture** my own car; **leurs propres enfants** their own children.

proprement adverb **1** properly; **mange proprement!** eat properly!; **2** à proprement parler strictly speaking.

propreté noun Fem. cleanliness.

propriétaire noun Masc. & Fem. **1** owner (usually of a building or a business); **2** landlord, landlady.

propriété noun Fem. **1** property; **propriété privée** private property; **2** ownership.

prospectus noun Masc. leaflet.

prospère adjective prosperous.

prostituée noun Fem. prostitute.

protecteur, **protectrice** noun Masc., Fem. protector.

protecteur (Fem. **protectrice**) adjective protective; **une crème protectrice** protective cream.

protection noun Fem. protection; **des lunettes de protection** protective goggles.

protéger verb [15] to protect; **pour protéger l'environnement** to protect the environment; **se**

a b c d e f g h i j k l m n o p q r s t u v w x y z

protéger du soleil to protect yourself from the sun.

protestant, protestante noun Masc., Fem., adjective Protestant.

protestation noun Fem. protest.

protester verb [1] to protest; **protester contre quelque chose** to protest against something.

prouver verb [1] to prove.

provenance noun Fem. origin; **du fromage en provenance de France** cheese from France; **un passager en provenance de Madrid** a passenger arriving from Madrid.

provençal (plural **provençaux**) adjective from Provence, Provençal.

proverbe noun Masc. proverb.

province noun Fem. province; **en province** in the provinces; **une ville de province** a provincial town.

provision noun Fem. 1 supply; **nous avons fait provision de bois** we've laid in a supply of wood; 2 **des provisions** food; **maman est partie prendre des provisions** Mum's gone off shopping for food.

provisoire adjective temporary.

provocateur, provocatrice noun Masc., Fem. agitator.

provocateur (Fem. **provocatrice**) adjective provocative.

provoquer verb [1] 1 to cause; **provoquer un accident** to cause an accident; **provoquer une discussion** to spark off a discussion; 2 **provoquer quelqu'un** to provoke somebody.

proximité noun Fem. nearness; **à proximité de** near.

prudemment adverb carefully.

prudence noun Fem. caution; **conduisez avec prudence!** drive carefully!

prudent adjective 1 careful; **soyez prudents par mauvais temps!** be careful in bad weather!; 2 wise; **il est plus prudent de réserver** it's wiser to book.

prune noun Fem. plum.

pruneau (plural **pruneaux**) noun Masc. prune.

prunier noun Masc. plum tree.

psychanalyste noun Masc. & Fem. psychoanalyst.

psychiatre noun Masc. & Fem. psychiatrist.

psychologie noun Fem. psychology.

psychologique adjective psychological.

psychologue noun Masc. & Fem. psychologist.

pu verb SEE **pouvoir**[1].

pub noun Fem. (informal) SHORT FOR **publicité** advert.

public noun Masc. 1 public; **en public** in public; **ouvert au public** open to the public; **'interdit au public'** 'no admission'; 2 audience, spectators; **pour un public jeune** for a young audience; 3 fans (of a performer).

public (Fem. **publique**) adjective public; **dans un lieu public** in a public place; **une école publique** a state school.

publicitaire *adjective*
1 advertising; **une campagne publicitaire** an advertising campaign; **2** promotional (*material*).

publicité *noun Fem.* **1** advertising; **elle travaille dans la publicité** she works in advertising; **faire de la publicité** to advertise; **2** advertisement, ad (*in a magazine, a newspaper, on television, or at the cinema*).

publier *verb* [1] to publish.

puce *noun Fem.* **1 une puce électronique** a microchip; **une carte à puce** a smart card; **2** flea; **un marché aux puces** a fleamarket.

puer *verb* [1] to stink.

puis *adverb* then; **nous allons à Cannes, puis à Nice** we're going to Cannes, then Nice.

puisque, puisqu' (*before a vowel or silent 'h'*) *conjunction* since; **puisqu'il pleut je prendrai le bus** since it's raining I'll take the bus.

puissance *noun Fem.* power; **un moteur d'une forte puissance** a high-power engine; **une puissance étrangère** a foreign power.

puissant *adjective* powerful, strong.

puits *noun Masc.* well.

pull, pull-over *noun Masc.* jumper.

pulvérisateur *noun Masc.* spray.

punaise *noun Fem.* **1** drawing-pin; **2** bug.

punir *verb* [2] to punish.

punition *noun Fem.* punishment.

pur *adjective* **1** pure; **un shampooing très doux, très pur** an ultra-mild, ultra-pure shampoo; **un croissant pur beurre** an all-butter croissant; **2** sheer, total; **c'est de la folie pure** it's sheer madness.

purée *noun Fem.* mashed potatoes.

puzzle *noun Masc.* jigsaw puzzle.

PV *noun Masc.* SHORT FOR **procès verbal** parking ticket.

pyjama *noun Masc.* (pair of) pyjamas; **où est mon pyjama?** where are my pyjamas?; **un pyjama propre** a clean pair of pyjamas.

pyramide *noun Fem.* pyramid.

Pyrénées *plural noun Fem.* Pyrenees.

Qq

qu'est-ce que SEE **que**.

qu'est-ce qui SEE **qui**.

quai *noun Masc.* **1** platform; **le train à destination de Paris va arriver au quai numéro trois** the train for Paris is about to arrive at platform number three; **2** quay.

qualifié *adjective* **1** qualified; **2** skilled.

qualifier *verb* [1] to qualify.

qualité *noun Fem.* quality; **des fruits de première qualité** top quality fruit.

quand *conjunction, adverb* when; **quand est-ce que ton frère arrive?** when is your brother arriving?; **quand tu auras dix-sept**

a
b
c
d
e
f
g
h
i
j
k
l
m
n
o
p
q
r
s
t
u
v
w
x
y
z

a
b
c
d
e
f
g
h
i
j
k
l
m
n
o
p
q
r
s
t
u
v
w
x
y
z

**ans, tu pourras apprendre à
conduire** when you're seventeen
you'll be able to learn to drive.

quand même *adverb* all the
same; **il pleut mais je vais sortir
quand même** it's raining but I'm
going to go out all the same; **quand
même!** honestly!

quant à *preposition* as for; **quant à
moi, je reste** as for me, I'm staying
here.

quantité *noun Fem.* amount.

quarantaine *noun Fem.* **1** about
forty; **une quarantaine de
personnes** about forty people;
j'approche la quarantaine I'll
soon be forty; **2** quarantine.

quarante *number* forty.

quart *noun Masc.* **1** (*in time
expressions*) quarter; **un quart
d'heure** a quarter of an hour; **dix
heures et quart** quarter past ten;
2 quarter; **le quart du gâteau** a
quarter of the cake; **un quart d'eau
minérale** a quarter-litre bottle of
mineral water; **trois quarts** three
quarters; **les trois quarts du
temps** most of the time.

quart de finale *noun Masc.*
quarter-final.

quartier *noun Masc.* area (*of a
town*); **un quartier résidentiel** a
residential area; **les gens du
quartier** the local people.

quartier général *Masc.*
headquarters.

quartz *noun Masc.* quartz.

quasi *adverb* almost; **quasi parfait**
almost perfect.

quasiment *adverb* **1** practically;
c'est quasiment neuf it's

practically new; **2 quasiment
jamais** hardly ever; **il n'est
quasiment jamais chez lui** he's
hardly ever at home.

quatorze *number* fourteen; **Céline
a quatorze ans** Céline's fourteen;
le quatorze juin the fourteenth of
June.

quatre *number* four; **Louis a
quatre ans** Louis is four; **le quatre
mars** the fourth of March.

quatre-vingt-dix *number* ninety;
quatre-vingt-dix-neuf ninety-nine.

quatre-vingts *number* eighty;
quatre-vingts personnes eighty
people; **quatre-vingt-trois** eighty-
three (*note that the 's' is dropped
when another number is added*);
quatre-vingt-seize ninety-six.

quatrième *noun Fem.* (*in a French
school*) the equivalent of Year 9.

quatrième *noun Masc.* **au
quatrième** on the fourth floor.

quatrième *adjective* fourth.

que *conjunction, pronoun, adverb*
1 that (*often left out in English*);
elle dit que c'est vrai she says
(that) it's true; **je sais qu'il y
habite** I know he lives there; **je
veux que tu sois heureux** I want
you to be happy; **2** whether; **qu'ils
arrivent demain ou mardi,
n'importe** whether they come
tomorrow or on Tuesday, it doesn't
matter; **3 que tout le monde se
lève!** everybody stand up!; **4 plus
...que** more ...than; **elle est plus
grande que Marie** she's taller than
Marie; **5 aussi ...que** as ...as; **elle
est aussi
grande que moi** she's as tall

as me; **6 ne ...que** only; **je n'ai que dix euros** I've only got ten euros; **7** that, which, whom (*often left out in English*); **le livre que je lis** the book (that) I'm reading; **la chemise qu'il a achetée** the shirt (which) he's bought; **8** what; **que veut-il?** what does he want?; **je ne sais pas ce qu'il veut** I don't know what he wants; **9 qu'est-ce que ...?** what ...?; **qu'est-ce que tu as trouvé?** what have you found?; **qu'est-ce que c'est?** what's that?; **qu'est-ce qu'il y a?** what's the matter?; **qu'est-ce qu'elle a?** what's the matter with her?; **10** how (*in an exclamation*); **que tu as grandi!** how you've grown!

Québec noun Masc. **le Québec** Quebec.

québécois noun Masc. Canadian French (*language*).

québécois adjective from Quebec, Quebecker.

Québécois, Québécoise noun Masc., Fem. French Canadian, Quebecker; **les Québécois** the French Canadians, the Quebeckers.

quel, quelle adjective **1** (*in a question*) what, which; **quel livre?** which book?; **quelle voiture?** which car?; **quelle heure est-il?** what time is it?; **quel âge as-tu?** how old are you?; **dans quels pays?** in which countries?; **pour quelles raisons?** for what reasons?; **2** (*in an exclamation*) what; **quel beau temps!** what lovely weather!; **quelle**

coïncidence! what a coincidence!; **quelle horreur!** how dreadful!

quelconque adjective any; **si tu as un problème quelconque** if you have any sort of a problem; **si pour une raison quelconque** if for any reason.

quelle adjective SEE **quel.**

quelque chose pronoun **1** something; **il faut manger quelque chose, Claire** you must eat something, Claire; **il y a quelque chose de bizarre** there's something strange; **voulez-vous boire quelque chose?** would you like something to drink?; **2** anything; **est-ce que tu as vu quelque chose?** did you see anything?

quelquefois adverb sometimes.

quelque part adverb **1** somewhere; **quelque part dans le jardin** somewhere in the garden; **2** anywhere; **est-ce que tu as vu mes lunettes quelque part?** have you seen my glasses anywhere?

quelques plural adjective **1** some; **je vais te donner quelques cerises** I'll give you some cherries; **2** a few; **il reste quelques fraises** there are a few strawberries left; **elle est partie pour quelques jours** she's gone away for a few days.

quelqu'un pronoun **1** somebody; **quelqu'un a appelé pour toi** somebody rang for you; **quelqu'un d'autre** somebody else; **2** anybody; **il y a quelqu'un?** is there anybody there?

a
b
c
d
e
f
g
h
i
j
k
l
m
n
o
p
q
r
s
t
u
v
w
x
y
z

quelques-uns, quelques-unes plural pronoun some; **quelques-uns des enfants** some of the children.

quels, quelles adjective SEE **quel**.

querelle noun Fem. quarrel.

question noun Fem. **1** question; **poser une question à quelqu'un** to ask somebody a question; **elle n'a pas répondu à mes questions** she didn't answer my questions; **2** matter, question; **c'est une question de goût** it's a matter of taste; **c'est hors de question** it's out of the question; **pas question!** no way!.

questionnaire noun Masc. questionnaire.

questionner verb [1] to question.

queue noun Fem. **1** tail; **la queue du chat** the cat's tail; **2** queue; **faire la queue** to queue; **3 la queue du train** the rear of the train; **4** stalk (of a flower or a fruit).

queue de cheval noun Fem. ponytail.

qui pronoun **1** who; **qui a fermé la porte?** who closed the door?; **qui voulez-vous voir?** who do you want to see?; **la personne qui vous a écrit n'est pas là aujourd'hui** the person who wrote to you is not here today; **2** that; **prends la casserole qui est sur l'évier** take the pan that's on the sink; **3 à qui?** whose?; **à qui est ce pull?** whose is this jumper?; **4 à qui parles-tu?** who are you talking to?; **5 qu'est-ce qui ...?** what ...?; **qu'est-ce qui t'amène?** what brings you here?

quincaillerie noun Fem. hardware shop.

quinzaine noun Fem. **1** about fifteen; **une quinzaine d'enfants** about fifteen children; **2 une quinzaine de jours** a fortnight; **dans une quinzaine** two weeks from now.

quinze number **1** fifteen; **Marise a quinze ans** Marise is fifteen; **le quinze juillet** the fifteenth of July; **2 quinze jours** two weeks; **tous les quinze jours** every two weeks.

quitter verb [1] **1** to leave; **je quitte le bureau à cinq heures** I leave the office at five; **j'ai quitté l'école à seize ans** I left school at sixteen; **2 se quitter** to part; **3 ne quittez pas** hold the line please (on the telephone).

quoi pronoun **1** what; **quoi encore?** what now?; **tu es sourd ou quoi?** are you deaf or what?; **à quoi penses-tu?** what are you thinking about?; **pour quoi faire?** what for?; **à quoi bon continuer?** what's the point in going on?; **il n'y a pas de quoi se fâcher** there's no reason to get angry; **il n'y a pas de quoi** don't mention it; **2** which; **après quoi, il est parti** after which, he left.

quoique conjunction although, though; **quoique petit, il est fort** although he's small he's strong.

quotidien (Fem. **quotidienne**) adjective daily; **la vie quotidienne** daily life; **sa visite quotidienne** her daily visit.

quotidien noun Masc. daily newspaper.

quotidiennement adverb daily; **les livraisons s'effectuent quotidiennement** deliveries are made daily.

Rr

rabais *noun Masc.* discount; **au rabais** at a discount.

raccompagner *verb* [1] **raccompagner quelqu'un** to see somebody home.

raccourci *noun Masc.* short cut.

raccourcir *verb* [2] to shorten.

raccrocher *verb* [1] to hang up (*telephone*).

race *noun Fem.* **1** race; **la race humaine** the human race; **2** breed; **un chien de race** a pedigree dog.

racheter *verb* [16] **1** to buy more; **il faut racheter du pain** we'll have to buy more bread; **2 il m'a racheté ma voiture** he bought my car off me.

racine *noun Fem.* root.

raciste *noun Masc. & Fem., adjective* racist; **des propos racistes** racist remarks.

racler *verb* [1] to scrape.

raconter *verb* [1] to tell (*a story*); **raconte-nous ce qui s'est passé** tell us what happened.

radar *noun Masc.* radar.

radeau (*plural* **radeaux**) *noun Masc.* raft.

radiateur *noun Masc.* radiator.

radio *noun Fem.* **1** radio; **je l'ai entendu à la radio** I heard it on the radio; **2** X-ray; **passer une radio** to have an X-ray.

radiocassette *noun Masc. OR Fem.* radio cassette player.

radio-réveil *noun Masc.* clock radio.

radis *noun Masc.* radish.

rafale *noun Fem.* gust (*of wind or rain*), flurry (*of snow*).

raffoler *verb* [1] **raffoler de** to be mad about; **je ne raffole pas des huîtres** I'm not mad about oysters.

rafraîchir *verb* [2] **1 le temps se rafraîchit** the weather's getting cooler; **2** to cool (*somebody*) down.

rafraîchissement *noun Masc.* **1** refreshment; **2** drop in temperature.

rage *noun Fem.* **1** rabies; **2 une rage de dents** raging toothache.

ragoût *noun Masc.* stew.

raide *adjective* **1** stiff (*body, arm, leg*); **2** straight (*hair*); **3 une pente raide** a steep slope.

raie *noun Fem.* **1** parting (*in your hair*); **2** skate (*the fish*).

rail *noun Masc.* rail (*for trains*); ★ **remettre quelque chose sur les rails** to put something back on the right track.

raisin *noun Masc.* grapes; **j'ai acheté du raisin noir** I bought some black grapes; **une grappe de raisin** a bunch of grapes; **un grain de raisin** a grape; **le jus de raisin** grape juice.

raisin de Corinthe *noun Masc.* currant.

raisin sec *noun Masc.* raisin.

raison *noun Fem.* **1** reason; **pour cette raison** for this reason; **pour raisons de santé** for health reasons; **2 avoir raison** to be right; **oui, tu as raison** yes, you're right.

raisonnable *adjective* sensible.

a
b
c
d
e
f
g
h
i
j
k
l
m
n
o
p
q
r
s
t
u
v
w
x
y
z

raisonnement noun Masc.
reasoning.

rajouter verb [1] to add; **on peut
rajouter de l'eau si on veut** you
can add water if you want.

ralentir verb [2] to slow down.

ralentissement noun Masc.
slowing down.

ralentisseur noun Masc. speed
bump.

râler verb [1] (informal) to moan;
arrête de râler! stop moaning!

rallonge noun Fem. **1** extension
cord; **2** extra leaf (for a table).

ramasser verb [1] **1** to pick up;
**est-ce que tu peux ramasser tous
ces papiers, s'il te plaît** can you
pick up all these papers please; **2** to
pick (fruit); **ils ont déjà ramassé
les framboises** they've already
picked the raspberries; **3** to collect;
**on va ramasser des châtaignes
dans les bois** we're going to go and
collect chestnuts in the woods;
4 collect in (books, homework);
**Anne, veux-tu ramasser tous les
cahiers?** Anne, would you collect
in all the exercise books?

rame noun Fem. **1** oar; **2 une rame
de métro** an underground train.

rameau (plural **rameaux**) noun
Masc. branch; **le dimanche des
Rameaux** Palm Sunday.

ramener verb [50] **1 ramener
quelqu'un (en voiture)** to give
somebody a lift home; **tu veux que
je te ramène?** do you want a lift
home?; **elle m'a ramené en
voiture** she gave me a lift back; **2** to
take back; **je dois ramener les**

livres à la bibliothèque I must take
these books back to the library.

ramer verb [1] to row.

rampe noun Fem. **1** banister;
2 ramp.

rançon noun Fem. ransom.

rancune noun Fem. resentment,
grudge.

randonnée noun Fem. hike, walk;
faire une randonnée pédestre to
go on a hike (on public footpaths);
**on a fait une randonnée de vingt
kilomètres** a twenty-
kilometre walk; **faire une
randonnée à cheval** to go pony-
trekking; **une randonnée à vélo** a
long-distance bike ride.

randonneur, randonneuse
noun Masc., Fem. **1** hiker, walker,
rambler; **2** touring cyclist.

rang noun Masc. row; **au cinquième
rang** in the fifth row.

rangée noun Fem. row; **une rangée
de maisons** a row of houses.

ranger verb [52] **1** to put away;
ranger la vaisselle to put away the
dishes; **2** to tidy; **je vais ranger ma
chambre** I'm going to tidy my
room; **3** to arrange; **il range ses
livres par ordre alphabétique** he
arranges his books alphabetically.

râper verb [1] to grate; **le fromage
râpé** grated cheese.

rapide noun Masc. express train.

rapide adjective quick; **prends le
métro, c'est plus rapide** take the
underground, it's quicker.

rapidement adverb quickly,
rapidly.

rappel noun Masc. **1** reminder (for a bill); **'dernier rappel'** 'final demand'; **2** booster (vaccination).

rappeler verb [18] **1** to remind; **rappelle-moi de passer par la banque** remind me to go to the bank; **le paysage me rappelle la France** the countryside reminds me of France; **2** to ring back (on the telephone); **il va te rappeler dans une heure** he'll ring you back in an hour; **3 se rappeler** to remember; **je ne me rappelle plus** I can't remember; **je me rappelle qu'elle avait les cheveux longs** I remember she had long hair.

rapport noun Masc. **1** report; **un rapport officiel** an official report; **2** connection; **je ne vois pas le rapport** I don't see the connection; **3 être en rapport avec quelqu'un** to be in touch with someone; **4 avoir de bons/mauvais rapports avec quelqu'un** to be on good/bad relations with someone; **5 par rapport à** compared with; **il a fait très beau par rapport à l'année dernière** the weather's been very good compared with last year.

rapporter verb [1] **1** to bring back; **est-ce que tu peux le rapporter demain?** can you bring it back tomorrow?; **2** to bring in; **son travail ne rapporte pas beaucoup** her job doesn't bring in much money.

rapprocher verb [1] **1** to move (something) closer; **peux-tu rapprocher la lampe de ma chaise?** can you move the lamp closer to my chair?; **2** to bring together (different people); **des**

efforts pour rapprocher les deux pays efforts to bring the two countries together; **3 se rapprocher** to come (or go) closer; **elle s'est rapprochée de la table** she moved closer to the table.

raquette noun Fem. **1** racket (for tennis); **2** bat (for ping-pong).

rare adjective rare; **une fleur rare** a rare flower; **il est rare qu'elle arrive à l'heure** she hardly ever arrives on time.

rarement adverb rarely.

ras adjective **1** short (hair or fur); **il a les cheveux coupés ras** his hair is cut short; **2 en rase campagne** in open country; **3 au ras de l'eau/du sol** at water/ground level; ★ **j'en ai ras le bol!** (informal) I'm fed up!

raser verb [1] **1** to shave, to shave off; **il a rasé sa barbe** he's shaved off his beard; **la mousse à raser** shaving foam; **2 se raser** to shave; **se raser les jambes** to shave your legs.

ras-le-cou noun Masc. crew-neck sweater.

rasoir noun Masc. razor.

rassemblement noun Masc. meeting, rally.

rassembler verb [1] to gather (together); **j'ai rassemblé les enfants près de l'entrée** I gathered all the children together by the main entrance; **tout le village s'est rassemblé pour l'écouter** the whole village gathered to listen to him.

rassis adjective **du pain rassis** stale bread.

a
b
c
d
e
f
g
h
i
j
k
l
m
n
o
p
q
r
s
t
u
v
w
x
y
z

a
b
c
d
e
f
g
h
i
j
k
l
m
n
o
p
q
r
s
t
u
v
w
x
y
z

rassurer verb [1] **1** to reassure; **ah, cela me rassure!** oh, that sets my mind at rest!; **2 rassure-toi** don't worry.

rat noun Masc. rat.

râteau (plural **râteaux**) noun Masc. rake.

rater verb [1] **1** to fail; **Sophie a raté son permis** Sophie failed her driving test; **2** to miss; **j'ai raté mon train** I've missed my train.

rationner verb [1] to ration.

RATP noun Fem. SHORT FOR **Régie autonome des transports parisiens** (Paris city-transport system).

rattacher verb [1] **1** to (re)fasten; **rattache ta ceinture** (re)fasten your seat-belt; **2** to attach; **plus rien ne me rattache ici** I no longer have any ties here.

rattraper verb [1] **1** to catch up with (a person); **ne t'inquiète pas, ils nous rattraperont** don't worry, they'll catch up with us; **2** to make up for (lost time); **3 se rattraper** to make up for it; **j'ai très peu joué cet été mais je vais me rattraper** I've played very little this summer but I'll make up for it.

rature noun Fem. crossing-out.

ravi adjective delighted; **je suis ravi de vous voir** I'm delighted to see you.

ravisseur, ravisseuse noun Masc., Fem. kidnapper.

rayé adjective striped (fabric).

rayer verb [59] **1** to cross out (a mistake); **j'ai rayé ton nom de la liste** I crossed your name off the list; **2** to scratch (a surface).

rayon noun Masc. **1** shelf; **un rayon pour mes livres** a shelf for my books; **2** department (in a department store); section (in a supermarket); **au rayon fraîcheur** in the chilled foods section; **3** ray; **un rayon de soleil** a ray of sunshine; **un rayon laser** a laser beam; **les rayons X** X-rays; **4** radius.

rayure noun Fem. **1** stripe; **2** scratch.

RC noun Masc. SHORT FOR **rez-de-chaussée** ground floor.

réacteur noun Masc. **1** un **réacteur nucléaire** a nuclear reactor; **2** jet engine.

réaction noun Fem. reaction.

réagir verb [2] to react; **elle n'a pas réagi** she didn't react.

réalisateur, réalisatrice noun Masc., Fem. director (of a film or TV programme).

réalisation noun Fem. **1** carrying out (of a plan or project); **2** production (of a film or a radio/TV programme).

réaliser verb [1] **1** to carry out (a project); **2** to fulfil; **réaliser un rêve** to fulfil a dream; **3** to make (a film); **4** to realize.

réaliste adjective realistic.

réalité noun Fem. reality; **en réalité** in reality.

réanimation noun Fem. resuscitation; **(service de) réanimation** intensive care (unit).

rebelle noun Masc. & Fem. rebel.

rébellion noun Fem. rebellion.

rebondir verb [2] to bounce.

rebord noun Masc. **1 le rebord de la fenêtre** the window ledge; **2** edge; **le rebord de la baignoire** the edge of the bath.

récemment adverb recently.

récent adjective recent.

réception noun Fem. **1** reception desk; **demandez la clé à la réception** ask for the key at the reception desk; **2** reception (party).

réceptionniste noun Masc. & Fem. receptionist.

recette noun Fem. recipe; **la recette du gâteau** the recipe for the cake.

recevoir verb [66] **1** to receive, to get; **j'ai reçu ta lettre** I got your letter; **2** to welcome (a visitor or guest); **3** to see (a patient or client); **le dentiste reçoit entre 9h et 17h** the dentist sees patients between 9 a.m. and 5 p.m.; **4 être reçu à un examen** to pass an exam; **elle a été reçue première à l'examen** she came top in the exam.

rechange noun Masc. **de rechange** spare; **une pièce de rechange** a spare part.

recharge noun Fem. refill.

réchaud noun Masc. stove.

réchauffer verb [1] **1** to warm up (food); **peux-tu mettre la soupe à réchauffer?** can you put the soup on to warm?; **2** to warm (hands or feet); **3 se réchauffer** to get warm; **va te réchauffer près du feu** go and get warm by the fire.

recherche noun Fem. **1** research; **2 être à la recherche de quelque chose** to be looking for something; **je suis à la recherche d'un** logement I'm looking for somewhere to live.

rechercher verb [1] to look for; **la police le recherche** the police are looking for him; **elle recherche un travail plus flexible** she's looking for a more flexible job.

récipient noun Masc. container.

réciproque adjective mutual.

récit noun Masc. story; **il nous a fait le récit de son voyage** he told us all about his journey.

réciter verb [1] to recite.

réclamation noun Fem. claim (for compensation).

réclame noun Fem. **1** advertisement; **une réclame pour le nouveau modèle** an advertisement for the new model; **2 en réclame** on (special) offer; **le jambon est en réclame cette semaine** the ham is on special offer this week.

réclamer verb [1] to demand; **ils réclament trois jours de plus de vacances** they're demanding three more days' holiday.

récolte noun Fem. **1** harvest; **2** crop; **faire la récolte** to get the harvest in.

récolter verb [1] **1** to harvest; **récolter le blé** to harvest the wheat; **2** to collect (money); **3** (informal) to get; **récolter une amende** to get a fine.

recommandation noun Fem. recommendation.

recommandé adjective registered; **une lettre recommandée** a registered letter; **je voudrais l'envoyer en**

a
b
c
d
e
f
g
h
i
j
k
l
m
n
o
p
q
r
s
t
u
v
w
x
y
z

recommandé I'd like to send it by registered post.

recommander *verb* [1] **1** to advise; **je te recommande de ne rien dire** I advise you to say nothing; **2** to recommend.

recommencer *verb* [61] **1** to start again; **j'ai recommencé ma lettre** I started my letter again; **il a recommencé à neiger** it's started snowing again; **2** to do it again; **si tu ne fais pas attention, elle va recommencer** if you don't watch out, she'll do it again; **ça recommence!** here we go again!

récompense *noun Fem.* reward.

récompenser *verb* [1] to reward.

réconcilier *verb* [1] **se réconcilier avec quelqu'un** to make it up with somebody.

réconfortant *adjective* comforting.

reconnaissable *adjective* recognizable.

reconnaissance *noun Fem.* **1** gratitude; **en reconnaissance de** in appreciation of; **2** recognition.

reconnaissant *adjective* grateful.

reconnaître *verb* [27] **1** to recognize; **je ne l'ai pas reconnue** I didn't recognize her; **je l'ai reconnu à sa voix** I recognized him by his voice; **2** to admit; **il faut reconnaître que c'est difficile** it must be admitted that it's difficult; **elle reconnaît qu'elle a menti** she admits she lied.

reconstruire *verb* [26] to rebuild.

recopier *verb* [1] to copy out.

record *noun Masc.* record; **un record mondial** a world record; **battre un record** to break a record.

recouvrir *verb* [30] to cover.

récréation *noun Fem.* break; **la cour de récréation** the playground.

rectangle *noun Masc.* rectangle.

rectangulaire *adjective* rectangular.

rectifier *verb* [1] to correct.

reçu *noun Masc.* receipt.

reçu *verb* SEE recevoir.

recueil *noun Masc.* collection (*of poems or essays*).

reculer *verb* [1] **1** to move back; **elle a reculé de quelques pas** she moved back a few steps; **2** to reverse (*in a car*); **3 reculer la date d'une réunion** to postpone a meeting.

reculons *in phrase* **à reculons** backwards.

récupérer *verb* [24] **1** to get back; **je vais chez Brigitte pour récupérer le bouquin que je lui ai prêté** I'm going round to Brigitte's to get back the book I lent her; **2** to recover (*from an illness*).

recycler *verb* [1] to recycle.

rédaction *noun Fem.* essay.

redemander *verb* [1] **1** to ask again; **tu devrais redemander** you should ask again; **2** to ask for more; **il faut qu'on redemande des cahiers** we'll have to ask for more exercise books.

redescendre *verb* [3] **1** to go (or come) back down; **elle est redescendue à la cave** she went back down to the cellar; **je monte à Glasgow demain et je redescends lundi** I'm going up to Glasgow tomorrow and I'm coming back down on Monday; **2 to bring or take back down; est-ce que tu peux redescendre ma valise?** can you bring my suitcase back down?

rédiger verb [52] to write (an article), to write up (notes).

redonner verb [1] to give again; **je leur ai redonné mon adresse** I gave them my address again; **est-ce que tu me redonne un peu de salade?** can I give you a bit more salad?

redoubler verb [1] to repeat a year (at school).

redresser verb [1] **1** to straighten up; **2** to put right; **3 se redresser** to recover.

réduction noun Fem. **1** reduction; **une réduction du nombre d'étudiants** a reduction in the number of students; **2** (price) reduction; **une réduction de 20%** a 20% reduction.

réduire verb [68] to cut (prices); **réduire les impôts** to cut taxes; **des vêtements à prix réduits** cut-price clothing.

rééducation noun Fem. physiotherapy.

réel (Fem. **réelle**) adjective real.

réellement adverb really.

refaire verb [10] **1** to redo; **je dois refaire mon devoir de maths** I have to redo my maths homework; **c'est tout à refaire** it has to be completely redone; **il ne faut pas refaire la même erreur** we mustn't

make the same mistake again; **2** to make more; **elle est en train de refaire du café** she's making some more coffee.

référence noun Fem. reference; **faire référence à quelque chose** to refer to something.

réfléchi adjective **1** reflexive (verb); **2** considered (decision).

réfléchir verb [2] to think; **il faut bien réfléchir avant d'accepter** you should think carefully before accepting; **j'ai réfléchi au problème** I've thought about the problem.

reflet noun Masc. **1** reflection; **2 des cheveux aux reflets blonds** hair with blond highlights.

refléter verb [24] to reflect.

réflexe noun Masc., adjective reflex.

réflexion noun Fem. **1** thought; **2** comment; **il m'a fait des réflexions désagréables** he made some nasty comments to me.

refrain noun Masc. chorus.

réfrigérateur noun Masc. refrigerator.

refroidir verb [2] to cool down.

refroidissement noun Masc. drop in temperature.

refuge noun Masc. **1** mountain hut (for climbers); **2** animal sanctuary; **3** traffic island; **4** refuge.

réfugié, réfugiée noun Masc., Fem. refugee.

réfugier verb [1] **se réfugier** to take shelter, to take refuge.

refus noun Masc. refusal; ★ ce n'est pas de refus I wouldn't say no; **'veux-tu boire quelque chose?' – 'ce n'est pas de refus'** 'would you like a drink?' – 'I wouldn't say no'.

refuser verb [1] 1 to refuse; **refuser de faire** to refuse to do; **elle a refusé de répondre** she refused to answer; 2 to turn down; **ils ont refusé sa candidature** they turned him down for the job.

regagner verb [1] **nous avons regagné nos places** we went back to our seats.

régal noun Masc. feast; **ça a été un véritable régal** it was a real feast.

régaler verb [1] **on s'est vraiment régalé!** the food was absolutely wonderful!

regard noun Masc. look.

regarder verb [1] 1 to look at; **je vais regarder la carte** I'll look at the map; 2 to watch; **regarder la télé** to watch telly; **veux-tu regarder le film?** do you want to watch the film?; 3 to look; **regarder par la fenêtre** to look out of the window; **regarde!** look!; 4 to concern; **cela ne nous regarde pas** that doesn't concern us; **cela ne le regarde pas** that's none of his business.

régate noun Fem. regatta.

régime noun Masc. 1 diet; **un régime sans sel** a salt-free diet; **je fais un régime** I'm on a diet; 2 **un régime de bananes** a bunch of bananas; 3 régime.

région noun Fem. region; **les vins de la région** the local wines.

régional (Masc. plural **régionaux**) adjective regional.

registre noun Masc. register.

réglable adjective adjustable.

règle noun Fem. 1 ruler; 2 rule; **selon les règles** according to the rules; **les règles de sécurité** the safety regulations; **en règle générale** as a general rule; 3 **en règle** in order (valid); 4 **les règles** period (menstruation); **j'ai mes règles** I've got my period.

règlement noun Masc. regulations.

régler verb [24] 1 to pay (a debt or a bill); **vous réglez comment, monsieur?** how would you like to pay, sir?; 2 to sort out (details or a problem); 3 to adjust; **on peut régler la hauteur** you can adjust the height.

réglisse noun Fem. liquorice.

règne noun Masc. reign.

régner verb [24] to reign.

regret noun Masc. regret; **avec/sans regret** with/without regret; **mille regrets** I'm terribly sorry.

regretter verb [1] 1 to be sorry; **je regrette** I'm sorry; **nous regrettons beaucoup de partir** we're very sorry to be leaving; 2 to regret; **elles regrettent avoir quitté Paris** they regret having left Paris; **je ne regrette rien** I have no regrets; 3 to miss; **je regrette la vie à Paris** I miss the Parisian way of life.

regrouper verb [1] 1 to group together; **les débutants sont regroupés ensemble** beginners are grouped together; 2 **se**

regrouper to regroup; **les enfants se sont regroupés autour d'elle** the children gathered around her.

régularité *noun Fem.* regularity.

régulier *(Fem.* **régulière)** *adjective* **1** regular; **à intervalles réguliers** at regular intervals; **2 vols réguliers à New York** scheduled flights to New York.

régulièrement *adverb* regularly.

rein *noun Masc.* **1** kidney; **2 les reins** the back; **j'ai mal aux reins** I've got back-ache.

reine *noun Fem.* queen; **la reine Elisabeth** Queen Elizabeth.

reine-claude *noun Fem.* greengage.

rejeter *verb* [48] to reject.

rejoindre *verb* [49] **1** to meet up with; **je vous rejoins au bar** I'll meet you in the bar; **2** to join *(other people, a group, or a movement)*; **3 se rejoindre** to meet up; **alors on se rejoint à onze heures?** so shall we meet up at eleven?; **4 se rejoindre** to merge *(motorways, lanes).*

rejouer *verb* [1] to replay.

relâcher *verb* [1] **1** to loosen *(a grip or hold)*; **2** to set free *(a prisoner, hostage, or animal)*; **3** to relax *(your attention or discipline).*

relais *noun Masc.* **1** restaurant, hotel; **2 prendre le relais (de quelqu'un)** to take over *(from someone)*; **il a pris le relais au volant** he took over the driving; **3** relay race.

relatif *(Fem.* **relative)** *adjective* relative.

relation *noun Fem.* **1** connection; **en relation avec** in connection with; **2** acquaintance; **une relation de mon frère** an acquaintance of my brother's; **3** relationship; **il a de bonnes relations avec son patron** he has a good relationship with his boss; **4 les relations publiques** public relations.

relativement *adverb* relatively; **relativement à** in relation to.

relax *adjective* *(informal)* casual, laid back.

relaxer *verb* [1] to relax.

relent *noun Masc.* lingering smell.

relevé *noun Masc.* **1 faire le relevé de quelque chose** to make a list of something; **2 un relevé de compte** a bank statement.

relever *verb* [50] **1** to raise; **2 relever la tête** to look up; **3** to notice *(details, mistakes, or interesting facts)*; **4 relever le compteur** to read the meter; **5 se relever** to pick yourself up *(after a fall).*

relier *verb* [1] **1** to link; **2** to match up.

religieux, religieuse *noun Masc., Fem.* monk, nun.

religieux *(Fem.* **religieuse)** *adjective* religious.

religion *noun Fem.* religion.

relire *verb* [51] to re-read, to read over.

remarié *adjective* remarried.

remarquable *adjective* remarkable, striking.

remarque *noun Fem.* remark, comment.

a b c d e f g h i j k l m n o p q r s t u v w x y z

a

remarquer verb [1] **1** to notice; **je n'ai rien remarqué** I didn't notice anything; **j'ai remarqué qu'elle est arrivée en retard** I noticed she arrived late; **2 se faire remarquer** to draw attention to yourself; **il n'aime pas se faire remarquer** he doesn't like drawing attention to himself; **3 faire remarquer quelque chose à quelqu'un** to point something out to somebody; **elle lui a fait remarquer que c'était déjà trop tard** she pointed out to him that it was already too late.

rembobiner verb [1] to rewind (a tape or video).

remboursement noun Masc. repayment, refund.

rembourser verb [1] **1** to pay back; **je te rembourserai demain** I'll pay you back tomorrow; **2** to refund the price of; **ils m'ont remboursé les billets** they refunded me the price of the tickets; **3** to reimburse; **nous vous rembourserons le voyage** we'll pay your travelling expenses.

remède noun Masc. remedy.

remerciement noun Masc. thanks; **tous mes remerciements** many thanks; **une lettre de remerciement** a thank-you letter.

remercier verb [1] **1** to thank; **je l'ai remerciée pour les fleurs** I thanked her for the flowers; **2 remercier quelqu'un d'avoir fait quelque chose** to thank somebody for doing something; **il nous a remerciés de l'avoir aidé** he thanked us for helping him.

remettre verb [11] **1** to put back; **remets la bouteille au frigo** put the bottle back in the fridge; **il a remis la photo sur la table** he put the photo back on the table; **as-tu remis tous les livres à leur place?** have you put all the books back in their place?; **2** to put back on; **je vais remettre ma veste** I'm going to put my jacket back on; **3** to hand over; **pouvez-vous me remettre les clés demain?** can you hand over the keys to me tomorrow?; **4** to put off; **ils ont remis la réunion à jeudi** they've put the meeting off until Thursday; **5 se remettre** to start again; **elle s'est remise au piano** she's started playing the piano again; **il s'est remis à pleuvoir** it's started raining again; **6 se remettre de** to recover; **ils ne se sont toujours pas remis du choc** they still haven't recovered from the shock.

remise noun Fem. **1** handing out; **la remise des prix** the prizegiving; **2** discount; **nous faisons une remise de 20% sur tous les CD** we're giving a 20% discount on all CDs; **3** garden shed.

remonte-pente noun Masc. ski lift.

remonter verb [1] **1** to go (or come) back up; **Nathalie est remontée dans sa chambre** Nathalie's gone back up to her room; **je descends à Londres ce soir et je remonte lundi** I'm going down to London tonight and coming back up on Monday; **2** to take (or bring) back up; **veux-tu remonter les chaises?** would you take the chairs back upstairs?; **3** to put back up; **il m'a remonté ma valise au filet** he put my case up in the luggage rack for me; **4** remonter la pente to get or climb back up the hill; **5** to get or climb back in; **ils sont remontés dans le car** they got back into the coach; **6** remonter quelqu'un, remonter le moral à quelqu'un to cheer someone up.

remords noun Masc. remorse.

remorque noun Fem. **1** trailer (for a car); **2** tow-rope.

remplaçant, remplaçante noun Masc., Fem. **1** replacement (for another person); **2** supply teacher.

remplacer verb [61] **1** to stand in for (a person); **2** to replace; **il faut remplacer les piles** you need to replace the batteries.

remplir verb [2] **1** to fill; **il a rempli son verre de vin** he filled his glass with wine; **la salle était remplie de jeunes** the hall was full of young people; **2** remplir un formulaire to fill in a form; **3** to carry out (a duty or a role).

remue-ménage noun Masc. commotion.

remuer verb [1] **1** to move (your head or hand, for example); **le vent remuait les branches** the wind was shaking the branches; **2** to stir; **peux-tu remuer la sauce, s'il te plaît?** can you stir the sauce, please?

rémunérer verb [24] to pay (a person), to pay for (work).

renard noun Masc. fox.

rencontre noun Fem. **1** meeting; **elle est venue à ma rencontre** she

came to meet me; **2** (in sport) match; **la rencontre entre la France et l'Allemagne** the match between France and Germany.

rencontrer verb [1] **1** to meet (a person); **je l'ai rencontrée en 1993** I met her in 1993; **2** to play (an opponent or a team); **3** se rencontrer to meet; **nous nous sommes rencontrés à Londres** we met in London.

rendez-vous noun Masc. **1** appointment; **prendre rendez-vous** to make an appointment; **j'ai rendez-vous chez le dentiste** I've got a dentist's appointment; **le médecin voit les malades sur rendez-vous** the doctor sees patients by appointment; **2** date; **Marc a rendez-vous avec sa copine à trois heures** Marc's got a date with his girlfriend at three; **3** donner rendez-vous à quelqu'un to arrange to meet somebody; **il m'a donné rendez-vous au café** he arranged to meet me at the cafe.

rendormir verb [37] se rendormir to go back to sleep; **elle s'est rendormie** she went back to sleep.

rendre verb [3] **1** to give back; **je te rendrai les clés demain** I'll give you back the keys tomorrow; **2** rendre quelqu'un heureux to make somebody happy; **3** to hand in (homework); **4** se rendre to give oneself up, to surrender; **les voleurs se sont rendus à la police** the thieves gave themselves up to the police; **5** se rendre compte de quelque chose to realize something; **je me suis rendu**

compte du fait que j'avais oublié mes clés I realized I had forgotten my keys.

renifler verb [1] to sniff.

renne noun Masc. reindeer.

renommé adjective famous.

renoncer verb [61] 1 to give up; **c'est trop difficile, je renonce!** it's too difficult, I give up!; 2 **renoncer à quelque chose** to give something up.

renouveler verb [18] to renew (a passport or a subscription, for example).

rénover verb [1] 1 to renovate (a house); 2 to restore (furniture).

renseignement noun Masc. 1 un renseignement a piece of information; **un renseignement utile** a useful piece of information; 2 **les renseignements** information; **je cherche des renseignements** I'm looking for information; **adressez-vous aux renseignements** ask at the information desk; 3 **renseignements** directory enquiries.

renseigner verb [1] 1 **renseigner quelqu'un** to give someone information; **la brochure vous renseigne sur les horaires** the brochure gives you timetable information; **il était très bien renseigné sur le projet** he was very well-informed about the project; 2 **se renseigner** to find out; **je vais me renseigner au bureau de tourisme** I'm going to find out at the tourist office.

rentable adjective profitable.

rentrée noun Fem. **la rentrée (des classes)** the start of the new school year.

rentrer verb [1] 1 to get home; **Maman sera à dix-huit heures** Mum will be home at six; **je vais rentrer chez moi** I'm going home; 2 to get back; **ils rentrent de Paris jeudi** they'll be back from Paris on Thursday; 3 to come (or go) in; **rentrez!** do come in!; **elles sont rentrées dans un magasin** they've gone into a shop; 4 **rentrer dans quelque chose** to go in something; **tout ça ne rentrera jamais dans ton sac!** all that will never go in your bag!; 5 **rentrer dans quelque chose** to crash into something; **la voiture est rentrée dans un mur** the car crashed into a wall; 6 **rentrer quelque chose** to bring something in (from outside); **rentre les chaises, il pleut!** bring the chairs in, it's raining!

renverser verb [1] 1 to knock over; **il a renversé sa chaise** he knocked his chair over; 2 **être renversé par une voiture** to be knocked down by a car; 3 to spill; **j'ai renversé mon thé** I've spilled my tea.

renvoyer verb [40] 1 to send back; **as-tu renvoyé le formulaire?** have you sent back the form?; **on m'a renvoyé à l'hôpital** they sent me back to hospital; 2 to throw back (a ball); 3 to dismiss; **la secrétaire a été renvoyée** the secretary has been dismissed.

réouverture noun Fem. reopening.

répandu adjective widespread.

réparation noun Fem. repair.

réparer verb [1] to repair.

repartir verb [58] **1** to go off again; **ils ont déposé les enfants et ils sont repartis** they dropped the children and went off again; **2** to go again; **je suis reparti chez moi** I went home again; **3** repartir à zéro to start from scratch.

repas noun Masc. meal; **le repas de midi** lunch; **le repas du soir** the evening meal.

repassage noun Masc. ironing.

repasser verb [1] **1** to drop in again; **il a dit qu'il repasserait demain** he said he'd drop in again tomorrow; **2** to iron; **Frank est en train de repasser sa chemise** Frank's busy ironing his shirt; **une planche à repasser** an ironing board; **3** to resit (an exam or test); **4** to replay (a video).

repeindre verb [60] to repaint.

repère noun Masc. **un point de repère** a landmark, a reference point.

repérer verb [24] **1** (informal) to spot; **j'ai repéré trois erreurs dans son article** I spotted three mistakes in his article; **2** to locate (a place).

répertoire noun Masc. notebook (with a thumb index); **un répertoire d'adresses** an address book.

répéter verb [24] **1** to repeat; **elle l'a répété trois fois** she repeated it three times; **faire des essais répétés** to make repeated attempts; **2** to rehearse (a play); **3** to practise (a piece of music); **4 se répéter** to repeat oneself; **5 se**

répéter to happen again; **espérons que cela ne se répétera pas** let's hope it doesn't happen again.

répétition noun Fem. **1** rehearsal; **la répétition générale** the dress rehearsal; **2** repetition.

replier verb [1] **1** to fold up; **elle a replié la carte** she folded up the map (a sheet); **2** elle a replié ses jambes she tucked her legs up (under her).

répondeur noun Masc. answering machine; **j'ai laissé un message sur le répondeur** I left a message on the answering machine.

répondre verb [3] **1** to answer; **il n'a pas répondu** he didn't answer; **je ne lui ai pas répondu** I didn't answer him; **2** répondre à une question to answer a question; **3** répondre à une lettre to reply to a letter.

réponse noun Fem. answer; **donner la bonne/mauvaise réponse** to give the right/wrong answer.

reportage noun Masc. **1** report; **un reportage sur la drogue** a report on drugs; **2** (news) story.

reporter[1] verb [1] to postpone; **on a reporté le match à jeudi** the match has been postponed until Thursday.

reporter[2] noun Masc. reporter.

repos noun Masc. rest; **dix jours de repos** ten days' rest.

reposant adjective restful.

reposer verb [1] **1** reposer quelque chose to put something back down; **elle a reposé le livre sur la table** she put the book back

repousser verb [1] 1 to grow again; tes cheveux ont vite repoussé your hair's grown quickly; 2 to push back; 3 to postpone; le match a été repoussé the match has been postponed.

reprendre verb [64] 1 to have some more (food or drink); reprends du poulet have some more chicken; 2 to take back; est-ce que je peux reprendre les verres que je t'avais prêtés? can I take back the glasses I lent you?; 3 to start again; l'école reprend en septembre school starts again in September; 4 reprendre le travail to go back to work; j'ai repris le travail lundi I went back to work on Monday; 5 reprendre la route to set off again.

représentant, représentante noun Masc., Fem. sales rep.

représentation noun Fem. performance (of a play); prochaine représentation à 20h next performance 8 p.m.

représenter verb [1] 1 to depict; 2 to represent.

réprimander verb [1] to tell off, to reprimand.

réprimer verb [1] to suppress.

reprise noun Fem. 1 resumption (of work or discussions); rerun (of a play or film), repeat (of a broadcast); 3 à plusieurs reprises on several occasions.

reproche noun Masc. criticism; il m'a fait des reproches he criticized me.

reprocher verb [1] to criticize; il a reproché à son fils de ne pas travailler he criticized his son for not working; 2 se reprocher to blame oneself.

reproduction noun Fem. reproduction.

reproduire verb [26] 1 to reproduce; 2 se reproduire to happen again.

républicain adjective republican.

république noun Fem. republic; la République française the French Republic.

répugnant adjective revolting.

réputation noun Fem. reputation; il a la réputation d'être très sévère he has a reputation for being very strict.

requin noun Masc. shark.

RER noun Masc. SHORT FOR réseau express régional (the fast suburban network on the Paris underground).

rescousse noun Fem. aller à la rescousse de quelqu'un to go to someone's rescue.

réseau (plural réseaux) noun Masc. network.

réservation noun Fem. reservation.

réservé adjective reserved.

réserve noun Fem. 1 stock; des réserves de charbon stocks of coal; j'ai deux bouteilles en réserve I have put aside two bottles; 2 reserve (for birds or *animals*); **une réserve ornithologique** a bird sanctuary.

réserver *verb* [1] **1** to reserve, to book; **j'ai réservé deux places pour ce soir** I've booked two seats for this evening; **2** to keep; **Philippe t'a réservé du poulet** Philippe's kept some chicken for you.

réservoir *noun Masc.* **1** tank; **réservoir à essence** petrol tank; **2** reservoir.

résidence *noun Fem.* **1** home, residence; **une résidence secondaire** a holiday home; **2** block of flats.

résidence universitaire *noun Fem.* hall of residence.

résident, résidente *noun Masc., Fem.* resident.

résidentiel (*Fem.* **résidentielle**) *adjective* residential.

résistant, résistante *noun Masc., Fem.* Resistance fighter (*in France during World War II*).

résistant *adjective* tough.

résister *verb* [1] **résister à** to resist.

résolu *adjective* **1** determined; **elle est résolue à démissionner** she is determined to resign; **2** resolved; **le problème est résolu** the problem is resolved.

résoudre *verb* [67] **1** to solve (*a problem*); **2 se résoudre à faire** to make up one's mind to do; **elle s'est résolue à partir** she made up her mind to leave.

respect *noun Masc.* respect.

respecter *verb* [1] to respect.

respectueux (*Fem.* **respectueuse**) *adjective* respectful.

respiration *noun Fem.* breathing.

respirer *verb* [1] to breathe.

responsabilité *noun Fem.* **1** responsibility; **2 avoir la responsabilité de quelque chose** to be responsible for something; **il a la responsabilité des livraisons** he's responsible for deliveries.

responsable *noun Masc. & Fem.* **1** person in charge; **le responsable du projet** the person in charge of the project; **2** person responsible; **les responsables de la catastrophe** those responsible for the disaster.

responsable *adjective* responsible; **il est responsable de l'accident** he's responsible for the accident.

ressemblance *noun Fem.* similarity.

ressembler *verb* [1] **1 ressembler à** to look like; **elle ressemble beaucoup à sa mère** she looks very like her mother; **cela ressemble à du bois mais c'est du plastique** it looks like wood but it's plastic; **2 se ressembler** to be alike; **les deux sœurs ne se ressemblent pas du tout** the two sisters are not at all alike.

ressentiment *noun Masc.* resentment.

resserrer *verb* [1] **1** to tighten (*a knot or screw, for example*); **2 se resserrer** to move closer together;

resservez-vous un peu! squeeze up a bit!

resservir verb [58] **1** to give another helping; **je vous ressers un peu?** shall I give you a little more?; **2 se resservir** to help yourself to more; **ressers-toi de la salade** help yourself to some more salad; **je me suis déjà resservi, merci** I've already helped myself to, thank you.

ressort noun Masc. spring (in a bed or a chair).

ressortir verb [58] to go out again; **il est revenu pour les clés et il est ressorti** he came back for the keys and went out again.

ressource noun Fem. **1** resource; **des ressources énergétiques** energy resources; **2 il est sans ressources** he has no means of support.

restaurant noun Masc. restaurant; **on mange au restaurant ce soir** we're going out for a meal tonight.

restauration noun Fem. **1** catering; **la restauration rapide** the fast-food industry; **2** restoration.

restaurer verb [1] to restore.

reste noun Masc. **1 le reste** the rest; **le reste du temps** the rest of the time; **et tout le reste, tu le sais déjà** and you know all the rest already; **2 les restes** the leftovers; **j'ai fait un curry avec les restes du poulet** I made a curry with the leftover chicken.

rester verb [1] **1** to stay; **reste là, je reviens tout de suite!** stay there,

I'll be right back!; **Camille est restée à la maison** Camille stayed at home; **je ne peux pas rester longtemps** I can't stay long; **hier je suis resté sans manger** I didn't have anything to eat yesterday; **2 rester debout** to remain standing; **je préfère rester debout** I prefer to stand; **3 rester assis** to remain seated; **je suis resté assis toute la journée** I've been sitting down all day; **4** to be left; **il reste du fromage** there's some cheese left; **il nous reste combien d'argent?** how much money have we got left?; **il ne reste pas beaucoup à faire** there's not much left to do.

restriction noun Fem. restriction.

résultat noun Masc. result; **les résultats des examens** the exam results.

résulter verb [1] **résulter de** to result from.

résumé noun Masc. summary, résumé.

résumer verb [1] to summarize, to sum up.

rétablir verb [2] **1** to restore; **2 se rétablir** to recover (after an illness).

retaper verb [1] to do up (a house).

retard noun Masc. **1** delay; **ils annoncent une heure de retard sur notre vol** they say there's an hour's delay on our flight; **sans retard** without delay; **2 avoir du retard** to be late; **excusez mon retard** I'm sorry I'm late; **ils sont arrivés avec trois heures de retard** they arrived three hours late; **3 être en retard** to be late;

back there; **2** to turn over; **est-ce que je retourne les steaks?** shall I turn the steaks over?; **3** to overturn.

retarder verb [1] **1** to hold up, to delay; **la grève nous a retardés** the strike held us up; **l'avion était retardé** the plane was delayed; **2** to put off, to postpone; **il a retardé son départ** he put off his departure.

retenir verb [77] **1** to hold up; **j'ai été retenu au bureau** I was held up at the office; **je ne vous retiendrai pas longtemps** I won't keep you long; **2 retenir son souffle** to hold your breath; **elle ne pouvait pas retenir ses larmes** she couldn't hold back her tears; **3** to book; **j'ai retenu des places** I've booked seats; **4** to remember; **je ne retiens jamais leur adresse** I can never remember their address.

réticence noun Fem. **1** reluctance; **2** reticence.

retirer verb [1] **1** to take off; **je vais d'abord retirer ma veste** I'll take my jacket off first; **2** to take away; **ils ont retiré son permis** they took away his licence; **3 retirer de l'argent** to take out some money (from your bank account).

retouche noun Fem. alteration (to a garment).

retour noun Masc. **1** return; **un billet aller-retour** a return ticket; **dès mon retour** as soon as I get back; **2 être de retour** to be back; **elle sera de retour vers onze heures** she'll be back about eleven.

retourner verb [1] **1** to go back; **elle est retournée à l'école** she went back to school; **je n'y suis jamais retourné** I've never been

retraite noun Fem. retirement; **prendre sa retraite** to retire; **une maison de retraite** an old people's home.

retraité, retraitée noun Masc., Fem. pensioner.

rétrécir verb [2] to shrink.

retrousser verb [1] **1** to hitch up; **2** to roll up; **il a retroussé ses manches** he rolled up his sleeves.

retrouver verb [1] **1** to find; **as-tu retrouvé tes clés?** did you find your keys?; **2** to meet; **je te retrouve à la sortie** I'll meet you at the exit; **3 se retrouver** to meet; **on se retrouve devant le cinéma?** shall we meet outside the cinema?; **on se retrouvera à Noël** we'll see each other again at Christmas; **4 se retrouver** to end up; **on s'est retrouvé chez Amanda** we ended up at Amanda's place; **5 se retrouver** to find one's way around; **je n'arrive jamais à me retrouver à Londres** I can never find my way around London.

rétroviseur, rétro noun Masc. rearview mirror.

réunion noun Fem. **1** meeting; **2** reunion; **3** gathering; **4** reunification.

réunir verb [2] **se réunir** to meet; **on s'est réuni pour discuter du problème** we met to discuss the problem.

réussi adjective successful.

réussir verb [2] **1** to succeed; j'espère qu'elle va réussir I hope she'll succeed; **2** réussir un examen to pass an exam; **3** to be successful; ça a très bien réussi that was very successful; **4** réussir à faire to manage to do; je n'ai pas réussi à les persuader I didn't manage to persuade them.

réussite noun Fem. success.

réutilisable adjective reusable.

revanche noun Fem. **1** return match; **2** prendre sa revanche to get your own back; **3** en revanche on the other hand.

rêve noun Masc. dream; faire un rêve to have a dream; votre maison de rêve your dream house.

réveil noun Masc. alarm clock.

réveille-matin noun Masc. alarm clock.

réveiller verb [1] **1** réveiller quelqu'un to wake somebody up; elle m'a réveillé à sept heures she woke me at seven; **2** se réveiller to wake up; d'habitude je me réveille à sept heures I usually wake up at seven.

réveillon noun Masc. le réveillon du Nouvel An the New Year's Eve celebrations.

réveillonner verb [1] **1** to celebrate Christmas Eve; **2** to see the New Year in.

révéler verb [24] to reveal.

revenant, revenante noun Masc., Fem. ghost.

revendre verb [3] to sell, to resell.

revenir verb [81] **1** to come back; elles sont revenues très tard they came back very late; tu reviendras nous voir? will you come back and see us?; **2** to come to; ça revient à quinze euros that comes to fifteen euros; ça revient au même it comes to the same thing; je n'en reviens pas! I can't get over it!

revenu noun Masc. income.

rêver verb [1] to dream.

réverbère noun Masc. street lamp.

revers noun Masc. **1** lapel (on a jacket); turn-up (of trousers); cuff (on a sleeve); **2** backhand (in tennis); **3** setback; **4** le revers de la médaille the other side of the coin.

réviser verb [1] **1** to revise; **2** to service (a car or machine).

révision noun Fem. **1** revision; **2** service (of a car).

revoici preposition (informal) me revoici! here I am again!

revoir[1] verb [13] **1** to see again; et nous ne l'avons jamais revue and we never saw her again; **2** to revise; je dois revoir ma chimie I have to revise my chemistry.

revoir[2] noun Masc. au revoir goodbye.

révoltant adjective appalling.

révolte noun Fem. revolt, rebellion.

révolter verb [1] to appal.

révolution noun Fem. revolution.

révolutionner verb [1] to revolutionize.

revolver noun Masc. revolver, handgun.

revouloir verb [14] to have a second helping of; est-ce que tu reveux des frites? would you like a second helping of chips?

revue noun Fem. magazine; **une revue d'art** an art magazine; **une revue scientifique** a scientific journal.

rez-de-chaussée noun Masc. ground floor (literally: level with the road); **la réception est au rez-de-chaussée** reception is on the ground floor.

RF SHORT FOR **République française** French Republic.

Rhin noun Masc. **le Rhin** the Rhine.

rhinocéros noun Masc. rhinoceros.

rhubarbe noun Fem. rhubarb.

rhum noun Masc. rum.

rhume noun Masc. cold; **attraper un rhume** to catch a cold; **un rhume de cerveau** a head cold.

rhume des foins noun Masc. hay fever.

ri verb SEE **rire**.

ricaner verb [1] to snigger, to giggle.

riche adjective **1** well-off; **nous ne sommes pas très riches** we're not terribly well-off; **2** rich; **riche en vitamines** rich in vitamins.

richesse noun Fem. **1** wealth; **2 les richesses naturelles** natural resources.

ride noun Fem. wrinkle (on skin), ripple (on water).

rideau (plural **rideaux**) noun Masc. curtain.

ridicule adjective ridiculous; **mais c'est totalement ridicule!** but that's completely ridiculous!

rien[1] pronoun **1** nothing; **'qu'est-ce qu'elle a dit?' – 'rien'** what did she say?' – 'nothing'; **il n'a rien** he has nothing; **je n'ai rien vu** I didn't see anything; **ce n'est rien** it's nothing; **il ne reste plus rien** there's nothing left; **rien du tout** nothing at all; **'merci' – 'de rien'** 'thank you' – 'it's nothing'; **rien d'autre** nothing else; **rien de bon** nothing good; **2 rien que** just; **rien que les livres pèsent 20 kilos** the books by themselves weigh 20 kilos; **'que reste-t-il à faire?' – 'rien que la vaisselle'** 'what's left to do?' – 'just the washing-up'; ★ **rien à faire!** it's no good!

rien[2] noun Masc. little thing; **elle se met à hurler pour un rien** the slightest thing starts her shouting.

rigide adjective rigid, stiff.

rigoler verb [1] (informal) **1** to laugh; **elle en a beaucoup rigolé** she had a good laugh about it; **2** to have a good time; **nous avons bien rigolé** we had a great time; **3** to be joking; **je rigolais!** I was only joking!

rigolo (Fem. **rigolote**) adjective (informal) funny.

rigoureux (Fem. **rigoureuse**) adjective **1** rigorous; **2** strict; **3** harsh.

rillettes plural noun Fem. **les rillettes de porc** potted pork.

rime noun Fem. rhyme.

rimer verb [1] to rhyme.

rincer verb [61] to rinse; **se rincer les cheveux** to rinse one's hair.

rire noun Masc. laughter; **un rire** a laugh.

rire verb [68] **1** to laugh; **il nous fait rire** he makes us laugh; **2** to have

a
b
c
d
e
f
g
h
i
j
k
l
m
n
o
p
q
r
s
t
u
v
w
x
y
z

fun; **on va rire ce soir** we'll have some fun this evening; **c'était pour rire** it was meant as a joke.

ris noun Masc. **les ris de veau** calf's sweetbreads.

risque noun Masc. risk; **risque d'incendie** fire risk; **c'est sans risque** it's safe.

risqué adjective risky.

risquer verb [1] 1 to risk; **vas-y, tu ne risques rien** go on, it's quite safe; 2 **il risque de pleuvoir** it might well rain; **tu risques de te brûler** you might burn yourself.

rivage noun Masc. shore.

rival, rivale noun Masc., Fem. (Masc. plural **rivaux**) rival.

rive noun Fem. 1 bank (of a river); **la Rive gauche** the Left Bank (when talking about the Seine in Paris and other rivers which flow through cities, the left bank is the left side of the river when you are facing downstream); 2 shore (by the sea).

rivière noun Fem. river.

riz noun Masc. rice; **riz cantonais** fried rice; **gâteau de riz** rice pudding.

RN noun Fem. SHORT FOR **route nationale** A road.

robe noun Fem. dress; **une robe d'été** a summer dress; **une robe de mariée** a wedding dress.

robe de chambre noun Fem. dressing gown.

robinet noun Masc. tap; **l'eau du robinet** tap water.

robot noun Masc. robot; **robot ménager** food processor.

robuste adjective robust, sturdy.

roche noun Fem. rock.

rocher noun Masc. rock.

rock noun Masc. rock (music).

rôder verb [1] to prowl.

rognons plural noun Masc. kidneys (for cooking).

roi noun Masc. king; **le roi Charles** King Charles; **les Rois mages** the Three Wise Men; **la fête des Rois** Twelfth Night.

rôle noun Masc. role.

roller noun Masc. 1 roller-skating; 2 roller-skate.

romain adjective Roman.

roman noun Masc. novel; **un roman** a detective story.

romancier, romancière noun Masc., Fem. novelist.

romantique adjective romantic.

romarin noun Masc. rosemary.

rompre verb [69] to split up; **Claire et David ont rompu** Claire and David have split up; **Anne a rompu avec son copain** Anne's broken up with her boyfriend; **rompre ses fiançailles** to break off your engagement.

ronce noun Fem. bramble.

rond noun Masc. circle; **tourner en rond** to go round in circles.

rond adjective round.

rondelle noun Fem. 1 slice; **une rondelle de tomate** a slice of tomato; 2 washer (for a tap or screw).

rond-point noun Masc. roundabout.

ronfler verb [1] to snore.

ronger *verb* [52] **1** to gnaw; **2 se ronger les ongles** to bite one's nails.

ronronner *verb* [1] to purr.

rosbif *noun Masc.* roast beef.

rose *noun Fem.* rose.

rose *adjective* pink; **rose pâle** pale pink.

rosé *noun Masc.* rosé (wine); **un verre de rosé** a glass of rosé.

rosée *noun Fem.* dew.

rosier *noun Masc.* rosebush.

rossignol *noun Masc.* nightingale.

rôti *noun Masc.* roast; **du rôti de bœuf** roast beef; **un rôti de bœuf** a joint of beef.

rôtir *verb* [2] to roast.

roucouler *verb* [1] to coo.

roue *noun Fem.* wheel; **la roue de secours** the spare wheel; ★ **faire la roue** to turn a cartwheel.

rouge *noun Masc.* **1** (the colour) red; **le rouge ne me va pas** red doesn't suit me; **2** red traffic light; **il est passé au rouge** he jumped the lights; **le feu est passé au rouge** the light changed to red; **3** red wine; **un verre de rouge** a glass of red wine.

rouge *adjective* red; **tes chaussettes rouges** your red socks.

rouge à lèvres *noun Masc.* lipstick.

rouge-gorge *noun Masc.* robin.

rougeur *noun Fem.* redness.

rougir *verb* [2] **1** to blush; **2** to turn red.

rouille *noun Fem.* rust.

rouillé *adjective* rusty.

rouiller, se rouiller *verb* [1] to go rusty.

roulade *noun Fem.* **1** stuffed rolled meat; **2** somersault, roll.

roulant *adjective* **un fauteuil roulant** a wheelchair.

rouleau (*plural* **rouleaux**) *noun Masc.* roll; **un rouleau d'essuie-tout** a roll of kitchen towel.

rouleau à pâtisserie *noun Masc.* rolling pin.

rouler *verb* [1] **1** to go; **nous roulons très vite** we're going very fast; **2** to drive; **il faut rouler à droite en France** in France you must drive on the right; **nous avons roulé toute la nuit** we drove all night; **3** to roll; **4** to roll up; **il faut rouler le tapis** we must roll up the carpet; **5** (*informal*) to cheat; **on m'a roulé!** I've been done!

Roumanie *noun Fem.* Romania.

rousse *adjective* SEE **roux**.

route *noun Fem.* **1** road; **une grande route** a main road; **un accident de la route** a road accident; **Rouen est à trois heures de route d'ici** Rouen is three hours' drive from here; **2** route; **il a changé de route à cause de la neige** he changed his route because of the snow; **3 en route** on the way; **être en route** to be on the way; **nous sommes en route pour Nice** we're on our way to Nice; **4 se mettre en route** to set off; **5 bonne route!** safe journey!

route à quatre voies *noun Fem.* dual carriageway.

route départementale *noun Fem.* secondary road, B road.

route nationale noun Fem. A road.

routier, routière noun Masc. Fem. lorry driver.

routier, routière adjective road; **le transport routier** road transport; **la gare routière** the bus station.

routine noun Fem. routine.

roux (Fem. **rousse**) adjective red-haired, ginger.

royal (plural **royaux**) adjective royal.

royaume noun Masc. kingdom.

Royaume-Uni noun Masc. United Kingdom.

ruban noun Masc. ribbon.

ruban adhésif noun Masc. sticky tape.

rubéole noun Fem. German measles.

ruche noun Fem. beehive.

rudement adverb (informal) really; **il est rudement bon ton gâteau** your cake's really good.

rue noun Fem. street; **une rue piétonne** a pedestrian street; ★ **mettre quelqu'un à la rue** to put someone out on the street.

rugby noun Masc. rugby; **jouer au rugby** to play rugby.

rugbyman (plural **rugbymen**) noun Masc. rugby player.

ruine noun Fem. ruin; **une maison en ruine(s)** a ruined house.

ruiner verb [1] to ruin.

ruisseau (plural **ruisseaux**) noun Masc. stream.

rumeur noun Fem. **1** rumour; **2** murmur.

rumsteck noun Masc. rump steak.

rupture noun Fem. break-up.

rural (Masc. plural **ruraux**) adjective country; **la vie rurale** country life.

ruse noun Fem. **1** trick; **les ruses du métier** the tricks of the trade; **2** cunning.

rusé adjective cunning, crafty.

russe noun Masc. Russian (language).

russe adjective Russian.

Russe noun Masc., Fem. Russian (person).

Russie noun Fem. Russia.

rythme noun Masc. rhythm; **marquer le rythme** to beat time.

Ss

s' pronoun SEE **se**.

sa adjective SEE **son**.

sable noun Masc. sand.

sablé noun Masc. shortbread biscuit.

sablé adjective **la pâte sablée** shortcrust pastry.

sac noun Masc. **1** bag; **un sac de sucre** a bag of sugar; **un sac de sport** a sports bag; **2** sack; **un sac de charbon** a sack of coal; ★ **vider son sac** (informal) to get something off one's chest (literally: to empty one's bag).

sac à dos noun Masc. rucksack.

sac à main noun Masc. handbag.

sac de congélation noun Masc. freezer bag.

sac de couchage noun Masc. sleeping bag.

sachet noun Masc. sachet; **un sachet de thé** a teabag.

sacoche noun Fem. **1** bag; **la sacoche du facteur** the postman's bag; **2** pannier (for a bike).

sacré adjective **1** (informal) **c'est un sacré problème** it's a hell of a problem; **elle a eu une sacrée chance** she's been damn lucky; **2** sacred.

sacrifice noun Masc. sacrifice.

sacrifier verb [1] to sacrifice.

sage adjective **1** wise, well-behaved; **Tom, sois sage** be a good boy, Tom; **2** wise, sensible; **il serait sage de se renseigner sur le prix** it would be wise to enquire about the price.

sage-femme noun Fem. midwife.

sagesse noun Fem. wisdom; **une dent de sagesse** a wisdom tooth.

Sagittaire noun Masc. Sagittarius (sign of the Zodiac).

saignant adjective rare (beef).

saigner verb [1] to bleed.

sain adjective healthy; ★ **sain et sauf** safe and sound.

saint, sainte noun Masc., Fem. saint.

saint adjective holy; **le Saint-Esprit** the Holy Spirit; **le vendredi saint** Good Friday; **la Sainte Vierge** the Virgin Mary.

Saint-Jacques noun **une coquille Saint-Jacques** a scallop.

Saint-Jean noun Fem. Midsummer's Day (June 24th).

Saint-Sylvestre noun Fem. New Year's Eve.

Saint-Valentin noun Fem. St Valentine's Day.

sais verb SEE savoir[1].

saisir verb [2] **1** to grab; **il m'a saisi par le bras** he grabbed my arm; **2 saisir l'occasion** to seize the opportunity; **3** to understand; **je n'ai pas tout à fait saisi ...** I didn't entirely understand ...; **4** to catch, (to hear); **je n'ai pas saisi votre nom** I didn't catch your name.

saison noun Fem. season; **il fait froid pour la saison** it's cold for the time of year.

sait verb SEE savoir[1].

salade noun Fem. **1** lettuce; **une salade** a lettuce ; **2** salad; **une salade de fruits** a fruit salad.

saladier noun Masc. salad bowl.

salaire noun Masc. salary, wages.

salarié, salariée noun Masc., Fem. salaried employee.

sale adjective **1** (after the noun) dirty; **les mains sales** dirty hands; **2** (before the noun) (informal) horrible; **quel sale temps!** what horrible weather!; **il a une sale tête** he looks awful.

salé adjective **1** salty; **la sauce est un peu trop salée** the sauce is a bit salty; **2** savoury; **des petits gâteaux salés** savoury biscuits; **3 du beurre salé** salt butter.

saler verb [1] to salt.

saleté noun Fem. dirt.

salir verb [2] to dirty, to get (something) dirty; **tu vas salir ta robe** you'll get your dress dirty.

salive noun Fem. saliva.

salle noun Fem. 1 room (*'salle' by itself is no longer used to mean a room in a house*); 2 dining-room (*in a restaurant*); 3 hall; 4 auditorium (*in a theatre or cinema*).

salle à manger noun Fem. 1 dining room; 2 dining-room suite.

salle d'attente noun Fem. waiting room.

salle d'eau noun Fem. shower room.

salle de bains noun Fem. bathroom.

salle de classe noun Fem. classroom.

salle de jeux noun Fem. games room.

salle d'embarquement noun Fem. departure lounge.

salle de séjour noun Fem. living room.

salle des fêtes noun Fem. community centre.

salon noun Masc. 1 sitting room; 2 living-room suite; 3 trade fair; 4 salon; **salon de coiffure** hair salon.

salon de thé noun Masc. tea-room.

salopette noun Fem. 1 dungarees; 2 overalls.

saluer verb [1] 1 to say hello to; **je l'ai salué, mais il ne m'a pas entendu** I said hello to him but he didn't hear; **elle l'a salué de la main** she waved at him; 2 to say goodbye to.

salut greeting Masc. Hi!

samedi noun Masc. 1 Saturday; **samedi prochain** next Saturday; **samedi dernier** last Saturday; 2 on Saturday; **samedi soir** on Saturday evening; 3 **le samedi** on Saturdays; **fermé le samedi** closed on Saturdays; 4 **tous les samedis** every Saturday.

SAMU noun Masc. SHORT FOR **Service d'assistance médicale d'urgence** ambulance service.

sandale noun Fem. sandal.

sandwich noun Masc. sandwich; **un sandwich au jambon** a ham sandwich.

sandwicherie noun Fem. snack bar.

sang noun Masc. blood; **être en sang** to be covered in blood.

sang-froid noun Masc. calm.

sanglier noun Masc. wild boar.

sanglot noun Masc. sob; **éclater en sanglots** to burst into tears.

sanisette™ noun Fem. automatic public lavatory.

sanitaire adjective **les conditions sanitaires** sanitary conditions; **les règlements sanitaires** health regulations.

sanitaire noun Masc. **les sanitaires** the toilet block (*in a campsite*).

sans preposition without; **une maison sans téléphone** a house without a telephone; **un café sans sucre** a coffee with no sugar; **sans hésiter** without hesitating.

sans-abri noun Masc. & Fem. homeless person; **les sans-abri** the homeless.

sans-emploi noun Masc. & Fem. unemployed person; **les sans-emploi** the unemployed.

santé noun Fem. **1** health; **être en bonne santé** to be in good health; **2 à votre santé!** cheers!

sapeur-pompier noun Masc. fireman; **appeler les sapeurs-pompiers** to call the fire brigade.

sapin noun Masc. fir tree; **un sapin de Noël** a Christmas tree.

sarcasme noun Masc. sarcasm.

sardine noun Fem. sardine.

satellite noun Masc. satellite.

satin noun Masc. satin.

satisfaction noun Fem. satisfaction.

satisfaire verb [10] to satisfy.

satisfaisant adjective satisfactory.

satisfait adjective satisfied; **êtes-vous satisfaits de votre séjour?** are you satisfied with your stay?

sauce noun Fem. **1** sauce; **2** gravy.

saucisse noun Fem. sausage.

saucisson noun Masc. salami.

sauf[1] preposition **1** except; **tous les jours sauf le lundi** every day except Monday; **sauf quand il pleut** except when it rains; **2 sauf si** unless; **c'est tout, sauf s'il y a des questions?** that's all, unless there are any questions? **3** except that; **tout va bien, sauf que ta sur n'est pas encore arrivée** everything's fine, except that your sister hasn't arrived yet.

sauf[2] adjective SEE **sain**.

saule noun Masc. willow; **un saule pleureur** a weeping willow.

saumon noun Masc. salmon.

saupoudrer verb [1] to sprinkle.

saut noun Masc. jump.

saut à la perche noun Masc. pole vault.

saut à l'élastique noun Masc. bungee jumping.

saut en hauteur noun Masc. high jump.

saut en longueur noun Masc. long jump.

sauter verb [1] **1** to jump, to jump over; **elle a sauté la barrière** she jumped over the gate; **elle a sauté dans un taxi** she jumped into a taxi; **2 sauter à la corde** to skip (with a rope); **3** to skip; **nous avons sauté trois pages** we've skipped three pages; **4** to blow up; **les terroristes ont fait sauter l'avion** the terrorists blew up the plane; **faire sauter les plombs** to blow the fuses; ★ **ça saute aux yeux!** it's blindingly obvious!

sauterelle noun Fem. grasshopper.

sauvage noun Masc., Fem. savage.

sauvage adjective **1** wild; **2** savage.

sauvegarder verb [1] **1** to safeguard; **2** to save, to back up (on a computer).

sauver verb [1] **1** to save; **vous m'avez sauvé la vie** you saved my life; **2 se sauver** to run away; **ils se sont sauvés** they ran away; **3 je me sauve!** (informal) I'm off!

sauvetage noun Masc. rescue, life-saving.

savent, savez verb SEE **savoir**[1].

savoir[1] *verb* [70] **1** to know; **je sais qu'il habite à Londres** I know he lives in London; **je ne savais pas qu'elle était médecin** I didn't know she was a doctor; **tu sais très bien que ...** you know very well that ...; **je n'en sais rien** I know nothing about it; **comment l'avez-vous su?** how did you find out about it?; **allez savoir!** who knows!; **2 savoir faire** to know how to do; **je ne sais pas le faire** I don't know how to do it; **savoir lire et écrire** to be able to read and write; **tu sais jouer du piano?** can you play the piano?.

savoir[2] *noun Masc.* knowledge.

savoir-faire *noun Masc.* know-how.

savon *noun Masc.* soap.

savonnette *noun Fem.* cake of soap.

savons *verb* SEE **savoir**[1].

savoureux (*Fem.* **savoureuse**) *adjective* tasty.

scandale *noun Masc.* scandal; **le discours du ministre a fait scandale** the minister's speech caused a scandal.

scandinave *adjective* Scandinavian.

Scandinavie *noun Fem.* Scandinavia.

scanner *noun Masc.* scanner (*in medicine and for documents*); **passer un scanneur** to have a scan.

scarabée *noun Masc.* beetle.

scénariste *noun Masc. & Fem.* scriptwriter.

scène *noun Fem.* **1** stage (*in a theatre*); **être sur scène** to be on stage; **mettre en scène** to stage (*a play*), to direct (*a film*); **2** scene; **sur la scène politique** on the political scene; **des scènes de panique** scenes of panic; **faire (toute) une scène** to throw a fit.

sceptique *adjective* sceptical.

schéma *noun Masc.* diagram.

scie *noun Fem.* saw.

science *noun Fem.* science.

sciences naturelles *plural noun Fem.* biology.

scientifique *noun Masc. & Fem.* scientist.

scientifique *adjective* scientific.

scier *verb* [1] to saw.

scolaire *adjective* school; **les vacances scolaires** the school holidays; **le livret scolaire** the school report.

scolarité *noun Fem.* schooling, education.

Scorpion *noun Masc.* Scorpio (*sign of the Zodiac*).

Scotch™ *noun Masc.* Sellotape™.

scout, scoute *noun Masc., Fem.* boy scout, girl guide.

scrutin *noun Masc.* **1** ballot; **2** polls; **le jour du scrutin** polling day.

sculpteur *noun Masc.* sculptor.

sculpteuse *noun Fem.* sculptress.

sculpture *noun Fem.* sculpture.

SDF *noun Masc. & Fem.* SHORT FOR **sans domicile fixe** of no fixed abode; **les SDF** the homeless.

se, s' (*before a vowel or silent 'h'*) *reflexive pronoun* **1** himself; **il se**

regarde he's looking at himself;
2 herself; **elle se regarde** she's
looking at herself; **3** itself; **le chien
s'est fait mal** the dog has hurt
itself; **4** themselves; **ils se sont fait
mal** they've hurt themselves;
5 each other; **ils se regardaient**
they were looking at each other;
6 yourself, oneself; **se faire mal** to
hurt yourself (or oneself);
7 (*sometimes not translated*)
Claudie se lave les cheveux
Claudie's washing her hair; **Jules
se brosse les dents** Jules is
brushing his teeth.

séance noun Fem. **1** session;
2 showing (*of a film*); **la séance de
vingt heures** the eight o'clock
showing.

seau (*plural* **seaux**) noun Masc.
bucket.

sec (Fem. **sèche**) adjective **1** dry;
mes cheveux ne sont pas secs
my hair's not dry; **un vin blanc sec**
a dry white wine; **2** dried; **des
abricots secs** dried apricots.

sèche-cheveux noun Masc. hair
dryer.

sèche-linge noun Masc. tumble
dryer.

sèche-mains noun Masc. hand
dryer.

sécher verb [1] to dry; **des fleurs
séchées** dried flowers.

sécheresse noun Fem. drought.

second noun Masc. **au second** on
the second floor; **il est arrivé en
second** he arrived second.

second adjective second; **la
seconde fois** the second time.

secondaire adjective secondary;
une école secondaire a secondary
school; **des effets secondaires**
side effects.

seconde noun Fem. **1** second; **je
reviens dans une seconde** I'll be
back in a moment; **2** second class;
voyager en seconde to travel
second class; **un billet de seconde**
a second class ticket; **3** (*in a French
school*) the equivalent of Year 11.

secouer verb [1] to shake; **secouer
la tête** to shake your head.

secourir verb [29] to rescue.

secourisme noun Masc. first aid.

secouriste noun Masc. & Fem. first
aider.

secours noun Masc. **1** help; **au
secours!** help!; **elle a crié au
secours** she shouted for help; **2** ;
les premiers secours first aid;
3 une sortie de secours an
emergency exit; **4 la roue de
secours** the spare wheel.

secret noun Masc. secret; **garder
un secret** to keep a secret; **en
secret** in secret.

secret (Fem. **secrète**) adjective
secret.

secrétaire[1] noun Masc., Fem.
secretary.

secrétaire[2] noun Masc. writing
desk.

secrétariat noun Masc.
secretary's office.

secteur noun Masc. sector; **dans le
secteur privé** in the private sector;
dans le secteur public in the
public sector.

sécu noun Fem. (*informal*) SHORT FOR
Sécurité sociale Social Security.

a b c d e f g h i j k l m n o p q r **s** t u v w x y z

sécurité *noun Fem.* **1** safety; **pour votre sécurité** for your own safety; **les règles de sécurité** safety regulations; **la sécurité routière** road safety; **une ceinture de sécurité** a seatbelt; **2 être en sécurité** to be safe; **3** security; **un système de sécurité** a security system; **la sécurité de l'emploi** job security.

Sécurité sociale *noun Fem.* Social Security.

séduisant *adjective* attractive, appealing.

seigle *noun Masc.* rye; **le pain de seigle** rye bread.

seigneur *noun Masc.* lord; **le Seigneur** the Lord.

sein *noun Masc.* **1** breast; **avoir un cancer du sein** to have breast cancer; **2** within; **au sein du gouvernement** within the government.

seize *number* sixteen; **Corinne a seize ans** Corinne's sixteen; **le seize juillet** the sixteenth of July.

seizième *number* sixteenth.

séjour *noun Masc.* **1** stay; **pendant votre séjour en France** during your stay in France; **2 la salle de séjour** the living room.

sel *noun Masc.* salt; **une pincée de sel** a pinch of salt.

sélection *noun Fem.* **1** selection; **2** choice; **3** team; **la sélection française** the French team.

sélectionner *verb* [1] to select.

self *noun Masc.* (*informal*) self-service restaurant.

self-service *noun Masc.* (*informal*) self-service restaurant.

selle *noun Fem.* saddle.

selon *preposition* according to; **selon la météo, il va pleuvoir** according to the forecast, it's going to rain.

semaine *noun Fem.* week; **cette semaine** this week; **la semaine prochaine/dernière** next/last week; **une/deux fois par semaine** once/twice a week; **elle est payée à la semaine** she's paid by the week.

semblable *adjective* similar.

semblant *noun Masc.* **faire semblant de faire** to pretend to do; **elle fait semblant de ne pas entendre** she's pretending not to hear.

sembler *verb* [1] to seem; **la maison semble vide** the house seems empty; **il semble bon d'attendre leur retour** it seems a good idea to wait till they get back.

semelle *noun Fem.* sole (*of a shoe*).

semer *verb* [1] **1** to sow (*seeds*); **2 semer la panique** to spread panic.

semestre *noun Masc.* semester.

semi-remorque *noun Masc.* articulated truck.

semoule *noun Fem.* semolina; **le sucre semoule** caster sugar.

sens *noun Masc.* **1** direction; **dans les deux sens** in both directions; **dans le sens Calais-Paris** in the Calais-Paris direction; **dans tous les sens** in all directions; **sens dessus dessous** upside down; **mets-le dans le bon sens!** put it the right way up!; **2** meaning; **le sens d'un mot** the meaning of a word; **cela n'a pas de sens** it doesn't make sense, it's absurd.

sensation noun Fem. **1** feeling; **2** sensation; **le film a fait sensation à Cannes** the film was a sensation at Cannes.

sensationnel (Fem. **sensationnelle**) adjective sensational, fantastic.

sens commun noun Masc. common sense.

sens de l'humour noun Masc. sense of humour; **avoir le sens de l'humour** to have a sense of humour.

sensé adjective sensible.

sensibiliser verb [1] **sensibiliser les gens à un problème** to increase people's awareness of a problem.

sensibilité noun Fem. **1** sensitivity; **2** sensibility.

sensible adjective **1** sensitive; **c'est une fille très sensible** she's a very sensitive girl; **je suis sensible au froid** I feel the cold; **2** noticeable; **une différence sensible** a noticeable difference.

sensiblement adverb noticeably.

sens interdit noun Masc. no entry sign, one-way street.

sens unique noun Masc. one-way street.

sentier noun Masc. path.

sentier de randonnée noun Masc. long-distance footpath (a marked route for ramblers).

sentiment noun Masc. feeling; **sentiments affectueux** best wishes; **veuillez croire à mes sentiments les meilleurs** yours sincerely, yours faithfully (one of a number of fixed formulae for ending a formal letter).

sentimental (Masc. plural **sentimentaux**) adjective sentimental.

sentir verb [58] **1** to smell; **ça sent bon!** that smells good!; **2** to smell of; **ça sent les roses** it smells of roses; **tu sens la cigarette** you smell of cigarettes; **3** to feel; **je ne sens rien** I can't feel anything; **on sent que l'hiver s'approche** you can feel it will soon be winter; **je sens qu'elle est sincère** I feel she's sincere; **4 se sentir** to feel; **je ne me sens pas bien** I don't feel well; ★ **je ne peux pas le sentir!** I can't stand him!

séparé adjective **1** separated; **mes parents sont séparés** my parents are separated; **2** separate; **dans une chambre séparée** in a separate bedroom.

séparément adverb separately.

séparer verb [1] **1** to separate; **séparez les œufs** separate the eggs; **séparer les filles des garçons** to separate the girls from the boys; **2 se séparer** to separate, to split up; **mes parents se sont séparés** my parents have separated.

sept number seven; **Yasmin a sept ans** Yasmin's seven; **il est sept heures** it's seven o'clock; **le sept mars** the seventh of March.

septante number seventy (used in Belgium and Switzerland, instead of soixante-dix); **septante-sept** seventy-seven.

a b c d e f g h i j k l m n o p q r s t u v w x y z

septembre noun Masc.
September; **en septembre, au
mois de septembre** in September.

septième noun Masc. **au
septième** on the seventh floor.

septième adjective seventh.

sera, serai, seras, serez verb
SEE **être**[1].

série noun Fem. series.

sérieusement adverb seriously.

sérieux noun **prendre quelque
chose au sérieux** to take
something seriously.

sérieux (Fem. **sérieuse**) adjective
1 serious; **vraiment? tu es
sérieux?** really? are you serious?;
2 responsible; **Camilla est une
jeune fille sérieuse** Camilla is a
responsible young woman;
3 reliable; **il n'est pas sérieux** he's
unreliable; 4 **un travail sérieux** a
careful piece of work; ★ **garder son
sérieux** to keep a straight face.

serin noun Masc. canary.

seringue noun Fem. syringe.

séronégatif (Fem. **séronégative**)
adjective HIV-negative.

serons, seront verb SEE **être**[1].

séropositif (Fem. **séropositive**)
adjective HIV-positive.

serpent noun Masc. snake.

serpillière noun Fem. floorcloth.

serre noun Fem. greenhouse; **l'effet
de serre** the greenhouse effect.

serré adjective 1 tight; **ma jupe est
trop serrée** my skirt's too tight; **un
budget serré** a tight budget;
2 close (match or competition).

serrer verb [1] 1 to grip; **elle
serrait le volant** she gripped the
steering wheel; **il m'a serrée dans
ses bras** he hugged me; 2 **serrer la
main à quelqu'un** to shake
somebody's hand; **nous nous
sommes serré la main** we shook
hands; 3 **serrer quelqu'un dans
ses bras** to hug somebody;
4 **serrer les poings** to clench your
fists; 5 to tighten (a screw or belt);
6 to be too tight; **mes chaussures
me serrent** my shoes are too tight;
7 to push closer together; **serrez
les tables** move the tables closer
together; 8 **se serrer** to squeeze up;
serrez-vous un peu! squeeze up a
bit!

serrure noun Fem. lock.

serveur noun Masc., **serveuse** noun Masc.,
Fem. waiter, waitress.

service noun Masc. 1 favour; **peux-
tu me rendre un petit service?**
could you do me a small favour?;
2 service (bus, train); **service de
dimanche** Sunday service; 3 **être
en service** to be working; **il n'y a
qu'un ascenseur en service**
there's only one lift working; **être
hors service** to be out of order;
l'ascenseur est hors service the
lift is out of order; 4 duty, service;
la pharmacie de service the duty
chemist; **je suis de service ce soir**
I am on duty this evening; **le
service militaire** national service;
5 service (charge); **le service est
compris** service is included;
6 department (in a town hall or
hospital, for example); **le service
des urgences** the casualty
department.

service après-vente noun
Masc. after-sales service.

service clientèle noun Masc. customer services.

serviette noun Fem. **1** towel; **une serviette de bain** a bath towel; **2** napkin; **3** briefcase.

serviette hygiénique noun Fem. sanitary towel.

servir verb [71] **1** to serve (in a shop, for example); **merci, on me sert** thank you, I'm being served; **2** to serve (with food or drink); **est-ce que je peux vous servir du poulet?** can I give you some chicken?; **'servir frais'** 'serve chilled'; **3 se servir** to help yourself; **sers-toi de riz** help yourself to rice; **4 se servir de** to use; **est-ce que tu sais te servir d'une machine à coudre?** do you know how to use a sewing machine?; **5** to serve (in tennis or in the army); **à toi de servir!** your service!; **6 servir à** to be used for; **à quoi ça sert?** what's it for?; **ça ne sert à rien!** it's no use!; **ça ne sert à rien de pleurer** there's no point in crying; **7 se servir** to be served (food or drink); **ce vin se sert frais** this wine should be served chilled.

ses adjective SEE **son**.

set de table noun Masc. place mat.

seul adjective **1** only; **la seule personne** the only person; **c'est le seul Anglais que je connaisse** he's the only English person I know; **j'étais le seul à aimer le film** I was the only one who liked the film; **2** alone; **il ne faut pas y aller seul** you mustn't go there alone; **j'étais tout seul à la maison** I was all alone in the house; **3 se**

sentir seul to feel lonely; **4 tout seul** all by yourself; **il l'a fait tout seul** he did it all by himself; **Sophie sait s'habiller toute seule maintenant** Sophie can get dressed all by herself now.

seulement adverb **1** only; **trois fois seulement** only three times; **2 non seulement …mais** not only …but; **non seulement elle n'est pas venue, mais elle n'a même pas appelé** not only did she not come, but she didn't even phone; **3 si seulement je l'avais su** if only I'd known.

sévère adjective strict.

sexe noun Masc. **1** sex; **2** genitals.

sexuel (Fem. **sexuelle**) adjective **1** sexual; **2 l'éducation sexuelle** sex education.

shampooing noun Masc. shampoo.

short noun Masc. (pair of) shorts; **où est mon short?** where are my shorts?; **trois shorts** three pairs of shorts.

si, s' (before 'il' or 'ils') conjunction if; **si tu veux** if you like; **s'il pleut** if it rains.

si adverb **1** so; **je suis si fatigué!** I'm so tired!; **tu chantes si bien!** you sing so well!; **2** yes (when you are contradicting somebody); **'tu ne viens pas avec nous?' –'si!'** 'you're not coming with us?' – 'yes I am!'; **'il ne reste pas manger' – 'mais si!'** 'he's not staying for a meal' – 'of course he is!'; **elle ne les aime pas du tout, moi si** she doesn't like them at all, but I do.

Sicile noun Fem. Sicily.

sida noun Masc. SHORT FOR **syndrome immuno-déficitaire acquis** AIDS; **avoir le sida** to have AIDS.

siècle noun Masc. century; **au vingtième siècle** in the twentieth century.

siège noun Masc. **1** seat; **le siège d'avant** the front seat; **2** head office (of a company); **3** siege (in war).

sien, sienne, siens, siennes pronoun **le sien, la sienne, les siens, les siennes 1** his; **j'ai prêté mon vélo à Paul, le sien est chez lui** I've lent Paul my bike, his is at home; **'est-ce que ces chaussures sont à Bernard?' – 'oui, ce sont les siennes'** 'are these shoes Bernard's?' – 'yes, they're his'; **2** hers; **j'ai prêté mon vélo à Annie, le sien est chez elle** I've lent Annie my bike, hers is at home; **'est-ce que ces chaussures sont à Nathalie?' – 'oui, ce sont les siennes'** 'are these shoes Nathalie's?' – 'yes, they're hers'.

sieste noun Fem. nap; **faire la sieste** to have a nap.

siffler verb [1] to whistle.

sifflet noun Masc. whistle.

signal (plural **signaux**) noun Masc. signal.

signaler verb [1] **1** to point out; **je vous signale que je serai absent ce jour-là** I'd like to point out that I shall be away that day; **2** to report; **3** to indicate (roadworks or danger; for example).

signalisation noun Fem. signalling, signals.

signalisation routière noun Fem. road signs and markings.

signature noun Fem. signature; **je vous demande une petite signature** just sign here, would you?

signe noun Masc. sign; **c'est bon/ mauvais signe** it's a good/bad sign; **faire signe à quelqu'un** to wave to someone; **il m'a fait signe de m'approcher** he beckoned me over to him; **d'un signe de main elle a montré la sortie** she pointed to the exit; **de quel signe êtes-vous?** what star sign are you?

signe astrologique noun Masc. star sign.

signer verb [1] **1** to sign; **2 se signer** to cross oneself.

signification noun Fem. meaning.

signifier verb [1] to mean.

silence noun Masc. silence; **en silence** in silence.

silencieux (Fem. **silencieuse**) adjective silent.

silhouette noun Fem. **1** silhouette, outline; **2** figure.

similarité noun Fem. similarity.

simple noun Masc. **le simple messieurs/dames** the men's/ women's singles (in tennis).

simple adjective simple; **un repas simple** a simple meal; **un simple coup de téléphone** just one telephone call.

simplement adverb simply.

simplicité noun Fem. simplicity.

simplifier verb [1] to simplify.

simuler verb [1] to simulate.

simultané adjective simultaneous.

sincère adjective sincere.

sincérité noun Fem. sincerity.

singe noun Masc. monkey; **un grand singe** an ape.

singulier noun Masc. singular; **au singulier** in the singular.

sinistre noun Masc. accident, disaster (for example, a fire or flood).

sinistre adjective **1** sinister; **2** gloomy.

sinistré, sinistrée noun Masc., Fem. disaster victim.

sinistrée adjective stricken; **de l'aide pour les familles sinistrées** help for the families stricken by the disaster.

sinon conjunction otherwise; **il faut partir, sinon on sera en retard** we must leave, otherwise we'll be late.

sirène noun Fem. **1** siren; **une sirène d'alarme** a fire alarm; **2** mermaid.

sirop noun Masc. **1** syrup; **sirop pectoral** cough mixture; **2** sirop de menthe mint cordial.

site noun Masc. site, area; **site touristique** place of interest (to visit); **site classé** conservation area.

site internet noun Masc. web site.

sitôt adverb as soon as; **sitôt rentrée, elle s'est couchée** as soon as she got home, she went to bed; **sitôt après** immediately afterwards; * **sitôt dit, sitôt fait** no sooner said than done.

situation noun Fem. **1** situation; **2** job; **il a perdu sa situation** he's lost his job.

situer verb [1] **1 être situé** to be situated; **l'hôtel est situé au bord** de la mer the hotel is situated by the sea; **bien situé** well situated; **2 se situer** to be situated; **la maison se situe dans un quartier résidentiel** the house is in a residential area; **3 se situer** to be set; **le roman se situe à Moscou** the novel is set in Moscow.

six number six; **Rosie a six ans** Rosie's six; **il est six heures** it's six o'clock; **le six juillet** the sixth of July.

sixième noun Fem. (in a French school) the equivalent of Year 7.

sixième noun Masc. **au sixième** on the sixth floor.

sixième adjective sixth.

skate noun Masc. **1** skate-boarding; **2** skate-board.

ski noun Masc. **1** ski; **où sont mes skis?** where are my skis?; **2** skiing; **il adore le ski** he loves skiing; **on va faire du ski ce week-end** we're going skiing this weekend.

ski de fond noun Masc. cross-country skiing.

ski de piste noun Masc. downhill skiing.

skier verb [1] to ski; **il skie plutôt bien** he skis pretty well; **skier hors piste** to ski off-piste.

skieur, skieuse noun Masc., Fem. skier.

ski nautique noun Masc. water-skiing.

slip noun Masc. **1** underpants; **2** knickers.

Slovaquie noun Fem. Slovakia.

Slovénie noun Fem. Slovenia.

SMIC noun Masc. SHORT FOR **Salaire minimum interprofessionnel de croissance** guaranteed minimum wage; **elle touche le SMIC** she's on the legal minimum wage.

smoking noun Masc. dinner jacket.

snack noun Masc. snack bar.

SNCF noun Fem. SHORT FOR **Société nationale des chemins de fer français** (French national railways).

snob noun Masc. & Fem. snob.

snob adjective snobbish (of a person), posh (of a restaurant).

sobre adjective sober.

sociable adjective friendly, sociable.

social (Masc. plural **sociaux**) adjective social.

socialiste noun Masc., Fem., adjective socialist.

société noun Fem. **1** society; **dans notre société** in our society; **2** company; **il travaille pour une grande société** he works for a big company.

société anonyme noun Fem. public company.

sociologie noun Fem. sociology.

socquette noun Fem. ankle sock.

sœur noun Fem. sister; **ma grande sœur** my big sister, my older sister.

soi pronoun **1** one, oneself; **des amis autour de soi** friends around one; **2 avoir confiance en soi** to have confidence in oneself; **3** itself; **pas très intéressant en soi** not very interesting in itself; **cela va de soi** that goes without saying.

soi-disant adjective **1** so-called; **c'est le soi-disant champion** he's the so-called champion; **2** supposedly; **elle est soi-disant malade** she's supposedly ill.

soie noun Fem. silk; **un foulard en soie** a silk scarf; **le papier de soie** tissue paper.

soif noun Masc. thirst; **avoir soif** to be thirsty.

soigner verb [1] to look after.

soigneusement adverb carefully.

soi-même pronoun yourself, oneself; **il faut le faire soi-même** you have to do it yourself.

soin noun Masc. **1** care; **2 prendre soin de quelque chose** to take care of something; **3 les soins** treatment; **4 les premiers soins** first aid.

soir noun Masc. evening, night; **ce soir** tonight; **hier soir** last night; **demain soir** tomorrow night; **je sors tous les samedis soirs** I go out every Saturday night; **par un beau soir d'été** one fine summer's evening; **à six heures du soir** at six in the evening; **à ce soir!** see you tonight!

soirée noun Fem. **1** evening; **pendant la soirée** during the evening; **2** party; **elle donne une petite soirée** she's having a little party; **3 en tenue de soirée** in evening dress.

soirée dansante noun Fem. dance.

sois verb SEE **être**[1]; **sois gentil** be good.

soit *conjunction* **soit ...soit** either ...or; **soit demain, soit jeudi** either tomorrow or Thursday.

soixantaine *noun Fem.* **1** about sixty; **une soixantaine de personnes** about sixty people; **2 avoir la soixantaine** to be in your sixties.

soixante *number* sixty.

soixante-dix *number* seventy; **soixante-dix-huit** seventy-eight.

soja *noun Masc.* soya bean; **la sauce de soja** soy sauce.

sol *noun Masc.* **1** floor; **2** soil.

solaire *adjective* **1** solar; **2 la crème solaire** sun cream.

soldat *noun Masc.* soldier.

solde *noun Masc.* **1 les soldes** the sales; **faire les soldes** to go round the sales; **2 être en solde** to be reduced; **les pulls sont en solde** the jumpers are reduced; **3** balance *(in a bank account)*.

soldé *adjective* reduced.

sole *noun Fem.* sole *(fish)*.

soleil *noun Masc.* sun; **au soleil** in the sun; **il fait soleil** it's sunny; **en plein soleil** in full sun; **attraper un coup de soleil** to get sunburnt.

solfège *noun Masc.* musical theory.

solide *adjective* **1** strong; **2** solid.

soliste *noun Masc. & Fem.* soloist.

solitaire *adjective* **1** lonely, isolated; **2 un navigateur solitaire** a solo yachtsman.

solitude *noun Fem.* **1** loneliness; **2** solitude.

solution *noun Fem.* solution.

sombre *adjective* dark, gloomy.

somme[1] *noun Fem.* sum; **une somme d'argent** a sum of money.

somme[2] *noun Masc.* nap; **faire un somme** to have a nap.

sommeil *noun Masc.* sleep; **avoir sommeil** to feel sleepy; **je n'ai plus sommeil** I'm not sleepy any more.

sommes *verb* SEE **être**[1].

sommet *noun Masc.* summit.

somnambule *noun Masc. & Fem.* sleepwalker; **être somnambule** to walk in your sleep.

son[1], **sa, ses** *adjective* **1** his; **son fils** his son; **sa fille** his daughter; **ses enfants** his children; **2** her; **son fils** her son; **sa fille** her daughter; **ses enfants** her children; **3** its; **le chat a perdu son collier** the cat's lost its collar.

son[2] *noun Masc.* **1** sound; **le son d'un piano** the sound of a piano; **2** volume *(on a radio or hi-fi)*; **baisser le son** to turn the volume down; **3** bran.

sondage *noun Masc.* survey; **un sondage d'opinion** an opinion poll.

sonner *verb* [1] to ring; **le téléphone sonne** the phone's ringing; **on sonne à la porte** somebody's ringing the doorbell.

sonnerie *noun Fem.* bell; **la sonnerie d'alarme** the alarm bell; **la sonnerie du téléphone** the ring of the telephone.

sonnette *noun Fem.* bell, doorbell.

sono *noun Fem.* *(informal)* sound system.

Sonotone™ *noun Masc.* hearing aid.

a b c d e f g h i j k l m n o p q r s t u v w x y z

a **sophistiqué** adjective
sophisticated.

b **sorbet** noun Masc. sorbet; **un sorbet au cassis** a blackcurrant sorbet.

c **sorcière** noun Fem. witch.

d **sort** noun Masc. fate; ★ **tirer au sort** to draw lots.

e **sorte** noun Fem. sort; **c'est une sorte de poudre** it's a sort of powder; **toutes sortes d'activités** all sorts of activities.

f **sortie** noun Fem. 1 exit; **il nous attend à la sortie** he's waiting for us at the exit; **sortie de secours** emergency exit; 2 outing; 3 launch (of a new product), release (of a film), publication (of a book).

g **sortir** verb [72] 1 to go out; **tout le monde est sorti dans la rue** everybody went out into the street; **ils sont sortis déjeuner** they've gone out for lunch; **elle est sortie en courant** she ran out; 2 to come out; **c'est l'heure où les gens sortent du cinéma** it's the time when people are coming out of the cinema; **son nouveau film sortira en mai** her new film is coming out in May; 3 to go out (for pleasure); **mes parents sortent peu** my parents don't go out much; 4 **sortir avec** to be going out with; **il sort avec ma sœur** he's going out with my sister; 5 to take out; **elle a sorti une bouteille du frigo** she took a bottle out of the fridge; **j'ai oublié de sortir le chien** I forgot to take the dog out; 6 **s'en sortir** to manage; **je m'en sortirai d'une manière ou d'une autre** I'll manage one way or another.

sottise noun Fem. 1 silliness; 2 **dire des sottises** to talk nonsense; **ne fais pas de sottises** don't do anything silly.

sou noun Masc. **j'ai dépensé tous mes sous** I've spent all my money; **je n'ai pas un sou** I'm broke; **une machine à sous** a fruit machine; ★ **être près de ses sous** to be tight-fisted.

souci noun Masc. 1 worry; **se faire du souci** to worry; **mon fils me donne bien des soucis** my son's a great worry to me; **j'ai d'autres soucis à présent** I've got other problems just now; 2 marigold.

soucieux (Fem. **soucieuse**) adjective worried.

soucoupe noun Fem. saucer.

soudain adjective sudden.

soudain adverb suddenly.

souffle noun Masc. breath; **être à bout de souffle** to be out of breath; **couper le souffle à quelqu'un** to take someone's breath away.

soufflé noun Masc. soufflé; **un soufflé au fromage** a cheese soufflé.

souffler verb [1] 1 to blow; **le vent soufflait fort** there was a strong wind; 2 to blow out (a candle); 3 to whisper; **elle me soufflait quelque chose à l'oreille** she was whispering something in my ear; ★ **souffler dans le ballon** (informal) to be breathalysed.

souffrance noun Fem. 1 suffering; 2 misery.

souffrir verb [73] 1 to suffer; **a-t-elle beaucoup souffert?** did she suffer much?; **il souffre souvent**

du dos he often has back pain; **2 je ne peux pas le souffrir!** (*informal*) I can't stand him!

souhait *noun Masc.* wish; **★ à tes souhaits!** bless you! (*when somebody sneezes*).

souhaiter *verb* [1] to wish; **je te souhaite bonne chance** I wish you luck; **il nous a souhaité la bienvenue** he welcomed us; **il souhaite se marier** he'd like to get married.

soûl *adjective* drunk.

soulagé *adjective* relieved.

soulagement *noun Masc.* relief.

soulager *verb* [52] to relieve.

soulever *verb* [50] **1** to lift; **je n'arrive pas à soulever ta valise** I can't lift your case; **2** to raise (*problems, objections, or difficulties*); **personne n'a soulevé la question** nobody raised the question.

soulier *noun Masc.* shoe.

souligner *verb* [1] **1** to underline; **2** to emphasize.

soupçon *noun Masc.* **1** suspicion; **2** spot, drop (*of food or drink*); **juste un soupçon de lait** just a drop of milk.

soupçonner *verb* [1] to suspect.

soupe *noun Fem.* soup; **la soupe aux oignons** onion soup.

souper *verb* [1] to have supper.

soupir *noun Masc.* sigh.

soupirer *verb* [1] to sigh.

souple *adjective* **1** supple (*person*); **2** flexible (*system*); **3** soft (*hair or clean washing*).

source *noun Fem.* spring; **l'eau de source** spring water.

sourcil *noun Masc.* eyebrow.

sourd *adjective* **1** deaf; **2** dull, muffled (*noise*); **★ faire la sourde oreille** to turn a deaf ear.

souriant *adjective* cheerful.

sourire *noun Masc.* smile; **il faut garder le sourire** you must keep smiling.

sourire *verb* [68] to smile; **sourire à quelqu'un** to smile at somebody.

souris *noun Fem.* mouse (*also for a computer*).

sous *preposition* under, underneath; **sous la chaise** under the chair; **sortir sous la pluie** to go out in the rain; **sous terre** underground; **★ sous peu** before long.

sous-entendu *noun Masc.* innuendo.

sous-entendu *adjective* implied.

sous-estimer *verb* [1] to underestimate.

sous-marin *noun Masc.* submarine.

sous-marin *adjective* under-water, deep-sea.

sous-sol *noun Masc.* basement; **au sous-sol** in the basement.

sous-tasse *noun Fem.* saucer.

sous-titre *noun Masc.* subtitle.

soustraction *noun Fem.* subtraction.

sous-vêtements *plural noun Masc.* underwear.

soutenir *verb* [77] **1** to support; **elle m'a soutenu à la réunion** she supported me at the meeting;

a b c d e f g h i j k l m n o p q r s t u v w x y z

2 soutenir que to maintain that; **3 soutenir une conversation** to keep up a conversation; **4** to withstand (*a shock or attack*).

souterrain *adjective* underground.

soutien *noun Masc.* support.

soutien-gorge *noun Masc.* bra.

soutif *noun Masc.* (*informal*) bra.

souvenir *noun Masc.* **1** memory; **mes souvenirs de Londres** my memories of London; **garder un bon souvenir de quelque chose** to have happy memories of something; **je n'ai aucun souvenir de l'avoir rencontrée** I have no memory of meeting her; **2** souvenir.

souvenir *verb* [81] **se souvenir de** to remember; **je me souviens d'elle** I remember her; **je me souviens de l'avoir rencontrée** I remember meeting her; **t'en souviens-tu?** do you remember that?

souvent *adverb* often; **je ne la vois pas très souvent** I don't see her very often; **le plus souvent** more often than not.

spacieux (*Fem.* **spacieuse**) *adjective* spacious.

spaghettis *plural noun Masc.* spaghetti; **manger des spaghettis** to have spaghetti.

sparadrap *noun Masc.* sticking plaster.

speaker, speakerine *noun Masc., Fem.* announcer.

spécial (*Masc. plural* **spéciaux**) *adjective* **1** special; **rien de spécial** nothing special; **les effets spéciaux** special effects; **2** odd; **il est vraiment très spécial** he's really very odd.

spécialement *adverb* specially.

spécialiser *verb* [1] **se spécialiser** to specialize; **elle se spécialise dans la génétique** she's specializing in genetics.

spécialiste *noun Masc. & Fem.* specialist.

spécialité *noun Fem.* speciality.

spécifier *verb* [1] to specify.

spectacle *noun Masc.* show.

spectaculaire *adjective* spectacular.

spectateur, spectatrice *noun Masc., Fem.* **1** member of the audience; **2** spectator.

spéléologie *noun Fem.* potholing.

spirituel, spirituelle *adjective* **1** witty; **2** spiritual.

splendeur *noun Fem.* splendour.

splendide *adjective* magnificent.

sponsoriser *verb* [1] to sponsor.

spontané *adjective* spontaneous.

sport *noun Masc.* sport, sports; **aimez-vous le sport?** do you like sport?; **il fait beaucoup de sport** he does a lot of sport; **mon maillot de sport** my sports shirt; **les sports d'hiver** winter sports; **être bon en sport** to be good at sports.

sportif, sportive *noun Masc., Fem.* sportsman, sportswoman.

sportif (*Fem.* **sportive**) *adjective* **1** sports; **un club sportif** a sports club; **une rencontre sportive** a sports meeting; **2** sporty, athletic.

spot *noun Masc.* **1** spotlight; **2 un spot publicitaire** a commercial.

square noun Masc. public garden.

squelette noun Masc. skeleton.

stable adjective 1 stable; 2 **un emploi stable** a steady job.

stade noun Masc. stadium.

stage noun Masc. 1 course; **un stage intensif d'anglais** an intensive English course; **faire un stage de formation** to go on a training course; **2 un stage professionnel** work experience; **j'aimerais faire un stage professionnel dans une société française** I'd like to do work experience in a French company.

stagiaire noun Masc. & Fem. 1 trainee; 2 person on a work experience placement.

stand noun Masc. 1 stand (in a market or an exhibition); 2 stall (in a fairground).

standard noun Masc. switchboard; **il faut passer par le standard** you have to go through the switchboard.

standardiste noun Masc. & Fem. switchboard operator.

standing noun Masc. **un appartement de standing** a luxury flat.

star noun Fem. star (in a film or show).

starter noun Masc. choke (in a car).

station noun Fem. 1 **une station de métro** an underground station; 2 **une station de taxis** a taxi rank; 3 resort; **une station de ski** a ski resort; 4 **une station de radio** a radio station.

station de travail noun Fem. (computer) work station.

stationnaire adjective 1 stationary; 2 stable.

stationnement noun Masc. parking; **'stationnement interdit'** 'no parking'.

stationner verb [1] to park.

station-service noun Fem. service station.

statistique noun Fem. statistic(s).

statue noun Fem. statue.

statut noun Masc. 1 statute; 2 status.

steak noun Masc. steak; **un steak frites** steak and chips; **un steak haché** a burger steak.

sténodactylo noun Masc. & Fem. shorthand typist.

stéréo noun Fem., adjective stereo.

stérile adjective sterile.

stériliser verb [1] to sterilize.

steward noun Masc. flight attendant (male).

stimulant adjective stimulating.

stock noun Masc. stock; **en stock** in stock.

stop noun Masc. 1 stop sign; 2 **faire du stop** to hitch-hike.

stopper verb [1] to stop.

store noun Masc. 1 blind; 2 awning.

strapontin noun Masc. fold-down seat.

stratégie noun Fem. strategy.

stratégique adjective strategic.

stress noun Masc. stress.

stressant adjective stressful.

stressé adjective stressed; **elle avait l'air stressé** she looked

a b c d e f g h i j k l m n o p q r s t u v w x y z

stressed; **je suis très stressé en ce moment** I'm stressed out at the moment.

strict adjective **1** strict; **2** severe.

studieux (Fem. **studieuse**) adjective studious.

studio noun Masc. **1** studio flat; **2** studio.

stupéfait adjective astounded.

stupéfiants plural noun Masc. narcotics.

stupeur noun Fem. astonishment.

stupide adjective stupid.

stupidité noun Fem. stupidity.

style noun Masc. style; **c'est bien son style!** that's just like him!

styliste noun Masc. & Fem. designer.

stylo noun Masc. fountain pen.

stylo-bille noun Masc. ball-point pen.

stylo-feutre noun Masc. felt pen.

stylo-plume noun Masc. fountain pen.

su verb SEE **savoir**[1].

subir verb [2] **1** to be subjected to (change, violence, or pressure); **2** to suffer (defeat or damage); **3** **subir une opération** to have an operation.

subitement adverb suddenly.

subjonctif noun Masc. subjunctive; **au subjonctif** in the subjunctive.

subordonné, subordonnée noun Masc., Fem. subordinate.

substituer verb [1] to substitute.

subtil adjective subtle.

subvention noun Fem. subsidy.

succès noun Masc. success; **c'est un grand succès!** it's a great success!

succursale noun Fem. branch (of a company).

sucer verb [61] to suck.

sucette noun Fem. lollipop.

sucre noun Masc. **1** sugar; **du jus d'orange sans sucre** unsweetened orange juice; **2** **un sucre** a lump of sugar.

sucré adjective sweet; **c'est trop sucré pour moi** it's too sweet for me.

sucre cristallisé noun Masc. granulated sugar.

sucre d'orge noun Masc. barley sugar.

sucre en morceaux noun Masc. sugar lumps.

sucre en poudre noun Masc. caster sugar.

sucre glace noun Masc. icing sugar.

sucrerie noun Fem. **des sucreries** sweet things.

sucre roux noun Masc. brown sugar.

sucrier noun Masc. sugar bowl.

sud noun Masc. south; **au sud de l'Écosse** in the south of Scotland; **au sud de Calais** south of Calais; **un vent du sud** a south wind.

sud adjective **1** south; **la côte sud** the south coast; **2** southern; **la partie sud** the southern part.

sud-africain *adjective* South African.

Sud-Africain, Sud-Africaine *noun Masc., Fem.* South African.

sud-américain *adjective* South American.

Sud-Américain, Sud-Américaine *noun Masc., Fem.* South American.

sud-est *noun Masc., adjective* south-east.

sud-ouest *noun Masc., adjective* south-west.

Suède *noun Fem.* Sweden.

suédois *noun Masc.* Swedish (*language*).

suédois *adjective* Swedish.

Suédois, Suédoise *noun Masc., Fem.* Swede.

suer *verb* [1] to sweat.

sueur *noun Fem.* sweat; **je suis en sueur** I'm sweating.

suffire *verb* [74] **1** to be enough; **un kilo suffit** one kilo's enough; **ça suffit!** that's enough!; **2 il suffit de faire** all you have to do is; **il suffit de nous téléphoner** all you have to do is give us a call.

suffisamment *adverb* enough; **ce n'est pas suffisamment cuit** it's not cooked enough; **il n'y a pas suffisamment de verres** there aren't enough glasses.

suffisant *adjective* **1** sufficient; **c'est bien suffisant!** that's quite enough!; **2** smug; **je la trouve un peu suffisante** I find her a bit smug.

suffoquer *verb* [1] to suffocate, to choke.

suggérer *verb* [24] to suggest.

suggestion *noun Fem.* suggestion.

suicider *verb* [1] **se suicider** to commit suicide.

suis *verb* SEE **être**[1]; SEE **suivre**.

suisse *adjective* Swiss.

Suisse *noun Fem.* Switzerland; **en Suisse** in (or to) Switzerland; **la Suisse romande** French-speaking Switzerland; **la Suisse allemande** German-speaking Switzerland.

suite *noun Fem.* **1** rest; **je te raconterai la suite plus tard** I'll tell you the rest later; **et on connaît la suite** and we all know what happened next; **2** continuation; **'suite page 67'** 'continued on page 67'; **regardez la suite jeudi** watch the next instalment on Thursday; **3** suite (*in a hotel*); **4** in succession; **trois fois de suite** three times in succession; **5 tout de suite** straightaway; **j'arrive tout de suite!** I'll be right there!; **6 par la suite** later; **on s'est rendu compte par la suite que c'était une erreur** we realized later that it was a mistake.

suivant, suivante *noun Masc., Fem.* next one; **pas ce lundi mais le suivant** not this Monday but the next.

suivant *adjective* following; **le jour suivant** the following day.

suivre *verb* [75] **1** to follow; **suivez-moi** follow me; **2 suivre l'actualité** to keep up with the news; **3 'à suivre'** 'to be continued'; **4 faire suivre son courrier** to have your mail forwarded; **5 suivre un cours**

a b c d e f g h i j k l m n o p q r s t u v w x y z

to do a course; **6** suivre un régime to be on a diet.

sujet noun Masc. **1** subject; **au sujet de** about; **c'est au sujet de votre fils** it's about your son; **c'est à quel sujet?** what's it about?; **un sujet de conversation** a topic of conversation; **2 un sujet d'examen** an exam question.

sujet adjective (Fem. **sujette**) **être sujet à** to suffer from; **elle est sujette à des crises d'asthme** she suffers from asthma attacks.

super noun Masc. four-star petrol.

super adjective (informal) fantastic; **mais c'est super!** but that's fantastic!

superficie noun Fem. area.

superficiel (Fem. **superficielle**) adjective superficial.

supérieur, supérieure noun Masc., Fem. superior.

supérieur adjective **1** upper; **l'étage supérieur** the upper floor; **la lèvre supérieure** the upper lip; **2** greater; **la taille supérieure** the bigger size; **à une vitesse supérieure** at a faster speed; **à une température supérieure** at a higher temperature; **un prix supérieur** a higher price; **3** better, superior (work, quality); **c'est de loin supérieur à l'autre!** it's much better than the other one!; **4 supérieur à** greater than; **un nombre supérieur à trois** a number higher than three.

superlatif noun Masc. superlative.

supermarché noun Masc. supermarket.

superposer verb [1] **1** to stack up; **des lits superposés** bunk beds; **2** to superimpose (an image).

superstitieux (Fem. **superstitieuse**) adjective superstitious.

superstition noun Fem. superstition.

supplément noun Masc. extra charge; **le vin est en supplément** wine is extra.

supplémentaire adjective **1** additional; **2 faire des heures supplémentaires** to do overtime.

supplice noun Masc. torture.

supplier verb [1] to beg.

support noun Masc. **1** support; **2** back-up (material); **un support audiovisuel** audiovisual aids.

supportable adjective bearable.

supporter verb [1] **1** to stand; **il ne supporte pas qu'on le critique** he can't stand being criticized; **je ne peux plus la supporter!** I can't stand any more of her!; **2** to support (a weight).

supposer verb [1] to suppose.

supprimer verb [1] **1** to get rid of; **2 supprimer des emplois** to cut jobs; **supprimer un train** to cancel a train.

sur preposition **1** on; **c'est sur ton lit** it's on your bed; **un débat sur le racisme** a discussion on racism; **le cinéma est sur la droite** the cinema's on the right; **2** over; **un pont sur la Loire** a bridge over the Loire; **3** by (in measurements); **c'est deux mètres sur trois** it's two metres by three; **4** out of; **trois femmes sur cinq** three women out of five; **5** out of; **j'ai eu douze sur vingt en géographie** I got twelve out of twenty in geography.

sûr *adjective* **1** sure; **tu es sûr?** are you sure?; **oui, bien sûr!** yes, of course!; **sûr et certain** certain; **j'en étais sûr!** I knew it!; **2 sûr de soi, de lui, d'elle** (*etc*) self-confident; **elle est très sûre d'elle** she's very self-confident; **3** safe; **en lieu sûr** in a safe place; **le plus sûr est de tout fermer à clé** the safest thing is to lock everything.

surcharger *verb* [52] to overload.

surdité *noun Fem.* deafness.

surdose *noun Fem.* overdose (*of medicine*).

sûrement *adverb* **1** certainly; **sûrement pas!** certainly not!; **2 il doit sûrement arriver à tout instant** he's bound to arrive at any moment; **elle est sûrement partie** she's bound to have left.

sûreté *noun Fem.* safety, security.

surf *noun Masc.* surfing; **faire du surf** to go surfing.

surface *noun Fem.* **1** surface; **2** area; **3 une grande surface** a hypermarket.

surface de réparation *noun Fem.* penalty area.

surf des neiges *noun Masc.* snowboarding; **faire du surf des neiges** to go snowboarding.

surfer *verb* [1] **surfer Internet/le web** to surf the Net/Web.

surfeur, surfeuse *noun Masc., Fem.* surfer (*on the sea*).

surgelé *noun Masc.* **les surgelés** frozen food.

surgelé *adjective* frozen; **les légumes surgelés** frozen vegetables.

sur-le-champ *adverb* right away.

surlendemain *noun Masc.* **elle est arrivée le surlendemain** she arrived two days later.

surmonter *verb* [1] to overcome.

surnaturel (*Fem.* **surnaturelle**) *adjective* supernatural.

surnom *noun Masc.* nickname.

surnommer *verb* [1] to nickname.

surpeuplé *adjective* overpopulated.

surprenant *adjective* surprising.

surprendre *verb* [64] **1** to surprise; **ça m'a beaucoup surpris** I found that really surprising; **2 surprendre quelqu'un en train de faire quelque chose** to catch somebody doing something; **je l'ai surprise en train de lire mon courrier** I caught her reading my mail.

surpris *adjective* surprised; **je suis surpris de te voir** I'm surprised to see you.

surprise *noun Fem.* surprise; **quelle surprise!** what a surprise!; **à ma grande surprise elle a accepté** to my great surprise she agreed; **faire une surprise à quelqu'un** to give somebody a surprise.

surréaliste *noun Masc. & Fem.* surrealist.

surréaliste *adjective* surreal.

surtout *adverb* **1** especially; **il y a beaucoup de touristes, surtout en été** there are lots of tourists, especially in the summer; **2** above

a
b
c
d
e
f
g
h
i
j
k
l
m
n
o
p
q
r
s
t
u
v
w
x
y
z

surveillant, see below.

surveillant, surveillante noun Masc., Fem. supervisor (in a school, responsible for maintaining school discipline outside the classroom).

surveiller verb [1] **1** to watch, to keep an eye on; **est-ce que tu peux surveiller mon sac deux secondes?** can you keep an eye on my bag for a couple of minutes?; **2 surveiller une maison** to keep a house under surveillance; **3** to supervise; **surveiller le travail des élèves** to supervise the students' work (work or progress); **4 surveiller un examen** to invigilate an exam; **5 je surveille ma ligne** I'm watching my figure.

survêtement noun Masc. tracksuit.

survie noun Fem. survival.

survivant, survivante noun Masc., Fem. survivor.

survivre verb [82] to survive; **survivre à un accident** to survive an accident.

survoler verb [1] to fly over.

suspect, suspecte noun Masc., Fem. suspect.

suspect adjective suspicious.

suspense noun Masc. suspense (as in a thriller).

suture noun Fem. **un point de suture** a stitch (in a wound).

svelte adjective slender.

SVP SHORT FOR **s'il vous plaît** please.

sweat noun Masc. SEE **sweatshirt**.

sweatshirt noun Masc. sweatshirt.

syllabe noun Fem. syllable.

symbole noun Masc. symbol.

symbolique adjective symbolic; **un geste symbolique** a token gesture.

sympa adjective (informal) nice; **je le trouve très sympa, ton copain** he's really nice, your boyfriend.

sympathie noun Fem. **j'ai beaucoup de sympathie pour elle** I like her a lot.

sympathique adjective nice; **c'est un type sympathique** he's a nice guy.

sympathiser verb [1] **sympathiser avec quelqu'un** to get on well with someone.

symptôme noun Masc. symptom.

synagogue noun Fem. synagogue.

syndicat noun Masc. trade union.

syndicat d'initiative noun Masc. tourist information office.

synthétique adjective synthetic.

synthétiseur noun Masc. synthesizer.

système noun Masc. system; **un système d'éclairage** a lighting system.

Tt

ta adjective SEE **ton**[1].

tabac noun Masc. **1** tobacco; **2 un bureau de tabac** a tobacconist's.

tabagisme noun Masc. addiction to tobacco.

table noun Fem. table; **à table!** dinner's ready!; **se mettre à table**

to sit down to eat; **mettre la table** to lay the table.

tableau noun Masc. **1** painting; **un tableau de Renoir** a painting by Renoir; **2 le tableau noir** the blackboard; **3 le tableau d'affichage** the notice board.

tableau de bord noun Masc. dashboard.

table de chevet, table de nuit noun Fem. bedside table.

table des matières noun Fem. (list of) contents (in a book).

tablette noun Fem. **une tablette de chocolat** a bar of chocolate.

tablier noun Masc. apron.

tabouret noun Masc. stool.

tache noun Fem. **1** stain; **2** spot.

tâche noun Fem. task.

tache de rousseur noun Fem. freckle.

tacher verb [1] to stain.

tacle noun Masc. tackle (in rugby).

tact noun Masc. tact; **il l'a fait avec beaucoup de tact** he did it very tactfully.

tactique noun Fem. tactics.

tactique adjective tactical.

tagueur noun Masc. graffiti artist.

taie noun Fem. **une taie d'oreiller** a pillowcase.

taille noun Fem. **1** size; **qu'est-ce que vous avez à ma taille?** what have you got in my size?; **quelle taille faites-vous?** what size are you?; **'taille unique'** 'one size'; **la taille au-dessus/au-dessous** the next size up/down; **2** height; **un homme de grande taille** a tall man;

3 waist; **avoir la taille fine** to have a slim waist.

taille-crayon noun Masc. pencil sharpener.

tailler verb [1] **1** to cut; **2** to carve; **3** to prune; **4** to sharpen (a pencil).

tailleur noun Masc. **1** suit (for a woman); **2** tailor; ★ **s'asseoir en tailleur** to sit cross-legged (literally: like a tailor).

taire verb [76] **se taire** to stop talking; **taisez-vous!** be quiet!

talent noun Masc. talent; **c'est un jeune musicien de talent** he's a talented young musician.

talon noun Masc. **1** heel (of your foot or a shoe); **2** stub (of a ticket or cheque book).

talon aiguille noun Masc. stiletto heel.

tambour noun Masc. drum.

tambourin noun Masc. tambourine.

Tamise noun Fem. **la Tamise** the Thames.

tampon noun Masc. **1** pad (for sponging); **un tampon à récurer** a scouring pad; **2 un tampon (hygiénique)** a tampon.

tamponneuse adjective **les autos tamponneuses** the dodgems.

tandis que conjunction while.

tant adverb **1** so much; **j'ai tant mangé que ...** I've eaten so much that ...; **ce qu'elle avait tant espéré** what she had so much hoped for; **je ne les aime pas tant que ça** I don't like them as much as that; **2 tant de** so much, so many; **tant d'argent**

a b c d e f g h i j k l m n o p q r s t u v w x y z

so much money; **tant d'amis** so many friends; **tant de monde** so many people; **3 tant pis** never mind; **4 tant mieux** so much the better; **5 tant que** while; **tant que tu y es, passe-moi un stylo** while you're there, pass me a pen; **6 tant que as long as; tant que Jacques ne sera pas rentré, je ne peux pas sortir** I can't go out until Jacques gets back.

tante noun Fem. aunt.

tantôt adverb sometimes; **tantôt chez elle, tantôt chez moi** sometimes at her place and sometimes at mine.

taper verb [1] **1 taper quelqu'un** to hit somebody; **ça tape aujourd'hui** the sun's really beating down today; **2 taper à la machine** to type; **taper une lettre** to type a letter; **3 taper des mains** to clap your hands; **4 taper à la porte** to knock on the door; **5** (informal) **se taper dessus** to knock each other about.

tapis noun Masc. carpet.

tapis de bain noun Masc. bathmat.

tapis roulant noun Masc. **1** walkway; **2** carousel (for airport luggage); **3** conveyor belt.

tapisser verb [1] **1** to wallpaper; **2** to upholster.

tapisserie noun Fem. **1** tapestry; **2** wallpaper.

taquiner verb [1] to tease.

tard adverb late; **couche-toi, il est tard** go to bed, it's late; **plus tard** later; **trop tard** too late; **pas plus tard que mardi** no later than

Tuesday; **ce sera pour plus tard** there'll be other times.

tarder verb [1] to be a long time; **ta mère ne va pas tarder** your mother won't be long.

tardif (Fem. **tardive**) adjective late.

tarif noun Masc. **1** rate; **tarif de nuit** night rate (for the phone); **2** fare; **plein tarif** full fare; **tarif réduit** reduced fare; **3** price list.

tarte noun Fem. tart; **une tarte aux abricots** an apricot tart.

tartine noun Fem. slice of bread and butter (and/or jam).

tartiner verb [1] to spread (on bread).

tas noun Masc. **1** pile; **un tas de bois** a pile of wood; **2** batch; **un tas de lettres** a batch of letters; **3** (informal) **un tas de** stacks of; **j'ai un tas de choses à faire ce soir** I've got stacks of things to do tonight.

tasse noun Fem. cup; **une tasse de thé** a cup of tea.

tatie noun Fem. (informal) auntie.

taupe noun Fem. mole (animal).

taupinière noun Fem. mole hill.

taureau (plural **taureaux**) noun Masc. bull.

Taureau noun Masc. Taurus (sign of the Zodiac).

taux noun Masc. rate; **le taux mensuel** the monthly rate; **le taux de change** the exchange rate.

taxe noun Fem. tax; **la boutique hors taxes** the duty-free shop.

taxi noun Masc. taxi; **appeler un taxi** to call a taxi.

tchèque *adjective* Czech; **la République tchèque** the Czech Republic.

te, t' (*before a vowel or silent 'h'*) *pronoun* you **1** Gaby te cherche Gaby's looking for you; **il t'a vu** he saw you; **il te l'a donné** he gave it to you; **2** to you; **3** yourself; **tu peux te faire une salade** you can make yourself a salad; **tu t'es blessé?** have you hurt yourself?; **tu te lèves quand?** what time do you get up?

technicien, technicienne *noun Masc., Fem.* technician.

technique *noun Fem.* technique.

technique *adjective* technical.

technologie *noun Fem.* technology.

teckel *noun Masc.* dachshund.

tee-shirt *noun Masc.* T-shirt.

teint *noun Masc.* complexion; **avoir le teint clair** to have a fair complexion.

teinturier, teinturière *noun Masc., Fem.* dry-cleaner's.

tel, telle *adjective* **1** such; **avec un tel intérêt** with such interest; **une telle aventure** such an adventure; **de tels mensonges** such lies; **2 tel que** such as; **les grandes villes telles que Paris et Lyon** large towns such as Paris and Lyons; **3 rien de tel que** nothing like; **il n'y a rien de tel qu'un bon repas** there's nothing like a good meal; **4 servir le saumon tel quel** serve the salmon just as it is; **je l'ai acheté tel quel** I bought it just as it was.

télé *noun Fem.* (*informal*) telly; **je l'ai vu à la télé** I saw it on telly.

télécabine *noun Masc.* cable car.

télécarte™ *noun Fem.* phonecard.

télécommande *noun Fem.* remote control.

télécopie *noun Fem.* fax.

télécopieur *noun Masc.* fax machine, fax.

téléphérique *noun Masc.* cable car.

téléphone *noun Masc.* telephone; **un numéro de téléphone** a phone number; **Bruno est au téléphone** Bruno's on the phone.

téléphone portable *noun Masc.* mobile phone.

téléphoner *verb* [1] to phone; **je vais téléphoner à Robert** I'll phone Robert.

téléphone sans fil *noun Masc.* cordless phone.

téléphonique *adjective* **une cabine téléphonique** a phone box; **un appel téléphonique** a phone call.

télésiège *noun Masc.* chairlift.

téléski *noun Masc.* ski-tow.

téléspectateur, téléspectatrice *noun Masc., Fem.* viewer (*of TV*).

téléviser *verb* [1] to televize.

téléviseur *noun Masc.* television (set); **un téléviseur couleur** a colour television.

télévision *noun Fem.* television; **à la télévision** on television.

telle *adjective* SEE **tel**.

a
b
c
d
e
f
g
h
i
j
k
l
m
n
o
p
q
r
s
t
u
v
w
x
y
z

a
b
c
d
e
f
g
h
i
j
k
l
m
n
o
p
q
r
s
t
u
v
w
x
y
z

tellement *adverb* **1** so; **c'est tellement compliqué!** it's so complicated!; **2** so much; **c'est tellement mieux payé** it's so much better paid; **'tu aimes lire?'** – **'pas tellement'** 'do you like reading?' – 'not much'; **3** tellement de so much, so many; **j'ai tellement de travail!** I've got so much work!; **il y a tellement de choses à voir!** there are so many things to see!; **il y avait tellement de monde** there were so many people there.

tels, **telles** *adjective* SEE **tel**.

témoignage *noun Masc.* **1** story, account; **selon les témoignages de l'accident** according to accounts of the accident; **2** evidence (*in court*); **3 un témoignage d'amitié** a token of friendship.

témoigner *verb* [1] to give evidence.

témoin *noun Masc.* witness.

température *noun Fem.* temperature.

tempête *noun Fem.* storm.

temple *noun Masc.* **1** temple; **2** (Protestant) church.

temporaire *adjective* temporary.

temps *noun Masc.* **1** weather; **quel temps fait-il?** what's the weather like?; **par temps de pluie** in rainy weather; **2** time; **je n'ai pas le temps** I haven't got time; **il est temps de partir** it's time to go; **arriver à temps** to arrive in (*or* on) time; **de temps en temps** from time to time; **en même temps** at the same time; **ça a pris beaucoup de temps** it took a long time; **il**

nous reste combien de temps? how much time do we have left?; **c'est du temps perdu** it's a waste of time; **il était temps!** about time too!; **ces derniers temps** recently; **un travail à plein temps** a full-time job; **un travail à temps partiel** a part-time job; **3** tense (*of a verb*).

tendance *noun Fem.* **1** tendency; **avoir tendance à faire** to tend to do; **2** trend.

tendre¹ *verb* [3] **1** to stretch (*something elastic*); **2** to hold out; **elle m'a tendu un crayon** she held out a pencil to me; **tendre la main à quelqu'un** to hold out one's hand to someone; **3** tendre le bras to reach out.

tendre² *adjective* tender.

tendresse *noun Fem.* tenderness.

tendu *adjective* tense.

tenir *verb* [77] **1** to hold; **peux-tu tenir la corde?** can you hold the rope?; **elle tenait l'enfant par la main** she was holding the child by the hand; **2** to run (*a shop, a business*); **le stand est tenu par des bénévoles** the stand is run by volunteers; **3** to keep; **elle tenait les yeux baissés** she kept her eyes down; **'tenir hors de la portée des enfants'** 'keep out of reach of children'; **4** to take up; **cela tient la place de deux personnes** it takes up the space of two people; **5** tenir à to be attached to; **elle tient beaucoup à ses petits-enfants** she's very attached to her grandchildren; **6 tenir à faire quelque chose** to be determined to do something; **je tiens à le finir aujourd'hui** I'm determined to finish it today; **7 tiens!** oh!; **tiens, il est déjà midi!** oh, it's twelve already!; **tiens! est-ce que je t'ai raconté ...?** listen! have I told you ...?; **tiens, tiens, c'est toi!** well, well, it's you!; **tiens, prends le mien** here, take mine; **8 tenir de quelqu'un** to take after someone; **elle tient de sa mère** she takes after her mother; **9 se tenir** to hold; **ils se tenaient par la main** they were holding each other by the hand; **10 se tenir** to stand; **elle se tenait devant l'entrée** she was standing by the entrance; **tiens-toi tranquille!** be quiet!; **tiens-toi droit!** stand up straight!; **11 se tenir pour** to think yourself; **il se tient pour un génie** he thinks he's a genius.

tennis noun Masc. **1** tennis; **jouer au tennis** to play tennis; **un terrain de tennis, un tennis** a tennis court; **tennis de table** table tennis; **2** tennis shoe.

tension noun Fem. **1** tension; **2** blood pressure.

tentant adjective tempting.

tentation noun Fem. temptation.

tentative noun Fem. attempt.

tente noun Fem. tent.

tenter verb [1] **1** to attempt; **il a tenté de s'échapper** he tried to escape; **tenter sa chance, tenter le coup** (informal) to give it a try; **2** to tempt.

tenu adjective **1** bien/mal tenu well/badly cared for; **2** être tenu de faire to be required to do.

tenue noun Fem. clothes; **être en tenue de sport** to be in sports kit;

en tenue de soirée in evening dress.

terme noun Masc. **1** word, term; **un terme technique** a technical term; **les termes du contrat** the terms of the contract; **2** end; **à court terme** short-term; **à long terme** long-term.

terminaison noun Fem. ending.

terminale noun Fem. (in a French school) the equivalent of Year 13.

terminer verb [1] **1** to finish; **2** to end; **la réunion s'est terminée à dix-huit heures** the meeting ended at six p.m.; **ça va mal se terminer!** it'll end in tears!

terminus noun Masc. terminus.

terrain noun Masc. **1** ground, land; **il a acheté du terrain** he's bought some land; **2** pitch, ground (for sports); **un terrain de football** a football pitch; **un terrain de golf** a golf course; **3** piece of ground; **un terrain à bâtir** a building plot.

terrain de camping noun Masc. campsite.

terrain de jeu(x) noun Masc. playground.

terrain de sport(s) noun Masc. sports ground.

terrain vague noun Masc. waste ground.

terrasse noun Fem. terrace.

terre noun Fem. **1** ground; **s'asseoir par terre** to sit on the floor; **tomber par terre** to fall down; **2 la Terre** the Earth; **3** soil; **4** land (not sea); **aller à terre** to go ashore.

terre cuite noun Fem. terracotta.

terrible *adjective* **1** terrible; **des événements terribles** terrible events; **2** (*informal*) terrific; **'c'était bien, le film?' – 'pas terrible'** 'was the film any good?' – 'not great'.

terrifiant *adjective* terrifying.

terrifier *verb* [1] terrify.

terrine *noun Fem.* pâté.

territoire *noun Masc.* **1** territory; **2** country; **il fera beau sur l'ensemble du territoire** the weather will be fine throughout the country.

terrorisme *noun Masc.* terrorism.

terroriste *noun Masc. & Fem.* terrorist.

tes *adjective* your; SEE **ton**[1].

test *noun Masc.* test.

testament *noun Masc.* will.

tester *verb* [1] to test.

tétanos *noun Masc.* tetanus.

têtard *noun Masc.* tadpole.

tête *noun Fem.* **1** head; **se laver la tête** to wash your hair; **j'ai la tête qui tourne** my head's spinning; **2** face; **je n'aime pas sa tête** I don't like his face; **3** top; **tu es en tête de la liste** you're first on the list; **4** mind; **j'ai quelque chose en tête** I have something in mind; **où avais-tu la tête?** what were you thinking of? **5** front (*of a train*); **les deux wagons de tête sont à destination de Bourges** the two front coaches are for Bourges; ★ **faire la tête** to sulk; ★ **un dîner en tête à tête** a private dinner for two; ★ **j'en ai par-dessus la tête!** I'm fed up to the back teeth!

têtu *adjective* stubborn.

texte *noun Masc.* text.

texto™ *noun Masc.* text message; **envoyer un texto à quelqu'un** to text someone.

TGV *noun Masc.* SHORT FOR **train à grande vitesse** high-speed train.

thalassothérapie *noun Fem.* sea-water treatment (*at a health spa*).

thé *noun Masc.* tea; **un thé au lait** tea with milk.

théâtre *noun Masc.* **1** theatre; **des costumes de théâtre** stage costumes; **un coup de théâtre** a dramatic turn of events; **2** plays; **le théâtre de Molière** Molière's plays; **3 faire du théâtre** to belong to a drama group.

théière *noun Fem.* teapot.

thème *noun Masc.* **1** subject; **2** prose (*a text to translate into the foreign language*).

théorie *noun Fem.* theory.

thérapie *noun Fem.* **1** (medical) treatment; **2** therapy.

thermal (*Masc. plural* **thermaux**) *adjective* thermal; **une station thermale** a spa.

thermomètre *noun Masc.* thermometer.

thermos™ *noun Masc.* vacuum flask, thermos™.

thon *noun Masc.* tuna.

thym *noun Masc.* thyme.

tibia *noun Masc.* **1** shin; **2** shinbone.

tic *noun Masc.* nervous twitch.

ticket *noun Masc.* **1** ticket; **un ticket de métro** an underground ticket; **2 un ticket de caisse** a till receipt.

tiède *adjective* **1** warm; **2** lukewarm.

tien, tienne, tiens, tiennes *pronoun* **le tien, la tienne, les tiens, les tiennes** yours; **est-ce que ce stylo est le tien?** is this pen yours?; **ma voiture et la tienne** my car and yours; **mes lettres et les tiennes** my letters and yours.

tiens *verb* SEE **tenir**.

tiens *pronoun* SEE **tien**.

tiers *noun Masc.* third; **les deux tiers de la population** two-thirds of the population.

tiers *(Fem. tierce) adjective* third.

tiers-monde *noun Masc.* Third World.

tige *noun Fem.* stem.

tigre *noun Masc.* tiger.

tilleul *noun Masc.* **1** lime tree; **2** lime flower tea.

timbre *noun Masc.* stamp.

timide *adjective* **1** shy; **2** self-conscious.

timidité *noun Fem.* shyness.

tiquer *verb* [1] **sans tiquer** without batting an eyelid.

tir *noun Masc.* **1** shooting; **2** shot (*in football*).

tirage *noun Masc.* **le tirage au sort** the draw (*in a lottery, for example*); **par tirage au sort** by drawing lots.

tir à l'arc *noun Masc.* archery.

tire-bouchon *noun Masc.* corkscrew.

tirelire *noun Fem.* money box.

tirer *verb* [1] **1** to pull; **il m'a tiré par le bras** he pulled my arm; **elle m'a tiré les cheveux** she pulled my hair; **2** to draw; **tirer les rideaux** to draw the curtains; **il a tiré la lettre de sa poche** he drew the letter from his pocket; **tirer un trait** to draw a line; **tirer des conclusions** to draw conclusions; **tirer au sort** to draw lots; **3** to fire; **ils ont tiré sur les policiers** they fired on the police; **tirer plusieurs coups de feu** to fire several shots.

tiret *noun Masc.* dash.

tiroir *noun Masc.* drawer.

tisane *noun Fem.* herbal tea.

tisonnier *noun Masc.* poker (*for fire*).

tissu *noun Masc.* material, fabric.

titre *noun Masc.* **1** title; **2** headline; **les titres de l'actualité** the news headlines; **3 à juste titre** quite rightly; **à titre d'exemple** as an example.

titre de transport *noun Masc.* travel ticket.

tituber *verb* [1] to stagger.

toast *noun Masc.* **1** piece of toast; **servir avec des toasts** serve with toast; **2** toast (*to someone's health*).

toboggan *noun Masc.* slide.

toi *pronoun* you; **c'est toi!** it's you!; **avec toi** with you; **plus grand que toi** bigger than you; **c'est à toi de jouer** it's your turn; **assieds-toi** sit down; **est-ce que ces chaussettes sont à toi?** are these socks yours?

toile *noun Fem.* **1** cloth; **toile de lin** linen; **une toile cirée** an oilcloth; **2** painting, canvas; **une toile de Picasso** a painting by Picasso.

a
b
c
d
e
f
g
h
i
j
k
l
m
n
o
p
q
r
s
t
u
v
w
x
y
z

Toile noun Fem. **la Toile** the Web.

toile d'araignée noun Fem. spider's web, cobweb.

toilette noun Fem. **1 faire sa toilette** to have a wash; **2** outfit; **je me suis acheté une toilette pour le mariage de ma sœur** I've bought an outfit for my sister's wedding.

toilettes plural noun Fem. toilet; **aller aux toilettes** to go to the toilet.

toi-même pronoun yourself; **l'as-tu fait toi-même?** did you make it yourself?

toit noun Masc. roof.

tolérant adjective tolerant.

tolérer verb [24] to tolerate.

tomate noun Fem. tomato; **une salade de tomates** a tomato salad.

tombe noun Fem. grave.

tombeau (plural **tombeaux**) noun Masc. tomb.

tomber verb [1] **1** to fall; **attention, tu vas tomber!** careful, you'll fall!; **la chaise est tombée** the chair fell over; **Noël tombe un lundi** Christmas falls on a Monday; **2 laisser tomber** to drop; **j'ai laissé tomber mon porte-monnaie** I've dropped my purse; **3 laisser tomber** to give up (an activity); **elle a laissé tomber l'espagnol** she's given up Spanish; **4 tomber malade** to fall ill; **tomber amoureux** to fall in love; **5 tomber sur** to bump into; **je suis tombé sur Georges devant la poste** I bumped into Georges outside the post office; **6 ça tombe bien** that's lucky; ★ **je tombe de sommeil** I

can't keep my eyes open (literally: I'm dropping with sleep).

tombola noun Fem. tombola, lottery.

ton¹, ta, tes adjective your; **ton chat** your cat; **ta sœur** your sister; **tes pieds** your feet.

ton² noun Masc. **1** tone of voice; **2** colour.

tondeuse noun Fem. lawnmower.

tondre verb [3] to mow.

tonique adjective bracing.

tonne noun Fem. tonne, metric ton (1,000 kg); ★ **j'ai des tonnes de choses à faire** (informal) I've loads of things to do.

tonneau (plural **tonneaux**) noun Masc. barrel.

tonnerre noun Masc. thunder.

tonton noun Masc. (informal) uncle.

tonus noun Masc. **1** energy (for a person); **2** tone (for your muscles).

toque noun Fem. chef's hat.

torchon noun Masc. cloth, tea towel.

tordre verb [3] to twist; **se tordre la cheville** to twist your ankle.

tordu adjective **1** bent; **2** crooked; **3** weird; **une histoire tordue** a weird story.

tornade noun Fem. tornado.

torrent noun Masc. waterfall, mountain stream.

torse noun Masc. chest, upper body; **il s'est mis torse nu** he stripped to the waist.

tort noun Masc. **1 avoir tort** to be wrong; **je crois que tu as tort** I think you're wrong; **il a tort de dire**

ça he's wrong to say that; **2 à tort** wrongly; **à tort ou à raison** rightly or wrongly.

torticolis noun Masc. stiff neck; **avoir le torticolis** to have a stiff neck.

tortiller verb [1] **se tortiller** to wriggle.

tortue noun Fem. tortoise, turtle.

torture noun Fem. torture.

torturer verb [1] to torture.

tôt adverb **1** early; **on va partir tôt** we're leaving early; **tôt le matin** early in the morning; **2** soon; **le plus tôt possible** as soon as possible; **tôt ou tard** sooner or later.

total (plural **totaux**) noun Masc. total; **au total** in total.

total (Masc. plural **totaux**) adjective total.

totalement adverb totally.

totalité noun Fem. **la totalité des élèves** all the pupils; **la totalité du groupe** the whole group.

touchant adjective touching.

touche noun Fem. **1** key (on a piano or keyboard); **2** button (on a machine); **la touche d'enregistrement** the record button; **appuyez sur la touche** press the button; **3** (ligne de) **touche** touchline.

toucher verb [1] **1** to touch; **ne touche pas à ma peinture** don't touch my painting; **2** to touch; **cette histoire m'a beaucoup touché** that story really touched me; **3** to affect, to concern; **ce problème nous touche tous** this problem affects us all; **4** to get

(money or wages); **il touche 350 euros par semaine** he's getting 350 euros a week.

touffu adjective bushy, thick.

toujours adverb **1** always; **il est toujours en retard** he's always late; **comme toujours** as always; **2** still; **nous habitons toujours au même endroit** we're still living in the same place; **ton paquet n'est toujours pas arrivé** your parcel still hasn't come; **3 pour toujours** for ever.

tour[1] noun Masc. **1 faire le tour de** to go round; **faire le tour des magasins** to go round all the shops; **faire le tour du monde** to go round the world; **2 faire un tour** to go for a walk; **on va faire un petit tour** we'll go for a little walk; **3 faire un tour à vélo** to go for a bike ride; **4 faire un tour en voiture** to go for a drive; **5** turn; **c'est ton tour de jouer** it's your turn to play; **à qui le tour?** whose turn is it?

tour[2] noun Fem. **1** tower; **la tour Eiffel** the Eiffel Tower; **2** tower block; **3** castle, rook (in chess).

tourbillon noun Masc. whirlwind, whirlpool.

tourisme noun Masc. tourism.

touriste noun Masc. & Fem. tourist.

touristique adjective **un guide touristique** a tourist guide(book); **une ville touristique** a town which attracts tourists.

tourmenter verb [1] to tease.

tournant noun Masc. **1** bend (in a road); **2** turning-point.

tourne-disque noun Masc. record player.

a
b
c
d
e
f
g
h
i
j
k
l
m
n
o
p
q
r
s
t
u
v
w
x
y
z

tournée noun Fem. **1** round (of a postman or baker, for example); **2** round (of drinks); **c'est ma tournée** it's my round; **3** tour (of a performer); **être en tournée** to be on tour.

tourner verb [1] **1** to turn; **tournez à gauche à l'église** turn left at the church; **2** to toss (a salad); **3** mal tourner to go wrong; **4** se tourner to turn; **elle s'est tournée vers moi** she turned to face me; **5** tourner le dos à quelqu'un to have your back to somebody.

tournesol noun Masc. sunflower.

tournevis noun Masc. screwdriver.

tournis noun Masc. avoir le tournis to feel dizzy; **j'ai le tournis** I'm feeling dizzy.

tournoi noun Masc. tournament.

tourterelle noun Fem. turtle dove.

tous adjective, pronoun SEE tout.

Toussaint noun Fem. All Saints' Day (November 1st).

tousser verb [1] to cough.

tout, toute, tous, toutes adjective **1** all; **tout le pain** all the bread; **toute la classe** all the class, the whole class; **tous les garçons** all the boys; **toutes les filles** all the girls; **tout le monde** everybody; **toute la journée** all day; **tous les deux** both; **je les achète tous les trois** I'll buy all three of them; **pendant toute une année** for a whole year; **2** any; **à tout âge** at any age; **à tout instant** at any moment; **'service à toute heure'** 'service at any time'; **3** every; **tous les jours** every day; **prenez un comprimé toutes les quatre heures** take one pill every four hours.

tout, toutes, tous, toutes pronoun **1** everything; **ils ont tout pris** they took everything; **tout va bien** everything's fine; **2** all; **tous ensemble** all together; **elles étaient toutes là** they were all there; **54 en tout** 54 in all; **et tout ça** and all that; **tout ce que je sais, c'est que ...** all I know is that ...; **3** pas du tout not at all.

tout adverb **c'est tout prêt** it's all ready; **il est tout seul** he's all alone; **tout doucement** very slowly; **tout droit** straight ahead.

tout à coup adverb suddenly.

tout à fait adverb completely, absolutely; **ce n'est pas tout à fait sec** it's not absolutely dry.

tout à l'heure adverb **1** just now; **je l'ai vu tout à l'heure** I saw him just now; **2** in a little while; **à tout à l'heure!** see you later!.

tout de même adverb all the same; **c'est tout de même bizarre** all the same, it is odd.

tout de suite adverb at once; **fais-le tout de suite!** do it at once!

tout d'un coup adverb suddenly.

toutefois adverb however.

toutes adjective, pronoun SEE tout.

toux noun Fem. cough.

toxicomane noun Masc. & Fem. drug addict.

toxique adjective poisonous, toxic.

trac noun Masc. (informal) avoir le trac to feel nervous.

trace noun Fem. **1** tracks; **des traces de skis** ski-tracks; **des**

traces de pas footprints; **2** mark; des traces de doigts finger marks.

tracer verb [61] to draw.

tracteur noun Masc. tractor.

tradition noun Fem. tradition.

traditionnel (Fem. **traditionnelle**) adjective traditional.

traducteur, traductrice noun Masc., Fem. translator.

traduction noun Fem. translation.

traduire verb [26] to translate; **traduire en français** to translate into French.

trafic noun Masc. **1** le trafic de drogue drug dealing; **2** traffic.

trafiquant, trafiquante noun Masc., Fem. dealer (in drugs or arms).

tragédie noun Fem. tragedy.

tragique adjective tragic.

trahir verb [2] to betray.

trahison noun Fem. betrayal.

train noun Masc. **1** train; **monter dans le train** to get on the train; **descendre du train** to get off the train; **le train de dix heures** the ten o'clock train; **2** être en train de faire to be (busy) doing; Henri est en train de faire la vaisselle Henri's doing the washing-up.

traîner verb [1] **1** to wander round; **2** to lie around; **il laisse ses affaires traîner partout** he leaves his things lying around everywhere; **3** to dawdle; **ne traînez pas, le train arrive** don't be long, the train's coming; **4** to drag on; **j'ai des projets qui traînent** I've got some projects that are dragging on; **5** to drag; **elle traînait sa valise**

derrière elle she was dragging her suitcase behind her; **6** traîner les pieds to drag your feet.

traire verb [78] to milk.

trait noun Masc. **1** line; **2 les traits** features (of a face); **avoir les traits fins** to have delicate features; **3 d'un seul trait** at one go; **il l'a bu d'un seul trait** he drank it all at one go.

trait d'union noun Masc. hyphen.

traité noun Masc. treaty.

traitement noun Masc. **1** treatment; **2** processing; **le traitement de texte** word processing; **3** salary.

traiter verb [1] **1** to treat; **il la traite très mal** he treats her very badly; **le médecin qui me traite** the doctor who's treating me; **2** to deal with (a question or problem); **3** traiter de to call; **il m'a traité de menteur** he called me a liar.

traiteur noun Masc. caterer.

trajet noun Masc. **1** journey; **c'est un trajet de deux heures** it's a two-hour journey; **2** route.

trampoline noun Masc. trampoline; **faire du trampoline** to trampoline.

tramway noun Masc. tram, tramway.

tranchant adjective sharp.

tranche noun Fem. **1** slice; **deux tranches de jambon** two slices of ham; **2** phase, period (of time).

trancher verb [1] **1** to slice; **2** to decide.

a
b
c
d
e
f
g
h
i
j
k
l
m
n
o
p
q
r
s
t
u
v
w
x
y
z

290

tranquille *adjective* **1** quiet; **une rue tranquille** a quiet street; **tiens-toi tranquille!** be quiet!; **2 laisse-moi tranquille!** leave me alone!; **3 maman n'est pas tranquille si je n'appelle pas** Mum worries if I don't ring.

tranquillité *noun Fem.* peace.

transat *noun Masc.* (*informal*) deck chair.

transférer *verb* [24] to transfer.

transfert *noun Masc.* transfer.

transformer *verb* [1] **1** to change; **ils ont transformé leur jardin** they've completely changed their garden; **nous avons transformé cette chambre en bureau** we've turned this bedroom into a study; **2 se transformer** to change into; **le têtard se transforme en grenouille** the tadpole changes into a frog.

transfusion *noun Fem.* **une transfusion sanguine** a blood transfusion.

transistor *noun Masc.* transistor.

transmettre *verb* [11] **1 transmettre quelque chose à quelqu'un** to pass something on to somebody; **2** to transmit.

transpiration *noun Fem.* perspiration, sweat.

transpirer *verb* [1] to sweat.

transplantation *noun Fem.* **1** transplant (*medical*); **2** transplantation (*of plants*).

transport *noun Masc.* **1** transport; **les frais de transport** transport costs; **2 les transports en commun** public transport.

transporter *verb* [1] **1** to transport; **2** to carry.

trappe *noun Fem.* trap door.

travail (*plural* **travaux**) *noun Masc.* **1** work; **j'ai beaucoup de travail à faire** I've got a lot of work to do; **2** job; **je cherche un travail** I'm looking for a job.

travailler *verb* [1] to work; **travailler dans la banque** to work in banking.

travailleur, travailleuse *noun Masc., Fem.* worker.

travailleur (*Fem.* **travailleuse**) *adjective* hard-working.

travailliste *adjective* Labour; **le parti travailliste** the Labour party (*in Britain*).

travaux *plural noun Masc.* **1** work; **des travaux de construction** building work; **ils font faire des travaux chez eux** they're having some work done on the house; **2** roadworks; **3 les travaux ménagers** housework; **4 les travaux dirigés** classwork; **les travaux manuels** handicrafts.

travée *noun Fem.* bay (*for coaches*).

travers *noun* **1 à travers** through; **j'ai regardé à travers les rideaux** I looked through the curtains; **voyager à travers le monde** to travel all over the world; **2 de travers** crooked; **le tableau est de travers** the picture's crooked; **3 de travers** wrongly; **c'est boutonné de travers** it's buttoned up wrongly.

traversée noun Fem. crossing; **une traversée de l'Atlantique** an Atlantic crossing.

traverser verb [1] **1** to cross; **regarde avant de traverser la rue** look before you cross the road; **2** to go through; **traverser la France pour aller en Italie** to go through France on the way to Italy; **la pluie a traversé ma veste** the rain's gone right through my jacket; **ils ont traversé une crise** they went through a crisis.

traversin noun Masc. bolster.

trébucher verb [1] to stumble.

trèfle noun Masc. **1** clover; **2** clubs (in cards); **la dame de trèfle** the queen of clubs.

treize number thirteen; **Aurélie a treize ans** Aurélie's thirteen; **à treize heures** at one p.m.; **le treize juillet** the thirteenth of July.

treizième number thirteenth.

tremblement de terre noun Masc. earthquake.

trembler verb [1] to shake, to tremble.

trempé adjective soaked.

tremper verb [1] to soak.

tremplin noun Masc. springboard.

trentaine noun Fem. **1** about thirty; **une trentaine de personnes** about thirty people; **2 elle a la trentaine** she's in her thirties.

trente number thirty; **elle a trente ans** she's thirty; **le trente juillet** the thirtieth of July.

très adverb very; **très heureux** very happy; **j'ai très faim** I'm very

hungry; **très bien fait** very well done.

trésor noun Masc. treasure.

tresse noun Fem. plait.

tréteau (plural **tréteaux**) noun Masc. trestle.

triangulaire adjective triangular.

tribu noun Fem. tribe.

tribunal (plural **tribunaux**) noun Masc. court; **paraître devant le tribunal** to appear in court (on a charge).

tricher verb [1] to cheat.

tricolore adjective three-coloured; **le drapeau tricolore** the French flag (which is three-coloured, blue, white, and red, in vertical stripes).

tricoter verb [1] to knit.

trier verb [1] to sort (out); **hier soir nous avons trié toutes les photos** last night we sorted out all the photographs.

trimestre noun Masc. term.

trinidadien (Fem. **trinidadienne**) adjective Trinidadian.

Trinidadien, Trinidadienne noun Masc., Fem. Trinidadian.

Trinité noun Fem. **(l'île de) la Trinité** Trinidad.

triomphe noun Masc. triumph.

triompher verb [1] to triumph.

tripes plural noun Fem. tripe.

triple noun Masc. **le triple** three times as much.

tripler verb [1] to treble; **le prix a triplé** the price has tripled.

triplés plural noun Masc. triplets.

triste *adjective* sad.

tristesse *noun Fem.* sadness.

trognon *noun Masc.* **un trognon de pomme** an apple core.

trois *number* three; **Tom a trois ans** Tom's three; **à trois heures** at three o'clock; **le trois mars** the third of March; ★ **être haut comme trois pommes** to be knee-high to a grasshopper (*literally: as tall as three apples*).

troisième *noun Fem.* (*in a French school*) the equivalent of Year 10.

troisième *noun Masc.* **au troisième** on the third floor.

troisième *adjective* third.

trombone *noun Masc.* **1** trombone; **2** paperclip (*because of its shape*).

trompe *noun Fem.* trunk (*elephant's*).

tromper *verb* [1] **1** to deceive; **2 se tromper** to make a mistake; **il s'est trompé** he made a mistake; **je me suis trompé de train** I got the wrong train; **vous vous êtes trompé de numéro** you've got the wrong number.

trompette *noun Fem.* trumpet; **jouer de la trompette** to play the trumpet.

tronc *noun Masc.* trunk (*of a tree*).

tronçonneuse *noun Fem.* chain saw.

trop *adverb* **1** too; **c'est trop loin** it's too far; **c'est beaucoup trop cher** it's much too expensive; **2** too much; **j'ai trop mangé** I've eaten too much; **tu m'en as donné trop** you've given me too much; **3 trop de** too much, too many; **trop de pain** too much bread; **trop de**

tomates too many tomatoes; **trop de monde** too many people; **4 de trop** too many, too much; **il y a une chaise de trop** there's one chair too many; **il y a dix euros de trop** that's ten euros too much.

tropique *noun Masc.* tropic.

trottoir *noun Masc.* pavement.

trou *noun Masc.* hole; **le trou dans la couche d'ozone** the hole in the ozone layer.

troublant *adjective* disturbing.

trou d'incendie *noun Masc.* fire hydrant.

trou de serrure *noun Masc.* keyhole.

trouer *verb* [1] to make a hole in; **des chaussettes trouées** socks with holes in them.

trouille *noun Fem.* **avoir la trouille** (*informal*) to be scared.

troupe *noun Fem.* **1 une troupe de théâtre** a theatre company; **2** flock (*of birds*); **3** troop (*of tourists or children*).

troupeau (*plural* **troupeaux**) *noun Masc.* herd (*of cattle*), flock (*of sheep*).

trousse *noun Fem.* pencil case.

trousseau (*plural* **trousseaux**) *noun Masc.* **un trousseau de clés** a bunch of keys.

trousse de maquillage *noun Fem.* make-up bag.

trousse de secours *noun Fem.* first-aid kit.

trousse de toilette *noun Masc.* toilet bag.

trouver *verb* [1] **1** to find; **as-tu trouvé ton passeport?** did you find your passport?; **2** to think; **j'ai trouvé le film passionnant** I thought the film was wonderful; **3 se trouver** to be (*in a place*); **les gens qui se trouvaient autour de moi** the people who were around me; **savez-vous où se trouve la gare routière?** do you know where the bus station is?

truc *noun* Masc. (*informal*) **1** thing; **un petit truc en bois** a little thing made of wood; **il y a un truc qui ne va pas** something's wrong; **le jazz, ce n'est pas mon truc** jazz just isn't my thing; **2** trick; **il doit y avoir un truc** there must be a trick to it.

truite *noun* Fem. trout.

tsigane *noun* Masc. & Fem. gipsy.

TSVP SHORT FOR **tournez s'il vous plaît** PTO (*please turn over*).

TTC SHORT FOR **toutes taxes comprises** inclusive of tax.

tu *pronoun* you ('*tu' is used when talking to family members, people you know well, and people of your own age; otherwise 'vous' is used for 'you'*).

tube *noun* Masc. **1** tube; **2** (*informal*) hit (*a pop song*).

tuer *verb* [1] **1** to kill; **2 se tuer** to be killed; **elle s'est tuée dans un accident de voiture** she was killed in a car accident; **3 se tuer** to kill yourself.

tue-tête *in phrase* **crier à tue-tête** to shout at the top of your voice.

tuile *noun* Fem. **1** tile; **2** thin almond biscuit.

tulipe *noun* Fem. tulip.

Tunisie *noun* Fem. Tunisia.

tunisien (*Fem.* **tunisienne**) *adjective* Tunisian.

tunnel *noun* Masc. tunnel; **le tunnel sous la Manche** the Channel Tunnel.

turban *noun* Masc. turban.

turc *noun* Masc. Turkish (*language*).

turc (*Fem.* **turque**) *adjective* Turkish.

Turc, Turque *noun* Masc., Fem. Turk.

Turquie *noun* Fem. Turkey.

tuteur, tutrice *noun* Masc., Fem. **1** guardian; **2** tutor.

tutoyer *verb* [39] to address somebody as 'tu' (*rather than 'vous'*); **il ne faut pas tutoyer ton professeur** you mustn't address your teacher as 'tu'; **et si on se tutoyait?** shall we say 'tu' to each other?

tuyau (*plural* **tuyaux**) *noun* Masc. **1** pipe; **2** (*informal*) tip (*a helpful hint*).

tuyau d'arrosage *noun* Masc. hosepipe.

TVA *noun* Fem. SHORT FOR **taxe à la valeur ajoutée** VAT.

type *noun* Masc. **1** kind; **quel type de papier?** what type of paper?; **2** (*informal*) guy; **le type qui a ouvert la porte** the guy who opened the door.

typique *adjective* typical.

tyranniser *verb* [1] to bully.

tzigane *noun* Masc. & Fem., *adjective* gipsy.

a b c d e f g h i j k l m n o p q r s t u v w x y z

Uu

ulcère noun Masc. ulcer.

un, une (plural **des**) article, pronoun, number **1** a, an; **un lion** a lion; **une fraise** a strawberry; **des cerises** (some) cherries; **2** one; **un pour moi** one for me; **un par un** one by one; **trente et une personnes** thirty-one people; **les uns pensent que …** some think that …; **un jour sur deux** every other day; **3** l'un(e) **et l'autre** the one and the other; **l'un est français et l'autre est allemand** one's French and the other's German; **4** l'un(e) ou **l'autre** either of them; **tu peux prendre l'un ou l'autre, ça n'a pas d'importance** you can take either of them, it doesn't matter.

uni adjective **1** close-knit (family or group); **2** plain (not patterned); **un tissu uni** a plain fabric.

uniforme noun Masc. uniform.

union noun Fem. union; **l'ex-Union soviétique** the former Soviet Union.

Union européenne noun Fem. European Union.

unique adjective **1** only; **elle est fille unique** she's an only child; **il est fils unique** he's an only child; **l'unique raison** the only reason; **2** single; **'prix unique'** 'all one price'; **3** unique.

uniquement adverb only.

unité noun Fem. **1** unity; **2** unit (of currency, measurement, etc).

unité de disques noun Fem. disk drive.

univers noun Masc. universe.

universitaire adjective university (degree, town), academic (work).

université noun Fem. university.

urbanisme noun Masc. town planning.

urgence noun Fem. **1** urgency; **il y a urgence** it's urgent!; **2** d'urgence immediately, at once; **il faut téléphoner d'urgence** you must phone at once; **3** emergency; **les urgences, le service des urgences** accident and emergency, the casualty department.

urgent adjective urgent.

USA plural noun Masc. USA; **aux USA** in (or to) the USA.

usage noun Masc. **1** use; **à l'usage** with use; **en usage** in use; **à usage externe** for external use only; **2** 'hors d'usage' 'not in service'.

usagé adjective **1** worn; **2** used.

usager noun Masc. user.

usé adjective worn.

user verb [1] to wear out (shoes, clothing).

usine noun Fem. factory.

ustensile noun Masc. utensil.

utile adjective useful.

utilisable adjective usable.

utilisateur, utilisatrice noun Masc., Fem. user.

utiliser verb [1] to use.

utilité noun Fem. usefulness; **un livre d'une grande utilité** a very useful book.

Vv

va verb SEE **aller**.

vacances plural noun Fem. holidays; **les vacances scolaires** the school holidays; **les grandes vacances** the summer holidays; **être en vacances** to be on holiday; **bonnes vacances!** have a good holiday!

vacancier, vacancière noun Masc., Fem. holiday-maker.

vacarme noun Masc. din; **ils faisaient un vacarme pas possible!** they were making an amazing din!

vaccination noun Fem. vaccination.

vacciner verb [1] to vaccinate; **se faire vacciner** to be vaccinated.

vache noun Fem. cow.

vache adjective mean.

vachement adverb (informal) really; **c'était vachement bien!** it was really good!

va-et-vient noun Masc. coming and going.

vagabond noun Masc. tramp.

vagin noun Masc. vagina.

vague[1] noun Fem. wave (in the sea).

vague[2] adjective vague.

vaguement adverb vaguely.

vain adjective 1 useless; 2 **en vain** in vain.

vaincre verb [79] 1 to defeat; 2 to overcome.

vainqueur noun Masc. winner.

vais verb SEE **aller**.

vaisseau (plural **vaisseaux**) noun Masc. vessel.

vaisselle noun Fem. dishes; **faire la vaisselle** to do the washing-up.

valable adjective valid.

valet noun Masc. jack; **le valet de pique** the jack of spades.

valeur noun Fem. value; **des objets de valeur** valuables; **c'est sans valeur** it's of no value.

valider verb [1] to stamp (a ticket).

valise noun Fem. suitcase; **faire ses valises** to pack.

vallée noun Fem. valley.

valoir verb [80] 1 to be worth; **ça vaut combien?** how much is it worth?; **ce tableau vaut cher** that painting's worth a lot; **2 valoir la peine** to be worth it; **ça ne vaut pas la peine d'y aller s'il pleut** it's not worth going if it's raining; **ça vaudrait la peine d'essayer** it would be worth a try; **3 il vaut mieux faire** it would be better to do; **il vaut mieux téléphoner avant** it would be better to phone first.

valse noun Fem. waltz.

vampire noun Masc. vampire.

vandalisme noun Masc. vandalism.

vanille noun Fem. vanilla; **une glace à la vanille** a vanilla ice cream.

vanter verb [1] **se vanter** to boast.

vapeur noun Fem. steam; **faire cuire des légumes à la vapeur** to steam vegetables.

vaporisateur noun Masc. (perfume) spray.

a
b
c
d
e
f
g
h
i
j
k
l
m
n
o
p
q
r
s
t
u
v
w
x
y
z

a

variable *adjective* variable, changeable.

b

varicelle *noun Fem.* chickenpox; **avoir la varicelle** to have chickenpox.

c

varié *adjective* varied, various; **'sandwichs variés'** 'a selection of sandwiches'.

d

e

varier *verb* [1] to vary.

f

variété *noun Fem.* 1 variety; 2 **un spectacle de variétés** a variety show.

g

h

vas *verb* SEE **aller.**

i

vase[1] *noun Masc.* vase.

j

vase[2] *noun Fem.* mud.

k

vaste *adjective* large, enormous.

va-vite *adverb Fem.* **à la va-vite** in a rush.

l

m

veau (*plural* **veaux**) *noun Masc.* 1 calf; 2 veal.

n

vécu *verb* SEE **vivre.**

o

vedette *noun Fem.* star; **une vedette de cinéma** a film star.

p

végétal *adjective* vegetable; **l'huile végétale** vegetable oil.

q

végétarien, végétarienne *noun Masc., Fem.*

r

végétarien (*Fem.* **végétarienne**) *adjective* vegetarian.

s

véhicule *noun Masc.* vehicle.

t

u

veille *noun Fem.* **la veille** the day before; **je l'avais rencontrée la veille de mon départ** I met her the day before my departure; **la veille de Noël** Christmas Eve; **la veille du jour de l'an** New Year's Eve.

v

w

veilleuse *noun Fem.* 1 night-light; 2 pilot light.

x

y

veinard *noun Masc.* (*informal*) **petit veinard!** you lucky little devil!

z

veine *noun Fem.* 1 **avoir de la veine** (*informal*) to be lucky; 2 vein.

vélo *noun Masc.* bike; **je suis venu à vélo** I came by bike; **faire du vélo** to go cycling.

vélodrome *noun Masc.* cycle-racing track, velodrome.

vélomoteur *noun Masc.* moped.

vélo tout-terrain *noun Masc.* mountain bike.

velours *noun Masc.* 1 velvet; 2 corduroy.

velouté *noun Masc.* cream soup; **velouté de champignons** cream of mushroom soup.

vendanges *plural noun Fem.* grape harvest.

vendeur, vendeuse *noun Masc., Fem.* 1 shop assistant; 2 salesperson; 3 seller.

vendre *verb* [3] to sell; **vendre quelque chose à quelqu'un** to sell somebody something; **j'ai vendu mon ordinateur à Colette** I've sold my computer to Colette; **'à vendre'** 'for sale'; **'vendu'** 'sold'.

vendredi *noun Masc.* 1 Friday; **nous sommes vendredi aujourd'hui** it's Friday today; **vendredi dernier** last Friday; **vendredi prochain** next Friday; 2 on Friday; **je l'ai vu vendredi soir** I saw him on Friday evening; 3 on Fridays; **fermé le vendredi** closed on Fridays; 4 **tous les vendredis** every Friday; **le vendredi saint** Good Friday.

vénéneux (*Fem.* **vénéneuse**) *adjective* poisonous (*plant*).

vengeance *noun Fem.* revenge.

venger verb [52] **se venger** to have your revenge.

venimeux (Fem. **venimeuse**) adjective poisonous (snake, spider).

venir verb [81] **1** to come; **il vient de Provence** he comes from Provence; **elles sont venues mardi** they came on Tuesday; **viens voir!** come and see!; **2 faire venir** to send for; **il faut faire venir le médecin** we must send for the doctor; **3 venir de faire** to have just done; **ils viennent d'arriver** they have just arrived; **elle venait de partir** she had just left.

vent noun Masc. wind; **un vent du sud** a south wind.

vente noun Fem. sale; **être en vente** to be on sale.

vente aux enchères noun Fem. auction sale.

ventilateur noun Masc. fan.

ventre noun Masc. stomach; **avoir mal au ventre** to have stomachache.

venu verb SEE **venir**.

ver noun Masc. worm.

verbe noun Masc. verb.

verdict noun Masc. verdict.

verger noun Masc. orchard.

verglas noun Masc. black ice.

vérifier verb [1] to check.

véritable adjective real.

vérité noun Fem. truth.

vernir verb [2] to varnish.

vernis à ongles noun Masc. nail varnish.

verre noun Masc. **1** glass; **un verre de vin** a glass of wine; **2** glass; **un**

vase en verre a glass vase; **3** lens (of spectacles).

verrou noun Masc. bolt (on a door).

verrouiller verb [1] to bolt (a door).

verrue noun Fem. wart.

vers[1] preposition **1** towards; **il montait vers l'église** he was going up towards the church; **2** about (a time); **vers midi** about twelve; **vers la fin du mois** around the end of the month.

vers[2] noun Masc. line of poetry; **des vers** poetry.

Verseau noun Masc. Aquarius (sign of the Zodiac).

versement noun Masc. payment.

verser verb [1] **1** to pour; **Sylvie m'a versé une tasse de thé** Sylvie poured me a cup of tea; **2** to pay in; **j'ai versé 300 euros sur mon compte** I paid 300 euros into my account.

version noun Fem. **1** version; **2** translation (into your own language).

verso noun Masc. back (of a piece of paper); **voir au verso** see overleaf.

vert adjective green; ★ **avoir la main verte** to have green fingers.

vertical (Masc. plural **verticaux**) adjective vertical, upright.

vertige noun Masc. vertigo.

verveine noun Fem. verbena tea.

veste noun Fem. jacket.

vestiaire noun Masc. **1** cloakroom (in a theatre, restaurant, etc); **2** changing room (in a gym, sports ground).

a
b
c
d
e
f
g
h
i
j
k
l
m
n
o
p
q
r
s
t
u
v
w
x
y
z

vêtement noun Masc. garment; les **vêtements** clothes; '**vêtements pour enfants**' 'children's wear'.

vétérinaire noun Masc. & Fem. vet.

veuf, veuve noun Masc., Fem. widower, widow.

vexer verb [1] to annoy, to offend.

viande noun Fem. meat.

vibrer verb [1] to vibrate.

victime noun Fem. victim.

victoire noun Fem. victory.

vide adjective empty.

vide noun Masc. **1** space; dans le vide in(to) space; **2** vacuum; emballé sous vide vacuum-packed.

vidéo noun Fem. video; une cassette vidéo a video cassette; une caméra vidéo a video camera; un jeu vidéo a video game.

vidéoclip noun Masc. music video.

vidéoclub noun Masc. video shop.

vidéothèque noun Fem. video library.

vider verb [1] to empty.

vie noun Fem. life; toute ma vie all my life; il est encore en vie he's still alive; ton mode de vie your lifestyle; ★ c'est la vie that's life, that's the way it goes.

vieil adjective SEE **vieux.**

vieillard, vieillarde noun Masc., Fem. old man, old woman.

vieille adjective SEE **vieux.**

vieillesse noun Fem. old age.

vieillir verb [2] to age; il a beaucoup vieilli récemment he's aged a lot recently.

vierge noun Fem. virgin; la Sainte Vierge the Virgin Mary.

vierge adjective **1** blank; une cassette vierge a blank cassette; **2** laine vierge pure new wool; l'huile d'olive vierge virgin olive oil.

Vierge noun Fem. Virgo (sign of the Zodiac).

vieux, vieil (before a vowel or silent 'h') (Fem. vieille) (Masc. plural vieux) adjective old; une vieille ville an old town; un vieil arbre an old tree.

vieux, vieille noun Masc., Fem. un vieux an old man; une vieille an old woman.

vieux garçon noun Masc. bachelor.

vif (Fem. vive) adjective **1** bright; rose vif bright pink; **2** lively; une vive discussion a lively discussion; **3** avoir l'esprit vif to be quick-witted.

vigne noun Fem. vine, vineyard.

vigneron, vigneronne noun Masc., Fem. wine-grower.

vignette noun Fem. **1** label; **2** tax disc.

vignoble noun Masc. vineyard.

vilain adjective **1** ugly; **2** naughty; c'est vilain, ça! that's naughty!

villa noun Fem. detached house, villa.

village noun Masc. village.

ville noun Fem. town, city; une grande ville a city; en ville in (or into) town.

vin noun Masc. wine.

vinaigre noun Masc. vinegar.

vinaigrette noun Fem. French dressing.

vingt *number* twenty; **Marion a vingt ans** Marion's twenty; **le vingt juillet** the twentieth of July; **à vingt heures** at 8 p.m.; **vingt et un** twenty-one.

vingtaine *noun Fem.* about twenty; **une vingtaine de personnes** about twenty people.

vingtième *adjective* twentieth.

viol *noun Masc.* rape.

violemment *adjective* violently.

violence *noun Fem.* violence.

violent *adjective* violent.

violer *verb* [1] to rape.

violet (*Fem.* **violette**[1]) *adjective* purple.

violette[2] *noun Fem.* violet (*the flower*).

violon *noun Masc.* violin; **jouer du violon** to play the violin.

violoncelle *noun Masc.* cello; **jouer du violoncelle** to play the cello.

vipère *noun Fem.* adder, viper.

virage *noun Masc.* bend (*in the road*).

virement *noun Masc.* transfer (*of money*).

virer *verb* [1] **1** to transfer (*money*); **2** to turn; **3** to turn (right) around.

virgule *noun Fem.* **1** comma; **2** decimal point; **sept virgule trois** seven point three.

virus *noun Masc.* virus.

vis[1] *verb SEE* **vivre.**

vis[2] *noun Fem.* screw.

visa *noun Masc.* visa.

visage *noun Masc.* face.

viser *verb* [1] **1** to aim; **2** to aim at (*a target*).

visibilité *noun Fem.* visibility.

visible *adjective* visible, obvious.

visite *noun Fem.* visite; **une visite chez nos cousins** a visit to our cousins; **rendre visite à quelqu'un** to visit somebody; **elle a de la visite** she's got visitors.

visiter *verb* [1] to visit (*a place*); **on peut visiter l'appartement?** can we see round the flat?

visiteur, visiteuse *noun Masc., Fem.* visitor.

visualisation graphique *noun Fem.* graphics.

vit *verb SEE* **vivre.**

vitamine *noun Fem.* vitamin.

vite *adverb* **1** fast; **tu conduis trop vite** you drive too fast; **parle moins vite** speak more slowly; **2** quick; **vite! le bus arrive!** quick! here's the bus!; **ce sera vite fait** it won't take long; **3** soon; **on sera vite arrivé** we'll soon be there; **elle a vite compris** she understood immediately.

vitesse *noun Fem.* **1** speed; **elle est partie à toute vitesse** she rushed off; **2** gear; **en deuxième vitesse** in second gear.

vitrail (*plural* **vitraux**) *noun Masc.* stained glass window.

vitre *noun Fem.* window.

vitrine *noun Fem.* shop window.

vivant *adjective* **1** living; **2** lively.

vive[1] *adjective SEE* **vif.**

vive[2] *exclamation* **Vive le roi!** Long live the king!

a
b
c
d
e
f
g
h
i
j
k
l
m
n
o
p
q
r
s
t
u
v
w
x
y
z

vivement *adverb* **1** réagir vivement to react strongly; **2** vivement les vacances! roll on the holidays!

vivre *verb* [82] to live; **ils vivent ensemble** they live together; **ils ont vécu dans plusieurs pays différents** they've lived in several different countries.

vocabulaire *noun Masc.* vocabulary.

vœu *noun (plural vœux) Masc.* **1** wish; **faire un vœu** to make a wish; **meilleurs vœux!** best wishes! (*especially at the New Year*); **2** vow.

vogue *noun Fem.* fashion; **en vogue** in fashion.

voici *preposition* **1** here is, here are; **voici l'addition** here's the bill; **voici les clés** here are the keys; **me voici!** here I am!; **2** this is; **voici ma sœur** this is my sister.

voie *noun Fem.* **1** way; **être sur la bonne voie** to be on the right track; **2** track (*for trains*); **la voie ferrée** the railway track; **le train de Bourges entre en gare voie dix** the train from Bourges is now arriving at platform ten; **3** lane (*on a main road*); **une route à trois voies** a three-lane road.

voilà *preposition* **1** there is, there are; **voilà tes lunettes, là-bas sur la table** there are your glasses, over there on the table; **la voilà devant la boulangerie** there she is outside the baker's; **2** here is, here are; **voilà Anna qui arrive** here's Anna coming now; **voilà ton café** here's your coffee; **voilà, c'est tout** right, that's all; **3** that is; **voilà ma**

fille that's my daughter; **et voilà pourquoi** and that's why.

voile[1] *noun Masc.* veil.

voile[2] *noun Fem.* sail; **des cours de voile** sailing lessons.

voilier *noun Masc.* sailing boat.

voir *verb* [13] **1** to see; **je ne vois rien** I can't see anything; **je viendrai te voir un de ces jours** I'll come and see you one of these days; **oui, je vois, tu veux dire que ...** yes, I see, you mean that ...; **un film à voir** a film worth seeing; **peut-être, on verra** perhaps, we'll see; **2 se voir** to be noticeable; **ça ne se verra pas** nobody will notice; **3 se voir** to see each other; **ils se voient à Noël** they see each other at Christmas; **4 faire voir quelque chose à quelqu'un** to show somebody something; **je te ferai voir mes photos de vacances** I'll show you my holiday photos; **fais voir!** let's have a look!; **5** **ça n'a rien à voir avec mon problème** that's got nothing to do with my problem; ★ **il ne voit pas plus loin que le bout de son nez** he can't see any further than the end of his nose; ★ **elle ne peut pas le voir (en peinture)** she can't stand him (*literally: she can't bear to see him (in a painting)*); ★ **j'en ai vu d'autres** I've seen worse.

voisin, voisine *noun Masc., Fem.* neighbour; **Claire est chez les voisins** Claire's round at the neighbours'; **ma voisine de table** the girl sitting next to me at table.

voisinage *noun Masc.* neighbourhood.

voiture noun Fem. **1** car; **en voiture** by car; **2** carriage (on a train).

voix noun Fem. **1** voice; **à haute voix** aloud; **à voix basse** softly; **2** vote; **elle a eu 20 voix** she got 20 votes.

vol noun Masc. **1** flight; **le vol pour Milan** the Milan flight; **2** theft; ★ **à vol d'oiseau** as the crow flies (literally: by bird flight).

volaille noun Fem. poultry; **les foies de volaille** chicken livers.

volant noun Masc. **1** steering wheel; **qui était au volant?** who was driving?; **2** shuttlecock.

volant adjective flying.

volcan noun Masc. volcano.

volée noun Fem. volley.

voler verb [1] **1** to fly; **2** to steal; **voler quelque chose à quelqu'un** to steal something from someone; **on leur a volé leur voiture** their car's been stolen; **3** **voler quelqu'un** to rob somebody.

volet noun Masc. shutter.

voleur, voleuse noun Masc., Fem. thief.

volley noun Masc. volleyball; **jouer au volley** to play volleyball.

volontaire noun Masc. & Fem. volunteer.

volonté noun Fem. **1** will; **la bonne volonté** goodwill; **2** **à volonté** unlimited; **'pizza à volonté'** 'as much pizza as you want'.

volontiers adverb gladly; **'tu viens avec nous?' – 'volontiers'** 'will you come too?' – 'I'd love to'; **'tu me le prêtes?' – 'volontiers'** 'will you lend it to me?' – 'of course'.

volume noun Masc. volume.

vomir verb [2] to be sick, to vomit.

vos adjective SEE **votre**.

voter verb [1] to vote; **elle vote toujours pour les Verts** she always votes for the Greens.

votre (plural **vos**) adjective your; **nous connaissons votre fils** we know your son; **vos billets, monsieur** your tickets, sir.

vôtre pronoun **le vôtre, la vôtre, les vôtres** yours; **une maison comme la vôtre** a house like yours; **mes parents et les vôtres** my parents and yours; ★ **à la vôtre!** cheers!

vouloir verb [14] **1** to want; **elle ne veut rien** she doesn't want anything; **veux-tu venir avec nous?** do you want to come with us?; **je n'ai pas voulu arriver trop tôt** I didn't want to arrive too early; **il veut qu'elle l'appelle** he wants her to phone him; **il m'a vexé sans le vouloir** he annoyed me without meaning to; **2** to like; **si tu veux** if you like; **je voudrais visiter Versailles** I'd like to go to Versailles; **'encore du café?' – 'oui, je veux bien'** 'more coffee?' – 'yes, I'd love some'; **3 voulez-vous m'excuser?** would you excuse me?; **veux-tu fermer la porte?** would you shut the door?; **veux-tu te taire!** will you be quiet!; **4 vouloir dire** to mean; **qu'est-ce que tu veux dire?** what do you mean?; **si tu vois ce que je veux dire** if you see what I mean; **qu'est-ce que ce mot veut dire?** what does this word mean?; **5 en vouloir à quelqu'un** to bear a grudge against someone;

a b c d e f g h i j k l m n o p q r s t u v w x y z

elle leur en veut she's never forgiven them; ★ **vouloir c'est pouvoir** where there's a will there's a way (*literally: to want is to be able*).

voulu verb SEE **vouloir**.

vous pronoun 1 you; **avec vous** with you; **est-ce que ce sac est à vous?** is this your bag?; **à vous de jouer!** your turn to play!; 2 to you; **je vous écrirai** I'll write to you; 3 yourself; **ne vous coupez pas!** don't cut yourself!

vous-même(s) pronoun yourself, yourselves; **vous me l'avez dit vous-même** you told me yourself; **est-ce que vous l'avez fait vous-mêmes?** did you make it yourselves?

voûte noun Fem. vault, arch.

vouvoyer verb [39] to use 'vous' to mean 'you' (*rather than 'tu' which you use when talking to friends, family, and people of your own age*); **ils se connaissent depuis des années mais ils continuent à se vouvoyer** they've known each other for years but they still address each other as 'vous'.

voyage noun Masc. journey; **bon voyage!** have a good trip!

voyage organisé noun Masc. package tour.

voyager verb [52] to travel.

voyageur, voyageuse noun Masc., Fem. passenger.

voyelle noun Fem. vowel.

voyou noun Masc. hooligan.

vrac adverb **acheter des olives en vrac** to buy olives loose (*as opposed to pre-packaged*).

vrai adjective 1 true; **c'est une histoire vraie** it's a true story; 2 real; **c'est un vrai problème** it's a real problem; **c'est vrai?** really?; **pour de vrai** for real; 3 **à vrai dire** to tell the truth.

vraiment adverb really.

vraisemblable adjective likely; **peu vraisemblable** unlikely.

vraisemblablement adverb probably.

VTT noun Masc. SHORT FOR **vélo tout-terrain** mountain bike.

vu verb SEE **voir**.

vu adjective 1 vu que seeing that; **vu qu'il pleut, ce n'est pas la peine d'y aller** seeing it's raining, there's no point in going; 2 **être mal vu** to be disapproved of; **il est plutôt mal vu** people don't think much of him; **c'est mal vu de faire beaucoup de bruit** they don't like people making a lot of noise; **cette critique a été mal vue** this criticism didn't go down well; 3 **être bien vu** to be well thought of; **elle est très bien vue dans la société** people think highly of her.

vue noun Fem. 1 eyesight; **perdre la vue** to lose your eyesight; 2 sight; **je le connais de vue** I know him by sight; **nous l'avons perdue de vue** we've lost touch with her; **rien qu'à la vue de la viande** at the very sight of meat; 3 view; **une chambre avec vue sur le lac** a room with a view of the lake.

vulgaire adjective 1 vulgar; 2 common.

Ww

wagon noun Masc. **1** railway carriage; **2** wagon.

wagon-lit noun Masc. sleeper (on a train).

wagon-restaurant noun Masc. restaurant car.

wallon noun Masc. Wallon (language).

wallon (Fem. **wallonne**) adjective Wallon (of French-speaking Belgium).

Wallon, Wallonne noun Masc., Fem. Wallon (French-speaking Belgian).

WC (pronounced 'vaysay') plural noun Masc. toilet; **aller aux WC** to go to the toilet; **il est aux WC** he's in the loo.

web noun Masc. **le web** the Web.

Xx

xylophone noun Masc. xylophone; **jouer du xylophone** to play the xylophone.

Yy

y pronoun,, adverb **1** there; **j'y vais demain** I'm going there tomorrow; **2 il y a** there is, there are; **il y a un café à côté** there's a cafe next door; **il y a des tomates dans le frigo** there are some tomatoes in the

fridge; **3 j'y pensais** I was thinking of it; **tu n'y peux rien** you can't do anything about it.

yaourt noun Masc. yoghurt.

yeux plural noun Masc. SEE **œil**.

yoga noun Masc. yoga.

yougoslave adjective Yugoslavian.

Yougoslavie noun Fem. Yugoslavia; **l'ex-Yougoslavie** the former Yugoslavia.

Zz

zapper verb [1] to channel hop.

zèbre noun Masc. zebra.

zéro noun Masc. zero, nil, love (in tennis); **trois à zéro** three-nil; **zéro heure** midnight; **elle a le moral à zéro** she's really depressed; ★ **il faut tout reprendre à zéro** we'll have to start again from scratch.

zézayer verb [59] to lisp.

zigzag noun Masc. zigzag; **une route en zigzag** a winding road; **faire des zigzags** to zigzag.

zodiaque noun Masc. zodiac.

zone noun Fem. **1** zone, area; **2 la zone** the slums; **un enfant de la zone** a child who grew up in the slums.

zone euro noun Fem. eurozone.

zone industrielle noun Fem. industrial estate.

zoo noun Masc. zoo.

zoologique adjective zoological.

zut exclamation (informal) damn!

VERB TABLES AND FORMS

French regular verbs (pages 306–309)
There are three regular verb families in French: **-er**, **-ir**, and **-re** verbs.

When you look up an entry in this dictionary, you will see a number in square brackets ([1], [2], etc.). This number tells you which verb model you need to follow for that verb.

[1] **-er**   e.g. **parler**   to speak
[2] **-ir**   e.g. **finir**   to finish
[3] **-re**   e.g. **attendre**   to wait

[4] **reflexive (-er)** e.g. **se laver**   to wash (oneself)

Main French irregular verbs (pages 310–319)
The following verbs are unlike the regular verbs. They are irregular and don't follow a particular pattern so their forms are given for you. Again, when you look up an entry, use the number in square brackets to bring you to these tables to see how to form the parts of the verb you need.

| [5] | **avoir** | to have |
[6]	**être**	to be
[7]	**aller**	to go
[8]	**devoir**	to have to
[9]	**dire**	to say
[10]	**faire**	to do or to make
[11]	**mettre**	to put
[12]	**pouvoir**	to be able
[13]	**voir**	to see
[14]	**vouloir**	to want

The main forms of other irregular verbs are given on pages 320–322.

il/elle/on and ils/elles/on
Use the **il** form in the tables for **il/elle** and **on**. Use the **ils** form for **ils/elles** and **on** forms.

Perfect tense
Some verbs take **avoir** in the perfect tense and some take **être**. In these tables the ✳ reminds you which ones take **être**.

1
parler
to speak
°

Imperative		Past participle	
parle	speak	parlé	spoken
parlons	let's speak		
parlez	speak		

Present

je parle	I speak or I am speaking
tu parles	
il parle	
nous parlons	
vous parlez	
ils parlent	

Present subjunctive ☆

je parle	I speak or I am speaking
tu parles	
il parle	
nous parlions	
vous parliez	
ils parlent	

Perfect ★

j' ai parlé	I have spoken or I spoke
tu as parlé	
il a parlé	
nous avons parlé	
vous avez parlé	
ils ont parlé	

Imperfect ○

je parlais	I spoke or I used to speak or I was speaking
tu parlais	
il parlait	
nous parlions	
vous parliez	
ils parlaient	

Future

je parlerai	I will speak
tu parleras	
il parlera	
nous parlerons	
vous parlerez	
ils parleront	

Conditional

je parlerais	I would speak
tu parlerais	
il parlerait	
nous parlerions	
vous parleriez	
ils parleraient	

★ uses *avoir* plus the past participle to describe completed events in the past

☆ usually used after *que*: **Il est possible que tu aimés le film.** It is possible that you will like the film.

○ used to describe what something was like, what used to happen, or what was happening

Imperative		Past participle	
finis	finish	fini	finished
finissons	let's finish		
finissez	finish		

2
finir
to finish

Present

je finis	I finish or I am finishing
tu finis	
il finit	
nous finissons	
vous finissez	
ils finissent	

Perfect ★

j' ai fini	I have finished or I finished
tu as fini	
il a fini	
nous avons fini	
vous avez fini	
ils ont fini	

Future

je finirai	I will finish
tu finiras	
il finira	
nous finirons	
vous finirez	
ils finiront	

Present subjunctive ☆

je finisse	I finish or I am finishing
tu finisses	
il finisse	
nous finissions	
vous finissiez	
ils finissent	

Imperfect ✪

je finissais	I finished or I used to finish or I was finishing
tu finissais	
il finissait	
nous finissions	
vous finissiez	
ils finissaient	

Conditional

je finirais	I would finish
tu finirais	
il finirait	
nous finirions	
vous finiriez	
ils finiraient	

★ uses *avoir* plus the past participle to describe completed events in the past

☆ usually used after *que*: **Le prof veut que je finisse ça pour demain.** The teacher wants me to finish this for tomorrow.

✪ used to describe what something was like, what used to happen, or what was happening

3

attendre
to wait

Imperative	Past participle
attends wait	attendu waited
attendons let's wait	
attendez wait	

Present

j'	attends	I wait or I am waiting
tu	attends	
il	attend	
nous	attendons	
vous	attendez	
ils	attendent	

Present subjunctive ☆

j'	attende	I wait or I am waiting
tu	attendes	
il	attende	
nous	attendions	
vous	attendiez	
ils	attendent	

Perfect ★

j'	ai attendu	I have waited or I waited
tu	as attendu	
il	a attendu	
nous	avons attendu	
vous	avez attendu	
ils	ont attendu	

Imperfect ✪

j'	attendais	I waited or I used to wait or I was waiting
tu	attendais	
il	attendait	
nous	attendions	
vous	attendiez	
ils	attendaient	

Future

j'	attendrai	I will wait
tu	attendras	
il	attendra	
nous	attendrons	
vous	attendrez	
ils	attendront	

Conditional

j'	attendrais	I would wait
tu	attendrais	
il	attendrait	
nous	attendrions	
vous	attendriez	
ils	attendraient	

★ uses *avoir* plus the past participle to describe completed events in the past

☆ usually used after *que*: **Il faut que tu attendes les autres.** You must wait for the others.

✪ used to describe what something was like, what used to happen, or what was happening

se laver
to wash (oneself)

Imperative

lave-toi
wash (yourself) or have a wash

lavons-nous
let's wash (ourselves) or let's have a wash

lavez-vous
wash (yourselves) or wash (yourself) or have a wash

Past participle

lavé washed

Present

je	me **lave**	I wash (myself) or I am washing (myself)
tu	te **laves**	
il	se **lave**	
nous	nous **lavons**	
vous	vous **lavez**	
ils	se **lavent**	

Perfect ✳

je	me **suis lavé**	I have washed (myself) or I washed (myself)
tu	t'es **lavé**	
il	s'est **lavé**	
elle	s'est **lavée**	
nous	nous **sommes lavés**	
vous	vous **êtes lavé(s)**	
ils	se **sont lavés**	
elles	se **sont lavées**	

Future

je	me **laverai**	I will wash (myself)
tu	te **laveras**	
il	se **lavera**	
nous	nous **laverons**	
vous	vous **laverez**	
ils	se **laveront**	

Present subjunctive ☆

je	me **lave**	I wash (myself) or I am washing (myself)
tu	te **laves**	
il	se **lave**	
nous	nous **lavions**	
vous	vous **laviez**	
ils	se **lavent**	

Imperfect ☉

je	me **lavais**	I washed (myself) or I used to wash (myself) or I was washing (myself)
tu	te **lavais**	
il	se **lavait**	
nous	nous **lavions**	
vous	vous **laviez**	
ils	se **lavaient**	

Conditional

je	me **laverais**	I would wash (myself)
tu	te **laverais**	
il	se **laverait**	
nous	nous **laverions**	
vous	vous **laveriez**	
ils	se **laveraient**	

✳ uses *être* plus the past participle to describe completed events in the past

☆ usually used after *que*: **Il est important que vous vous laviez les mains.** It is important that you wash your hands.

☉ used to describe what something was like, what used to happen, or what was happening

5
avoir
to have

Imperative		Past participle	
aie	have	eu	had
ayons	let's have		
ayez	have		

Present

j'	ai	I have or I am having
tu	as	
il	a	
nous	avons	
vous	avez	
ils	ont	

Present subjunctive ☆

j'	aie	I have or I am having
tu	aies	
il	ait	
nous	ayons	
vous	ayez	
ils	aient	

Perfect ★

j'	ai eu	I have had or I had
tu	as eu	
il	a eu	
nous	avons eu	
vous	avez eu	
ils	ont eu	

Imperfect ⊙

j'	avais	I had or I used to have or I was having
tu	avais	
il	avait	
nous	avions	
vous	aviez	
ils	avaient	

Future

j'	aurai	I will have
tu	auras	
il	aura	
nous	aurons	
vous	aurez	
ils	auront	

Conditional

j'	aurais	I would have
tu	aurais	
il	aurait	
nous	aurions	
vous	auriez	
ils	auraient	

★ uses *avoir* plus the past participle to describe completed events in the past
☆ usually used after *que*: **Il faut que j'aie ce jeu.** I must have that game.
⊙ used to describe what something was like, what used to happen, or what was happening

Imperative		Past participle	
sois	be	**été**	been
soyons	let's be		
soyez	be		

6
être
to be

Present

je	**suis**	I am
tu	**es**	
il	**est**	
nous	**sommes**	
vous	**êtes**	
ils	**sont**	

Present subjunctive ☆

je	**sois**	I am
tu	**sois**	
il	**soit**	
nous	**soyons**	
vous	**soyez**	
ils	**soient**	

Perfect ★

j'	**ai été**	I have been or I was
tu	**as été**	
il	**a été**	
nous	**avons été**	
vous	**avez été**	
ils	**ont été**	

Imperfect ✿

j'	**étais**	I was or I used to be or I was being
tu	**étais**	
il	**était**	
nous	**étions**	
vous	**étiez**	
ils	**étaient**	

Future

je	**serai**	I will be
tu	**seras**	
il	**sera**	
nous	**serons**	
vous	**serez**	
ils	**seront**	

Conditional

je	**serais**	I would be
tu	**serais**	
il	**serait**	
nous	**serions**	
vous	**seriez**	
ils	**seraient**	

★ uses *avoir* plus the past participle to describe completed events in the past
☆ usually used after *que*: **J'ai peur qu'elle soit là.** I'm afraid she may be here.
✿ used to describe what something was like, what used to happen, or what was happening

7
aller
to go

Imperative		Past participle	
va	go	allé	gone
allons	let's go		
allez	go		

Present

je **vais**	I go or I am going
tu **vas**	
il **va**	
nous **allons**	
vous **allez**	
ils **vont**	

Present subjunctive ☆

j' **aille**	I go or I am going
tu **ailles**	
il **aille**	
nous **allions**	
vous **alliez**	
ils **aillent**	

Perfect ✻

je **suis allé**	I have gone or I went
tu **es allé**	
il **est allé**	
elle **est allée**	
nous **sommes allés**	
vous **êtes allé(s)**	
ils **sont allés**	
elles **sont allées**	

Imperfect ⦿

j' **allais**	I went or I used to go or I was going
tu **allais**	
il **allait**	
nous **allions**	
vous **alliez**	
ils **allaient**	

Conditional

j' **irais**	I would go
tu **irais**	
il **irait**	
nous **irions**	
vous **iriez**	
ils **iraient**	

Future

j' **irai**	I will go
tu **iras**	
il **ira**	
nous **irons**	
vous **irez**	
ils **iront**	

✻ uses *être* plus the past participle to describe completed events in the past
☆ usually used after *que*: **Mamie veut que tu ailles faire des courses avec elle.** Gran wants you to go shopping with her.
⦿ used to describe what something was like, what used to happen, or what was happening

Imperative	Past participle	**8**
The imperative of	**dû** had to	
devoir is not used.		**devoir**
		to have to

Present

je **dois**	I have to or I must
tu **dois**	
il **doit**	
nous **devons**	
vous **devez**	
ils **doivent**	

Present subjunctive ☆

je **doive**	I have to or I must
tu **doives**	
il **doive**	
nous **devions**	
vous **deviez**	
ils **doivent**	

Perfect ★

j' **ai dû**	I have had to or
	I had to
tu **as dû**	
il **a dû**	
nous **avons dû**	
vous **avez dû**	
ils **ont dû**	

Imperfect ✷

je **devais**	I had to or I used to
	have to
tu **devais**	
il **devait**	
nous **devions**	
vous **deviez**	
ils **devaient**	

Future

je **devrai**	I will have to
tu **devras**	
il **devra**	
nous **devrons**	
vous **devrez**	
ils **devront**	

Conditional

je **devrais**	I ought to
tu **devrais**	
il **devrait**	
nous **devrions**	
vous **devriez**	
ils **devraient**	

★ uses *avoir* plus the past participle to describe completed events in the past

☆ usually used after *que*: **J'ai bien peur que nous devions aller le voir.** I'm afraid we may have to visit him.

✷ used to describe what something was like, what used to happen, or what was happening

9
dire
to say

Imperative		Past participle	
dis	say	dit	said
disons	let's say		
dites	say		

Present

je	**dis**	I say or I am saying
tu	**dis**	
il	**dit**	
nous	**disons**	
vous	**dites**	
ils	**disent**	

Perfect ★

j'	ai **dit**	I have said or I said
tu	as **dit**	
il	a **dit**	
nous	avons **dit**	
vous	avez **dit**	
ils	ont **dit**	

Future

je	**dir**ai	I will say
tu	**dir**as	
il	**dir**a	
nous	**dir**ons	
vous	**dir**ez	
ils	**dir**ont	

Present subjunctive ☆

je	**dise**	I say or I am saying
tu	**dises**	
il	**dise**	
nous	**disions**	
vous	**disiez**	
ils	**disent**	

Imperfect ✿

je	**dis**ais	I said or I used to say or I was saying
tu	**dis**ais	
il	**dis**ait	
nous	**dis**ions	
vous	**dis**iez	
ils	**dis**aient	

Conditional

je	**dir**ais	I would say
tu	**dir**ais	
il	**dir**ait	
nous	**dir**ions	
vous	**dir**iez	
ils	**dir**aient	

★ uses *avoir* plus the past participle to describe completed events in the past
☆ usually used after *que*: **Il faut que tu le lui dises.** You must tell her.
✿ used to describe what something was like, what used to happen, or what was happening

Imperative		Past participle	
fais	do or make	**fait**	done or made
faisons	let's do or let's make		
faites	do or make		

Present

je	**fais**	I do or I make or I am doing or I am making
tu	**fais**	
il	**fait**	
nous	**faisons**	
vous	**faites**	
ils	**font**	

Perfect ★

j'	ai **fait**	I have done or I have made or I did or I made
tu	as **fait**	
il	a **fait**	
nous	avons **fait**	
vous	avez **fait**	
ils	ont **fait**	

Future

je	**ferai**	I will do or I will make
tu	**feras**	
il	**fera**	
nous	**ferons**	
vous	**ferez**	
ils	**feront**	

Present subjunctive ☆

je	**fasse**	I do or I make or I am doing or I am making
tu	**fasses**	
il	**fasse**	
nous	**fassions**	
vous	**fassiez**	
ils	**fassent**	

Imperfect ⊙

je	**faisais**	I did or I made or I used to do or I used to make or I was doing or I was making
tu	**faisais**	
il	**faisait**	
nous	**faisions**	
vous	**faisiez**	
ils	**faisaient**	

Conditional

je	**ferais**	I would do or I would make
tu	**ferais**	
il	**ferait**	
nous	**ferions**	
vous	**feriez**	
ils	**feraient**	

★ uses *avoir* plus the past participle to describe completed events in the past

☆ usually used after *que*: **Le prof veut que nous fassions tous nos devoirs.** The teacher wants us to do all our homework.

⊙ used to describe what something was like, what used to happen, or what was happening

11
mettre
to put

Imperative		Past participle	
mets	put	mis	put
mettons	let's put		
mettez	put		

Present

je	**mets**	I put or I am putting
tu	**mets**	
il	**met**	
nous	**mettons**	
vous	**mettez**	
ils	**mettent**	

Perfect ★

j'	ai **mis**	I have put or I put
tu	as **mis**	
il	a **mis**	
nous	avons **mis**	
vous	avez **mis**	
ils	ont **mis**	

Future

je	**mettrai**	I will put
tu	**mettras**	
il	**mettra**	
nous	**mettrons**	
vous	**mettrez**	
ils	**mettront**	

Present subjunctive ☆

je	**mette**	I put or I am putting
tu	**mettes**	
il	**mette**	
nous	**mettions**	
vous	**mettiez**	
ils	**mettent**	

Imperfect ๏

je	**mettais**	I put or I used to put or I was putting
tu	**mettais**	
il	**mettait**	
nous	**mettions**	
vous	**mettiez**	
ils	**mettaient**	

Conditional

je	**mettrais**	I would put
tu	**mettrais**	
il	**mettrait**	
nous	**mettrions**	
vous	**mettriez**	
ils	**mettraient**	

★ uses *avoir* plus the past participle to describe completed events in the past

☆ usually used after *que*: **Il faut qu'elle mette aussi un casque.** She must also wear a helmet.

๏ used to describe what something was like, what used to happen, or what was happening

Imperative
The imperative of **pouvoir** is not used.

Past participle
pu been able to

12

pouvoir
to be able to

Present

je	**peux**	I am able to *or* I can
tu	**peux**	
il	**peut**	
nous	**pouvons**	
vous	**pouvez**	
ils	**peuvent**	

Perfect ★

j'	**ai pu**	I have been able to *or* I was able to *or* I could
tu	**as pu**	
il	**a pu**	
nous	**avons pu**	
vous	**avez pu**	
ils	**ont pu**	

Future

je	**pourrai**	I will be able to
tu	**pourras**	
il	**pourra**	
nous	**pourrons**	
vous	**pourrez**	
ils	**pourront**	

Present subjunctive ☆

je	**puisse**	I am able to *or* I can
tu	**puisses**	
il	**puisse**	
nous	**puissions**	
vous	**puissiez**	
ils	**puissent**	

Imperfect ○

je	**pouvais**	I was able to *or* I could *or* I used to be able to
tu	**pouvais**	
il	**pouvait**	
nous	**pouvions**	
vous	**pouviez**	
ils	**pouvaient**	

Conditional

je	**pourrais**	I would be able to *or* I could
tu	**pourrais**	
il	**pourrait**	
nous	**pourrions**	
vous	**pourriez**	
ils	**pourraient**	

★ uses *avoir* plus the past participle to describe completed events in the past

☆ usually used after *que*: **Ça m'étonnerait qu'elle puisse le faire**. I'd be surprised if she could do it.

○ used to describe what something was like, what used to happen, or what was happening

13
voir
to see

Imperative		Past participle	
vois	see	**vu**	seen
voyons	let's see		
voyez	see		

Present

je **vois**	I see or I am seeing
tu **vois**	
il **voit**	
nous **voyons**	
vous **voyez**	
ils **voient**	

Present subjunctive ☆

je **voie**	I see or I am seeing
tu **voies**	
il **voie**	
nous **voyions**	
vous **voyiez**	
ils **voient**	

Perfect ★

j' **ai vu**	I have seen or I saw
tu **as vu**	
il **a vu**	
nous **avons vu**	
vous **avez vu**	
ils **ont vu**	

Imperfect ✺

je **voyais**	I saw or I used to see or I was seeing
tu **voyais**	
il **voyait**	
nous **voyions**	
vous **voyiez**	
ils **voyaient**	

Future

je **verrai**	I will see
tu **verras**	
il **verra**	
nous **verrons**	
vous **verrez**	
ils **verront**	

Conditional

je **verrais**	I would see
tu **verrais**	
il **verrait**	
nous **verrions**	
vous **verriez**	
ils **verraient**	

★ uses *avoir* plus the past participle to describe completed events in the past

☆ usually used after *que*: **Il faut que vous voyiez mon nouveau VTT.** You must see my new cross-country bike.

✺ used to describe what something was like, what used to happen, or what was happening

Imperative	Past participle
The **veuille** and the **veuillons** form of the imperative are not used.	voul**u** wanted
veuillez please	

14
vouloir
to want

Present

je	**veux**	I want or I am wanting
tu	**veux**	
il	**veut**	
nous	**voulons**	
vous	**voulez**	
ils	**veulent**	

Perfect ★

j'	ai **voulu**	I have wanted or I wanted
tu	as **voulu**	
il	a **voulu**	
nous	avons **voulu**	
vous	avez **voulu**	
ils	ont **voulu**	

Future

je	**voudrai**	I will want
tu	**voudras**	
il	**voudra**	
nous	**voudrons**	
vous	**voudrez**	
ils	**voudront**	

Present subjunctive ☆

je	**veuille**	I want or I am wanting
tu	**veuilles**	
il	**veuille**	
nous	**voulions**	
vous	**vouliez**	
ils	**veuillent**	

Imperfect ✪

je	**voulais**	I wanted or I used to want or I was wanting
tu	**voulais**	
il	**voulait**	
nous	**voulions**	
vous	**vouliez**	
ils	**voulaient**	

Conditional

je	**voudrais**	I would like
tu	**voudrais**	
il	**voudrait**	
nous	**voudrions**	
vous	**voudriez**	
ils	**voudraient**	

★ uses *avoir* plus the past participle to describe completed events in the past

☆ usually used after *que*: **Ça m'étonnerait qu'il veuille venir avec nous.** I'd be surprised if he wanted to come.

✪ used to describe what something was like, what used to happen, or what was happening

French irregular verb forms

The list shows the main forms of other irregular verbs. The number before the infinitive is the number given after verbs in the dictionary which follow this pattern.

(1) = Present   **(3)** = Imperfect

(2) = Past participle   **(4)** = Future

15 **abréger** (1) j'abrège, nous abrégeons, ils abrègent (2) abrégé (3) j'abrégeais (4) j'abrégerai

16 **acheter** (1) j'achète, nous achetons, ils achètent (2) acheté (3) j'achetais (4) j'achèterai

17 **acquérir** (1) j'acquiers, il acquiert, nous acquérons, vous acquérez ils acquièrent (2) acquis (3) j'acquérais (4) j'acquerrai

18 **appeler** (1) j'appelle, nous appelons, appelé (2) (3) j'appelais (4) j'appellerai

19 **apprendre** (1) j'apprends, nous apprenons, vous apprenez, ils apprennent (2) appris (3) j'apprenais (4) j'apprendrai

20 **s'asseoir** (1) je m'assieds, nous nous asseyons, vous vous asseyez, ils s'asseyent (2) assis (3) je m'asseyais (4) je m'assiérai

21 **battre** (1) je bats, il bat, nous battons (2) battu (3) je battais (4) je battrai

22 **boire** (1) je bois, nous buvons, ils boivent (2) bu (3) je buvais (4) je boirai

23 **bouillir** (1) je bous, nous bouillons (2) bouilli (3) je bouillais (4) je bouillirai

24 **céder** (1) je cède, nous cédons, ils cèdent (2) cédé (3) je cédais (4) je céderai

25 **conclure** (1) je conclus, nous concluons (2) conclu (3) je concluais (4) je conclurai

26 **conduire** (1) je conduis, nous conduisons (2) conduit (3) je conduisais (4) je conduirai

27 **connaître** (1) je connais, nous connaissons (2) connu (3) je connaissais (4) je connaîtrai

28 **coudre** (1) je couds, nous cousons, vous cousez, ils cousent (2) cousu (3) je cousais (4) je coudrai

29 **courir** (1) je cours, nous courons (2) couru (3) je courais (4) je courrai

30 **couvrir** (1) je couvre, nous couvrons (2) couvert (3) je couvrais (4) je couvrirai

31 **craindre** (1) je crains, nous craignons (2) craint (3) je craignais (4) je craindrai

32 créer (1) je crée, nous créons **(2)** créé **(3)** je créais **(4)** je créerai

33 croire (1) je crois, nous croyons, ils croient **(2)** cru **(3)** je croyais **(4)** je croirai

34 croître (1) je croîs, nous croissons **(2)** crû, crue **(3)** je croissais **(4)** je croîtrai

35 cueillir (1) je cueille, nous cueillons **(2)** cueilli **(3)** je cueillais **(4)** je cueillerai

36 cuire (1) je cuis, nous cuisons, ils cuisent **(2)** cuit **(3)** je cuisais **(4)** je cuirai

37 dormir (1) je dors, nous dormons **(2)** dormi **(3)** je dormais **(4)** je dormirai

38 écrire (1) j'écris, nous écrivons **(2)** écrit **(3)** j'écrivais **(4)** j'écrirai

39 employer (1) j'emploie, nous employons, vous employez, ils emploient **(2)** employé **(3)** j'employais **(4)** j'emploierai

40 envoyer (1) j'envoie, nous envoyons, vous envoyez, ils envoient **(2)** envoyé **(3)** j'envoyais **(4)** j'enverrai

41 essuyer (1) j'essuie, nous essuyons, vous essuyez, ils essuient **(2)** essuyé **(3)** j'essuyais **(4)** j'essuierai

42 faillir (1) je faille **(2)** failli

43 falloir (1) je il faut **(2)** fallu **(3)** il fallait **(4)** il faudra

44 fuir (1) je fuis, nous fuyons, ils fuient **(2)** fui **(3)** je fuyais **(4)** je fuirai

45 geler (1) je gèle, nous gelons, vous gelez, ils gèlent **(2)** gelé **(3)** je gelais **(4)** je gèlerai

46 haïr (1) je hais, nous haïssons, ils haïssent **(2)** haï **(3)** je haïssais **(4)** je haïrai

47 interdire (1) j'interdis, nous interdisons, vous interdisez **(2)** interdit **(3)** j'interdisais **(4)** j'interdirai

48 jeter (1) je jette, nous jetons, ils jettent **(2)** jeté **(3)** je jetais **(4)** je jetterai

49 joindre (1) je joins, nous joignons **(2)** joint **(3)** je joignais **(4)** je joindrai

50 lever (1) je lève, nous levons, ils lèvent **(2)** levé **(3)** je levais **(4)** je lèverai

51 lire (1) je lis, nous lisons **(2)** lu **(3)** je lisais **(4)** je lirai

52 manger (1) je mange, nous mangeons **(2)** mangé **(3)** je mangeais **(4)** je mangerai

53 mentir (1) je mens, nous mentons **(2)** menti **(3)** je mentais **(4)** je mentirai

54 mourir (1) je meurs, nous mourons, ils meurent **(2)** mort **(3)** je mourais **(4)** je mourrai

55 naître (1) je nais, il naît, nous naissons **(2)** né **(3)** je naissais **(4)** je naîtrai

56 offrir (1) j'offre, nous offrons **(2)** offert **(3)** j'offrais **(4)** j'offrirai

57 paraître (1) je parais, il paraît, nous paraissons **(2)** paru **(3)** je paraissais **(4)** je paraîtrai

58 partir (1) je pars, nous partons **(2)** parti **(3)** je partais **(4)** je partirai

59 payer (1) je paie/je paye, nous payons, vous payez, ils paient/ils payent **(2)** payé **(3)** je payais **(4)** je paierai/je payerai

60 peindre (1) je peins, nous peignons **(2)** peint **(3)** je peignais **(4)** je peindrai

61 placer (1) je place, nous plaçons **(2)** placé **(3)** je plaçais **(4)** je placerai

62 plaire (1) je plais, il plaît, nous plaisons **(2)** plu **(3)** je plaisais **(4)** je plairai

63 pleuvoir (1) je il pleut **(2)** plu **(3)** il pleuvait **(4)** il pleuvra

64 prendre (1) je prends, nous prenons, ils prennent **(2)** pris **(3)** je prenais **(4)** je prendrai

65 prévoir (1) je prévois, nous prévoyons, vous prévoyez, ils prévoient **(2)** prévu **(3)** je prévoyais **(4)** je prévoirai

66 recevoir (1) je reçois, il reçoit, ils reçoivent **(2)** reçu **(3)** je recevais **(4)** je recevrai

67 résoudre (1) je résous, nous résolvons, vous résolvez, ils résolvent **(2)** résolu **(3)** je résolvais **(4)** je résoudrai

68 rire (1) je ris, nous rions **(2)** ri **(3)** je riais **(4)** je rirai

69 rompre (1) je romps, il rompt, nous rompons **(2)** rompu **(3)** je rompais **(4)** je romprai

70 savoir (1) je sais, nous savons, ils savent **(2)** su **(3)** je savais **(4)** je saurai **(5)** pres subj je sache

71 servir (1) je sers, nous servons **(2)** servi **(3)** je servais **(4)** je servirai

72 sortir (1) je sors, nous sortons **(2)** sorti **(3)** je sortais **(4)** je sortirai

73 souffrir (1) je souffre, nous souffrons **(2)** souffert **(3)** je souffrais **(4)** je souffrirai

74 suffire (1) je suffis, nous suffisons **(2)** suffi **(3)** je suffisais **(4)** je suffirai

75 suivre (1) je suis, nous suivons **(2)** suivi **(3)** je suivais **(4)** je suivrai

76 taire (1) je me tais, nous nous taisons **(2)** tu **(3)** je me taisais **(4)** je me tairai

77 tenir (1) je tiens, nous tenons, ils tiennent **(2)** tenu **(3)** je tenais **(4)** je tiendrai

78 traire (1) je trais, nous trayons, ils traient **(2)** trait **(3)** je trayais **(4)** je trairai

79 vaincre (1) je vaincs, il vainc, nous vainquons **(2)** vaincu **(3)** je vainquais **(4)** je vaincrai

80 valoir (1) je vaux, il vaut, nous valons **(2)** valu **(3)** je valais **(4)** je vaudrai

81 venir (1) je viens, nous venons, ils viennent **(2)** venu **(3)** je venais **(4)** je viendrai

82 vivre (1) je vis, nous vivons **(2)** vécu **(3)** je vivais **(4)** je vivrai

Aa

a *indefinite article* **1** (*before a noun which is masculine in French*) un; **a tree** un arbre; **2** (*before a noun which is feminine in French*) une; **a table** une table; **3 five euros a kilo** cinq euros le kilo; **4 fifty kilometres an hour** cinquante kilomètres l'heure; **5 three times a day** trois fois par jour.

abandon *verb* abandonner [1].

abbey *noun* abbaye *Fem.*; **Westminster Abbey** l'Abbaye de Westminster.

abbreviation *noun* abréviation *Fem.*

abide *verb* **I can't abide ...** je ne supporte pas ....

ability *noun* capacité *Fem.*; **the ability to do** la capacité de faire.

able *adjective* **to be able to do** pouvoir [12] faire; **she wasn't able to come** elle n'a pas pu venir.

abnormal *adjective* anormal (*Masc. plural* anormaux).

abolish *verb* abolir [2].

abortion *noun* avortement *Masc.*

about *preposition* **1** (*on the subject of*) sur; **a film about Picasso** un film sur Picasso; **2 what's it about?**; **3** (*concerning or in relation to*) au sujet de; **he wants to talk to you about your exam** il veut te parler au sujet de ton examen; **4 to talk about something** parler de quelque chose; **what is she talking about?** de quoi parle-t-elle?; **5 to think about something/somebody** penser à quelque

chose/quelqu'un; **I'm thinking about you** je pense à toi.

about *adverb* **1** (*approximately*) environ, à peu près; **there are about sixty people** il y a environ soixante personnes, il y a à peu près soixante personnes; **2** (*when talking about the time*) vers; **about three o'clock** vers trois heures; ★ **to be about to do** être sur le point de faire; **I'm (just) about to leave** je suis sur le point de partir.

above *preposition* **1** au dessus de; **above the table** au dessus de la table; **2 above all** surtout.

abroad *adverb* à l'étranger; **to go abroad** aller à l'étranger; **to live abroad** vivre à l'étranger.

abscess *noun* abcès *Masc.*

abseiling *noun* descente *Fem.* en rappel.

absent *adjective* absent; **to be absent from** être absent de.

absent-minded *adjective* distrait.

absolute *adjective* complet (*Fem.* complète); **an absolute disaster** un désastre complet.

absolutely *adverb* **1** absolument; **it's absolutely dreadful** c'est absolument affreux; **2** tout à fait; **you're absolutely right** tu as tout à fait raison.

absorb *verb* absorber [1].

abuse *noun* **1 alcohol abuse** abus *Masc.* d'alcool; **drug abuse** usage *Masc.* des stupéfiants; **2** (*violent treatment of a person*) mauvais traitement *Masc.*; **3** (*insulting words*) injures *Fem. plural*.

a b c d e f g h i j k l m n o p q r s t u v w x y z

a

abuse *verb* to abuse somebody maltraiter [1] quelqu'un.

academic *adjective* the academic year l'année universitaire.

accelerate *verb* accélérer [24].

accelerator *noun* accélérateur *Masc.*

accent *noun* accent *Masc.*; **she has a French accent** elle a l'accent français.

accept *verb* accepter [1].

acceptable *adjective* acceptable.

acceptance *noun* acceptation *Fem.*

access *noun* accès *Masc.*

access *verb* to access something accéder [24] à quelque chose.

accessory *noun* accessoire *Masc.*

accident & emergency *noun* les urgences *Fem.* plural.

accident *noun* **1** accident *Masc.*; **to have an accident** avoir un accident; **a road accident** un accident de la route; **a car accident** un accident de voiture; **2** (*chance*) hasard *Masc.*; **by accident** par hasard; **I found it by accident** je l'ai trouvé par hasard.

accidental *adjective* fortuit; **an accidental discovery** une découverte fortuite.

accidentally *adverb* **1** (*without meaning to*) accidentellement; **I accidentally knocked over his glass** j'ai accidentellement renversé son verre; **2** (*by chance*) par hasard; **I accidentally discovered that …** j'ai découvert par hasard que ....

accommodate *verb* recevoir [66]; **the centre can accommodate sixty people** le centre peut recevoir soixante personnes.

accommodation *noun* logement *Masc.*; **I'm looking for accommodation** je cherche un logement.

accompany *verb* to accompany somebody accompagner [1] quelqu'un.

according *in phrase* according to selon; **according to Sophie** selon Sophie.

accordion *noun* accordéon *Masc.*

account *noun* **1** (*in a bank, shop, or post office*) compte *Masc.*; **a bank account** un compte bancaire; **to open an account** ouvrir un compte; **I have fifty pounds in my account** j'ai cinquante livres sur mon compte; **2** (*a description of an experience or event*) compte rendu *Masc.*; **3** on account of à cause de; **the station is closed on account of the strike** la gare est fermée à cause de la grève; **4** to take something into account tenir compte de quelque chose; **we will take his illness into account** nous tiendrons compte de sa maladie.

accountant *noun* comptable *Masc. & Fem.*; **she is an accountant** elle est comptable.

accuracy *noun* précision *Fem.*

accurate *adjective* précis.

accurately *adverb* avec précision.

accuse *verb* accuser [1]; **to accuse somebody of something**

accuser quelqu'un de quelque chose ; **to accuse someone of doing something** accuser quelqu'un d'avoir fait quelque chose ; **she accused me of stealing her pen** elle m'a accusé d'avoir volé son stylo.

accustomed to *adjective* ; **to be accustomed to something** être [6] habitué à ; **she's accustomed to having lots of homework** elle a l'habitude d'avoir beaucoup de devoirs.

ace *noun* as *Masc.* ; **the ace of hearts** l'as de cœur.

ace *adjective* super (*informal*) ; **he's an ace drummer** c'est un super batteur.

ache *verb* **my arm aches** j'ai mal au bras ; **my head aches** j'ai mal à la tête.

achieve *verb* **1** accomplir [2] ; **she's achieved a great deal** elle a beaucoup accompli ; **2 to achieve an ambition** réaliser [1] une ambition ; **3 to achieve an aim** atteindre [60] un objectif ; **4 to achieve success** réussir [2].

achievement *noun* **1** réussite *Fem.* ; **it's a great achievement** c'est une grande réussite ; **2 a sense of achievement** un sentiment de satisfaction.

acid *noun* acide *Masc.*

acid rain *noun* pluies *Fem. plural* acides.

acne *noun* acné *Fem.*

acorn *noun* gland *Masc.*

acrobat *noun* acrobate *Masc. & Fem.*

across *preposition* **1** (*over to the other side of*) **to walk across something** traverser [1] quelque chose ; **we walked across the park** nous avons traversé le parc ; **to run across the road** traverser la route en courant ; **2** (*on the other side of*) de l'autre côté de ; **the house across the street** la maison de l'autre côté de la rue ; **3 across from** en face de ; **she was sitting across from me** elle était assise en face de moi.

acrylic *noun* acrylique *Masc.*

act *noun* acte *Masc.*

act *verb* **1** (*in a play or film*) jouer [1] ; **to act the part of** jouer le rôle de ; **2** (*to take action*) agir [2].

acting *noun* jeu *Masc.* ; **she wants to go into acting** elle veut devenir actrice ; **the acting was terrible/sensational** les acteurs jouaient très mal/bien.

action *noun* action *Fem.*

action replay *noun* répétition *Fem.* d'une séquence.

active *adjective* actif (*Fem.* active).

activity *noun* activité *Fem.*

activity holiday *noun* vacances *Fem. plural* sportives.

actor *noun* acteur *Masc.* ; **who's your favourite actor?** qui est votre acteur préféré ?

actress *noun* actrice *Fem.* ; **she's my favourite actress** c'est mon actrice préférée.

actual *adjective* **his actual words** ses paroles précises ; ★ **in actual fact** en fait.

actually *adverb* **1** (*in fact, as it happens*) en fait ; **actually, I've**

a b c d e f g h i j k l m n o p q r s t u v w x y z

a b c d e f g h i j k l m n o p q r s t u v w x y z

changed my mind en fait, j'ai changé d'avis; **he's not actually here at the moment** en fait il n'est pas là en ce moment; **2** (*really and truly*) vraiment; **did she actually say that?** est-ce qu'elle a vraiment dit ça?

acupuncture noun acupuncture *Fem.*

acute adjective **1** (*pain*) vif (*Fem.* vive); **2 an acute accent** un accent aigu.

ad noun **1** pub *Fem.* (*informal*); **2** (*in a newspaper*) annonce *Fem.*; **to put an ad in the paper** mettre une annonce dans le journal; **the small ads** les petites annonces.

AD abbreviation après Jésus-Christ, apr. J-C; **in 400 AD** en quatre cents après Jésus-Christ.

adapt verb **1 to adapt something** adapter [1] quelque chose (*a book or film*); **2 to adapt to something** s'adapter [1] à quelque chose; **she's adapted to the new system** elle s'est adaptée au nouveau système.

adaptor noun adaptateur *Masc.*

add verb ajouter [1]; **add three eggs** ajoutez trois œufs.

• **to add something up** additionner [1] quelque chose.

addict noun **1** (*drug addict*) drogué, droguée *Masc., Fem.*; **2** accro *Masc. & Fem.* (*informal*); **she's a telly addict** c'est une accro de la télé; **he's a football addict** c'est un accro du foot.

addicted adjective **1 to become addicted to heroin** former une dépendance à l'héroïne; **2 I'm**

addicted to tomatoes je raffole des tomates.

addition noun **1** (*adding up*) addition *Fem.*; **2 in addition** en plus; **3 in addition to** en plus de.

additional adjective supplémentaire; **additional costs** les frais supplémentaires.

additive noun additif *Masc.*

address noun adresse *Fem.*; **what's your address?** quelle est ton adresse?; **to change address** changer d'adresse.

address book noun carnet *Masc.* d'adresses.

adequate adjective suffisant.

adhesive noun colle *Fem.*

adhesive adjective collant; **adhesive tape** du papier collant.

adjective noun adjectif *Masc.*

adjust verb **1 to adjust something** régler [24] quelque chose; **to adjust the height** régler la hauteur; **2 to adjust to something** s'adapter [1] à quelque chose.

adjustable adjective réglable.

administration noun administration *Fem.*

admiral noun amiral *Masc.*

admiration noun admiration *Fem.*

admire verb admirer [1].

admission noun entrée *Fem.*; **'no admission'** 'entrée interdite'; **'admission free'** 'entrée gratuite'.

admit verb **1** (*confess*) reconnaître [27]; **she admits she lied** elle reconnaît qu'elle a menti; **2** (*concede*) admettre [11]; **I must admit that ...** j'admets que ...; **3** (*allow to enter*) laisser [1] entrer;

to admit somebody to a restaurant laisser entrer quelqu'un dans un restaurant; **4 to be admitted to hospital** être [6] hospitalisé.

adolescence noun adolescence Fem.

adolescent noun adolescent Masc., adolescente Fem.

adopt verb adopter [1].

adopted adjective adoptif (Fem. adoptive).

adoption noun adoption Fem.

adore verb adorer [1].

Adriatic Sea noun the Adriatic Sea la mer Adriatique.

adult noun adulte Masc. & Fem.

adult adjective adulte; **the adult population** la population adulte.

Adult Education noun enseignement Masc. pour adultes.

advance noun progrès Masc.; **advances in technology** des progrès dans le domaine de la technologie.

advance verb **1** (make progress) progresser [1]; **2** (move forward) avancer [61].

advanced adjective avancé.

advantage noun **1** avantage Masc.; **there are several advantages** il y a plusieurs avantages; **2 to take advantage of something** profiter de quelque chose; **I took advantage of the sales to buy myself some shoes** j'ai profité des soldes pour m'acheter des chaussures; **3 to take advantage of somebody** (unfairly) exploiter quelqu'un.

Advent noun Avent Masc.

adventure noun aventure Fem.

adventurous adjective aventureux (Fem. aventureuse).

adverb noun adverbe Masc.

advert, advertisement noun **1** (at the cinema or on television) publicité Fem.; **2** (commercial advertisement in a newspaper) annonce Fem.; **3** (small ad in a newspaper advertising a job, an article for sale, etc) petite annonce Fem.

advertise verb **1 to advertise something in the newspaper** (in the small ads) mettre [11] une annonce pour quelque chose dans le journal; **I saw a bike advertised in the paper** j'ai vu une annonce pour un vélo dans le journal; **2 to advertise a product** faire [10] de la publicité pour un produit.

advertising noun publicité Fem.

advice noun conseils Masc. plural; **to ask for advice about something** demander des conseils à propos de quelque chose; **a piece of advice** un conseil.

advise verb conseiller [1]; **to advise somebody to do** conseiller à quelqu'un de faire; **I advised him to stop** je lui ai conseillé d'arrêter; **I advised her not to wait** je lui ai conseillé de ne pas attendre.

adviser noun conseiller Masc., conseillère Fem.

aerial noun antenne Fem.

aerobics noun aérobic Masc.; **to do aerobics** faire de l'aérobic.

aeroplane noun avion Masc.

aerosol noun **an aerosol can** une bombe.

a
b
c
d
e
f
g
h
i
j
k
l
m
n
o
p
q
r
s
t
u
v
w
x
y
z

a

affair noun **1** (event) affaire Fem.;
international affairs les affaires
internationales; **2 a love affair** une
aventure amoureuse.

affect verb affecter [1].

affectionate adjective affectueux
(Fem. affectueuse).

afford verb **to be able to afford to
do** avoir [5] les moyens de faire; **we
can't afford to go out much** nous
n'avons pas les moyens de sortir
beaucoup; **I can't afford a new
bike** je n'ai pas les moyens de
m'acheter un nouveau vélo.

afraid adjective **1 to be afraid of
something** avoir peur de quelque
chose; **she's afraid of dogs** elle a
peur des chiens; **2 I'm afraid
there's no milk left** je suis désolé
mais il ne reste plus de lait; **I'm
afraid so** hélas oui; **I'm afraid not**
hélas non.

Africa noun Afrique Fem.; **in Africa**
en Afrique; **to Africa** en Afrique.

African noun Africain Masc.,
Africaine Fem.

African adjective africain (Fem.
africaine).

after preposition, adverb,
conjunction après; **after 10 o'clock**
après dix heures; **after lunch** après
le déjeuner; **after school** après
l'école; **the day after tomorrow**
après-demain; **soon after** peu
après; **after I've finished my
homework** après que j'aurai fini
mes devoirs; **to run after
somebody** courir après quelqu'un.

after all adverb après tout; **after
all, she's only six** elle n'a que six
ans après tout.

afternoon noun après-midi Masc.
or Fem.; **this afternoon** cet après-
midi; **tomorrow afternoon** demain
après-midi; **yesterday afternoon**
hier après-midi; **on Saturday
afternoon** samedi après-midi; **on
Saturday afternoons** le samedi
après-midi; **at four o'clock in the
afternoon** à quatre heures de
l'après-midi; **every afternoon** tous
les après-midi.

afters noun dessert Masc.

after-shave noun après-rasage
Masc.

afterwards adverb après; **shortly
afterwards** peu de temps après.

again adverb **1** (one more time)
encore une fois; **try again** essaie
encore une fois; **I've forgotten it
again** je l'ai oublié encore une fois;
2 (once more) de nouveau; **she's ill
again** elle est de nouveau malade;
3 I saw her again yesterday je l'ai
revue hier; **you should ask again**
tu devrais redemander; **4 I don't
want to see her again** je ne veux
plus la revoir; **never again!** jamais
plus!

against preposition contre;
against the wall contre le mur; **to
lean against the wall** s'appuyer
contre le mur; **I'm against the idea**
je suis contre l'idée; **the fight
against racism** la lutte contre le
racisme.

age noun âge Masc. **1 at the age of
fifteen** à l'âge de quinze ans; **she's
the same age as me** elle a le même
âge que moi; **to be under age** être
mineur; **2 I haven't seen Johnny
for ages** ça fait une éternité que je
n'ai pas vu Johnny; **I haven't been**

to London for ages ça fait une éternité que je ne suis pas allé à Londres.

aged *adjective* âgé de; **a woman aged thirty** une femme âgée de trente ans.

agenda *noun* ordre *Masc.* du jour.

agent *noun* agent *Masc.*; **an estate agent** un agent immobilier; **a travel agent's** une agence de voyage.

aggressive *adjective* agressif (*Fem.* agressive).

ago *adverb* **an hour ago** il y a une heure; **three days ago** il y a trois jours; **five years ago** il y a cinq ans; **a long time ago** il y a longtemps; **not long ago** il n'y a pas longtemps; **how long ago was it?** c'était il y a combien de temps?

agree *verb* **1 to agree with somebody** être [6] d'accord avec quelqu'un; **I agree with Laura** je suis d'accord avec Laura; **I don't agree** je ne suis pas d'accord; **2 I agree that** ... je suis d'accord sur le fait que ...; **I agree that it's too late now** je suis d'accord sur le fait qu'il est maintenant trop tard; **3 to agree to do** accepter [1] de faire; **Steve's agreed to help me** Steve a accepté de m'aider; **4 coffee doesn't agree with me** je ne supporte pas le café.

agreement *noun* accord *Masc.*

agricultural *adjective* agricole.

agriculture *noun* agriculture *Fem.*

ahead *adverb* **1 go ahead!** allez-y!; **2 straight ahead** tout droit; **go straight ahead until you get to the crossroads** allez tout droit jusqu'au carrefour; **3 our team was ten points ahead** notre équipe avait dix points d'avance; **4 to be ahead of time** être en avance.

aid *noun* **1** aide *Fem.*; **aid to developing countries** l'aide aux pays en voie de développement; **2 in aid of** au profit de; **in aid of the homeless** au profit des sans-abri.

AIDS *noun* sida *Masc.* (short for: syndrome immunodéficitaire acquis); **to have AIDS** avoir le sida.

aim *noun* objectif *Masc.*; **their aim is to control pollution** leur objectif est de contrôler la pollution.

aim *verb* **1 to aim to do** avoir [5] l'intention de faire; **we're aiming to finish it today** nous avons l'intention de le finir aujourd'hui; **2 a campaign aimed at young people** une campagne qui vise les jeunes; **3 to aim a gun at somebody** braquer [1] un révolver sur quelqu'un.

air *noun* **1** air *Masc.*; **in the open air** en plein air; **to go out for a breath of air** sortir prendre l'air; **2 to travel by air** voyager en avion.

airbag *noun* (in a car) airbag *Masc.*

air-conditioned *adjective* climatisé.

air conditioning *noun* climatisation *Fem.*

Air Force *noun* Armée *Fem.* de l'air.

air hostess *noun* hôtesse *Fem.* de l'air; **she's an air hostess** elle est hôtesse de l'air.

a b c d e f g h i j k l m n o p q r s t u v w x y z

a

airline noun compagnie Fem. aérienne.

b

airmail noun by airmail par avion.

c

airport noun aéroport Masc.

aisle noun allée Fem. centrale.

d

e

alarm noun alarme Fem.; **a fire alarm** une alarme incendie; **a burglar alarm** une alarme contre le vol.

f

g

alarm clock noun réveil Masc.

h

album noun album Masc.

i

alcohol noun alcool Masc.

alcoholic noun alcoolique Masc. & Fem.

j

k

alcoholic adjective alcoolisé; **alcoholic drinks** les boissons alcoolisées.

l

m

alert adjective vif (Fem. vive) noun **on the alert: you must be on the alert for pickpockets** faites attention aux pickpockets.

n

o

A levels noun plural baccalauréat Masc., bac Masc. (informal) (Students take 'le bac' at the same age as A levels are taken in Britain. You can explain A levels briefly as follows: Les A levels sont répartis en deux niveaux, AS et A2. On passe les examens AS au bout d'une année de préparation, généralement dans quatre ou cinq matières. On passe les examens A2 un an plus tard, dans un plus petit nombre de matières, en choisissant parmi celles qui ont déjà fait l'objet d'un examen AS. La meilleure note que l'on peut obtenir est A et la note la plus basse est N. Les A levels permettent de s'inscrire à l'université). SEE baccalauréat.

p

q

r

s

t

u

v

w

x

y

z

Algeria noun Algérie Fem.; **to Algeria** en Algérie; **in Algeria** en Algérie.

alibi noun alibi Masc.

alien noun 1 (foreigner) étranger Masc., étrangère Fem.; 2 (from outer space) extra-terrestre Masc. & Fem.

alike adjective pareil (Fem. pareille) 1 **they're all alike** ils sont tous pareils; 2 **to look alike** se ressembler; **the two brothers look alike** les deux frères se ressemblent.

alive adjective vivant.

all along adverb depuis le début; **I knew it all along** je le savais depuis le début.

allergic adjective allergique; **to be allergic to something** être allergique à quelque chose.

allergy noun allergie Fem.; **she has an allergy to cats** elle est allergique aux chats.

alligator noun alligator Masc.

allow verb 1 **to allow somebody to do** permettre [11] à quelqu'un de faire; **the teacher allowed them to go out** le prof leur a permis de sortir; 2 **to be allowed to do** avoir [5] le droit de faire; **I'm not allowed to go out during the week** je n'ai pas le droit de sortir en semaine.

all right adverb 1 (yes) d'accord; **'come round to my house around six'–'all right'** 'passe chez moi vers six heures'–'d'accord'; 2 (fine) bien; **is everything all right?** est-ce que tout va bien?; **she's all right now** elle va bien maintenant; **it's all right by me** ça ne me dérange pas; 3 (not bad) pas mal; **the meal was**

all right le repas n'était pas mal; **4 are you all right?** ça va?; **5 is it all right to ...?** est-ce qu'on peut ...?; **is it all right to leave the door open?** est-ce qu'on peut laisser la porte ouverte?

ally noun allié Masc., alliée Fem.

almond noun amande Fem.

almost adverb presque; **almost every day** presque tous les jours; **almost everybody** presque tout le monde; **she's almost five** elle a presque cinq ans.

alone adjective **1** seul; **he lives alone** il habite seul; **2 leave me alone!** laisse-moi tranquille!; **3 leave these papers alone!** ne touche pas à ces papiers!

along preposition **1** le long de; **there are trees all along the road** il y a des arbres tout le long de la route; **2** (there is often no direct translation for 'along' so the sentence has to be expressed differently) **she lives along the road from me** elle habite dans la même rue que moi; **to go for a walk along the beach** aller se promener sur la plage.

aloud adverb à haute voix; **to read something aloud** lire quelque chose à haute voix.

alphabet noun alphabet Masc.

alphabetical adjective alphabétique; **in alphabetical order** par ordre alphabétique.

Alps plural noun the Alps les Alpes.

already adverb déjà; **they've already left** ils sont déjà partis; **it's**

six o'clock already! il est déjà six heures!

Alsatian noun (dog) berger Masc. allemand.

also adverb aussi; **I've also invited Karen** j'ai aussi invité Karen.

alter verb changer [52].

alternate adjective **on alternate days** un jour sur deux.

alternative noun **1** possibilité Fem.; **there are several alternatives** il y a plusieurs possibilités; **2 we have no alternative** nous n'avons pas le choix.

alternative adjective autre; **to find an alternative solution** trouver une autre solution.

alternatively adverb sinon; **alternatively, we could go together on Saturday** sinon, on pourrait y aller ensemble samedi.

alternative medicine noun médecine Fem. douce.

although conjunction bien que (followed by subjunctive); **although she's ill, she's willing to help us** bien qu'elle soit malade, elle est prête à nous aider.

altitude noun altitude Fem.

altogether adverb **1** en tout; **I've spent thirty pounds altogether** j'ai dépensé trente livres en tout; **2** (completely) complètement; **I'm not altogether convinced** je ne suis pas complètement convaincu.

aluminium noun aluminium Masc.

always adverb toujours; **I always leave at five** je pars toujours à cinq heures.

am verb SEE be.

a b c d e f g h i j k l m n o p q r s t u v w x y z

a.m. *abbreviation* du matin; **at 8 a.m.** à huit heures du matin.

amateur *noun* amateur *Masc.*; **amateur dramatics** théâtre *Masc.* amateur.

amaze *verb* surprendre [64]; **what amazes me is** ... ce qui me surprend c'est ....

amazed *adjective* stupéfait; **I was amazed to see her** j'étais stupéfait de la voir.

amazement *noun* stupéfaction *Fem.*; **to my amazement: to my amazement she agreed** à ma grande surprise elle s'est mise d'accord.

amazing *adjective* 1 (*terrific*) fantastique; **your dress is amazing!** ta robe est fantastique!; **they've got an amazing house** ils ont une maison fantastique; 2 (*extraordinary*) extraordinaire; **she has an amazing number of friends** elle a un nombre extraordinaire d'amis; **he told me an amazing story** il m'a raconté une histoire extraordinaire.

ambassador *noun* ambassadeur *Masc.*, ambassadrice *Fem.*.

ambition *noun* ambition *Fem.*

ambitious *adjective* ambitieux (*Fem.* ambitieuse).

ambulance *noun* ambulance *Fem.*

ambulance driver *noun* ambulancier *Masc.*, ambulancière *Fem.*

amenities *plural noun* équipements *Masc. plural.*

America *noun* Amérique *Fem.*; **in America** en Amérique; **to America** en Amérique.

American *noun* Américain *Masc.*, Américaine *Fem.*.

American *adjective* américain (*Fem.* américaine).

ammunition *noun* munition *Fem.*

among, amongst *preposition* 1 parmi; **I found it amongst my books** je l'ai trouvé parmi les livres; 2 (*between*) entre; **you can decide amongst yourselves** vous pouvez décider entre vous.

amount *noun* 1 quantité *Fem.*; **an enormous amount of bread** une énorme quantité de pain; **a huge amount of work** un travail énorme; 2 (*of money*) somme *Fem.*; **a large amount of money** une grosse somme d'argent.

amount *verb* **to amount to** s'élever [50] à; **the bill amounts to five hundred euros** la facture s'élève à cinq cents euros.

amp *noun* 1 (*electricity*) ampère *Masc.*; 2 (*amplifier*) ampli *Masc.* (*informal*).

amplifier *noun* amplificateur *Masc.*

amuse *verb* amuser [1].

amusement arcade *noun* salle *Fem.* de jeux électroniques.

amusing *adjective* amusant.

an *article* SEE **a**.

anaesthetic *noun* anesthésie *Fem.*

analyse *verb* analyser [1].

analysis *noun* analyse *Fem.*

ancestor *noun* ancêtre *Masc.* & *Fem.*

anchor *noun* ancre *Fem.*

anchovy *noun* anchois *Masc.*

ancient *adjective* **1** (*historic*) ancien (*Fem.* ancienne); **an ancient abbey** une abbaye ancienne; **2** (*very old*) très vieux (*Fem.* très vieille); **an ancient pair of jeans** un très vieux jean; **3 ancient Greece** la Grèce antique.

and *conjunction* **1** et; **Sean and Anna** Sean et Anna; **Rosie and I** Rosie et moi; **your shoes and socks** tes chaussures et tes chaussettes; **2 louder and louder** de plus en plus fort.

angel *noun* ange *Masc.*

anger *noun* colère *Fem.*

angle *noun* angle *Masc.*

angrily *adverb* avec colère.

angry *adjective* **to be angry** être en colère; **she was angry with me** elle était en colère contre moi; **to get angry** se fâcher [1].

animal *noun* animal *Masc.* (*plural* animaux).

ankle *noun* cheville *Fem.*; **to break your ankle** se casser la cheville.

anniversary *noun* anniversaire *Masc.*; **a wedding anniversary** un anniversaire de mariage.

announce *verb* annoncer [61].

announcement *noun* annonce *Fem.*

annoy *verb* agacer [61]; **to be annoyed** être [6] agacé; **to get annoyed** se fâcher [1]; **she got annoyed** elle s'est fâchée.

annoying *adjective* agaçant.

annual *adjective* annuel (*Fem.* annuelle).

anorak *noun* anorak *Masc.*

anorexia *noun* anorexie *Fem.*

another *adjective* **1** un autre (*Fem.* une autre); **would you like another cup of tea?** voulez-vous une autre tasse de thé?; **2** encore; **another two years** encore deux ans; **we need another three chairs** il nous faut encore trois chaises.

answer *noun* **1** réponse *Fem.*; **the right answer** la bonne réponse; **the wrong answer** la mauvaise réponse; **2 the answer to a problem** la solution à un problème.

answer *verb* **1** répondre [3] à; **he hasn't answered our letter** il n'a pas répondu à notre lettre; **2 to answer the door** aller [5] ouvrir la porte.

answering machine *noun* répondeur *Masc.*; **to leave a message on the answering machine** laisser un message au répondeur.

ant *noun* fourmi *Fem.*

Antarctic *noun* Antarctique *Masc.*

anthem *noun* **the national anthem** l'hymne national.

antibiotic *noun* antibiotique *Fem.*

antique *noun* **antiques** les antiquités *Fem.*

antique *adjective* ancien (*Fem.* ancienne); **an antique table** une table ancienne.

antique shop *noun* magasin *Masc.* d'antiquités.

antiseptic *noun* antiseptique *Masc.*

anxious *adjective* inquiet (*Fem.* inquiète).

anxiously *adverb* avec inquiétude.

a b c d e f g h i j k l m n o p q r s t u v w x y z

any adjective, adverb, pronoun
1 du, de l', de la, des; **is there any butter?** y a-t-il du beurre?; **is there any oil?** y a-t-il de l'huile?; **is there any flour?** y a-t-il de la farine?; **are there any eggs?** y a-t-il des œufs?; 2 de (used in negative sentences); **there isn't any flour** il n'y a pas de farine; **there aren't any eggs** il n'y a pas d'œufs; 3 en (when 'any' is used on its own without a noun); **I don't want any** je n'en veux pas; 4 **not ...any more** ne ...plus; **there isn't any more butter** il n'y a plus de beurre; **I don't go there any more** je n'y vais plus.

anybody, anyone pronoun 1 (in questions and after 'if') quelqu'un; **is anybody in?** est-ce qu'il y a quelqu'un?; **if anybody wants some beer, it's in the fridge** si quelqu'un veut de la bière, elle est au frigo; **does anybody want some tea?** qui veut du thé?; 2 **not ...anybody** ne ...personne; **there isn't anybody in his office** il n'y a personne dans son bureau; 3 (absolutely anybody) n'importe qui; **anybody can go** n'importe qui peut y aller.

anyhow adverb SEE anyway.

anyone pronoun SEE anybody.

anything pronoun 1 (in questions) quelque chose; **is there anything I can do to help?** est-ce que je peux faire quelque chose pour t'aider?; 2 **not ...anything** ne ...rien; **there isn't anything on the table** il n'y a rien sur la table; 3 (anything at all) n'importe quoi; **anything could happen** il pourrait arriver n'importe quoi.

anyway, anyhow adverb de toute façon; **anyway, I'll ring you before I leave** de toute façon, je t'appellerai avant de partir.

anywhere adverb 1 (in questions) quelque part; **have you seen my keys anywhere?** est-ce que tu as vu mes clés quelque part?; **are you going anywhere tomorrow?** est-ce que tu vas quelque part demain?; 2 **not ...anywhere** ne ...nulle part; **I can't find my keys anywhere** je ne trouve nulle part mes clés; 3 (absolutely anywhere) n'importe où; **put your cases down anywhere** pose tes valises n'importe où.

apart adjective, adverb 1 (separate) séparé; **we don't like being apart** nous n'aimons pas être séparés; 2 **to be two metres apart** être à deux mètres l'un de l'autre; 3 **apart from** à part; **apart from Judy everybody was there** à part Judy tout le monde y était.

apartheid noun apartheid Masc.

apartment noun appartement Masc.

ape noun (grand) singe Masc.

apologize verb s'excuser [1]; **he apologizes for his behaviour** il s'excuse de son comportement; **he apologized to Tanya** il s'est excusé auprès de Tanya.

apology noun excuses Fem. plural.

apostrophe noun apostrophe Fem.

apparatus noun 1 (in a gym) agrès Masc. plural; 2 (in a lab) matériel Masc.

apparent adjective apparent.

apparently *adverb* apparemment.

appeal *noun* appel Masc.

appeal *verb* **1 to appeal for** lancer [61] un appel pour; **2 to appeal to somebody** tenter [1] quelqu'un; **horror films don't appeal to me** les films d'épouvante ne me tentent pas.

appear *verb* **1** apparaître [57]; **Mick appeared at the door** Mick est apparu à la porte; **2 to appear on television** passer [1] à la télévision; **3** (*seem*) paraître [57]; **it appears that somebody has stolen the key** il paraît que quelqu'un a volé la clé.

appendicitis *noun* appendicite Fem.

appendix *noun* **1** (*of book*) annexe Fem.; **2** (*organ*) appendice Masc.

appetite *noun* appétit Masc.; **it'll spoil your appetite** ça te coupera l'appétit.

applaud *verb* applaudir [2].

applause *noun* applaudissements Masc. plural.

apple *noun* pomme Fem.

apple core *noun* trognon Masc. de pomme.

apple tree *noun* pommier Masc.

applicant *noun* candidat Masc., candidate Fem.

application *noun* **a job application** une candidature.

application form *noun* (*for a job*) dossier Masc. de candidature.

apply *verb* **1 to apply for a job** poser [1] sa candidature à un poste; **2 to apply for a course** faire [10] une demande d'inscription à un cours; **3 to apply to** s'appliquer [1] à; **that doesn't apply to students** cela ne s'applique pas aux étudiants.

appointment *noun* rendez-vous Masc.; **to make a dental appointment** prendre rendez-vous chez le dentiste; **I've got a hair appointment at four** j'ai rendez-vous chez le coiffeur à seize heures.

appreciate *verb* **I appreciate your advice** je vous suis reconnaissant de vos conseils; **I'd appreciate it if you could tidy up afterwards** je te serais reconnaissant de ranger après.

apprentice *noun* apprenti Masc., apprentie Fem.

apprenticeship *noun* apprentissage Masc.

approach *verb* (*come near to*) **1** s'approcher de [1]; **we were approaching Paris** nous nous approchions de Paris; **2** (*tackle*) aborder [1] (*a task or problem*).

appropriate *adjective* approprié.

approval *noun* approbation Fem.

approve *verb* **to approve of** apprécier [1]; **they don't approve of her friends** ils n'apprécient pas ses amis.

approximate *adjective* approximatif (Fem. approximative).

approximately *adverb* environ; **approximately fifty people** environ cinquante personnes.

apricot *noun* abricot Masc.

apricot tree *noun* abricotier Masc.

April *noun* avril Masc.; **in April** en avril.

a b c d e f g h i j k l m n o p q r s t u v w x y z

a
b
c
d
e
f
g
h
i
j
k
l
m
n
o
p
q
r
s
t
u
v
w
x
y
z

April Fool noun poisson Masc. d'avril.

April Fool's Day noun le premier avril.

apron noun tablier Masc.

aquarium noun aquarium Masc.

Aquarius noun Verseau Masc.; **Sharon's Aquarius** Sharon est Verseau.

Arab noun Arabe Masc. & Fem.

Arab adjective arabe; **the Arab countries** les pays arabes.

arch noun arche Fem.

archaeologist noun archéologue Masc. & Fem.; **she's an archaeologist** elle est archéologue.

archaeology noun archéologie Fem.

archbishop noun archevêque Masc.

architect noun architecte Masc. & Fem.; **he's an architect** il est architecte.

architecture noun architecture Fem.

Arctic noun Arctique Masc.

are verb SEE be.

area noun 1 (part of a town) quartier; **a nice area** un quartier bien; **a rough area** un quartier mal fréquenté; 2 (region) région Fem.; **in the Leeds area** dans la région de Leeds.

argue verb se disputer [1] 1 **there's no point in arguing** ce n'est pas la peine de se disputer; 2 **to argue about something** discuter [1] de quelque chose; **they're arguing**

about the result ils sont en train de discuter du résultat.

argument noun dispute Fem.; **to have an argument** se disputer.

Aries noun Bélier Masc.; **Pauline's Aries** Pauline est Bélier.

arithmetic noun arithmétique Fem.

arm noun bras Masc.; **to fold your arms** croiser les bras; **arm in arm** bras dessus bras dessous; **to break your arm** se casser le bras.

armchair noun fauteuil Masc.

armed adjective armé.

armpit noun aisselle Fem.

army noun armée Fem.; **to join the army** s'engager dans l'armée.

around preposition, adverb 1 (with time) vers; **we'll be there around ten** on va arriver vers dix heures; 2 (with ages or amounts) environ; **she's around fifteen** elle a environ quinze ans; **we need around six kilos** il nous faut environ six kilos; 3 (surrounding) autour de; **the countryside around Edinburgh** le paysage autour d'Édimbourg; 4 (near) **is there a post office around here?** est-ce qu'il y a un bureau de poste près d'ici?; **is Phil around?** est-ce que Phil est là?; 5 (wrapped around) autour de; **she had a scarf around her neck** elle avait une écharpe autour du cou.

arrange verb **to arrange to do** prévoir [65] de faire; **we've arranged to see a film on Saturday** nous avons prévu de voir un film samedi.

arrangement noun **1** (of things) disposition Fem.; **2** (agreement) accord Masc.

arrest noun **to be under arrest** être en état d'arrestation.

arrest verb arrêter [1].

arrival noun arrivée Fem.

arrive verb arriver [1]; **they arrived at 3 p.m.** ils sont arrivés à quinze heures.

arrow noun flèche Fem.

art noun **1** art Masc.; **modern art** l'art moderne; **2** (school subject) dessin Masc.; **the art class** le cours de dessin.

artery noun artère Fem.

art gallery noun (public) musée Masc. des beaux arts.

artichoke noun artichaut Masc.

article noun article Masc.

artificial adjective artificiel (Fem. artificielle).

artist noun artiste Masc. & Fem.; **he's an artist** c'est un artiste.

artistic adjective artistique.

art school noun école Fem. de beaux arts.

as conjunction, adverb, preposition **1** comme; **as you know** comme vous le savez; **as usual** comme d'habitude; **as I told you** comme je t'avais dit; **2** (because) puisque; **as there were no trains, we took the bus** puisqu'il n'y avait pas de trains, nous avons pris le bus; **3** as ...as aussi ...que; **he's as tall as his brother** il est aussi grand que son frère; **you must be as tired as I am** tu dois être aussi fatigué que moi; **4 as much ...as** autant de ...que; **you have as much time as I do** tu as autant de temps que moi; **5 as many ...as** autant de ...que; **we have as many problems as he does** nous avons autant de problèmes que lui; **6 as long as** pourvu que (with subjunctive); **we'll go tomorrow, as long as it's a nice day** on va y aller demain, pourvu qu'il fasse beau; **7 for as long as** aussi longtemps que; **you can stay for as long as you like** tu peux rester aussi longtemps que tu veux; **8 as soon as possible** dès que possible; **9 to work as** travailler comme; **he works as a taxi driver in the evenings** il travaille comme chauffeur de taxi le soir.

asbestos noun amiante Fem.

ash noun cendre Fem.

ashamed adjective **to be ashamed** avoir honte; **you should be ashamed of yourself!** tu devrais avoir honte!

ashtray noun cendrier Masc.

Asia noun Asie Fem.; **in Asia** en Asie.

Asian noun **1** (from the Far East) Asiatique Masc. & Fem.; **2** (from India) Indien Masc., Indienne Fem.; **3** (from Pakistan) Pakistanais Masc., Pakistanaise Fem.

Asian adjective **1** asiatique (from Asia); **2** (from India) indien (Fem. indienne); **3** (from Pakistan) pakistanais (Fem. pakistanaise).

ask verb **1** demander [1]; **you can ask at reception** tu peux demander à l'accueil; **to ask somebody something** demander quelque chose à quelqu'un; **I asked him where he lives** je lui ai

a
b
c
d
e
f
g
h
i
j
k
l
m
n
o
p
q
r
s
t
u
v
w
x
y
z

demandé où il habite; **to ask for something** demander quelque chose; **I asked for three coffees** j'ai demandé trois cafés; **to ask somebody for something** demander quelque chose à quelqu'un; **to ask somebody to do something** demander à quelqu'un de faire; **ask Danny to give you a hand** demande à Danny de te donner un coup de main; **2 to ask somebody a question** poser [1] une question à quelqu'un; **I asked you a question!** je t'ai posé une question!; **3** inviter [1]; **they've asked us to a party at their house** ils nous ont invité à une soirée chez eux; **4 Paul's asked Janie out on Friday** Paul a invité Janie à sortir avec lui vendredi.

asleep adjective **to be asleep** dormir [37]; **the baby's asleep** le bébé dort; **to fall asleep** s'endormir [37].

asparagus noun asperges Fem. plural.

aspirin noun aspirine Fem.

assembly noun (at school) rassemblement Masc.

assess verb évaluer [1].

assignment noun (at school) devoir Masc.

assist verb aider [1].

assistance noun aide Fem.

assistant noun **1** assistant Masc., assistante Fem.; **2 a shop assistant** un vendeur, une vendeuse.

association noun association Fem.

assorted adjective variés (Fem. variées).

assortment noun mélange Masc.

assume verb supposer [1].

assure verb assurer [1].

asterisk noun astérisque Masc.

asthma noun asthme Masc.; **she has asthma** elle souffre de l'asthme.

astonishing adjective étonnant; **her knowledge is astonishing** elle a des connaissances incroyables.

astrologer noun astrologue Masc. & Fem.

astrology noun astrologie Fem.

astronaut noun astronaute Masc. & Fem.

astronomer noun astronome Masc. & Fem.

astronomy noun astronomie Fem.

at preposition **1** à (note that 'à + le' always becomes 'au' and 'à + les' always becomes 'aux'); **at home** à la maison; **at school** à l'école; **at my office** à mon bureau; **at the market** au marché; **at meetings** aux réunions; **2** (talking about the time) à; **at eight o'clock** à huit heures; **3 at night** la nuit; **at the weekend** le weekend; **4 at Emma's house** chez Emma; **she's at her brother's this evening** elle est chez son frère ce soir; **at the hairdresser's** chez le coiffeur; **5 at last** enfin; **he's found a job at last** il a enfin trouvé un emploi; **4** (@ in e-mail addresses) arobase Masc.; **john-dot-smith@easycom-dot-com** john-dot-smith-arobase-easycom-point-com.

athlete noun athlète Masc. & Fem.

athletic adjective athlétique.

athletics noun athlétisme Masc.

Atlantic noun Atlantique Masc.

atlas noun atlas Masc.

atmosphere noun atmosphère Fem.

atom noun atome Masc.

atomic adjective atomique.

attach verb attacher [1].

attached adjective to be attached to être [6] attaché à.

attachment noun pièce Fem. jointe.

attack noun attaque Fem.

attack verb attaquer [1].

attacker noun agresseur Masc.

attempt noun tentative Fem.; at the first attempt à la première tentative.

attempt verb to attempt to do essayer [59] de faire.

attend verb assister [1] à; to attend a class assister à un cours.

attention noun attention Fem.; to pay attention to faire attention à; I wasn't paying atttention je ne faisais pas attention.

attic noun grenier Masc.; in the attic au grenier.

attitude noun attitude Fem.

attract verb attirer [1].

attraction noun attraction Fem.

attractive adjective séduisant.

aubergine noun aubergine Fem.

auction noun vente Fem. aux enchères.

audience noun public Masc.

August noun août Masc.; in August en août.

aunt, auntie noun tante Fem.

au pair noun jeune fille Fem. au pair; I'm looking for a job as an au pair je cherche un emploi de jeune fille au pair.

Australia noun Australie Fem.; in Australia en Australie; to Australia en Australie.

Australian noun Australien Masc., Australienne Fem.

Australian adjective australien (Fem. australienne).

Austria noun Autriche Fem.; in Austria en Autriche; to Austria en Autriche.

Austrian noun Autrichien Masc., Autrichienne Fem.

Austrian adjective autrichien (Fem. autrichienne).

author noun auteur Masc.

autobiography noun autobiographie Fem.

autograph noun autographe Masc.

automatic adjective automatique.

automatically adverb automatiquement.

autumn noun automne Masc.; in autumn en automne.

availability noun disponibilité Fem.

available adjective disponible.

avalanche noun avalanche Fem.

avenue noun avenue Fem.

average noun moyenne Fem.; on average en moyenne; above average au-dessus de la moyenne.

average adjective moyen (Fem. moyenne); the average height la hauteur moyenne.

avocado noun avocat Masc.

a b c d e f g h i j k l m n o p q r s t u v w x y z

a
b
c
d
e
f
g
h
i
j
k
l
m
n
o
p
q
r
s
t
u
v
w
x
y
z

avoid verb éviter [1]; **she avoided me** elle m'a évité; **to avoid doing** éviter de faire; **I avoid speaking to him** j'évite de lui parler.

awake adjective **is Lola awake?** est-ce que Lola est réveillée?; **are you still awake?** tu ne dors pas?

award noun prix Masc.; **to win an award** remporter un prix.

aware adjective **to be aware of a noise** être conscient d'un bruit; **to be aware of a problem** être au courant d'un problème; **as far as I'm aware** à ma connaissance.

away adverb **1 to be away** être absent; **I'll be away next week** je serai absent la semaine prochaine; **2 to go away** partir; **Laura's gone away for a week** Laura est partie pour une semaine; **go away!** va-t-en!; **3 to run away** partir en courant; **the thieves ran away** les voleurs sont partis en courant; **4 the school is two kilometres away** l'école est à deux kilomètres d'ici; **how far away is it?** c'est à quelle distance d'ici?; **not far away** pas loin d'ici; **5 to put something away** ranger quelque chose; **I'll just put my books away** je vais juste ranger mes livres; **6 to give something away** donner quelque chose; **she's given away all her tapes** elle a donné toutes ses cassettes.

away match noun match Masc. à l'extérieur.

awful adjective **1** affreux (Fem. affreuse); **the film was awful!** le film était affreux!; **2 I feel awful** (ill) je ne me sens pas bien du tout;

3 I feel awful about it ça m'ennuie vraiment; **4 an awful lot of** énormément de.

awkward adjective **1** difficile; **it's an awkward situation** c'est une situation difficile; **it's a bit awkward** c'est un peu difficile; **an awkward child** un enfant difficile; **2 an awkward question** une question gênante.

axe noun hache Fem.

Bb

baby noun bébé Masc.

babysit verb faire [10] du babysitting.

babysitter noun babysitter Masc. & Fem.

babysitting noun babysitting Masc.

bachelor noun célibataire Masc.

back noun **1** (of a person or animal) dos Masc.; **to do something behind someone's back** faire quelque chose dans le dos de quelqu'un; **2** (of a piece of paper, your hand, or a garment) dos Masc.; **on the back** au dos; **3** (of a car, a plane, or a building) arrière Masc.; **we have seats at the back** nous avons des places à l'arrière; **a garden at the back of the house** un jardin à l'arrière de la maison; **4 the children at the back of the room** les enfants au fond de la salle; **5** (of a chair or sofa) dossier Masc.; **6** (in football or hockey) arrière Masc.; **left back** arrière gauche.

back adjective **1** arrière (a wheel or seat); **the back seat of the car** le siège arrière de la voiture; **2 the back gate** la porte de derrière; **the back garden** le jardin de derrière.

back adverb **1 to go back** rentrer; **to go back to school** rentrer à l'école; **Lisa's gone back to London** Lisa est rentrée à Londres; **2 to come back** rentrer; **they've come back from Italy** ils sont rentrés d'Italie; **she's back at work** elle a repris le travail; **Sue's not back yet** Sue n'est pas encore rentrée; **we went by bus and walked back** nous avons pris le bus pour y aller et nous sommes rentrés à pied; **3 to phone back** rappeler; **I'll ring back later** je rappellerai plus tard; **4 to give something back to somebody** rendre quelque chose à quelqu'un; **I gave him back his cassettes** je lui ai rendu ses cassettes; **give it back!** rends-le-moi!

back verb **1** (to support) soutenir [81] (a candidate, for example); **2** (to bet on) parier [1] sur (a horse).

● **to back up** (computing) **to back up a file** sauvegarder [1] un fichier sur disquette.

● **to back somebody up** soutenir [77] quelqu'un.

backache noun mal Masc. de dos.

backbone noun colonne Fem. vertébrale.

back door noun **1** (of a building) porte Fem. de derrière; **2** (of a car) porte Fem. arrière.

backfire verb (turn out badly) échouer [1].

background noun **1** (of a person) (social) milieu Masc.; **2** (of events or a situation) contexte Masc.; **3** (in a picture or view) arrière-plan Masc.; **the trees in the background** les arbres à l'arrière-plan; **4 background music** la musique d'ambiance; **5 background noise** les bruits Masc. plural de fond.

backhand noun revers Masc.

backing noun **1** (on sticky-back plastic, for example) revêtement Masc. intérieur; **2** (moral support) soutien Masc.; **3** (in music) **a backing group** un groupe d'accompagnement.

backpack noun sac Masc. à dos.

backpack verb **to go backpacking** partir [58] en voyage avec son sac à dos.

back seat noun siège Masc. arrière.

backside noun derrière Masc.

backstage adverb **to go backstage** aller dans les coulisses.

backstroke noun dos Masc. crawlé.

back to front adverb à l'envers; **your jumper's back to front** ton pull est à l'envers.

backup noun **1** (support) soutien Masc.; **2** (in computing) **a backup disk** un disque de sauvegarde.

backwards adverb (to lean or fall) en arrière.

bacon noun **1** (French streaky bacon) lard Masc.; **2** (thin-sliced British-type) bacon Masc.; **bacon and eggs** œufs au bacon.

bad adjective **1** (not good) mauvais (goes before the noun) **bad work** du mauvais travail; **a bad meal** un mauvais repas; **his new film's not bad** son nouveau film n'est pas mauvais; **it's bad for your health** c'est mauvais pour la santé; **I'm bad at physics** je suis mauvais en physique; **2** (*serious*) grave; **a bad accident** un accident grave; **a bad cold** un gros rhume; **3** (*rotten*) pourri; **a bad apple** une pomme pourrie; **to go bad** se gâter; **4** (*rude*) **bad language** du langage grossier; **5** (*naughty*) vilain; **bad dog!** vilain!; **bad girl!** vilaine!; ★ **too bad!** (*I'm sorry for you*) pas de chance!; (*I don't care*) tant pis!

badge *noun* badge *Masc.*

badly *adverb* **1** mal; **he writes badly** il écrit mal; **I slept badly** j'ai mal dormi; **the exam went badly** l'examen s'est mal passé; **2** (*seriously*) (*to hurt or damage*) gravement; **the car was badly damaged** la voiture a été gravement endommagée; **badly hurt** grièvement blessé.

bad-mannered *adjective* mal élevé.

badminton *noun* badminton *Masc.*; **to play badminton** jouer au badminton.

bad-tempered *adjective* **1** (*for a little while*) irrité; **2** (*always*) **she's very bad-tempered** elle a très mauvais caractère.

bag *noun* sac *Masc.*

baggage *noun* bagages *Masc. plural.*

baggage allowance *noun* franchise *Fem.* de bagages.

baggage reclaim *noun* réception *Fem.* des bagages.

bagpipes *plural noun* cornemuse *Fem.*; **to play the bagpipes** jouer de la cornemuse.

bags *plural noun* bagages *Masc. plural*; **to pack your bags** faire ses bagages; ★ **to have bags under your eyes** avoir des valises sous les yeux (*informal*) .

Bahaman *adjective* des Bahamas.

Bahamas *noun* (*plural*) **the Bahamas** les Bahamas; **the Bahamas Islands** les îles Bahamas.

bake *verb* **to bake a cake** faire [10] un gâteau; **to bake vegetables** faire [10] cuire des légumes au four.

baked *adjective* **1** (*fish or fruit*) au four; **baked apples** les pommes au four; **2 a baked potato** une pomme de terre au four.

baked beans *plural noun* les haricots blancs à la sauce tomate.

baker *noun* boulanger *Masc.*, boulangère *Fem.*; **to go to the baker's** aller à la boulangerie.

bakery *noun* boulangerie *Fem.*

balance *noun* **1** équilibre *Masc.*; **lose your balance** perdre l'équilibre; **2** (*money in your bank account*) solde *Masc.*

balanced *adjective* équilibré.

balcony *noun* balcon *Masc.*

bald *adjective* chauve.

ball *noun* **1** (*for tennis or golf*) balle *Fem.*; **2** (*for football or volleyball*) ballon *Masc.*; **3** (*of string or wool*) pelote *Fem.*

ballet *noun* ballet *Masc.*

ballet dancer noun danseur Masc. de ballet, danseuse Fem. de ballet.

ballet shoe noun chausson Masc. de danse.

balloon noun 1 (for money) ballon Masc.; 2 (hot air) montgolfière Fem.

ballot noun scrutin Masc.

ballpoint (pen) noun stylo Masc. à bille.

ban noun interdiction Fem.; **a ban on smoking** une interdiction de fumer.

ban verb interdire [47].

banana noun banane Fem.; **a banana yoghurt** un yaourt à la banane.

band noun 1 (playing music) groupe Masc.; **a rock band** un groupe de rock; **2 a jazz band** un orchestre de jazz; **3 a brass band** une fanfare; **4 a rubber band** un élastique.

bandage noun bandage Masc.

bandage verb bander [11] un bandage à.

bang noun 1 (noise) boum Masc.; **2** (of a door, shutter, or window, etc) claquement Masc.

bang verb 1 (to hit) taper [1] sur (a drum, for example); **he banged his fist on the table** il a tapé du poing sur la table; **2** (to knock) cogner [1]; **to bang on the door** cogner à la porte; **I banged my head on the door** je me suis cogné la tête contre la porte; **I banged into the table** j'ai heurté la table; **3 to bang the door** claquer [1] la porte.

bang exclamation (like a gun) pan!

bangle noun bracelet Masc.

banister(s), bannister(s) (plural) noun rampe Fem. (d'escalier).

bank noun 1 (for money) banque Fem.; **I'm going to the bank** je vais à la banque; **2** (of a river or lake) bord Masc.

bank account noun compte Masc. bancaire.

bank balance noun solde Masc. bancaire.

bank card noun carte Fem. bancaire.

bank holiday noun jour Masc. férié.

banking noun banque Fem; milieu Masc. bancaire.

banknote noun billet Masc. de banque.

bank statement noun relevé Masc. de compte.

baptize verb baptiser [1].

bar noun 1 (selling drinks) bar Masc.; **Janet works in a bar** Janet travaille dans un bar; **2** (the counter) comptoir Masc.; **on the bar** sur le bar; **3 a bar of chocolate** une tablette de chocolat; **4 a bar of soap** une savonnette; **5** (made of wood or metal) barre Fem.; **a metal bar** une barre en métal; **6** (in music) mesure Fem.

bar verb 1 (to block physically) barrer [1]; **to bar someone's way** barrer le passage à quelqu'un; **2** (to ban from an activity) exclure [25].

Barbadian noun Barbadien Masc., Barbadienne Fem.

Barbadian adjective de la Barbade.

Barbados noun la Barbade.

a
b
c
d
e
f
g
h
i
j
k
l
m
n
o
p
q
r
s
t
u
v
w
x
y
z

barbecue noun barbecue Masc.;
there's a barbecue tonight il y a
un barbecue ce soir.

barbecue verb to barbecue a
chicken faire [10] griller un poulet
au barbecue; **barbecued chicken**
du poulet grillé au barbecue.

barbed wire noun barbelé Masc.

bare adjective nu.

barefoot adjective to be barefoot
être nu-pieds; **to walk barefoot**
marcher pieds nus.

bargain noun (a good buy) affaire
Fem.; **I got a bargain** j'ai fait une
affaire; **it's a bargain!** c'est une
bonne affaire!

barge noun péniche Fem.

bark noun 1 (of a tree) écorce Fem.;
2 (of a dog) aboiement Masc.

bark verb aboyer [39].

barley noun orge Masc.

barmaid noun barmaid Fem.

barman noun barman Masc.

barn noun grange Fem.

barometer noun baromètre Masc.

barrel noun tonneau Masc. (plural
tonneaux).

barrier noun barrière Fem.

base noun base Fem.

baseball noun base-ball Masc.; **a
baseball cap** une casquette de
base-ball.

based adjective 1 to be based on
être fondé sur; **the film is based on
a true story** le film est fondé sur
une histoire vraie; 2 to be based
in être basé à; **he's based in Bristol**
il est basé à Bristol.

basement noun sous-sol Masc.; **in
the basement** au sous-sol.

bash noun 1 bosse Fem.; **it's got a
bash on the wing** il y a une bosse à
l'aile; 2 I'll have a bash je vais
essayer un coup.

bash verb cogner [1]; **I bashed my
head** je me suis cogné la tête.

basic adjective 1 de base; **basic
knowledge** des connaissances de
base; **her basic salary** son salaire
de base; 2 the basic facts les faits
essentiels; 3 (not luxurious)
rudimentaire; **the flat's a bit basic**
l'appartement est un peu
rudimentaire.

basically adverb 1 au fond; **it's
basically all right** au fond ça va;
2 à vrai dire; **basically, I don't
want to go** à vrai dire, je ne veux
pas y aller.

basics noun rudiments Masc. plural.

basin noun (washbasin) lavabo
Masc.

basis noun 1 base Fem.; 2 on the
basis of sur la base de; **on a
regular basis** régulièrement.

basket noun 1 (for shopping)
panier Masc.; 2 (other) corbeille
Fem.; **a waste-paper basket** une
corbeille à papier; **a linen basket**
une corbeille à linge.

basketball noun basketball Masc.;
to play basketball jouer au
basketball.

bass noun 1 basse Fem.; **to play
bass** jouer de la basse; 2 a double
bass une contrebasse.

bass drum noun grosse caisse
Fem.

bass guitar noun guitare Fem.
basse.

bassoon noun basson Masc.; **to play the bassoon** jouer du basson.

bat noun **1** (for cricket or baseball) batte Fem.; **2** (for table tennis) raquette Fem.; **3** (animal) chauve-souris Fem.

batch noun **1** (of cakes) fournée Fem.; **2** (of letters) tas Masc.; **a batch of letters** un tas de lettres; **3** (in computing) lot Masc.

bath noun **1** bain Masc.; **to have a bath** prendre un bain; **I was in the bath** j'étais dans mon bain; **2** (bathtub) baignoire Fem.; **the bath's pink** la baignoire est rose.

bathe verb **1** laver [1] (a wound); **2** (go swimming) se baigner [1].

bathroom noun salle Fem. de bains (plural salles de bains).

baths plural noun piscine Fem.

bath towel noun serviette Fem. de bain.

batter noun (for frying) pâte Fem. à frire; **fish in batter** des beignets de poisson; **pancake batter** la pâte à crêpes.

battery noun **1** (for a torch or radio, for example) pile Fem.; **2** (for a car) batterie Fem.

battle noun bataille Fem.

bay noun **1** (on the coast) baie Fem.; **2** (for coaches) travée Fem.

B.C. (short for: before Christ) av. J.-C.

be verb **1** être [6]; **Melanie is in the kitchen** Melanie est dans la cuisine; **where is the butter?** où est le beurre?; **I'm tired** je suis fatigué; **when we were in France** quand nous étions en France; **2** (with jobs and professions) être;

she's a teacher elle est professeur (note that 'a' is not translated); **he's a taxi driver** il est chauffeur de taxi; **3** (in clock times) être; **it's three o'clock** il est trois heures; **it's half past five** il est cinq heures et demie; **4** (days of the week and dates) **what day is it today?** nous sommes quel jour aujourd'hui?; **it's Tuesday today** nous sommes mardi aujourd'hui; **it's the twentieth of May** nous sommes le vingt mai; **5** (talking about age) avoir [5]; **how old are you?** quel âge as-tu?; **I'm fifteen** j'ai quinze ans; **Harry's twenty** Harry a vingt ans; **6** (cold, hot, hungry) avoir [5]; **I'm hot** j'ai chaud; **I'm cold** j'ai froid; **I'm hungry** j'ai faim; **7** (weather) faire [10]; **it's cold today** il fait froid aujourd'hui; **it's a nice day** il fait beau; **8** I've never been to Paris je ne suis jamais allé à Paris; **have you been to Britain before?** est-ce que tu es déjà venu en Grande Bretagne?; **9 to be loved** être aimé; **he has been killed** il a été tué.

beach noun plage Fem.; **to go to the beach** aller à la plage; **on the beach** sur la plage.

bead noun perle Fem.

beak noun bec Masc.

beam noun **1** (of light) rayon Masc.; **2** (for a roof) poutre Fem.

bean noun haricot Masc.; **baked beans** les haricots à la sauce tomate; **green beans** les haricots verts.

bear noun ours Masc.

bear verb **1** supporter [1]; **I can't bear him** je ne peux pas le supporter; **I can't bear the idea** je ne supporte pas l'idée; **2 to bear something in mind** tenir [77] compte de quelque chose; **I'll bear it in mind** je ne l'oublierai pas.

● **to bear up** tenir [77] le coup.

beard noun barbe Fem.

bearded adjective barbu.

bearings plural noun **to get one's bearings** se repérer [24].

beast noun **1** (animal) bête Fem.; **2 you beast!** chameau!

beat noun rythme Masc.

beat verb **1** (defeat) battre [21]; **we beat them!** on les a battus!; **2 to beat the eggs** battre les œufs; **3 you can't beat a good meal** rien ne vaut un bon repas.

● **to beat somebody up** tabasser [1] quelqu'un (informal).

beautician noun esthéticien Masc., esthéticienne Fem.

beautiful adjective beau (Fem. belle) (Masc. plural beaux) (goes before the noun); **a beautiful day** un beau jour; **a beautiful girl** une belle fille; **beautiful pictures** de beaux tableaux; **a beautiful place** un bel endroit ('bel' for masculine nouns beginning with a vowel or silent 'h').

beautifully adverb admirablement.

beauty noun beauté Fem.

beauty spot noun (for tourists) beau site Masc.

because conjunction **1** parce que; **because it's you** parce que c'est toi; **because it's cold** parce qu'il fait froid; **2 because of** à cause de; **because of the accident** à cause de l'accident.

become verb devenir [81].

bed noun **1** lit Masc.; **a double bed** un grand lit; **in bed** au lit; **to go to bed** aller se coucher; **2** (flower bed) parterre Masc.

bedclothes plural noun couvertures Fem. plural.

bedding noun literie Fem.

bedroom noun chambre Fem.; **bedroom furniture** les meubles de chambre; **my bedroom window** la fenêtre de ma chambre.

bedside noun **a bedside table** une table de chevet.

bedsit, bedsitter noun chambre Fem. meublée.

bedspread noun dessus-de-lit Masc.

bedtime noun **it's bedtime** c'est l'heure d'aller se coucher.

bee noun abeille Fem.

beech noun hêtre Masc.

beef noun bœuf Masc.; **we had roast beef** on a mangé du rôti de bœuf.

beefburger noun hamburger Masc.

beer noun bière Fem.; **two beers please** deux bières s'il vous plaît; **a beer can** une canette de bière.

beetle noun scarabée Masc.

beetroot noun betterave Fem.

before preposition, adverb **1** avant; **before Monday** avant lundi; **he left before me** il est parti avant moi; **2 the day before** la veille; **the day before the wedding** la veille du mariage; **the day before yesterday** avant-hier; **the week before** la semaine d'avant; **3** (already) déjà; **I've seen him**

before somewhere je l'ai déjà vu quelque part; **I had seen the film before** j'avais déjà vu le film.

before *conjunction* **1** avant de; **before doing** avant de faire; **I closed the windows before leaving** (or **before I left**) j'ai fermé les fenêtres avant de partir; **2** avant que; **phone me before they leave** appelle-moi avant qu'ils s'en aillent; **oh, before I forget** … avant que j'oublie ….

beforehand *adverb* (*ahead of time*) à l'avance; **phone beforehand** appelle à l'avance.

beg *verb* **1** (*ask for money*) mendier [1]; **2** (*ask*) supplier [1]; **she begged me not to leave** elle m'a supplié de ne pas partir; **I beg your pardon** je vous demande pardon.

begin *verb* **1** commencer [61]; **the meeting begins at ten** la réunion commence à dix heures; **the words beginning with P** les mots qui commencent par un P; **2 to begin to do** commencer à faire; **I'm beginning to understand** je commence à comprendre.

beginner *noun* débutant *Masc.*, débutante *Fem.*

beginning *noun* début *Masc.*; **at the beginning** au début; **at the beginning of the holidays** au début des vacances.

behalf *noun* **on behalf of** pour.

behave *verb* **1** se comporter [1]; **he behaved badly** il s'est mal comporté; **2 to behave yourself** être sage; **behave yourselves!** soyez sages!

behaviour *noun* comportement *Masc.*

behind *adverb, preposition* **1** derrière; **behind the sofa** derrière le canapé; **behind them** derrière eux; **the car behind** la voiture de derrière; **2** (*not making progress*) **he's behind in class** il a du retard en classe; **3 to leave something behind** oublier quelque chose; **I've left my keys behind** j'ai oublié mes clés.

behind *noun* derrière *Masc.*

beige *adjective* beige.

Belgian *noun* Belge *Masc. & Fem.*

Belgian *adjective* belge.

Belgium *noun* Belgique *Fem.*; **to Belgium** en Belgique; **in Belgium** en Belgique.

belief *noun* conviction *Fem.*; **his political beliefs** ses convictions politiques.

believe *verb* **1** croire [33]; **I believe you** je te crois; **they believed what I said** ils ont cru ce que j'ai dit; **I don't believe you!** ce n'est pas vrai!; **2 to believe in** croire à; **to believe in ghosts** croire aux fantômes; **to believe in God** croire en Dieu.

bell *noun* **1** (*in a church*) cloche *Fem.*; **2** (*on a door*) sonnette *Fem.*; **ring the bell!** appuyez sur la sonnette!; **3** (*for a cat or toy*) grelot *Masc.*; ★ **that name rings a bell** ce nom me dit quelque chose (*literally: says something to me*).

belong *verb* **1 to belong to** appartenir [81] à; **that belongs to Richard** cela appartient à Richard; **2 to belong to a club** faire [10] partie d'un club; **3** (go) aller [5]; **that chair belongs in the study** cette chaise va dans le bureau; **where does this vase belong?** ce vase va où?

belongings plural noun affaires Fem. plural; **all my belongings are in London** toutes mes affaires sont à Londres.

below preposition au-dessous de; **below the window** au-dessous de la fenêtre; **the flat below yours** l'appartement au-dessous du tien.

below adverb **1** (further down) en bas; **shouts came from below** des cris venaient d'en bas; **2 the flat below** l'appartement de dessous.

belt noun ceinture Fem.

bench noun banc Masc.

bend noun **1** (in a road) virage Masc.; **2** (in a river) courbe Fem.

bend verb **1** (to make a bend in) plier [1] (your arm or leg, or a wire); **2** (to curve) (a road or path) tourner [1]; **3 to bend down** or forwards se pencher [1]; **she bent down to look** elle s'est penchée pour regarder.

beneath preposition sous.

benefit noun **1** avantage Masc.; **2 unemployment benefit** les allocations Fem. plural de chômage.

bent adjective tordu.

beret noun béret Masc.

berry noun baie Fem.

berth noun couchette Fem.

beside preposition (next to) à côté de; **she was sitting beside me** elle était assise à côté de moi; **that's beside the point** ça n'a rien à voir.

besides adverb **1** (anyway) d'ailleurs; **besides, it's too late**

d'ailleurs, il est trop tard; **2** (as well) en plus; **four dogs, and six cats besides** quatre chiens et six chats en plus.

best adjective **1** meilleur; **it's the best** c'est le meilleur; **that's the best car** cette voiture-là est la meilleure; **she's my best friend** c'est ma meilleure amie; **2 she's the best at tennis** c'est elle la meilleure en tennis; **the best thing to do is to phone them** la meilleure chose à faire, c'est de les appeler.

best adverb le mieux; **he plays best** il joue le mieux; **I like Paris best** c'est Paris que j'aime le mieux; **best of all** mieux que tout; ★ **all the best!** (good luck!) bonne chance! (cheers!) à ta santé!; ★ **it's the best I can do** je ne peux pas faire mieux; ★ **to do your best to** do faire de son mieux pour faire;; **I did my best to help her** j'ai fait de mon mieux pour l'aider.

best man noun garçon Masc. d'honneur.

bet noun pari Masc.

bet verb parier [1]; **to bet on a horse** parier sur un cheval; **I bet you he'll forget!** je te parie qu'il va oublier!

better adjective, adverb **1** meilleur; **she's found a better flat** elle a trouvé un meilleur appartement; **this road's better than the other one** cette route est meilleure que l'autre; **2** mieux; **this pen writes better** ce stylo écrit mieux; **it works better than the other one** ça fonctionne mieux que l'autre; **3 even better** encore mieux; **it's even better than before** c'est encore mieux qu'avant; **4** (less ill) **to be better** aller mieux; **he's a bit better today** il va un peu mieux aujourd'hui; **to feel better** se sentir mieux; **I feel better** je me sens mieux; **5 to get better** s'améliorer; **my French is getting better** mon français s'améliore; **6 so much the better** tant mieux; **the sooner the better** le plus vite possible.

better adverb **you had better phone at once** tu ferais mieux d'appeler tout de suite; **he'd better not go** il ferait mieux de ne pas y aller; **I'd better go now** je dois partir maintenant.

better off adjective **1** (richer) plus riche; **they're better off than us** ils sont plus riches que nous; **2** (more comfortable) mieux; **you'd be better off in bed** tu serais mieux au lit.

between preposition entre; **between London and Dover** entre Londres et Douvres; **between Monday and Friday** entre lundi et vendredi; **between the two** entre les deux.

beware verb **beware of the dog!** attention au chien!

beyond preposition **1** (in space and time) au-delà de; **beyond the border** au-delà de la frontière; **2 it's beyond me!** ça me dépasse!

Bible noun **the Bible** la Bible.

bicycle noun vélo Masc.; **by bicycle** à vélo.

bicycle lane noun piste Fem. cyclable.

big adjective **1** grand (goes before the noun); **a big house** une grande maison; **a big city** une grande ville; **my big sister** ma grande sœur; **it's too big for me** c'est trop grand pour moi; **2** gros (Fem. grosse) (before the noun); **a big dog** un gros chien; **a big car** une grosse voiture; **a big mistake** une grosse erreur.

bigheaded adjective **to be bigheaded** avoir la grosse tête.

big screen noun grand écran Masc.

big toe noun gros orteil Masc.

bike noun **1** (with pedals) vélo Masc.; **by bike** à vélo; **2** (with motor) moto Fem.

bikini noun bikini Masc.

bilingual adjective bilingue.

bill noun **1** (in a restaurant) addition Fem.; **can we have the bill, please** l'addition, s'il vous plait; **2** (for gas, electricity, etc.) facture Fem.

billiards noun billard Masc.; **to play billiards** jouer au billard.

billion noun milliard Masc.

bin noun poubelle Fem.

binoculars noun jumelles Fem. plural.

biochemistry noun biochimie Fem.

biography noun biographie Fem.

biologist noun biologiste Masc. & Fem.

biology noun biologie Fem.

bird noun oiseau Masc. (plural oiseaux).

bird sanctuary noun réserve Fem. ornithologique.

a
b
c
d
e
f
g
h
i
j
k
l
m
n
o
p
q
r
s
t
u
v
w
x
y
z

birdwatching noun to go
birdwatching observer les oiseaux.

Biro™ noun bic™ Masc.

birth noun naissance Fem.

birth certificate noun acte Masc.
de naissance.

birth control noun contraception
Fem.

birthday noun 1 anniversaire
Masc.; happy birthday! joyeux
anniversaire!; 2 a birthday
present un cadeau d'anniversaire.

birthday party noun 1 (for a
child) goûter Masc. d'anniversaire;
2 (for an adult) soirée Fem.
d'anniversaire.

biscuit noun biscuit Masc.

bishop noun évêque Masc.

bit noun 1 (of bread, cheese, wood)
morceau Masc.; a bit of chocolate
un morceau de chocolat; 2 (of
string, paper, garden) bout Masc.; a
bit of string un bout de ficelle; with
a little bit of garden avec un petit
bout de jardin; 3 (a small amount)
a bit of un peu de; a bit of sugar un
peu de sucre; with a bit of luck
avec un peu de chance; a bit of
news une nouvelle; to have a bit of
trouble with avoir un petit
problème avec; 4 (in a book or film,
for example) passage Masc.; this bit
is brilliant! ce passage est génial!;
5 to fall to bits tomber en
morceaux; 6 a bit un peu; a bit hot
un peu chaud; a bit early un peu
trop tôt; wait a bit! attends un peu!;
7 (for a horse) mors Masc; ★ bit by
bit petit à petit.

bite noun 1 (snack) morceau Masc.;
I'll just have a bite before I go je

vais juste manger un morceau
avant de partir; 2 (from an insect)
piqûre Fem.; a mosquito bite une
piqûre de moustique; 3 (from a
dog) morsure Fem.

bite verb 1 (a person or a dog)
mordre [3]; 2 (an insect) piquer [1];
★ to bite one's nails se ronger [52]
les ongles.

bitter adjective (taste) amer (Fem.
amère).

black adjective 1 noir; my black
jacket ma veste noire; to turn
black noircir [2]; 2 a Black man un
Noir; a Black woman une Noire;
3 a black coffee un café noir.

blackberry noun mûre Fem.

blackbird noun merle Masc.

blackboard noun tableau Masc.
noir.

blackcurrant noun cassis Masc.

black eye noun œil Masc. au
beurre noir.

black pudding noun boudin
Masc. noir.

blade noun lame Fem.

blame noun responsabilité Fem.; to
take the blame for something
prendre la responsabilité de
quelque chose.

blame verb to blame someone for
something tenir [77] quelqu'un
responsable de quelque chose; they
blamed him for the accident ils
l'ont tenu responsable de
l'accident; she is to blame for it
elle en est responsable; I blame the
parents! à mon avis c'est la faute
des parents!; I don't blame you! je
te comprends!

blank noun blanc Masc.

blank adjective 1 (a page or piece of paper, or a cheque) blanc (Fem. blanche); (a tape or disk) vierge (a screen) vide; **2 my mind went blank** j'ai eu un trou de mémoire.

blanket noun couverture Fem.

blast noun 1 (an explosion) explosion Fem.; **2** (of air) souffle Masc.; **3 to play music at full blast** jouer de la musique à plein volume.

blaze noun incendie Masc.

blaze verb brûler [1].

blazer noun blazer Masc.

bleach noun eau Fem. de javel.

bleed verb saigner [1]; **my nose is bleeding** je saigne du nez.

blend noun mélange Masc.

blender noun mixer Masc.

bless verb bénir [2]; **bless you!** (after a sneeze) à tes souhaits!

blind noun (in a window) store Masc.

blind adjective aveugle; **to go blind** perdre la vue.

blindness noun cécité Fem.

blink verb (your eyes) cligner [1] des yeux.

blister noun ampoule Fem.

blizzard noun tempête Fem. de neige.

blob noun goutte Fem.

block noun 1 **a block of flats** un immeuble; **an office block** un immeuble de bureaux; **2** (a square group of buildings) **to run** (or **drive**) **round the block** faire le tour du pâté de maisons.

block verb 1 bloquer [1] (an exit or a road); **2** boucher [1] (a drain or a hole); **the sink's blocked** l'évier est bouché.

blonde adjective blond.

blood noun sang Masc.

blood test noun prise Fem. de sang.

blossom noun fleurs Fem. plural; **to be in blossom** être en fleurs.

blot noun tache Fem.

blotchy adjective (skin) marbré.

blouse noun chemisier Masc.

blow noun coup Masc.

blow verb 1 (the wind or a person) souffler [1]; **2** (in an explosion) **the bomb blew a hole in the wall** la bombe a fait un trou dans le mur; **3 to blow your nose** se moucher [1].

● **to blow something out** souffler [1] (a candle), éteindre [60] (flames).

● **to blow up** (explode) exploser [1].

● **to blow something up** gonfler [1] (a balloon or tyre), faire [10] sauter (a building); **they blew up the president's residence** ils ont fait sauter la résidence du président.

blow-dry noun brushing Masc.; **a cut and blow dry** une coupe brushing.

blue adjective bleu; **blue eyes** les yeux bleus.

bluebell noun jacinthe Fem. des bois.

blues plural noun le blues Masc. singular.

blunder noun gaffe Fem.

blunt adjective 1 (a knife or scissors) émoussé; **2** (a pencil) mal taillé; **3** (person) brusque.

blurred adjective **1** indistinct; **2** (photo) flou.

blush verb rougir [2].

board noun **1** (plank) planche Fem.; **2** (blackboard) tableau Masc. noir; **3** (notice board) panneau Masc. d'affichage; **4** (for a board game) jeu Masc.; **5 a chess board** un échiquier; **6** (accommodation in a hotel) **full board** pension Fem. complète; **half board** demi-pension Fem.; **7 on board** à bord; **they were on board the ferry** ils étaient à bord du ferry.

boarder noun (in a school) interne Masc. & Fem.

board game noun jeu Masc. de société (plural jeux de société).

boarding noun embarquement Masc.

boarding card noun carte Fem. d'embarquement.

boarding school noun école Fem. privée avec internat.

boast verb se vanter [1]; **he was boasting about his new bike** il se vantait de son nouveau vélo.

boat noun **1** (in general) bateau Masc.; **2** (sailing boat) voilier Masc.; **3** (rowing boat) barque Fem.

body noun **1** corps Masc.; **2** (corpse) cadavre Masc.

bodybuilding noun culturisme Masc.

bodyguard noun garde Masc. du corps.

boil noun **1 bring the water to the boil** portez l'eau à ébullition; **2** (swelling) furoncle Masc.

boil verb **1** bouillir [23]; **the water's boiling** l'eau bout; **2** faire [10]

bouillir; **I'm going to boil some water** je vais faire bouillir de l'eau; **to boil vegetables** faire [10] cuire des légumes à l'eau bouillante; **to boil an egg** faire cuire un œuf.

● **to boil over** déborder [1].

boiled egg noun œuf Masc. à la coque.

boiler noun (for central heating) chaudière Fem.

boiling adjective **1** (water) bouillant; **2 it's boiling hot today!** il fait une chaleur infernale aujourd'hui!

bolt noun (on a door) verrou Masc.

bolt verb (to lock) verrouiller [1] (a door).

bomb noun bombe Fem.

bomb verb bombarder [1].

bombing noun **1** (in a war) bombardement Masc.; **2** (a terrorist attack) attentat Masc. à la bombe.

bone noun **1** os Masc.; **2** (of a fish) arête Fem.

bonfire noun **1** (for rubbish) feu Masc. de jardin; **2** (for a celebration) feu Masc. de joie.

bonnet noun capot Masc. (of a car).

bony adjective **1** (fish) plein d'arêtes; **2** (body) anguleux (Fem. anguleuse); **3** (knee) osseux (Fem. osseuse).

boo verb huer [1]; **the crowd booed the referee** la foule a hué l'arbitre.

book noun **1** (that you read) livre Masc.; **a book about dinosaurs** un livre sur les dinosaures; **a biology book** un livre de biologie; **an exercise book** un cahier; **3** (of cheques, stamps, tickets, etc) carnet

Masc.; **a cheque book** un carnet de chèques.

book verb réserver [1]; **I booked a table for 8 p.m.** j'ai réservé une table pour vingt heures.

bookcase noun bibliothèque Fem.

booking noun (for a theatre or a holiday, for example) réservation Fem.

booking office noun bureau Masc. de location.

booklet noun brochure Fem.

bookshelf noun étagère Fem.

bookshop noun librairie Fem.

boom noun 1 (of a sail) bôme Fem.; 2 (time of prosperity) boom Masc.

boot noun 1 (for football, walking, climbing, or skiing) chaussure Fem.; **walking boots** des chaussures de randonnée; 2 (short fashion boot) bottine Fem.; 3 (knee-high boots or wellingtons) botte Fem.; 4 (of a car) coffre Masc.

border noun (between countries) frontière Fem.; **we crossed the border at Basel** nous avons passé la frontière à Bâle.

bore noun 1 (a boring person) raseur Masc., raseuse Fem. (informal); 2 (a nuisance) **what a bore!** quelle barbe!

bored adjective **to be bored** s'ennuyer; **je m'ennuie** I'm bored; **to get bored** s'ennuyer.

boring adjective ennuyeux (Fem. ennuyeuse).

born adjective né; **to be born** naître [55]; **she was born in June** elle est née en juin.

borrow verb emprunter [1]; **can I borrow your bike?** puis-je

t'emprunter ton vélo?; **to borrow something from someone** emprunter quelque chose à quelqu'un; **I'll borrow some money from Dad** je vais emprunter de l'argent à Papa.

Bosnia noun Bosnie Fem.

boss noun patron Masc., patronne Fem.

bossy adjective autoritaire.

both pronoun 1 (of people) tous les deux (Fem. toutes les deux); **they both came** ils sont venus tous les deux; **both my sisters were there** mes sœurs y étaient toutes les deux; 2 (of things) les deux; **they are both sold** ils sont tous vendus; **both my feet** mes deux pieds; 3 **both at home and at school** à la maison comme à l'école; **both in summer and in winter** en été comme en hiver.

bother noun ennui Masc.; **I've had a lot of bother with the car** j'ai eu beaucoup d'ennuis avec la voiture; **it's too much bother** c'est trop de tracas; **it's no bother** ce n'est pas un problème; **without any bother** sans aucune difficulté.

bother verb 1 (to disturb) déranger [52]; **I'm sorry to bother you** je suis désolé de vous déranger; 2 (to worry) inquiéter [24]; **that doesn't bother me at all** ça ne m'inquiète pas du tout; **don't bother about dinner** ne t'inquiète pas pour le dîner; 3 **she didn't even bother to come** elle n'a même pas pris la peine de venir; **don't bother!** ce n'est pas la peine!

bottle noun bouteille Fem.

bottle bank noun conteneur Masc. à verre.

bottle opener noun ouvre-bouteille Masc.

bottom noun 1 (of a hill, a wall, or steps) pied Masc.; **at the bottom of the ladder** au pied de l'échelle; 2 (of a bag or a table, a hole, a stretch of water, or a garden) fond Masc.; **at the bottom of the lake** au fond du lac; **at the bottom of the page** en bas de la page; 4 (buttocks) derrière Masc.

bottom adjective 1 inférieur; **the bottom shelf** le rayon inférieur; 2 (a division, team, or place) dernier (Fem. dernière); 3 **the bottom sheet** le drap de dessous; **the bottom flat** l'appartement du rez-de-chaussée.

bounce verb rebondir [2].

bouncer noun videur Masc.

bound adjective (certain) **he's bound to be late** il va sûrement être en retard; **that was bound to happen** cela devait arriver.

boundary noun limite Fem. (for sports) limites Fem. plural du terrain.

bow noun 1 (in a shoelace or ribbon) nœud Masc.; 2 (for a violin) archet Masc.; 3 **a bow and arrow** un arc et une flèche.

bowels plural noun intestins Masc. plural.

bowl noun 1 (for cereal, for example) bol Masc.; 2 (larger, for salad or mixing) saladier Masc.; 3 (for washing up) cuvette Fem.

bowl verb lancer [61] (a ball).

bowler noun (in cricket) lanceur Masc.

bowling noun (tenpin) bowling Masc.; **to go bowling** jouer au bowling.

bow tie noun nœud Masc. papillon.

box noun 1 boîte Fem.; **a box of chocolates** une boîte de chocolats; 2 **a cardboard box** un carton; 3 (on an application form) case Fem.

boxer noun 1 (fighter) boxeur Masc.; 2 (dog) boxer Masc.

boxer shorts plural noun caleçon Masc. singular.

boxing noun 1 boxe Fem.; 2 **a boxing match** un match de boxe.

Boxing Day noun le lendemain de Noël.

box office noun guichet Masc.

boy noun garçon Masc.; **a little boy** un petit garçon.

boyfriend noun copain Masc.

bra noun soutien-gorge Masc.

brace noun (for teeth) appareil Masc.

bracelet noun bracelet Masc.

bracket noun **in brackets** entre parenthèses.

brain noun cerveau Masc. (plural cerveaux).

brainwave noun idée Fem. géniale.

brake noun frein Masc.

brake verb freiner [1].

bramble noun ronce Fem.

branch noun 1 (of a tree) branche Fem.; 2 (of a shop) succursale Fem.; **our Oxford branch** notre succursale à Oxford; 3 (of a bank) agence Fem.

brand noun marque Fem.

brand new adjective tout neuf (Fem. toute neuve).

brandy noun cognac Masc.

brass noun laiton Masc., cuivre Masc. jaune; **a brass candlestick** un chandelier en cuivre jaune.

brass band noun fanfare Fem.

brave adjective courageux (Fem. courageuse).

bravery noun courage Masc.

Brazilian noun Brésilien Masc., Brésilienne Fem.

Brazilian adjective brésilien (Fem. brésilienne).

bread noun pain Masc.; **a slice of bread** une tranche de pain.

break noun 1 (a short rest) pause Fem.; **fifteen minutes' break** une pause de quinze minutes; **to take a break** faire une pause; 2 (in school) récréation Fem.; 3 **the Christmas break** les vacances de Noël.

break verb 1 casser [1]; **he broke a glass** il a cassé un verre; **I broke a tooth/my arm** je me suis cassé une dent/le bras; 2 se casser [1]; **the eggs broke** les œufs se sont cassés; 3 **to break your arm** se casser le bras; 4 **to break your promise** manquer [1] à sa promesse; **he broke the rules** il n'a pas respecté les règlements; **you mustn't break the rules** il faut respecter les règlements; 5 **to break a record** battre [21] un record; 6 **to break the news** annoncer [61] la nouvelle.

● **to break down** tomber [1] en panne; **the car broke down** la voiture est tombée en panne.

● **to break in** (a thief) entrer [1] par effraction.

● **to break out** 1 (a fire) se déclarer [1]; 2 (a fight or a storm) éclater [1]; 3 (a prisoner) s'évader [1].

● **to break up** 1 (a family or couple) se séparer [1]; 2 (a crowd or clouds) se disperser [1]; 3 (for the holidays) **we break up on Thursday** les cours finissent jeudi.

breakdown noun 1 (of a vehicle) panne Fem.; **we had a breakdown on the motorway** nous sommes tombés en panne sur l'autoroute; 2 (in talks or negotiations) rupture Fem.; 3 (a nervous collapse) dépression Fem.; **to have a (nervous) breakdown** faire une dépression.

breakdown truck noun camion Masc. de dépannage.

breakfast noun petit déjeuner Masc.; **we have breakfast at eight** nous prenons le petit déjeuner à huit heures.

break-in noun cambriolage Masc.

breast noun 1 (a woman's) sein Masc.; 2 (of a chicken or other fowl) blanc Masc.

breaststroke noun brasse Fem.

breath noun 1 (when you breathe in) souffle Masc.; **out of breath** à bout de souffle; **to get one's breath back** reprendre son souffle; **to take a deep breath** respirer profondément; 2 (when you breathe out) haleine Fem.; **to have bad breath** avoir mauvaise haleine.

breathe verb respirer [1].

breathing noun respiration Fem.

a
b
c
d
e
f
g
h
i
j
k
l
m
n
o
p
q
r
s
t
u
v
w
x
y
z

breed noun (of dog, for example) race Fem.

breed verb 1 élever [50] (animals); 2 (to have babies) se reproduire [26]; **rabbits breed fast** les lapins se reproduisent vite.

breeze noun brise Fem.

brew verb 1 préparer [1] (tea); 2 brasser [1] (beer).

brewery noun brasserie Fem.

brick noun brique Fem.; **a brick wall** un mur de briques.

bride noun mariée Fem.; **the bride and groom** les mariés Masc. plural.

bridegroom noun marié Masc.

bridesmaid noun demoiselle Fem. d'honneur.

bridge noun 1 (over a river) pont Masc.; **a bridge over the Thames** un pont sur la Tamise; 2 (card game) bridge Masc.; **to play bridge** jouer au bridge.

bridle noun bride Fem.

brief adjective bref (Fem. brève).

briefcase noun serviette Fem.

briefly adverb brièvement.

briefs plural noun slip Masc.

bright adjective 1 (colour, light) vif (Fem. vive); **bright green socks** des chaussettes vert vif; 2 **bright sunshine** un soleil éclatant; 3 (clever) intelligent; **she's not very bright** elle n'est pas très intelligente; ★ **to look on the bright side** voir le bon côté des choses.

brighten up verb **the weather's brightening up** le temps s'éclaircit.

brilliant adjective 1 (very clever) brillant; **a brilliant surgeon** un chirurgien brillant; **he's brilliant at maths** il est très doué en maths; 2 (wonderful) génial (Masc. plural géniaux) (informal); **the party was brilliant!** la boum était géniale!

bring verb 1 apporter [1] (something you carry); **they brought a present** ils ont apporté un cadeau; **bring your camera!** apporte ton appareil-photo!; **it brings good luck** ça porte bonheur; 2 amener [50] (a person or an animal); **she's bringing all the children** elle va amener tous les enfants; 3 **to bring something back** rapporter [1] quelque chose; 4 **to bring up** élever [50] (children); **he was brought up by his aunt** il a été élevé par sa tante.

bristle noun poil Masc.

Britain, Great Britain noun Grande-Bretagne Fem.; **in Britain** en Grande-Bretagne; **to Britain** en Grande-Bretagne; **Britain is sending aid** la Grande-Bretagne envoie de l'aide.

British plural noun the British les Britanniques; **the British love animals** les Britanniques adorent les animaux.

British adjective britannique; **the British army** l'armée britannique; **the British Isles** les îles Britanniques.

Brittany noun Bretagne Fem.; **in Brittany** en Bretagne; **to Brittany** en Bretagne.

broad adjective (wide) large.

broad bean noun fève Fem.

broadcast noun émission Fem.

broadcast verb diffuser [1] (a programme).

broccoli noun brocolis Masc. plural; **to eat broccoli** manger des brocolis.

brochure noun brochure Fem.

broke adjective **to be broke** (no money) être fauché (informal).

broken adjective cassé; **the window's broken** la vitre est cassée; **to have a broken leg** avoir la jambe cassée.

bronchitis noun bronchite Fem.; **to have bronchitis** avoir une bronchite.

brooch noun broche Fem.

broom noun 1 (for sweeping) balai Masc.; 2 (bush) genêt Masc.

brother noun frère Masc.; **my little brother** mon petit frère; **my mother's brother** le frère de ma mère.

brother-in-law noun beau-frère Masc. (plural beaux-frères).

brown adjective marron (does not change in the feminine or plural); **my brown jacket** ma veste marron; **your brown shoes** tes chaussures marron; **light brown** marron clair; **dark brown** marron foncé; 2 châtain (hair); 3 (tanned in the sun) bronzé; **to go brown** bronzer.

brown bread noun pain Masc. complet.

brown sugar noun sucre Masc. brun.

bruise noun 1 (on a person) bleu Masc.; 2 (on fruit) tache Fem.

brush noun 1 (for your hair, clothes, nails, or shoes) brosse Fem.; my hair brush ma brosse à cheveux; 2 (for sweeping) balai Masc.; 3 (paintbrush) pinceau Masc.

brush verb brosser [1] (the floor or your clothes); **to brush your hair** se brosser les cheveux; **she brushed her hair** elle s'est brossé les cheveux; **to brush your teeth** se brosser les dents.

Brussels noun Bruxelles.

Brussels sprout noun chou Masc. de Bruxelles.

bubble noun bulle Fem.

bubble bath noun bain Masc. moussant.

bucket noun seau Masc. (plural seaux).

buckle noun boucle Fem.

Buddhism noun bouddhisme Masc.

Buddhist noun bouddhiste Masc. & Fem.

budget noun budget Masc.

budgie noun perruche Fem.

buffet noun buffet Masc.

buffet car noun voiture Fem. bar.

bug noun 1 (insect) bestiole Fem. (informal); 2 (germ) microbe Masc.; **a stomach bug** une gastroentérite; 3 (in a computer) bug Masc.

build verb construire [26]; **they are building three houses over there** ils construisent trois maisons là-bas.

builder noun maçon Masc.

building noun bâtiment Masc.; (with offices or flats) immeuble Masc.

building site noun chantier Masc.

a
b
c
d
e
f
g
h
i
j
k
l
m
n
o
p
q
r
s
t
u
v
w
x
y
z

building society noun société Fem. d'investissement et de crédit immobilier.

built-up adjective urbanisé; **a built-up area** une agglomération.

bulb noun **1** (for a light) ampoule Fem.; **2** (that you plant) bulbe Masc.

bull noun taureau Masc. (plural taureaux).

bulldozer noun bulldozer Masc.

bullet noun balle Fem.

bulletin noun bulletin Masc.; **a news bulletin** un bulletin d'informations.

bullfight noun corrida Fem.

bully noun brute Fem.; **he's a bully** c'est une brute.

bully verb tyranniser [1].

bum noun (bottom) derrière Masc.

bump noun **1** (that sticks up) bosse Fem.; **a bump on the head** une bosse à la tête; **a bump in the road** une bosse sur la route; **2** (jolt) secousse Fem.; **3** (noise) bruit Masc. sourd.

bump verb **1** (to bang) cogner [1]; **I bumped my head** je me suis cogné la tête; **2 to bump into something** rentrer [1] dans quelque chose; **3 to bump into somebody** (meet by chance) croiser [1] quelqu'un.

bumper noun pare-chocs Masc.

bumpy adjective **1** accidenté (road); **2** agité (plane landing).

bun noun **1** (for a burger) petit pain Masc.; **2** (sugary) petit cake Masc.

bunch noun **1** (of flowers) bouquet Masc.; **2** (of carrots or radishes) botte Fem.; **3** (of keys) trousseau Masc.; **4 a bunch of grapes** une grappe de raisin.

bundle noun tas Masc.

bungalow noun pavillon Masc.

bunk noun **1** (on a train or boat) couchette Fem.; **2 bunk beds** des lits superposés.

bureau noun agence Fem.

burger noun hamburger Masc.

burglar noun cambrioleur Masc.

burglar alarm noun sonnerie Fem. d'alarme.

burglary noun cambriolage Masc.

burn noun brûlure Fem.

burn verb **1** brûler [1]; **I've burned the rubbish** j'ai brûlé les ordures; **the fire's burning well** le feu brûle bien; **she burnt herself on the grill** elle s'est brûlée au grill; **you'll burn your finger!** tu vas te brûler le doigt!; **2** laisser [1] brûler (something you're cooking); **Mum's burnt her cake** maman a laissé brûler son gâteau; **3** (through sunburn) **I burn easily** j'attrape facilement des coups de soleil.

burnt adjective brûlé.

burst verb **1** crever [50] (a balloon or tyre, for example); **a burst tyre** un pneu crevé; **2 to burst out laughing** éclater [1] de rire; **3 to burst into tears** fondre [3] en larmes; **4 to burst into flames** prendre [64] feu.

bury verb enterrer [1].

bus noun (public transport) autobus Masc., bus Masc.; **we'll take the bus** on va prendre le bus; **on the bus** dans le bus; **a bus ticket** un ticket de bus; **2** (coach) car Masc.; **to go to London by bus** aller à Londres en car.

bus conductor noun receveur Masc. d'autobus.

bus driver noun conducteur de bus Masc., conductrice de bus Fem.

bush noun buisson Masc.

business noun 1 (commercial dealings) affaires Fem. plural; **to be in business** être dans les affaires; **he's in Leeds on business** il est à Leeds en voyage d'affaires; **he's in the insurance business** il travaille dans l'assurance; **a business letter** une lettre d'affaires; 2 (firm or company) entreprise Fem.; **small businesses** les petites entreprises; 3 **mind your own business!** occupe-toi de tes affaires!; **that's my business!** ça me regarde!

business class noun classe Fem. affaires.

businessman noun homme Masc. d'affaires.

business trip noun voyage Masc. d'affaires.

businesswoman noun femme Fem. d'affaires.

bus lane noun couloir Masc. d'autobus.

bus pass noun carte Fem. de bus.

bus route noun ligne Fem. d'autobus.

bus shelter noun abribus™ Masc.

bus station noun gare Fem. routière.

bus stop noun arrêt Masc. de bus.

bust noun bust size tour Masc. de poitrine.

busy adjective 1 occupé (a person), chargé (a day or week); 2 **don't disturb him, he's busy** ne le dérange pas, il est occupé; **a busy day** une journée chargée; 3 (full of cars or people) très fréquenté (a road); **the shops were busy** il y avait beaucoup de monde dans les magasins; 4 (phone) **the line's busy** la ligne est occupée.

but conjunction mais; **small but strong** petit mais fort; **not Thursday but Friday** pas jeudi mais vendredi; **I'll try, but it's difficult** j'essaierai, mais c'est difficile.

but preposition sauf; **anything but that** tout, sauf ça; **everyone but Roger** tout le monde sauf Roger; **the last but one** l'avant-dernier.

butcher noun boucher Masc.; **he's a butcher** il est boucher; **the butcher's** la boucherie.

butter noun beurre Masc.

butter verb beurrer [1].

buttercup noun bouton Masc. d'or.

butterfly noun papillon Masc.

button noun bouton Masc.; **the record button** la touche d'enregistrement.

buttonhole noun boutonnière Fem.

buy noun **a good buy** une bonne affaire; **a bad buy** une mauvaise affaire.

buy verb acheter [16]; **I bought the tickets** j'ai acheté les billets; **to buy something for somebody** acheter quelque chose à quelqu'un; **Sarah bought him a sweater** Sarah lui a acheté un pull; **to buy something from someone** acheter quelque chose à quelqu'un; **I bought my**

a b c d e f g h i j k l m n o p q r s t u v w x y z

bike from Tim j'ai acheté mon vélo à Tim.

buyer noun acheteur Masc., acheteuse Fem.

buzz verb (a fly or bee) bourdonner [1].

buzzer noun sonnerie Fem.

by preposition 1 par; **to take somebody by telephone** par téléphone; **to take somebody by the hand** prendre quelqu'un par la main; **eaten by a dog** mangé par un chien; **by mistake** par erreur; 2 (travel) en; **to come by bus** venir en bus; **to leave by train** partir en train; **by bike** en vélo; 3 (near) à côté de; **by the fire** à côté du feu; **by the sea** au bord de la mer; **close by** tout près; 4 (before) avant; **ready by Monday** prêt avant lundi; **Kevin was back by four** Kevin est rentré avant quatre heures; 5 **by yourself** tout seul; **I was by myself in the house** j'étais tout seul chez moi; **she did it by herself** elle l'a fait toute seule; 6 **by the way** au fait; 7 **to go by** passer.

bye exclamation au revoir; **bye for now!** à bientôt!

bypass noun rocade Fem.

Cc

cab noun 1 taxi Masc.; **to call a cab** appeler un taxi; 2 (on a lorry) cabine Fem.

cabbage noun chou Masc. (plural choux).

cabin noun cabine Fem.

cable noun câble Masc.

cable car noun téléférique Masc.

cable television noun télévision Fem. par câble.

cactus noun cactus Masc.

cafe noun café Masc.

cage noun cage Fem.

cagoule noun K-way™ Masc.

cake noun gâteau Masc. (plural gâteaux); **would you like a piece of cake?** veux-tu un morceau de gâteau?

calculate verb calculer [1].

calculation noun calcul Masc.

calculator noun calculatrice Fem.

calendar noun calendrier Masc.

calf noun 1 (animal) veau Masc.; 2 (of your leg) mollet.

call noun (telephone) appel Masc.; **I had several calls this morning** j'ai eu plusieurs appels ce matin; **thank you for your call** merci de votre appel; **a phone call** un coup de téléphone.

call verb 1 appeler [18]; **to call a taxi** appeler un taxi; **to call the doctor** appeler le médecin; **they called the police** ils ont appelé la police; **call this number** appelez ce numéro; **thank you for calling** merci de votre appel; **I'll call you back later** je te rappellerai plus tard; 2 appeler [18]; **they've called the baby Julie** ils ont appelé le bébé Julie; 3 **to be called** s'appeler [18]; **she has a brother called Dan** elle a un frère qui s'appelle Dan; **what's he called?** il s'appelle comment?

● **to call in** passer [1]; **I'll call in on the way back from school** je passerai en rentrant de l'école.

call box noun cabine Fem. téléphonique.

calm adjective calme.

calm verb calmer [1].

● **to calm down** se calmer; **he's calmed down a bit** il s'est calmé un peu.

● **to calm somebody down** calmer quelqu'un; **I tried to calm her down** j'ai essayé de la calmer.

calmly adverb calmement.

calorie noun calorie Fem.

camcorder noun caméscope Masc.

camel noun chameau Masc. (plural chameaux).

camera noun **1** appareil Masc. photo (plural appareils photo); **2** (film or TV camera) caméra.

cameraman noun caméraman Masc.

camp noun camp Masc.

camp verb camper [1].

campaign noun campagne Fem.

camper van noun camping-car Masc.

camping noun camping Masc.; **to go camping** faire du camping; **we're going camping in Brittany this summer** nous allons faire du camping en Bretagne cet été.

campsite noun terrain Masc. de camping.

can[1] noun **1** boîte Fem.; **a can of tomatoes** une boîte de tomates; **2** (for petrol or oil) bidon Masc.

can[2] verb **1** pouvoir [12]; **I can't/cannot be there before ten** je ne peux pas y être avant dix heures; **you can leave your bag here** to

peux laisser ton sac ici; **can you open the door, please?** peux-tu ouvrir la porte, s'il te plaît?; **can I help you?** est-ce que je peux vous aider?; **they couldn't come** ils n'ont pas pu venir; **you could ring back tomorrow** tu pourrais rappeler demain; **you could have told me** tu aurais pu me le dire; **2** (not translated) **can you hear me?** est-ce que tu m'entends?; **I can't see him** je ne le vois pas; **I can't remember** je ne me souviens pas; **I can't find my keys** je ne trouve pas mes clés; **3** (know how to) savoir [70]; **she can't drive** elle ne sait pas conduire; **can you play the piano?** est-ce que tu sais jouer du piano?

Canada noun Canada Masc.; **to Canada** au Canada; **in Canada** au Canada.

Canadian noun Canadien Masc., Canadienne Fem..

Canadian adjective canadien (Fem. canadienne).

canal noun canal Masc. (plural canaux).

canary noun canari Masc.

cancel verb annuler [1]; **the concert's been cancelled** le concert a été annulé.

cancer noun cancer Masc.; **to have lung cancer** avoir un cancer du poumon.

Cancer noun Cancer Masc.; **I'm Cancer** je suis Cancer.

candidate noun candidat Masc., candidate Fem.

candle noun bougie Fem.

candlestick noun bougeoir Masc.

a b c d e f g h i j k l m n o p q r s t u v w x y z

candyfloss noun barbe Fem. à papa.

canned adjective en conserve; **canned tomatoes** les tomates en conserve.

cannon noun canon Masc.

cannot verb can².

canoe noun canoë Masc.

canoeing noun to go canoeing faire du canoë; **I like canoeing** j'aime faire du canoë.

can-opener noun ouvre-boîte Masc.

canteen noun cantine Fem.

canvas noun toile Fem.

cap noun 1 (hat) casquette Fem.; **a baseball cap** une casquette de baseball; 2 (on a bottle or tube) bouchon Masc.

capable adjective capable.

capacity noun capacité Fem.

capital noun 1 (city) capitale Fem.; **Paris is the capital of France** Paris est la capitale de la France; 2 (letter) majuscule Fem.; **in capitals** en majuscules.

capitalism noun capitalisme Masc.

Capricorn noun Capricorne Masc.; **Linda's Capricorn** Linda est Capricorne.

capsize verb chavirer [1].

captain noun capitaine Masc.

captivity noun captivité Fem.; **to be kept in captivity** être gardé en captivité.

capture verb capturer [1].

car noun voiture Fem.; **in the car** dans la voiture; **to park the car** garer la voiture; **we're going by**

car nous y allons en voiture; **a car crash** un accident de voiture.

caramel noun caramel Masc.

caravan noun caravane Fem.

card noun carte Fem.; **un jeu de cartes** a card game, a pack of cards; **faire une partie de cartes** to have a game of cards.

cardboard noun carton Masc.

cardigan noun cardigan Masc.

cardphone noun téléphone à carte.

care noun 1 soin Masc.; **to take care to do** prendre soin de faire; 2 **to take care of somebody** s'occuper de quelqu'un; 3 **take care!** (be careful) fais attention!, (when saying goodbye) à bientôt!

care verb 1 **to care about** se soucier de [1]; **to care about pollution** se soucier de la pollution; 2 **she doesn't care** ça lui est égal; **I couldn't care less!** ça m'est complètement égal!

career noun carrière Fem.

careful adjective prudent 1 **a careful driver** un conducteur prudent; 2 **be careful!** fais attention!

carefully adverb 1 **read the instructions carefully** lisez attentivement les instructions; **listen carefully** écoutez bien; 2 (handle) avec précaution; **she put the vase down carefully** a posé le vase avec précaution; 3 **to copy something carefully** recopier soigneusement quelque chose; 4 **drive carefully!** sois prudent!

careless adjective **1** he's very careless il ne fait pas du tout attention à ce qu'il fait; **2** this is careless work c'est du travail peu soigné; a careless mistake une faute d'inattention; **3** careless driving la conduite imprudente.

caretaker noun gardien Masc., gardienne Fem.

car ferry noun ferry Masc.

cargo noun cargaison Fem.

car hire noun location Fem. de voitures.

Caribbean noun **1** the Caribbean (islands) les Caraïbes; **2** the Caribbean (sea) la mer des Caraïbes.

carnation noun œillet Masc.

carnival noun carnaval Masc.

car park noun parking Masc.

carpenter noun menuisier Masc.

carpentry noun menuiserie Fem.

carpet noun **1** (fitted) moquette Fem.; **2** (loose) tapis Masc.

car phone noun téléphone Masc. de voiture.

car radio noun autoradio Masc.

carriage noun (of a train) voiture Fem.

carrier bag noun sac Masc. en plastique.

carrot noun carotte Fem.

carry verb **1** porter [1]; she was carrying a parcel elle portait un paquet; **2** (vehicle, plane) transporter [1]; the coach was carrying schoolchildren le car transportait des écoliers

● to carry on continuer [1]; they carried on talking ils ont continué à parler.

carrycot noun porte-bébé Masc.

carsick adjective to be carsick avoir le mal de la route.

cart noun charrette Fem.

carton noun **1** (of cream or yoghurt) pot Masc.; **2** (of milk or orange) brique Fem.

cartoon noun **1** (a film) dessin Masc. animé; **2** (a comic strip) bande Fem. dessinée; **3** (an amusing drawing) dessin Masc. humoristique.

cartridge noun (for a pen or a video) cartouche Fem.

carve verb découper [1] (meat).

case¹ noun **1** (suitcase) valise Fem.; to pack a case faire une valise; **2** (a large wooden box, for wine for example) caisse Fem.; **3** (for spectacles or small things) étui Masc.

case² noun **1** cas Masc.; in that case en ce cas; that's not the case ce n'est pas le cas; a case of flu un cas de grippe; **2** in case au cas où; in case he's late au cas où il serait en retard; check first, just in case vérifie d'abord, au cas où; **3** in any case de toute façon; in any case, it's too late de toute façon, c'est trop tard.

cash noun **1** (money in general) argent Masc.; I haven't any cash on me je n'ai pas d'argent; **2** (money rather than a cheque) espèces Fem. plural; to pay in cash payer en espèces; £50 in cash cinquante livres en espèces.

a b c d e f g h i j k l m n o p q r s t u v w x y z

cash card noun carte Fem. de retrait.

cash desk noun caisse Fem.; **pay at the cash desk** payez à la caisse.

cash dispenser noun guichet Masc. automatique.

cashew noun cajou Masc.

cashier noun caissier Masc., caissière Fem.

cash point noun = cash dispenser.

cassette noun cassette Fem.

cassette recorder noun magnétophone Masc. à cassettes.

cast noun les acteurs Masc. plural; **the cast were on stage** les acteurs étaient sur scène.

castle noun 1 (in an accident) château Masc. (plural **châteaux**); 2 (in chess) tour Fem.

casual adjective décontracté.

casualty noun 1 (in an accident) victime Fem.; **there are 47 casualties** il y a 47 victimes; 2 (hospital department) urgences Fem. plural; **he's in casualty** il est aux urgences.

cat noun chat Masc.; (female) chatte Fem.; **a big black cat** un gros chat noir; ★ **it's raining cats and dogs** il pleut des cordes (literally: it's raining in ropes).

catalogue noun catalogue Masc.

catastrophe noun catastrophe Fem.

catch noun 1 (on a door) fermeture Fem.; 2 (a drawback) piège Masc.; **what's the catch?** où est le piège?

catch verb 1 attraper [1]; **Tom caught the ball** Tom a attrapé le ballon; **you can't catch me!** vous ne m'attraperez pas!; **can you catch hold of the branch?** peux-tu attraper la branche?; 2 **to catch somebody doing** attraper quelqu'un en train de faire; **he was caught stealing money** il a été attrapé en train de voler de l'argent; 3 prendre [64] (a bus or plane); **did Tim catch his plane?** est-ce que Tim a pris son avion?; 4 attraper [1] (an illness); **he's caught chickenpox** il a attrapé la varicelle; **I've caught a cold** j'ai attrapé un rhume; 5 saisir [2] (what somebody says); **I didn't catch your name** je n'ai pas saisi votre nom.

● **to catch up with somebody** rattraper [1] quelqu'un.

category noun catégorie Fem.

catering noun restauration Fem.

caterpillar noun chenille Fem.

cathedral noun cathédrale Fem.; **Winchester cathedral** la cathédrale de Winchester.

Catholic noun, adjective catholique Masc. & Fem.

cattle plural noun bétail Masc. singular.

cauliflower noun chou-fleur Masc. (plural **choux-fleurs**); **cauliflower cheese** un gratin de chou-fleur.

cause noun cause Fem.; **the cause of the accident** la cause de l'accident; **for a good cause** pour une bonne cause.

cause verb 1 causer [1] (damage or problems); **to cause problems** causer des problèmes; 2 provoquer [1] (chaos or disease); **the strike**

caused delays la grève a provoqué des retards.

caution noun prudence Fem.

cautious adjective prudent.

cave noun grotte Fem.

caving noun spéléologie Fem.; **to go caving** faire de la spéléologie.

CD noun CD Masc.

CD player noun platine Fem. laser.

CD-ROM noun CD-ROM Masc.

ceiling noun plafond Masc.; **on the ceiling** au plafond.

celebrate verb fêter [1]; **I'm celebrating my birthday** je fête mon anniversaire.

celebrity noun célébrité Fem.

celery noun céleri Masc.

cell noun cellule Fem.

cellar noun cave Fem.

cello noun violoncelle Masc.; **to play the cello** jouer du violoncelle.

cement noun ciment Masc.

cemetery noun cimetière Masc.

cent noun **1** (in euro system) centime Masc. (d'euro) (unofficial term); cent Masc. (official term); **2** (in dollar system) cent Masc.

centenary noun centenaire Masc.

centigrade adjective centigrade; **ten degrees centigrade** dix degrés centigrade.

centimetre noun centimètre Masc.

central adjective central (Masc. plural centraux); **central London** le centre de Londres; **the office is very central** le bureau est en plein centre-ville.

central heating noun chauffage Masc. central.

centre noun centre Masc.; **in the centre of** au centre de; **in the town centre** en centre-ville; **a shopping centre** un centre commercial.

century noun siècle Masc.; **in the twentieth century** au vingtième siècle; **the twenty-first century** le vingt-et-unième siècle.

cereal noun breakfast cereal céréales Fem. plural pour le petit déjeuner; **to have cereal for breakfast** prendre des céréales au petit déjeuner.

ceremony noun cérémonie Fem.

certain adjective certain; **a certain number of** un certain nombre de; **are you certain of the address?** es-tu certain de l'adresse?; **I'm certain of it** j'en suis certain; **to be certain that** être sûr que; **Nicola's certain you're wrong** Nicola est sûre que tu as tort; **nobody knows for certain** personne ne sait au juste.

certainly adverb certainement; **certainly not** certainement pas.

certificate noun **1** certificat Masc.; **2 a birth certificate** un acte de naissance.

chain noun chaîne Fem.

chair noun **1** (upright) chaise Fem.; **a kitchen chair** une chaise de cuisine; **2** (with arms) fauteuil Masc.

chair lift noun télésiège Masc.

chalet noun **1** (in the mountains) chalet Masc.; **2** (in a holiday camp) bungalow Masc.

chalk noun craie Fem.

a
b
c
d
e
f
g
h
i
j
k
l
m
n
o
p
q
r
s
t
u
v
w
x
y
z

challenge noun 1 (that excites you) challenge Masc.; **the challenge of new ideas** le challenge des nouvelles idées; 2 (that is difficult) épreuve Fem.; **the exam was a real challenge** l'examen était une vraie épreuve.

champion noun champion Masc., championne Fem.; **world champion** champion du monde.

chance noun 1 (an opportunity) occasion Fem.; **to have the chance to do** avoir l'occasion de faire; **if you have the chance to go to New York** si tu as l'occasion d'aller à New York; **I haven't had the chance to write to him** je n'ai pas eu l'occasion de lui écrire; 2 (likelihood) chance Fem.; **there's little chance of winning** il y a peu de chance de gagner; 3 (luck) by **chance** par hasard; **do you have her address, by any chance?** aurais-tu par hasard son adresse?

change noun 1 changement Masc.; **a change of plan** un changement de programme; **they've made some changes to the house** ils ont fait des changements dans la maison; **for a change, let's eat out** mangeons au restaurant pour changer; **it makes a change from hamburgers** cela change un peu des hamburgers; 2 **a change of clothes** des vêtements de rechange; 3 (cash) monnaie Fem.; **I haven't any change** je n'ai pas de monnaie.

change verb 1 (transform completely) changer [52]; **it changed my life** cela m'a changé la vie; **Liz never changes** Liz ne

change jamais; 2 (to switch from one thing to another) changer [52] de; **we changed trains at Crewe** nous avons changé de train à Crewe; **I must change my shirt** je dois changer de chemise; **they changed places** ils ont changé de place; **to change your mind** changer d'avis; 3 (to exchange in a shop) échanger [52]; **can I change it for the larger size?** puis-je l'échanger contre la taille au-dessus?; 4 (to change your clothes) se changer [52]; **Mike's gone up to change** Mike est monté se changer.

changing room noun (for sport or swimming) 1 vestiaire Masc.; 2 (in a shop) salon Masc. d'essayage.

channel noun 1 (on TV) chaîne Fem.; **to change channels** changer de chaîne; 2 **the Channel** la Manche.

Channel Islands plural noun îles Fem. plural Anglo-Normandes.

Channel Tunnel noun tunnel Masc. sous la Manche.

chaos noun pagaille Fem. (informal); **it was chaos!** c'était la pagaille!

chapel noun chapelle Fem.

chapter noun chapitre Masc.; **in chapter two** au chapitre deux.

character noun 1 (personality) caractère Masc.; **a house with a lot of character** une maison qui a du caractère; 2 (somebody in a book, play, or film) personnage Masc.; **the main character** le personnage principal.

characteristic *adjective* caractéristique.

charcoal *noun* 1 (*for burning*) charbon *Masc.* de bois; 2 (*for drawing*) fusain *Masc.*

charge *noun* 1 (*what you pay*) frais *Masc. plural*; **a booking charge** des frais de réservation; **an extra or additional charge** un supplément; **there's no charge** c'est gratuit; 2 **to be in charge** être responsable; **who's in charge of these children?** qui est responsable de ces enfants?; 3 **to be on a charge of theft** être inculpé de vol.

charge *verb* 1 (*to ask a specific sum*) prendre [64]; **they charge fifteen pounds an hour** ils prennent quinze livres de l'heure; **how much do you charge for one day?** combien prenez-vous pour une journée?; 2 (*to ask people to pay*) faire [10] payer; **we don't charge, it's free** nous ne faisons pas payer les gens, c'est gratuit; 3 **to charge somebody with** inculper [1] quelqu'un de (*a crime*).

charity *noun* organisation *Fem.* caritative.

charm *noun* charme *Masc.*

charming *adjective* charmant.

chart *noun* 1 (*table*) tableau *Masc.*; 2 **the weather chart** la carte du temps; 3 **the charts** le hit-parade; **number one in the charts** numéro un au hit-parade.

charter flight *noun* vol *Masc.* charter.

chase *noun* poursuite *Fem.*; **a car chase** une poursuite en voiture.

chase *verb* pourchasser [1] (*a person or animal*).

chat *noun* conversation *Fem.*; **to have a chat with somebody** bavarder avec quelqu'un.

chatroom *noun* chatroom *Masc.*

chat show *noun* talk-show *Masc.*

chatter *verb* 1 (*gossip*) bavarder [1]; 2 **my teeth are chattering** je claque des dents.

cheap *adjective* pas cher (*Fem.* pas chère); **cheap shoes** des chaussures pas chères; **that's very cheap!** ce n'est vraiment pas cher!

cheaper *adjective* moins cher (*Fem.* moins chère).

cheaply *adverb* pas cher; **to eat cheaply** manger pas cher.

cheap rate *adjective* à tarif réduit; **a cheap rate phone call** un appel à tarif réduit.

cheat *noun* tricheur *Masc.*, tricheuse *Fem.*

cheat *verb* tricher [1].

check *noun* 1 (*in a factory or at border controls*) contrôle *Masc.*; **passport check** contrôle des passeports; 2 (*by a doctor*) examen *Masc.*; 3 (*in chess*) **check!** échec au roi!

check *verb* (*to make sure*) vérifier [1]; **he checked the time** il a vérifié l'heure; **check they're all back** vérifiez qu'ils sont tous rentrés; **check with your father** demande à ton père.

● **to check in** 1 (*at the airport*) enregistrer [1]; 2 (*at a hotel*) arriver [1] à l'hôtel; **he checked in at five o'clock** il est arrivé à l'hôtel à cinq heures.

a
b
c
d
e
f
g
h
i
j
k
l
m
n
o
p
q
r
s
t
u
v
w
x
y
z

a

● **to check out** quitter [1] l'hôtel; **he checked out at 8.30** il a quitté l'hôtel à 8h30.

b

c

check-in *noun* enregistrement *Masc.*

d

checkout *noun* caisse *Fem.*; **at the checkout** à la caisse.

e

check-up *noun* examen *Masc.* médical.

f

cheek *noun* **1** (*part of face*) joue *Fem.*; **2** (*nerve*) **what a cheek!** quel culot! (*informal*).

g

cheeky *adjective* **1** coquin; **2** (*rude*) impoli.

h

i

cheer *noun* **1** three cheers for Tom! faisons un ban à Tom!; **2** (*when you have a drink*) **cheers!** à la vôtre!

j

k

cheer *verb* (*to shout hurray*) applaudir [2].

l

m

● **to cheer on** encourager.

● **to cheer up: cheer up!** courage!

n

● **to cheer somebody up** remonter [1] le moral à quelqu'un; **your visit's cheered me up** ta visite m'a remonté le moral.

o

p

cheerful *adjective* gai.

cheese *noun* fromage *Masc.*; **blue cheese** le fromage bleu; **a cheese sandwich** un sandwich au fromage.

q

r

s

cheesecake *noun* cheesecake *Masc.*

t

u

chef *noun* chef *Masc.* cuisinier.

v

chemical *noun* produit *Masc.* chimique.

w

x

chemical *adjective* chimique.

chemist *noun* **1** pharmacien *Masc.*, pharmacienne *Fem.*; **2** chemist's pharmacie *Fem.*; **at the**

y

z

chemist's à la pharmacie; **3** (*scientist*) chimiste *Masc. & Fem.*

chemistry *noun* chimie *Fem.*

cheque *noun* chèque *Masc.*; **to pay by cheque** payer par chèque; **to write a cheque** faire un chèque.

chequebook *noun* carnet *Masc.* de chèques.

cherry *noun* cerise *Fem.*

chess *noun* échecs *Masc. plural*; **to play chess** jouer aux échecs.

chessboard *noun* échiquier *Masc.*

chest *noun* **1** (*part of the body*) poitrine *Fem.*; **2** (*box*) coffre *Masc.*; **3 a chest of drawers** une commode.

chestnut *noun* marron *Masc.*

chestnut tree *noun* **1** (*horse-chestnut*) marronnier *Masc.*; **2** (*sweet chestnut*) châtaignier *Masc.*

chew *verb* mâcher [1] (*food*).

chewing gum *noun* chewing-gum *Masc.*

chick *noun* (*of a hen*) poussin *Masc.*

chicken *noun* poulet *Masc.*; **roast chicken** du poulet rôti; **chicken thighs** des cuisses de poulet; **a chicken sandwich** un sandwich au poulet.

chickenpox *noun* varicelle *Fem.*

chicory *noun* endive *Fem.*

chief *noun* chef *Masc.*; **the chief of police** le préfet de police.

child *noun* enfant *Masc. & Fem.*; **Jenny's children** les enfants de Jenny.

childish *adjective* puéril.

child-minder *noun* nourrice *Fem.*

chill *noun* fraîcheur *Fem.*

chilled *adjective* (*wine*) bien frais.

chilli noun piment Masc.

chilly adjective frisquet (Fem. frisquette); **it's chilly today** il fait frisquet aujourd'hui.

chimney noun cheminée Fem.

chimpanzee noun chimpanzé Masc.

chin noun menton Masc.

China noun Chine Fem.; **in China** en Chine.

china noun porcelaine Fem.; **a china plate** une assiette en porcelaine.

Chinese noun 1 **the Chinese** (people) les Chinois; 2 (language) chinois Masc.

Chinese adjective chinois; **a Chinese man** un Chinois; **a Chinese woman** une Chinoise; **a Chinese meal** un repas chinois.

chip noun 1 (fried potato) frite Fem.; **I'd like some chips** j'aimerais des frites; 2 (microchip) puce Fem.; 3 (in glass or china) ébréchure Fem.

chipped adjective ébréché.

chives noun ciboulette Fem. singular.

chocolate noun chocolat Masc.; **a chocolate ice cream** une glace au chocolat; **hot chocolate** chocolat Masc. chaud; **a box of chocolates** une boîte de chocolats.

choice noun choix Masc.; **you have a choice of two flights** vous avez le choix entre deux vols.

choir noun 1 (in a school) chorale Fem.; **I sing in the choir** je fais partie de la chorale; 2 (professional) chur Masc.

choke noun (on a car) starter Masc.

choke verb 1 (by yourself) s'étouffer [1]; **she was choking on a bone** elle s'éttouffait avec une arête; 2 (smoke or fumes) étouffer [1].

choose verb choisir [2]; **you chose well** tu as bien choisi; **Cathy chose the red one** Cathy a choisi le rouge; **it's hard to choose from all these colours** il est difficile de choisir parmi toutes ces couleurs.

chop noun côtelette Fem.; **a lamb chop** une côtelette d'agneau.

chop verb hacher [1].

chopstick noun baguette Fem.

chord noun accord Masc.

chorus noun 1 (when you all join in the song) refrain Masc.; 2 (a group of singers) chœur Masc.

Christ noun le Christ.

christening noun baptême Masc.

Christian noun, adjective chrétien Masc., chrétienne Fem.

Christian name noun prénom Masc.

Christmas noun Noël Masc.; **at Christmas** à Noël; **Happy Christmas!** Joyeux Noël!

Christmas card noun carte Fem. de Noël.

Christmas carol noun chant Masc. de Noël.

Christmas cracker noun diablotin Masc.

Christmas Day noun jour Masc. de Noël.

Christmas dinner noun repas Masc. de Noël.

a
b
c
d
e
f
g
h
i
j
k
l
m
n
o
p
q
r
s
t
u
v
w
x
y
z

Christmas Eve noun veille Fem. de Noël; **on Christmas Eve** la veille de Noël.

Christmas present noun cadeau Masc. de Noël.

Christmas tree noun sapin Masc. de Noël.

chunk noun morceau Masc.

church noun église Fem.; **to go to church** aller à l'église.

churchyard noun cimetière Masc.

chute noun (in a swimming pool or playground) toboggan Masc.

cider noun cidre Masc.

cigar noun cigare Masc.

cigarette noun cigarette Fem.; **to light a cigarette** allumer une cigarette.

cinema noun cinéma Masc.; **to go to the cinema** aller au cinéma.

circle noun cercle Masc.; **to sit in a circle** s'asseoir en cercle; **to go round in circles** tourner en rond.

circuit noun 1 (for athletes) piste Fem.; 2 (for cars) circuit Masc.

circumference noun circonférence Fem.

circumflex noun accent Masc. circonflexe.

circumstances plural noun **under the circumstances** dans ces circonstances.

circus noun cirque Masc.

citizen noun citoyen Masc., citoyenne Fem.

city noun (grande) ville Fem.; **the city of Paris** la ville de Paris.

city centre noun centre-ville Masc.; **in the city centre** au centre-ville.

civilian noun civil Masc., civile Fem.

civilization noun civilisation Fem.

civil servant noun fonctionnaire Masc. & Fem.; **he's a civil servant** il est fonctionnaire.

civil service noun fonction Fem. publique.

civil war noun guerre Fem. civile.

claim noun 1 (statement) déclaration Fem.; 2 (for compensation) réclamation Fem.; **to make a claim on insurance** faire une demande de remboursement auprès d'une compagnie d'assurance.

claim verb prétendre [3]; **he claimed to know** il prétendait savoir.

clap verb 1 applaudir [2]; **everyone clapped** tout le monde a applaudi; 2 **to clap your hands** battre [21] des mains.

clapping noun applaudissements Masc. plural.

clarinet noun clarinette Fem.; **to play the clarinet** jouer de la clarinette.

clash noun (for example, between police and demonstrators) affrontement Masc.

clash verb 1 (rival groups) s'affronter [1]; 2 (colours) jurer [1]; **the curtains clash with the wallpaper** les rideaux jurent avec le papier peint.

clasp noun (of a necklace) fermoir Masc.

class noun 1 (a group of students or pupils) classe Fem.; **she's in the same class as me** elle est dans la même classe que moi; **2** (*a lesson*) cours Masc.; **an art class** un cours de dessin; **in class** en cours; **3** (*division*) classe Fem.; **a social class** une classe sociale.

classic *adjective* classique.

classical *adjective* classique; **classical music** la musique classique.

classmate *noun* camarade Masc. & Fem. de classe.

classroom *noun* classe Fem.

claw *noun* **1** (*of a cat or dog*) griffe Fem.; **2** (*of a crab*) pince Fem.

clay *noun* **1** (*for modelling*) argile Fem.; **2 a clay court** (*in tennis*) un terrain en terre battue.

clean *adjective* propre; **a clean shirt** une chemise propre; **my hands are clean** j'ai les mains propres; **2** (*germ-free*) pur (*air or water*).

clean *verb* nettoyer [39] **1 I cleaned the whole house** j'ai nettoyé toute la maison; **2 to clean your teeth** se laver [1] les dents; **I'm going to clean my teeth** je vais me laver les dents.

cleaner *noun* **1** (*in a public place*) agent Masc. de nettoyage; **2** (*cleaning lady*) femme Fem. de ménage; **3 a dry cleaner's** un pressing.

cleaning *noun* **to do the cleaning** faire le ménage.

cleanser *noun* **1** (*for the house*) produit Masc. d'entretien; **2** (*for your face*) démaquillant Masc.

clear *adjective* **1** (*that you can see through*) transparent; **clear glass** du verre transparent; **2** (*cloudless*)

clair; **3** (*easy to understand*) clair; **clear instructions** des instructions claires; **is that clear?** est-ce que c'est clair?; **it's clear that** ... il est clair que ....

clear *verb* **1** enlever [50] (*papers, rubbish, or clothes*); **have you cleared your stuff out of your room?** as-tu enlevé tes affaires de ta chambre?; **2** débarrasser [1] (*a table or a room*); **can I clear the table?** puis-je débarrasser la table?; **3** dégager [52] (*a road or path*); **4** (*fog or snow*) se dissiper [1]; **and then the fog cleared et puis le brouillard s'est dissipé; **5 to clear your throat** se racler [1] la gorge.

● **to clear something up** ranger [52] quelque chose; **I'll just clear up my books** je vais juste ranger mes livres.

clearly *adverb* **1** (*to think, speak, or hear*) clairement; **2** (*obviously*) manifestement; **she was clearly worried** manifestement, elle était inquiète.

clementine *noun* clémentine Fem.

clever *adjective* **1** intelligent; **their children are all very clever** leurs enfants sont tous très intelligents; **2** (*ingenious*) astucieux (Fem. astucieuse); **a clever idea** une idée astucieuse.

click *noun* **1** (*noise*) petit bruit Masc.; déclic Masc.; **2** (*with mouse*) clic Masc.; **a double-click** un double-clic.

click *verb* **to click on something**: cliquer [1] sur quelque chose; **click on the icon twice** cliquer deux fois sur l'icône.

a b c d e f g h i j k l m n o p q r s t u v w x y z

client noun client Masc., cliente Fem.

cliff noun falaise Fem.

climate noun climat Masc.

climb verb 1 monter [1] (a hill, stairs); 2 faire [10] l'escalade de (a mountain); we climbed Mont Blanc nous avons fait l'escalade du Mont Blanc.

climber noun alpiniste Masc. & Fem.

climbing noun escalade Fem.; they go climbing in Italy ils font de l'escalade en Italie.

clinic noun centre Masc. médical (plural centres médicaux).

clip noun 1 (from a film) extrait Masc.; 2 (for your hair) barrette Fem.

clip verb 1 (to cut) couper [1]; 2 (to fasten) attacher [1].

cloakroom noun (for coats) vestiaire Masc.

clock noun (large) horloge Fem.; (smaller) pendule Fem.; an alarm clock un réveil; to put the clocks forward an hour avancer les pendules d'une heure; to put the clocks back reculer les pendules.

clock radio noun radio-réveil Masc.

clockwise adverb dans le sens des aiguilles d'une montre; it turns clockwise ça tourne dans le sens des aiguilles d'une montre.

close[1] adjective, adverb 1 (result) serré; 2 (friend or relation) proche; 3 (near) près; the station's very close la gare est tout près; she lives close by elle habite tout près; close to the cinema près du cinéma; not very close pas très près.

close[2] noun fin Fem.; at the close à la fin.

close verb fermer [1]; close your eyes! ferme les yeux!; she closed the door elle a fermé la porte; the post office closes at six la poste ferme à six heures.

closed adjective fermé; 'closed on Mondays' 'fermé le lundi'.

closely adverb de près; to examine something closely regarder quelque chose de près.

closing date noun date Fem. limite; the closing date for entries la date limite pour les inscriptions.

closing-down sale noun liquidation Fem.

closing time noun heure Fem. de fermeture.

cloth noun 1 (for the floor) serpillière Fem.; 2 (for polishing) chiffon Masc.; 3 (for drying up) torchon Masc.; 4 (fabric by the metre) tissu Masc.

clothes plural noun vêtements Masc. plural; to put your clothes on s'habiller; to take your clothes off se déshabiller; to change your clothes se changer.

clothes hanger noun cintre Masc.

clothes line noun corde Fem. à linge.

clothes peg noun pince Fem. à linge.

clothing noun vêtements Masc. plural.

cloud noun nuage Masc.

- **to cloud over** se couvrir [30]; **it clouded over in the afternoon** ça s'est couvert dans l'après-midi.

cloudy *adjective* nuageux (*Fem.* nuageuse).

clove *noun* **1** clou *Masc.* de girofle; **2 a clove of garlic** une gousse d'ail.

clown *noun* clown *Masc.*

club *noun* **1** (*association*) club *Masc.*; **he's in the football club** il fait partie du club de foot; **2** (*in cards*) trèfle *Masc.*; **the four of clubs** le quatre de trèfle; **3** (*golfing iron*) crosse *Fem.*

clue *noun* **1** indice *Masc.*; **they have a few clues** ils ont quelques indices; **2** (*in a crossword*) définition *Fem.*; ★ **I haven't a clue** je n'ai aucune idée.

clumsy *adjective* maladroit.

clutch *noun* (*in a car*) embrayage *Masc.*

clutch *verb* **to clutch something** tenir [77] quelque chose fermement.

coach *noun* **1** (*bus*) car *Masc.*; **by coach** en car; **on the coach** dans le car; **to travel by coach** voyager en car; **2** (*sports trainer*) entraîneur *Masc.*, entraîneuse *Fem.*; **3** (*railway carriage*) wagon *Masc.*

coach station *noun* gare *Fem.* routière.

coach trip *noun* excursion *Fem.* en car; **to go on a coach trip** faire une excursion en car.

coal *noun* charbon *Masc.*

coal mine *noun* mine *Fem.* de charbon.

coal miner *noun* mineur *Masc.*

coarse *adjective* grossier (*Fem.* grossière).

coast *noun* côte *Fem.*; **on the east coast** sur la côte est.

coat *noun* **1** manteau *Masc.* (*plural* manteaux*); **2 a coat of paint** une couche de peinture.

coat hanger *noun* cintre *Masc.*

cobweb *noun* toile *Fem.* d'araignée.

cockerel *noun* coq *Masc.*

cocoa *noun* (*drink*) chocolat *Masc.* (chaud); (*powder*) cacao *Masc.*

coconut *noun* noix *Fem.* de coco.

cod *noun* cabillaud *Masc.*

code *noun* **1** code *Masc.*; **the highway code** le code de la route; **2 the dialling code for Cambridge** l'indicatif pour Cambridge.

coffee *noun* café *Masc.*; **a cup of coffee** un café; **a black coffee, please** un café, s'il vous plaît; **a white coffee** un café au lait.

coffee break *noun* pause-café *Fem.*

coffee cup *noun* tasse *Fem.* à café.

coffee machine *noun* cafetière *Fem.*; (*electric*) cafetière *Fem.* électrique.

coffee table *noun* table *Fem.* basse.

coffin *noun* cercueil *Masc.*

coin *noun* pièce *Fem.* de monnaie; **a pound coin** une pièce d'une livre.

coincidence *noun* coïncidence *Fem.*

Coke™ *noun* coca *Masc.*; **two Cokes™ please** deux cocas s'il vous plaît.

colander *noun* passoire *Fem.*

a
b
c
d
e
f
g
h
i
j
k
l
m
n
o
p
q
r
s
t
u
v
w
x
y
z

cold noun **1** (cold weather) froid Masc.; **to be out in the cold** être dehors dans le froid; **2** (illness) rhume Masc.; **to have a cold** être enrhumé; **Carol's got a cold** Carol est enrhumée; **a bad cold** un gros rhume.

cold adjective **1** froid; **your hands are cold** tu as les mains froides; **cold milk** du lait froid; **2** (weather, temperature) **it's cold today** il fait froid aujourd'hui; **it's cold in the kitchen** il fait froid dans la cuisine; **3** (feeling) **I'm cold** j'ai froid.

cold sore noun bouton Masc. de fièvre.

collapse verb **1** (a roof or a wall) s'écrouler [1]; **2** (a person) **he collapsed in his office** il a eu un malaise dans son bureau.

collar noun **1** (on a garment) col Masc.; **2** (for a dog) collier Masc.

collarbone noun clavicule Fem.

colleague noun collègue Masc. & Fem.

collect verb **1** (as a hobby) collectionner [1]; **I collect stamps** je collectionne les timbres; **2** aller [7] chercher (a person); **she collects the children from school** elle va chercher les enfants à la sortie de l'école; **3** passer [64] prendre (thing); **I have to collect a book at the library** je dois passer prendre un livre à la bibliothèque; **4** encaisser [1] (fares or money); **5 to collect in the exercise books** ramasser [1] les cahiers.

collection noun **1** (of stamps, CDs, etc) collection Fem.; **2** (of money) collecte Fem.

collector noun collectionneur Masc., collectionneuse Fem.

college noun **1** (for higher education) établissement Masc. d'études supérieures; **to go to college** faire des études supérieures; **2** (a school) collège Masc.

collie noun colley Masc.

collision noun collision Fem.

colonel noun colonel Masc.

colour noun couleur Fem.; **what colour is your car?** de quelle couleur est ta voiture?; **what colour is it?** c'est de quelle couleur?; **do you have it in a different colour?** est-ce que vous l'avez dans une autre couleur?.

colour verb (with paints or crayons) colorier [1]; **to colour something red** colorier quelque chose en rouge.

colour blind adjective daltonien (Fem. daltonienne).

colour film noun pellicule Fem. couleur (plural pellicules couleur)

colourful adjective en couleurs vives.

colouring book noun album Masc. à colorier.

colour scheme noun couleurs Fem. plural.

colour supplement noun supplément Masc. illustré.

column noun colonne Fem.

comb noun peigne Masc.

comb verb **to comb your hair** se peigner [1]; **I'll just comb my hair** je vais juste me peigner.

combination noun combinaison Fem.

combine verb combiner [1] (two separate things); **they don't combine well** ils ne se combinent pas bien.

come verb 1 venir [81]; **come quick!** viens vite!; **come and see!** venez voir!; **Nick came by bike** Nick est venu à vélo; **did Jess come to school yesterday?** est-ce que Jess est venue à l'école hier?; **Alan comes from Scotland** Alan vient de l'Ecosse; **can you come over for a coffee?** peux-tu venir prendre un café?; **2** arriver [1]; **coming!** j'arrive!; **the bus is coming** le bus arrive; **3 to come down** descendre [3] (the stairs or the street); **4 to come up** monter [1]; **can you come up a moment?** peux-tu monter un instant?; **5 to come in** entrer [1]; **come in! entrez!**; **she came into the kitchen** elle est entrée dans la cuisine; **6 to come for** passer [1] prendre (a person); **my father's coming for me** mon père passe me prendre; **7 come along!** dépêche-toi!

● **to come apart** (to break) se casser [1]; **the door handle came apart in my hands** la poignée m'est restée dans la main; (a book) se déchirer [1].

● **to come back** revenir [81]; **he's coming back to collect us** il revient nous chercher.

● **to come off** (a button or handle, for example) se détacher [1], (a lid) s'enlever [50].

● **to come out 1** sortir [72]; **they came out when I called** ils sont sortis quand j'ai appelé; **the CD's coming out soon** le CD sort bientôt; **2** (the sun or moon) se montrer [1].

● **to come up to somebody** aborder [1] quelqu'un.

comedian noun comique Masc.

comedy noun comédie Fem.

comfortable adjective 1 confortable; **this chair's really comfortable** ce fauteuil est très confortable; **2 to feel comfortable** (a person) se sentir à l'aise; **are you comfortable there?** êtes-vous bien là?

comfortably adverb confortablement.

comic noun (magazine) illustré Masc.

comic strip noun bande Fem. dessinée.

comma noun virgule Fem.

command noun ordre Masc.

comment noun (in a conversation) remarque Fem.; **he made some rude comments about my friends** il a fait des remarques impolies sur mes amis.

commentary noun reportage Masc. en direct; **the commentary of the match** le reportage du match.

commentator noun commentateur Masc., commentatrice Fem.; **a sports commentator** un commentateur sportif.

commercial noun spot Masc. publicitaire.

a b c d e f g h i j k l m n o p q r s t u v w x y z

commercial adjective commercial (Masc. plural commerciaux).

commit verb 1 commettre [11] (a crime); 2 to commit yourself s'engager [52].

committee noun comité Masc.

common adjective 1 courant; it's a common problem c'est un problème courant; 2 in common en commun; they have nothing in common ils n'ont rien en commun.

common sense noun bon sens Masc.

communicate verb communiquer [1].

communication noun 1 (message) communication Fem.; 2 communications communications Fem (plural); the communications are good les communications sont bonnes.

communion noun communion Fem.

communism noun communisme Masc.

communist noun, adjective communiste Masc. & Fem.

community noun communauté Fem.; the European Community la Communauté Européenne.

commute verb to commute between Oxford and London faire [10] le trajet entre Oxford et Londres tous les jours.

commuter noun navetteur Masc., navetteuse Fem.

compact disc noun disque Masc. compact.

compact disc player noun platine Fem. laser.

company noun 1 (business) société Fem.; an insurance company une société d'assurances; she's set up a company elle a monté une société; 2 compagnie Fem.; an airline company une compagnie aérienne; a theatre company une compagnie théâtrale; 3 to keep somebody company tenir compagnie à quelqu'un; the dog keeps me company le chien me tient compagnie.

comparatively adverb relativement.

compare verb comparer [1]; if you compare the French with the English si on compare les Français aux Anglais; our house is small compared with yours notre maison est petite par rapport à la vôtre.

comparison noun comparaison Fem.; in comparison with par rapport à.

compartment noun compartiment Masc.

compass noun boussole Fem.

compatible adjective (computing) compatible.

compensation noun indemnisation Fem.

compete verb 1 to compete in something participer [1] à quelque chose (race, event); 2 to compete for something se disputer [1] quelque chose (jobs, places); thirty people competing for one job trente personnes qui se disputent un seul emploi.

competent adjective compétent.

competition *noun* concours Masc.; **a fishing competition** un concours de pêche.

competitor *noun* concurrent Masc., concurrente Fem.

complain *verb* se plaindre [31]; **we complained about the hotel and the meals** nous nous sommes plaints de l'hôtel et des repas.

complaint *noun* plainte Fem.; **to make a complaint** se plaindre [31]; **she made a complaint to the manager about the poor service** elle s'est plainte de la qualité du service auprès du responsable.

complete *adjective* complet (Fem. complète); **the complete collection** la collection complète.

complete *verb* (to finish) compléter [24].

completely *adverb* complètement.

complexion *noun* teint Masc.

complicated *adjective* compliqué.

compliment *noun* compliment Masc.; **to pay somebody a compliment** faire un compliment à quelqu'un.

compose *verb* composer [1]; **composed of** composé de.

composer *noun* compositeur Masc., compositrice Fem.

comprehension *noun* compréhension Fem.; **a comprehension test** un test de compréhension.

compromise *noun* compromis Masc.

compulsory *adjective* obligatoire.

computer *noun* ordinateur Masc.; **to work on a computer** travailler sur ordinateur; **to have something on computer** avoir quelque chose sur ordinateur.

computer engineer *noun* technicien Masc. en informatique, technicienne Fem. en informatique.

computer game *noun* jeu Masc. électronique (*plural* jeux électroniques).

computer program *noun* programme Masc. informatique, logiciel Masc.

computer programmer *noun* programmeur Masc., programmeuse Fem.

computer science *noun* informatique Fem.

computing *noun* informatique. Fem.

conceited *adjective* vaniteux (Fem. vaniteuse).

concentrate *verb* se concentrer [1]; **I can't concentrate** je n'arrive pas à me concentrer; **I was concentrating on the film** je me concentrais sur le film.

concentration *noun* concentration Fem.

concern *noun* (worry) inquiétude Fem.; **there is no cause for concern** il n'y a pas lieu de s'inquiéter.

concern *verb* **1** (to affect) concerner [1]; **this doesn't concern you** ceci ne te concerne pas; **2 as far as I'm concerned** en ce qui me concerne.

a
b
c
d
e
f
g
h
i
j
k
l
m
n
o
p
q
r
s
t
u
v
w
x
y
z

concert noun **1** concert Masc.; **to go to a concert** aller à un concert; **2 a concert ticket** un billet de concert.

conclusion noun conclusion Fem.

concrete noun béton Masc.; **a concrete floor** un sol en béton.

condemn verb condamner [1].

condition noun **1** condition Fem.; **in good condition** en bonne condition; **weather conditions** les conditions météorologiques; **2** (something you agree to) condition Fem.; **the conditions of sale** les conditions de vente; **on condition that you let me pay** à condition que tu me laisses payer.

conditional noun conditionnel Masc.

conditioner noun (for your hair) après-shampooing Masc.

condom noun préservatif Masc.

conduct noun conduite Fem.

conduct verb diriger [52] (an orchestra or a piece of music).

conductor noun (of an orchestra) chef Masc. d'orchestre.

cone noun **1** (for ice cream) cornet Masc.; **2** (for traffic) balise Fem.

confectionery noun confiserie Fem.

conference noun conférence Fem.

confess verb avouer [1].

confession noun confession Fem.

confidence noun **1** (self-confidence) assurance Fem.; **to be lacking in confidence** manquer d'assurance; **2** (faith in somebody else) confiance Fem.; **to have**

confidence in somebody avoir confiance en quelqu'un.

confident adjective **1** (sure of yourself) assuré; **2** (sure that something will happen) sûr.

confirm verb confirmer [1]; **we'll confirm the date** nous confirmerons la date.

confuse verb **1** troubler [1] (a person); **2** confondre [69]; **I confuse him with his brother** je le confonds avec son frère.

confused adjective **1** confus; **he gave us a confused story** il nous a raconté une histoire confuse; **2 I'm confused about the holiday dates** je ne comprends pas bien les dates des vacances; **now I'm completely confused!** là je ne comprends plus rien!

confusing adjective pas clair; **the instructions are confusing** les instructions ne sont pas claires.

confusion noun confusion Fem.

congratulate verb féliciter [1]; **I congratulated Tim on his success** j'ai félicité Tim de son succès; **we congratulate you on winning** nous vous félicitons d'avoir gagné.

congratulations plural noun félicitations Fem. plural; **congratulations on the baby!** félicitations pour le bébé!

conjurer noun prestidigitateur Masc.

connect verb (to plug in to the mains) brancher [1] (a dishwasher or TV, for example).

connection noun **1** (between two ideas or events) rapport Masc.;

there's no connection between his letter and my decision il n'y a auccun rapport entre sa lettre et ma décision; **2** (*between trains or planes*) correspondance *Fem.*; **Sally missed her connection** Sally a raté sa correspondance; **3** (*electrical*) contact; **a faulty connection** un mauvais contact.

conscience *noun* conscience *Fem.*; **to have a guilty conscience** avoir mauvaise conscience.

conscious *adjective* conscient.

consequence *noun* conséquence *Fem.*

consequently *adverb* par conséquent.

conservation *noun* (*of nature*) protection *Fem.*

conservative *noun, adjective* conservateur *Masc.*, conservatrice *Fem.*

conservatory *noun* jardin *Masc.* d'hiver.

consider *verb* **1** (*to give thought to*) considérer [24] (*a suggestion or idea*); **2** (*to think you might do*) envisager [52]; **we are considering buying a flat** nous envisageons d'acheter un appartement; **3** all things considered tout compte fait.

considerable *adjective* considérable; **a considerable number of the students** un pourcentage considérable des étudiants.

considerate *adjective* attentionné (*person*).

consideration *noun* considération *Fem.*; **no**

consideration was given to their safety on ne s'est pas soucié de leur sécurité.

considering *preposition* étant donné; **considering her age** étant donné son âge; **considering he did it all himself** étant donné qu'il a tout fait lui-même.

consist *verb* **to consist of** être [6] composé de.

consistent *adjective* régulier, constant.

consonant *noun* consonne *Fem.*

constant *adjective* permanent.

constipated *adjective* constipé.

construct *verb* construire [26].

construction *noun* construction *Fem.*

consul *noun* consul *Masc.*

consulate *noun* consulat *Masc.*

consult *verb* consulter [1].

consumer *noun* consommateur *Masc.*, consommatrice *Fem.*

consumption *noun* consommation *Fem.*

contact *noun* **1** (*touch*) contact *Masc.*; **to be in contact with somebody** être en contact avec quelqu'un; **we've lost contact** nous avons perdu contact; **2** (*a person you know*) connaissance *Fem.*; **Rob has contacts in the music business** Rob a des connaissances dans le monde de la musique.

contact *verb* contacter [1]; **I'll contact you tomorrow** je te contacterai demain.

a
b
c
d
e
f
g
h
i
j
k
l
m
n
o
p
q
r
s
t
u
v
w
x
y
z

a
contact lens noun lentille Fem. de contact (plural **lentilles de contact**).

b
contain verb contenir [77].

c
container noun récipient Masc.

d
contaminate verb contaminer [1].

e
contemporary adjective **1** (around today) contemporain; **2** (modern) moderne.

f
g
contents plural noun contenu Masc.; **the contents of my suitcase** le contenu de ma valise.

h
contest noun concours Masc.

i
contestant noun concurrent Masc., concurrente Fem.

j
context noun contexte Masc.

k
continent noun continent Masc.; **on the Continent** en Europe continentale.

l
m
continental adjective **a continental holiday** des vacances en Europe continentale.

n
o
continue verb continuer [1]; **we continued (with) our journey** nous avons continué notre voyage; **Jill continued chatting** Jill a continué de bavarder; **'to be continued'** 'à suivre'.

p
q
r
s
continuous adjective continu; **continuous assessment** le contrôle continu.

t
u
contraception noun contraception Fem.

v
contraceptive noun contraceptif Masc.

w
x
contract noun contrat Masc.

contradict verb contredire [47].

y
z
contradiction noun contradiction Fem.

contrary noun contraire Masc.; **on the contrary** au contraire.

contrast noun contraste Masc.

contribute verb donner [1] (money).

contribution noun (to charity or an appeal) don Masc.

control noun (of a crowd or animals) contrôle Masc.; **the police have lost control** la police a perdu le contrôle; **keep your dogs under control** maîtrisez vos chiens; **everything's under control** tout va bien; **the fire was out of control** on ne maîtrisait plus l'incendie.

control verb **1** maîtriser [1] (a crowd, animals, or a fire, for example); **2 to control oneself** se contrôler [1].

controversial adjective discutable; **a controversial decision** une décision discutable.

convenient adjective **1** commode; **frozen vegetables are very convenient** les légumes congelés sont très commodes; **2 to be convenient for somebody** convenir à quelqu'un; **if that's convenient for you** si cela vous convient; **3 the house is convenient for shops and schools** la maison est bien située par rapport aux magasins et aux écoles.

convent noun couvent Masc.

conventional adjective **1** conventionnel (Fem. conventionnelle); **2** (person) conformiste.

conversation noun conversation Fem.

convert verb transformer [1]; **we're going to convert the garage into a workshop** nous allons transformer le garage en atelier.

convince verb convaincre [79]; **I'm convinced you're wrong** je suis convaincu que tu as tort.

convincing adjective convaincant.

cook noun cuisinier Masc., cuisinière Fem.

cook verb 1 faire [10] la cuisine; **who's cooking tonight?** qui fait la cuisine ce soir?; **I like cooking** j'aime faire la cuisine; 2 faire [10] cuire (vegetables, pasta, etc); **cook the carrots for five minutes** faites cuire les carottes pendant cinq minutes; 3 préparer [1] (a meal); **Fran's busy cooking supper** Fran est en train de préparer le dîner; 4 (food) cuire [36]; **the sausages are cooking** les saucisses sont en train de cuire; **is the chicken cooked?** est-ce que le poulet est cuit?

cooker noun cuisinière Fem.; **an electric cooker** une cuisinière électrique; **a gas cooker** une cuisinière à gaz.

cookery noun cuisine Fem.

cookery book noun livre Masc. de cuisine.

cooking noun cuisine Fem.; **to do the cooking** faire la cuisine; **Italian cooking** la cuisine italienne.

cool noun 1 (coldness) fraîcheur Fem.; **stay in the cool** reste à la fraîcheur; 2 (calm) to lose one's

cool perdre son sang-froid; **he kept his cool** il a gardé son sang-froid.

cool adjective 1 (cold) frais (Fem. fraîche); **a cool drink** une boisson fraîche; **it's cool inside** il fait frais dans la maison; 2 (laid-back) décontracté; 3 (sophisticated) branché (informal).

cool verb refroidir [2]; **while the engine was cooling (down)** pendant que le moteur refroidissait.

cooperate verb coopérer [24].

cop noun flic Masc. (informal).

cope verb 1 (to manage) se débrouiller [1]; **she copes well** elle se débrouille bien; 2 **to cope with** s'occuper [1] de (children or work); **I'll cope with the dishes** je m'occuperai de la vaisselle; 3 faire [10] face à (problems); **she's had a lot to cope with** elle a été obligée de faire face à beaucoup de choses; **he can't cope any more** il n'arrive plus à faire face.

copper noun cuivre Masc.

copy noun 1 copie Fem.; **make ten copies of this letter** faites dix copies de cette lettre; 2 (of a book) exemplaire Masc.

copy verb copier [1]; **I copied (down) the address** j'ai copié l'adresse.

cord noun (for a blind, for example) cordon Masc.

cordless telephone noun téléphone Masc. sans fil.

core noun (of an apple or a pear) trognon Masc.

cork noun 1 (in a bottle) bouchon Masc.; 2 (material) liège Masc.

a
b
c
d
e
f
g
h
i
j
k
l
m
n
o
p
q
r
s
t
u
v
w
x
y
z

corkscrew noun tire-bouchon Masc.

corn noun 1 (wheat) blé Masc.; 2 (sweetcorn) maïs Masc.

corner noun coin Masc.; **in a corner of the kitchen** dans un coin de la cuisine; **at the corner of the street** au coin de la rue; **out of the corner of your eye** du coin de l'œil; **it's just round the corner** c'est tout près.

cornflakes noun corn-flakes Masc. plural.

Cornwall noun Cornouailles Fem.; **in Cornwall** en Cornouailles.

corpse noun cadavre Masc.

correct adjective 1 exact; **yes, that's correct** oui, c'est exact; 2 bon (Fem. bonne); **the correct sum** la bonne somme; **the correct answer** la bonne réponse; **the correct choice** le bon choix.

correct verb corriger [52].

correction noun correction Fem.

correctly adverb correctement; **have you filled in the form correctly?** est-ce que vous avez rempli le formulaire correctement?; **she answered correctly** elle a donné la bonne réponse.

correspond verb correspondre [3].

corridor noun couloir Masc.

Corsica noun Corse Fem.; **to Corsica** en Corse.

cosmetics plural noun produits Masc. plural de beauté.

cost noun prix Masc.; **the cost of a new computer** le prix d'un nouvel ordinateur; **the cost of living** le coût de la vie.

cost verb coûter [1]; **how much does it cost?** combien est-ce que ça coûte?; **the tickets cost £10** les billets coûtent dix livres; **it costs too much** cela coûte trop cher.

costume noun costume Masc.

cosy adjective (a bed or room) douillet (Fem. douillette); **it's cosy by the fire** on est bien à côté du feu.

cot noun lit Masc. d'enfant.

cottage noun petite maison Fem.

cotton noun 1 (fabric) coton Masc.; **a cotton shirt** une chemise en coton; 2 (thread) fil Masc. de coton.

cotton wool noun ouate Fem. de coton.

couch noun canapé Masc.

cough noun toux Fem.; **a nasty cough** une mauvaise toux; **to have a cough** tousser.

cough verb tousser [1].

could verb 1 if he could pay s'il pouvait payer; **I couldn't open it** je ne pouvais pas l'ouvrir; **they couldn't smoke there** ils ne pouvaient pas fumer là; **she did all she could** elle a fait tout ce qu'elle pouvait; 2 (knew how to) **he couldn't drive** il ne savait pas conduire; **I couldn't swim** je ne savais pas nager; 3 (with seeing, hearing, or smelling) **I could hear the police car** j'entendais la voiture de police; **she couldn't see anything** elle ne voyait rien; 4 (might) **could I speak to David?** pourrais-je parler à David?; **you could try telephoning** tu pourrais téléphoner.

council noun conseil Masc.; **the town council** le conseil municipal.

councillor noun 1 (of town council) membre Masc., du conseil municipal; 2 (local council) membre Masc., du conseil régional.

count verb 1 (reckon up) compter [1]; **I counted my money** j'ai compté mon argent; **thirty-five not counting the children** trente-cinq sans compter les enfants; 2 **to count as** être [6] considéré comme; **children over twelve count as adults** les enfants au-dessus de douze ans sont considérés comme adultes; 3 (to be allowed) compter [1]; **that doesn't count** ça ne compte pas.

counter noun 1 (in a shop or café) comptoir Masc.; 2 (in a post office or bank) guichet Masc.; 3 (in a big store) rayon Masc.; **on the cheese counter** au rayon fromagerie; 4 (for board games) jeton Masc.

country noun 1 (France, England, etc) pays Masc.; **a foreign country** un pays étranger; **from another country** d'un autre pays; 2 (not town) campagne Fem.; **to live in the country** vivre à la campagne; **a country walk** une promenade à la campagne; **a country road** une route de campagne.

country dancing noun danse Fem. folklorique.

countryside noun campagne Fem.

county noun comté Masc.

couple noun 1 (a pair) couple Masc.; 2 **a couple of** deux ou trois; **a couple of times** deux ou trois

fois; **I've got a couple of things to do** j'ai deux ou trois choses à faire.

courage noun courage Masc.

courgette noun courgette Fem.

courier noun 1 (on a package holiday) accompagnateur Masc., accompagnatrice Fem.; 2 (delivery service) coursier Masc.; **by courier** par coursier.

course noun 1 (lessons) cours Masc.; **a beginners' course** un cours pour débutants; **a computer course** un cours d'informatique; **to go on a course** suivre un cours; 2 (part of a meal) plat Masc.; **the main course** le plat principal; **a golf course** un golf; 3 **of course** bien sûr; **yes, of course!** oui, bien sûr!; **he's forgotten, of course** il a oublié, bien sûr.

court noun 1 (for tennis or squash) court Masc.; 2 (for basketball) terrain Masc.

courtyard noun cour Fem.

cousin noun cousin Masc., cousine Fem.; **my cousin Sonia** ma cousine Sonia.

cover noun 1 (for a book) couverture Fem.; 2 (for a duvet or cushion) housse Fem.; **a duvet cover** une housse de couette.

cover verb 1 (to protect or cover up) couvrir [30]; **cover the wound** couvrez la blessure; **he was covered in spots** il était couvert de boutons; 2 (with leaves, snow, or fabric) recouvrir [30]; **the ground was covered with snow** le sol était recouvert de neige.

a b c d e f g h i j k l m n o p q r s t u v w x y z

cow noun vache Fem.; **mad cow disease** maladie Fem. de la vache folle.

coward noun lâche Masc. & Fem.

cowboy noun cowboy Masc.

crab noun crabe Masc.

crack noun 1 (in a wall or cup) fêlure Fem.; 2 (a cracking noise) craquement Masc.

crack verb 1 (to make a crack in) fêler [1] (a cup, a chair, or a bone); 2 (to break) casser [1] (a nut or an egg); 3 (to split by itself: ice, for example) se fêler [1]; 4 (to make a noise) (a twig) craquer [1].

cracker noun 1 (biscuit) cracker Masc.; 2 (Christmas cracker) diablotin Masc.

crackle verb crépiter [1].

craft noun (at school) travaux Masc. plural manuels.

crafty adjective ingénieux (Fem. ingénieuse); **she was very crafty of her** c'était très ingénieux de sa part.

cramp noun crampe Fem.; **to have cramp in your leg** avoir une crampe à la jambe.

crane noun grue Fem.

crash noun 1 (an accident) accident Masc.; **a car crash** un accident de voiture; 2 (smashing noise) fracas Masc.; **a crash of broken glass** un fracas de verre brisé.

crash verb 1 (a car or plane) s'écraser [1]; **the plane crashed** l'avion s'est écrasé; 2 **to crash into something** rentrer [1] dans quelque chose; **the car crashed into a tree** la voiture est rentrée dans un arbre.

crash course noun cours Masc. intensif.

crash helmet noun casque Masc.

crate noun 1 (for bottles or china) caisse Fem.; 2 (for fruit) cageot Masc.

crawl noun (in swimming) crawl Masc.

crawl verb 1 (a person, a baby) marcher [1] à quatre pattes; 2 (cars in a jam) rouler [1] au pas; **we were crawling along** nous roulions au pas.

crayon noun 1 (wax) crayon Masc. gras; 2 (coloured pencil) crayon Masc. de couleur.

craze noun vogue Fem.; **the craze for rollerblades** la vogue des rollers.

crazy adjective fou (Fem. folle).

creak verb grincer [61] (a hinge) (a floorboard) craquer [1].

cream noun crème Fem.; **strawberries and cream** des fraises à la crème.

cream cheese noun fromage Masc. à tartiner.

crease noun pli Masc.

creased adjective froissé.

create verb créer [32].

creative adjective créatif (Fem. créative) (a person).

creature noun créature Fem.

crèche noun crèche Fem.

credit noun crédit Masc.; **to buy something on credit** acheter quelque chose à crédit.

credit card noun carte Fem. de crédit.

cress noun cresson Masc.

crew noun **1** (on a ship or plane) équipage Masc.; **2** (rowing or filming) équipe Fem.

crew cut noun cheveux Masc. plural en brosse.

cricket noun **1** (game) cricket Masc.; **to play cricket** jouer au cricket; **2** (insect) grillon Masc.

cricket bat noun batte Fem. de cricket.

crime noun **1** crime Masc.; **murder is a crime** le meurtre est un crime; **2** (within society) criminalité Fem.; **the fight against crime** la lutte contre la criminalité.

criminal noun, adjective criminel Masc., criminelle Fem.

crimson adjective pourpre.

crisis noun crise Fem.

crisp noun chip Fem.; **a packet of (potato) crisps** un sachet de chips.

crisp adjective **1** (biscuit) croustillant; **2** (apple) croquant.

critical adjective **1** critique (a remark or somebody's condition); **2** décisif (Fem. décisive) (a moment).

criticism noun critique Fem.

criticize verb critiquer [1].

Croatia noun Croatie Fem.

crockery noun vaisselle Fem.

crocodile noun crocodile Masc.

crook noun (criminal) escroc Masc.

crooked adjective de travers; **the picture is crooked** le tableau est de travers; **a crooked line** une ligne pas droite.

crop noun récolte Fem.

cross noun croix Fem.

cross adjective fâché; **she's very cross** elle est très fâchée; **I'm cross with you** je suis fâché contre toi.

cross verb **1** (to cross over) traverser [1]; **to cross the road** traverser la rue; **2 to cross your legs** croiser [1] les jambes; **3 to cross into Italy** passer [1] en Italie; **4** (to cross each other) se croiser [1]; **the two roads cross here** les deux routes se croisent ici.

● **to cross out** rayer [59] (a mistake, for example).

cross-Channel adjective trans-Manche; **a cross-Channel ferry** un ferry trans-Manche.

cross-country noun **1** cross Masc.; **2 cross-country skiing** le ski de fond.

crossing noun **1** (from one place to another) traversée Fem.; **a Channel crossing** une traversée trans-Manche; **2 a pedestrian crossing** un passage piétons; **a level crossing** un passage à niveau.

cross-legged adjective **to sit cross-legged** être assis en tailleur.

crossroads noun carrefour Masc.; **at the crossroads** au carrefour.

crossword noun mots Masc. plural croisés; **to do the crossword** faire les mots croisés.

crouch verb s'accroupir [2].

crow noun corbeau Masc.; ★ **ten kilometres as the crow flies** dix kilomètres à vol d'oiseau.

crow verb (a cock) chanter [1].

crowd noun foule Fem.; **in the crowd** dans la foule; **a crowd of 5,000** une foule de cinq mille.

crowd verb **to crowd into** or **onto** s'entasser [1] dans (a room or bus, for example); **we all crowded into the train** nous nous sommes tous entassés dans le train.

crowded adjective bondé.

crown noun couronne Fem.

crude adjective **1** (rough and ready) rudimentaire; **2** (vulgar) grossier (Fem. grossière).

cruel adjective cruel (Fem. cruelle).

cruelty noun cruauté Fem.; **they were treated with great cruelty** ils ont été traités avec beaucoup de cruauté.

cruise noun croisière Fem.; **to go on a cruise** faire une croisière.

crumb noun miette Fem.

crumple verb froisser [1].

crunch verb croquer [1] (an apple).

crunchy adjective croquant.

crush verb écraser [1].

crust noun croûte Fem.

crusty adjective croustillant (bread).

crutch noun béquille Fem.; **to be on crutches** marcher avec des béquilles.

cry noun cri Masc.

cry verb **1** (weep) pleurer [1]; **2** (call out) crier [1].

crystal noun cristal Masc.

cub noun **1** (animal) petit Masc.; **2** (scout) louveteau Masc.

Cuba noun Cuba Masc.

Cuban noun Cubain Masc., Cubaine Fem.

Cuban adjective cubain.

cube noun cube Masc.; **an ice cube** un glaçon.

cubic adjective (for measurements) cube; **three cubic metres** trois mètres cube.

cubicle noun **1** (in a changing room) cabine Fem.; **2** (in a public lavatory) cabinet Masc.

cuckoo noun coucou Masc.

cucumber noun concombre Masc.

cuddle noun **to give somebody a cuddle** faire un câlin à quelqu'un.

cuddle verb câliner [1].

cue noun (billiards, pool, snooker) queue Fem. de billard.

cuff noun (on a shirt) manchette Fem.

cul-de-sac noun impasse Fem.

culture noun culture Fem.

cunning adjective rusé.

cup noun **1** (for drinking) tasse Fem.; **a cup of tea** une tasse de thé; **2** (a trophy) coupe Fem.

cupboard noun placard Masc.; **in the kitchen cupboard** dans le placard de la cuisine.

cup tie noun match Masc. de coupe.

cure noun remède Masc.

cure verb guérir [2].

curiosity noun curiosité Fem.

curious adjective curieux (Fem. curieuse).

curl noun boucle Fem.

curl verb friser [1] (hair).

currant noun raisin Masc. de Corinthe.

currency noun **foreign currency** les devises étrangères.

current noun (of electricity or water) courant Masc.

current adjective actuel (Fem. actuelle) (a situation, for example).

current affairs noun actualité Fem.

curriculum noun programme Masc.

curry noun curry Masc.; **chicken curry** le curry de poulet.

cursor noun curseur Masc.

curtain noun rideau Masc. (plural rideaux).

cushion noun coussin Masc.

custard noun 1 (runny) crème Fem. anglaise; 2 (baked) flan Masc.

custom noun coutume Fem.

customer noun client Masc., cliente Fem.; **customer services** le service clientèle.

customs plural noun douane Fem. singular; **to go through customs** passer à la douane.

customs hall noun douane Fem.

customs officer noun douanier Masc., douanière Fem.

cut noun 1 (injury) coupure Fem.; 2 (haircut) coupe Fem.

cut verb 1 couper [1]; **I've cut the bread** j'ai coupé le pain; **you'll cut yourself!** tu vas te couper!; **Kevin's cut his finger** Kevin s'est coupé le doigt; 2 **to cut the grass** tondre [3] le gazon; 3 **to get your hair cut** se faire [10] couper les cheveux; **Anne's had her hair cut** Anne s'est fait couper les cheveux; 4 **to cut prices** baisser les prix.

● **to cut down something** abattre [21] (a tree).

● **to cut out something** 1 découper [1] (a shape, a newspaper article); 2 supprimer (sugar, fatty food, etc.).

● **to cut up something** couper [1] (food).

cutlery noun couverts Masc. plural.

CV noun CV Masc.

cycle noun (bike) vélo Masc.

cycle verb faire [10] du vélo; **do you like cycling?** est-ce que tu aimes faire du vélo?; **we cycle to school** nous allons à l'école à vélo.

cycle lane noun piste Fem. cyclable.

cycle race noun course Fem. cycliste.

cycling noun cyclisme Masc.

cycling holiday noun vacances Fem. plural à vélo.

cyclist noun cycliste Masc. & Fem.

cylinder noun cylindre Masc.

Dd

dad noun 1 père Masc.; **Anna's dad** le père d'Anna; **my dad works in a bank** mon père travaille dans une banque; 2 (within the family) papa Masc.; **Dad's not home yet** Papa n'est pas encore rentré.

daffodil noun jonquille Fem.

daily adjective quotidien (Fem. quotidienne); **his daily visit** sa visite quotidienne.

daily adverb quotidiennement; **she visits him daily** elle lui rend visite tous les jours.

a b c d e f g h i j k l m n o p q r s t u v w x y z

a
b
c
d
e
f
g
h
i
j
k
l
m
n
o
p
q
r
s
t
u
v
w
x
y
z

dairy products plural noun les produits Masc. plural laitiers.

daisy noun paquerette Fem.

dam noun barrage Masc.

damage verb abimer [1].

damage noun dégâts Masc. plural; **there's no damage** il n'y a pas de dégâts.

damage verb endommager [52].

damn noun **he doesn't give a damn** il s'en fiche complètement (informal).

damn exclamation **damn!** zut! (informal).

damp adjective humide.

damp noun humidité Fem.; **because of the damp** à cause de l'humidité.

dance noun **1** (art form) danse Fem.; **a folk dance** une danse traditionnelle; **2** (occasion) soirée Fem. dansante.

dance verb danser [1].

dancer noun danseur Masc., danseuse Fem.

dancing noun danse Fem.; **I like dancing** j'aime danser.

dancing class noun cours Masc. de danse; **to go to dancing classes** suivre des cours de danse.

dandruff noun pellicules Fem. plural.

danger noun danger Masc.; **to be in danger** être en danger.

dangerous adjective dangereux (Fem. dangereuse); **it's dangerous to drive too fast** il est dangereux de conduire trop vite.

Danish noun danois Masc.

Danish adjective danois.

dare verb **1** oser [1]; **to dare to do** oser faire; **I didn't dare suggest it** je n'ai pas osé le suggérer; **2 don't you dare tell her I'm here!** je t'interdis de lui dire que je suis là!; **3 I dare you!** chiche que tu y vas! (informal); **I dare you to tell him!** chiche que tu le lui dises! (informal).

daring adjective osé; **that was a bit daring!** c'était un peu osé!

dark noun **in the dark** dans l'obscurité; **after dark** après la tombée de la nuit; **to be afraid of the dark** avoir peur du noir.

dark adjective **1** (colour) foncé; **a dark blue skirt** une jupe bleu foncé; **2 she has dark brown hair** elle est brune; **3 it's dark already** il fait nuit déjà; **it gets dark around five** la nuit commence à tomber vers cinq heures; **4** (room) sombre; **the kitchen's a bit dark** la cuisine est plutôt sombre; **it's dark in here** il fait sombre ici.

darkness noun obscurité Fem.; **in darkness** dans l'obscurité.

darling noun chéri Masc., chérie Fem.; **see you later, darling!** à tout à l'heure, chéri!

dart noun fléchette Fem.; **to play darts** jouer aux fléchettes.

data plural noun données Fem. plural.

database noun base Fem. de données.

date noun **1** date Fem.; **the date of the meeting** la date de la réunion; **to fix a date for** fixer une date pour; **2 what's the date today?** nous sommes le combien aujourd'hui?; **3** out of date (*passport, driving licence, etc*) périmé; (*technology, method, information, etc*) dépassé; **my passport's out of date** mon passeport est périmé; **4** (*appointment*) **Laura's got a date with Frank tonight** Laura sort avec Frank ce soir; **5** (*fruit*) datte Fem.

date of birth noun date Fem. de naissance.

daughter noun fille Fem.; **Tina's daughter** la fille de Tina.

daughter-in-law noun belle-fille Fem. (*plural* **belles-filles**).

dawn noun aube Fem.

day noun **1** jour Masc.; **three days later** trois jours plus tard; **the day I went to London** le jour où je suis allé à Londres; **2** (*just from morning until evening*) journée Fem.; **we spent the day in London** nous avons passé la journée à Londres; **it rained all day** il a plu pendant toute la journée; **3** **it's going to be a nice day tomorrow** il va faire beau demain; **4** **the day after** le lendemain; **the day after the wedding** le lendemain du mariage; **the day after tomorrow** après-demain; **my sister's arriving the day after tomorrow** ma sœur arrive après-demain; **5** **the day before** la veille; **the day before the wedding** la veille du mariage; **the day before yesterday** avant-hier; **my sister arrived the day before yesterday** ma sœur est arrivée avant-hier.

day off noun jour Masc. de congé; **when's your day off?** quel est ton jour de congé?

dead adjective mort; **her father's dead** son père est mort.

dead adverb (*really*) vachement (*informal*); **he's dead nice** il est vachement gentil; **it was dead good** c'était vachement bien; **it's dead easy** c'est vachement facile; **you're dead right** tu as absolument raison; **she arrived dead on time** elle est arrivée à l'heure pile.

dead end noun impasse Fem.

deadline noun date Fem. limite.

deaf adjective sourd.

deafening adjective assourdissant.

deal noun **1** (*involving money*) affaire Fem.; **it's a good deal** c'est une bonne affaire; **2** marché Masc.; **I'll make a deal with you** je te ferai un marché avec toi; **it's a deal!** marché conclu!; **3 a great deal of** beaucoup de; **I don't have a great deal of time** je n'ai pas beaucoup de temps.

deal verb (*in cards*) donner [1]; **it's you to deal** c'est à toi de donner.

● **to deal with something** s'occuper [1] de quelque chose; **Linda deals with the accounts** Linda s'occupe de la comptabilité; **I'll deal with it as soon as possible** je m'en occuperai dès que possible.

dear adjective **1** cher (*Fem.* chère); **Dear Sylvie** Chère Sylvie; **2** (*expensive*) cher (*Fem.* chère).

death noun mort Fem.; **after his father's death** après la mort de son père; ★ **you'll frighten him to death** tu lui feras une peur bleue; ★ **I'm bored to death** je m'ennuie à mourir; ★ **I'm sick to death of it** j'en ai marre (*informal*) .

death penalty *noun* peine *Fem.* de mort.

debate *noun* débat *Masc.*

debate *verb* débattre [21].

debt *noun* dette *Fem.*; **to get into debt** s'endetter.

decade *noun* décennie *Fem.*

decaffeinated *adjective* décaféiné.

deceive *verb* tromper [1].

December *noun* décembre *Masc.*; **in December** en décembre.

decent *adjective* **1** convenable; **a decent salary** un salaire convenable; **2 a decent meal** un bon repas; **3 he seems a decent enough guy** il semble être un type plutôt bien (*informal*).

decide *verb* décider [1]; **to decide to do** décider de faire; **she's decided to buy a car** elle a décidé d'acheter une voiture; **she's decided not to buy a car** elle a décidé de ne pas acheter une voiture.

decimal *adjective* décimal (*Masc. plural* décimaux).

decimal point *noun* virgule *Fem.*

decision *noun* décision *Fem.*; **the right decision** la bonne décision; **the wrong decision** la mauvaise décision; **to make a decision** prendre une décision.

deck *noun* (*on a ship*) pont *Masc.*

deckchair *noun* transat *Masc.*

declare *verb* déclarer [1].

decorate *verb* **1** décorer [1]; **to decorate the Christmas tree**

décorer le sapin de Noël; **2** peindre; **we're decorating the kitchen this weekend** on va peindre la cuisine ce weekend.

decoration *noun* décoration *Fem.*

decorator *noun* peintre-décorateur *Masc.*

decrease *noun* diminution *Fem.*; **a decrease in the number of** une diminution du nombre de.

decrease *verb* diminuer [1].

deduct *verb* déduire [26].

deep *adjective* profond; **a deep feeling of gratitude** un profond sentiment de reconnaissance; **the river is very deep here** la rivière est très profonde ici; **how deep is the swimming pool?** quelle est la profondeur de la piscine?; **a hole two metres deep** un trou de deux mètres de profondeur.

deep end *noun* the deep end (*of a swimming pool*) le grand bassin.

deep freeze *noun* congélateur *Masc.*

deeply *adverb* profondément.

deer *noun* **1** (*red deer*) cerf *Masc.*; **2** (*roe deer*) chevreuil *Masc.*; **3** (*fallow deer*) daim *Masc.*

defeat *noun* défaite *Fem.*

defeat *verb* battre [21].

defect *noun* défaut *Masc.*

defence *noun* défense *Fem.*

defend *verb* défendre [3].

defender *noun* défenseur. *Masc.*

define *verb* définir [2].

definite *adjective* **1** net (*Fem.* nette) (*before the noun*); **a definite change** un net changement; **a definite improvement** une nette amélioration; **2** (*certain*) sûr; **it's not definite yet** ce n'est pas encore sûr; **3** (*exact*) précis; **a definite answer** une réponse précise; **I don't have a definite idea of what I want** je n'ai pas une idée précise de ce que je veux.

definite article *noun* article *Masc.* défini.

definitely *adverb* **1** (*when giving your opinion about something*) sans aucun doute; **the blue one is definitely the biggest** le bleu est sans aucun doute le plus grand; **your French is definitely better than mine** ton français est sans aucun doute meilleur que le mien; **'are you sure you like this one better?' – 'definitely!'** 'tu es sûr que tu préfères celui-ci?' – 'sans aucun doute!'; **she's definitely going to be there** elle va y être, c'est sûr; **I'm definitely not going** c'est décidé, je n'y vais pas.

definition *noun* définition *Fem.*

degree *noun* **1** degré *Masc.*; **thirty degrees** trente degrés; **2 a university degree** un diplôme universitaire.

delay *noun* retard *Masc.*; **a two-hour delay** un retard de deux heures.

delay *verb* **1** (*make late*) retarder [1]; **the flight was delayed by bad weather** le vol a été retardé par le mauvais temps; **2** (*postpone*) différer [24]; **the decision has been delayed until Thursday** la décision a été différée juqu'à jeudi.

delete *verb* effacer [61].

deliberate *adjective* délibéré.

deliberately *adverb* exprès; **you did it deliberately** tu l'as fait exprès; **he left it there deliberately** il a fait exprès de le laisser là.

delicate *adjective* délicat.

delicatessen *noun* épicerie *Fem.* fine.

delicious *adjective* délicieux (*Fem.* délicieuse).

delighted *adjective* ravi; **they're delighted with their new flat** ils sont ravis de leur nouvel appartement; **I'm delighted to hear you can come** je suis ravi d'apprendre que vous pouvez venir.

deliver *verb* **1** livrer [1]; **they're delivering the washing machine tomorrow** ils vont livrer la machine à laver demain; **2** distribuer [1] (*mail*).

delivery *noun* livraison *Fem.*

demand *noun* demande *Fem.*

demand *verb* exiger [52].

demo *noun* (*protest*) manif *Fem.* (*informal*).

democracy *noun* démocratie *Fem.*

democratic *adjective* démocratique.

demolish *verb* démolir [2].

demonstrate *verb* **1** faire [10] la démonstration de (*a machine, product, or technique*); **2** (*protest*) manifester [1]; **to demonstrate against something** manifester contre quelque chose.

demonstration *noun* **1** (*of machine, product, technique*)

a
b
c
d
e
f
g
h
i
j
k
l
m
n
o
p
q
r
s
t
u
v
w
x
y
z

démonstration Fem.; **2** (*protest*) manifestation.

demonstrator *noun* (*in protest*) manifestant Masc., manifestante Fem.

denim *noun* jean Masc.; **a denim jacket** un blouson en jean.

Denmark *noun* Danemark Masc.; **in Denmark** au Danemark; **to Denmark** au Danemark.

dense *adjective* dense.

dent *noun* bosse Fem.

dent *verb* cabosser [1].

dental *adjective* **1** dentaire; **dental floss** du fil dentaire; **dental hygiene** l'hygiène dentaire; **2 a dental appointment** un rendez-vous chez le dentiste.

dental surgeon *noun* chirurgien-dentiste Masc.

dentist *noun* dentiste Masc. & Fem.; **my mum's a dentist** ma mère est dentiste.

deny *verb* nier [1].

deodorant *noun* déodorant Masc.

depart *verb* partir [58].

department *noun* **1** (*in school, university*) département Masc.; **the language department** le département de langues; **2** (*in a shop*) rayon Masc.; **the men's department** le rayon hommes.

department store *noun* grand magasin Masc.

departure *noun* départ Masc.

departure lounge *noun* salle Fem. d'embarquement.

depend *verb* **to depend on** dépendre [3] de; **it depends on the price** ça dépend du prix; **it**

depends on what you want ça dépend de ce que tu veux; **it depends** ça dépend.

deposit *noun* **1** (*when renting or hiring*) caution Fem.; **2** (*when booking a holiday or hotel room*) arrhes Fem. plural; **to pay a deposit** verser des arrhes; **3** (*on a bottle*) consigne Fem.

depressed *adjective* déprimé.

depressing *adjective* déprimant.

depth *noun* profondeur Fem.

deputy *noun* adjoint Masc., adjointe Fem..

deputy head *noun* directeur Masc. adjoint, directrice Fem. adjointe.

descend *verb* descendre [3].

describe *verb* décrire [38].

description *noun* description Fem.

desert *noun* désert Masc.; **in the desert** dans le désert.

desert island *noun* île Fem. déserte.

deserve *verb* mériter [1].

design *noun* **1** conception Fem.; **the design of the plane** la conception de l'avion; **2** (*artistic design*) design Masc.; **fashion design** le stylisme; **3** (*pattern*) motif Masc.; **a floral design** un motif floral.

design *verb* **1** concevoir [66] (*a machine, plane, system*); **2** créer [32] (*costumes, clothes, fabric, scenery*).

designer *noun* **1** (*fashion designer*) styliste Masc. & Fem.; **2** (*graphic designer*) graphiste Masc. & Fem.

desire noun désir Masc.

desire verb désirer [1].

desk noun **1** (in office or at home) bureau Masc.; **2** (pupil's) table Fem.; **3** the reception desk la réception; the information desk le bureau des renseignements.

despair noun désespoir Masc.

despair verb to despair of doing désespérer [24] de faire.

desperate adjective **1** désespéré; a desperate attempt une tentative désespérée; **2** to be desperate to do avoir très envie de faire; I'm desperate to see you j'ai très envie de te voir.

despise verb mépriser [1].

dessert noun dessert Masc.; what's for dessert? qu'est-ce qu'il y a comme dessert?

destination noun destination Fem.

destroy verb détruire [26].

destruction noun destruction Fem.

detached house noun maison Fem. individuelle.

detail noun détail Masc.

detailed adjective détaillé.

detective noun **1** (police) inspecteur Masc. de police; **2** a private detective un détective.

detective story noun roman Masc. policier.

detention noun retenue Fem.

detergent noun détergent Masc.

determined adjective résolu; he's determined to leave il est résolu de partir.

detour noun détour Masc.

develop verb **1** développer [1]; to get a film developed faire développer une pellicule; **2** se développer; how children develop comment les enfants se développent.

developing country noun pays Masc. en voie de développement.

development noun développement Masc.

devil noun diable Masc.

devoted adjective dévoué.

dew noun rosée Fem.

diabetes noun diabète Masc.

diabetic noun, adjective diabète Masc. & Fem.; to be (a) diabetic être diabète.

diaeresis noun tréma Masc.

diagnosis noun diagnostic Masc.

diagonal adjective diagonal (Masc. plural diagonaux).

diagram noun schéma Masc.

dial verb composer [1] le numéro; lift the receiver and dial 142 décrochez et composez le 142; dial 00 33 for France faites le 00 33 pour la France.

dialling tone noun tonalité Fem.

dialogue noun dialogue Masc.

diameter noun diamètre Masc.

diamond noun **1** diamant Masc.; **2** (in cards) carreau; the jack of diamonds le valet de carreau; **3** (shape) losange Masc.

diarrhoea noun diarrhée Fem.; to have diarrhoea avoir la diarrhée.

diary noun **1** agenda Masc.; j'ai marqué la date de la réunion dans mon agenda I've noted the date of the meeting in my diary;

2 journal intime; **to keep a diary** tenir un journal (intime).

dice noun dé Masc.; **to throw the dice** jeter le dé.

dictation noun dictée Fem.

dictionary noun dictionnaire Masc.; **to look up a word in the dictionary** chercher un mot dans le dictionnaire.

did verb SEE **do**.

die verb 1 mourir [54]; **my grannie died in January** ma grand-mère est morte en janvier; 2 **to be dying to do** mourir d'envie de faire; **I'm dying to see them!** je meurs d'envie de les voir!

• **to die out** disparaître [27].

diesel noun 1 gazole Masc.; 2 **a diesel engine** un moteur diesel; **a diesel car** une voiture diesel.

diet noun 1 alimentation Fem.; **to have a healthy diet** avoir une alimentation saine; 2 (slimming or special) régime Masc.; **to be on a diet** être au régime; **a salt-free diet** un régime sans sel.

difference noun 1 différence Fem.; **I can't see any difference between the two** je ne vois pas la différence entre les deux; **what's the difference between ...?** quelle est la différence entre ...?; 2 **it makes a difference** ça change quelque chose; **it makes no difference** ça ne change rien; **it makes no difference what I say** je peux dire ce que je veux, ça ne change rien.

different adjective différent; **the two sisters are very different** les deux sœurs sont très différentes;

she's very different from her sister elle est très différente de sa sœur.

difficult adjective difficile; **it's really difficult** c'est vraiment difficile; **it's difficult to decide** il est difficile de décider.

difficulty noun 1 difficulté Fem.; 2 **to have difficulty doing** avoir du mal à faire; **I had difficulty finding your house** j'ai eu du mal à trouver ta maison.

dig verb **to dig a hole** creuser [1] un trou.

digestion noun digestion Fem.

digital adjective numérique; **a digital recording** un enregistrement numérique; **a digital watch** une montre à affichage numérique.

dim adjective 1 **a dim light** une lumière faible; 2 **she's a bit dim** elle est un peu bouchée (informal).

dimension noun dimension Fem.

din noun vacarme Masc.; **they were making a dreadful din** ils faisaient un vacarme pas possible; **stop making such a din!** arrétez de faire ce vacarme!

dinghy noun 1 **a sailing dinghy** un dériveur; 2 **a rubber dinghy** un canot pneumatique.

dining room noun salle Fem. à manger; **in the dining room** dans la salle à manger.

dinner noun 1 (evening) dîner Masc.; **to invite somebody to dinner** inviter quelqu'un à dîner; 2 (midday) déjeuner Masc.; **to have school dinner** manger à la cantine.

dinner party noun dîner Masc.

dinner time noun 1 (evening) l'heure du dîner; 2 (midday) l'heure du déjeuner.

dinosaur noun dinosaure Masc.

diploma noun diplôme Masc.

direct adjective direct; **a direct flight** un vol direct.

direct adverb directement; **the bus goes direct to the airport** le bus est direct pour l'aéroport.

direct verb 1 réaliser [1] (programme, film); 2 mettre en scène (play); 3 régler (traffic).

direction noun 1 direction Fem.; **in the other direction** dans l'autre direction; 2 **to ask somebody for directions** demander son chemin à quelqu'un; 3 **directions for use** mode Masc. d'emploi.

directly adverb 1 directement, 2 **directly afterwards** immédiatement après.

director noun 1 (of a company) directeur Masc., directrice Fem.; 2 (of a programme or film) réalisateur Masc., réalisatrice Fem.; 3 (of a play) metteur Masc. en scène.

directory noun annuaire Masc.; **to be ex-directory** être sur la liste rouge.

dirt noun saleté Fem.

dirty adjective sale; **my hands are dirty** j'ai les mains sales; **to get something dirty** salir quelque chose; **you'll get your dress dirty** tu vas salir ta robe; **to get dirty** se salir; **the curtains get dirty quickly** les rideaux se salissent vite.

disability noun infirmité Fem., handicap Masc.; **does he have a disability?** est-il infirme?

disabled adjective handicapé; **disabled people** les handicapés.

disadvantage noun 1 désavantage Masc.; 2 **to be at a disadvantage** être désavantagé.

disagree verb 1 disagree je ne suis pas d'accord; **I disagree with James** je ne suis pas d'accord avec James.

disappear verb disparaître [27].

disappearance noun disparition Fem.

disappointed adjective déçu; **I was disappointed with my marks** j'ai été déçu par mes notes.

disappointment noun déception Fem.

disaster noun désastre Masc.; **it was a complete disaster** ça a été un désastre complet.

disastrous adjective désastreux (Fem. désastreuse).

disc noun 1 **a compact disc** un disque compact; 2 **a slipped disc** une hernie discale; 3 **a tax disc** (for a vehicle) une vignette.

discipline noun discipline Fem.

disc-jockey noun disc-jockey Masc.

disco noun 1 soirée Fem. disco; **they're having a disco** ils font une soirée disco; 2 (club) discothèque.

disconnect verb 1 (the telephone, electricity) couper [1]; **have you disconnected the electricity?** est-ce que vous avez coupé l'électricité?; 2 (appliance) débrancher [1].

a
b
c
d
e
f
g
h
i
j
k
l
m
n
o
p
q
r
s
t
u
v
w
x
y
z

discount noun réduction Fem.

discourage verb décourager [52].

discover verb découvrir [30].

discovery noun découverte Fem.

discreet adjective discret (Fem. discrète).

discrimination noun discrimination Fem.; **racial discrimination** la discrimination raciale.

discuss verb **to discuss something** discuter [1] de quelque chose; **we'll discuss the problem tomorrow** nous discuterons du problème demain; **I'm going to discuss it with Phil** je vais en discuter avec Phil.

discussion noun discussion Fem.

disease noun maladie Fem.

disgraceful adjective scandaleux (Fem. scandaleuse).

disguise noun déguisement Masc.; **to be in disguise** être déguisé.

disguise verb déguiser [1]; **disguised as a woman** déguisé en femme.

disgust noun dégoût Masc.

disgusted adjective dégoûté.

disgusting adjective dégoûtant.

dish noun **1** plat Masc.; **a large white dish** un grand plat blanc; **he cooked my favourite dish** il a préparé mon plat favori; **2 to do the dishes** faire la vaisselle.

dishcloth noun (for drying up) torchon Masc.

dishonest adjective malhonnête.

dishonesty noun malhonnêteté Fem.

dish towel noun torchon Masc.

dishwasher noun lave-vaisselle Masc.

disinfect verb désinfecter [1].

disinfectant noun désinfectant Masc.

disk noun disque Masc.; **a floppy disk** une disquette; **the hard disk** le disque dur.

disk drive noun unité Fem. de disque; **the floppy disk drive** le lecteur de disquettes.

diskette noun disquette Fem.

dislike verb ne pas aimer [1]; **I dislike sport** je n'aime pas le sport.

dismay noun consternation Fem.

dismiss verb licencier [1] (an employee).

disobedient adjective désobéissant.

disobey verb désobéir à [2] (a person); enfreindre [60] (a rule); **she disobeyed the rules** elle a enfreint les règles.

display noun **1** exposition Fem.; **a handicrafts display** une exposition d'artisanat; **to be on display** être exposé; **2 a window display** une vitrine; **3 a firework display** un feu d'artifice.

display verb exposer [1].

disposable adjective jetable.

dispute noun dispute Fem.

disqualify verb disqualifier [1].

disrupt verb perturber [1].

dissolve verb dissoudre [67].

distance noun distance Fem.; **from a distance** de loin; **in the distance** au loin; **it's within walking distance** on peut y aller à pied.

distant adjective lointain.

distinct *adjective* net (*Fem.* nette).

distinctly *adverb* **1** distinctement;
2 it's distinctly odd c'est vraiment
bizarre.

distract *verb* distraire [78].

distribute *verb* distribuer [1].

district *noun* **1** (*in town*) quartier
Masc.; **a poor district of Paris** un
quartier pauvre de Paris; **2** (*in the
country*) région *Fem.*

disturb *verb* déranger [52]; **sorry
to disturb you** je suis désolé de
vous déranger; **do not disturb** ne
pas déranger.

ditch *noun* fossé *Masc.*

ditch *verb* **to ditch somebody**
plaquer [1] quelqu'un (*informal*).

dive *noun* plongeon *Masc.*

dive *verb* plonger [52].

diver *noun* plongeur *Masc.*,
plongeuse *Fem.*.

diversion *noun* (*traffic*) déviation
Fem.

divide *verb* diviser [1].

diving *noun* plongée *Fem.*

diving board *noun* plongeoir
Masc.

division *noun* division *Fem.*

divorce *noun* divorce *Masc.*

divorce *verb* divorcer [61]; **they
divorced in Mexico** ils ont divorcé
au Mexique.

divorced *adjective* divorcé; **my
parents are divorced** mes parents
sont divorcés.

DIY *noun* bricolage *Masc.*; **to do DIY**
faire du bricolage; **a DIY shop** un
magasin de bricolage.

dizzy *adjective* **I feel dizzy** j'ai la
tête qui tourne.

DJ *noun* disc jockey *Masc.*

do *verb* **1** faire [10]; **what are you
doing?** qu'est-ce que tu fais?; **I'm
doing my homework** je fais mes
devoirs; **what have you done with
the hammer?** qu'est-ce que tu as
fait du marteau?; **2** (*questions in
French are formed either with 'est-ce
que' or by putting the pronoun
subject after the verb and a hyphen
between them*) **do you want some
strawberries?** est-ce que tu veux
des fraises?, veux-tu des fraises?;
when does it start? quand est-ce
que ça commence?; **how did you
open the door?** comment as-tu
ouvert la porte?; **3** (*in negative
sentences*) **don't, doesn't, didn't** ne
...pas; **I don't like mushrooms** je
n'aime pas les champignons; **Rosie
doesn't like spinach** Rosie n'aime
pas les épinards; **you didn't shut
the door** tu n'as pas fermé la porte;
it doesn't matter ça ne fait rien;
4 (*when it refers back to another
verb, 'do' is not translated*) **'do you
live here?' – 'yes, I do'** est-ce que
tu habites ici? – 'oui'; **she has
more money than I do** elle a plus
d'argent que moi; **'I live in Oxford'
– 'so do I'** 'j'habite à Oxford' – 'moi
aussi'; **'I didn't phone Gemma' –
'neither did I'** 'je n'ai pas appelé
Gemma' – 'moi non plus'; **5 don't
you?, doesn't he?** etc. n'est-ce
pas?; **you know Helen, don't you?**
tu connais Helen, n'est-ce pas?; **she
left on Thursday, didn't she?** elle
est partie jeudi, n'est-ce pas?;
6 that'll do ça ira; **it'll do like that**
ça ira comme ça.

● **to do something up 1** lacer [61]

a (*shoes*); **2** boutonner [1] (*cardigan, jacket*); **3** retaper [1] (*house*).

● **to do with 1** regarder [1]; **it has nothing to do with him/you** ça ne le/te regarde pas; **2 to do with something: I could do with a rest** j'aurai bien besoin de me reposer.

● **to do without** se passer [1] de; **we can do without knives** on peut se passer de couteaux.

doctor *noun* médecin *Masc.*; **her mother's a doctor** sa mère est médecin.

document *noun* document *Masc.*

documentary *noun* documentaire *Masc.*

dodgems *plural noun* **the dodgems** les autos *Fem. plural* tamponneuses.

dog *noun* chien *Masc.*; (*female*) chienne *Fem.*

do-it-yourself *noun* bricolage *Masc.*

dole *noun* allocations *Fem. plural* chômage; **to be on the dole** être au chômage.

doll *noun* poupée *Fem.*

dollar *noun* dollar *Masc.*

dolphin *noun* dauphin *Masc.*

Dominican *noun* Dominicain *Masc.*, Dominicaine *Fem.*

Dominican *adjective* dominicain.

Dominican Republic *noun* République *Fem.* dominicaine.

domino *noun* domino *Masc.*; **to play dominoes** jouer aux dominos.

don't SEE do.

donation *noun* don *Masc.*

donkey *noun* âne *Masc.*

door *noun* **1** porte *Fem.*; **to open the door** ouvrir la porte; **to shut the door** fermer la porte; **2** (*of a vehicle or train*) portière *Fem.*

doorbell *noun* sonnerie *Fem.*; **to ring the doorbell** sonner à la porte; **there's the doorbell!** on sonne!

doorstep *noun* pas *Masc.* de la porte.

dormitory *noun* dortoir *Masc.*

dot *noun* **1** (*written*) point *Masc.*; **2** (*on fabric*) pois *Masc.*; **3 at ten on the dot** à dix heures pile.

double *adjective, adverb* **1** double; **a double helping** une double portion; **a double whisky** un double whisky; **2** le double; **double the time** le double du temps; **double the price** le double du prix; **3 a double room** une chambre pour deux personnes; **4 a double bed** un grand lit.

double bass *noun* contrebasse *Fem.*; **to play the double bass** jouer de la contrebasse.

double-breasted *adjective* **a double-breasted jacket** une veste croisée.

double-decker bus *noun* autobus *Masc.* à impériale.

double glazing *noun* double vitrage *Masc.*

doubles *noun* (*in tennis*) doubles *Masc.*; **to play a game of doubles** faire un double.

doubt *noun* doute *Masc.*; **there's no doubt about it** il n'y a aucun doute là-dessus; **I have my doubts** j'ai des doutes.

doubt *verb* **to doubt something** douter [1] de quelque chose; **I doubt**

it j'en doute; **I doubt that** douter que (+ *subjunctive*); **I doubt they'll do it** je doute qu'ils le fassent.

doubtful *adjective* **1** pas sûr; **it's doubtful** ce n'est pas sûr; **2 to be doubtful about doing** hésiter à faire; **I'm doubtful about inviting them together** j'hésite à les inviter ensemble.

dough *noun* pâte *Fem*.

doughnut *noun* beignet *Masc*.

Dover *noun* Douvres; **to Dover** à Douvres.

down *adverb, preposition* **1** en bas; **he's down in the cellar** il est en bas dans la cave; **2 down the road** (*nearby*) à côté; **there's a chemist's just down the road** il y a une pharmacie juste à côté; **3 to go down** descendre; **I went down to the kitchen** je suis descendu dans la cuisine; **to walk down the street** descendre la rue; **to run down the stairs** descendre les escaliers en courant; **4 to come down** descendre; **she came down from her bedroom** elle est descendue de sa chambre; **5 to sit down** s'asseoir; **she sat down on the sofa** elle s'est assise sur le canapé.

downstairs *adverb* **1** en bas; **she's downstairs in the sitting-room** elle est en bas dans le salon; **the dog sleeps downstairs** le chien dort en bas; **2** du dessous; **the flat downstairs** l'appartement du dessous; **the people downstairs** les voisins du dessous.

doze *verb* sommeiller [1].

dozen *noun* douzaine *Fem*.; **a dozen eggs** une douzaine d'œufs.

drag *noun* **what a drag!** quelle barbe! (*informal*); **she's a bit of a drag** elle n'est pas marrante (*informal*).

drag *verb* traîner [1].

dragon *noun* dragon *Masc*.

drain *noun* égout *Masc*.

drain *verb* égoutter [1] (*vegetables*).

drama *noun* **1** (*subject*) art *Masc*. dramatique; **2 he made a big drama about it** il en a fait tout un cinéma (*informal*).

dramatic *adjective* spectaculaire.

draught *noun* courant *Masc*. d'air.

draughts *noun* dames *Fem*. plural; **to play draughts** jouer aux dames.

draw *noun* **1** (*in a match*) match nul *Masc*.; **it was a draw** on a fait match nul; **2** (*lottery*) tirage *Masc*. au sort.

draw *verb* **1** dessiner [1]; **I can't draw horses** je ne sais pas dessiner les chevaux; **she can draw really well** elle dessine vraiment bien; **2 to draw a picture** faire [10] un dessin; **3 to draw the curtains** tirer [1] les rideaux; **4 to draw a crowd** attirer [1] une foule de spectateurs; **5** (*in a match*) faire [10] match nul; **we drew three all** nous avons fait match nul trois à trois; **6 to draw lots** tirer [1] au sort.

drawback *noun* inconvénient *Masc*.

drawer *noun* tiroir *Masc*.

drawing *noun* dessin *Masc*.

drawing pin *noun* punaise *Fem*.

dreadful *adjective* affreux (*Fem*. affreuse).

a b c d e f g h i j k l m n o p q r s t u v w x y z

a

b

c

d

e

f

g

h

i

j

k

l

m

n

o

p

q

r

s

t

u

v

w

x

y

z

dreadfully adverb terriblement;
I'm dreadfully late je suis
terriblement en retard; **I'm
dreadfully sorry** je suis vraiment
navré.

dream noun rêve Masc.; **to have a
dream** faire un rêve; **I had a
horrible dream last night** j'ai fait
un rêve horrible cette nuit.

dream verb rêver [1]; **to dream
about something** rêver de quelque
chose.

drenched adjective trempé; **to get
drenched** se faire tremper; **we got
drenched on the way home** on
s'est fait tremper en rentrant.

dress noun robe Fem.

dress verb **to dress a child**
habiller [1] un enfant.

● **to dress up** se déguiser [1]; **to
dress up as a vampire** se déguiser
en vampire.

dressed adjective **1** habillé; **is
Tom dressed yet?** est-ce que Tom
est habillé?; **she was dressed in
black trousers and a yellow shirt**
elle était habillée d'un pantalon
noir et d'une chemise jaune; **2 to
get dressed** s'habiller; **I got
dressed quickly** je me suis vite
habillé.

dresser noun (for dishes)
vaisselier Masc.

dressing gown noun robe Fem.
de chambre.

dressing table noun coiffeuse
Fem.

drier noun **a hair drier** un sèche-
cheveux; **a tumble drier** un sèche-
linge.

drift noun **a snow drift** une
congère.

drill noun perceuse Fem.

drink noun **1** boisson Fem.; **a hot
drink** une boisson chaude; **a cold
drink** une boisson fraîche; **2 would
you like a drink?** tu veux boire
quelque chose?; **3 to go out for a
drink** aller prendre un pot
(informal).

drink verb boire [22]; **he drank a
glass of water** il a bu un verre
d'eau.

drive noun **1 to go for a drive** faire
un tour en voiture; **2** (up to a
house) allée Fem.

drive verb **1** conduire [26]; **she
drives very fast** elle conduit très
vite; **to drive a car** conduire une
voiture; **I'd like to learn to drive**
j'aimerais apprendre à conduire;
can you drive? tu sais conduire?;
2 aller en voiture; **we drove to
Paris** nous somes allés à Paris en
voiture; **3 to drive somebody (to a
place)** emmener [50] quelqu'un en
voiture; **Mum drove me to the
station** Maman m'a emmené en
voiture à la gare; **to drive
somebody home** raccompagner
[1] quelqu'un; ★ **she drives me
mad!** elle me rend folle!

driver noun **1** conducteur Masc.,
conductrice Fem.; **2** (of a taxi or
bus) chauffeur Masc.

driving instructor noun
moniteur Masc. d'auto-école.

driving lesson noun leçon Fem.
de conduite.

driving licence noun permis
Masc. de conduite.

driving school noun école Fem. de conduite.

driving test noun permis Masc. de conduite; **to take your driving test** passer son permis; **Jenny's passed her driving test** Jenny a eu son permis.

drop noun goutte Fem.

drop verb **1 to drop something** laisser [1] tomber quelque chose; **I dropped my glasses** j'ai laissé tomber mes lunettes; **I'm going to drop history next year** je vais laisser tomber l'histoire l'année prochaine; **drop it!** laisse tomber!; **2** déposer [1] (a person); **could you drop me at the station?** est-ce que tu peux me déposer à la gare?

drought noun sécheresse Fem.

drown verb se noyer [39]; **she drowned in the lake** elle s'est noyée dans le lac.

drug noun **1** (medicine) médicament Masc.; **2** (illegal) **drugs** la drogue.

drug abuse noun usage Masc. des stupéfiants.

drug addict noun toxicomane Masc. & Fem.

drug addiction noun toxicomanie Fem.

drum noun **1** tambour Masc.; **2 drums** la batterie; **to play drums** jouer de la batterie.

drum kit noun batterie Fem.

drummer noun batteur Masc., batteuse Fem.

drunk noun ivrogne Masc. & Fem.

drunk adjective ivre.

dry adjective sec (Fem. sèche).

dry verb **1** sécher [24]; **to let something dry** laisser [1] sécher quelque chose; **2 to dry your hair** se sécher les cheveux; **3 to dry your hands** s'essuyer [41] les mains; **to dry the dishes** s'essuyer [41] la vaisselle; **4 to dry the washing** faire [10] sécher le linge.

dry cleaner's noun teinturerie Fem.

dryer noun SEE **drier**.

dual carriageway noun route Fem. à quatre voies.

dubbed adjective **a dubbed film** un film doublé.

duck noun canard Masc.

due adjective, adverb **1 to be due to do something** devoir faire; **we're due to leave on Thursday** nous devons partir jeudi; **Paul's due back soon** Paul doit bientôt revenir; **2 due to** en raison de; **the match has been cancelled due to bad weather** le match a été annulé en raison du mauvais temps.

duke noun duc Masc.

dull adjective **1 dull weather** un temps maussade; **it's a dull day today** il fait un temps maussade aujourd'hui; **2** (boring) ennuyeux (Fem. ennuyeuse).

dumb adjective **1** muet (Fem. muette); **to be deaf and dumb** être sourd-muet; **2** (stupid) bête; **he asked some dumb questions** il a posé des questions bêtes.

dummy noun (for a baby) tétine Fem.

dump verb **1** jeter [48] (rubbish); **2** plaquer [1] (a person) (informal);

a b c d e f g h i j k l m n o p q r s t u v w x y z

a

she's dumped her boyfriend elle a plaqué son copain.

b

dune noun dune Fem.

c

dungarees plural noun salopette Fem. singular.

dungeon noun cachot Masc.

d

Dunkirk noun Dunkerque.

e

Dunkirk noun Dunkerque.

f

during preposition pendant; **during the night** pendant la nuit; **I saw her during the holidays** je l'ai vue pendant les vacances.

g

dusk noun **at dusk** à la nuit tombante.

h

dust noun poussière Fem.

i

j

dust verb épousseter [48].

k

dustbin noun poubelle Fem.; **to put something in the dustbin** jeter quelque chose à la poubelle.

l

dustman noun éboueur Masc.

m

dusty adjective poussiéreux (Fem. poussiéreuse).

n

Dutch noun 1 (language) hollandais Masc.; 2 the Dutch (people) les Hollandais Masc. plural.

o

Dutch adjective hollandais.

p

duty noun 1 devoir Masc.; **to have a duty to do** avoir le devoir de faire; **you have a duty to inform us** vous avez le devoir de nous informer; 2 **to be on duty** être de service; **to be on night duty** être de service de nuit; **I'm off duty tonight** je ne suis pas de service ce soir.

q

r

s

t

u

duty-free adjective hors taxes; **the duty-free shops** les boutiques hors taxes; **duty-free purchases** les achats hors taxes.

v

w

duvet noun couette Fem.

x

y

duvet cover noun housse Fem. de couette.

z

DVD noun DVD Masc.

dwarf noun nain Masc., naine Fem.

dye noun teinture Fem.

dye verb teindre [60]; **to dye your hair** se teindre les cheveux; **I'm going to dye my hair pink** je vais me teindre les cheveux en rose.

dynamic adjective dynamique.

dyslexia noun dyslexie Fem.

dyslexic adjective dyslexique.

Ee

each adjective chaque; **each time** chaque fois; **curtains for each window** des rideaux pour chaque fenêtre.

each pronoun chacun (Fem. chacune); **my sisters each have a computer** mes sœurs ont chacune un ordinateur; **she gave us an apple each** elle nous a donné une pomme à chacun; **each of you** chacun de vous, chacune de vous; **we each got a present** chacun de nous a reçu un cadeau; **the tickets cost ten pounds each** les billets coûtent dix livres chacun.

each other pronoun ('each other' is usually translated using a reflexive pronoun) **they love each other** ils s'aiment; **we know each other** nous nous connaissons; **do you often see each other?** est-ce que vous vous voyez souvent?

eagle noun aigle Masc.

ear noun oreille Fem.

earache noun **to have earache** avoir une otite.

earlier adverb 1 (a while ago) tout à l'heure; **your brother phoned earlier** ton frère a appelé tout à l'heure; 2 (not as late) plus tôt; **we should have started earlier** nous aurions dû commencer plus tôt; **earlier in the morning** plus tôt le matin.

early adverb 1 (in the morning) tôt; **to get up early** se lever tôt; **it's too early** il est trop tôt; 2 (for an appointment) en avance; **we're early, the train doesn't leave until ten** nous sommes en avance, le train ne part qu'à dix heures; **Grandma likes to be early** Grand-mère aime être en avance.

early adjective 1 (one of the first) premier (Fem. première); **in the early months** pendant les premiers mois; **I'm getting the early train** je prends le premier train; 2 **to have an early lunch** déjeuner tôt; **Jan's having an early night** Jan va se coucher tôt; **we're making an early start** nous partons tôt; 3 **in the early afternoon** en début d'après-midi; **in the early hours** au petit matin.

earn verb gagner [1] (money); **Richard earns four pounds an hour** Richard gagne quatre livres de l'heure.

earnings plural noun salaire Masc.

earphones noun casque Masc.

earring noun boucle Fem. d'oreille.

earth noun terre Fem.; **life on earth** la vie sur terre; ★ **what on earth are you doing?** mais qu'est-ce que tu fais là?

earthquake noun tremblement Masc. de terre.

easily adverb 1 (without difficulty) facilement; 2 (by far) de loin; **he's easily the best** il est de loin le meilleur.

east noun est Masc.; **in the east** à l'est.

east adjective, adverb est; **the east side** le côté est; **an east wind** un vent d'est; **east of Paris** à l'est de Paris.

Easter noun Pâques Masc.; **they're coming at Easter** ils viennent à Pâques; **Happy Easter** Joyeuses Pâques.

Easter Day noun dimanche Masc. de Pâques.

Easter egg noun œuf Masc. de Pâques.

Eastern Europe noun Europe Fem. de l'Est.

easy adjective facile; **it's easy!** c'est facile!; **it was easy to make** c'était facile à faire.

eat verb 1 manger [52]; **he was eating a banana** il mangeait une banane; **we're going to have something to eat** nous allons manger quelque chose; 2 prendre [64] (a meal); **we were eating breakfast** nous prenions le petit déjeuner; 3 **to eat out** manger au restaurant.

EC noun (short for European Community) CE Fem., Communauté Fem. européenne.

earphones noun casque Masc.

echo noun écho Masc.

echo verb retentir [2].

eclipse noun éclipse Fem.

ecological adjective écologique.

ecologist noun écologiste Masc. & Fem.

a b c d e f g h i j k l m n o p q r s t u v w x y z

a **ecology** noun écologie Fem.

b **economic** adjective 1 (to do with the economy) économique;
c 2 (profitable) rentable.

economical adjective 1 économe
d (a person); 2 économique (way of doing something); **it's more**
e **economical to buy a big one** c'est plus économique d'acheter un
f grand.

g **economics** noun économie Fem.

h **economy** noun économie Fem.

i **eczema** noun eczéma Masc.

j **edge** noun 1 bord Masc.; **the edge of the table** le bord de la table; **at**
k **the edge of the lake** au bord du lac; 2 **to be on edge** être énervé.

l **edible** adjective comestible.

Edinburgh noun Édimbourg.
m
edit verb éditer [1].
n
editor noun (of a newspaper) rédacteur Masc. en chef, rédactrice
o Fem. en chef.

p **educate** verb (a teacher) instruire [26].

q **education** noun éducation Fem.

r **educational** adjective éducatif (Fem. éducative).

s **effect** noun effet Masc.; **the effect of the accident** l'effet de
t l'accident; **to have an effect on** avoir un effet sur; **it had a good**
u **effect on the whole family** ça a eu un bon effet sur toute la famille;
v **special effects** les effets spéciaux.

w **effective** adjective efficace.

x **efficient** adjective efficace.

y **effort** noun effort Masc.; **to make an effort** faire un effort; **David**
z **made an effort to help us** David a

fait un effort pour nous aider; **he didn't even make the effort to apologize** il n'a même pas fait l'effort pour s'excuser.

e.g. par ex.

egg noun œuf Masc.; **a dozen eggs** une douzaine d'œufs; **a fried egg** un œuf au plat; **two boiled eggs** deux œufs à la coque; **a hard-boiled egg** un œuf dur; **scrambled eggs** les œufs brouillés.

egg-cup noun coquetier Masc.

eggshell noun coquille Fem. d'œuf.

egg-white noun blanc Masc. d'œuf.

egg-yolk noun jaune Masc. d'œuf.

eight number huit Masc.; **Maya's eight** Maya a huit ans; **at eight o'clock** à huit heures.

eighteen number dix-huit Masc.; **Jason's eighteen** Jason a dix-huit ans.

eighth number 1 huitième; 2 **the eighth of July** le huit juillet; **on the eighth floor** au huitième étage.

eighty number quatre-vingts; **eighty-five** quatre-vingt-cinq (note that the 's' disappears when another number follows).

Eire noun la République d'Irlande; **in Eire** en République d'Irlande.

either pronoun 1 (one or the other) l'un ou l'autre; **choose either (of them)** choisis l'un ou l'autre; **I don't like either (of them)** je n'aime ni l'un ni l'autre; 2 (both) les deux; **either is possible** tous les deux sont possibles.

either conjunction 1 **either ... or** ou ... ou; **either Thursday or Friday** ou jeudi ou vendredi; **either Susie or Judy** ou Susie ou Judy; **he either wrote or phoned** il a ou écrit ou appelé; **2** (*with a negative*) non plus; **he doesn't want to either** il ne veut pas non plus; **I don't know them either** je ne les connais pas non plus.

elastic *noun, adjective* élastique *Masc.*

elastic band *noun* élastique *Masc.*

elbow *noun* coude *Masc.*

elder *adjective* aîné; **her elder brother** son frère aîné.

elderly *adjective* âgé; **the elderly** les personnes *Fem. plural* âgées.

eldest *adjective* aîné; **her eldest brother** son frère aîné.

elect *verb* élire [51]; **she has been elected** elle a été élue.

election *noun* élection *Fem.*; **in the election** aux élections; **to call a general election** fixer les élections législatives.

electric *adjective* électrique.

electrical *adjective* électrique.

electrician *noun* électricien *Masc.*, électricienne *Fem.*

electricity *noun* électricité *Fem.*; **to turn off the electricity** couper le courant.

electronic *adjective* électronique.

electronic mail *noun* courrier *Masc.* électronique.

electronics *noun* électronique *Fem.*

elegant *adjective* élégant.

element *noun* élément *Masc.*

elephant *noun* éléphant *Masc.*

eleven *number* onze *Masc.*; **Josh is eleven** Josh a onze ans; **at eleven o'clock** à onze heures; **a football eleven** une équipe de football.

eleventh *number* onzième; **the eleventh of May** le onze mai; **on the eleventh floor** à l'onzième étage.

eliminate *verb* éliminer [1].

else *adverb* **1** d'autre; **somebody else** quelqu'un d'autre; **did you see anyone else?** as-tu vu quelqu'un d'autre?; **nothing else** rien d'autre; **I don't want anything else** je ne veux rien d'autre; **2 something else** autre chose; **would you like something else?** désirez-vous autre chose?; **3 somewhere else** ailleurs; **4 or else** sinon; **hurry up, or else we'll be late** dépêche-toi, sinon nous serons en retard.

e-mail *noun* courrier *Masc.* électronique.

embankment *noun* **1** (*by a river*) quai *Masc.*; **2** (*by a railway*) remblai *Masc.*

embarrassed *adjective* gêné; **I was terribly embarrassed** j'étais très gêné.

embarrassing *adjective* gênant.

embarrassment *noun* embarras *Masc.*, gêne *Fem.*

embassy *noun* ambassade *Fem.*; **the French Embassy** l'ambassade de France.

embroider *verb* broder [1].

embroidery *noun* broderie *Fem.*

emergency *noun* cas *Masc.* d'urgence; **in an emergency, break the glass** en cas d'urgence,

a
b
c
d
f
g
h
i
j
k
l
m
n
o
p
q
r
s
t
u
v
w
x
y
z

a b c d e f g h i j k l m n o p q r s t u v w x y z

cassez la vitre; **it's an emergency!** c'est urgent!

emergency exit noun sortie Fem. de secours.

emergency landing noun atterrissage Masc. d'urgence.

emotion noun émotion Fem.

emotional adjective **1** ému (a person); **she was quite emotional** elle était tout émue; **2** (a speech or an occasion) chargé d'émotion.

emperor noun empereur Masc.

emphasis noun accent Masc.

emphasize verb he emphasized that it wasn't compulsory il a insisté sur le fait que ce n'était pas obligatoire.

empire noun empire Masc.; **the Roman Empire** l'Empire Romain.

employ verb employer [39].

employee noun salarié Masc., salariée Fem.

employer noun employeur Masc., employeuse Fem.

employment noun travail Masc.

empress noun impératrice Fem.

empty adjective vide; **an empty bottle** une bouteille vide; **the room was empty** la pièce était vide.

empty verb vider [1]; **I emptied the teapot into the sink** j'ai vidé la théière dans l'évier.

enchanting adjective ravissant.

enclose verb (in a letter) joindre [49]; **please find enclosed a cheque** veuillez trouver ci-joint un chèque.

encore noun bis Masc.; **to give an encore** jouer un bis.

encourage verb encourager [52]; **to encourage somebody to do something** encourager quelqu'un à faire quelque chose; **Mum encouraged me to try again** Maman m'a encouragé à recommencer.

encouragement noun encouragement Masc.

encouraging adjective encourageant.

encyclopedia noun encyclopédie Fem.

end noun **1** (last part) fin Fem.; **'The End' 'Fin';** **at the end of the film** à la fin du film; **by the end of the day** à la fin de la journée; **in the end** I went home finalement je suis rentré chez moi; **Sally's coming at the end of June** Sally viendra fin juin; **2** (of a table, garden, stick, or road, for example) bout Masc.; **hold the other end** tiens l'autre bout; **at the end of the street** au bout de la rue; **3** (in tennis or football) côté Masc.; **to change ends** changer de côté.

end verb **1** (to put an end to) mettre [11] fin à (an arrangement); **they've ended the strike** ils ont mis fin à la grève; **2** (to come to an end) se terminer [1]; **the day ended with a dinner** la journée s'est terminée par un dîner.

● **to end up 1 to end up doing** finir [2] par faire; **we ended up taking a taxi** nous avons fini par prendre un taxi; **2 to end up somewhere** se retrouver [1] quelque part; **Rob ended up in San Francisco** Rob s'est retrouvé à San Francisco.

endangered *adjective* menacé; **an endangered species** une espèce en voie d'extinction.

ending *noun* fin *Fem.*

endless *adjective* interminable (*a day or a journey, for example*).

enemy *noun* ennemi *Masc.*, ennemie *Fem.*; **to make enemies** se faire des ennemis.

energetic *adjective* énergique.

energy *noun* énergie *Fem.*

engaged *adjective* **1** (*to be married*) fiancé; **they're engaged** ils sont fiancés; **to get engaged** se fiancer [61]; **2** (*a phone or toilet*) occupé; **it's engaged, I'll ring later** c'est occupé, j'appellerai plus tard.

engagement *noun* (*to marry*) fiançailles *Fem. plural*.

engagement ring *noun* bague *Fem.* de fiançailles.

engine *noun* **1** (*in a car*) moteur *Masc.*; **2** (*pulling a train*) locomotive *Fem.*

engineer *noun* **1** (*who comes for repairs*) technicien *Masc.*; **2** (*who builds roads and bridges*) ingénieur *Masc.*

engineering *noun* ingénierie *Fem.*; **to study engineering** faire des études d'ingénierie.

England *noun* Angleterre *Fem.*; **in England** en Angleterre; **to England** en Angleterre; **I am from England** je suis anglais.

English *noun* **1** (*the language*) anglais *Masc.*; **do you speak English?** parlez-vous anglais?; **he answered in English** il a répondu en anglais; **2** (*English people*) **the English** les Anglais *Masc. plural*.

English *adjective* **1** (*of or from England*) anglais; **the English team** l'équipe anglaise; **2 an English lesson** un cours d'anglais; **our English teacher** notre professeur d'anglais.

English Channel *noun* the **English Channel** la Manche.

Englishman *noun* Anglais *Masc.*

Englishwoman *noun* Anglaise *Fem.*

enjoy *verb* **1** aimer [1]; **did you enjoy the party?** as-tu aimé la soirée?; **we really enjoyed the concert** nous avons beaucoup aimé le concert; **2 to enjoy doing** aimer faire; **I enjoy swimming** j'aime nager; **do you enjoy living in York?** aimez-vous vivre à York?; **3 to enjoy oneself** s'amuser [1]; **we really enjoyed ourselves** nous nous sommes très bien amusés; **enjoy yourselves!** amusez-vous bien!; **did you enjoy yourself?** tu t'es bien amusé?

enjoyable *adjective* agréable.

enlarge *verb* agrandir [2] (*a photo, for example*).

enlargement *noun* (*of a photo*) agrandissement *Masc.*

enormous *adjective* énorme.

enough *adverb, pronoun* **1** assez; **there's enough for everyone** il y en a assez pour tout le monde; **2** (*followed by a noun*) assez de; **is there enough bread?** est-ce qu'il y a assez de pain?; **3** (*followed by an adjective or adverb*) suffisamment; **big enough** suffisamment grand; **slowly enough** suffisamment

a b c d e f g h i j k l m n o p q r s t u v w x y z

lentement; **4 that's enough** ça suffit.

enquire verb se renseigner [1]; **I'm going to enquire about the trains** je vais me renseigner sur les trains.

enquiry noun demande Fem. de renseignements; **to make enquiries about something** demander des renseignements sur quelque chose.

enrol verb s'inscrire [38]; **I want to enrol on the course** je veux m'inscrire au cours.

enter verb **1** (to go inside) entrer [1] dans (a room or building); **we all entered the church** nous sommes tous entrés dans l'église; **2 to enter for** s'inscrire [38] à (an exam or competition); s'inscrire pour (a race).

entertain verb **1** (to keep amused) divertir [2]; **something to entertain the children** quelque chose pour divertir les enfants; **2** (to have people round) recevoir [66]; **they don't entertain much** ils reçoivent peu.

entertaining noun **they do a lot of entertaining** ils reçoivent beaucoup.

entertaining adjective amusant.

entertainment noun (fun) distractions Fem. plural; **there wasn't much entertainment in the evenings** il n'y avait pas beaucoup de distractions le soir.

enthusiasm noun enthousiasme Masc.

enthusiast noun passionné Masc., passionnée Fem.; **he's a rugby**

enthusiast c'est un passionné de rugby.

enthusiastic adjective enthousiaste.

entire adjective entier (Fem. entière); **the entire class** la classe entière.

entirely adverb complètement.

entrance noun entrée Fem.

entry noun (the way in) entrée Fem.; **'no entry'** 'défense d'entrer'.

entry phone noun interphone Masc.

envelope noun enveloppe Fem.

envious adjective envieux (Fem. envieuse); **he's envious of my exam results** il est jaloux de mes résultats d'examen.

environment noun environnement Masc.

environmental adjective écologique.

environment-friendly adjective écologique.

envy noun envie Fem.

epidemic noun épidémie Fem.

epileptic noun épileptique Masc. & Fem.

episode noun épisode Masc.

equal adjective égal (Masc. plural égaux); **in equal quantities** en quantités égales.

equal verb égaler [1].

equality noun égalité Fem.

equalize verb égaliser [1]; **they equalized in the last minute** ils ont égalisé dans la dernière minute.

equally adverb (to share) en parts égales; **we divided it equally** nous l'avons divisé en parts égales.

equator noun équateur Masc.

equip verb équiper [1]; **well equipped for the hike** bien équipé pour la randonnée; **equipped with rucksacks** équipés de sacs à dos.

equipment noun 1 (for sport) équipement Masc.; 2 matériel Masc.; **laboratory equipment** le matériel de laboratoire; 3 (for sports) équipement Masc.

equivalent adjective **to be equivalent to** être équivalent à.

error noun 1 (in spelling or typing) faute Fem.; **a spelling error** une faute d'orthographe; 2 (in maths or on a computer) erreur Fem.

error message noun message Masc. d'erreur.

escalator noun escalier Masc. mécanique.

escape noun (from prison) évasion Fem.

escape verb 1 (a person) s'évader [1]; 2 (an animal) s'échapper [1].

escort noun escorte Fem.; **a police escort** une escorte de police.

especially adjective 1 (above all) surtout; **there are lots of tourists, especially in August** il y a beaucoup de touristes, surtout en août; 2 (unusually) particulièrement; **'is he rich?' – 'not especially'** 'est-il riche?' – 'pas particulièrement'.

essay noun rédaction Fem.; **an essay on pollution** une rédaction sur la pollution.

essential adjective essentiel (Fem. essentielle); **it's essential to reply quickly** il est essentiel de répondre vite.

establishment noun (an organization) établissement Masc.

estate noun 1 (a housing estate) cité Fem.; 2 (a big house and grounds) domaine Masc.

estate agent's noun agence Fem. immobilière.

estate car noun break Masc.

estimate noun 1 (a quote for work) devis Masc.; 2 (a rough guess) estimation Fem.

estimate verb évaluer [1].

etc etc.

ethnic adjective ethnique; **an ethnic minority** une minorité ethnique.

EU noun (SHORT FOR **European Union**) Union Fem. européenne.

euro noun euro Masc.; **the euro is divided into cents** l'euro est divisé en centimes.

Europe noun Europe Fem.; **in Europe** en Europe; **to Europe** to Europe.

European noun Européen Masc., Européenne Fem.

European adjective européen (Fem. européenne).

European Union noun Union Fem. européenne.

eurozone noun zone Fem. euro.

evacuate verb faire [10] évacuer; **the police evacuated the building** la police a fait évacuer l'immeuble.

evaporate verb s'évaporer [1].

a
b
c
d
e
f
g
h
i
j
k
l
m
n
o
p
q
r
s
t
u
v
w
x
y
z

eve noun **Christmas Eve** la veille de Noël; **New Year's Eve** la Saint-Sylvestre.

even[1] adverb **1** même; **even Lisa didn't like it** même Lisa ne l'a pas aimé; **without even asking** sans même demander; **2 even if** même si; **even if they arrive** même s'ils arrivent; **3 not even** même pas; **I don't like animals, not even dogs** je n'aime pas les animaux, même pas les chiens; **4 even bigger** encore plus grand; **even more embarrassing** encore plus gênant; **even faster** encore plus vite; **5 even more than** encore plus que; **I liked the song even more than their last one** j'ai aimé la chanson encore plus que leur dernière; **6 even so** quand même; **even so, we had a good time** nous nous sommes bien amusés quand même.

even[2] adjective **1** (a surface or layer) régulier (Fem. régulière); **2** (a number) pair; **six is an even number** six est un numéro pair; **3** (with the same score) à égalité (competitors); **Lee and Blair are even** Lee et Blair sont à égalité.

evening noun **1** soir Masc.; **this evening** ce soir; **at six o'clock in the evening** à six heures du soir; **tomorrow evening** demain soir; **on Thursday evening** jeudi soir; **the evening before** la veille au soir; **every evening** tous les soirs; **I work in the evening(s)** je travaille le soir; **the evening meal** le repas du soir; **2** (from beginning to end) soirée Fem.; **during the evening** pendant la soirée; **an evening with** Pavarotti une soirée avec Pavarotti.

evening class noun cours Masc. du soir.

event noun **1** (a happening) évènement Masc.; **2** (in athletics) épreuve Fem.; **track events** les épreuves de vitesse; **3 in any event, at all events** de toute façon.

eventful adjective mouvementé (a day or an outing).

eventually adverb finalement.

ever adverb **1** (at any time) jamais; **hardly ever** presque jamais; **have you ever noticed that?** est-ce que tu l'as jamais remarqué ça?; **no-one ever came** personne n'est jamais venu; **hotter than ever** plus chaud que jamais; **more slowly than ever** plus lentement que jamais; **2** (always) toujours; **as cheerful as ever** toujours aussi gai; **the same as ever** toujours le même; **3 ever since** depuis; **and it's been raining ever since** et depuis il pleut tout le temps.

every adjective **1** tous (Fem. toutes); **every house has a garden** toutes les maisons ont un jardin; **every day** tous les jours; **every Monday** tous les lundis; **every ten kilometres** tous les dix kilomètres; **I've seen every one of his films** j'ai vu tous ses films; **2** (each) chaque; **every time** chaque fois; **3 every now and then** de temps en temps.

everybody, everyone pronoun tout le monde; **everybody knows that** ... tout le monde sait que ...; **everyone else** tous les autres.

everything pronoun tout;
everything is ready tout est prêt;
everything's fine tout va bien;
everything else tout le reste;
everything you said tout ce que tu as dit.

everywhere adverb partout;
there was mud everywhere il y avait de la boue partout;
everywhere she went partout où elle allait; **everywhere else** partout ailleurs.

evidently adverb manifestement.

evil noun mal Masc.

evil adjective mauvais.

exact adjective exact; **the exact amount** la somme exacte; **it's the exact opposite** c'est exactement le contraire.

exactly adverb exactement;
they're exactly the same age ils ont exactement le même âge; **yes, exactly** oui, exactement.

exaggerate verb exagérer [24].

exaggeration noun exagération Fem.

exam noun examen Masc.; **a history exam** un examen d'histoire; **to sit an exam** passer un examen; **to pass an exam** réussir un examen; **to fail an exam** échouer à un examen.

examination noun examen Masc.

examine verb examiner [1].

examiner noun examinateur Masc., examinatrice Fem.

example noun exemple Masc.; **for example** par exemple; **to set a good example** donner l'exemple.

excellent adjective excellent.

except preposition 1 sauf; **except in March** sauf au mois de mars; **every day except Tuesday** tous les jours sauf le mardi; **except when it rains** sauf quand il pleut; 2 **except for** sauf; **except for the children** sauf les enfants.

exception noun exception Fem.;
without exception sans exception;
with the exception of à l'exception de.

exchange noun échange Masc.; **in exchange for his help** en échange de son aide; **an exchange visit** un voyage d'échange.

exchange verb échanger [52]; **can I exchange this shirt for a smaller one?** puis-je échanger cette chemise contre une plus petite?

exchange rate noun taux Masc. d'échange.

excite verb exciter [1].

excited adjective 1 excité (a person or animal); **the children are excited** les enfants sont excités; 2 **to get excited** s'exciter; **the dogs get excited when they hear the car** les chiens s'excitent quand ils entendent la voiture.

excitement noun excitation Fem.

exciting adjective passionnant; **a really exciting film** un film vraiment passionnant.

exclamation mark noun point Masc. d'exclamation.

excursion noun excursion Fem.

excuse noun excuse Fem.; **Gary has a good excuse** Gary a une bonne excuse; **that's no excuse** ce n'est pas une excuse.

a
b
c
d
e
f
g
h
i
j
k
l
m
n
o
p
q
r
s
t
u
v
w
x
y
z

excuse verb (apologizing) **excuse me!** excusez-moi!

execute verb exécuter [1].

exercise noun exercice Masc.; **a maths exercise** un exercice de maths; **physical exercise** l'exercice physique.

exercise bicycle noun vélo Masc. d'appartement.

exercise book noun cahier Masc.; **my French exercise book** mon cahier de français.

exhaust (pipe) noun pot Masc. d'échappement.

exhausted adjective épuisé.

exhaust fumes noun gaz Masc. plural d'échappement.

exhibition noun exposition Fem.; **the Cézanne exhibition** l'exposition Cézanne.

exist verb exister [1].

exit noun sortie Fem.

expand verb s'agrandir [2]; **the town is expanding** la ville se développe.

expect verb 1 attendre [3] (guests or a baby); **we're expecting thirty people** nous attendons trente personnes; 2 s'attendre [3] à (something to happen); **I didn't expect that** je ne m'attendais pas à ça; **I didn't expect it at all** je ne m'y attendais pas du tout; 3 (as a supposition) imaginer [1]; **I expect you're tired** j'imagine que tu es fatigué; **I expect she'll bring her boyfriend** j'imagine qu'elle amènera son copain; **yes, I expect so** oui, j'imagine.

expedition noun expédition Fem.

expel verb to be expelled (from school) se faire [10] renvoyer.

expenses noun frais Masc. plural.

expensive adjective cher (Fem. chère); **those shoes are too expensive for me** ces chaussures sont trop chères pour moi; **the most expensive CDs** les CDs les plus chers.

experience noun expérience Fem.

experienced adjective expérimenté.

experiment noun expérience Fem.; **to do an experiment** faire une expérience.

expert noun spécialiste Masc. & Fem.; **he's a computer expert** c'est un spécialiste en informatique.

expire verb expirer [1].

expiry date noun date Fem. d'expiration.

explain verb expliquer [1].

explanation noun explication Fem.

explode verb exploser [1].

explore verb explorer [1].

explosion noun explosion Fem.

export noun exportation Fem.; **our chief export is wool** la laine est notre premier produit d'exportation.

export verb exporter [1]; **Russia exports a lot of oil and timber** la Russie exporte beaucoup de pétrole et de bois.

exposure noun (of a film) pose Fem.; **a 24-exposure film** une pellicule de vingt-quatre poses.

express noun (a train) rapide Masc.

express *verb* **1** exprimer [1]; **2 to express yourself** s'exprimer.

expression *noun* expression *Fem.*

extend *verb* agrandir [2] (*a building*).

extension *noun* **1** (*to a house*) addition *Fem.*; **2** (*telephone*) poste *Masc.*; **can I have extension 2347 please?** est-ce que je peux avoir le poste vingt-trois quarante-sept, s'il vous plaît? (*note that in spoken French telephone numbers are usually broken down into groups of two figures; this applies to longer numbers as well*); **3** (*electrical*) rallonge *Fem.*

extension lead *noun* rallonge *Fem.*

extension number *noun* numéro *Masc.* de poste.

exterior *adjective* extérieur.

extinct *adjective* **1** (*species*) disparu; **2** (*volcano*) éteint.

extinguish *verb* éteindre [60].

extinguisher *noun* (*fire extinguisher*) extincteur *Masc.*

extra *adjective* supplémentaire; **extra homework** des devoirs supplémentaires; **wine is extra** le vin est en supplément; **you have to pay extra** il faut payer un supplément; **at no extra charge** sans supplément.

extra *adverb* extra; **extra hot** extra-chaud; **extra large** extra-grand.

extraordinary *adjective* extraordinaire.

extra-special *adjective* exceptionnel (*Fem.* exceptionnelle).

extra time *noun* (*in football*) prolongation *Fem.*; **to go into extra time** jouer les prolongations.

extravagant *adjective* dépensier (*Fem.* dépensière) (*a person*).

extreme *noun* extrême *Masc.*; **to go to extremes** pousser les choses à l'extrême.

extreme *adjective* extrême.

extremely *adverb* extrêmement; **extremely fast** extrêmement vite.

eye *noun* œil *Masc.* (*plural* yeux); **my left eye** mon œil gauche; **a girl with blue eyes** une fille aux yeux bleus; **shut your eyes!** ferme les yeux!; ★ **to keep an eye on something** surveiller quelque chose; ★ **to make eyes at somebody** faire les yeux doux à quelqu'un.

eyebrow *noun* sourcil *Masc.*

eyelash *noun* cil *Masc.*

eyelid *noun* paupière *Fem.*

eyeliner *noun* eye-liner *Masc.*

eye make-up *noun* maquillage *Masc.* pour les yeux.

eye shadow *noun* fard *Masc.* à paupières.

eyesight *noun* vue *Fem.*

Ff

fabric *noun* (*cloth*) tissu *Masc.*

fabulous *adjective* sensationnel (*Fem.* sensationnelle).

face *noun* **1** (*of a person*) visage *Masc.*; **you've got chocolate on your face** tu as du chocolat sur le visage; **2 to pull a face** faire une

a b c d e f g h i j k l m n o p q r s t u v w x y z

grimace; **3** (of a clock or watch) cadran Masc.

face verb **1** (a person) faire [10] face à; **she faced her attacker** elle a fait face à son agresseur; **2 the house faces the garden** la maison donne sur le jardin public; **3** (to stand the idea of) avoir [5] le courage de; **I can't face going back** je n'ai pas le courage de rentrer; **4** to face up to something faire face à quelque chose.

face cloth noun gant Masc. de toilette.

facilities plural noun **1 the school has good sports facilities** l'école dispose d'un bon ensemble sportif; **2 the flat has cooking facilities** l'appartement a une cuisine équipée.

fact noun fait Masc.; **the fact is that ...** le fait est que ...; **in fact** en fait; **is that a fact?** vraiment?

factory noun usine Fem.

fade verb **1** (fabric) se décolorer [1]; **faded jeans** un jean délavé; **2 the colours have faded** les couleurs ont passé.

fail verb **1** rater [1] (a test or exam); **I failed my driving test** j'ai raté mon permis; **2** échouer [1]; **three students failed** trois étudiants ont échoué; **3** (not to do) to fail to do manquer [1] de faire; **he failed to contact us** il a manqué de nous contacter; **★ without fail** sans faute; **ring me without fail** appelle-moi sans faute.

failure noun **1** échec Masc.; **it was a terrible failure** c'était un échec terrible; **2** (a breakdown in a machine) panne Fem.; **a power failure** une panne de courant.

faint adjective **1 to feel faint** se sentir [58] mal; **2** (slight) léger (Fem. légère); **a faint smell of gas** une légère odeur de gaz; **I haven't the faintest idea** je n'en ai pas la moindre idée; **3** (a voice or sound) faible.

faint verb s'évanouir [2]; **Lisa fainted** Lisa s'est évanouie.

fair noun foire Fem.

fair adjective **1** (not unfair) juste; **it's not fair!** ce n'est pas juste!; **2** (hair) blond; **he's fair-haired** il a les cheveux blonds; **3** (skin) clair; **people with fair skin** les gens qui ont la peau claire; **4** (fairly good) assez bon (Fem. assez bonne) (a chance, condition, or performance) **her history is fair** son histoire est assez bonne; **5** (weather) **if it's fair tomorrow** s'il ne pleut pas demain.

fairground noun champ Masc. de foire.

fairly adverb (quite) assez; **she's fairly happy** elle est assez contente.

fairy noun fée Fem.

fairy tale noun conte Masc. de fées.

faith noun **1** (trust) confiance Fem.; **to have faith in somebody** avoir confiance en quelqu'un; **2** (religious belief) foi Fem.

faithful adjective fidèle.

faithfully adverb **yours faithfully** veuillez agréer, Monsieur (or Madame) mes salutations distinguées.

fake noun faux Masc.; **the diamonds were fakes** les diamants étaient des faux.

fake *adjective* faux (*Fem.* fausse) (*goes before the noun*); **a fake passport** un faux passeport.

fall *noun* chute *Fem.*; **to have a fall** tomber.

fall *verb* 1 tomber [1]; **mind, you'll fall** attention, tu vas tomber; **Tony fell off his bike** Tony est tombé de son vélo; **she fell downstairs** elle est tombée dans l'escalier; **my jacket fell on the floor** ma veste est tombée par terre; 2 (*the temperature*) descendre [3]; **it fell to minus eleven last night** il est descendu à moins onze cette nuit; 3 (*prices*) baisser [1].

false *adjective* faux (*Fem.* fausse) (*goes before the noun*); **a false alarm** une fausse alerte.

false teeth *plural noun* dentier *Masc.*

fame *noun* renommée *Fem.*

familiar *adjective* familier (*Fem.* familière); **your face is familiar** votre visage m'est familier.

family *noun* famille *Fem.*; **a family of six** une famille de six personnes; **Ben's one of the family** Ben fait partie de la famille; **the Barnes family** la famille Barnes.

family name *noun* nom *Masc.* de famille.

famous *adjective* célèbre.

fan *noun* 1 fan *Masc.* & *Fem.* (*informal*;); **Diana's an Oasis fan** Diana est une fan d'Oasis; 2 (*of a team*) supporter *Masc.*; **Brian's a Chelsea fan** Brian est un supporter de Chelsea; 3 (*electric, for cooling*) ventilateur *Masc.*;

4 (*that you hold in your hand*) éventail *Masc.*

fanatic *noun* fanatique *Masc.* & *Fem.*

fancy *noun* **to take someone's fancy** faire envie à quelqu'un; **the picture took his fancy** le tableau lui a fait envie.

fancy *adjective* (*equipment*) sophistiqué.

fancy *verb* 1 (*to want*) (**do you**) **fancy a coffee?** tu veux un café?; **do you fancy going to the new film?** ça te dirait d'aller voir le nouveau film?; 2 **I really fancy him** il me plaît beaucoup; 3 (*just*) **fancy that!** pas possible!; **fancy you being here!** tiens donc, toi ici!

fancy dress *noun* **in fancy dress** déguisé; **a fancy-dress party** une soirée déguisée.

fantastic *adjective* génial (*Masc. plural* géniaux) (*informal*); **really? that's fantastic!** vraiment? c'est génial!; **a fantastic holiday** des vacances géniales.

far *adverb, adjective* 1 loin; **it's not far** ce n'est pas loin; **is it far to Carlisle?** est-ce que Carlisle est loin d'ici?; **how far is it to Bristol?** Bristol est à quelle distance d'ici?; **he took us as far as Newport** il nous a accompagnés jusqu'à Newport; 2 **by far** de loin; **the prettiest by far** de loin le plus joli; 3 (*much*) beaucoup; **far better** beaucoup mieux; **far faster** beaucoup plus vite; **far too many people** beaucoup trop de monde; 4 **so far** jusqu'ici; **so far everything's going well** jusqu'ici

a
b
c
d
e
f
g
h
i
j
k
l
m
n
o
p
q
r
s
t
u
v
w
x
y
z

tout va bien; **★ as far as I know** pour autant que je sache.

fare noun **1** (on a bus or the underground) prix Masc. du ticket; **2** (on a train or plane) prix Masc. du billet; **half fare** demi-tarif Masc.; **full fare** plein tarif Masc.; **the return fare to Cardiff** le prix d'un aller-retour à Cardiff.

Far East noun Extrême-Orient Masc.

farm noun ferme Fem.

farmer noun agriculteur Masc., agricultrice Fem.

farmhouse noun ferme Fem.

farming noun agriculture Fem.

farthest adjective le plus éloigné; **the farthest hill** la colline la plus éloignée.

farthest adverb le plus loin; **that's the farthest we went that day** nous ne sommes pas allés plus loin ce jour-là.

fascinating adjective fascinant.

fashion noun mode Fem.; **in fashion** à la mode; **out of fashion** démodé.

fashionable adjective à la mode.

fashion model noun mannequin Masc.

fashion show noun présentation Fem. de collection.

fast adjective **1** rapide; **a fast car** une voiture rapide; **2 my watch is fast** ma montre avance; **you're ten minutes fast** ta montre avance de dix minutes.

fast adverb **1** vite; **he swims fast** il nage vite; **2 to be fast asleep** être profondément endormi.

fast food noun fast-food Masc.

fast forward noun avance Fem. rapide.

fat noun **1** (butter, cream, etc) matières Fem. plural grasses; **2** (on meat) gras Masc.; **3** (on your body) graisse Fem.

fat adjective gros (Fem. grosse) (goes before the noun); **a fat man** un gros monsieur; **to get fat** grossir.

fatal adjective (accident) mortel (Fem. mortelle).

Father's Day noun fête Fem. des Pères.

father noun père Masc.; **my father's office** le bureau de mon père.

Father Christmas noun le père Noël.

father-in-law noun beau-père Masc.

fault noun **1** (when you are responsible) faute Fem.; **it's Stephen's fault** c'est la faute de Stephen; **it's not my fault** ce n'est pas ma faute; **2** (a defect) défaut Masc.; **there's a fault in this sweater** il y a un défaut dans ce pull; **3** (in tennis) faute Fem.

favour noun **1** (a kindness) service Masc.; **to do somebody a favour** rendre service à quelqu'un; **can you do me a favour?** peux-tu me rendre service?; **to ask a favour of somebody** demander un service à quelqu'un; **2 to be in favour of something** être pour quelque chose.

favourite adjective préféré; **my favourite band** mon groupe préféré.

fax noun fax Masc.

fear noun peur Fem.

fear verb craindre [31]; **to fear the worst** craindre le pire.

feather noun plume Fem.

feature noun 1 (of your face) trait Masc.; **to have delicate features** avoir les traits délicats; 2 (of a car or a machine) caractéristique Fem.

February noun février Masc.; **in February** en février.

fed up adjective **I'm fed up** j'en ai marre (informal); **I'm fed up with working every day** j'en ai marre de travailler tous les jours.

feed verb donner [1] à manger à; **have you fed the dog?** est-ce que tu as donné à manger au chien?

feel verb 1 se sentir [58]; **I feel tired** je me sens fatigué; **I don't feel well** je ne me sens pas bien; 2 sentir [58]; **I didn't feel a thing** je n'ai rien senti; 3 **to feel afraid** avoir [5] peur; **to feel cold** avoir froid; **to feel thirsty** avoir soif; 4 **to feel like doing** avoir envie de faire; **I feel like going to the cinema** j'ai envie d'aller au cinéma; 5 (touch) toucher [1].

feeling noun 1 (in your mind) sentiment Masc.; **a feeling of embarrassment** un sentiment de gêne; **to show your feelings** montrer ses sentiments; **to hurt somebody's feelings** blesser quelqu'un; 2 (in your body) sensation Fem.; **a dizzy feeling** une sensation de vertige; 3 (an impression or intuition) impression Fem.; **I have the feeling James doesn't like me** j'ai l'impression que James ne m'aime pas.

felt-tip (pen) noun feutre Masc.

female noun (animal) femelle Fem.

female adjective 1 féminin (person, population); 2 femelle (animal, insect).

feminine adjective féminin.

feminist noun, adjective féministe Masc. & Fem.

fence noun (round a field) clôture Fem.

fern noun fougère Fem.

ferry noun ferry Masc.

fertilizer noun engrais Masc.

festival noun (for films, art, or music) festival Masc.

fetch verb aller [7] chercher; **Tom's fetching the children** Tom est allé chercher les enfants; **fetch me the other knife!** va me chercher l'autre couteau!

fever noun fièvre Fem.

few adjective, pronoun 1 peu de; **few people think that ...** peu de gens pensent que ...; **very few houses have a swimming-pool** très peu de maisons ont une piscine; 2 **a few** (followed by a noun) quelques; **a few weeks earlier** quelques semaines plus tôt; **in a few minutes** dans quelques minutes; 3 **a few** (by itself) quelques-uns (Fem. quelques-unes); **have you any tomatoes? we want a few for the salad** avez-vous des tomates? nous en voulons quelques-unes pour la salade; 4 **quite a few** pas mal de; **there were quite a few questions** il y avait pas mal de questions.

fewer adjective moins de; **there are fewer tourists this year** il y a moins de touristes cette année.

fiancé noun fiancé Masc.

fiancée noun fiancée Fem.

fiction noun I read a lot of fiction je lis beaucoup de romans.

field noun 1 (with grass or crops) champ Masc.; a field of wheat un champ de blé; 2 (for sport) terrain Masc.; 3 (the kind of work you do) domaine Masc.

fierce adjective 1 féroce (an animal or person); 2 violent (a storm or a battle).

fifteen number quinze; Lara's fifteen Lara a quinze ans.

fifth number cinquième; the fifth of January le cinq janvier; on the fifth floor au cinquième étage.

fifty number cinquante Masc.; my uncle's fifty mon oncle a cinquante ans.

fig noun figue Fem.

fight noun 1 (a scuffle) bagarre Fem.; 2 (in boxing) combat Masc.; 3 (against illness) lutte Fem.

fight verb 1 (to have a fight) se battre [21]; they were fighting ils se battaient; 2 (to quarrel) se disputer [1]; they're always fighting ils sont toujours en train de se disputer; 3 (struggle against) lutter [1] contre (poverty or a disease).

fighting noun 1 (in the streets or a pub, for example) bagarre Fem.; 2 (in war) combat Masc.

figure noun 1 (number) chiffre Masc.; a four-figure number un nombre de quatre chiffres; 2 (body shape) ligne Fem.; good for your figure bon pour la ligne; 3 (a person) personnage Masc.; a

familiar figure un personnage familier; 4 (diagram) figure Fem.

file noun 1 (for records of a person or case) dossier Masc.; 2 (ring binder) classeur Masc.; 3 (cardboard folder) chemise Fem.; 4 (on a computer) fichier Masc.; 5 a nail file une lime.

file verb 1 classer [1] (documents); 2 to file your nails se limer [1] les ongles.

fill verb remplir [2] (a container); she filled my glass elle a rempli mon verre; a smoke-filled room une pièce remplie de fumée.

● to fill in remplir [2] (a form).

● to fill in for someone remplacer [61] quelqu'un.

filling noun 1 (for a sandwich) garniture Fem.; (of meat, vegetables) farce Fem.; with an apricot filling fourré à l'abricot; 2 (in tooth) plombage Masc.

film noun 1 (in a cinema) film Masc.; shall we go and see a film? si on allait voir un film?; the new film about Picasso le nouveau film au sujet de Picasso; 2 (for a camera) pellicule Fem.; a 24-exposure colour film une pellicule couleur de 24 poses.

film star noun vedette Fem. de cinéma.

filter noun filtre Masc.

filthy adjective dégoûtant.

fin noun nageoire Fem.

final noun (in sport) finale Fem.

final adjective dernier (Fem. dernière); the final instalment le dernier épisode; the final result le résultat final.

finally adverb finalement.
find verb trouver [1]; **did you find your passport?** as-tu trouvé ton passeport?; **I can't find my keys** je ne trouve pas mes clefs.

● **to find out 1** (to enquire) se renseigner [1]; **I don't know, I'll find out** je ne sais pas, je me renseignerai; **2 to find something out** découvrir [30] (the facts or an answer); **when Lucy found out the truth** quand Lucy a découvert la vérité.

fine noun amende Fem. (for parking or speeding) contravention Fem.

fine adjective **1** (in good health) bien; **'how are you?' – 'fine, thanks'** 'comment ça va?' – 'très bien merci'; **2** (very good) excellent; **she's a fine athlete** c'est une excellente athlète; **ten o'clock? yes, that's fine** dix heures? oui, très bien; **Friday will be fine** vendredi sera très bien; **4** (sunny) beau (Fem. belle) (weather or a day); **if it's fine** s'il fait beau; **5** (not coarse or thick) fin; **in fine wool** en laine fine.

finely adjective (chopped or grated) finement.

finger noun doigt Masc.; ★ **I'll keep my fingers crossed for you** je croise les doigts pour toi.

fingernail noun ongle Masc.

finish noun **1** (end) fin Fem.; **2** (in a race) arrivée Fem.

finish verb **1** finir [2]; wait, I haven't finished attends, je n'ai pas fini; **when does school finish?** à quelle heure finit l'école?; **2** (to finish off) terminer [1] (work or a project); **have you finished the**

book? est-ce que tu as terminé le livre?; **3 to finish doing** finir de faire; **have you finished telephoning?** as-tu fini de téléphoner?

● **to finish with** finir avec; **have you finished with the computer?** as-tu fini avec l'ordinateur?.

finishing line noun ligne Fem. d'arrivée.

Finland noun Finlande Fem.; **in Finland** en Finlande; **to Finland** en Finlande.

Finnish noun finnois Masc. (the language).

Finnish adjective finlandais.

fire noun **1** (in a grate) feu Masc.; **to light a fire** allumer un feu; **sitting by the fire** assis près du feu; **2 to catch fire** prendre feu; **3** (accidental) incendie Masc.; **a fire in a factory** un incendie dans une usine.

fire verb **1** (to shoot) tirer [1]; **the soldiers were firing** les soldats tiraient; **to fire at somebody** tirer sur quelqu'un; **2** décharger (a gun).

fire alarm noun alarme Fem. incendie.

fire brigade noun pompiers Masc. plural.

fire engine noun voiture Fem. des pompiers.

fire escape noun escalier Masc. de secours.

fire extinguisher noun extincteur Masc.

fire fighter noun pompier Masc.

fireplace noun cheminée Fem.

fire station noun caserne Fem. de pompiers.

a **firework** noun feu Masc. d'artifice (plural **feux d'artifice**); **there will be a firework display** il y aura un feu d'artifice.

b
c **firm** noun (business) entreprise Fem.

d **firm** adjective ferme.

e **first** adjective, adverb **1** premier (Fem. première); **Susan's the first** Susan est la première; **the first of May** le premier mai; **for the first time** pour la première fois; **I came first in the 200 metres** je suis arrivé premier aux 200 mètres; **2** (to begin with) d'abord; **first, I'm going to make some tea** d'abord je vais faire du thé; **3 at first** au début; **at first he was shy** au début il était timide.

f
g
h
i
j
k **first aid** noun premiers secours Masc. plural.

l
m **first-aid kit** noun trousse Fem. de secours.

n **first class** adjective **1** de première classe (a ticket, carriage, or hotel); **a first-class compartment** un compartiment de première classe; **he always travels first class** il voyage toujours en première; **2** au tarif rapide (a letter or stamp); **six first-class stamps** six timbres au tarif rapide.

o
p
q
r
s **first floor** noun premier étage Masc.; **on the first floor** au premier étage.

t
u **firstly** adverb premièrement.

v **first name** noun prénom Masc.

w **fir tree** noun sapin Masc.

x **fish** noun poisson Masc.; **do you like fish?** aimez-vous le poisson?

y
z

fish verb pêcher [1]; **Dad was fishing for trout** Papa pêchait la truite.

fish and chips noun poisson Masc. frit avec des frites.

fisherman noun pêcheur Masc.

fishing noun pêche Fem.; **I love fishing** j'adore la pêche; **to go fishing** aller à la pêche.

fishing rod noun canne Fem. à pêche.

fishing tackle noun matériel Masc. de pêche.

fist noun poing Masc.

fit noun **1** (of rage) **to have a fit** piquer une crise; **your dad'll have a fit when he sees your hair!** ton père va piquer une crise quand il va voir tes cheveux!; **2 an epileptic fit** une crise d'épilepsie.

fit adjective (healthy) en forme; **I feel really fit** je me sens vraiment en forme; **to keep fit** se maintenir en forme.

fit verb **1** (to be the right size for) (a garment) être [6] de la taille de (a person); (shoes) être à la pointure de; **this skirt doesn't fit me** cette jupe n'est pas à ma taille; **2** (be able to be put into) aller [7] dans; **will my cases all fit in the car?** est-ce que mes valises iront dans la voiture?; **the key doesn't fit in the lock** la clé ne va pas dans la serrure; **3** (install) installer [1]; **they've fitted an alarm** ils ont installé une alarme.

fitness noun forme Fem.; **fitness training** exercices Masc. plural de mise en forme.

fitted carpet noun moquette Fem.

fitted kitchen noun cuisine Fem. intégrée.

fitting room noun cabine Fem. d'essayage.

five number cinq Masc.; **Belinda's five** Belinda a cinq ans; **it's five o'clock** il est cinq heures.

fix verb 1 (repair) réparer [1]; **Mum's fixed the computer** Maman a réparé l'ordinateur; 2 (to decide on) fixer [1]; **to fix a date** fixer une date; **at a fixed price** à prix fixe; 3 préparer [1] (a meal); **I'll fix supper** c'est moi qui vais préparer le repas du soir.

fizzy adjective gazeux (Fem. gazeuse); **fizzy water** eau Fem. gazeuse.

flag noun drapeau Masc. (plural drapeaux).

flame noun flamme Fem.

flamingo noun flamant Masc. rose.

flan noun tarte Fem.; **an onion flan** une tarte à l'oignon.

flap verb battre [21]; **the bird flapped its wings** l'oiseau battait des ailes.

flash noun 1 **a flash of lightning** un éclair; 2 **to do something in a flash** faire quelque chose en un clin d'œil; 3 (on a camera) flash Masc.

flash verb 1 (a light) clignoter [1]; 2 **to flash by or past** passer [1] comme un éclair; 3 **to flash your headlights** faire [10] un appel de phares.

flashback noun flash-back Masc.

flask noun 1 (insulated bottle) thermos™ Masc. or Fem.; 2 (container) flacon Masc.

flat noun appartement Masc.; **a third-floor flat** un appartement au troisième étage.

flat adjective plat; **flat shoes** des chaussures plates; **a flat landscape** un paysage plat; 2 **a flat tyre** un pneu crevé.

flatmate noun colocataire Masc. & Fem.

flatter verb flatter [1].

flattering adjective flatteur (Fem. flatteuse).

flavour noun 1 (taste) goût Masc.; **the sauce had no flavour** la sauce n'avait aucun goût; 2 (of drink, ice cream, etc.) parfum Masc.; **what flavour of ice cream would you like?** tu veux quel parfum de glace?

flavour verb parfumer [1]; **vanilla-flavoured** parfumé à la vanille.

flea noun puce Fem.

flea market noun marché Masc. aux puces.

fleet noun 1 (of ships) flotte Fem.; 2 (of vehicles) parc Masc.

flesh noun chair Fem.

flex noun fil Masc.

flexible adjective flexible (an arrangement).

flight noun 1 vol Masc.; **a charter flight** un vol charter; **the flight from Moscow is delayed** le vol de Moscou est retardé; 2 **a flight of stairs** un escalier; **four flights of stairs** quatre étages.

flight attendant noun 1 (male) steward Masc.; 2 (female) hôtesse Fem. de l'air.

fling verb lancer [61].

flipper noun (for a swimmer) palme Fem.

flirt verb flirter [1].

float verb flotter [1].

flood noun **1** (of water) inondation Fem.; **the floods in the south** les inondations au sud; **to be in floods of tears** verser des torrents de larmes; **2** (of letters or complaints) déluge Masc.

flood verb inonder [1].

floodlight noun projecteur Masc.

floor noun **1** (wooden) plancher Masc. (concrete) sol Masc.; **to sweep the floor** balayer; **to sweep the kitchen floor** balayer la cuisine; **your glasses are on the floor** tes lunettes sont par terre; **2** (a storey) étage Masc.; **on the second floor** au deuxième étage.

floppy disk noun disquette Fem.

florist noun fleuriste Masc. & Fem.

flour noun farine Fem.

flow verb couler [1].

flower noun fleur Fem.; **a bunch of flowers** un bouquet.

flower verb fleurir [2].

flu noun grippe Fem.; **to have flu** avoir la grippe.

fluent adjective **she speaks fluent Italian** elle parle couramment l'italien.

fluently adverb couramment.

fluid noun liquide Masc.

flush verb **1** (to go red) rougir [2]; **2** to flush the lavatory tirer [1] la chasse.

flute noun flûte Fem.; **to play the flute** jouer de la flûte.

fly noun mouche Fem.

fly verb **1** (a bird, a bee, or a plane) voler [1]; **2** (in a plane) prendre [64]

l'avion; **we flew to Edinburgh** nous sommes allés à Édimbourg en avion; **we flew from Gatwick** nous sommes partis de Gatwick; **3** faire [10] voler (a kite); **4** (to pass quickly) (time) passer [1] très vite.

fly spray noun bombe Fem. insecticide.

foam noun **1** (foam rubber) mousse Fem.; **a foam mattress** un matelas mousse; **2** (on a drink) mousse Fem.

focus noun **to be in focus** être au point; **to be out of focus** être flou.

focus verb mettre [11] au point (a camera).

fog noun brouillard Masc.

foggy adjective brumeux (Fem. brumeuse) (weather); **it was foggy** il y avait du brouillard.

foil noun (kitchen foil) papier Masc. aluminium.

fold noun pli Masc.

fold verb **1** plier [1]; **to fold something up** plier quelque chose; **2** to fold your arms croiser [1] les bras.

folder noun chemise Fem.

folding adjective pliant; **a folding table** une table pliante.

follow verb suivre [75]; **follow me!** suivez-moi!; **followed by a dinner** suivi d'un dîner; **do you follow me?** vous me suivez?

following adjective suivant; **the following year** l'année suivante.

fond adjective **to be fond of somebody** aimer beaucoup quelqu'un; **I'm very fond of him** je l'aime beaucoup.

food noun **1** nourriture Fem.; **to buy food** acheter à manger; **I like**

French food j'aime la cuisine française; **2** (*stocks*) provisions *Fem. plural*; **we bought food for the holiday** nous avons acheté des provisions pour les vacances.

food poisoning *noun* intoxication *Fem.* alimentaire.

fool *noun* idiot *Masc.*, idiote *Fem.*

foot *noun* **1** pied *Masc.*; **Lucy came on foot** Lucy est venue à pied; **2** (*the bottom*) **at the foot of the stairs** en bas de l'escalier.

football *noun* **1** (*the game*) football *Masc.*; **to play football** jouer au football; **2** (*ball*) ballon *Masc.* de football.

footballer *noun* joueur *Masc.* de football, joueuse *Fem.* de football.

footpath *noun* sentier *Masc.*

footprint *noun* empreinte *Fem.*

footstep *noun* pas *Masc.*

for *preposition* **1** pour; **a present for my mother** un cadeau pour ma mère; **petrol for the car** de l'essence pour la voiture; **sausages for lunch** des saucisses pour le déjeuner; **it's for cleaning** c'est pour nettoyer; **what's it for?** c'est pour quoi faire?; **2** (*time expressions in the past or future*) pendant; **I studied French for six years** (*but I no longer do*) j'ai étudié le français pendant six ans; **I'll be away for four days** je serai absent pendant quatre jours; **3** (*time expressions in the past but continuing in the present*) depuis; **I've been waiting here for an hour** (*and I'm still waiting*) j'attends ici depuis une heure; **my brother's been living in Paris for three** years (*and he still lives there*) mon frère habite à Paris depuis trois ans; **4 I sold my bike for fifty pounds** j'ai vendu mon vélo cinquante livres; **5 what's the French for 'bee'?** comment dit-on 'bee' en français?

forbid *verb* défendre [3]; **to forbid somebody to do something** défendre à quelqu'un de faire quelque chose; **I forbid you to go out** je te défends de sortir.

forbidden *adjective* défendu.

force *noun* force *Fem.*

force *verb* forcer [61]; **to force somebody to do** forcer quelqu'un à faire.

forecast *noun* (*weather forecast*) météo *Fem.*

forefinger *noun* index *Masc.*

foreground *noun* premier plan *Masc.*; **in the foreground** au premier plan.

forehead *noun* front *Masc.*

foreign *adjective* étranger (*Fem.* étrangère); **in a foreign country** dans un pays étranger.

foreigner *noun* étranger *Masc.*, étrangère *Fem.*

foresee *verb* prévoir [65].

forest *noun* forêt *Fem.*

forever *adverb* **1** pour toujours; **I'd like to stay here forever** j'aimerais rester là pour toujours; **2** (*non-stop*) sans arrêt; **he's forever asking questions** il pose sans arrêt des questions.

forgery *noun* **1** (*picture*) faux *Masc.*; **2** (*signature, banknote*) contrefaçon *Fem.*

a **forget** verb oublier [1]; **I forget his name** j'oublie son nom; **we've forgotten the bread!** nous avons oublié le pain!; **to forget to do** oublier de faire; **I forgot to phone** j'ai oublié d'appeler; **to forget about something** oublier quelque chose.

forgive verb pardonner [1] à; **to forgive somebody** pardonner à quelqu'un; **I forgave him** je lui ai pardonné; **to forgive somebody for doing** pardonner à quelqu'un d'avoir fait; **I forgave her for losing my ring** je lui ai pardonné d'avoir perdu ma bague.

fork noun fourchette Fem.

form noun **1** formulaire Masc.; **to fill in a form** remplir un formulaire; **2** (shape or kind) forme Fem.; **in the form of** sous forme de; **3 to be on form** être en forme; **4** (in school) classe Fem.

form verb former [1].

formal adjective officiel (Fem. officielle) (invitation, event, complaint, etc.).

format noun format Masc.

former adjective ancien (Fem. ancienne) (goes before the noun); **a former pupil** un ancien élève.

formula noun formule Fem.

fortnight noun quinze jours Masc. plural; **we're going to Spain for a fortnight** nous allons passer quinze jours en Espagne.

fortress noun forteresse Fem.

fortunate adjective **to be fortunate** avoir [5] de la chance.

fortunately adverb heureusement.

fortune noun fortune Fem.; **to make a fortune** gagner [1] beaucoup d'argent.

forty number quarante; **my aunt's forty** ma tante a quarante ans.

forward noun (in sport) avant Masc.

forward adverb **to move forward** avancer; **a seat further forward** une place plus en avant.

foster child noun enfant Masc. adoptif, enfant Fem. adoptive.

foul noun (in sport) faute Fem.

foul adjective infect; **the weather's foul** il fait un temps infect.

fountain noun fontaine Fem.

fountain pen noun stylo Masc. à encre.

four number quatre Masc.; **Simon's four** Simon a quatre ans; **it's four o'clock** il est quatre heures; ★ **on all fours** à quatre pattes.

fourteen number quatorze Masc.; **Susie's fourteen** Susie a quatorze ans.

fourth number quatrième; **the fourth of July** le quatre juillet; **on the fourth floor** au quatrième étage.

fox noun renard Masc.

fracture noun fracture Fem.

fragile adjective fragile.

frame noun **1** (of picture) cadre Masc.; **2** (of door) encadrement Masc.

franc noun franc Masc.; (the currency of Switzerland; name of the currencies used in France, Belgium and Luxembourg until replaced by the euro; 100 French francs = 15.24 euros).

France noun France Fem.; **in France** en France; **to France** en France; **I like France** j'aime la France; **Nadine's from France** Nadine est française.

frantic adjective 1 (very upset) fou (Fem. folle); **Mum was frantic with worry** Maman était folle d'inquiétude; 2 (desperate) désespéré (efforts or a search).

freckle noun tache Fem. de rousseur.

free adjective 1 (when you don't pay) gratuit; **the bus is free** le bus est gratuit; **a free ticket** un billet gratuit; 2 (not occupied) libre; **are you free on Thursday?** es-tu libre jeudi?; 3 **sugar-free** sans sucre; **lead-free** sans plomb.

free verb libérer [24].

freedom noun liberté Fem.

free gift noun cadeau Masc. (plural cadeaux).

free kick noun coup Masc. franc.

freeze verb 1 (in a freezer) congeler [45]; **frozen peas** des petits pois congelés; 2 (in cold weather) geler [45]; **it's freezing outside** il gèle dehors.

freezer noun congélateur Masc.

freezing noun zéro Masc.; **three degrees below freezing** trois degrés en-dessous de zéro.

freezing adjective **I'm freezing** je suis gelé (informal); **it's freezing outside** il fait très froid dehors.

French noun 1 (the language) français Masc.; **to speak French** parler français; **say it in French** dis-le en français; **to learn French** apprendre le français; 2 (the

people) **the French** les Français Masc. plural; **most of the French** la plupart des Français.

French adjective 1 français; **Jean-Marc is French** Jean-Marc est français; 2 de français (a teacher or a lesson); **the French class** le cours de français.

French bean noun haricot Masc. vert.

French dressing noun vinaigrette Fem.

French fries plural noun frites Fem. plural.

Frenchman noun Français Masc.

French stick noun baguette Fem.

French window noun porte-fenêtre Fem. (plural portes-fenêtres).

Frenchwoman noun Française Fem.

frequent adjective fréquent.

frequently adverb souvent.

fresh adjective frais (Fem. fraîche); **fresh eggs** des œufs frais; **I'm going out for some fresh air** je vais prendre de l'air.

Friday noun vendredi Masc.; **next Friday** vendredi prochain; **last Friday** vendredi dernier; **on Friday** vendredi; **I'll phone you on Friday evening** je t'appellerai vendredi soir; **on Fridays** le vendredi; **closed on Fridays** fermé le vendredi; **every Friday** tous les vendredis; **Good Friday** le Vendredi saint.

fridge noun frigo Masc. (informal); **put it in the fridge** mets-le au frigo.

friend noun ami Masc., amie Fem.; **a friend of mine** un ami (or une

a
b
c
d
e
f
g
h
i
j
k
l
m
n
o
p
q
r
s
t
u
v
w
x
y
z

a

amie) à moi; **to make friends** (*in a general way*) se faire des amis; **he made friends with Danny** il est devenu ami avec Danny.

friendly *adjective* sympathique.

friendship *noun* amitié *Fem.*

fries *plural noun* frites *Fem. plural.*

fright *noun* peur *Fem.*; **to have or get a fright** avoir peur; **you gave me a fright!** tu m'as fait peur!

frighten *verb* effrayer [59].

frightened *adjective* **to be frightened** avoir peur; **Martin's frightened of snakes** Martin a peur des serpents.

frightening *adjective* effrayant.

fringe *noun* frange *Fem.*

frog *noun* grenouille *Fem.*

from *preposition* de; **a letter from Tom** une lettre de Tom; **100 metres from the cinema** à cent mètres du cinéma; **from Monday to Friday** du lundi jusqu'au vendredi; **he comes from Dublin** il vient de Dublin; **two years from now** d'ici deux ans; **from seven o'clock onwards** à partir de sept heures.

front *noun* **1** (*of a building, a garment, or a cupboard*) devant *Masc.*; **2** (*of a car*) avant *Masc.*; **sitting in the front** assis à l'avant; **3** (*of a train or a queue*) tête *Fem.*; **there are seats at the front of the train** il y a des places en tête du train; **4** (*of a card or envelope*) recto *Masc.*; **the address is on the front** l'adresse est au recto; **5** (*in a theatre, cinema, or class*) premier rang *Masc.*; **seats at the front** des places au premier rang; **6 in front of** devant; **in front of the TV**

devant la télé; **in front of me** devant moi.

front *adjective* **1** de devant; **his front paw** sa patte de devant; **in the front row** au premier rang; **2** avant; **the front seat** (*of a car*) le siège avant; **the front wheel** la roue avant.

front door *noun* porte *Fem.* d'entrée.

frontier *noun* frontière *Fem.*

frost *noun* gel *Masc.*

frosty *adjective* **1 it's frosty this morning** il gèle ce matin; **2** couvert de givre (*windscreen, grass, etc.*).

frown *verb* froncer [61] les sourcils; **he frowned at us** il nous a regardés en fronçant les sourcils.

frozen *adjective* (*in a freezer*) surgelé; **a frozen pizza** une pizza surgelée.

fruit *noun* fruits *Masc. plural* (*note that in French 'un fruit' is a piece of fruit, whereas 'fruit' in English meaning several pieces of fruit always has to be 'fruits' in the plural in French*) **we bought cheese and fruit** nous avons acheté du fromage et des fruits; **fruit juice** le jus de fruits.

fruit machine *noun* machine *Fem.* à sous.

fruit salad *noun* salade *Fem.* de fruits.

frustrated *adjective* frustré.

frustrating *adjective* frustrant.

fry *verb* faire [10] frire; **we fried the fish** nous avons fait frire les poissons; **a fried egg** un œuf au plat.

frying pan *noun* poêle *Fem.*

fuel noun (for a vehicle or plane) carburant Masc.

full adjective **1** plein; **this glass is full** ce verre est plein; **the train was full of tourists** le train était plein de touristes; **2** complet (Fem. complète) (a hotel or flight); **3** (top) **at full speed** à toute vitesse; **at full volume** à plein volume; **4** I'm full j'ai assez mangé; **5** to write something out in full écrire quelque chose en toutes lettres.

full stop noun point Masc.

full-time adjective **a full-time job** un travail à plein temps.

full time noun (in sport) fin Fem. du match.

fully adjective entièrement.

fun noun plaisir Masc.; **to have fun** s'amuser; **have fun!** amusez-vous bien!; **we had fun catching the ponies** nous nous sommes beaucoup amusés en attrapant les poneys; **skiing is fun** c'est amusant de faire du ski; **I do it for fun** je le fais pour m'amuser; ★ **to make fun of somebody** se moquer de quelqu'un.

funds plural noun fonds Masc. plural.

funeral noun enterrement Masc.

funfair noun fête Fem. foraine.

funny adjective **1** (when you laugh) drôle; **how funny you are!** que tu es drôle!; **a funny story** une histoire drôle; **2** (strange) bizarre; **that's funny, I'm sure I paid** c'est bizarre, je suis certain que j'ai payé; **a funny noise** un bruit bizarre.

fur noun **1** (on an animal) poils Masc. plural; **2** (for a coat) fourrure Fem.; **a fur coat** un manteau de fourrure.

furious adjective furieux (Fem. furieuse); **she was furious with Steve** elle était furieuse contre Steve.

furniture noun meubles Masc. plural; **to buy some furniture** acheter des meubles; **a piece of furniture** un meuble.

further adverb plus loin; **further than the station** plus loin que la gare; **ten kilometres further on** dix kilomètres plus loin; **further forward** plus en avant; **further back** plus en arrière.

fuse noun fusible Masc.

fuss noun histoires Fem. plural; **to make a fuss** faire des histoires; **to make a fuss about the bill** faire toute une histoire à propos de l'addition.

fussy adjective **to be fussy about something** être difficile sur quelque chose (food, for example).

future noun **1** avenir Masc.; **in future** à l'avenir; **in the future** dans l'avenir; **2** (in grammar) futur Masc.; **a verb in the future** un verbe au futur.

Gg

gadget noun gadget Masc.

gain verb gagner [1]; **in order to gain time** pour gagner du temps; **we have nothing to gain** nous n'avons rien à gagner; **2 to gain**

speed prendre de la vitesse; **to gain weight** prendre du poids.

galaxy noun galaxie Fem.

gale noun vent Masc. violent.

gallery noun **an art gallery** (public) un musée; (private) une galerie.

gamble verb jouer [1].

gambling noun jeu Masc.

game noun **1** (jeu Masc.; **children's games** les jeux d'enfant; **a game of chance** un jeu de hasard; **a board game** un jeu de société; **2 a game of** une partie de; **to have a game of cards** faire une partie de cartes; **3** match Masc.; **a game of football** un match de foot; **to be good at games:** Jack's **very good at games** Jack est très bon en sport.

gang noun bande Fem.; **all the gang were there** toute la bande y était.

gangster noun gangster Masc.

gap noun **1** (hole) trou Masc.; **2** (in time) intervalle Masc.; **a two-year gap** un intervalle de deux ans; **an age gap** une différence d'âge.

gap year noun année Fem. sabbatique avant d'entrer à l'université.

garage noun garage Masc.

garden noun jardin Masc.

gardener noun jardinier Masc.; **he wants to be a gardener** il veut être jardinier.

gardening noun jardinage Masc.

garlic noun ail Masc.

garlic mayonnaise noun aïoli Masc.

garment noun vêtement Masc.

gas noun gaz Masc.

gas cooker noun cuisinière Fem. à gaz.

gas fire noun radiateur Masc. à gaz.

gas meter noun compteur Masc. à gaz.

gate noun **1** (garden) portail Masc.; **2** (field) barrière Fem.; **3** (at the airport) porte Fem.

gather verb **1** (people) se rassembler [1]; **a crowd gathered** une foule s'est rassemblée; **2** cueillir [35] (fruit, vegetables, flowers); **3 as far as I can gather** autant que je sache.

gay adjective homosexuel (Fem. homosexuelle).

gaze verb **to gaze at something** regarder [1] quelque chose.

GCSEs noun plural You can explain GCSEs briefly as follows: Ce sont des examens que l'on passe à environ 16 ans dans un certain nombre de matières (12 au maximum). La meilleure note que l'on peut obtenir est A-star et la note la plus basse est N. Une fois qu'ils ont obtenu leurs GCSEs, de nombreux étudiants se préparent pour les A levels. SEE **A levels.**

gear noun **1** (in a car) vitesse Fem.; **to change gear** changer de vitesse; **2** (equipment) matériel Masc.; **camping gear** du matériel de camping; **3** (things) affaires; **I've left all my gear at Gary's** j'ai laissé toutes mes affaires chez Gary.

gear lever noun levier Masc. de vitesses.

gel noun **hair gel** le gel pour les cheveux.

Gemini noun Gémeaux Masc. plural; **Steph's Gemini** Steph est Gémeaux.

gender noun (of a word) genre Masc.; **what is the gender of 'maison'?** quel est le genre de 'maison'?

general noun général Masc. (plural généraux); **General Jackson** le général Jackson.

general adjective général (Masc. plural généraux); **in general** en général.

general election noun élections Fem. plural législatives.

general knowledge noun connaissances Fem. plural générales.

generally adverb généralement.

generation noun génération Fem.

generator noun générateur Masc.

generous adjective généreux (Fem. généreuse).

genetics noun génétique Fem.

Geneva noun Genève; **to Geneva** à Genève; **in Geneva** à Genève; **Lake Geneva** le lac Léman.

genius noun génie Masc.; **Lisa, you're a genius!** Lisa, tu es un génie!

gentle adjective doux (Fem. douce).

gentleman noun monsieur Masc. (plural messieurs); **ladies and gentlemen** mesdames et messieurs.

gently adverb doucement.

gents noun toilettes Fem. plural, (marked on the door) 'Messieurs'; **where's the gents?** où sont les toilettes?

genuine adjective 1 (real) véritable; **a genuine diamond** un véritable diamant; 2 (authentic) authentique; **a genuine signature** une signature authentique; 3 sincère (person); **she's very genuine** elle est très sincère.

geography noun géographie Fem.

geology noun géologie Fem.

geometry noun géométrie Fem.

germ noun microbe Masc.

German noun 1 Allemand Masc., Allemande Fem.; 2 (language) allemand.

German adjective allemand.

Germany noun Allemagne Fem.; **to Germany** en Allemagne; **in Germany** en Allemagne.

get verb 1 (have, receive) avoir [5]; **he's got lots of money** il a beaucoup d'argent; **she's got long hair** elle a les cheveux longs; **I got a bike for my birthday** j'ai eu un vélo pour mon anniversaire; **I got your letter yesterday** j'ai eu ta lettre hier; **I got fifteen for my French homework** j'ai eu quinze pour mon devoir français; 2 (fetch) chercher [1]; **I'll go and get some bread** j'irai chercher du pain; **I'll get your bag for you** je te chercherai ton sac; 3 (obtain) trouver [1]; **Fred's got a job** Fred a trouvé un emploi; **where did you get that jacket?** où est-ce que tu as trouvé cette veste? 4 **to have got to do** devoir [8] faire; **I've got to phone before midday** je dois appeler avant midi; 5 **to get to somewhere** arriver [1] quelque part; **when we got to London** quand nous sommes arrivés à Londres; **to get here** (or there)

a
b
c
d
e
f
g
h
i
j
k
l
m
n
o
p
q
r
s
t
u
v
w
x
y
z

arriver; **we got here this morning** nous sommes arrivés ce matin; **what time did they get there?** ile sont arrivés à quelle heure?; **6** (*become*) commencer à être; **I'm getting tired** je commence à être fatigué; **it's getting late** il commence à être tard; **it's getting dark** il commence à faire nuit; **I'm getting hungry** je commence à avoir faim; **7 to get something done** faire [10] faire quelque chose; **I'm getting my hair cut this afternoon** je vais me faire couper les cheveux cet après-midi.

● **to get back** rentrer [1]; **Mum gets back at six** Maman rentre à six heures.

● **to get something back** récupérer [24] quelque chose; **did you get your books back?** est-ce que tu as récupéré tes livres?

● **to get into something** monter [1] dans quelque chose (*a vehicle*); **he got into the car** il est monté dans la voiture.

● **to get off something** descendre [3] de quelque chose; **I got off the train at Banbury** je suis descendu du train à Banbury.

● **to get on** aller [7]; **how's Amanda getting on?** comment va Amanda?

● **to get on something** monter [1] dans quelque chose (*vehicle*); **she got on the train at Reading** elle est montée dans le train à Reading.

● **to get on with somebody** s'entendre [3] avec quelqu'un; **she doesn't get on with her brother** elle ne s'entend pas avec son frère.

● **to get out of something** descendre [3] de quelque chose

(*vehicle*); **Laura got out of the car** Laura est descendue de la voiture.

● **to get something out** [72] quelque chose; **Robert got his guitar out** Robert a sorti sa guitare.

● **to get together** se voir; [13]; **we must get together soon** il faut qu'on se voie bientôt.

● **to get up** se lever; [50]; **I get up at seven** je me lève à sept heures.

ghost noun fantôme Masc.

giant noun géant Masc., géante Fem.

giant adjective énorme; **a giant lorry** un énorme camion.

giddy adjective **to feel giddy** avoir [5] le tournis; **I'm feeling giddy** j'ai le tournis.

gift noun **1** cadeau Masc. (*plural* cadeaux); **a Christmas gift** un cadeau de Noël; **2 to have a gift for something** être doué pour quelque chose; **Jo has a real gift for languages** Jo est vraiment douée pour les langues.

gifted adjective doué.

gig noun concert Masc. de rock.

gigabyte noun gigaoctet Masc.; **a twenty gigabyte hard disk** un disque dur de 20 gigaoctets.

gigantic adjective gigantesque.

gin noun gin Masc.

ginger noun gingembre Masc.

gipsy noun **1** (*in general*) bohémien Masc., bohémienne Fem.; **2** (*from Spain*) gitan Masc., gitane Fem.; **3** (*from Eastern Europe*) tsigane Masc. & Fem.

giraffe noun giraffe Fem.

girl noun **1** fille Fem.; **three boys and four girls** trois garçons et quatre filles; **a little girl** une petite fille; **when I was a little girl** quand j'étais petite; **2** (*a teenager or young woman*) jeune fille Fem.; **an eighteen-year-old girl** une jeune fille de dix-huit ans.

girlfriend noun copine Fem.; **Darren's gone out with his girlfriend** Darren est sorti avec sa copine; **Lizzie and her girlfriends have gone to the cinema** Lizzie et ses copines sont allées au cinéma.

give verb donner [1]; **to give something to somebody** donner quelque chose à quelqu'un; **I'll give you my address** je te donnerai mon adresse; **give me the key** donne-moi la clé; **Yasmin's dad gave her the money** le père de Yasmin lui a donné l'argent.

● **to give something away** donner quelque chose; **she's given away all her books** elle a donné tous ses livres.

● **to give something back to somebody** rendre [3] quelque chose à quelqu'un; **I gave her back the keys** je lui ai rendu les clés.

● **to give in** céder [24]; **my mum said no but she gave in in the end** maman a dit non, mais elle a fini par céder.

● **to give up** abandonner [1]; **I give up!** j'abandonne!

● **to give up doing** arrêter [1] de faire; **she's given up smoking** elle a arrêté de fumer.

glacier noun glacier Masc.

glad adjective content; **I'm glad to hear he's better** je suis content d'apprendre qu'il va mieux; **I'm**

glad to be back je suis content d'être de retour.

glamorous adjective **1** (*life*) luxueux (Fem. luxueuse); **2** (*job*) prestigieux (Fem. prestigieuse); **3** (*woman*) élégant.

glance noun coup d'œil Masc.

glance verb **to glance at something** jeter [48] un coup d'œil à quelque chose; **Sara glanced at the envelope** Sara a jeté un coup d'œil à l'enveloppe.

glass noun verre Masc.; **a glass of water** un verre d'eau; **a glass table** une table en verre.

glasses plural noun lunettes Fem. plural; **to wear glasses** porter des lunettes.

glider noun planeur Masc.

global adjective mondial (Masc. plural mondiaux).

global warming noun le réchauffement de la planète.

globe noun globe Masc.

gloomy adjective **1** (*expression*) lugubre; **2** (*weather*) déprimant.

glory noun gloire Fem.

glove noun gant Masc.; **a pair of gloves** une paire de gants.

glove compartment noun boîte Fem. à gants.

glue noun colle Fem.

go noun **1** (*in a game*) whose go is it? c'est à qui de jouer?; **it's my go** c'est à moi de jouer; **2 to have a go at doing** essayer de faire; **I'll have a go at mending it for you** j'essaierai de le réparer pour toi.

go verb **1** aller [7]; **we're going to London tomorrow** nous allons à Londres demain; **Mark's gone to**

the dentist's Mark est allé chez le dentiste; **to go for a walk** aller se promener; **2** *(with another verb)* aller; **I'm going to make some tea** je vais faire du thé; **he was going to phone me** il allait m'appeler; **3** *(leave)* partir [58]; **Pauline's already gone** Pauline est déjà partie; **we're going on holiday tomorrow** nous partons en vacances demain; **4** *(an event)* se passer [1]; **did the party go well?** est-ce que la soirée s'est bien passée?

● **to go away** s'en aller [7]; **go away!** va-t-en!

● **to go back** retourner [1]; **I'm going back to France in March** je retourne en France en mars; **I'm not going back there again!** je n'y retourne plus!; **2** *(to home, school, office)* rentrer [1]; **I went back home** je suis rentré chez moi

● **to go down** 1 descendre [3]; **she's gone down to the kitchen** elle est descendue dans la cuisine; **to go down the stairs** descendre l'escalier; **2** *(price, temperature)* baisser [1]; **prices have gone down** les prix ont baissé; **3** *(tyre, balloon, airbed)* se dégonfler [1].

● **to go in** entrer [1]; **he went in and shut the door** il est entré et il a fermé la porte.

● **to go into** 1 *(person)* entrer dans; **Fran went into the kitchen** Fran est entrée dans la cuisine; **2** *(object)* rentrer [1] dans; **this file won't go into my bag** ce classeur ne rentre pas dans mon sac

● **to go off** 1 *(bomb)* exploser [1]; **2** *(alarm clock)* sonner [1]; **my**

alarm clock went off at six mon réveil a sonné à six heures; **3** *(fire or burglar alarm)* se déclencher [1]; **the fire alarm went off** l'alarme d'incendie s'est déclenchée

● **to go on** 1 se passer [1]; **what's going on?** qu'est-ce qui se passe?; **2** to go on doing continuer [1] à faire; **she went on talking** elle a continué à parler; **3** to go on about something ne pas arrêter [1] de parler de quelque chose; **he's always going on about his dog** il n'arrête pas de parler de son chien

● **to go out** 1 sortir [72]; **I'm going out tonight** je sors ce soir; **she went out of the kitchen** elle est sortie de la cuisine; **2** to be going out with somebody sortir avec quelqu'un; **she's going out with my brother** elle sort avec mon frère; **3** *(light, fire)* s'éteindre [60]; **the light went out** la lumière s'est éteinte

● **to go past something** passer [1] devant quelque chose; **we went past your house** nous sommes passés devant chez toi.

● **to go round: to go round to somebody's house** aller [7] chez quelqu'un; **I went round to Fred's last night** je suis allé chez Fred hier soir.

● **to go round something** 1 faire [10] le tour de *(building, park, garden)*; **2** visiter [1] *(museum, monument)*.

● **to go through** passer [1] par; **the train went through Dijon** le train est passé par Dijon; **you can go through my office** tu peux passer par mon bureau.

● **to go up 1** (*person*) monter [1]; **she's gone up to her room** elle est montée dans sa chambre; **to go up the stairs** monter l'escalier; **2** (*prices*) augmenter [1]; **the price of petrol has gone up** le prix de l'essence a augmenté

goal *noun* but *Masc.*; **to score a goal** marquer un but; **to win by three goals to two** gagner trois buts à deux.

goalkeeper *noun* gardien *Masc.* de but.

goat *noun* chèvre *Fem.*; **goat's cheese** le fromage de chèvre.

God *noun* Dieu *Masc.*; **to believe in God** croire en Dieu.

god *noun* dieu *Masc.* (*plural* **dieux**).

godchild *noun* filleul *Masc.*, filleule *Fem.*

goddaughter *noun* filleule *Fem.*

goddess *noun* déesse *Fem.*

godfather *noun* parrain *Masc.*

godmother *noun* marraine *Fem.*

godson *noun* filleul *Masc.*

goggles *plural noun* lunettes *Fem. plural*; **swimming goggles** les lunettes de plongée; **skiing goggles** les lunettes de ski.

go-karting *noun* karting *Masc.*; **to go go-karting** faire du karting.

gold *noun* or *Masc.*; **a gold bracelet** un bracelet en or.

goldfish *noun* poisson *Masc.* rouge.

golf *noun* golf *Masc.*; **to play golf** jouer au golf.

golf club *noun* **1** (*place*) club *Masc.* de golf; **2** (*iron*) crosse *Fem.* de golf.

golf course *noun* terrain *Masc.* de golf.

golfer *noun* golfeur *Masc.*, golfeuse *Fem.*

good *adjective* **1** bon (*Fem.* bonne); **she's a good teacher** c'est un bon professeur; **the cherries are very good** les cerises sont très bonnes; **2 to be good for you** être bon pour la santé; **tomatoes are good for you** les tomates sont bonnes pour la santé; **3 to be good at** être bon en; **she's good at art** elle est bonne en dessin; **4** (*well-behaved*) sage; **be good!** sois sage!; **5** (*kind*) gentil (*Fem.* gentille); **she's been very good to me** elle a été très gentille avec moi; **6 for good** pour de bon; **I've stopped smoking for good** j'ai arrêté de fumer pour de bon.

good afternoon *exclamation* bonjour.

goodbye *exclamation* au revoir.

good evening *exclamation* bonsoir.

Good Friday *noun* le Vendredi saint.

good-looking *adjective* beau (*Fem.* belle) (*Masc. plural* beaux); **Maya's boyfriend's really good-looking** le copain de Maya est très beau.

good morning *exclamation* bonjour.

goodness *exclamation* mon Dieu!; **for goodness sake!** au nom du ciel!

goodnight *exclamation* bonne nuit.

goods *plural noun* marchandises *Fem. plural*.

a b c d e f g h i j k l m n o p q r s t u v w x y z

a

goods train noun train Masc. de
marchandises.

b

goose noun oie Fem.

c

goose pimples noun chair Fem.
de poule.

d

gorgeous adjective superbe; **a
gorgeous dress** une robe superbe;
it's a gorgeous day il fait un temps
superbe.

e

f

g

gorilla noun gorille Masc.

h

gorse noun ajoncs Masc. plural.

i

gosh exclamation ça alors!

j

gossip noun 1 (person) bavard
Masc., bavarde Fem.; 2 (news)
nouvelles Fem. plural; **what's the
latest gossip?** quoi de neuf?

k

l

gossip verb bavarder [1].

m

government noun gouvernement
Masc.

n

o

grab verb 1 saisir [2]; **she grabbed
my arm** elle m'a saisi par le bras;
2 **to grab something from
somebody** arracher [1] quelque
chose à quelqu'un; **he grabbed the
book from me** il m'a arraché le
livre.

p

q

r

graceful adjective élégant.

s

grade noun (mark) note Fem.; **to
get good grades** avoir de bonnes
notes.

t

gradual adjective progressif (Fem.
progressive).

u

v

gradually adverb petit à petit; **the
weather got gradually better** le
temps s'est amélioré petit à petit.

w

x

graffiti plural noun graffiti Masc.
plural.

y

grain noun grain Masc.

z

grammar noun grammaire Fem.

grammar school noun (from age
11 to 15) collège Masc.; (from age 15
to 18) lycée Masc.

grammatical adjective **a
grammatical error** une faute de
grammaire.

gramme noun gramme Masc.

gran noun mamie Fem. (informal).

grandchildren plural noun
petits-enfants Masc. plural.

granddad noun papy Masc.
(informal).

granddaughter noun petite-fille
Fem.

grandfather noun grand-père
Masc.

grandma noun mamie Fem.
(informal).

grandmother noun grand-mère
Fem.

grandpa noun papi Masc.
(informal).

grandparents plural noun
grandparents Masc. plural.

grandson noun petit-fils Masc.

granny noun mamie Fem.
(informal).

grape noun **a grape** un grain de
raisin; **to buy some grapes**
acheter du raisin; **do you like
grapes?** est-ce que tu aimes le
raisin?; **a bunch of grapes** une
grappe de raisin.

grapefruit noun pamplemousse
Masc.

graph noun graphique Masc.

graphic designer noun
graphiste Masc. & Fem.

graphics noun visualisation Fem.
graphique.

grasp verb saisir [2].

grass noun **1** herbe Fem.; **sitting on the grass** assis sur l'herbe; **2** (lawn) pelouse Fem.; **to cut the grass** tondre la pelouse.

grasshopper noun sauterelle Fem.

grate verb râper [1]; **grated cheese** du fromage râpé.

grateful adjective reconnaissant.

grater noun râpe Fem.

grave[1] noun tombe Fem.

grave[2] noun accent Masc. grave.

gravel noun gravillons Masc. plural.

graveyard noun cimetière Masc.

gravity noun pesanteur Fem.

gravy noun sauce Fem. au jus de rôti.

grease noun graisse Fem.

greasy adjective gras (Fem. grasse); **to have greasy skin** avoir la peau grasse; **I hate greasy food** je déteste la nourriture grasse.

great adjective **1** grand; **a great poet** un grand poète; **2** (terrific) génial (Masc. plural géniaux); **it was a great party!** ça a été une soirée géniale!; **great!** génial!; **3 a great deal of** beaucoup de; **a great many** beaucoup de; **there are a great many things still to be done** il reste beaucoup de choses à faire.

Great Britain noun Grande-Bretagne Fem.; **in Great Britain** en Grande-Bretagne; **to Great Britain** en Grande-Bretagne; **to be from Great Britain** être britannique.

Greece noun Grèce Fem.; **to Greece** en Grèce; **in Greece** en Grèce.

greedy adjective (with food) gourmand.

Greek noun **1** (person) Grec Masc., Grecque Fem.; **2** (language) grec Masc.

Greek adjective grec (Fem. grecque).

green noun **1** (colour) vert Masc.; **a pale green** un vert pâle; **2 greens** (vegetables) les légumes verts; **3 the Greens** (ecologists) les Verts Masc. plural.

green adjective **1** vert; **a green door** une porte verte; **2** écologiste; **the Green Party** le parti écologiste.

greengrocer noun marchand Masc. de fruits et légumes.

greenhouse noun serre Fem.

greenhouse effect noun effet Masc. de serre.

greetings plural noun **Season's Greetings** meilleurs vœux Masc. plural.

greetings card noun carte Fem. de vœux.

grey adjective gris; **a grey skirt** une jupe grise; **to have grey hair** avoir les cheveux gris.

greyhound noun lévrier Masc.

grid noun **1** (grating) grille Fem.; **2** (network) réseau Masc. (plural réseaux).

grief noun chagrin Masc.

grill noun (of a cooker) gril Masc.

grill verb **to grill something** faire [10] griller quelque chose; **I grilled the sausages** j'ai fait griller les saucisses.

grim adjective sinistre.

grin noun sourire Masc.

grin verb sourire [68].

a
b
c
d
e
f
g
h
i
j
k
l
m
n
o
p
q
r
s
t
u
v
w
x
y
z

grip noun prise Fem.

grip verb serrer [1].

grit noun (for roads) gravillons Masc. plural.

groan noun **1** (of pain) gémissement Masc.; **2** (of disgust, boredom) grognement Masc.

groan verb **1** (in pain) gémir [2]; **2** (in disgust, boredom) grogner [1].

grocer's noun épicerie Fem.; **I met Jake in the grocer's** j'ai rencontré Jake à l'épicerie.

grocer noun épicier Masc.; **my dad's a grocer** mon père est épicier.

groceries plural noun provisions Fem. plural; **to buy some groceries** acheter des provisions.

groom noun (bridegroom) marié Masc.; **the bride and groom** les jeunes mariés.

gross adjective **1** a gross injustice une injustice flagrante; **2** a gross error une erreur grossière; **3** (disgusting) dégoûtant; **the food was gross!** la nourriture était dégoûtante!

ground noun **1** terre Fem.; **to sit on the ground** s'asseoir par terre; **to throw something on the ground** jeter quelque chose par terre; **2** (for sport) terrain Masc.; **a football ground** un terrain de foot.

ground adjective moulu; **ground coffee** du café moulu.

ground floor noun rez-de-chaussée Masc.; **they live on the ground floor** ils habitent au rez-de-chaussée.

group noun groupe Masc.

grow verb **1** (plant, hair) pousser [1]; **you hair's grown!** tes cheveux ont poussé!; **2** (person) grandir [2]; **my little sister's grown a lot this year** ma petite sœur a beaucoup grandi cette année; **3** (number) augmenter [1]; **the number of students has grown** le nombre d'étudiants a augmenté; **4** faire [10] pousser (fruit, vegetables); **our neighbours grow strawberries** nos voisins font pousser des fraises; **5 to grow a beard** se laisser [1] pousser la barbe; **6 to grow old** vieillir [2].

- **to grow up** grandir [2]; **the children are growing up** les enfants grandissent; **she grew up in Scotland** elle a grandi en Écosse.

growl verb grogner [1].

grown-up noun adulte Masc. & Fem.

growth noun croissance Fem.

grudge noun **to bear a grudge against somebody** en vouloir à quelqu'un; **she bears me a grudge** elle m'en veut.

gruesome adjective horrible.

grumble verb se plaindre [31]; **she's always grumbling** elle est toujours en train de se plaindre; **to grumble about something** se plaindre de quelque chose.

guarantee noun garantie Fem.; **a year's guarantee** une garantie d'un an.

guarantee verb garantir [2].

guard noun **1** a prison guard un gardien de prison; **2** (on a train) chef Masc. de train; **3** a security guard un vigile.

guard verb surveiller [1]

guard dog noun chien Masc. de garde.

guardian noun (of child) tuteur Masc., tutrice Fem.

guess noun **have a guess!** devine!; **it's a good guess** tu as deviné.

guess verb deviner [1]; **guess who I saw last night!** devine qui j'ai vu hier soir!; **you'll never guess!** tu ne devineras jamais!

guest noun 1 invité Masc., invitée Fem.; **we've got guests coming tonight** nous avons des invités ce soir; **2** (in a hotel) client Masc., cliente Fem.; **3 a paying guest** un hôte payant.

guesthouse noun pension Fem. de famille.

guide noun 1 (person or book) guide Masc.; **2** (girl guide) guide Fem., (belonging to a church company of girl guides) éclaireuse Fem.

guidebook noun guide Masc.

guide dog noun chien Masc. d'aveugle.

guideline noun indication Fem.

guilty adjective coupable; **to feel guilty** se sentir coupable.

guinea pig noun (pet) cochon Masc. d'Inde; (in an experiment) cobaye Masc.; **they want me to be a guinea pig** ils veulent que je serve de cobaye.

guitar noun guitare Fem.; **to play the guitar** jouer de la guitare; **on the guitar** à la guitare.

guitarist noun guitariste Masc. & Fem.

gum noun 1 (in mouth) gencive Fem.; **2** (chewing gum) chewing-gum Masc.

gun noun 1 revolver Masc.; **2** (rifle) fusil Masc.

gust noun **a gust of wind** une rafale de vent.

gutter noun (in the street) caniveau (plural caniveaux).

guy noun type Masc. (informal); **he's a nice guy** c'est un type sympa; **a guy from Newcastle** un type qui vient de Newcastle.

guy rope noun corde Fem. d'attache.

gym noun gym Fem.; **to go to the gym** aller à la gym.

gymnasium noun gymnase Masc.

gymnast noun gymnaste Masc. & Fem.

gymnastics noun gymnastique Fem.

gym shoe noun tennis Masc.

Hh

habit noun habitude Fem.; **to be in the habit of doing** avoir l'habitude de faire; **it's a bad habit** c'est une mauvaise habitude.

haddock noun églefin Masc.; **smoked haddock** haddock Masc.

hail noun grêle Fem.

hailstone noun grêlon Masc.

hailstorm noun averse Fem. de grêle.

hair noun 1 cheveux Masc. plural; **to have short hair** avoir les cheveux

a
b
c
d
e
f
g
h
i
j
k
l
m
n
o
p
q
r
s
t
u
v
w
x
y
z

courts; **to brush your hair** se brosser les cheveux; **to wash your hair** se laver les cheveux; **to have your hair cut** se faire couper les cheveux; **she's had her hair cut** elle s'est fait couper les cheveux; **2 a hair** (from the head) un cheveu; (from the body) un poil.

hairbrush noun brosse Fem. à cheveux.

haircut noun **1** coupe Fem.; **I like your new haircut** j'aime bien ta nouvelle coupe; **2 to have a haircut** se faire couper les cheveux.

hairdresser noun coiffeur Masc., coiffeuse Fem.; **she's a hairdresser** elle est coiffeuse; **at the hairdresser's** chez le coiffeur.

hair drier noun sèche-cheveux Masc.

hair gel noun gel Masc. pour les cheveux.

hairgrip noun pince Fem. à cheveux.

hair remover noun crème Fem. dépilatoire.

hairslide noun barrette Fem.

hairspray noun laque Fem.

hairstyle noun coiffure Fem.

hairy adjective poilu.

Haiti noun Haïti Masc.
Haitian noun Haïtien Masc., Haïtienne Fem.

Haitian adjective haïtien (Fem. haïtienne).

half noun **1** moitié Fem.; **half of a** moitié de; **I gave him half of the money** je lui ai donné la moitié de l'argent; **half an apple** la moitié d'une pomme; **you've only eaten half of it** tu n'en as mangé que la

moitié; **half the people** la moitié des gens; **2 to cut something in half** couper quelque chose en deux; **3** (as a fraction) demi; **three and a half** trois et demi; **she's five and a half** elle a cinq ans et demi; **4** (in time) demi, demie; **half an hour** une demi-heure; **an hour and a half** une heure et demie; **it's half past three** il est trois heures et demie; **5** (in weights and measures) demi, demie; **half a litre** un demi-litre; **half a cup** une demi-tasse.

half hour noun demi-heure Fem.; **every half hour** toutes les demi-heures.

half price adjective, adverb à moitié prix; **half-price CDs** des CD à moitié prix; **I bought it half price** je l'ai acheté à moitié prix.

half-time noun mi-temps Fem.; **at half-time** à la mi-temps.

halfway adverb **1** à mi-chemin; **halfway between Paris and Dijon** à mi-chemin entre Paris et Dijon; **2 to be halfway through doing** avoir à moitié fini de faire; **I'm halfway through my homework** j'ai à moitié fini mes devoirs.

hall noun **1** (in a house) entrée Fem.; **2** (public) salle Fem.; **the village hall** la salle des fêtes; **a concert hall** une salle de concert.

Hallowe'en noun la veille de la Toussaint (the French do not have any particular customs for this date).

ham noun jambon Masc.; **a slice of ham** une tranche de jambon; **a ham sandwich** un sandwich au jambon.

hamburger *noun* hamburger Masc.

hammer *noun* marteau Masc. (*plural* **marteaux**).

hammock *noun* hamac Masc.

hamster *noun* hamster Masc.

hand *noun* 1 main Fem.; **to have something in your hand** avoir quelque chose à la main; **to hold somebody's hand** tenir quelqu'un par la main; **2 to give somebody a hand** donner un coup de main à quelqu'un; **can you give me a hand to move the table?** est-ce que tu peux me donner un coup de main pour déplacer la table?; **do you need a hand?** est-ce que tu as besoin d'un coup de main?; **3 on the other hand** ... par contre ...; **4** (*of a watch or clock*) aiguille Fem.; **the hour hand** l'aiguille des heures.

hand *verb* **to hand something to somebody** passer [1] quelque chose à quelqu'un; **I handed him the keys** je lui ai passé les clés.

● **to hand something in** rendre [3] quelque chose; **I've handed in my homework** j'ai rendu mon devoir.

● **to hand something out** distribuer [1] quelque chose; **Claire handed out the exercise books** Claire a distribué les cahiers.

handbag *noun* sac Masc. à main (*plural* **sacs** à main).

handcuffs *plural noun* menottes Fem. plural.

handful *noun* **a handful of** une poignée de.

handicapped *adjective* handicapé.

handkerchief *noun* mouchoir Masc.

handle *noun* 1 (*of a door or drawer*) poignée Fem.; **2** (*on a cup or basket*) anse Fem.; **3** (*of a knife, tool, or saucepan*) manche Masc.; **4** (*of a frying pan*) queue Fem.

handle *verb* **1** s'occuper [1] de; **Gina handles the accounts** Gina s'occupe de la comptabilité; **2 she's good at handling people** elle a un bon contact avec les gens; **3 I can't handle any more problems!** j'ai assez de problèmes comme ça!

handlebars *plural noun* guidon Masc.

hand luggage *noun* bagages Masc. à main.

handmade *adjective* fait à la main.

handsome *adjective* beau (Fem. belle); **he's a handsome guy** c'est un beau type.

handwriting *noun* écriture Fem.

handy *adjective* **1** pratique; **this little knife's very handy** ce petit couteau est très pratique; **2 sous la main**; **I always keep a notebook handy** je garde toujours un calepin sous la main.

hang *verb* **1** être [6] accroché; **there was a mirror hanging on the wall** il y avait un miroir accroché au mur; **2 to hang something** accrocher [1] quelque chose; **we hung the mirror on the wall** nous avons accroché le miroir au mur.

● **to hang around** traîner [1]; **we were hanging around outside the cinema** on traînait devant le cinéma.

● **to hang down** pendre [3].

● **to hang on** attendre [3]; **hang on a second!** attends une seconde!.

● **to hang up** (*on the phone*) raccrocher [1]; **she hung up on me** elle m'a raccroché au nez (*literally: she hung up on my nose*).

● **to hang something up** accrocher [1] quelque chose; **you can hang your coat up in the hall** tu peux accrocher ton manteau dans l'entrée.

hang-gliding *noun* deltaplane *Masc.*; **to go hang-gliding** faire du deltaplane.

hangover *noun* gueule *Fem.* de bois; **to have a hangover** avoir la gueule de bois.

happen *verb* 1 se passer [1]; **what's happening?** qu'est-ce qui se passe?; **it happened in June** ça s'est passé en juin; **what's happened to the can-opener?** où est l'ouvre-boîte?; **3 if you happen to see Jill** si par hasard tu vois Jill.

happily *adverb* 1 joyeusement; **she smiled happily** elle a souri joyeusement; 2 (*willingly*) volontiers; **I'll happily do it for you** je le ferai pour toi volontiers.

happiness *noun* bonheur *Masc.*

happy *adjective* heureux (*Fem.* heureuse); **a happy child** un enfant heureux; **Happy Birthday!** Bon anniversaire!

harbour *noun* port *Masc.*

hard *adjective* 1 dur; **to go hard** durcir; 2 (*difficult*) difficile; **a hard question** une question difficile; **it's hard to know ...** il est difficile de savoir ....

hard *adverb* 1 **to work hard** travailler dur; 2 **to try hard** faire beaucoup d'efforts.

hard-boiled egg *noun* œuf *Masc.* dur.

hard disk *noun* (*in a computer*) disque *Masc.* dur.

hardly *adverb* 1 à peine; **I can hardly hear him** je l'entends à peine; 2 **hardly any** presque pas de; **there's hardly any milk** il n'y a presque pas de lait; 3 **hardly ever** presque jamais; **I hardly ever see them** je ne les vois presque jamais; 4 **there was hardly anybody** il n'y avait presque personne.

hard up *adjective* fauché (*informal*).

hare *noun* lièvre *Masc.*

harm *noun* **it won't do you any harm** ça ne te fera pas de mal.

harm *verb* **to harm somebody** faire [10] du mal à quelqu'un; **they did not harm him** ils ne lui ont pas fait de mal; **a cup of coffee won't harm you** une tasse de café ne te fera pas de mal.

harmful *adjective* nuisible.

harmless *adjective* inoffensif (*Fem.* inoffensive).

harvest *noun* récolte *Fem.*; **to get the harvest in** faire [10] la récolte.

hat *noun* chapeau *Masc.* (*plural* chapeaux).

hate *verb* détester [1]; **I hate geography** je déteste la géographie.

hatred *noun* haine *Fem.*

haunted *adjective* hanté.

have *verb* 1 avoir [5]; **Anna has three brothers** Anna a trois frères;

how many sisters do you have? tu as combien de sœurs?; **2 to have got** avoir [5]; **we've got a dog** nous avons un chien; **what have you got in your hand?** qu'est-ce que tu as à la main?; **3** (*to form past tenses, some verbs in French take 'avoir' and some 'être'*) **I've finished** j'ai fini; **have you seen the film?** est-ce que tu as vu le film?; **Rosie hasn't arrived yet** Rosie n'est pas encore arrivée; **he had left** il était parti; **4 to have to do** devoir [8] faire; **I have to phone my mum** je dois appeler ma mère; **5** prendre [64] (*food, drink, a shower*); **we had a coffee** nous avons pris un café; **what will you have?** qu'est-ce que tu prends?; **I'll have an omelette** je prends une omelette; **I'm going to have a shower** je vais prendre une douche; **6 to have lunch** déjeuner [1]; **to have dinner** (*in the evening*) dîner [1]; **7 to have something done** faire [10] quelque chose; **I'm going to have my hair cut** je vais me faire couper les cheveux.

hawk *noun* faucon *Masc.*

hay *noun* foin *Masc.*

hay fever *noun* rhume *Masc.* des foins.

hazelnut *noun* noisette *Fem.*

he *pronoun* il; **he lives in Manchester** il habite à Manchester; **he's my brother** c'est mon frère.

head *noun* 1 tête *Fem.*; **he had a cap on his head** il avait une casquette sur la tête; **at the head of the queue** à la tête de la queue; **2** (*of school*) directeur *Masc.*, directrice *Fem.*; **3** (*when tossing a coin*) **"heads or tails?"** – 'heads' 'pile ou face?' – 'face' (*note that it is in fact 'tails or heads' in French*).

● **to head for something** se diriger [52] vers quelque chose; **Liz headed for the door** Liz s'est dirigée vers la porte.

headache *noun* **I've got a headache** j'ai mal à la tête.

headlight *noun* phare *Masc.*

headline *noun* gros titre *Masc.*; **to hit the headlines** faire la une.

headmaster *noun* directeur *Masc.*

headmistress *noun* directrice *Fem.*

headphones *plural noun* casque *Masc. singular.*

headquarters *noun* **1** (*of organization*) siège *Masc.* social; **2** (*military*) quartier *Masc.* général.

headteacher *noun* directeur *Masc.*, directrice *Fem.*

health *noun* santé *Fem.*

health centre *noun* centre *Masc.* médico-social.

healthy *adjective* **1** (*person*) **to be healthy** être en bonne santé; **2 a healthy diet** une alimentation saine.

heap *noun* tas *Masc.*; **I've got heaps of things to do** j'ai un tas de choses à faire.

hear *verb* **1** entendre [3]; **I can't hear you** je ne t'entends pas; **I can't hear anything** je n'entends rien; **2** apprendre [64] (*news*); **I hear you've bought a dog** j'apprends que tu as acheté un chien.

● **to hear about something**

entendre [3] parler de quelque chose; **have you heard about the concert?** as-tu entendu parler du concert?

● **to hear from somebody** avoir [5] des nouvelles de quelqu'un; **have you heard from Amanda?** as-tu des nouvelles d'Amanda?

hearing aid noun Sonotone™ Masc.

heart noun 1 cœur Masc.; **to learn something by heart** apprendre quelque chose par cœur; 2 (in cards) cœur Masc.; **the jack of hearts** le valet de cœur.

heart attack noun crise Fem. cardiaque.

heat noun chaleur Fem.

heat verb 1 chauffer [1]; **the soup's heating** la soupe est en train de chauffer; 2 **to heat something** faire [10] chauffer quelque chose; **I'll go and heat the soup** je vais faire chauffer la soupe.

● **to heat something up** faire [10] réchauffer quelque chose; **I'm heating up the sauce** je fais réchauffer la sauce.

heater noun radiateur Masc.

heather noun bruyère Fem.

heating noun chauffage Masc.

heatwave noun vague Fem. de chaleur.

heaven noun paradis Masc.

heavy adjective 1 lourd; **my rucksack's really heavy** mon sac à dos est très lourd; 2 (busy) chargé; **I've got a heavy day tomorrow** j'ai une journée chargée demain; 3 **heavy rain** des pluies fortes.

heavy metal noun (music) hard rock Masc.

hectic adjective **a hectic day** une journée mouvementée.

hedge noun haie Fem.

hedgehog noun hérisson Masc.

heel noun talon Masc.

height noun 1 (of a person) taille Fem.; 2 (of a building) hauteur Fem.; 3 (of a mountain) altitude Fem.

helicopter noun hélicoptère Masc.

hell noun enfer Masc.; **it's hell here!** c'est infernal ici!

hello exclamation 1 (polite) bonjour!; 2 (informal) salut!; 3 (on the telephone) allô!

helmet noun casque Masc.

help noun aide Fem.; **do you need any help?** est-ce que tu as besoin d'aide?

help verb 1 aider [1]; **to help somebody to do** aider quelqu'un à faire; **can you help me move the table?** peux-tu m'aider à déplacer la table?; 2 **to help yourself to something** se servir [71] de quelque chose; **help yourselves to vegetables** servez-vous de légumes; **help yourself!** sers-toi!; 3 help! au secours!

helper noun aide Masc. & Fem.; **helpers are needed to run charity stalls** on a besoin de bénévoles pour tenir les stands de la fête de charité.

helpful adjective (person) serviable.

helping noun portion Fem.; **would you like a second helping of chips?** est-ce que tu veux reprendre des frites?

ENGLISH-FRENCH 443 **hide**

hem noun ourlet Masc.

hen noun poule Fem.

her pronoun 1 la, l' (before a vowel or silent 'h'); **I know her** je la connais; **I can hear her** je l'entends; **listen to her!** écoute-la!; **I saw her last week** je l'ai vue la semaine dernière; **2** (to her) lui; **I gave her my address** je lui ai donné mon adresse; **3** (after a preposition) elle; **without her** sans elle; (in comparisons) **he's older than her** il est plus âgé qu'elle.

her adjective **1** (before a masculine noun) son; **her brother** son frère; **her book** son livre; **2** (before a feminine noun) sa; **her sister** sa sœur; **her house** sa maison (but 'sa' becomes 'son' before a feminine noun beginning with a vowel or silent 'h') **her address** son adresse; **3** (before a plural noun) ses; **her children** ses enfants; **4** (with parts of the body) le, la, les; **she had a glass in her hand** elle avait un verre à la main; **she's washing her hands** elle se lave les mains.

herb noun herbe Fem.

herd noun troupeau Masc (plural troupeaux).

here adverb **1** ici; **not far from here** pas loin d'ici; **2** là; **Tom isn't here at the moment** Tom n'est pas là en ce moment; **3 here is** voilà; **here's my address** voilà mon adresse; **4 here are** voilà; **here are the photos** voilà les photos; **and here they are!** et les voilà!

hero noun héros Masc.

heroin noun héroïne Fem.

heroine noun héroïne Fem.

herring noun hareng Masc.

hers pronoun **1** (for a masculine noun) le sien; **I took my hat and she took hers** j'ai pris mon chapeau et elle a pris le sien; **2** (for a feminine noun) la sienne; **I gave her my address and she gave me hers** je lui ai donné mon adresse et elle m'a donné la sienne; **3** (for a masculine plural noun) les siens; **I've invited my parents and Karen's invited hers** j'ai invité mes parents et Karen a invité les siens; **4** (for a feminine plural noun) les siennes; **I showed her my photos and she showed me hers** je lui ai montré mes photos et elle m'a montré les siennes; **5** à elle; **the green one's hers** le vert est à elle; **it's hers** c'est à elle.

herself pronoun **1 she's hurt herself** elle s'est blessée; **2 she said it herself** elle l'a dit elle-même; **3 she did it by herself** elle l'a fait toute seule.

hesitate verb hésiter [1]; **to hesitate to do** hésiter à faire.

heterosexual adjective, noun hétérosexuel Masc., hétérosexuelle Fem.

hi exclamation salut!

hiccups plural noun **to have the hiccups** avoir le hoquet.

hidden adjective caché.

hide verb **1** (person) se cacher [1]; **she hid behind the door** elle s'est cachée derrière la porte; **2 to hide something** cacher [1] quelque chose; **who's hidden the**

a b c d e f g h i j k l m n o p q r s t u v w x y z

chocolate? qui a caché le chocolat?

hide-and-seek noun **to play hide-and-seek** jouer à cache-cache.

hi-fi noun chaîne Fem. hi-fi.

high adjective **1** haut; **on a high shelf** sur une étagère haute; **the wall is very high** le mur est très haut; **how high is the wall?** quelle est la hauteur du mur?; **the wall is two metres high** le mur fait deux mètres de hauteur; **2** (number, price, temperature) élevé; **food prices are very high** les prix de la nourriture sont très élevés; **3 at high speed** à grande vitesse; **4 high winds** des vents violents; **5 a high voice** une voix aiguë.

Highers, Advanced Highers noun plural baccalauréat Masc., bac Masc. (informal) (Students take 'le bac' at the end of their secondary education. You can explain Highers briefly as follows: Les Highers sont un examen qui sanctionne l'avant-dernière année d'école secondaire en Écosse. On passe les Highers dans cinq matières au maximum. En dernière année, certains lycéens passent également les Advance Highers dans un maximum de trois matières, qui ont déjà fait l'objet de l'un de leurs Highers. Ces deux examens sont notés de A à C et permettent de s'inscrire à l'université).

high-heeled adjective à hauts talons; **high-heeled shoes** des chaussures à hauts talons.

high jump noun saut Masc. en hauteur.

highly adverb extrêmement.

hijack verb **to hijack a plane** détourner [1] un avion.

hijacker noun pirate Masc. de l'air.

hijacking noun détournement Masc.

hike noun randonnée Fem.; **to go on a hike** faire une randonnée.

hiker noun randonneur Masc., randonneuse Fem.

hiking noun randonnée Fem.

hilarious adjective hilarant.

hill noun **1** (in landscape) colline Fem.; **you can see the hills** on voit les collines; **2** (hillside) coteau Masc. (plural coteaux); **the houses on the hill** les maisons sur le coteau; **3** (sloping street or road) **to go up the hill** monter; **you go up the hill to the church and then turn right** vous montez jusqu'à l'église et vous tournez à droite.

him pronoun **1** le, l' (before a vowel or silent 'h'); **I know him** je le connais; **I can hear him** je l'entends; **listen to him!** écoute-le!; **I saw him last week** je l'ai vu la semaine dernière; **2** (to him) lui; **I gave him my address** je lui ai donné mon adresse; **3** (after a preposition) lui; **with him** avec lui; **without him** sans lui; (in comparisons) **she's older than him** elle est plus âgée que lui.

himself pronoun **1 he's hurt himself** il s'est blessé; **2 he said it himself** il l'a dit lui-même; **3 he did it by himself** il l'a fait tout seul.

Hindu adjective hindou.

hip noun hanche Fem.

hippie noun hippie Masc. & Fem.

hippopotamus noun
hippopotame Masc.

hire noun location Fem.; **car hire**
location de voitures; **for hire** à
louer.

hire verb louer [1]; **we're going to
hire a car** nous allons louer une
voiture.

his adjective **1** (before a masculine
noun) son; **his brother** son frère;
his book son livre; **2** (before a
feminine noun) sa; **his sister** sa
sœur; **his house** sa maison (but
'sa' becomes 'son' before a feminine
noun beginning with a vowel or
silent 'h') **his address** son adresse;
3 (before a plural noun) ses; **his
children** ses enfants; **4** (with parts
of the body) le, la, les; **he had a
glass in his hand** il avait un verre
à la main; **he's washing his hands**
il se lave les mains.

his pronoun **1** (for a masculine
noun) le sien; **I took my hat and he
took his** j'ai pris mon chapeau et il
a pris le sien; **2** (for a feminine
noun) la sienne; **I gave him my
address and he gave me his** je lui
ai donné mon adresse et il m'a
donné la sienne; **3** (for a masculine
plural noun) les siens; **I've invited
my parents and Steve's invited
his** j'ai invité mes parents et Steve
a invité les siens; **4** (for a feminine
plural noun) les siennes; **I showed
him my photos and he showed
me his** je lui ai montré mes photos
et il m'a montré les siennes; **5** à lui;
the green car's his la voiture verte
est à lui; **it's his** c'est à lui.

historic adjective historique.

history noun histoire Fem.

hit noun **1** (song) tube Masc.
(informal); **their latest hit** leur
dernier tube; **2** (success) succès
Masc.; **the film is a huge hit** le film
a un succès fou.

hit verb **1** frapper [1]; **to hit the ball**
frapper la balle; **2 to hit your head
on something** se cogner [1] la tête
contre quelque chose; **3** heurter [1];
the car hit a tree la voiture a
heurté un arbre; **4 to be hit by a
car** (person) être [6] renversé par
une voiture.

hitch noun problème Masc.; **there's
been a slight hitch** il y a eu un
petit problème.

hitch verb **to hitch a lift** faire [10]
du stop (informal).

hitchhike verb faire [10] du stop
(informal); **we hitchhiked to Dijon**
nous sommes allés à Dijon en stop.

hitchhiker noun autostoppeur
Masc., autostoppeuse Fem.

hitchhiking noun autostop Masc.

HIV-negative adjective
séronégatif (Fem. séronégative).

HIV-positive adjective séropositif
(Fem. séropositive).

hobby noun passe-temps Masc.

hockey noun hockey Masc.; **to play
hockey** jouer au hockey.

hockey stick noun crosse Fem. de
hockey.

hold verb **1** tenir [77]; **to hold
something in your hand** tenir
quelque chose à la main; **can you
hold the torch?** est-ce que tu peux
tenir la lampe?; **2** (contain)
contenir [77]; **a jug which holds a
litre** un pichet qui contient un
litre; **3 to hold a meeting**

a
b
c
d
e
f
g
h
i
j
k
l
m
n
o
p
q
r
s
t
u
v
w
x
y
z

a
b
c
d
e
f
g
h
i
j
k
l
m
n
o
p
q
r
s
t
u
v
w
x
y
z

organiser [1] une réunion; **4 can
you hold the line, please** ne
quittez pas, s'il vous plaît; **5 hold
on!** (*wait*) attends!; (*on telephone*)
ne quittez pas!

● **to hold somebody up** (*delay*)
retenir [77] quelqu'un; **I was held
up at the dentist's** j'ai été retenu
chez le dentiste.

● **to hold something up** (*raise*) lever
[50] quelque chose; **he held up his
glass** il a levé son verre.

hold-up *noun* **1** retard *Masc.*;
2 (*traffic jam*) bouchon *Masc.*;
3 (*robbery*) hold-up *Masc.*

hole *noun* trou *Masc.*

holiday *noun* **1** vacances *Fem.
plural*; **where are you going for
your holiday?** où est-ce que vous
partez en vacances?; **have a good
holiday!** bonnes vacances!; **to be
away on holiday** être en vacances;
to go on holiday partir en
vacances; **the school holidays** les
vacances scolaires; **2** (*from work*)
congé *Masc.*; **I'm taking two days'
holiday next week** je prends deux
jours de congé la semaine
prochaine; **3 a public holiday** un
jour férié; **Monday's a holiday**
lundi est férié.

holiday home *noun* résidence
Fem. secondaire.

Holland *noun* Hollande *Fem.*; **to
Holland** en Hollande; **in Holland** en
Hollande.

hollow *adjective* creux (*Fem.*
creuse).

holly *noun* houx *Masc.*

holy *adjective* saint.

home *noun* maison *Fem.*; **I was at
home** j'étais à la maison; **to stay at
home** rester à la maison; **make
yourself at home** fais comme chez
toi.

home *adverb* **1** chez soi; **Susie's
gone home** Susie est rentrée chez
elle; **I'll call in and see you on my
way home** je passerai te voir en
rentrant chez moi; **2 to get home**
rentrer; **we got home at midnight**
nous sommes rentrés à minuit.

homeless *adjective* sans abri; **the
homeless** les sans-abri *Masc. plural*.

homemade *adjective* fait maison;
homemade cakes des gâteaux
faits maison.

home match *noun* match *Masc.* à
domicile.

homeopathic *adjective*
homéopathique.

homesick *adjective* **to be
homesick** avoir le mal du pays.

homework *noun* devoirs *Masc.
plural*; **I did my homework** j'ai fait
mes devoirs; **my French
homework** mes devoirs de
français; (*written*) mon devoir de
français.

homosexual *adjective, noun*
homosexuel (*Fem.* homosexuelle).

honest *adjective* honnête.

honestly *adverb* franchement.

honesty *noun* honnêteté *Fem.*

honey *noun* miel *Masc.*

honeymoon *noun* voyage *Masc.* de
noces; **they're going to Paris on
their honeymoon** ils partent à
Paris en voyage de noces.

honeysuckle *noun* chèvrefeuille
Masc.

honour noun honneur Masc.

hood noun capuchon Masc.

hook noun 1 crochet Masc.; 2 to take the phone of the hook décrocher le téléphone.

hooligan noun voyou Masc.

hooray exclamation hourra!

Hoover™ noun aspirateur Masc.

hoover verb passer [1] l'aspirateur; I hoovered my bedroom j'ai passé l'aspirateur dans ma chambre.

hope noun espoir Masc.; to give up hope perdre espoir.

hope verb espérer [24]; we hope you'll be able to come nous espérons que vous allez pouvoir venir; hoping to see you on Friday en espérant te voir vendredi; here's hoping! espérons que ça marchera!; I hope so je l'espère; I hope not j'espère que non.

hopefully adverb avec un peu de chance; hopefully, the film won't have started avec un peu de chance, le film n'aura pas commencé.

hopeless adjective nul (Fem. nulle) (informal); I'm completely hopeless at geography je suis complètement nul en géographie.

horizon noun horizon Masc.

horizontal adjective horizontal (Masc. plural horizontaux).

horn noun 1 (of an animal) corne Fem.; 2 (of a car) klaxon Masc.; to sound your horn klaxonner; 3 (musical instrument) cor; to play the horn jouer du cor.

horoscope noun horoscope Masc.

horrible adjective 1 affreux (Fem. affreuse); the weather was horrible il a fait un temps affreux; 2 (person) désagréable; she's really horrible! elle est vraiment désagréable; he was really horrible to me il a été vraiment désagréable avec moi.

horrific adjective terrible; a horrific accident un terrible accident.

horror noun horreur Fem.

horror film noun film Masc. d'épouvante.

horse noun cheval Masc. (plural chevaux).

horse chestnut noun 1 (tree) marronnier Masc.; 2 (nut) marron Masc.

horse racing noun courses Fem. plural hippiques.

horseshoe noun fer Masc. à cheval.

hose noun tuyau Masc. (plural tuyaux).

hosepipe noun tuyau Masc. d'arrosage.

hospital noun hôpital Masc. (plural hôpitaux); to be in hospital être à l'hôpital; to be taken into hospital être hospitalisé.

hospitality noun hospitalité Fem.

host noun hôte Masc., hôtesse Fem.; my host family is very nice ma famille d'accueil est très sympathique.

hostage noun otage Masc.

hostel noun youth hostel auberge Fem. de jeunesse.

hostess noun hôtesse Fem.; an air hostess une hôtesse de l'air.

a

hot *adjective* **1** chaud; **a hot drink** une boisson chaude; **be careful, the plates are hot!** fais attention, les assiettes sont très chaudes!; **2** (*a person*) **to be hot** avoir chaud; **I'm hot** j'ai chaud; **I'm very hot** j'ai très chaud; **I'm too hot** j'ai trop chaud; **3** (*the weather or temperature in a room*) **it's hot today** il fait chaud aujourd'hui; **it's very hot in the kitchen** il fait très chaud dans la cuisine; **4** (*food: spicy*) épicé; **the curry's too hot for me** le curry est trop épicé pour moi.

hot dog *noun* hot-dog *Masc.*

hotel *noun* hôtel *Masc.*

hour *noun* heure *Fem.*; **two hours later** deux heures plus tard; **we waited for two hours** nous avons attendu pendant deux heures; **two hours ago** il y a deux heures; **to be paid by the hour** être payé à l'heure; **every hour** toutes les heures; **half an hour** une demi-heure; **a quarter of an hour** un quart d'heure; **an hour and a half** une heure et demie.

hourly *adjective* toutes les heures; **there is an hourly bus** il y a un bus par heure; **the trains leave hourly** il y a des trains toutes les heures.

house *noun* **1** maison *Fem.*; **to buy a house** acheter une maison; **2 at somebody's house** chez quelqu'un; **I'm at Judy's house** je suis chez Judy; **I'm going to Judy's house tonight** je vais chez Judy ce soir; **I phoned from Judy's house** j'ai téléphoné de chez Judy.

housewife *noun* femme *Fem.* au foyer.

housework *noun* ménage *Masc.*; **to do the housework** faire le ménage.

how *adverb* **1** comment; **how did you do it?** comment l'as-tu fait?; **how are you?** comment allez-vous?; **2 how much?** combien?; **how much money do you have?** tu as combien d'argent?; **how much is it?** (*price*) ça coûte combien?; **3 how many?** combien?; **how many brothers do you have?** tu as combien de frères?; **4 how old are you?** quel âge as-tu?; **5 how far is it?** c'est à quelle distance d'ici?; **how far is it to Paris?** Paris est à quelle distance d'ici?; **6 how long will it take?** ça va prendre combien de temps?; **how long have you known her?** tu la connais depuis combien de temps?

however *adverb* cependant.

hug *noun* **to give somebody a hug** serrer quelqu'un dans ses bras; **she gave me a hug** elle m'a serré dans ses bras.

huge *adjective* immense.

hum *verb* fredonner [1].

human *adjective* humain.

human being *noun* être *Masc.* humain.

humour *noun* humour *Masc.*; **to have a sense of humour** avoir le sens de l'humour.

hundred *number* **1** cent; **two hundred** deux cents; **two hundred and ten** deux cent dix (*note that there is no 's' on 'cent' when it is followed by another number*); **a hundred people** cent personnes; **2 about a hundred** une centaine.

b
c
d
e
f
g
h
i
j
k
l
m
n
o
p
q
r
s
t
u
v
w
x
y
z

about a hundred people une centaine de personnes; **hundreds of people** des centaines de personnes.

Hungary noun Hongrie Fem.

hunger noun faim Fem.

hungry adjective **to be hungry** avoir faim; **I'm hungry** j'ai faim.

hunt verb **1** chasser [1] (an animal); **2** rechercher [1] (person).

hunting noun chasse Fem.; **fox-hunting** la chasse au renard.

hurricane noun ouragan Masc.

hurry noun **to be in a hurry** être pressé; **I'm in a hurry** je suis pressé.

hurry verb se dépêcher [50]; **I must hurry** je dois me dépêcher; **he hurried home** il s'est dépêché de rentrer chez lui; **hurry up!** dépêche-toi!

hurt verb **1 to hurt somebody** faire [10] mal à quelqu'un; **you're hurting me!** tu me fais mal!; **that hurts!** ça fait mal!; **2 my back hurts** j'ai mal au dos; **3 to hurt yourself** se faire [10] mal; **did you hurt yourself?** est-ce que tu t'es fait mal?

hurt adjective **1** (in an accident) blessé; **three people were hurt** trois personnes ont été blessées; **2** (in feelings) blessé; **she felt hurt** elle était blessée.

husband noun mari Masc.

hutch noun clapier Masc.

hygienic adjective hygiénique.

hymn noun cantique Masc.

hypermarket noun hypermarché Masc.

hyphen noun trait Masc. d'union.

hypnotize verb hypnotiser [1].

Ii

I pronoun **1** je, j' (before a vowel or a silent 'h'); **I am Scottish** je suis écossais; **I have two sisters** j'ai deux sœurs; **2** moi; **Robert and I** Robert et moi; **Tony and I left before you** Tony et moi sommes partis avant vous.

ice noun **1** glace Fem.; **2** (on the roads) verglas Masc.; **3** (in a drink) glaçons Masc. plural.

iceberg noun iceberg Masc.

ice cream noun glace Fem.; **a chocolate ice cream** une glace au chocolat.

ice-cube noun glaçon Masc.

ice hockey noun hockey Masc. sur glace.

ice rink noun patinoire Fem.

ice-skating noun **to go ice-skating** faire [10] du patin à glace.

icing noun glaçage Masc.

icon noun icône Fem.

icy adjective **1** verglacé (a road); **2** (very cold) glacial; **an icy wind** un vent glacial.

idea noun idée Fem.; **what a good idea!** quelle bonne idée!; **I've no idea** je n'ai aucune idée.

ideal adjective idéal (Masc. plural idéaux).

identical adjective identique; **identical twins** des vrais jumeaux.

identification noun identification Fem.

a **identify** verb identifier [1].

identity card noun carte Fem. d'identité.

b **idiom** noun idiome Masc.

c **idiot** noun idiot Masc., idiote Fem.

idiotic adjective bête.

d **idyllic** adjective idyllique.

e **i.e.** c-à-d (short for: c'est-à-dire).

f **if** conjunction 1 si, s' (before 'il' and 'ils'); **if Sue's there** si Sue est là; **if it rains** s'il pleut; **if I won the lottery** si je gagnais la loterie; **if not** sinon; 2 **if only** ... si seulement ...; **if only you'd told me** si seulement tu me l'avais dit; 3 **even if** même si; **even if it snows** même s'il neige; 4 **if I were you** ... à ta place ...; **if I were you, I'd forget it** à ta place je n'y penserais plus.

g

h

i

j

k **ignore** verb 1 ignorer [1] (a person); 2 **ne pas écouter** [1] (what somebody says); 3 **just ignore it** ne fais pas attention.

l

m **ill** adjective malade; **to fall ill, to be taken ill** tomber [1] malade; **I feel ill** je ne me sens pas bien.

n

o **illegal** adjective illégal (Masc. plural illégaux).

p **illegible** adjective illisible.

q **illness** noun maladie Fem.

illusion noun illusion Fem.

r **illustrated** adjective illustré.

s **illustration** noun illustration Fem.

t **image** noun image Fem.; ★ **he's the spitting image of his father** c'est son père tout craché.

u

v **imagination** noun imagination Fem.; **to show imagination** faire preuve d'imagination.

w

x

y

z

imaginative adjective plein d'imagination.

imagine verb imaginer [1]; **imagine that you're very rich** imagine que tu es très riche; **you can't imagine how hard it was!** tu ne peux pas t'imaginer combien c'était difficile!

imitate verb imiter [1].

imitation noun imitation Fem.

immediate adjective immédiat.

immediately adverb immédiatement; **I rang them immediately** je les ai appelés immédiatement; **immediately before** juste avant; **immediately after** juste après.

immigrant noun immigré Masc., immigrée Fem..

immigration noun immigration Fem.

impact noun impact Masc.

impatience noun impatience Fem.

impatient adjective 1 impatient; 2 **to get impatient with somebody** s'impatienter [1] contre quelqu'un.

impatiently adverb avec impatience.

imperfect noun (of a verb) imparfait Masc.; **in the imperfect** à l'imparfait.

import noun produit Masc. importé.

import verb importer [1].

importance noun importance Fem.

important adjective important.

impossible adjective impossible; **it's impossible to find a telephone**

il est impossible de trouver un téléphone.

impressed *adjective*
impressionné.

impression *noun* impression
Fem.; **to make a good impression
on somebody** faire bonne
impression sur quelqu'un; **I got
the impression he was hiding
something** j'avais l'impression
qu'il cachait quelque chose.

impressive *adjective*
impressionnant.

improve *verb* **1** to improve
something améliorer [1] quelque
chose; **2** (*get better*) s'améliorer [1];
the weather is improving le temps
s'améliore.

improvement *noun* **1** (*a clear
change for the better*) amélioration
Fem.; **2** (*gradual progress*) progrès
Masc. plural (*in schoolwork, for
example*).

in *preposition, adverb* **1** dans; **in my
pocket** dans ma poche; **in the
newspaper** dans le journal; **in the
kitchen** dans la cuisine; **in my
class** dans ma classe; **I was in the
bath** j'étais dans mon bain; **2** à; **in
Oxford** à Oxford; **a house in the
country** une maison à la
campagne; **in school** à l'école; **in
the sun** au soleil; **the girl in the
pink shirt** la fille à la chemise rose;
3 en; **in France** en France (*BUT*) **in
Portugal** au Portugal ('*en*' *for
feminine countries, '*au*' for most
masculine countries*); **in town** en
ville; **in French** en français; **4** (*time
expressions*) **in May** en mai; **in '94**
en quatre-vingt-quatorze; **in winter**
en hiver; **in summer** en été; (*BUT*)

in spring au printemps; **in the
morning** le matin; **at eight in the
morning** à huit heures du matin; **in
the night** pendant la nuit; **I'll
phone you in ten minutes** je
t'appellerai dans dix minutes; **she
did it in five minutes** elle l'a fait en
cinq minutes; **5** (*talking about a
group*) de; **the tallest boy in the
class** le garçon le plus grand de la
classe; **the biggest city in the
world** la ville la plus grande du
monde; **6** in time à temps; **7** in the
photo sur la photo; **8** in the rain
sous la pluie; **9** dressed in white
habillé en blanc; **10** to come in
entrer; **to go in** entrer; **we went
into the cinema** nous sommes
entrés dans le cinéma; **to run in**
entrer en courant; **11** to be in être
là; **Mick's not in at the moment**
Mick n'est pas là en ce moment.

incident *noun* incident Masc.

include *verb* comprendre [64];
dinner is included in the price le
dîner est compris dans le prix;
service included service compris.

including *preposition* (y) compris;
£50 including VAT cinquante
livres TVA comprise; **everyone,
including children** tout le monde, y
compris les enfants; **including
Sundays** y compris les dimanches;
not including Sundays sans
compter les dimanches.

income *noun* revenu Masc.

income tax *noun* impôt Masc. sur
le revenu.

inconvenient *adjective*
1 incommode (*a place or an
arrangement*); **2** inopportun (*a
time*).

increase noun augmentation Fem. (in price, for example).

increase verb augmenter [1]; **the price has increased by £10** le prix a augmenté de dix livres.

incredible adjective incroyable.

incredibly adverb (very) extrêmement; **the film's incredibly boring** le film est extrêmement ennuyeux.

indeed adverb 1 (to emphasize) vraiment; **she's very pleased indeed** elle est vraiment très contente; **I'm very hungry indeed** j'ai vraiment très faim; **thank you very much indeed** merci beaucoup; 2 (certainly) bien sûr; **'can you hear his radio?' – 'indeed I can!'** 'entends-tu sa radio?' – 'bien sûr que oui!'

indefinite article noun (in grammar) article Masc. indéfini.

independence noun indépendance Fem.

independent adjective indépendant; **an independent school** une école privée.

index noun index Masc.

index finger noun index Masc.

India noun Inde Fem.; **in India** en Inde; **to India** en Inde.

Indian noun Indien Masc., Indienne Fem.

Indian adjective indien (Fem. indienne).

indicate verb indiquer [1].

indication noun indication Fem.

indigestion noun indigestion Fem.; **to have indigestion** avoir une indigestion.

indirect adjective indirect.

individual noun individu Masc.

individual adjective 1 individuel (Fem. individuelle) (a serving or a contribution, for example); 2 **individual tuition** des cours particuliers.

indoor adjective couvert; **an indoor swimming pool** une piscine couverte.

indoors adverb à l'intérieur; **it's cooler indoors** il fait plus frais à l'intérieur; **to go indoors** rentrer.

industrial adjective industriel (Fem. industrielle).

industrial estate noun zone Fem. industrielle.

industry noun industrie Fem.; **the advertising industry** l'industrie de la publicité.

inefficient adjective inefficace.

inevitable adjective inévitable.

inevitably adverb inévitablement.

inexperienced adjective inexpérimenté.

infant school noun école Fem. maternelle.

infected adjective qui s'est infecté.

infection noun infection Fem.; **an eye infection** une infection de l'œil; **a throat infection** une angine.

infectious adjective contagieux (Fem. contagieuse).

infinitive noun infinitif Masc.; **in the infinitive** à l'infinitif.

inflammable adjective inflammable.

inflatable adjective pneumatique (a mattress or a boat).

inflate *verb* gonfler [1] (*a mattress or boat*).

inflation *noun* inflation *Fem.*

influence *noun* influence *Fem.*; **to be a good influence on somebody** avoir une bonne influence sur quelqu'un.

influence *verb* influencer [61].

inform *verb* informer [1]; **to inform somebody that** informer quelqu'un du fait que; **they informed us that there was a problem** ils nous ont informés du fait qu'il y avait un problème; **to inform somebody of something** informer quelqu'un de quelque chose.

informal *adjective* **1** simple (*a meal or event, for example*); **2** (*language*) familier (*Fem.* familière); **an informal expression** une expression familière.

information *noun* renseignements *Masc. plural*; **I need some information about flights to Paris** j'ai besoin de quelques renseignements sur les vols vers Paris; **a piece of information** un renseignement.

information desk, **information office** *noun* bureau *Masc.* des renseignements.

information technology *noun* informatique *Fem.*

infuriating *adjective* exaspérant.

ingredient *noun* ingrédient *Masc.*

inhabitant *noun* habitant *Masc.*, habitante *Fem.*

initials *plural noun* initiales *Fem. plural*; **put your initials here** marquez vos initiales ici.

initiative *noun* initiative *Fem.*

injection *noun* piqûre *Fem.*; **to give somebody an injection** faire [10] une piqûre à quelqu'un.

injure *verb* blesser [1].

injured *adjective* blessé.

injury *noun* blessure *Fem.*

ink *noun* encre *Fem.*

in-laws *noun* beaux-parents *Masc. plural*.

inner *adjective* intérieur.

innocent *adjective* innocent.

insane *adjective* fou (*Fem.* folle).

inscription *noun* inscription *Fem.*

insect *noun* insecte *Masc.*; **an insect bite** une piqûre d'insecte.

insect repellent *noun* insectifuge *Masc.*

insert *verb* insérer [24].

inside *noun* intérieur *Masc.*; **the inside of the oven** l'intérieur du four.

inside *preposition* à l'intérieur de; **inside the cinema** à l'intérieur du cinéma.

inside *adverb* à l'intérieur; **she's inside, I think** elle est à l'intérieur, je crois; **to go inside** rentrer.

inside out *adjective, adverb* à l'envers.

insincere *adjective* peu sincère.

insist *verb* **1** insister [1]; **if you insist** puisque tu insistes; **to insist on doing** insister pour faire; **he insisted on paying** il a insisté pour payer; **2 to insist that** affirmer [1] que; **Ruth insisted I was wrong** Ruth a affirmé que j'avais tort.

insomnia *noun* insomnie *Fem.*

a
b
c
d
e
f
g
h
i
j
k
l
m
n
o
p
q
r
s
t
u
v
w
x
y
z

inspector noun inspecteur Masc., inspectrice Fem.

install verb installer [1].

instalment noun (of a story or serial) épisode Masc.

instance noun for instance par exemple.

instant noun instant Masc.; **come here this instant!** viens ici tout de suite!

instant adjective 1 instantané (coffee or soup); 2 (immediate) immédiat (an effect or a success, for example).

instantly adverb immédiatement.

instead adverb 1 Ted couldn't go, so I went instead Ted ne pouvait pas y aller, donc je suis allé à sa place; 2 instead of au lieu de; **we didn't go to the concert, we went to Lucy's instead** au lieu d'aller au concert, nous sommes allés chez Lucy; 2 instead of au lieu de; **instead of pudding I had cheese** j'ai pris le fromage au lieu d'un dessert; **instead of playing tennis we went swimming** au lieu de jouer au tennis nous sommes allés à la piscine.

instinct noun instinct Masc.

institute noun institut Masc.

institution noun institution Fem.

instruct verb to instruct somebody to do donner [1] l'ordre à quelqu'un de faire; **the teacher instructed us to stay together** le professeur nous a donné l'ordre de rester en groupe.

instructions plural noun instructions Fem. plural; **follow the instructions on the packet** suivez les instructions sur l'emballage; **'instructions for use'** 'mode d'emploi'.

instructor noun moniteur Masc., monitrice Fem.; **my skiing instructor** mon moniteur de ski.

instrument noun instrument Masc.; **to play an instrument** jouer d'un instrument.

insulin noun insuline Fem.

insult noun insulte Fem.

insult verb insulter [1].

insurance noun assurance Fem.; **travel insurance** l'assurance voyage; **do you have medical insurance?** est-ce que vous avez une assurance maladie?

intelligence noun intelligence Fem.

intelligent adjective intelligent.

intend verb 1 vouloir [14]; **as I intended** comme je le voulais; 2 to intend to do avoir [5] l'intention de faire; **we intend to spend the night in Rome** nous avons l'intention de passer la nuit à Rome.

intensive adjective intensif (Fem. intensive).

intensive care noun in intensive care en réanimation.

intention noun intention Fem.; **I have no intention of paying** je n'ai aucune intention de payer.

interest noun 1 (hobby) centre Masc. d'intérêt; **what are your interests?** quels sont vos centres d'intérêt?; 2 (keenness) intérêt Masc.; **he has an interest in jazz** il a un intérêt pour le jazz.

interest verb intéresser [1]; **that doesn't interest me** ça ne m'intéresse pas.

interested adjective **to be interested in** s'intéresser à; **Sean's very interested in cooking** Sean s'intéresse beaucoup à la cuisine.

interesting adjective intéressant.

interfere verb **1 to interfere with something** (to fiddle with it) toucher [1] quelque chose; **don't interfere with my computer!** ne touche pas mon ordinateur; **2 to interfere in** se mêler [1] à (someone else's affairs).

interior adjective intérieur.

interior designer noun designer Masc. & Fem.

international adjective international (Masc. plural internationaux).

Internet noun Internet Masc.; **on the Internet** sur Internet.

Internet cafe noun cybercafé Masc.; **where is there an Internet cafe?** où est-ce qu'il y a un cybercafé?

interpret verb (act as an interpreter) faire [10] l'interprète.

interpreter noun interprète Masc. & Fem.

interrupt verb interrompre [69].

interruption noun interruption Fem.

interval noun entracte Masc. (in a play or concert).

interview noun **1** (for a job) entretien Masc.; **a job interview** un entretien; **2** (in a newspaper, on TV or radio) interview Fem.

interview verb interviewer [1] (on TV, radio).

interviewer noun interviewer Masc.

into preposition **1** dans; **he's gone into the bank** il est entré dans la banque; **I put the cat into his basket** j'ai mis le chat dans son panier; **we all got into the car** nous sommes tous montés dans la voiture; **2 to go into town** aller en ville; **Mum's gone into town** Maman est allée en ville; **to get into bed** se mettre au lit; **to translate into French** traduire en français; **to change pounds into euros** changer des livres sterling en euros; **3 to be into jazz** être fana du jazz (informal).

introduce verb présenter [1]; **she introduced me to her brother** elle m'a présenté à son frère; **can I introduce you to my mother?** je te présente ma mère.

introduction noun (in a book) introduction Fem.

intuition noun intuition Fem.

invade verb envahir [2].

invalid noun malade Masc. & Fem.

invasion noun invasion Fem.

invent verb inventer [1].

invention noun invention Fem.

inventor noun inventeur Masc., inventrice Fem.

inverted commas plural noun guillemets Masc. plural; **in inverted commas** entre guillemets.

investigation noun (by police) enquête Fem.; **an investigation into the fire** une enquête sur l'incendie.

invisible adjective invisible.

a
b
c
d
e
f
g
h
i
j
k
l
m
n
o
p
q
r
s
t
u
v
w
x
y
z

a

b

c

d

e

f

g

h

i

j

k

l

m

n

o

p

q

r

s

t

u

v

w

x

y

z

invitation noun invitation Fem.;
an invitation to dinner une
invitation à dîner.

invite verb inviter [1]; **Kirsty
invited me to lunch** Kirsty m'a
invité à déjeuner; **he's invited me
out on Tuesday** il m'a invitée à
sortir avec lui mardi.

inviting adjective **1** appétissant (a
meal); **2** accueillant (a room).

invoice noun facture Fem.

involve verb **1** nécessiter [1]; **it
involves a lot of work** cela
nécessite beaucoup de travail; **2** (to
affect) concerner [1]; **the play will
involve everybody** le spectacle va
concerner tout le monde; **two cars
were involved** deux voitures ont
été concernées; **3 to be involved in**
participer [1] à; **I am involved in
the new project** je participe au
nouveau projet.

Iran noun Iran Masc.

Iraq noun Iraq Masc.

Ireland noun Irlande Fem.; **in
Ireland** en Irlande; **to Ireland** en
Irlande; **the Republic of Ireland** la
République d'Irlande.

Irish noun **1** (the language)
irlandais Masc.; **2** (the people) **the
Irish** les Irlandais Masc. plural.

Irish adjective irlandais.

Irishman noun Irlandais Masc.

Irish Sea noun mer Fem. d'Irlande.

Irishwoman noun Irlandaise Fem.

iron noun **1** (for clothes) fer Masc. à
repasser; **2** (the metal) fer Masc.

iron verb repasser [1].

ironing noun repassage Masc.; **to
do the ironing** faire le repassage.

ironing board noun planche Fem.
à repasser.

ironmonger's noun quincaillerie
Fem.

irregular adjective irrégulier
(Fem. irrégulière).

irresponsible adjective
irresponsable.

irritable adjective irritable.

irritate verb irriter [1].

irritating adjective irritant.

Islam noun Islam Masc.

Islamic adjective islamique.

island noun île Fem.

isolated adjective isolé.

Israel noun Israël Masc.

Israeli noun Israélien Masc.,
Israélienne Fem.

Israeli adjective israélien (Fem.
israélienne).

issue noun **1** (something you
discuss) question Fem.; **a political
issue** une question politique; **2** (of
a magazine) numéro Masc.

issue verb (hand out) distribuer [1].

IT noun (short for information
technology) informatique Fem.

it pronoun **1** (as the subject) il (when
it stands for a masculine noun); elle
(when it stands for a feminine
noun); **'where is my bag?' – 'it's in
the kitchen'** 'où est mon sac?' – 'il
est dans la cuisine'; **'how old is
your car?'** – **'it's five years old'**
'quel âge a ta voiture?' – 'elle a cinq
ans'; **2** (as the object) le (when it
stands for a masculine noun); la
(when it stands for a feminine
noun); l' (before a vowel or silent
'h'); **his new book? I know it** son

nouveau livre? je le connais; **his address? I know it** son adresse? je la connais; **where's my book? I've lost it** où est mon livre? je l'ai perdu; **3 yes, it's true** oui, c'est vrai; **it doesn't matter** ça ne fait rien; **4 who is it?** qui c'est?; **it's me** c'est moi; **what is it?** qu'est-ce que c'est?; **5 it's raining** il pleut; **it's a nice day** il fait beau; **it's two o'clock** il est deux heures.

Italian noun **1** (the language) italien Masc.; **2** (person) Italien Masc., Italienne Fem.

Italian adjective **1** italien (Fem. italienne); **Italian food** la cuisine italienne; **2** d'italien (a teacher or a lesson); **my Italian class** mon cours d'italien.

italics noun italique Masc.; **in italics** en italique.

Italy noun Italie Fem.; **in Italy** en Italie; **to Italy** en Italie.

itch verb **my back is itching** j'ai le dos qui me démange; **this sweater itches** ce pull me gratte.

item noun article Masc.

its determiner son (before a masculine noun or a feminine noun beginning with a vowel or silent 'h'); sa (before a feminine noun); ses (before a plural noun); **the dog has lost its collar** le chien a perdu son collier; **the dog's in its kennel** le chien est dans sa niche; **its ear** son oreille; **its toys** ses jouets.

itself pronoun **1** se, s' (before a vowel or silent 'h'); **the cat is washing itself** le chat se lave; **2 he left the dog by itself** il a laissé le chien tout seul.

ivory noun ivoire Masc.

ivy noun lierre Masc.

Jj

jack noun **1** (in cards) valet Masc.; **the jack of clubs** le valet de trèfle; **2** (for a car) cric Masc.

jacket noun veste Fem.

jacket potato noun pomme Fem. de terre en robe des champs.

jackpot noun gros lot Masc.; **to win the jackpot** gagner le gros lot.

jagged adjective dentelé.

jail noun prison Fem.

jail verb emprisonner [1].

jam noun **1** (that you eat) confiture Fem.; **raspberry jam** la confiture de framboises; **2 a traffic jam** un embouteillage.

Jamaica noun Jamaïque Fem.

Jamaican noun Jamaïquain Masc., Jamaïquaine Fem.

Jamaican adjective jamaïquain.

jammed adjective coincé.

January noun janvier Masc.; **in January** en janvier.

Japan noun Japon Masc.; **in Japan** au Japon.

Japanese noun **1** (the language) japonais Masc.; **2** (person) Japonais Masc., Japonaise Fem.; **the Japanese** les Japonais Masc. plural.

Japanese adjective japonais.

jar noun (small) pot Masc.; (large) bocal Masc. (plural bocaux); **a jar of jam** un pot de confiture.

javelin noun javelot Masc.

jaw noun mâchoire Fem.

jazz noun jazz Masc.

jealous adjective jaloux (Fem. jalouse).

jealousy noun jalousie Fem.

jeans noun jean Masc.; **my jeans** mon jean; **a pair of jeans** un jean.

jelly noun gelée Fem.

jellyfish noun méduse Fem.

jersey noun 1 (a pullover) pull-over Masc.; 2 (for football) maillot Masc.

Jersey noun Jersey Fem.

Jesus noun Jésus Masc.; **Jesus Christ** Jésus-Christ.

jet noun jet Masc.

jet lag noun décalage Masc. horaire.

jetty noun jetée Fem.

Jew noun Juif Masc., Juive Fem.

jewel noun bijou Masc. (plural bijoux).

jeweller's noun bijouterie Fem.

jeweller noun bijoutier Masc., bijoutière Fem.

jewellery noun bijoux Masc. plural.

Jewish adjective juif (Fem. juive).

jigsaw noun puzzle Masc.

job noun 1 (paid work) emploi Masc.; **a job as a secretary** un emploi comme secrétaire; **he's got a job** il a trouvé un emploi; **out of a job** sans emploi; **what's your job?** qu'est-ce que vous faites comme travail?; **a job offer** une offre d'emploi; 2 (a task) travail Masc.; **it's not an easy job** ce n'est pas un travail facile; **she made a good job of it** elle a fait un bon travail.

jobless adjective sans emploi.

jockey noun jockey Masc.

jog verb **to go jogging** faire [10] du jogging.

join verb 1 (become a member of) s'inscrire [38] à; **I've joined the judo club** je me suis inscrit au club de judo; 2 (to meet up with) rejoindre [49]; **I'll join you later** je vous rejoindrai plus tard.

● **to join in** 1 participer [1]; **Ruth never joins in** Ruth ne participe jamais; 2 **to join in something** participer [1] à quelque chose; **won't you join in the game?** veux-tu participer au jeu?

joiner noun menuisier Masc.

joint noun 1 (of meat) rôti Masc.; **a joint of beef** un rôti de bœuf; 2 (in your body) articulation Fem.

joint adjective 1 **the joint winners** les lauréats ex aequo.

joke noun (a funny story) plaisanterie Fem.; **to tell a joke** raconter une plaisanterie.

joke verb plaisanter [1]; **you must be joking!** tu plaisantes!

joker noun (in cards) joker Masc.

Jordan noun Jordanie Fem.

journalism noun journalisme Masc.

journalist noun journaliste Masc. & Fem.; **Sean's a journalist** Sean est journaliste.

journey noun 1 (a long one) voyage Masc.; **our journey to Turkey** notre voyage en Turquie; 2 (shorter: to work or school) trajet Masc.; **a bus journey** un trajet en bus.

joy noun joie Fem.

joy-riding noun rodéo Masc. à la voiture volée.

a
b
c
d
e
f
g
h
i
j
k
l
m
n
o
p
q
r
s
t
u
v
w
x
y
z

joystick noun (for computer games) manette Fem. de jeu.

Judaism noun judaïsme Masc.

judge noun juge Masc.

judge verb estimer [1] (a time or distance).

judgement noun jugement Masc.

judo noun judo Masc.; **he does judo** il fait du judo.

jug noun pot Masc.

juggle verb jongler [1].

juice noun jus Masc.; **two orange juices please** deux jus d'orange s'il vous plaît.

juicy adjective juteux (Fem. juteuse).

jukebox noun jukebox Masc.

July noun juillet Masc.; **in July** en juillet.

jumble sale noun vente Fem. de charité.

jumbo jet noun gros-porteur Masc.

jump noun saut Masc.; **a parachute jump** un saut en parachute.

jump verb sauter [1].

jumper noun pull Masc.

junction noun 1 (of roads) carrefour Masc.; 2 (of motorways) échangeur Masc.; 3 (on railway) nœud Masc. ferroviaire.

June noun juin Masc.; **in June** en juin.

jungle noun jungle Fem.

junior adjective primaire; **a junior school** une école primaire; **the juniors** les élèves du primaire.

junk noun (real rubbish) bric-à-brac Masc.

junk food noun **you shouldn't eat junk food** tu devrais manger

correctement (there is no word for junk food in French, so you will need to express it differently, according to the context).

junk shop noun magasin Masc. de brocante.

jury noun jury Masc.

just adverb 1 juste; **just before midday** juste avant midi; **just after the church** juste après l'église; **just for fun** juste pour rire; 2 **to have just done** venir de faire; **Tom has just arrived** Tom vient d'arriver; **Helen had just called** Helen venait d'appeler; 3 **to be just doing** être en train de faire; **I'm just finishing the ironing** je suis en train de finir le repassage; 4 (only) ne ...que; **he's just a child** il n'est qu'un enfant; **there's just me and Justine** il n'y a que moi et Justine; 5 **just coming!** j'arrive!

justice noun justice Fem.

justify verb justifier [1].

Kk

kangaroo noun kangourou Masc.

karaoke noun karaoké Masc.

karate noun karaté Masc.

kebab noun brochette Fem.

keen adjective 1 (enthusiastic) enthousiaste; **you don't look too keen** tu n'as pas l'air très enthousiaste; 2 (committed) passionné; **he's a keen photographer** c'est un photographe passionné; 3 **I'm not keen on fish** je n'aime pas trop le

a

poisson; **4 to be keen on doing (or to do)** avoir très envie de faire; **I'm not keen on camping** je n'ai pas très envie de faire du camping.

b

c

keep verb **1** garder [1]; **I kept the letter** j'ai gardé la lettre; **will you keep my seat?** veux-tu garder ma place?; **they kept her in hospital** ils l'ont gardée à l'hôpital; **to keep a secret** garder un secret; **2 to keep somebody waiting** faire [10] attendre quelqu'un; **3** (*to store*) ranger [52]; **I keep my bike in the garage** je range mon vélo dans le garage; **where do you keep saucepans?** où rangez-vous les casseroles?; **4 to keep on doing** continuer [1] à faire; **she kept on talking** elle a continué à parler; **keep straight on** continuez tout droit; **5 to keep on doing** (*time after time*) **he keeps on ringing me up** il n'arrête pas de m'appeler; **6** (*stay*) rester [1]; **keep calm! restez calme!; keep out of the sun** reste à l'abri du soleil; **7 to keep a promise** tenir [77] sa promesse.

d

e

f

g

h

i

j

k

l

keep fit noun gymnastique Fem. d'entretien.

m

kennel noun **1** (*for one dog*) niche Fem.; **2** (*for boarding*) **kennels** chenil Masc.

n

o

kerb noun bord Masc. du trottoir.

p

ketchup noun ketchup Masc.

q

kettle noun bouilloire Fem.; **to put the kettle on** mettre l'eau à chauffer.

r

s

t

key noun **1** (*for a lock*) clé Fem.; **a bunch of keys** un trousseau de clés; **2** (*on a piano or typewriter*) touche Fem.

u

v

w

x

y

z

keyboard noun (*for a piano or a computer*) clavier Masc.

keyhole noun trou Masc. de serrure.

keyring noun porte-clés Masc.

kick noun **1** (*from a person or a horse*) coup Masc. de pied; **to give somebody a kick** donner un coup de pied à quelqu'un; **2** (*in football*) tir Masc.; ★ **to get a kick out of doing** prendre plaisir à faire.

kick verb **to kick somebody** donner [1] un coup de pied à quelqu'un; **to kick the ball** donner un coup de pied dans le ballon.

● **to kick off** donner [1] le coup d'envoi.

kick-off noun coup Masc. d'envoi.

kid noun gosse Masc. & Fem. (*child*); **Dad's looking after the kids** Dad s'occupe des gosses.

kidnap verb enlever [50].

kidnapper noun ravisseur Masc., ravisseuse Fem.

kidney noun **1** (*part of your body*) rein Masc.; **2** (*for eating*) rognon Masc.

kill verb tuer [1]; **she was killed in an accident** elle a été tuée dans un accident.

killer noun (*murderer*) meurtrier Masc., meurtrière Fem.

kilo noun kilo Masc.; **a kilo of sugar** un kilo de sucre; **five euros a kilo** cinq euros le kilo.

kilogramme noun kilogramme Masc.

kilometre noun kilomètre Masc.

kilt noun kilt Masc.

kind noun sorte Fem.; **all kinds of people** toutes sortes de gens.

kind adjective gentil (Fem. gentille); **Marion was very kind to me** Marion a été très gentille avec moi.

kindness noun gentillesse Fem.

king noun roi Masc.; **King George** le roi Georges; **the king of hearts** le roi de cœur.

kingdom noun royaume Masc.; **the United Kingdom** le Royaume-Uni.

kiosk noun 1 (for newspapers or snacks) kiosque Masc.; 2 (for a phone) cabine Fem.

kipper noun hareng Masc. fumé.

kiss noun baiser Masc.; **to give somebody a kiss** embrasser quelqu'un.

kiss verb embrasser [1]; **kiss me!** embrasse-moi!; **we kissed each other** nous nous sommes embrassés.

kit noun 1 (of tools) trousse Fem.; **a tool kit** une trousse à outils; 2 (clothes) affaires Fem. plural; **where's my football kit?** où sont mes affaires de foot?; 3 (for making a model, a piece of furniture, etc) kit Masc.

kitchen noun cuisine Fem.; **the kitchen table** la table de la cuisine.

kitchen foil noun papier Masc. d'aluminium.

kitchen garden noun jardin Masc. potager.

kitchen roll noun essuie-tout Masc.

kite noun (toy) cerf-volant Masc.; **to fly a kite** faire voler un cerf-volant.

kitten noun chaton Masc.

kiwi fruit noun kiwi Masc.

knack noun don Masc.

knee noun genou Masc. (plural genoux); **on (your) hands and knees** à quatre pattes.

kneel verb se mettre [11] à genoux.

knickers plural noun petite culotte Fem.

knife noun couteau Masc. (plural couteaux).

knight noun (in chess) cavalier Masc.

knit verb tricoter [1].

knitting noun tricot Masc.

knob noun bouton Masc.

knock noun coup Masc.; **a knock on the head** un coup à la tête; **a knock at the door** un coup à la porte.

knock verb 1 (to bang) cogner [1]; **I knocked my arm on the table** je me suis cogné le bras contre la table; 2 **to knock on something** (a person) frapper [1] à (the door).

● **to knock down** 1 (in a traffic accident) renverser [1] (a person); 2 (to demolish) démolir [2] (an old building).

● **to knock out** 1 (to make unconscious) assommer [1]; 2 (in sport, to eliminate) éliminer [1].

knocker noun heurtoir Masc.

knot noun nœud Masc.; **to tie a knot in something** nouer [1] quelque chose.

know verb 1 (know a fact) savoir [70]; **do you know where Tim is?** sais-tu où est Tim?; **I know they've moved house** je sais qu'ils ont déménagé; **he knows it by heart** il le sait par cœur; **yes, I know** oui, je

a b c d e f g h i j k l m n o p q r s t u v w x y z

sais; **you never know!** on ne sait jamais!; **2** (*be personally acquainted with*) connaître [27] (*a person, place, book, or music, for example*); **do you know the Jacksons?** est-ce que tu connais les Jacksons?; **all the people I know** tous les gens que je connais; **I don't know his mother** je ne connais pas sa mère; **3 to know how to do** savoir [70] faire; **Steve knows how to make couscous** Steve sait faire du couscous; **Liz knows how to mend it** Liz sait le réparer; **4 to know about** être [6] au courant de (*the latest news*); **5 to know about** s'y connaître [27] en (*machines, cooking, etc*); **Lindy knows about computers** Lindy s'y connaît en informatique.

knowledge noun connaissance Fem.

knuckle noun articulation Fem. des doigts.

koala noun koala Masc.

Koran noun Coran Masc.

kosher adjective kascher.

Ll

lab noun labo Masc.

label noun étiquette Fem.

laboratory noun laboratoire Masc.

Labour noun les travaillistes Masc. plural; **to vote for the Labour party** voter pour les travaillistes; **the Labour Party** le parti travailliste.

lace noun **1** (*for a shoe*) lacet Masc.; **2** (*for curtains, for example*) dentelle Fem.

lad noun gars Masc.

ladder noun (*for climbing, or in your tights*) échelle Fem.

ladies noun (*lavatory*) toilettes Fem. plural; (*on a sign*) **'Ladies'** 'Dames'.

lady noun dame Fem.; **ladies and gentlemen** mesdames et messieurs.

ladybird noun coccinelle Fem.

lager noun bière Fem. blonde.

laid-back adjective relaxe.

lake noun lac Masc.; **Lake Geneva** le lac Léman.

lamb noun agneau Masc. (*plural agneaux*); **a leg of lamb** un gigot.

lame adjective boiteux (Fem. boiteuse); **he is lame** il boite.

lamp noun lampe Fem.

lamp-post noun réverbère Masc.

lampshade noun abat-jour Masc. (*plural abat-jour*).

land noun **1** terre Fem.; **I can see land** je vois la terre; **2** (*property*) terrain Masc.; **a piece of land** un terrain.

land verb **1** (*plane, passenger*) atterrir [2]; **2** (*leave a ship*) débarquer [1].

landing noun **1** (*on the stairs*) palier Masc.; **2** (*of a plane*) atterrissage Masc.; **3** (*from a boat*) débarquement Masc.

landlady noun propriétaire Fem.

landlord noun propriétaire Masc.

landscape noun paysage Masc.

lane noun **1** (a country path) chemin Masc.; **2** (of a motorway) voie Fem.

language noun **1** (French, Italian, etc) langue Fem.; **a foreign language** une langue étrangère; **2** (way of speaking) langage Masc.; **bad language** un langage grossier.

language lab noun laboratoire Masc. de langues.

language school noun école Fem. de langue.

lap noun **1** (your knees) genoux Masc. plural; **on my lap** sur mes genoux; **2** (in races) tour Masc. de piste.

laptop noun portable Masc.

larder noun garde-manger Masc.

large adjective **1** grand (goes before the noun); **a large number** un grand nombre; **a large house** une grande maison; **2** gros (Fem. grosse) (a piece, part, animal) (goes before the noun); **a large piece of cake** un gros morceau de gâteau; **3** nombreux (Fem. nombreuse) (crowd or family); **I come from a large family** je viens d'une famille nombreuse.

laser noun laser Masc.

laser beam noun rayon Masc. laser.

laser printer noun imprimante Fem. laser.

last adjective dernier (Fem. dernière); **the last time** la dernière fois; **last week** la semaine dernière; **last night** (in the evening) hier soir; (in the night) cette nuit.

last adverb **1** (in final position) (to arrive or leave) en dernier; **Rob arrived last** Rob est arrivé en dernier; **at last!** enfin!; **2** (most recently) **I last saw him in May** la dernière fois que je l'ai vu était en mai.

last verb durer [1]; **the play lasted two hours** le spectacle a duré deux heures.

late adjective, adverb **1** en retard; **we're late** nous sommes en retard; **they arrived late** ils sont arrivés en retard; **to be late for something** être en retard pour quelque chose; **we were late for the film** nous étions en retard pour le film; **2** to be late (a bus or train) avoir du retard; **the train was an hour late** le train a eu une heure de retard; **3** (late in the day) tard; **we got up late** nous nous sommes levés tard; **the chemist is open late** la pharmacie est ouverte tard; **late last night** tard hier soir; **too late!** trop tard!

lately adverb ces derniers temps.

later adverb plus tard; **I'll explain later** j'expliquerai plus tard; **see you later!** à tout à l'heure!

latest adjective **1** dernier (Fem. dernière); **the latest news** les dernières nouvelles; **2 at the latest** au plus tard.

latest noun **the latest in audio equipment** le dernier cri en matière d'équipement hifi.

Latin noun latin Masc.

laugh noun rire Masc.; **to do something for a laugh** faire quelque chose pour rigoler (informal).

laugh verb rire [68]; **everybody laughed** tout le monde a ri; **2 to**

a
b
c
d
e
f
g
h
i
j
k
l
m
n
o
p
q
r
s
t
u
v
w
x
y
z

laugh at se moquer [1] de; **I tried to explain but they laughed at me** j'ai essayé d'expliquer mais ils se sont moqués de moi.

laughter noun rire Masc.

launch noun (of a ship, product, spacecraft) lancement Masc.

launch verb **1** (product, spacecraft) lancer [61]; **2** (ship) mettre [11] à l'eau.

launderette noun laverie Fem. automatique.

laundry noun **1** (in hotel etc) laverie Fem.; **2** (shop) blanchisserie Fem.

lavatory noun toilettes Fem. plural; **to go to the lavatory** aller aux toilettes.

lavender noun lavande Fem.

law noun **1** loi Fem.; **it's against the law** c'est interdit; **2** (subject of study) droit Masc.

lawn noun pelouse Fem.

lawnmower noun tondeuse Fem. à gazon.

lawyer noun avocat Masc., avocate Fem.

lay verb **1** (put) poser [1]; **she laid the card on the table** elle a posé la carte sur la table; **2** (spread out) étaler [1]; **we laid newspaper on the floor** nous avons étalé du papier journal sur le parquet; **3** to **lay the table** mettre [11] la table.

lay-by noun aire Fem. de stationnement.

layer noun couche Fem.

laziness noun paresse Fem.

lazy adjective paresseux (Fem. paresseuse).

lead[1] noun **1** (when you are ahead) **to be in the lead** être en tête; **Baxter's in the lead** Baxter est en tête; **we have a lead of three points** nous avons trois points d'avance; **2** (electric) fil Masc.; **3** (for a dog) laisse Fem.; **on a lead** en laisse.

lead adjective (a role or a singer) principal (Masc. plural principaux).

lead verb **1** mener [50]; **the path leads to the sea** le chemin mène à la mer; **2** to **lead the way** montrer [1] le chemin; **3** to **lead to something** entraîner [1] quelque chose (an accident or problems, for example).

lead[2] noun (the metal) plomb Masc.

leader noun **1** (of a gang) chef Masc.; **2** (of a political party) dirigeant Masc., dirigeante Fem.; **3** (in a competition) premier Masc., première Fem.

lead-free petrol noun essence Fem. sans plomb.

lead singer noun chanteur principal Masc., chanteuse principale Fem.

leaf noun feuille Fem.

leaflet noun dépliant Masc.

league noun (in sport) championnat Masc.

leak noun fuite Fem.; **a gas leak** une fuite de gaz.

leak verb (a bottle or a roof) fuir [44].

lean adjective (meat) maigre.

lean verb **1** to **lean on something** s'appuyer [41] contre quelque chose; **2** (prop) appuyer [41]; **lean**

the ladder against the tree! appuie l'échelle contre l'arbre!; **3** (a person) se pencher [1]; **to lean out of the window** se pencher par la fenêtre; **lean forward a bit** penche-toi un peu en avant.

leap verb sauter [1].

leap year noun année Fem. bissextile.

learn verb apprendre [64]; **to learn Russian** apprendre le russe; **to learn (how) to drive** apprendre à conduire.

learner noun apprenant Masc., apprenante Fem.; **to be a fast learner** apprendre vite.

learner driver noun élève Masc. & Fem. d'auto-école.

least adverb, adjective, pronoun **1** le moins; **I like the blue shirt least** c'est la chemise bleue que j'aime le moins; **2** (followed by a noun) le moins de; **Tony has the least money** c'est Tony qui a le moins d'argent; **3** (followed by an adjective) le moins, la moins, les moins (according to the gender and number of the noun going with the adjective); **the least expensive hotel** l'hôtel le moins cher; **the least expensive car** la voiture la moins chère; **the least expensive shoes** les chaussures les moins chères; **4 the least** (the slightest) le moindre, la moindre (according to the gender of the noun that follows); **I haven't the least idea** je n'ai pas la moindre idée; **5 at least** (at a minimum) au moins; **at least twenty people** au moins vingt personnes; **6 at least** (at any rate) du moins; **at least, I think she's a** teacher du moins, je crois qu'elle est professeur.

leather noun cuir Masc.; **a leather jacket** un blouson en cuir.

leave noun congé Masc.; **three days' leave** trois jours de congé.

leave verb **1** (go away) partir [58]; **they're leaving tomorrow** ils vont partir demain; **we left at six** nous sommes partis à six heures; **2** (go away from) quitter [1]; **I left the office at five** j'ai quitté le bureau à cinq heures; **Guy left school at sixteen** Guy a quitté l'école à seize ans; **3** (go out of) sortir [72] de; **she left the cinema at ten** elle est sortie du cinéma à dix heures; **4** (deposit) laisser [1]; **you can leave your coats in the hall** vous pouvez laisser vos manteaux dans l'entrée; **5** (not do) laisser [1]; **let's leave the washing up!** laissons la vaisselle!; **6** (forget) oublier [1]; **he left his umbrella on the train** il a oublié son parapluie dans le train; **7 be left** rester [1]; **there are two pancakes left** il reste deux crêpes; **we have ten minutes left** il nous reste dix minutes; **I don't have any money left** il ne me reste plus d'argent.

lecture noun **1** (at university) cours Masc. magistral (plural cours magistraux); **2** (public) conférence Fem.

lecturer noun professeur Masc. à l'université.

ledge noun **1** (of a window) rebord Masc.; **2** (on a cliff) corniche Fem.

leek noun poireau Masc. (plural poireaux).

a
b
c
d
e
f
g
h
i
j
k
l
m
n
o
p
q
r
s
t
u
v
w
x
y
z

left noun gauche Fem.; **to drive on the left** conduire à gauche; **turn left at the church** tournez à gauche à l'église; **on my left** à ma gauche.

left adjective gauche; **his left foot** son pied gauche.

left-click noun clic Masc. sur le bouton gauche de la souris.

left-click verb **to left-click the icon** cliquer [1] en appuyant sur le bouton gauche de la souris.

left-hand adjective **the left-hand side** la gauche.

left-handed adjective gaucher Masc., gauchère Fem.

left luggage office noun consigne Fem.

leftovers plural noun restes Masc. plural.

leg noun **1** (of a person or a horse) jambe Fem.; **my left leg** ma jambe gauche; **to break your leg** se casser la jambe; **2** (of other animals) patte Fem.; **3** (of a table or chair) pied Masc.; **4** (in cooking) **a leg of chicken** une cuisse de poulet; **a leg of lamb** un gigot; ★ **to pull somebody's leg** faire [10] marcher quelqu'un.

legal adjective légal (Masc. plural légaux).

legend noun **1** (story) légende Fem.; **2** (person) légende Fem.

leggings plural noun caleçon Masc.

leisure noun loisirs Masc. plural; **in my leisure time** pendant mes loisirs.

leisure centre noun centre Masc. de loisirs.

lemon noun citron Masc.; **a lemon yoghurt** un yaourt au citron.

lemonade noun limonade Fem.

lemon juice noun jus Masc. de citron.

lend verb prêter [1]; **to lend something to somebody** prêter quelque chose à quelqu'un; **I lent Judy my bike** j'ai prêté mon vélo à Judy; **will you lend it to me?** veux-tu me le prêter?

length noun longueur Fem.

lens noun **1** (in a camera) objectif Masc.; **2** (in spectacles) verre Masc.; **3 contact lenses** les lentilles Fem. plural de contact.

Lent noun Carême Masc.

lentil noun lentille Fem.

Leo noun Lion Masc.; **I'm Leo** je suis Lion.

leotard noun justaucorps Masc.

lesbian noun lesbienne Fem.

less pronoun, adjective, adverb **1** moins; **Richard eats less** Richard mange moins; **2** (before a noun) moins de; **less traffic** moins de circulation; **less time** moins de temps; **3** (before an adjective or adverb) moins; **less interesting** moins intéressant; **less quickly than us** moins vite que nous; **4 less than** moins de; **less than three hours** moins de trois heures; **less than a kilo** moins d'un kilo; **5 less than** (in comparisons) moins que; **you spent less than me** tu as dépensé moins que moi.

lesson noun **1** (class) cours Masc.; **the history lesson** le cours d'histoire; **to take tennis lessons** prendre des cours de tennis; **2** (one

in a planned series) leçon Fem.; a
driving lesson une leçon de
conduite.

let[1] verb **1** (allow) to let somebody
do laisser [1] quelqu'un faire; **she
lets me borrow her bike** elle me
laisse emprunter son vélo; **will you
let me go alone?** veux-tu me
laisser y aller toute seule?; **the
police let us through** la police
nous a laissés passer; **let me see**
(show me) laisse-moi voir; **2** (as a
suggestion or a command) **let's go!**
allons-y!; **let's not talk about it**
n'en parlons pas; **let's see, if
Tuesday is the third** ... voyons, si
mardi est le trois ...; **let's eat out** si
on mangeait au restaurant?

● **to let off 1** tirer [1] (fireworks);
2 faire [10] exploser (a bomb); **3** (to
excuse from) dispenser [1] de
(homework).

let[2] verb (to rent out) louer [1]; **'flat
to let'** 'appartement à louer'.

lethal adjective mortel (Fem.
mortelle)

letter noun lettre Fem.; **a letter for
you from Delia** une lettre pour toi
de Delia; **G is the letter after F** G
est la lettre après F.

letter box noun boîte Fem. à
lettres.

lettuce noun salade Fem.; **two
lettuces** deux salades.

leukaemia noun leucémie Fem.

level noun niveau Masc. (plural
niveaux); **at street level** au niveau
de la rue.

level adjective **1** droit (a shelf or
floor); **2** plat (ground).

level crossing noun passage
Masc. à niveau.

lever noun levier Masc.

liar noun menteur Masc., menteuse
Fem.

liberal adjective libéral (Masc.
plural libéraux); **the Liberal
Democrats** le parti libéral-
démocrate.

liberty noun liberté Fem.

Libra noun Balance Fem.; **Sean's
Libra** Sean est Balance.

librarian noun bibliothécaire
Masc. & Fem.; **Mark's a librarian**
Mark est bibliothécaire.

library noun bibliothèque Fem.; **the
public library** la bibliothèque
municipale.

licence noun **1** (for driving or
fishing) permis Masc.; **a driving
licence** un permis de conduire;
2 (for a TV) redevance Fem.

lick verb lécher [24].

lid noun couvercle Masc.; **she took
the lid off** elle a enlevé le
couvercle.

lie noun mensonge Masc.; **to tell a
lie** (or lies) mentir [53].

lie verb **1** (to be stretched out) être [6]
allongé; **Jimmy was lying on the
bed** Jimmy était allongé sur le lit;
my coat lay on the bed mon
manteau était sur le lit; **2** to lie
down se coucher [1]; (for a little
while) s'allonger [52]; **come and lie
down in the sun** viens t'allonger
au soleil; **3** (not to tell the truth)
mentir [53].

lie-in noun **to have a lie-in** faire la
grasse matinée.

lieutenant noun lieutenant Masc.

a
b
c
d
e
f
g
h
i
j
k
l
m
n
o
p
q
r
s
t
u
v
w
x
y
z

life noun vie Fem.; **all her life** toute sa vie; **full of life** plein de vie; **that's life!** c'est la vie!

lifebelt noun bouée Fem. de sauvetage.

lifeboat noun canot Masc. de sauvetage.

lifeguard noun maître nageur Masc.; **is there a lifeguard at the pool?** est-ce que la piscine est surveillée?

life jacket noun gilet Masc. de sauvetage.

life-style noun style Masc. de vie.

lift noun **1** ascenseur Masc.; **let's take the lift** prenons l'ascenseur; **2** (a ride) **to give somebody a lift to the station** déposer quelqu'un à la gare; **Tom gave me a lift home** Tom m'a déposé chez moi; **can I give you a lift?** puis-je vous déposer quelque part?

lift verb soulever [50]; **he lifted the box** il a soulevé le carton.

light noun **1** (electric) lumière Fem.; **will you turn the light on?** veux-tu allumer la lumière?; **to turn off the light** éteindre la lumière; **2** (streetlight) réverbère Masc.; **3** (a headlight for a car) phare Masc.; **are your lights on?** as-tu allumé tes phares?; **4** (an indicator on a machine) voyant Masc.; **5 traffic lights** les feux Masc. plural; **the lights were green** le feu était au vert; **6 have you got a light?** tu as du feu?

light adjective **1** (in colour) clair; **light blue eyes** des yeux bleu clair; **2** (not night) **it gets light at six** il fait jour à six heures; **3** (not heavy) léger (Fem. légère); **a light sweater** un pull léger; **a light breeze** une brise légère.

light verb **1** allumer [1] (the oven, the fire, or a cigarette); **we lit a fire** nous avons fait un feu; **2** craquer [1] (a match).

light bulb noun ampoule Fem.

lighter noun briquet Masc.

lighthouse noun phare Masc.

lightning noun éclairs Masc. plural; **a flash of lightning** un éclair; **to be struck by lightning** être frappé par la foudre.

light switch noun interrupteur Masc.

like[1] preposition, conjunction **1** comme; **like me** comme moi; **like this** comme ça; **like a duck** comme un canard; **like I said** comme j'ai dit; **what's it like?** c'est comment?; **what was the weather like?** quel temps faisait-il?; **2 to look like** ressembler [1] à (qch); **Cindy looks like her father** Cindy ressemble à son père.

like[2] verb **1** aimer [1] (bien); **I like fish** j'aime bien le poisson; **I don't like snakes** je n'aime pas les serpents; **Mum likes travelling** Maman aime bien voyager; **I like Renoir best** je préfère Renoir; **2 I would like** je voudrais; **would you like a coffee?** est-ce que tu voudrais un café?; **what would you like to eat?** qu'est-ce que tu veux manger?; **yes, if you like** oui, si tu veux.

likely adjective probable; **it's not very likely** ce n'est pas très probable; **she's likely to phone** elle va probablement appeler.

lilac noun lilas Masc.

lily noun lys Masc.

lily of the valley noun muguet Masc.

lime noun citron Masc. vert.

limit noun limitation Fem.; **the speed limit** la limitation de vitesse.

limp noun **to have a limp** boiter [1].

line noun **1** ligne Fem.; **a straight line** une ligne droite; **six lines of text** six lignes de texte; **to draw a line** tirer un trait; **2** a railway line (from one place to another) une ligne de chemin de fer; **on the railway line** (the track) sur la voie ferrée; **3** (a queue of people or cars) file Fem.; **to stand in line** faire la queue; **4** (telephone) ligne Fem.; **the line's bad** la ligne est mauvaise; **hold the line, please** ne quittez pas.

line verb doubler [1] (a coat).

linen noun lin Masc.; **a linen jacket** une veste en lin.

lining noun doublure Fem.

link noun rapport Masc.; **what's the link between the two?** quel est le rapport entre les deux?.

link verb relier [1] (two places); **the terminals are linked by a shuttle service** les terminaux sont reliés par une navette.

lino noun linoléum Masc.

lion noun lion Masc.

lip noun lèvre Fem.

lip-read verb lire [51] sur les lèvres.

lipstick noun rouge Masc. à lèvres.

liquid noun, adjective liquide Masc.

liquidizer noun mixer Masc.

list noun liste Fem.

listen verb **1** écouter [1]; **I wasn't listening** je n'écoutais pas; **2** **to listen to** écouter [1]; **listen to the music** écoutez la musique; **you're not listening to me** tu ne m'écoutes pas.

listener noun (to the radio) auditeur Masc., auditrice Fem.

literally adverb littéralement.

literature noun littérature Fem.

litre noun litre Masc.; **a litre of milk** un litre de lait.

litter noun (rubbbish) détritus Masc. plural.

litter bin noun poubelle Fem.

little adjective, pronoun **1** (small) petit (goes before the noun); **a little boy** un petit garçon; **a little break** une petite pause; **2** (not much) peu (de); **they have little money** ils ont peu d'argent; **we have very little time** nous avons très peu de temps; **3 a little** un peu (de); **4 we have a little money** nous avons un peu d'argent; **just a little, please** juste un peu, s'il vous plaît; **it's a little late** c'est un peu tard; **a little more** un peu plus; **a little less** un peu moins; **★ little by little** petit à petit.

little finger noun petit doigt Masc.

live[1] verb **1** (in a house or town) habiter [1]; **Susan lives in York** Susan habite à York; **we live in a flat** nous habitons dans un appartement; **they live at number 57** ils habitent au numéro cinquante-sept; **we're living in the country now** nous habitons à la campagne maintenant; **2** (be or stay alive, spend one's life) vivre

[82]; **lions live in Africa** les lions vivent en Afrique; **they live on fruit** ils vivent de fruits; **they live together** ils vivent ensemble.

live² *adjective* **1** en direct (*a broadcast*); **a live concert** un concert en direct; **a broadcast live from Wembley** une émission en direct de Wembley; **2** (*alive*) vivant.

lively *adjective* animé (*a party or restaurant, for example*).

liver *noun* foie *Masc.*

living *noun* vie *Fem.*; **to earn a living** gagner sa vie.

living room *noun* salle *Fem.* de séjour.

lizard *noun* lézard *Masc.*

load *noun* **1** (*on a lorry*) chargement *Masc.*; **a (lorry-)load of bricks** un camion de briques; **2 a bus-load of tourists** un autobus plein de touristes; **3 loads of** des tas de (*informal*); **loads of people** des tas de gens; **they've got loads of money** ils sont bourrés de fric (*informal*).

load *verb* charger [52]; **a lorry loaded with wood** un camion chargé de bois.

loaf *noun* pain *Masc.*; **a loaf of wholemeal bread** un pain complet.

loan *noun* prêt *Masc.*

loan *verb* prêter [1].

loathe *verb* détester [1]; **I loathe getting up early** je déteste me lever tôt.

lobster *noun* homard *Masc.*

local *noun* **1** (*a pub*) pub *Masc.* du coin; **2 the locals** (*people*) les gens du coin.

local *adjective* **the local library** la bibliothèque du coin; **the local newspaper** le journal local.

locally *adverb* de façon locale; **they only advertise locally** ils ne font de publicité que dans la région.

lock *noun* **1** (*with a key*) serrure *Fem.*; **2** (*on a canal*) écluse *Fem.*

lock *verb* **to lock the door** fermer [1] à clé; **the door was locked** la porte était fermée à clé.

locker *noun* casier *Masc.*

locker room *noun* vestiaire *Masc.*

lodger *noun* locataire *Masc. & Fem.*

loft *noun* grenier *Masc.*

log *noun* bûche *Fem.*; **a log fire** un feu de bois.

logical *adjective* logique.

lollipop *noun* sucette *Fem.*

London *noun* Londres; **to London** à Londres; **a day in London** une journée à Londres; **the London streets** les rues de Londres.

Londoner *noun* Londonien *Masc.*, Londonienne *Fem.*

loneliness *noun* solitude *Fem.*

lonely *adjective* **1** seul; **to feel lonely** se sentir [53] seul; **2** (*a place*) isolé.

long *adjective, adverb* **1** long (*Fem.* longue); **a long film** un film long; **a long day** une longue journée; **it's an hour long** ça dure une heure; **a long time** longtemps; **he stayed for a long time** il est resté longtemps; **I've been here for a long time** je suis là depuis longtemps; **a long time ago** il y a longtemps; **this won't take long** ça ne prendra pas longtemps; **3 how long?** combien de temps?; **how long have you been here?** tu es là depuis combien de temps?; **long ago** il y a longtemps; **4 a long way** loin; **it's a long way to the cinema** le cinéma est loin d'ici; **5 all night long** toute la nuit.

long *verb* to long to do avoir [5] très envie de faire; **I'm longing to see you** j'ai très envie de te voir.

long-distance call *noun (within the country)* appel Masc. interurbain.

longer *adverb* **no longer** ne ...plus; **I no longer know** je ne sais plus; **they no longer live here** ils n'habitent plus ici.

long jump *noun* saut Masc. en longueur.

longlife milk *noun* lait Masc. longue conservation.

loo *noun* toilettes Fem. plural.

look *noun* **1** *(a glance)* coup Masc. d'œil; **to have a look at something** jeter un coup d'œil à quelque chose; **2** *(a tour)* **to have a look round the town** faire un tour dans la ville; **to have a look round the shops** faire les magasins; **3 to have a look for** chercher *(something you've lost)*.

look *verb* **1** regarder [1]; **I wasn't looking** je ne regardais pas; **to look out of the window** regarder par la fenêtre; **2 to look at** regarder [1]; **Andy was looking at the photos** Andy regardait les photos; **3** *(to seem)* avoir [5] l'air; **Melanie looks pleased** Melanie a l'air contente; **the salad looks delicious** la salade a l'air

délicieuse; **4 to look like** ressembler [1] à; **Sally looks like her aunt** Sally ressemble à sa tante; **they look like each other** ils se ressemblent; **what does the house look like?** comment est la maison?; **it looks like rain** on dirait qu'il va pleuvoir.

● **to look after 1** s'occuper [1] de; **Dad's looking after the baby** Papa s'occupe du bébé; **2** surveiller [1] *(luggage)*; **to look for** chercher [1]; **I'm looking for the keys** je cherche les clés.

● **to look forward to something** attendre [3] quelque chose avec impatience *(a party or a trip, for example)*.

● **to look out** *(to be careful)* faire [10] attention; **look out, it's hot!** (fais) attention, c'est chaud!

● **to look something up** chercher [1] quelque chose *(in a dictionary or directory)*; **you can look it up in the dictionary** tu peux le chercher dans le dictionnaire.

loose *adjective* **1** *(a screw or knot)* desserré; **2** *(a garment)* ample; **3 loose change** la petite monnaie; ★ **I'm at a loose end** je ne sais pas trop quoi faire.

lorry *noun* camion Masc.

lorry driver *noun* routier Masc.

lose *verb* **1** perdre [3]; **we lost** nous avons perdu; **we lost the match** nous avons perdu le match; **Sam's lost his watch** Sam a perdu sa montre; **2 to get lost** se perdre [3]; **we got lost in the woods** nous nous sommes perdus dans les bois.

loss *noun* perte Fem.

a
b
c
d
e
f
g
h
i
j
k
l
m
n
o
p
q
r
s
t
u
v
w
x
y
z

lost adjective perdu; **I'm lost** je suis perdu; **are you lost?** vous êtes perdu?

lost property noun objets Masc. plural trouvés.

lot noun 1 **a lot** beaucoup; **Jason eats a lot** Jason mange beaucoup; **I spent a lot** j'ai beaucoup dépensé; **he's a lot better** il va beaucoup mieux; 2 **a lot of** beaucoup de; **a lot of coffee** beaucoup de café; **lots of people** beaucoup de gens; **'what are you doing tonight?' – 'not a lot'** 'qu'est-ce que tu fais ce soir?' – 'pas grand-chose'.

lottery noun loterie Fem.; **to win the lottery** gagner à la loterie.

loud adjective 1 fort; **in a loud voice** d'une voix forte; 2 **to say something out loud** dire quelque chose à haute voix.

loudly adverb fort.

loudspeaker noun haut-parleur Masc. (plural **haut-parleurs**).

lounge noun 1 (in a house or hotel) salon Masc.; 2 (in an airport) **the departure lounge** la salle d'embarquement.

love noun 1 amour Masc.; **to be in love with somebody** être amoureux (Fem. amoureuse) de quelqu'un; **she's in love with Jake** elle est amoureuse de Jake; **Gina sends her love** Gina t'embrasse; **with love from Charlie** amitiés, Charlie; 2 (in tennis) zéro Masc.

love verb 1 aimer [1] (a person) **I love you** je t'aime; 2 aimer beaucoup (place, suggestion); **she loves London** elle aime beaucoup Londres; **I'd love to come**

j'aimerais beaucoup venir; 3 adorer [1] (activity, thing); **I love dancing** j'adore danser; **Wayne loves seafood** Wayne adore les fruits de mer.

lovely adjective 1 (to look at) joli; **a lovely dress** une jolie robe; **their garden is lovely** leur jardin est très joli; **a lovely house** une belle maison; 2 **it's a lovely day** il fait très beau; **we had lovely weather** il a fait très beau; 3 (food, meal) délicieux (Fem. délicieuse).

lover noun 1 (general) partenaire Masc. & Fem.; 2 (of married man) maîtresse Fem.; (of married woman) amant Masc.

low adjective bas (Fem. basse); **a low table** une table basse; **at a low price** à prix bas; **in a low voice** à voix basse.

lower adjective (not as high) inférieur.

lower verb baisser [1].

low-fat milk noun lait Masc. écrémé.

loyalty noun loyauté Fem.; **loyalty card** carte Fem. de fidélité.

luck noun chance Fem.; **good luck!** bonne chance!; **bad luck!** pas de chance!; **with a bit of luck** avec un peu de chance.

luckily adverb heureusement; **luckily for them** heureusement pour eux.

lucky adjective 1 **to be lucky** (a person) avoir de la chance; **we were lucky** nous avons eu de la chance; 2 **to be lucky** (bringing luck) porter bonheur; **it's supposed to be lucky** c'est censé porter bonheur; **my lucky number** mon numéro porte-bonheur.

luggage *noun* bagages *Masc. plural*; **my luggage is in the boot** mes bagages sont dans le coffre.

lump *noun* **1** (*of earth*) motte *Fem.*; **2** (*piece*) morceau *Masc.* (*plural* morceaux); **3** (*swelling*) grosseur *Fem.*

lunch *noun* déjeuner *Masc.*; **to have lunch** déjeuner [1]; **we had lunch in Oxford** nous avons déjeuné à Oxford.

lunch break *noun* pause-déjeuner *Fem.*

lunch hour, lunch time *noun* heure *Fem.* du déjeuner.

lung *noun* poumon *Masc.*

Luxembourg *noun* **1** (*country*) Luxembourg *Masc.*; **to Luxembourg** au Luxembourg; **in Luxembourg** au Luxembourg; **2** (*city*) Luxembourg; **in Luxembourg** à Luxembourg.

luxurious *adjective* luxueux (*Fem.* luxueuse).

luxury *noun* luxe *Masc.*; **a luxury hotel** un hôtel de luxe.

lyrics *plural noun* paroles *Fem. plural.*

Mm

mac *noun* imper *Masc.* (*informal*).

macaroni *noun* macaronis *Masc. plural*; **we had macaroni** nous avons mangé des macaronis.

machine *noun* machine *Fem.*

machinery *noun* machines *Fem. plural.*

mackerel *noun* maquereau *Masc.* (*plural* maquereaux).

mad *adjective* **1** fou (*Fem.* folle); **she's completely mad!** elle est complètement folle!; **2** (*angry*) furieux (*Fem.* furieuse); **my mum will be mad!** ma mère sera furieuse!; **3 to be mad about something** adorer quelque chose; **she's mad about horses** elle adore les chevaux.

madam *noun* madame *Fem.*

madman *noun* fou *Masc.*

madness *noun* folie *Fem.*

magazine *noun* magazine *Masc.*

maggot *noun* asticot *Masc.*

magic *noun* magie *Fem.*

magic *adjective* **1** magique; **a magic wand** une baguette magique; **2** (*great*) super.

magician *noun* **1** (*wizard*) magicien *Masc.*; **2** (*conjurer*) prestidigitateur *Masc.*

magnet *noun* aimant *Masc.*

magnificent *adjective* magnifique.

magnifying glass *noun* loupe *Fem.*

magnolia *noun* magnolia *Masc.*

mahogany *noun* acajou *Masc.*

maiden name *noun* nom *Masc.* de jeune fille.

mail *noun* courrier *Masc.*; **email** (*electronic mail*) courrier *Masc.* électronique.

a
b
c
d
e
f
g
h
i
j
k
l
m
n
o
p
q
r
s
t
u
v
w
x
y
z

mail order *noun* to buy something by mail order acheter quelque chose par correspondance; **a mail order catalogue** un catalogue de vente par correspondance.

main *adjective* principal (*Masc. plural* principaux); **the main entrance** l'entrée principale.

main course *noun* plat *Masc.* principal.

mainly *adverb* principalement.

main road *noun* route *Fem.* principale.

maize *noun* maïs *Masc.*

major *adjective* majeur.

major *noun* commandant *Masc.*

Majorca *noun* Majorque *Fem.*

majority *noun* majorité *Fem.*

make *noun* marque *Fem.*; **what make is your bike?** de quelle marque est ton vélo?

make *verb* **1** faire [10]; **I made an omelette** j'ai fait une omelette; **she made her bed** elle a fait son lit; **he made me wait** il m'a fait attendre; **she makes me laugh** elle me fait rire; **two and three make five** deux et trois font cinq; **2** fabriquer [1]; **they make computers** ils fabriquent des ordinateurs; **'made in France'** 'fabriqué en France'; **3** rendre [3]; **to make somebody happy** rendre quelqu'un heureux; **that makes me hungry** ça me donne faim; **4** gagner [1] (*money*); **he makes forty pounds a day** il gagne quarante livres par jour; **to make a living** gagner sa vie; **5** (*force*) **to make**

somebody do something obliger [52] quelqu'un à faire quelque chose; **she made him give the money back** elle l'a obligé à rendre l'argent; **6 to make a meal** préparer [1] un repas; **7 to make a phone call** passer [1] un coup de fil; **I have to make a few phone calls** je dois passer quelques coups de fil; **8 I can't make it tonight** je ne peux pas venir ce soir.

● **to make something up**
1 inventer [1] quelque chose; **she made up an excuse** elle a inventé une excuse; **2 to make it up** (*after a quarrel*) se réconcilier [1]; **they've made it up now** ils se sont maintenant réconciliés

make-up *noun* maquillage *Masc.*; **to put on your make-up** se maquiller; **Jo's putting on her make-up** Jo est en train de se maquiller; **I don't wear make-up** je ne me maquille pas.

male *adjective* **1** mâle (*animal*); **a male rat** un rat mâle; **2** (*sex : on a form*) masculin; **3 a male rôle** un rôle pour homme; **a male voice** une voix d'homme; **a male student** un étudiant.

male chauvinist *noun* macho *Masc.*

mall *noun* centre *Masc.* commercial.

Malta *noun* Malte *Fem.*

mammal *noun* mammifère *Masc.*

man *noun* homme *Masc.*; **modern man is taller than his ancestors** l'homme moderne est plus grand que ses ancêtres.

manage verb 1 diriger [52] (business, team); **she manages a travel agency** elle dirige une agence de voyages; 2 (cope) se débrouiller [1]; **I can manage** je me débrouille; 3 **to manage to do** réussir [2] à faire; **he managed to open the door** il a réussi à ouvrir la porte; **I didn't manage to get in touch with her** je n'ai pas réussi à la contacter.

management noun 1 gestion Fem.; **a management course** un cours de gestion; 2 direction; **a meeting with management** une réunion avec la direction.

manager noun 1 (of a company or a bank) directeur Masc., directrice Fem.; 2 (of a shop or restaurant) gérant Masc., gérante Fem.; 3 (in sport and entertainment) manager Masc.

manageress noun gérante Fem.

managing director noun directeur Masc. général, directrice Fem. générale.

mandarin (orange) noun mandarine Fem.

mango noun mangue Fem.

mania noun manie Fem.

maniac noun fou Masc., folle Fem.; **she drives like a maniac!** elle conduit comme une folle!

mankind noun humanité Fem.

man-made adjective (fibre) synthétique.

manner noun 1 **in a manner of speaking** pour ainsi dire; 2 **to have good manners** être poli; **it's bad manners to talk like that** ce n'est pas poli de parler comme ça.

manpower noun main-d'œuvre Fem.

mansion noun demeure Fem.

mantelpiece noun cheminée Fem.

manual noun manuel Masc.

manufacture verb fabriquer [1].

manufacturer noun fabricant Masc.

manure noun fumier Masc.

many adjective, pronoun
1 beaucoup (de); **does she have many friends?** est-ce qu'elle a beaucoup d'amis?; **we didn't see many people** nous n'avons pas vu beaucoup (de) gens; **not many** pas beaucoup; **there aren't many onions left** il ne reste pas beaucoup d'oignons; **many of them forgot** beaucoup d'entre eux ont oublié; 2 **very many** beaucoup (de); **there aren't very many glasses** il n'y a pas beaucoup de verres; 3 **so many** tant; **I have so many things to do!** j'ai tant de choses à faire!; 4 **so many** autant de; **I've never eaten so many strawberries** je n'ai jamais mangé autant de fraises; 5 **as many as** autant que; **you can take as many as you like** tu peux en prendre autant que tu veux; 6 **too many** trop (de); **I've got too many things to do** j'ai trop de choses à faire; **there were too many people** il y avait trop de monde; **that's far too many!** c'est beaucoup trop!; 7 **how many?** combien?; **how many are there?** il y en a combien?; **how many sisters have you got?** tu as combien de sœurs?; **how many are there left?** il en reste combien?

a
b
c
d
e
f
g
h
i
j
k
m
n
o
p
q
r
s
t
u
v
w
x
y
z

map 476 ENGLISH-FRENCH

a

map noun 1 carte Fem.; **a road map** une carte routière; 2 (of a town) plan Masc.

b

marathon noun marathon Masc.

c

marble noun 1 marbre Masc.; **a marble fireplace** une cheminée en marbre; 2 bille; **to play marbles** jouer aux billes.

d

e

march noun (demonstration) manifestation Fem.

f

g

march verb (demonstrators) défiler [1].

h

March noun mars Masc.; **in March** en mars.

i

mare noun jument Fem.

j

margarine noun margarine Fem.

margin noun marge Fem.

k

marijuana noun marijuana Fem.

l

mark noun 1 (at school) note Fem.; **I got a good mark for my French homework** j'ai eu une bonne note pour mon devoir de français; **what mark did you get for French?** tu as eu combien en français?; 2 (stain) tache Fem.

m

n

o

mark verb corriger [52]; **the teacher marks our homework** le professeur corrige nos devoirs.

p

market noun marché Masc.

q

marketing noun marketing Masc.

r

marmalade noun confiture Fem. d'oranges amères.

s

maroon adjective bordeaux; **a maroon jumper** un pull bordeaux.

t

u

marriage noun mariage Masc.

v

married adjective marié; **a married couple** un couple marié; **they've been married for twenty years** ils sont mariés depuis vingt ans.

w

x

y

z

marry verb 1 **to marry somebody** épouser [1] quelqu'un; **she married a Frenchman** elle a épousé un Français; 2 **to get married** se marier [1]; **they got married in July** ils se sont mariés en juillet.

marvellous adjective merveilleux (Fem. merveilleuse); **the weather's marvellous** il fait un temps merveilleux.

marzipan noun pâte Fem. d'amandes.

mascara noun mascara Masc.

masculine noun (in French and other grammars) masculin Masc.; **in the masculine** au masculin.

mash verb écraser [1] (vegetables).

mashed potatoes noun purée Fem. de pommes de terre.

mask noun masque Masc.

mass noun 1 **a mass of** une masse de; 2 **masses of** beaucoup de; **they've got masses of money** ils ont beaucoup d'argent; **there's masses left over** il en reste beaucoup; 3 (religious) messe Fem.; **to go to mass** aller à la messe.

massacre noun massacre Masc.

massage noun massage Masc.

massive adjective énorme.

master verb maîtriser [1].

masterpiece noun chef-d'œuvre Masc. (plural chefs-d'œuvre).

mat noun 1 (doormat) paillasson Masc.; 2 (to put under a hot dish) dessous-de-plat Masc.; 3 **a table mat** un set de table.

match noun 1 allumette Fem.; **a box of matches** une boîte d'allumettes; 2 (sports) match Masc. (plural matchs); **a football match**

a
b
c
d
e
f
g
h
i
j
k
l
m
n
o
p
q
r
s
t
u
v
w
x
y
z

un match de foot; **to watch the match** regarder [1] le match; **to win the match** gagner [1] le match; **to lose the match** perdre [3] le match.

match verb être [6] assorti à; **the jacket matches the skirt** la veste est assortie à la jupe.

matching adjective **matching curtains and cushions** des rideaux et des coussins assortis.

mate noun copain Masc., copine Fem. (informal); **I'm going out with my mates tonight** je sors avec mes copains ce soir.

material noun **1** (fabric) tissu Masc.; **2** (information) documentation Fem.; **3** (substance) matière Fem.; **raw materials** les matières Fem. plural premières.

mathematics noun mathématiques Fem. plural.

maths noun maths Fem. plural; **I like maths** j'aime bien les maths; **Anna's good at maths** Anna est forte en maths.

matter noun **what's the matter?** qu'est-ce qu'il y a?

matter verb **1** the things that matter les choses importantes; **it matters a lot to me** c'est très important pour moi; **2 it doesn't matter** ça ne fait rien; **it doesn't matter if it rains** ça ne fait rien s'il pleut; **3 it doesn't matter** (whether one thing or another) ça n'a pas d'importance; **you can write it in French or English, it doesn't matter** tu peux l'écrire en français ou en anglais, ça n'a pas d'importance.

mattress noun matelas Masc.

mature adjective mûr.

maximum noun maximum Masc.; **the maximum possible** le maximum possible.

maximum adjective maximum (does not change in the feminine or plural); **the maximum temperature** la température maximum; **maximum profits** les bénéfices maximum.

May noun mai Masc.; **in May** en mai.

may verb **1 she may be ill** elle est peut-être malade; **we may go to Spain** nous irons peut-être en Espagne; **2** (asking permission) **may I close the door?** est-ce que je peux fermer la porte?

maybe adverb peut-être; **maybe not** peut-être pas; **maybe he's forgotten** il a peut-être oublié; **maybe they've got lost** ils se sont peut-être perdus.

May Day noun le Premier Mai.

mayonnaise noun mayonnaise Fem.

mayor noun maire Masc.

mayoress noun mairesse Fem.

me pronoun **1** me, m' (before a vowel or silent 'h'); **she knows me** elle me connaît; **can you help me, please?** est-ce que tu peux m'aider, s'il te plaît?; **can you lend me a pen?** peux-tu me prêter un stylo?; **can you give me your address?** peux-tu me donner ton adresse?; **2** (after a preposition) moi; **I took her with me** je l'ai emmenée avec moi; **they left without me** ils sont partis sans moi; **3** (in commands) moi; **listen to me!** écoute-moi!; **wait for me!** attends-moi!; **excuse me!** excusez-moi!; **4** (*in comparisons*) **than me** que moi; **she's older than me** elle est plus âgée que moi; **5 me too!** moi aussi!

meadow *noun* pré Masc.

meal *noun* repas Masc.; **they have three meals a day** ils mangent trois fois par jour.

mean *verb* **1** vouloir [14] dire; **what do you mean?** qu'est-ce que tu veux dire?; **what does that mean?** qu'est-ce que ça veut dire?; **that's not what I meant** ce n'est pas ce que je voulais dire; **2 to mean to do** avoir [5] l'intention de faire; **I meant to phone my mother** j'avais l'intention d'appeler ma mère; **3 to be meant to do** devoir faire; **she was meant to be here at six** elle devait être là à six heures.

mean *adjective* **1** (*with money*) radin (*informal*); **2** (*unkind*) méchant; **she's really mean to her brother** elle est vraiment méchante avec son frère; **what a mean thing to do!** c'est vraiment méchant!

meaning *noun* sens Masc.

means *noun* moyen Masc.; **a means of transport** un moyen de transport; **a means of doing** un moyen de faire; **we have no means of contacting him** nous n'avons aucun moyen de le contacter; **by means of** au moyen de; **by all means** certainement.

meantime *noun* **for the meantime** pour le moment; **in the meantime** pendant ce temps.

meanwhile *adverb* pendant ce temps; **meanwhile she was**

waiting at the station pendant ce temps, elle attendait à la gare.

measles *noun* rougeole Fem.

measure *verb* mesurer [1].

measurements *plural noun* **1** (*of a room or an object*) dimensions Fem. *plural*; **the measurements of the room** les dimensions de la pièce; **2** (*of a person*) mensurations Fem. *plural*; **my chest measurement** mon tour de poitrine; **my waist measurement** mon tour de taille.

meat *noun* viande Fem.

Mecca *noun* Mecque Fem.

mechanic *noun* mécanicien Masc.; **he's a mechanic** il est mécanicien.

mechanical *adjective* mécanique.

medal *noun* médaille Fem.; **the gold medal** la médaille d'or.

media *noun* **the media** les médias Masc. *plural*.

medical *noun* visite Fem. médicale; **to have a medical** passer une visite médicale.

medical *adjective* médical (Masc. *plural* médicaux); **do you have medical insurance?** est-ce que vous avez une assurance-maladie?

medicine *noun* **1** médicament Masc.; **I'd like some cough medecine** je voudrais un médicament pour la toux; **2** (*subject of study*) médecine Fem.; **she's studying medicine** elle fait des études de médecine; **3 alternative medecine** la médecine douce.

medieval *adjective* médiéval, du moyen-âge.

Mediterranean noun the Mediterranean la Méditerranée.

medium adjective moyen (Fem. moyenne).

medium-sized noun de taille moyenne.

meet verb 1 (by chance) rencontrer [1]; **I met Rosie outside the baker's** j'ai rencontré Rosie devant la boulangerie; 2 (by appointment) retrouver [1]; **I'll meet you outside the cinema at six** je te retrouverai devant le cinéma à six heures; 3 se retrouver [1]; **we're meeting at six** nous allons nous retrouver à six heures; 4 (get to know) faire [10] la connaissance de; **I met a French girl last week** j'ai fait la connaissance d'une Française la semaine dernière; 5 **Tom, have you met Oskar?** Tom, est-ce que tu connais Oskar?; 6 (off a train, bus, etc) venir [81] chercher; **my dad's meeting me at the station** mon père vient me chercher à la gare.

meeting noun réunion Fem.; **there's a meeting at ten o'clock** il y a une réunion à dix heures; **she's in a meeting** elle est en réunion.

megabyte noun mégaoctet Masc.

melody noun mélodie Fem.

melon noun melon Masc.

melt verb 1 fondre [3]; **it melts in your mouth** ça fond dans la bouche; 2 **to melt something** faire [10] fondre quelque chose; **melt the butter in a saucepan** faites fondre le beurre dans une casserole.

member noun membre Masc.; **she's a member of the Labour Party** elle est membre du parti travailliste.

Member of Parliament noun député Masc.

membership noun adhésion Fem.

membership card noun carte Fem. de membre.

membership fee noun cotisation Fem.

memorial noun **a war memorial** un monument aux morts.

memorial service noun messe Fem. commémorative.

memorize verb **to memorize something** apprendre [64] quelque chose par cur.

memory noun 1 (of a person or computer) mémoire Fem.; **you have a good memory!** tu as bonne mémoire!; **I have a bad memory** je n'ai pas de mémoire; 2 (of the past) souvenir Masc.; **I have good memories of my stay in France** j'ai de bons souvenirs de mon séjour en France.

mend verb réparer [1].

meningitis noun méningite Fem.

mental adjective mental (Masc. plural mentaux); **a mental illness** une maladie mentale; **a mental hospital** un hôpital psychiatrique.

mention verb mentionner [1].

menu noun menu Masc.; **on the menu** au menu; **is there a set menu?** est-ce qu'il y a un menu à prix fixe?

mercy noun pitié Fem.

merge verb 1 (roads) se rejoindre [49]; 2 (documents) fusionner [1].

meringue noun meringue Fem.

a
b
c
d
e
f
g
h
i
j
k
l
m
n
o
p
q
r
s
t
u
v
w
x
y
z

a **merit** noun mérite Masc.

   mermaid noun sirène Fem.

b **merry** adjective **1** joyeux (Fem.
c joyeuse); **Merry Christmas** Joyeux
   Noël; **2** (from drinking) éméché
d (informal).

e **merry-go-round** noun manège
   Masc.

f **mess** noun désordre Masc.; **my**
g **papers are in a mess** mes papiers
   sont dans le désordre; **to make a**
h **mess** mettre du désordre; **to clear**
   up the mess mettre de l'ordre;
i **what a mess!** quelle pagaille!
   (informal).
j
   ● **to mess about** faire [10]
k l'imbécile; **stop messing about!**
   arrête de faire l'imbécile!
l
   ● **to mess about with something**
m jouer [1] avec quelque chose; **it's**
   dangerous to mess about with
n **matches** il est dangereux de jouer
   avec les allumettes.
o
   ● **to mess something up** mettre [11]
p la pagaille dans quelque chose
   (informal); **you've messed up all**
q **my papers** tu as mis la pagaille
   dans tous mes papiers.
r
   message noun message Masc.; **a**
s **telephone message** un message
   téléphonique.
t
   messenger noun messager Masc.
u
   messy adjective **1** **it's a messy job**
v c'est un travail salissant; **2** **he's a**
   messy eater il mange n'importe
w comment; **her writing's really**
   messy elle écrit n'importe
x comment.

y **metal** noun métal Masc. (plural
   métaux).
z

meter noun **1** (electricity, gas, taxi)
compteur Masc.; **to read the meter**
relever le compteur; **2 a parking**
meter un parcmètre.

method noun méthode Fem.

Methodist noun méthodiste Masc.
& Fem.; **I'm a Methodist** je suis
méthodiste.

metre noun mètre Masc.

metric adjective métrique.

Mexican noun Mexicain Masc.,
Mexicaine Fem.

Mexican adjective mexicain.

Mexico noun Mexique Masc.; **in**
Mexico au Mexique; **to Mexico** au
Mexique.

microchip noun puce Fem.

microphone noun microphone
Masc.

microscope noun microscope
Masc.

microwave oven noun four
Masc. à micro-ondes.

midday noun midi Masc.; **at**
midday à midi.

middle noun **1** milieu Masc.; **in the**
middle of the room au milieu de la
pièce; **in the middle of the night** au
milieu de la nuit; **2 to be in the**
middle of doing être en train de
faire; **when she phoned I was in**
the middle of washing my hair
quand elle a appelé j'étais en train
de me laver les cheveux.

middle-aged adjective d'un
certain âge; **a middle-aged lady**
une dame d'un certain âge.

middle-class adjective de la
classe moyenne; **a middle-class**
family une famille de la classe
moyenne.

Middle-East noun Moyen-Orient Masc.; **in the Middle East** au Moyen-Orient.

middle finger noun majeur Masc.

midge noun moucheron Masc.

midnight noun minuit Masc.; **at midnight** à minuit.

Midsummer's Day noun la Saint Jean.

midwife noun sage-femme Fem.

might verb **'are you going to phone him?' – 'I might'** est-ce que tu vas l'appeler? – 'peut-être'; **I might invite Jo** j'inviterai peut-être Jo; **Amanda might know** Amanda le saurait peut-être; **he might have forgotten** il a peut-être oublié.

migraine noun migraine Fem.

mike noun micro Masc. (informal).

mild adjective doux (Fem. douce); **it's quite mild today** il fait plutôt doux aujourd'hui.

mile noun **1** mille Masc. (the French use kilometres for distances; to convert miles roughly to kilometres, multiply by 8 and divide by 5) **the village is ten miles from Oxford** le village est à seize kilomètres d'Oxford; **2 it's miles better!** c'est dix fois meilleur!

mileage noun kilométrage Masc.; **what's the mileage on your car?** elle a combien de kilomètres, votre voiture?

military adjective militaire.

milk noun lait Masc.; **full-cream milk** le lait entier; **skimmed milk** le lait écrémé; **semi-skimmed milk** le lait demi-écrémé.

milk verb traire [78].

milk chocolate noun chocolat Masc. au lait.

milk jug noun pot Masc. à lait.

milkman noun laitier Masc.

milk shake noun milk-shake Masc.

millennium noun millénaire Masc.

millimetre noun millimètre Masc.

million noun million Masc.; **a million people** un million de personnes; **two million people** deux millions de personnes.

millionaire noun millionnaire Masc.

mimic verb imiter [1].

mince noun viande Fem. hachée.

mind noun **1** esprit Masc.; **it crossed my mind that ...** il m'est venu à l'esprit que ...; **2 to change your mind** changer d'avis; **I've changed my mind** j'ai changé d'avis; **I can't make up my mind** je n'arrive pas à me décider.

mind verb **1** surveiller [1]; **can you mind my bag for me?** est-ce que tu peux surveiller mon sac?; **2** s'occuper [1] de (baby); **could you mind the baby for ten minutes?** est-ce que tu peux t'occuper du bébé pendant dix minutes?; **3 do you mind if ...?** est-ce que cela vous dérange si ...?; **do you mind if I close the door?** est-ce que cela vous dérange si je ferme la porte?; **I don't mind** cela ne me dérange pas; **I don't mind the heat** la chaleur ne me dérange pas; **4 mind the step!** attention à la marche!; **5 never mind!** peu importe!

a b c d e f g h i j k l m n o p q r s t u v w x y z

mine[1] *noun* mine Fem.; **a coal mine** une mine de charbon.

mine[2] *pronoun* **1** (*for a masculine noun*) le mien; **she took her hat and I took mine** elle a pris son chapeau et j'ai pris le mien; **2** (*for a feminine noun*) la mienne; **she gave me her address and I gave her mine** elle m'a donné son adresse et je lui ai donné la mienne; **3** (*for a masculine plural noun*) les miens; **Karen's invited her parents and I've invited mine** Karen a invité ses parents et j'ai invité les miens; **4** (*for a feminine plural noun*) les miennes; **she showed me her photos and I showed her mine** elle m'a montré ses photos et je lui ai montré les miennes; **5** à moi; **the green one's mine** le vert est à moi; **it's mine** c'est à moi.

miner *noun* mineur Masc.

mineral water *noun* eau Fem. minérale.

miniature *noun, adjective* miniature Fem.

minibus *noun* minibus Masc.

minimum *noun* minimum Masc.; **a minimum of** un minimum de.

minimum *adjective* minimum (*does not change in the feminine or plural*); **the minimum age** l'âge minimum; **minimum safety measures** des mesures de sécurité minimum; **the minimum amount** le minimum.

miniskirt *noun* mini-jupe Fem.

minister *noun* **1** (*in government*) ministre Masc.; **2** (*of a church*) pasteur Masc.

ministry *noun* ministère Masc.

minor *adjective* mineur.

minority *noun* minorité Fem.

mint *noun* **1** (*herb*) menthe Fem.; **2** (*sweet*) bonbon Masc. à la menthe.

minus *preposition* moins; **seven minus three is four** sept moins trois égale quatre; **it was minus ten this morning** il a fait moins dix ce matin.

minute[1] *noun* minute Fem.; **just a minute!** une minute!; **I'll be ready in two minutes** je serai prêt dans deux minutes; **it's five minutes' walk from here** c'est à cinq minutes à pied d'ici.

minute[2] *adjective* minuscule; **the bedrooms are minute** les chambres sont minuscules.

miracle *noun* miracle Masc.

mirror *noun* **1** glace Fem.; **I looked at myself in the mirror** je me suis regardé dans la glace; **2** (*rearview mirror in a car*) rétroviseur Masc.

misbehave *verb* se conduire [26] mal.

mischief *noun* **to get up to mischief** faire des bêtises.

mischievous *adjective* coquin.

miser *noun* avare Masc. & Fem.

miserable *adjective* **1** malheureux (Fem. malheureuse); **he was miserable without her** il était malheureux sans elle; **I feel really miserable today** je n'ai vraiment pas le moral aujourd'hui; **2** it's miserable weather il fait un sale temps; **3** she gets paid a miserable wage elle gagne un salaire de misère.

misery noun souffrance *Fem.*; **he was in misery** il était extrêmement malheureux.

misfire verb tomber [1] à plat; **our plans misfired** nos projets sont tombés à plat.

misfortune noun malheur *Masc.*

misjudge verb 1 mal évaluer [1]; **she misjudged the distance** elle a mal évalué la distance; 2 mal juger [52] (*a person*); **everybody had misjudged her** tout le monde l'avait mal jugée.

mislay verb égarer [1]; **I've mislaid my keys** j'ai égaré mes clés.

misleading adjective trompeur (*Fem.* trompeuse); **it's a misleading advertisement** c'est une publicité trompeuse.

Miss noun Mademoiselle; **Miss Jones** Mademoiselle Jones; (*written as*) Mlle Jones.

miss verb 1 rater [1]; **she missed her train** elle a raté son train; **I missed the film** j'ai raté le film; **the ball missed the goal** le ballon a raté le but; **missed!** raté!; 2 manquer [1]; **he's missed several classes** il a manqué plusieurs cours; **to miss an opportunity** manquer une occasion; 3 **I miss you** tu me manques; **she's missing her sister** sa sœur lui manque; **I miss France** la France me manque.

missile noun missile *Masc.*

missing adjective 1 manquant; **she's found the missing pieces** elle a trouvé les pièces manquantes; **the missing link** le chaînon manquant; 2 **there's a plate missing** il manque une assiette; **there are three forks missing** il manque trois fourchettes; 3 **to go missing** disparaître; **several things have gone missing lately** plusieurs choses ont disparu récemment; **three people are missing** trois personnes ont disparu.

missionary noun missionnaire *Masc. & Fem.*

mist noun brume *Fem.*

mistake noun 1 erreur *Fem.*; **by mistake** par erreur; **it was my mistake** c'était une erreur de ma part; 2 faute *Fem.*; **a spelling mistake** une faute d'orthographe; **you've made lots of mistakes** tu as fait beaucoup de fautes; 3 **to make a mistake** (*be mistaken*) se tromper; **sorry, I made a mistake** je suis désolé, je me suis trompé.

mistake verb **I mistook you for your brother** je vous ai pris pour votre frère.

mistaken adjective **to be mistaken** se tromper; **you're mistaken** tu te trompes.

mistletoe noun gui *Masc.*

misty adjective brumeux (*Fem.* brumeuse); **a misty morning** un matin brumeux; **it's misty this morning** il y a de la brume ce matin.

misunderstand verb mal comprendre [64]; **I misunderstood** j'ai mal compris.

misunderstanding noun malentendu *Masc.*; **there's been a misunderstanding** il y a eu un malentendu.

a b c d e f g h i j k l m n o p q r s t u v w x y z

mix noun 1 mélange Masc.; **a good mix of people** un bon mélange de gens; **2 a cake mix** une préparation pour gâteau.

mix verb 1 mélanger [52]; **mix all the ingredients together** mélangez tous les ingrédients; **2 to mix with** fréquenter [1]; **she mixes with lots of interesting people** elle fréquente beaucoup de gens intéressants.

● 1 mélanger [52]; **you've mixed up all my papers** tu as mélangé tous mes papiers; **you've got it all mixed up!** tu mélanges tout! (story); **2** (confuse) confondre [69]; **I get him mixed up with his brother** je le confonds avec son frère

mixed adjective varié; **a mixed programme** un programme varié.

mixed salad noun salade Fem. composée.

mixed school noun école Fem. mixte.

mixer noun batteur Masc. électrique.

mixture noun mélange Masc.; **it's a mixture of jazz and rock** c'est un mélange de jazz et de rock.

moan verb râler [1] (informal); **stop moaning!** arrête de râler!

mobile home noun mobile home Masc.

mobile phone noun téléphone Masc. portable.

mock noun (mock exam) examen Masc. blanc.

mock verb se moquer [1] de; **stop mocking me!** arrête de te moquer de moi!

model noun 1 (type) modèle Masc.; **the latest model** le dernier modèle; **2** (fashion model) mannequin Masc.; **she's a model** elle est mannequin de luxe; **3** (of a plane, car, etc) modèle Masc. réduit; **he makes models** il fait des modèles réduits; **4** (of a building) maquette Fem.; **a model of Westminster Abbey** une maquette de l'Abbaye de Westminster.

model aeroplane noun modèle Masc. réduit d'avion.

model railway noun chemin Masc. de fer miniature.

model village noun village Masc. miniature.

modem noun modem Masc.

moderate adjective modéré.

modern adjective moderne.

modernize verb moderniser [1].

modern languages noun langues Fem. plural vivantes.

modest adjective modeste.

modify verb modifier [1].

moisture noun humidité Fem.

moisturizer noun 1 (lotion) lait hydratant Masc.; **2** (cream) crème Fem. hydratante.

mole noun 1 (animal) taupe Fem.; **2** (on skin) graine Fem. de beauté.

molecule noun molécule Fem.

molehill noun taupinière Fem.

moment noun 1 instant Masc.; **he'll be here in a moment** il sera là dans un instant; **at any moment** à tout instant; **at the moment** en ce moment; **at the right moment** au bon moment.

Monaco noun Monaco.

monarchy noun monarchie Fem.

monastery noun monastère Masc.

Monday noun lundi Masc.; **on Monday** lundi; **I'm going out on Monday** je sors lundi; **see you on Monday!** à lundi!; **on Mondays** le lundi; **the museum is closed on Mondays** le musée est fermé le lundi; **every Monday** tous les lundis; **last Monday** lundi dernier; **next Monday** lundi prochain.

money noun argent Masc.; **I don't have enough money** je n'ai pas assez d'argent; **to make money** gagner de l'argent; **they gave me my money back** (in a shop) ils m'ont remboursé.

money box noun tirelire Fem.

mongrel noun chien Masc. bâtard.

monitor noun (on computer) moniteur Masc.

monk noun moine Masc.

monkey noun 1 singe Masc.; 2 **you little monkey!** petit galopin! (informal).

monotonous adjective monotone.

monster noun monstre Masc.

month noun mois Masc.; **in the month of May** au mois de mai; **this month** ce mois-ci; **next month** le mois prochain; **we're leaving next month** nous allons partir le mois prochain; **last month** le mois dernier; **every month** tous les mois; **in two months' time** dans deux mois; **at the end of the month** à la fin du mois.

monthly adjective mensuel (Fem. mensuelle); **a monthly payment** une mensualité.

monument noun monument Masc.

mood noun humeur Fem.; **to be in a good mood** être de bonne humeur; **to be in a bad mood** être de mauvaise humeur; **I'm not in the mood** ça ne me dit rien.

moody adjective lunatique.

moon noun lune Fem.; **by the light of the moon** au clair de lune; ★ **to be over the moon** être aux anges (literally: to be at the level of the angels).

moonlight noun clair Masc. de lune; **by moonlight** au clair de lune.

moor noun lande Fem.; **the Yorkshire moors** les landes du Yorkshire.

moor verb amarrer [1] (a boat).

moped noun mobylette™ Fem.

moral noun morale Fem.; **the moral of the story** la morale de l'histoire.

moral adjective moral (Masc. plural moraux).

morale noun moral Masc.; **to boost somebody's morale** remonter le moral à quelqu'un; **he's been trying to boost morale** il essaie de leur remonter le moral.

morals noun moralité Fem.

more adverb 1 plus; **more interesting** plus intéressant; **more difficult** plus difficile; **more slowly** plus lentement; **more easily** plus facilement; 2 **more ...than** plus ...que; **the book's more interesting than the film** le livre est plus intéressant que le film.

more adjective 1 plus de; **they have more money than we do** ils ont plus d'argent que nous; **I'll**

have a little more milk je prendrai un peu plus de lait; **2** (of something you have already) **would you like some more cake?** voulez-vous encore du gâteau?; **a few more glasses** encore quelques verres.

more pronoun **1** plus; **he eats more than me** il mange plus que moi; **2** (of something you have already) **I don't want any more** je n'en veux plus; **3 more and more** de plus en plus; **books are getting more and more expensive** les livres coûtent de plus en plus cher; **it takes more and more time** ça prend de plus en plus de temps; **4 more or less** plus ou moins; **it's more or less finished** c'est plus ou moins fini.

morning noun **1** matin Masc.; **this morning** ce matin; **tomorrow morning** demain matin; **yesterday morning** hier matin; **in the morning** le matin; **she doesn't work in the morning** elle ne travaille pas le matin; **on Friday mornings** le vendredi matin; **at six o'clock in the morning** à six heures du matin; **2** (as a period of time spent doing something) matinée; **I spent the whole morning doing the washing-up** j'ai passé toute la matinée à faire la vaisselle.

Morocco noun Maroc Masc.; **to Morocco** au Maroc; **in Morocco** au Maroc.

mortgage noun crédit Masc. (immobilier).

Moscow noun Moscou; **in Moscow** à Moscou.

Moslem noun musulman Masc., musulmane Fem.

mosque noun mosquée Fem.

mosquito noun moustique Masc.; **a mosquito bite** une piqûre de moustique.

most adjective, adverb, pronoun **1** (followed by a plural noun) la plupart de; **most children like chocolate** la plupart des enfants aiment le chocolat; **most of my friends** la plupart de mes amis; **2** (followed by a singular noun) presque tout; **they've eaten most of the chocolate** ils ont mangé presque tout le chocolat; **3 most of the time** la plupart du temps; **4 the most** (followed by adjective) le plus, la plus, les plus; **the most interesting film** le film le plus intéressant; **the most exciting story** l'histoire la plus passionnante; **the most boring books** les livres les plus ennuyeux; **5 the most** (followed by noun) le plus de; **I've got the most time** c'est moi qui ai le plus de temps; **6 the most** (after verb) le plus; **what I hate most is the noise** ce que je déteste le plus, c'est le bruit.

moth noun **1** (butterfly) papillon Masc. de nuit; **2** (clothes moth) mite Fem.

Mother's Day noun la fête des Mères (in France the last Sunday in May).

mother noun mère Fem.; **my mother** ma mère; **Kate's mother** la mère de Kate.

mother-in-law noun belle-mère Fem. (plural **belles-mères**).

motion noun mouvement Masc.

motivated adjective motivé.

motivation noun motivation Fem.

motor noun moteur Masc.

motorbike noun moto Fem.

motorboat noun bateau Masc. à moteur.

motorcyclist noun motocycliste Masc. & Fem.

motorist noun automobiliste Masc. & Fem.

motor racing noun course Fem. automobile.

motorway noun autoroute Fem.

mouldy adjective moisi.

mountain noun montagne Fem.; **in the mountains** à la montagne.

mountain bike noun VTT Masc. (short for 'vélo tout-terrain').

mountaineer noun alpiniste Masc. & Fem.

mountaineering noun alpinisme Masc.; **to go mountaineering** faire de l'alpinisme.

mountainous adjective montagneux (Fem. montagneuse).

mouse noun souris Fem. (both the animal and for a computer).

mousse noun mousse Fem.; **chocolate mousse** la mousse au chocolat.

moustache noun moustache Fem.; **a man with a moustache** un moustachu.

mouth noun bouche Fem.

mouthful noun bouchée Fem.

mouth organ noun harmonica Masc.; **to play the mouth organ** jouer de l'harmonica.

move noun **1** (to a different house) déménagement Masc.; **2** (in a game) **your move!** à toi de jouer!

move verb **1** bouger [52]; **she didn't move** elle n'a pas bougé; **2 move up a bit** pousse-toi un peu; **3** enlever [50] (an object); **can you move your bag, please?** peux-tu enlever ton sac, s'il te plaît?; **4** (car, traffic) avancer [61]; **the traffic was moving slowly** la circulation avançait lentement; **5 to move forward** avancer [61]; **he moved forward a step** il s'est avancé d'un pas; **6** (move house) déménager [52]; **we're moving on Tuesday** nous déménageons mardi; **they've moved to France** ils se sont installés en France.

● **to move in** emménager [52]; **when are you moving in?** quand est-ce que tu emménages?

● **to move out** déménager [52]; **we're moving out next week** nous déménageons la semaine prochaine.

movement noun mouvement Masc.

movie noun film Masc.; **to go to the movies** aller au cinéma.

moving adjective **1** en marche; **a moving vehicle** un véhicule en marche; **2** (emotionally) émouvant; **it's a very moving film** c'est un film très émouvant.

a b c d e f g h i j k l n o p q r s t u v w x y z

mow verb tondre [3]; **to mow the grass** tondre la pelouse.

mower noun tondeuse Fem. à gazon.

MP noun député Masc.; **she is an MP** elle est député.

Mr noun Monsieur (usually abbreviated to 'M.'); **Mr Angus Brown** M. Angus Brown.

Mrs noun Madame (usually abbreviated to 'Mme'); **Mrs Mary Hendry** Mme Mary Hendry.

Ms noun Madame (usually abbreviated to 'Mme'; note that there is no direct equivalent to 'Ms' in French, but 'Madame' may be used whether the woman is married or not).

much adjective, adverb, pronoun
1 beaucoup; **she doesn't eat much** elle ne mange pas beaucoup; **we don't go out much** nous ne sortons pas beaucoup; **much more** beaucoup plus; **much shorter** beaucoup plus court; **2** (followed by a noun) de; **we don't have much time** nous n'avons pas beaucoup de temps; **there isn't much butter left** il ne reste pas beaucoup de beurre; **3 very much** beaucoup; **thank you very much** merci beaucoup; **I don't watch television very much** je ne regarde pas beaucoup la télé; **4 very much** (followed by a noun) beaucoup de; **there isn't very much milk** il n'y a pas beaucoup de lait; **5 not much** pas beaucoup; **'do you have a lot of homework?' – 'no, not much'** 'est-ce que tu as beaucoup de devoirs?' – 'non, pas

beaucoup'; **6 so much** tellement; **we liked it so much!** nous l'avons tellement aimé!; **I have so much to do!** j'ai tellement de choses à faire!; **7 so much** autant; **you shouldn't have given me so much** tu n'aurais pas dû m'en donner autant; **8 as much as** autant que; **you can take as much as you like** tu peux en prendre autant que tu veux; **9 too much** trop (de); **her parents give her too much money** ses parents lui donnent trop d'argent; **that's far too much!** c'est beaucoup trop!; **10 how much?** combien (de)?; **how much is it?** ça coûte combien?; **how much do you want?** tu en veux combien?; **how much sugar do you want?** tu veux combien de sucre?

mud noun boue Fem.

muddle noun désordre Masc.; **to be in a muddle** être en désordre.

muddy adjective **1** (path, road) boueux (Fem. boueuse); **2** (shoes, clothes) couverts de boue; **your boots are all muddy** tes bottes sont couvertes de boue.

mug noun grande tasse Fem.; **a mug of coffee** une grande tasse de café.

mug verb **to mug somebody** agresser [1] quelqu'un; **to be mugged** se faire [10] agresser; **my brother was mugged in the park** mon frère s'est fait agresser au parc.

mugging noun agression Fem.

multiplication noun multiplication Fem.

multiply verb multiplier [1]; **to multiply six by four** multiplier six par quatre.

mum, mummy noun **1** mère Fem.; **Tom's mum** la mère de Tom; **I'll ask my mum** je vais demander à ma mère; **2** (within the family or as a name) maman Fem.; **mum's not back yet** maman n'est pas encore rentrée.

mumps noun oreillons Masc. plural.

murder noun meurtre Masc.

murder verb assassiner [1].

murderer noun assassin Masc.

muscle noun muscle Masc.

muscular adjective musclé.

museum noun musée Masc.; **to go to the museum** aller au musée.

mushroom noun champignon Masc.; **a mushroom salad** une salade aux champignons.

music noun musique Fem.; **pop music** la musique pop; **classical music** la musique classique.

musical noun comédie Fem. musicale.

musical adjective **1** a musical instrument un instrument de musique; **2** they're a very musical family ils sont très musiciens dans la famille.

musician noun musicien Masc., musicienne Fem.

Muslim noun musulman Masc., musulmane Fem.

mussel noun moule Fem.

must verb **1** falloir [43] (to express obligation 'falloir' is used as an impersonal verb) **we must leave now** il faut partir maintenant (the construction 'il faut que' is followed by a verb in the subjunctive) **I must tell you something** il faut que je te dise quelque chose; **you must be there at eight** il faut que tu sois là à huit heures; **you must learn the vocabulary** il faut que tu apprennes le vocabulaire; **2** (expressing probability) devoir [8]; **you must be tired** tu dois être fatigué; **it must be five o'clock** il doit être cinq heures; **he must have forgotten** il a dû oublier.

mustard noun moutarde Fem.

mutter verb marmonner [1].

my adjective **1** (before a masculine noun) mon; **my brother** mon frère; **my book** mon livre; **2** (before a feminine noun) ma; **my sister** ma sœur; **my house** ma maison (but 'ma' becomes 'mon' before a feminine noun beginning with a vowel or silent 'h') **my address** mon adresse; **3** (before a plural noun) mes; **my children** mes enfants; **4** (with parts of the body) le, la, les; **I had a glass in my hand** j'avais un verre à la main; **I'm washing my hands** je me lave les mains.

myself pronoun **1** I've hurt myself je me suis blessé; **2** I said it myself je l'ai dit moi-même; **3** by myself tout seul; **I did it by myself** je l'ai fait tout seul.

mysterious adjective mystérieux (Fem. mystérieuse).

mystery noun **1** mystère Masc.; **2** (book) roman Masc. policier.

myth noun mythe Masc.

mythology noun mythologie Fem.

a
b
c
d
e
f
g
h
i
j
k
l
m
n
o
p
q
r
s
t
u
v
w
x
y
z

Nn

nail noun **1** (on finger or toe) ongle Masc.; **to bite your nails** se ronger [52] les ongles; **2** (metal) clou Masc.

nail verb clouer [1].

nailbrush noun brosse Fem. à ongles.

nailfile noun lime Fem. à ongles.

nail scissors noun ciseaux Masc. plural à ongles.

nail varnish noun vernis Masc. à ongles.

nail varnish remover noun dissolvant Masc.

naked adjective nu.

name noun **1** nom Masc.; **I've forgotten her name** j'ai oublié son nom; **what's your name?** comment vous appelez-vous?; **my name is Joy** je m'appelle Joy; **2** (of a book or film) titre Masc.

nanny noun nurse Fem.

nap noun petit somme Masc.; **to have a nap** faire un petit somme.

napkin noun serviette Fem.

nappy noun couche Fem.

narrow adjective étroit; **a narrow street** une rue étroite.

nasty adjective **1** (mean) méchant; **that was a nasty thing to do** c'était méchant; **2** (unpleasant) désagréable; **that's a nasty job** c'est une tâche désagréable; **3** (bad) mauvais; **a nasty smell** une mauvaise odeur.

nation noun nation Fem.

national adjective national (Masc. plural nationaux).

national anthem noun hymne Masc. national.

nationality noun nationalité Fem.

national park noun parc Masc. national (plural parcs nationaux).

Nativity noun nativité Fem.

natural adjective naturel (Fem. naturelle).

naturally adverb naturellement.

nature noun nature Fem.

nature reserve noun réserve Fem. naturelle.

naughty adjective vilain.

nausea noun nausée Fem.

navel noun nombril Masc.

navigate verb naviguer [1].

navy noun marine Fem.; **my uncle's in the navy** mon oncle est dans la marine.

navy-blue adjective bleu marine; **navy-blue gloves** des gants bleu marine.

near adjective proche; **the nearest shop** le magasin le plus proche.

near adverb, preposition **1** près; **they live quite near** ils habitent tout près; **to come nearer** s'approcher; **2 near (to)** près de; **near the station** près de la gare.

nearby adverb tout près; **there's a park nearby** il y a un parc tout près.

nearly adverb presque; **nearly empty** presque vide; **we're nearly there** nous sommes presque arrivés.

neat adjective **1** (well-organized) bien rangé; **a neat desk** un bureau bien rangé; **2** soigné (a garden, your clothes, or the way you look).

neatly *adverb* avec soin.

necessarily *adverb* not necessarily pas forcément.

necessary *adjective* nécessaire; **if necessary** si besoin est.

neck *noun* **1** (*of a person*) cou *Masc.*; **2** (*of a garment*) encolure *Fem.*

necklace *noun* collier *Masc.*

nectarine *noun* nectarine *Fem.*

need *noun* there's no need, I've done it already inutile, c'est fait; **there's no need to wait** inutile d'attendre.

need *verb* **1** avoir [5] besoin de; **we need bread** nous avons besoin de pain; **they need help** ils ont besoin d'aide; **everything you need** tout ce qu'il vous faut; **2** (*to have to*) devoir [8]; **I need to drop in at the bank** je dois passer par la banque; **3** you needn't decide today tu n'es pas obligé de décider aujourd'hui; **you needn't wait** tu n'es pas obligé d'attendre.

needle *noun* aiguille *Fem.*

negative *noun* (*of a photo*) négatif *Masc.*

neglected *adjective* mal entretenu.

neighbour *noun* voisin *Masc.*, voisine *Fem.*; **we're going round to the neighbours'** on va chez les voisins.

neighbourhood *noun* quartier *Masc.*; **a nice neighbourhood** un quartier agréable.

neither *conjunction* **1** neither ... nor ni ...ni; **I have neither the time nor the money** je n'ai ni le temps ni l'argent; **2** neither do I moi non plus; **'I don't like fish'** – **'neither do I'** 'je n'aime pas le poisson' – 'moi non plus' (*translations using 'non plus' can be used for many similar replies*) **'I wasn't invited'** – **'neither was I'** 'je n'ai pas été invité' – 'moi non plus'; **"I didn't like the film"** – **'neither did Kirsty'** 'je n'ai pas aimé le film' – 'Kirsty non plus'; **3 'which do you like?'** – **'neither'** 'lequel aimes-tu?' – 'ni l'un ni l'autre'.

nephew *noun* neveu *Masc.* (*plural* neveux).

nerve *noun* **1** (*in the body*) nerf *Masc.*; **2 to lose one's nerve** perdre son courage; **3 you've got a nerve!** tu as un sacré culot! (*informal*); ★ **he gets on my nerves** il me tape sur les nerfs (*informal*).

nervous *adjective* nerveux (*Fem.* nerveuse); **to feel nervous** (*before a performance or an exam*) avoir le trac (*informal*).

nervous breakdown *noun* dépression *Fem.* nerveuse.

nest *noun* nid *Masc.*

net *noun* **1** (*for fishing or in tennis*) filet *Masc.*; **2** (*in football*) filets *Masc. plural*.

Netherlands *noun* Pays-Bas *Masc. plural*; **in the Netherlands** aux Pays-Bas.

nettle *noun* ortie *Fem.*

network *noun* réseau *Masc.* (*plural* réseaux).

a
b
c
d
e
f
g
h
i
j
k
l
m
o
p
q
r
s
t
u
v
w
x
y
z

neutral noun (in a gearbox) point Masc. mort; **to be in neutral** être au point mort.

neutral adjective neutre.

never adjective **1** ne ... jamais; **Ben never smokes** Ben ne fume jamais; **I've never seen the film** je n'ai jamais vu le film; **2** jamais; **'have you ever been to Spain?' – 'no, never'** 'est-ce que tu es déjà allé en Espagne?' – 'non, jamais'; **3** never again plus jamais; **4** never mind! peu importe!

new adjective **1** (different or unknown to you) nouveau (Fem. nouvelle); **have you seen their new house?** as-tu vu leur nouvelle maison?; **Debbie's new boyfriend** le nouveau copain de Debbie; **2** (brand new) neuf (Fem. neuve); **it's a new car** c'est une voiture neuve.

newcomer noun nouveau venu Masc. (plural nouveaux venus), nouvelle venue Fem (plural nouvelles venues).

news plural noun **1** (everyday gossip) nouvelle Fem., nouvelles Fem. plural; **a piece of good news** une bonne nouvelle; **I've got good news** j'ai de bonnes nouvelles; **any news?** y a-t-il des nouvelles?; **2** (on TV) journal Masc.; **the midday news** le journal de midi; **3** (on the radio) the news les informations.

newsagent noun marchand Masc. de journaux; **at the newsagent's** chez le marchand de journaux.

newspaper noun journal Masc. (plural journaux).

newsreader noun présentateur Masc., présentatrice Fem.

New Year noun le Nouvel An; **Happy New Year!** Bonne Année!

New Year's Day noun le jour de l'An.

New Year's Eve noun la Saint-Sylvestre.

New Zealand noun Nouvelle-Zélande Fem.

New Zealander noun Néo-Zélandais Masc., Néo-Zélandaise Fem.

next adjective **1** prochain; **the next train is at ten** le prochain train est à dix heures; **next week** la semaine prochaine; **next Thursday** jeudi prochain; **next year** l'année prochaine; **the next time I see you** la prochaine fois que je te verrai; **2** (following) suivant; **I saw her the next week** je l'ai vue la semaine suivante; **the next day** le lendemain; **the letter arrived the next day** la lettre est arrivée le lendemain; **3** (next-door) voisin; **in the next room** dans la pièce voisine.

next adverb **1** (afterwards) ensuite; **what did he say next?** qu'est-ce qu'il a dit ensuite?; **2** (now) maintenant; **what shall we do next?** qu'est-ce qu'on fait maintenant?; **3 next to** à côté de; **the girl next to Pat** la fille à côté de Pat; **it's next to the baker's** c'est à côté de la boulangerie.

next door adverb à côté; **they live next door** ils habitent à côté; **the girl next door** la fille d'à côté.

nice adjective **1** (pleasant) agréable; **we had a nice evening** nous avons passé une soirée agréable; **Brighton's a nice town**

Brighton est une ville agréable; **have a nice time!** amusez-vous bien!; 2 *(attractive to look at)* joli; **that's a nice dress** elle est jolie, cette robe; 3 *(kind, friendly)* sympathique *(a person)*; **she's really nice** elle est vraiment sympathique; 4 **to be nice to somebody** être gentil avec quelqu'un; **she's been very nice to me** elle a été très gentille avec moi; 5 *(tasting good)* bon *(Fem. bonne)*; **let's have a cup of tea** si on prenait une bonne tasse de thé; 6 *(weather)* **it's a nice day** il fait beau; **we had nice weather** il a fait beau.

nick *verb (steal)* piquer [1] *(informal)*.

nickname *noun* surnom Masc.

niece *noun* nièce Fem.

night *noun* 1 *(before you go to bed)* soir Masc.; **what are you doing tonight?** qu'est-ce que tu fais ce soir?; **see you tonight!** à ce soir!; **I saw Greg last night** j'ai vu Greg hier soir; 2 *(after bedtime)* nuit Fem.; **it's cold at night** il fait froid la nuit; **to stay the night with somebody** coucher chez quelqu'un.

night club *noun* boîte Fem. de nuit.

nightie *noun* chemise Fem. de nuit.

nightingale *noun* rossignol Masc.

nightmare *noun* cauchemar Masc.; **to have a nightmare** faire un cauchemar.

night-time *noun* nuit Fem.

nil *noun* zéro Masc.; **they won four-nil** ils ont gagné quatre à zéro.

nine *number* neuf Masc.; **Jake's nine** Jake a neuf ans.

nineteen *number* dix-neuf Masc.; **Kate's nineteen** Kate a dix-neuf ans.

ninety *number* quatre-vingt-dix Masc.

ninth *number* neuvième; **on the ninth floor** au neuvième étage; **the ninth of June** le neuf juin.

nitrogen *noun* azote Masc.

no *adverb* non; **I said no** j'ai dit non; **no thank you** non merci.

no *adjective* 1 pas de; **we've got no bread** nous n'avons pas de pain; **no problem!** pas de problème!; 2 *(on a notice)* **'no smoking'** 'défense de fumer'; **'no parking'** 'stationnement interdit'.

nobody *pronoun* personne; **'who's there?' – 'nobody'** 'qui est là?' – 'personne'; **there's nobody in the kitchen** il n'y a personne dans la cuisine; **nobody knows me** personne ne me connaît; **nobody answered** personne n'a répondu.

nod *verb (to say yes)* faire [10] oui de la tête; **he nodded** il a fait oui de la tête.

noise *noun* bruit Masc.; **to make a noise** faire du bruit.

noisy *adjective* bruyant.

none *pronoun* 1 *(not one)* aucun *(Fem. aucune)*; **'how many students failed the exam?' – 'none'** 'combien d'étudiants ont raté l'examen?' – 'aucun'; **none of the girls knows him** aucune des filles ne le connaît; 2 **there's none left** il n'y en a plus; **there are none left** il n'y en a plus.

nonsense noun bêtises Fem. plural;
to talk nonsense dire des bêtises;
nonsense! she's at least thirty! tu
dis des bêtises! elle a au moins
trente ans!

non-smoker noun non-fumeur
Masc.

non-stop adjective direct (a train
or flight).

non-stop adverb sans arrêt; she
talks non-stop elle parle sans
arrêt.

noodles plural noun nouilles Fem.
plural.

noon noun midi Masc.; at (twelve)
noon à midi.

no-one pronoun personne; 'who's
there?' – 'no-one' 'qui est là?' –
'personne'; there's no-one in the
kitchen il n'y a personne dans la
cuisine; no-one knows me
personne ne me connaît; no-one
answered personne n'a répondu.

nor conjunction 1 neither ...nor ni
...ni; I have neither the time nor
the money je n'ai ni le temps ni
l'argent; 2 nor do I moi non plus; 'I
don't like fish' – 'nor do I' 'je
n'aime pas le poisson' – 'moi non
plus'; (translations using 'non plus'
can be used for many similar
replies) 'I wasn't invited' – 'nor
was I' 'je n'ai pas été invité' –
'moi non plus'.

normal adjective 1 normal (Masc.
plural normaux); 2 (usual)
habituel (Fem. habituelle).

normally adverb normalement.

Normandy noun Normandie Fem.;
in Normandy en Normandie.

north noun nord Masc.; in the
north au nord.

north adjective, adverb nord (never
agrees); the north side le côté nord;
a north wind un vent du nord;
north of Paris au nord de Paris.

North America noun Amérique
Fem. du Nord.

North American noun Nord-
Américain Masc., Nord-Américaine
Fem.

North American adjective nord-
américain.

northeast noun nord-est Masc.

northeast adjective in northeast
England au nord-est de
l'Angleterre.

Northern Ireland noun Irlande
Fem. du Nord.

North Pole noun pôle Masc. Nord.

North Sea noun the North Sea la
mer du Nord.

northwest noun nord-ouest Masc.

northwest adjective in northwest
England au nord-ouest de
l'Angleterre.

Norway noun Norvège Fem.; in
Norway en Norvège.

Norwegian noun 1 (person)
Norvégien Masc., Norvégienne
Fem.; 2 (language) norvégien Masc.

Norwegian adjective norvégien
(Fem. norvégienne).

nose noun nez Masc.; to blow your
nose se moucher [1].

nosebleed noun to have a
nosebleed saigner [1] du nez.

nostril noun narine Fem.

not adverb 1 pas; **not on Saturdays** pas le samedi; **not all alone!** pas tout seul!; **not bad** pas mal; **not at all** pas du tout; **not yet** pas encore; 2 (when used with a verb) ne ...pas; **it's not my car** ce n'est pas ma voiture; **I don't know** je ne sais pas; **Sam didn't phone** Sam n'a pas appelé; **we decided not to wait** nous avons décidé de ne pas attendre; 3 **I hope not** j'espère que non.

note noun 1 (a short letter) mot Masc.; **she left me a note** elle m'a laissé un mot; 2 **to take notes** prendre [64] des notes; 3 (a banknote) billet Masc.; **a ten-pound note** un billet de dix livres; 4 (in music) note Fem.; (on the keyboard) touche Fem.

notebook noun carnet Masc.

notepad noun bloc-notes Masc. (plural blocs-notes).

nothing pronoun 1 rien; **'what did you say?' – 'nothing'** 'qu'est-ce que tu as dit?' – 'rien'; 2 (with an adjective) **nothing new** rien de nouveau; **there's nothing new** il n'y a rien de nouveau; 3 (when used with a verb) ne ...rien; **she knows nothing** elle ne sait rien; but **there was nothing there** mais il n'y avait rien; **I saw nothing** je n'ai rien vu; **nothing's happening** il ne se passe rien; 4 **nothing has changed** rien n'a changé.

notice noun 1 (a sign) panneau Masc. (plural **panneaux**); 2 (an advertisement) annonce Fem.; 3 **don't take any notice of her!** ne fais pas attention à elle!; 4 **to do**

something at short notice faire quelque chose à la dernière minute.

notice verb remarquer [1]; **I didn't notice anything** je n'ai rien remarqué.

noticeable adjective visible.

notice board noun panneau Masc. d'affichage.

nought noun zéro Masc.

noun noun nom Masc.

novel noun roman Masc.

novelist noun romancier Masc., romancière Fem.

November noun novembre Masc.; **in November** en novembre.

now adverb 1 maintenant; **where is he now?** où est-il maintenant?; **they've got six children now** ils ont six enfants maintenant; 2 **he's busy just now** il est occupé en ce moment; **I saw her just now in the corridor** je viens de la voir dans le couloir; 3 **do it right now!** fais-le tout de suite!; 4 **now and then** de temps en temps.

nowadays adverb de nos jours; **nowadays they are quite common** de nos jours, ils sont assez fréquents.

nowhere adjective 1 nulle part; **nowhere in France** nulle part en France; 2 **there's nowhere to park** il n'y a pas d'endroit pour se garer.

nuclear adjective nucléaire; **a nuclear power station** une centrale nucléaire.

nude noun **in the nude** nu.

nude adjective nu.

nuisance noun **it's a nuisance** c'est embêtant.

a

numb adjective **1** (with cold) engourdi; **my fingers are numb with cold** j'ai les doigts engourdis par le froid; **2** (with an anaesthetic) insensible.

b

c

d

number noun **1** (of a house, telephone, or account) numéro Masc.; **I live at number thirty-one** j'habite au numéro trente-et-un; **my new phone number** mon nouveau numéro de téléphone; **2** (a written figure) chiffre Masc.; **the third number is a 7** le troisième chiffre est un 7; **3** (an amount) nombre Masc.; **a large number of visitors** un grand nombre de visiteurs.

e

f

g

h

i

j

k

number plate noun plaque Fem. d'immatriculation.

l

nun noun religieuse Fem.

m

nurse noun infirmier Masc., infirmière Fem.; **Janet's a nurse** Janet est infirmière.

n

o

p

nursery noun **1** (for children) crèche Fem.; **2** (for plants) pépinière Fem.

q

nursery school noun école Fem. maternelle.

r

s

nursing noun profession Fem. d'infirmier/d'infirmière; **she went into nursing** elle est devenue infirmière.

t

u

nut noun **1** (walnut) noix Fem.; **2** (almond) amande Fem.; **3** (peanut) cacahuète Fem.; **4** (for a bolt) écrou Masc.

v

w

x

nutmeg noun noix Fem. de muscade.

y

z

nylon noun nylon Masc.

Oo

oak noun chêne Masc.

oar noun rame Fem.

oasis noun oasis Fem.

oats noun avoine Fem.; **porridge oats** les flocons d'avoine.

obedient adjective obéissant.

obey verb obéir [2] à (a person); **to obey the rules** respecter [1] les règlements.

object noun objet Masc.

object verb soulever [50] des objections; **if you don't object** si vous n'avez pas d'objection.

objection noun objection Fem.

oblong adjective rectangulaire.

oboe noun hautbois Masc.; **to play the oboe** jouer du hautbois.

obscene adjective obscène.

observe verb observer [1].

obsessed adjective obsédé; **she's obsessed with her diet** elle est obsédée par son régime.

obsession noun obsession Fem.; **she has an obsession with cleanliness** elle est obsédée par la propreté.

obstacle noun obstacle Masc.

obstinate adjective têtu.

obstruct verb gêner [1] (people or the traffic).

obtain verb obtenir [77].

obvious adjective évident.

obviously adverb **1** (of course) évidemment; **'do you want to come too?' – 'obviously, but it's a bit difficult'** 'veux-tu nous accompagner?' – 'évidemment,

mais c'est un peu difficile';
2 (*looking at something*)
manifestement; **the house is
obviously empty** la maison est
manifestement vide.

occasion *noun* occasion *Fem.*; **a
special occasion** une grande
occasion.

occasional *adjective* **he sends us
the occasional card** il nous envoie
une carte de temps en temps.

occasionally *adverb* de temps en
temps.

occupation *noun* 1 (*job*)
profession *Fem.*; 2 (*of territory*)
occupation *Fem.*

occupied *adjective* occupé.

occur *verb* 1 **it occurs to me that
my cousins live nearby** il me vient
à l'esprit que mes cousins habitent
tout près; **it never occurred to me**
cela ne m'est pas venu à l'idée;
2 (*happen*) avoir [5] lieu; **the
accident occurred on Monday**
l'accident a eu lieu lundi.

ocean *noun* océan *Masc.*

o'clock *adverb* **at ten o'clock** à dix
heures; **it's three o'clock** il est
trois heures.

October *noun* octobre *Masc.*; **in
October** en octobre.

octopus *noun* pieuvre *Fem.*

odd *adjective* 1 (*strange*) bizarre;
**that's odd, I'm sure I heard the
phone** c'est bizarre, je suis sûr
d'avoir entendu le téléphone;
2 (*number*) impair; **three is an odd
number** trois est un chiffre impair;
3 **to be the odd one out** être
l'exception.

odds and ends *plural noun*
bricoles *Fem. plural*.

of *preposition* 1 de; **a kilo of
tomatoes** un kilo de tomates; **the
end of my work** la fin de mon
travail; 2 (*note that 'de le' becomes
'du' and 'de les' becomes 'des'*) **the
beginning of the concert** le début
du concert; **the name of the flower**
le nom de la fleur; **the parents of
the children** les parents des
enfants; 3 **Ray has four horses but
he's selling three of them** Ray a
trois chevaux mais il en vend trois;
we ate a lot of it nous en avons
mangé beaucoup; 4 **two of us** deux
d'entre nous; 5 **the sixth of June** le
six juin; 6 **made of** en; **a bracelet
made of silver** un bracelet en
argent.

off *adverb, adjective, preposition*
1 (*switched off*) éteint; **is the telly
off?** est-ce que la télé est éteinte?;
to turn off the lights éteindre la
lumière; 2 (*tap, water, gas*) fermé;
to turn off the tap fermer le
robinet; 3 (*turned off at the meter*)
coupé; **the gas and electricity
were off** le gaz et l'électricité
étaient coupés; 4 **to be off** (*to leave*)
s'en aller [7]; **I'm off** je m'en vais;
5 **a day off** un jour de congé;
Caroline took three days off work
Caroline a pris trois jours de congé;
to be off sick être malade; **Maya's
off school today** Maya n'est pas à
l'école aujourd'hui; 6 (*cancelled*)
annulé; **the match is off** le match
est annulé; 7 '20% off shoes' '20%
de remise sur les chaussures'.

offence *noun* 1 (*crime*) délit *Masc.*;
2 **to take offence** s'offenser [1]; **he**

a

takes offence easily il s'offense facilement.

b

offer noun **1** offre Fem.; **a job offer** une offre d'emploi; **2 'on (special) offer'** 'en promotion'.

c

d

offer verb **1** offrir [56] (a present, or a reward, or a job) **he offered her a chair** il lui a offert une chaise; **2 to offer to do** proposer [1] de faire; **Blake offered to drive me to the station** Blake m'a proposé de me conduire à la gare.

e

f

g

h

office noun bureau Masc. (plural bureaux); **he's still at the office** il est toujours au bureau; **Sue works in the same office** Sue travaille dans le même bureau.

i

j

k

office block, office building noun immeuble Masc. de bureaux.

officer noun officier Masc.

l

official adjective officiel (Fem. officielle); **the official version** la version officielle.

m

n

off-licence noun magasin Masc. de vins et de spiritueux.

o

offside adjective hors jeu.

p

often adverb souvent; **he's often late** il est souvent en retard; **how often do you see Rosie?** est-ce que tu vois Rosie souvent?; **I'd like to see Eric more often** j'aimerais voir Eric plus souvent.

q

r

s

t

oil noun **1** huile Fem.; **olive oil** l'huile d'olive; **suntan oil** l'huile solaire; **2** (crude oil) pétrole Masc.

u

v

oil painting noun peinture Fem. à l'huile (both the activity and the object).

w

x

oil rig noun plateforme Fem. pétrolière.

y

z

oil slick noun marée Fem. noire.

oil tanker noun pétrolier Masc.

ointment noun pommade Fem.

okay adjective **1** d'accord; **okay, tomorrow at ten** d'accord, demain à dix heures; **is it okay with you if I don't come till Friday?** ça te va si je ne viens que vendredi?; **2** (person) sympa (informal); **Daisy's okay** Daisy est sympa; **3** (nothing special) **the film was okay** le film n'était pas mal; **4** (not ill) **are you okay?** ça va?; **I've been ill but I'm okay now** j'ai été malade, mais ça va mieux maintenant.

old adjective **1** (not young, not new) vieux, vieil (before a vowel or silent 'h') (Fem. vieille); **an old man** un vieux monsieur; **an old lady** une vieille dame; **an old tree** un vieil arbre; **old people** les personnes âgées; **bring some old clothes** apporte de vieux vêtements; **2** (previous) ancien (Fem. ancienne); **our old car was a Rover** notre ancienne voiture était une Rover; **I've only got their old address** je n'ai que leur ancienne adresse; **3** (talking about age) **how old are you?** tu as quel âge?; **James is ten years old** James a dix ans; **a two-year-old child** un enfant de deux ans; **4 my older sister** ma sœur aînée; **she's older than me** elle est plus âgée que moi; **he's a year older than me** il a un an de plus que moi.

old age noun vieillesse Fem.

old age pensioner noun retraité Masc., retraitée Fem.

old-fashioned noun **1** (clothes, music, style) démodé; **2** (a person)

vieux jeu (*never agrees*); **my
parents are so old-fashioned** mes
parents sont si vieux jeu.

olive *noun* olive Fem.

olive oil *noun* huile Fem. d'olive.

Olympic Games, Olympics
plural noun Jeux Olympiques
Masc. plural.

omelette *noun* omelette Fem.; **a
cheese omelette** une omelette au
fromage.

omit *verb* omettre [11].

on *preposition* **1** sur; **on the desk**
sur le bureau; **on the road** sur la
route; **on the beach** sur la plage;
2 (*in expressions of time*) **on March
21st** le 21 mars; **he's arriving on
Tuesday** il arrive mardi; **it's shut
on Saturdays** c'est fermé le
samedi; **on rainy days** quand il
pleut; **3** (*for buses, trains, etc*) **she
arrived on the bus** elle est arrivée
en bus; **I met Jackie on the bus**
j'ai vu Jackie dans le bus; **I slept
on the plane** j'ai dormi dans
l'avion; **let's go on our bikes!**
allons-y à vélo!; **4 on TV** à la télé;
on the radio à la radio; **on video**
en vidéo; **5 on holiday** en
vacances; **on strike** en grève.

on *adjective* **1** (*switched on*) **to be on**
(*TV, light, oven*) être [6] allumé;
(*radio, machine*) être en marche; **all
the lights were on** toutes les
lumières étaient allumées; **is the
radio on?** est-ce que la radio est en
marche?; **I've put the oven on** j'ai
allumé le four; **2** (*happening*)
what's on on TV? qu'est-ce qu'il y
a à la télé?; **what's on this week at
the cinema?** qu'est-ce qui passe
cette semaine au cinéma?

once *adverb* **1** une fois; **I've tried
once already** j'ai déjà essayé une
fois; **try once more** essaie encore
une fois; **once a day** une fois par
jour; **more than once** plus d'une
fois; **2 at once** (*immediately*) tout
de suite; **the doctor came at once**
le médecin est venu tout de suite;
3 at once (*at the same time*) à la
fois; **I can't do two things at once**
je ne peux pas faire deux choses à la
fois.

one's *determiner* son, sa, ses; **one
does one's best** on fait de son
mieux; **to pay for one's car** payer
sa voiture; **to love one's children**
aimer ses enfants; **to wash one's
hands** se laver les mains.

one *number* un (*Fem.* une); **one
son** un fils; **one apple** une pomme;
if you want a pen I've got one si
tu veux un stylo j'en ai un; **at one
o'clock** à une heure.

one *pronoun* **1** on; **one never
knows** on ne sait jamais; **2 this
one** celui-ci (*Fem.* celle-ci); **I like
that bike, but this one's cheaper**
j'aime bien ce vélo-là, mais celui-ci
est moins cher; **do you want the
red tie or this one?** veux-tu la
cravate rouge ou celle-ci?; **3 that
one** celui-là (*Fem.* celle-là); **'which
video?' – 'that one'** 'quelle vidéo?'
– 'celle-là'; **4 which one?** lequel?
(*Fem.* laquelle?); **'my foot's hurting'
– 'which one?'** 'j'ai mal au pied' –
'auquel?'; **'she borrowed a skirt
from me' – 'which one?'** 'elle m'a
emprunté une jupe' – 'laquelle?'

oneself *noun* **1 to wash oneself** se
laver; **to hurt oneself** se blesser;
2 (*for emphasis*) soi-même; **one has**

a
b
c
d
e
f
g
h
i
j
k
l
m
n
o
p
q
r
s
t
u
v
w
x
y
z

a

to do everything oneself il faut tout faire soi-même; **3** (all) by oneself tout seul (Fem. toute seule).

one-way street noun sens Masc. unique.

onion noun oignon Masc.; **onion soup** la soupe à l'oignon.

only adjective **1** seul; **the only free seat** la seule place libre; **the only thing to do** la seule chose à faire; **2 an only child** un enfant unique.

only adverb, conjunction **1** (with a verb) ne ...que; **they've only got two bedrooms** ils n'ont que deux chambres; **Anne's only free on Fridays** Anne n'est libre que le vendredi; **there are only three left** il n'en reste que trois; **2** 'how long did they stay?' – 'only two days' 'ils sont restés combien de temps?' – 'deux jours seulement'; **3** (but) mais; **I'd walk, only it's raining** j'irais à pied, mais il pleut.

onto preposition sur.

open noun **in the open** en plein air.

open adjective **1** (not shut) ouvert; **the door's open** la porte est ouverte; **the baker's is not open** la boulangerie n'est pas ouverte; **2 in the open air** en plein air.

open verb **1** ouvrir [30]; **can you open the door for me?** est-ce que tu peux ouvrir la porte?; **Sam opened his eyes** Sam a ouvert les yeux; **the bank opens at nine** la banque ouvre à neuf heures; **2 the door opened slowly** la porte s'est ouverte lentement.

open-air adjective en plein air; **an open-air swimming pool** une piscine en plein air.

opener noun **1** (for bottles) décapsuleur Masc.; **2** (for cans) ouvre-boîte Masc.

opening noun **1** (space) ouverture Fem.; **2** (opportunity) occasion Fem.; **there are few openings for recent graduates** il y a peu de débouchés pour les jeunes diplômés.

opera noun opéra Masc.

operate verb (medically) opérer [24]; **will they have to operate?** est-ce qu'il va falloir qu'ils opèrent?

operation noun opération Fem.; **to have an operation** se faire opérer; **she's had an operation** elle s'est fait opérer.

opinion noun avis Masc.; **in my opinion** à mon avis.

opinion poll noun sondage Masc.

opponent noun adversaire Masc. & Fem.

opportunity noun occasion Fem.; **to have the opportunity of doing** avoir l'occasion de faire; **I took the opportunity to visit the museum** j'ai profité de l'occasion pour visiter le musée.

opposed adjective **to be opposed to something** être [6] opposé à quelque chose; **they are opposed to any change of the rules** ils s'opposent à un changement des règles.

opposite noun contraire Masc.; **no, quite the opposite** non, tout le contraire.

opposite adjective **1** opposé (a direction, side, or view, for

example); **she went off in the opposite direction** elle est partie dans la direction opposée;
2 (*facing*) d'en face; **in the house opposite** dans la maison d'en face.

opposite *adverb* en face; **they live opposite** ils habitent en face.

opposite *preposition* en face de; **opposite the station** en face de la gare.

opposition *noun* opposition *Fem.*

optician *noun* opticien *Masc.*, opticienne *Fem.*

optimistic *adjective* optimiste.

option *noun* choix *Masc.*; **we have no option** nous n'avons pas le choix.

optional *adjective* facultatif (*Fem.* facultative).

or *conjunction* **1** ou; **English or French?** anglais ou français?; **today or Tuesday?** aujourd'hui ou mardi?; **2** (*in negatives*) **I don't have a cat or a dog** je n'ai ni un chat ni un chien; **not in June or July** ni en juin ni en juillet; **3** (*or else*) sinon; **phone Mum, or she'll worry** appelle maman, sinon elle va s'inquiéter.

oral *noun* (*an exam*) oral *Masc.* (*plural* oraux); **the French oral** l'oral de français.

orange *noun* (*the fruit*) orange *Fem.*; **an orange juice** un jus d'orange.

orange *adjective* orange (*never changes*); **my orange socks** mes chaussettes orange.

orchard *noun* verger *Masc.*

orchestra *noun* orchestre *Masc.*

order *noun* **1** (*arrangement*) ordre *Masc.*; **in the right order** dans le bon ordre; **in the wrong order** dans le mauvais ordre; **in alphabetical order** dans l'ordre alphabétique; **2** (*in a restaurant or café*) commande *Fem.*; **can I take your orders?** puis-je prendre vos commandes?; **3** 'out of order' 'en panne'; **4 in order to do** pour faire; **we hurried in order to be on time** nous nous sommes dépêchés pour arriver à l'heure.

order *verb* **1** (*in a restaurant or a shop*) commander [1]; **we ordered steaks** nous avons commandé des steaks; **2** réserver [1] (*a taxi*).

ordinary *adjective* ordinaire.

organ *noun* **1** (*in music*) orgue *Masc.*; **to play the organ** jouer de l'orgue; **2** (*of body*) organe *Masc.*

organic *adjective* biologique (*food*).

organization *noun* organisation *Fem.*

organize *verb* organiser [1].

orienteering *noun* course *Fem.* d'orientation.

original *adjective* original (*Masc. plural* originaux); **the original version was better** la version originale était meilleure; **it's a really original novel** c'est un roman très original.

originally *adverb* à l'origine; **originally we wanted to take the car** à l'origine nous voulions prendre la voiture.

Orkneys *plural noun* **the Orkneys** les Orcades *Fem. plural.*

ornament *noun* bibelot *Masc.*

a b c d e f g h i j k l m n o p q r s t u v w x y z

orphan noun orphelin Masc., orpheline Fem.

ostrich noun autruche Fem.

other adjective **1** autre; **the other day** l'autre jour; **we took the other road** nous avons pris l'autre route; **give me the other one** donne-moi l'autre; **where are the others?** où sont les autres?; **the other two cars** les deux autres voitures; **2** every other week une semaine sur deux; **3** somebody or other quelqu'un; **something or other** quelque chose; **somewhere or other** quelque part.

otherwise adverb (in other ways) à part ça; **the flat's a bit small but otherwise it's lovely** l'appartement n'est pas très grand mais à part ça il est très bien.

otherwise conjunction (or else) sinon; **I'll phone home, otherwise they'll worry** je vais appeler chez moi, sinon ils vont s'inquiéter.

ought verb ('ought' is translated by the conditional tense of 'devoir' [8]) **I ought to go now** je devrais partir maintenant; **they ought to know the address** ils devraient savoir l'adresse; **you oughtn't to have any problems** vous ne devriez pas avoir des problèmes.

our adjective **1** notre; **our house** notre maison; **2** (before a plural noun) nos; **our parents** nos parents; **3** (with parts of the body) le, la, les; **we'll go and wash our hands** on va se laver les mains.

ours pronoun **1** (for a masculine noun) le nôtre; **their garden's bigger than ours** leur jardin est plus grand que le nôtre; **2** (for a

feminine noun) la nôtre; **their house is smaller than ours** leur maison est plus petite que la nôtre; **3** (for a plural noun) les nôtres; **they've invited their friends and we've invited ours** ils ont invité leurs amis et nous avons invité les nôtres; **4** à nous; **the green one's ours** le vert est à nous; **it's ours** c'est à nous; **a friend of ours** un ami à nous.

ourselves pronoun **1** nous; **we introduced ourselves** nous nous sommes présentés; **2** (for emphasis) nous-mêmes; **in the end we did it ourselves** finalement nous l'avons fait nous-mêmes.

out adverb **1** (outside) dehors; **it's cold out there** il fait froid dehors; **out in the rain** sous la pluie; **they're out in the garden** ils sont dans le jardin; **2** to go out sortir [72]; **she went out an hour ago** elle est sortie il y a une heure; **Mr. Barnes is out** Monsieur Barnes est sorti; **are you going out this evening?** est-ce que tu sors ce soir?; **Alison's going out with Danny at the moment** Alison sort avec Danny en ce moment; **he's asked me out** il m'a invitée à sortir avec lui; **3** to go out of the room sortir de la pièce; **he threw it out of the window** il l'a jeté par la fenêtre; **to drink out of a glass** boire dans un verre; **she took the photo out of her bag** elle a pris la photo dans son sac.

out adjective (light, fire) éteint; **are all the lights out?** est-ce que toutes les lumières sont éteintes?; **the fire was out** le feu était éteint.

outdoor *adjective (an activity or sport)* de plein air; **an outdoor restaurant** un restaurant en plein air.

outdoors *adverb* en plein air.

outing *noun* sortie *Fem.*; **to go on an outing** faire une sortie.

outline *noun (of an object)* contour *Masc.*

out-of-date *adjective* **1** *(no longer valid)* périmé; **my passport's out of date** mon passeport est périmé; **2** *(old-fashioned)* démodé; **they played out-of-date music** ils ont joué la musique démodée.

outside *noun* extérieur *Masc.*; **it's blue on the outside** c'est bleu à l'extérieur.

outside *adjective* extérieur.

outside *adverb* dehors; **it's cold outside** il fait froid dehors.

outside *preposition (a building)*; **I'll meet you outside the cinema** on se retrouve devant le cinéma.

outskirts *noun* périphérie *Fem.*; **on the outskirts of York** à la périphérie de York.

outstanding *adjective* exceptionnel (*Fem.* exceptionnelle).

oval *adjective* ovale.

oven *noun* four *Masc.*; **I've put it in the oven** je l'ai mis au four.

over *preposition* **1** *(above)* au-dessus de; **there's a mirror over the sideboard** il y a un miroir au-dessus du buffet; **2** *(involving movement)* par-dessus; **she jumped over the fence** elle a sauté par-dessus la clôture; **he threw the ball over the wall** il a jeté la balle par-dessus le mur; **3 over here** par ici; **the drinks are over here** les boissons sont par ici; **4 over there** là-bas; **she's over there talking to Julian** elle est là-bas en train de discuter avec Julian; **5** *(more than)* plus de; **it will cost over a hundred pounds** ça coûtera plus de cent livres; **he's over sixty** il a plus de soixante ans; **6** *(during)* pendant; **over the weekend** pendant le weekend; **over Christmas** à Noël; **7** *(finished)* terminé; **when the meeting's over** quand la réunion sera terminée; **it's all over now** c'est terminé maintenant; **8 over the phone** par téléphone; **to ask someone over** inviter quelqu'un; **can you come over on Saturday?** peux-tu venir chez moi samedi?; **9 all over the place** partout; **all over the house** partout dans la maison.

overcast *adjective* couvert.

overcrowded *adjective* bondé.

overdose *noun* **1** *(of drugs)* overdose *Fem.*; **2** *(of medicine)* surdose *Fem.*

overflow *verb* déborder [1].

overseas *adverb* à l'étranger; **Dave works overseas** Dave travaille à l'étranger.

oversleep *verb* se réveiller [1] trop tard.

overtake *verb* doubler [1] *(another car)*.

overtime *noun* **to work overtime** faire [10] des heures supplémentaires.

a b c d e f g h i j k l m n o p q r s t u v w x y z

a
b
c
d
e
f
g
h
i
j
k
l
m
n
p
q
r
s
t
u
v
w
x
y
z

overweight adjective (a person) trop gros (Fem. trop grosse).

owe verb devoir [8]; **I owe Rick ten pounds** je dois dix livres à Rick.

owing adjective **1** (to pay) à payer; **there's five pounds owing** il y a cinq livres à payer; **2 owing to** en raison de; **owing to the snow** en raison de la neige.

owl noun hibou Masc. (plural hiboux).

own adjective **1** propre (goes before the noun); **my own computer** mon propre ordinateur; **I've got my own room** j'ai une chambre à moi; **2 on your own** tout seul (Fem. toute seule); **Annie did it on her own** Annie l'a fait toute seule.

own verb posséder [24].

owner noun propriétaire Masc. & Fem.

oxygen noun oxygène Masc.

oyster noun huître Fem.

ozone layer noun couche Fem. d'ozone.

Pp

pace noun **1** (a step) pas Masc.; **2** (the speed you walk at) allure Fem.; **at a brisk pace** à vive allure.

Pacific noun **the Pacific Ocean** l'océan Masc. Pacifique.

pack noun **1** paquet Masc.; **2 a pack of cards** un jeu de cartes.

pack verb **1** faire [10] ses bagages; **I haven't packed yet** je n'ai pas encore fait mes bagages; **2 I'll pack my case tonight** je ferai ma valise

ce soir; **have you packed my red shirt?** as-tu mis ma chemise rouge dans la valise?

package noun paquet Masc.

package holiday, **package tour** noun voyage Masc. organisé.

packed lunch noun panier-repas Masc.

packet noun **1** paquet Masc.; **a packet of biscuits** un paquet de biscuits; **2** (bag) sachet Masc.; **a packet of crisps** un sachet de chips.

packing noun **to do your packing** faire vos bagages.

pad noun (of paper) bloc-notes Masc.

paddle noun (for a canoe) pagaie Fem.

paddle verb (at the seaside) **to go paddling** faire [10] trempette.

padlock noun cadenas Masc.

page noun page Fem.; **on page seven** à la page sept.

pain noun douleur Fem.; **I've got a pain in my leg** j'ai mal à la jambe; **to be in pain** souffrir [73]; ★ **Eric's a real pain (in the neck)** Eric est vraiment pénible.

painful adjective douloureux (Fem. douloureuse).

painkiller noun analgésique Masc.

paint noun peinture Fem.; **'wet paint'** 'peinture fraîche'.

paint verb peindre [60]; **to paint something pink** peindre quelque chose en rose.

paintbrush noun pinceau Masc. (plural pinceaux).

painter noun peintre Masc.

painting noun (picture) tableau Masc. (plural tableaux); **a painting by Monet** un tableau de Monet.

pair noun **1** paire Fem.; **a pair of socks** une paire de chaussettes; **a pair of scissors** une paire de ciseaux; **2 a pair of jeans** un jean; **a pair of trousers** un pantalon; **a pair of knickers** un slip; **3 to work in pairs** travailler en groupes de deux.

Pakistan noun Pakistan Masc.; **in Pakistan** au Pakistan; **to Pakistan** au Pakistan.

Pakistani noun Pakistanais Masc., Pakistanaise Fem..

Pakistani adjective pakistanais.

palace noun palais Masc.

pale adjective pâle; **pale green** vert pâle (never changes); **pale green curtains** des rideaux vert pâle; **to turn pale** pâlir [2].

palm noun **1** (of your hand) paume Fem.; **2** (a palm tree) palmier Masc.

pan noun (saucepan) casserole Fem. **1 a pan of water** une casserole d'eau; **2** (frying pan) poêle Fem.

pancake noun crêpe Fem.

panel noun **1** (on radio or TV) (for a discussion) invités Masc. plural (i.e. guests); (for a quiz show) jury Masc.; **2** (for a wall or a bath, for example) panneau Masc. (plural **panneaux**).

panel game noun jeu Masc. (plural **jeux**).

panic noun panique Fem.

panic verb s'affoler [1]; **don't panic!** pas de panique!

pannier noun (on a bike) sacoche Fem.

panther noun panthère Fem.

panties noun petite culotte Fem.

pantomime noun spectacle Masc. pour enfants.

pants plural noun slip Masc.

paper noun **1** papier Masc.; **a sheet of paper** une feuille de papier; **2 a paper cup** un gobelet en carton; **a paper hanky** un mouchoir en papier; **3** (newspaper) journal Masc. (plural journaux); **it was in the paper** c'était dans le journal.

paperback noun livre Masc. de poche.

paperclip noun trombone Masc. (because of its shape).

paper shop noun magasin Masc. de journaux.

paper towel noun essuie-tout Masc.

parachute noun parachute Masc.

parachuting noun parachutisme Masc.; **to go parachuting** faire du parachutisme.

parade noun défilé Masc.

paradise noun paradis Masc.

paraffin noun pétrole Masc.

paragraph noun paragraphe Masc.; **'new paragraph'** 'à la ligne'.

parallel adjective parallèle.

paralysed adjective paralysé.

parcel noun paquet Masc.

pardon noun **I beg your pardon** pardon; **pardon?** pardon?

parent noun parent Masc.; **my parents are Scottish** mes parents sont écossais; **a parents' evening** une réunion pour les parents d'élèves.

Paris noun Paris; **Marie lives in Paris** Marie habite à Paris.

a b c d e f g h i j k l m n o p q r s t u v w x y z

Parisian noun Parisien Masc., Parisienne Fem.

Parisian adjective parisien (Fem. parisienne).

park noun 1 parc Masc.; **a theme park** un parc à thème; 2 **a car park** un parking.

park verb 1 se garer [1]; **you can park outside the house** vous pouvez vous garer devant la maison; 2 **to park a car** garer [1] une voiture; **where did you park the car?** où as-tu garé la voiture?

parking noun stationnement Masc.; **'no parking'** 'stationnement interdit'.

parking meter noun parcmètre Masc.

parking space noun place Fem.

parking ticket noun PV Masc. (informal).

parliament noun parlement Masc.

parrot noun perroquet Masc.

parsley noun persil Masc.

part noun 1 partie Fem.; **part of the garden** une partie du jardin; **the last part of the concert** la dernière partie du concert; **that's part of your job** ça fait partie de votre travail; 2 **to take part in something** participer à quelque chose; 3 (a role in a play) rôle Masc.; 4 **spare parts** pièces Fem. plural détachées.

particular adjective particulier (Fem. particulière); **nothing in particular** rien de particulier.

particularly adverb 1 (unusually) spécialement; **not particularly interesting** pas spécialement intéressant; 2 (in particular)

surtout; **particularly as it's our last day** surtout que c'est notre dernier jour.

parting noun (in your hair) raie Fem.

partly adverb en partie.

partner noun 1 (in a game) partenaire Masc.; 2 (the person you live with) partenaire Masc. & Fem.; 3 (in business) associé Masc., associée Fem.

partridge noun perdrix Fem.

part-time adjective, adverb à temps partiel; **part-time work** du travail à temps partiel; **to work part-time** travailler à temps partiel.

party noun 1 fête Fem.; **a Christmas party** une fête de Noël; **to have a birthday party** faire une fête d'anniversaire; 2 (more formal, in the evening) soirée Fem.; **we've been invited to a party at the Smiths' house** nous sommes invités à une soirée chez les Smith; 3 (group) groupe Masc.; **a party of schoolchildren** un groupe d'élèves; **a rescue party** une équipe de secouristes; 4 (in politics) parti Masc.; **the Labour party** le parti travailliste.

party game noun jeu Masc. de société (plural jeux de société).

pass noun 1 (to let you in) laisser-passer Masc. (plural laisser-passer); 2 **a bus pass** une carte de bus; 3 (a mountain pass) col Masc.; 4 (in an exam) **to get a pass in history** être reçu en histoire.

pass verb 1 (go past) passer [1] devant (a place or building); **we**

passed your house nous sommes passés devant chez toi; **2** (*to overtake*) doubler [1] (*a car*); **3** (*give*) passer [1]; **could you pass me the paper please?** peux-tu me passer le journal s'il te plaît?; **4** (*time*) passer [1]; **the time passed slowly** le temps passait lentement; **5** (*in an exam*) être [6] reçu; **did you pass?** as-tu été reçu?; **to pass an exam** être reçu à un examen.

passage noun **1** (*a corridor*) couloir *Masc.*; **2** (*a piece of text*) passage *Masc.*

passenger noun **1** (*in a car, plane, or ship*) passager *Masc.*, passagère *Fem.*; **2** (*in a train, bus, or underground*) voyageur *Masc.*, voyageuse *Fem.*

passerby noun passant *Masc.*, passante *Fem.*

passion noun passion *Fem.*

passionate adjective passionné.

passive noun passif *Masc.*

passive adjective passif (*Fem.* passive).

Passover noun Pâque *Fem.* juive.

passport noun passeport *Masc.*; **an EU passport** un passeport de l'UE.

password noun mot *Masc.* de passe.

past noun passé *Masc.*; **in the past** au passé.

past adjective **1** (*recent*) dernier (*Fem.* dernière) (*goes before the noun*); **in the past few weeks** pendant les dernières semaines; **2** (*over*) fini; **winter is past** l'hiver est fini.

past preposition, adverb **1 to walk or drive past something** passer devant quelque chose; **we went past the school** nous sommes passés devant l'école; **Ray went past in his new car** Ray est passé dans sa nouvelle voiture; **2** (*the other side of*) après; **it's just past the post office** c'est juste après la poste; **3** (*talking about time*) **ten past six** six heures dix; **half past four** quatre heures et demie; **a quarter past two** deux heures et quart.

pasta noun pâtes *Fem.* plural; **I don't like pasta** je n'aime pas les pâtes.

paste verb coller [1]; **to cut and paste the table** copier-coller le tableau.

pasteurized adjective pasteurisé.

pastry noun pâte *Fem.*

patch noun **1** (*fabric, for mending*) pièce *Fem.*; **2** (*of snow or ice*) plaque *Fem.*; **3** (*of blue sky*) coin *Masc.*

path noun chemin *Masc.*; (*very narrow*) sentier *Masc.*

pathetic adjective (*useless, hopeless*) lamentable.

patience noun **1** patience *Fem.*; **2** (*card game*) réussite *Fem.*

patient noun patient *Masc.*, patiente *Fem.*

patient adjective patient.

patiently adverb avec patience.

patio noun terrasse *Fem.*

patrol noun patrouille *Fem.*

patrol car noun voiture *Fem.* de police.

pattern noun **1** (*on wallpaper or fabric*) motif *Masc.*; **2** (*dressmaking*)

a b c d e f g h i j k l m n o p q r s t u v w x y z

patron Masc.; **3** (knitting) modèle Masc.

pause noun pause Fem.

pavement noun trottoir Masc.; **on the pavement** sur le trottoir.

paw noun patte Fem.

pawn noun pion Masc.

pay noun salaire Masc.

pay verb **1** payer [59]; **I'm paying** c'est moi qui paie; **to pay cash** payer comptant; **2 to pay for something** payer [59] quelque chose; **Tony paid for the drinks** Tony a payé les boissons; **it's all paid for** c'est tout payé; **3 to pay by credit card** régler [24] par carte de crédit; **to pay by cheque** régler par chèque; **4 to pay somebody back** (money) rembourser [1] quelqu'un; **5 to pay attention** faire [10] attention; **6 to pay a visit to somebody** rendre [3] visite à quelqu'un.

paydesk noun caisse Fem.

payment noun paiement Masc. (of a bill) règlement Masc.

pay phone noun téléphone Masc. public.

PC noun (computer) PC Masc.

pea noun petit pois Masc.

peace noun paix Fem.

peaceful adjective paisible (day, scene).

peach noun pêche Fem.

peacock noun paon Masc.

peak noun (of a mountain) pic Masc.

peak period (for holidays) période Fem. de pointe.

peak rate noun (for phoning) tarif Masc. rouge.

peak time noun (for traffic) heures Fem. plural de pointe.

peanut noun cacahuète Fem.

peanut butter noun beurre Masc. de cacahuètes.

pear noun poire Fem.

pearl noun perle Fem.

peasant noun paysan Masc., paysanne Fem.

pebble noun **1** (on the road) caillou Masc. (plural **cailloux**); **2** (on a beach) galet Masc.

peculiar adjective bizarre.

pedal noun pédale Fem.

pedal verb pédaler [1].

pedal boat noun pédalo™ Masc.

pedestrian noun piéton Masc.

pedestrian crossing noun passage Masc. pour piétons.

pedestrian precinct noun zone Fem. piétonne.

pee noun **to have a pee** faire [10] pipi (informal).

peel noun **1** (of an apple) peau Fem.; **2** (of an orange) écorce Fem.

peel verb éplucher [1] (fruit, vegetables).

peer verb **to peer at something** regarder [1] quelque chose attentivement.

peg noun **1** (hook) patère Fem.; **2** a **clothes peg** une pince à linge; **3** a **tent peg** un piquet.

pen noun stylo Masc.; **a felt pen** un stylo-feutre.

penalty noun **1** (a fine) amende Fem.; **2** (in football) penalty Masc.; **3** (in rugby) pénalité Fem.

penalty area noun surface Fem. de réparation.

pence *plural noun* pence Masc. plural.

pencil *noun* crayon Masc.; **to write in pencil** écrire au crayon.

pencil case *noun* trousse Fem.

pencil sharpener *noun* taille-crayon Masc.

pendant *noun* pendentif Masc.

penfriend *noun* correspondant Masc., correspondante Fem.; **my French pen-friend is called Christelle** ma correspondante française s'appelle Christelle.

penguin *noun* pingouin Masc.

penis *noun* pénis Masc.

penknife *noun* canif Masc.

penny *noun* penny Masc.

pension *noun* retraite Fem.

pensioner *noun* retraité Masc., retraitée Fem.

people *plural noun* 1 gens Masc. plural; **people round here** les gens d'ici; **nice people** des gens sympathiques; 2 (*when you're counting them*) personnes Fem. plural; **ten people** dix personnes; **several people** plusieurs personnes; **how many people have you asked?** tu as invité combien de personnes?; 3 **people say he's very rich** on dit qu'il est très riche.

pepper *noun* 1 (*spice*) poivre Masc.; 2 (*vegetable*) poivron Masc.; **a green pepper** un poivron vert.

peppermill *noun* moulin Masc. à poivre.

peppermint *noun* menthe Fem.; **peppermint tea** le thé à la menthe.

per *preposition* par; **ten pounds per person** dix livres par personne.

per cent *adverb* pour cent; **sixty per cent of students** soixante pour cent des étudiants.

percentage *noun* pourcentage Masc.

percussion *noun* percussion Fem.; **to play percussion** jouer des percussions.

perfect *adjective* 1 parfait; **she speaks perfect English** elle parle un anglais parfait; 2 (*ideal*) idéal (Masc. plural idéaux); **the perfect place for a picnic** l'endroit idéal pour un pique-nique.

perfectly *adverb* parfaitement.

perform *verb* 1 jouer [1] (*a piece of music or a play*); 2 chanter [1] (*a song*).

performance *noun* 1 (*playing or acting*) interprétation Fem.; **a wonderful performance of Macbeth** une superbe interprétation de Macbeth; 2 (*show*) spectacle Masc.; **the performance starts at eight** le spectacle commence à huit heures; 3 (*the results of a team or company*) performance Fem.

performer *noun* artiste Masc. & Fem.

perfume *noun* parfum Masc.

perhaps *adverb* peut-être; **perhaps it's in the drawer?** c'est peut-être dans le tiroir?; **perhaps he's missed the train** il a peut-être raté le train.

period *noun* 1 période Fem.; **a two-year period** une période de deux ans; 2 (*in school*) cours Masc.; a

a
b
c
d
e
f
g
h
i
j
k
l
m
n
o
p
q
r
s
t
u
v
w
x
y
z

a
b
c
d
e
f
g
h
i
j
k
l
m
n
o
p
q
r
s
t
u
v
w
x
y
z

forty-five-minute period un cours de quarante-cinq minutes; **3** (menstruation) règles Fem. plural; **during your period** pendant vos règles.

perm noun permanente Fem.

permanent adjective permanent.

permanently adverb en permanence.

permission noun permission Fem.; **to get permission to do** obtenir la permission de faire.

permit noun permis Masc.

permit verb permettre [11]; **to permit somebody to do** permettre à quelqu'un de faire; **smoking is not permitted** il est interdit de fumer; **weather permitting** si le temps le permet.

person noun personne Fem.; **there's room for one more person** il y a de la place pour une autre personne; **in person** en personne.

personal adjective personnel (Fem. personnelle).

personality noun personnalité Fem.

personally adverb personnellement; **personally, I'm against it** personnellement, je suis contre.

personal stereo noun baladeur Masc.

perspiration noun transpiration Fem.

persuade verb persuader [1]; **to persuade somebody to do** persuader quelqu'un de faire; **we persuaded Tim to wait a bit** nous avons persuadé Tim d'attendre un peu.

pessimistic adjective pessimiste.

pest noun **1** (greenfly for example) insecte Masc. nuisible; **2** (annoying person) casse-pieds Masc. & Fem.

pester verb harceler [45].

pet noun **1** animal Masc. de compagnie (plural animaux de compagnie); **do you have a pet?** avez-vous un animal de compagnie?; **a pet dog** un chien; **2** (favourite person) chouchou Masc., chouchoute Fem.; **Julie is teacher's pet** Julie est la chouchoute du prof.

petal noun pétale Masc.

pet name noun petit nom Masc.

petrol noun essence Fem.; **to fill up with petrol** faire le plein d'essence; **to run out of petrol** tomber en panne d'essence.

petrol station noun station Fem. d'essence.

petticoat noun jupon Masc.

pharmacist noun pharmaciste Masc. & Fem.

pharmacy noun pharmacie Fem.

pheasant noun faisan Masc.

philosophy noun philosophie Fem.

phone noun téléphone Masc.; **she's on the phone** elle est au téléphone; **I was on the phone to Sophie** j'étais au téléphone avec Sophie; **you can book by phone** on peut réserver par téléphone.

phone verb **1** téléphoner [1]; **while I was phoning** pendant que je téléphonais; **2 to phone somebody** appeler [18] quelqu'un; **I'll phone you tonight** je t'appellerai ce soir.

phone book noun annuaire Masc.

phone box noun cabine Fem. téléphonique.

phone call noun appel Masc.; **phone calls are free** ces appels sont gratuits; **to make a phone call** téléphoner.

phone card noun télécarte Fem.

phone number noun numéro Masc. de téléphone.

photo noun photo Fem.; **to take a photo** prendre une photo; **to take a photo of somebody** prendre quelqu'un en photo; **I took a photo of their house** j'ai pris leur maison en photo.

photocopier noun photocopieuse Fem.

photocopy noun photocopie Fem.

photocopy verb photocopier [1].

photograph noun photo Fem.; **to take a photograph** prendre une photo; **to take a photograph of somebody** prendre quelqu'un en photo.

photograph verb photographier [1].

photographer noun photographe Masc. & Fem.

photography noun photographie Fem.

phrase noun expression Fem.

phrase-book noun manuel Masc. de conversation.

physical adjective physique.

physicist noun physicien Masc., physicienne Fem.

physics noun physique Fem.

physiotherapist noun kinésithérapeute Masc. & Fem.

physiotherapy noun kinésithérapie Fem.

pianist noun pianiste Masc. & Fem.

piano noun piano Masc.; **to play the piano** jouer du piano; **Steve played it on the piano** Steve l'a joué au piano; **a piano lesson** une leçon de piano.

pick noun take your pick! choisis!

pick verb 1 (to choose) choisir [2]; **pick a card** choisis une carte; 2 (for a team) sélectionner [1]; **I've been picked for Saturday** j'ai été sélectionné pour samedi; 3 cueillir [35] (fruit or flowers).

● **to pick up** 1 (lift) prendre [64]; he **picked up the papers and went out** il a pris les papiers et il est sorti; 2 (collect together) ramasser [1]; **I'll pick up the toys** je ramasserai les jouets; 3 (to collect) venir [81] chercher; **I'll pick you up at six** je viendrai te chercher à six heures; **I'll pick up the keys tomorrow** je viendrai chercher les clés demain; 4 (learn) apprendre [64]; **you'll soon pick it up** tu vas vite l'apprendre.

pickpocket noun pickpocket Masc.

picnic noun pique-nique Masc.; **to have a picnic** pique-niquer.

picture noun 1 (a painting) tableau Masc. (plural tableaux); **a picture by Renoir** une tableau de Renoir; **he painted a picture of a horse** il a peint un cheval; 2 (a drawing) dessin Masc.; **draw me a picture of your little sister** dessine-moi ta petite sœur; 3 (in a book) illustration Fem.; **a book**

with lots of pictures un livre avec beaucoup d'illustrations; **4** (*the cinema*) **the pictures** le cinéma; **to go to the pictures** aller au cinéma.

pie noun **1** (*sweet*) tarte Fem.; **an apple pie** une tarte aux pommes; **2** (*savoury*) tourte Fem.; **a meat pie** une tourte à la viande.

piece noun **1** (*a bit*) morceau Masc. (*plural* **morceaux**); **a big piece of cheese** un gros morceau de fromage; **2** (*that you fit together*) pièce Fem.; **the pieces of a jigsaw** les pièces d'un puzzle; **to take something to pieces** démonter [1] quelque chose; **3 a piece of furniture** un meuble; **four pieces of luggage** quatre valises; **a piece of information** un renseignement; **that's a piece of luck!** c'est un coup de chance!; **4** (*coin*) pièce Fem.; **a two-euro piece** une pièce de deux euros.

pier noun jetée Fem.

pierced adjective percé; **to have pierced ears** avoir les oreilles percées.

pig noun cochon Masc.

pigeon noun pigeon Masc.

piggy bank noun tirelire Fem.

pigsty noun porcherie Fem.; **your room is a pigsty** ta chambre est une vraie porcherie.

pigtail noun natte Fem.

pile noun **1** (*a neat stack*) pile Fem.; **a pile of plates** une pile d'assiettes; **2** (*a heap*) tas Masc.; **a pile of dirty shirts** un tas de chemises sales.

● **to pile something up** (*neatly*) empiler [1] quelque chose; (*in a heap*) entasser [1] quelque chose.

pilgrimage noun pèlerinage Masc.; **to go on a pilgrimage** faire [10] un pèlerinage.

pill noun comprimé Masc.; **the pill** (*contraceptive*) la pilule.

pillar noun pilier Masc.

pillar box noun boîte Fem. aux lettres.

pillow noun oreiller Masc.

pillowcase noun taie Fem. d'oreiller.

pilot noun pilote Masc.

pimple noun bouton Masc.

pin noun **1** (*for sewing*) épingle Fem.; **2 a three-pin plug** une prise à trois fiches.

● **to pin up 1** épingler [1] (*a hem*); **2** accrocher [1] (*a notice*).

PIN noun (*personal identification number*) code Masc. confidentiel.

pinball noun flipper Masc.; **to play pinball** jouer au flipper; **a pinball machine** un flipper.

pinch noun (*of salt, for example*) pincée Fem.

pinch verb **1** (*steal*) piquer [1]; **somebody's pinched my bike** on m'a piqué mon vélo; **2 to pinch somebody** pincer [61] quelqu'un.

pine noun pin Masc.; **a pine table** une table en pin.

pineapple noun ananas Masc.

pine cone noun pomme Fem. de pin.

ping-pong noun ping-pong Masc.; **to play ping-pong** jouer au ping-pong.

pink adjective rose.

pip noun (in a fruit) pépin Masc.

pipe noun 1 (for gas or water) tuyau Masc. (plural tuyaux); 2 (to smoke) pipe Fem.; **he smokes a pipe** il fume la pipe.

pirate noun pirate Masc.

pirated adjective piraté; **a pirated video** une vidéo piratée.

Pisces noun Poissons Masc. plural; **Amanda is Pisces** Amanda est Poissons.

pistachio noun pistache Fem.

pit noun fosse Fem.

pitch noun terrain Masc.; **a football pitch** un terrain de foot.

pitch verb **to pitch a tent** dresser [1] une tente.

pity noun 1 **what a pity!** quel dommage!; **it would be a pity to miss the beginning** ce serait dommage de rater le début; 2 (feeling sorry for somebody) pitié Fem.

pity verb **to pity somebody** plaindre [31] quelqu'un.

pizza noun pizza Fem.

place noun 1 endroit Masc.; **in a warm place** dans un endroit chaud; **Rome is a wonderful place** Rome est un endroit merveilleux; **all over the place** partout; 2 (a space) place Fem.; **a place for the car** une place pour la voiture; **is there a place for me?** y a-t-il une place pour moi?; **will you keep my place?** veux-tu me garder ma place?; **to change places** changer de place; 3 (in a race) place Fem.; **in first place** à la première place; 4 **at your place** chez toi; **we'll go round**

to Zafir's place on ira chez Zafir; 5 **to take place** avoir [5] lieu; **the competition will take place at four** le concours aura lieu à quatre heures.

place verb mettre [11]; **he placed his cup on the table** il a mis sa tasse sur la table.

plain noun plaine Fem.

plain adjective 1 simple; **plain cooking** une cuisine simple; 2 (unflavoured) nature; **a plain yoghurt** un yaourt nature; 3 (not patterned) uni; **plain curtains** des rideaux unis.

plait noun natte Fem.

plan noun 1 projet Masc.; **what are your plans for this summer?** quels sont vos projets pour cet été?; **to go according to plan** se passer comme prévu; **everything went according to plan** tout s'est passé comme prévu; 2 (a map) plan Masc.

plan verb 1 **to plan to do** avoir [5] l'intention de faire; **we're planning to leave at eight** nous avons l'intention de partir à huit heures; 2 (make plans for) préparer [1]; **Ricky's planning a trip to Italy** Ricky prépare un voyage en Italie; 3 (organize) organiser [1]; **I'm planning my day** j'organise ma journée; 4 (to design) concevoir [66] (a house or garden); **a well-planned kitchen** une cuisine bien conçue.

plane noun avion Masc.; **we went by plane** nous avons pris l'avion.

planet noun planète Fem.

plank noun planche Fem.

plant noun plante Fem.; **a house plant** une plante d'intérieur.

plant verb planter [1].

a b c d e f g h i j k l m n o p q r s t u v w x y z

plaster noun **1** (*sticking plaster*) pansement Masc. adhésif.; **2** (*for walls*) plâtre Masc.; **3 to have your leg in plaster** avoir la jambe dans le plâtre.

plastic noun plastique Masc.; **a plastic bag** un sac en plastique.

plate noun assiette Fem.

platform noun **1** (*in a station*) quai Masc.; **the train arriving at platform six** le train qui entre en gare quai numéro six; **2** (*for lecturing or performing*) estrade Fem.

play noun pièce Fem.; **a play by Molière** une pièce de Molière; **our school is putting on a play** notre école monte une pièce.

play verb **1** jouer [1]; **the children were playing with a ball** les enfants jouaient avec un ballon; **they play all kinds of music** ils jouent toutes sortes de musique; **who's playing Hamlet?** qui est-ce qui joue Hamlet?; **2** jouer [1] à (*a game*); **to play tennis** jouer au tennis; **they were playing cards** ils jouaient aux cartes; **3** jouer [1] de (*a musical instrument*); **Helen plays the violin** Helen joue du violon; **4** mettre [11] (*a tape, CD, or record*); **play me your new CD** mets-moi ton nouveau CD.

player noun **1** (*in sport*) joueur Masc., joueuse Fem.; **a football player** un joueur de foot; **2** (*musician*) musicien Masc., musicienne Fem.

playground noun cour Fem. de récréation.

playgroup noun halte-garderie Fem.

playing card noun carte Fem. à jouer.

playing field noun terrain Masc. de sport.

playroom noun salle Fem. de jeux.

plaza noun **a shopping plaza** un centre commercial.

pleasant adjective agréable.

please adverb s'il vous plaît; (*less formal*) s'il te plaît; **two coffees, please** deux cafés, s'il vous plaît; **could you turn the TV off, please?** est-ce que tu peux éteindre la télé s'il te plaît?

pleased adjective content; **I was really pleased!** j'étais très content!; **she was pleased with her present** elle était contente de son cadeau; **pleased to meet you!** enchanté!

pleasure noun plaisir Masc.

plenty pronoun **1** (*lots*) beaucoup; **there's plenty of bread** il y a beaucoup de pain; **he's got plenty of money** il a beaucoup d'argent; **2** (*quite enough*) **we've got plenty of time for a coffee** nous avons largement le temps de prendre un café; **thank you, that's plenty!** merci, ça suffit largement!

pliers noun pince Fem.

plot noun (*of a film or novel*) intrigue Fem.

plough verb labourer [1].

plug noun **1** (*electrical*) prise Fem.; **2** (*in a bath or sink*) bonde Fem.; **to pull out the plug** retirer la bonde.

plum noun prune Fem.; **a plum tart** une tarte aux prunes.

plumber noun plombier Masc.; he's a plumber il est plombier.

plump adjective potelé.

plunge verb plonger [52].

plural noun pluriel Masc.; in the plural au pluriel.

plus preposition plus; three children plus the baby trois enfants plus le bébé.

p.m. adverb (French people usually express times after midday in terms of the 24-hour clock) 1 at two p.m. à quatorze heures; at nine p.m. à vingt-et-une heures; 2 (however, you can also use 'de l'après-midi', for times up to six, and 'du soir' for times after that) at two p.m. à deux heures de l'après-midi; at nine p.m. à neuf heures du soir.

poached egg noun œuf Masc. poché.

pocket noun poche Fem.

pocket money noun 1 (for child) argent Masc. de poche; 2 (for small purchases) petites dépenses Fem. plural.

poem noun poème Masc.

poet noun poète Masc.

poetry noun poésie Fem.

point noun 1 (tip) pointe Fem.; the point of a nail la pointe d'un clou; 2 (in time) moment Masc.; at that point the police arrived à ce moment-là, la police est arrivée; 3 to get the point comprendre; I don't get the point je ne comprends pas; what's the point of waiting? à quoi bon attendre?; there's no point phoning, he's out ça ne sert à rien d'appeler, il est sorti; that's not the point il ne

s'agit pas de ça; 4 that's a good point! c'est vrai!; 5 from my point of view de mon point de vue; 6 her strong point son point fort; 7 (in scoring) point Masc.; fifteen points to eleven quinze points à onze; 8 (in decimals) (in French, a comma is used for the decimal point, so 6,75) 6 point 4 6 virgule 4 (this is how you say it aloud).

point verb 1 indiquer [1]; a notice pointing to the station un panneau qui indiquait la gare; James pointed out the cathedral James nous a montré la cathédrale; 2 (with finger) montrer [1] du doigt; he pointed at one of the children il a montré l'un des enfants du doigt; 3 I'd like to point out that I'm paying je vous signale que c'est moi qui paie.

pointless adjective inutile; it's pointless to keep on ringing c'est inutile de continuer de sonner.

poison noun poison Masc.

poison verb empoisonner [1].

poisonous adjective 1 toxique (chemical or gas); 2 vénéneux (Fem. vénéneuse) (toadstools or berries); 3 venimeux (Fem. venimeuse) (snake or insect).

poker noun 1 (for fire) tisonnier Masc.; 2 (card game) poker Masc.

Poland noun Pologne Fem.; in Poland en Pologne.

polar bear noun ours Masc. polaire.

pole noun 1 (for a tent) mât Masc.; 2 (for skiing) bâton Masc.; 3 the North Pole le pôle Nord.

a
b
c
d
e
f
g
h
i
j
k
l
m
n
o
p
q
r
s
t
u
v
w
x
y
z

Pole noun (a Polish person)
Polonais Masc., Polonaise Fem.

police noun the police la police;
the police are coming la police
arrive (note that a singular verb is
used after 'la police').

police verb surveiller [1].

police car noun voiture Fem. de
police.

policeman noun agent Masc. de
police.

police station noun
commissariat Masc. de police.

policewoman noun femme Fem.
policier.

policy noun 1 (plan of action)
politique Fem.; 2 (document) police
Fem.

polish noun 1 (for furniture) cire
Fem.; 2 (for shoes) cirage Masc.

polish verb cirer [1] (shoes or
furniture).

Polish noun, adjective polonais
Masc.

polite adjective poli; to be polite to
somebody être poli avec
quelqu'un.

political adjective politique.

politician noun homme Masc.
politique, femme Fem. politique.

politics noun politique Fem.

polluted adjective pollué.

pollution noun pollution Fem.

polo-necked adjective à col roulé;
a polo-necked jumper un pull à
col roulé.

polythene bag noun sac Masc. en
plastique.

pond noun 1 (large) étang Masc.;
2 (smaller) mare Fem.; 3 (in a
garden) bassin Masc.

pony noun poney Masc.

ponytail noun queue Fem. de
cheval.

poodle noun caniche Masc.

pool noun 1 (swimming pool)
piscine Fem.; 2 (in the country)
étang Masc.; 3 (puddle) flaque Fem.;
4 (game) billard Masc. américain;
to have a game of pool jouer au
billard américain; 5 the football
pools le loto sportif; to do the
pools jouer au loto sportif.

poor adjective 1 pauvre; a poor
area un quartier pauvre; a poor
family une famille pauvre; poor
Tanya's failed her exam la pauvre
Tanya a raté son examen; 2 (bad)
mauvais; this is poor work c'est du
mauvais travail; the weather was
pretty poor le temps était assez
mauvais.

pop noun pop Masc.; a pop concert
un concert de pop; a pop star un
pop star; a pop song une chanson
pop.

● to pop into faire [10] un saut à; I'll
just pop into the bank je vais juste
faire un saut à la banque.

popcorn noun pop-corn Masc.

pope noun pape Masc.

poppy noun coquelicot Masc.

popular adjective populaire.

population noun population Fem.

porch noun porche Masc.

pork noun porc Masc.; a pork chop
une côtelette de porc.

porridge noun porridge Masc.

port noun **1** port Masc.; **the ferry was in port** le ferry était au port; **2** (wine) porto Masc.

portable computer noun ordinateur Masc. portable.

porter noun **1** (at a station or airport) porteur Masc.; **2** (in a hotel) portier Masc.

portion noun (of food) portion Fem.

portrait noun portrait Masc.

Portugal noun Portugal Masc.; **to Portugal** au Portugal; **in Portugal** au Portugal.

Portuguese noun **1** (language) portugais Masc.; **2** (a person) Portugais Masc., Portugaise Fem.

Portuguese adjective portugais.

posh adjective chic (never changes); **a posh house** une maison chic.

position noun position Fem.

positive adjective **1** (sure) sûr; **I'm positive he's left** je suis sûr qu'il est parti; **2** (enthusiastic) positif (Fem. positive); **her reaction was very positive** sa réaction était très positive; **try to be more positive** essaie d'être plus positif.

possess verb posséder [24].

possessions plural noun affaires Fem. plural; **all my possessions are in the flat** toutes mes affaires sont dans l'appartement.

possibility noun possibilité Fem.

possible adjective possible; **it's possible** c'est possible; **if possible** si possible; **as quickly as possible** le plus vite possible.

possibly adverb **1** (maybe) peut-être; **'will you be at home at midday?' – 'possibly'** 'est-ce que tu seras chez toi à midi?' – 'peut-être';

2 (for emphasis) **how can you possibly believe that?** mais comment donc peux-tu croire ça?; **I can't possibly arrive before Thursday** je ne peux vraiment pas arriver avant jeudi.

post noun **1** (poste Fem.; **to send something by post** envoyer quelque chose par la poste; **2** (letters) courrier Masc.; **is there any post for me?** y a-t-il du courrier pour moi?; **3** (a pole) poteau Masc.; **4** (a job) poste Masc.

post verb **to post a letter** mettre [11] une lettre à la poste.

postbox noun boîte Fem. à lettres.

postcard noun carte Fem. postale.

postcode noun code Masc. postal.

poster noun **1** (for decoration) poster Masc.; **I've bought an Oasis poster** j'ai acheté un poster d'Oasis; **2** (advertising) affiche Fem.; **I saw a poster for the concert** j'ai vu une affiche pour le concert.

postman noun facteur Masc.; **has the postman been?** est-ce que le facteur est passé?

post office noun poste Fem.; **the post office is on the right** la poste est à droite.

postpone verb **to postpone something** remettre [11] quelque chose à plus tard.

postwoman noun factrice Fem.

pot noun **1** (jar) pot Masc.; **a pot of honey** un pot de miel; **2** (teapot) théière Fem.; **I'll make a pot of tea** je vais faire du thé; **3** **the pots and pans** les casseroles Fem. plural; ★ **to**

a
b
c
d
e
f
g
h
i
j
k
l
m
n
o
p
q
r
s
t
u
v
w
x
y
z

take pot luck manger à la fortune du pot.

potato noun pomme Fem. de terre; **fried potatoes** des pommes de terre sautées; **mashed potatoes** de la purée.

potato crisps plural noun chips Masc. plural.

pottery noun poterie Fem.

pound noun 1 (money) livre Fem.; **fourteen pounds** quatorze livres; **how much is that in pounds?** c'est combien en livres sterling?; 2 (in weight) livre Fem.; **a pound of apples** une livre de pommes.

pour verb 1 verser [1] (liquid); **he poured the milk into the pan** il a versé le lait dans la casserole; 2 servir [71] (a drink); **to pour the tea** servir le thé; **I poured him a drink** je lui ai servi à boire; 3 (with rain) **it's pouring** il pleut à verse.

poverty noun pauvreté Fem.

powder noun poudre Fem.

power noun 1 (electricity) courant Masc.; 2 (energy) énergie Fem.; **nuclear power** l'énergie nucléaire; 3 (over other people) pouvoir Masc.; **to be in power** être au pouvoir.

power cut noun coupure Fem. de courant.

powerful adjective puissant.

power point noun prise Fem. de courant.

power station noun centrale Fem. électrique.

practical adjective pratique.

practical joke noun farce Fem.

practically adverb pratiquement.

practice noun 1 (for sport) entraînement Masc.; **hockey practice** l'entraînement de hockey; 2 (for an instrument) **to do your piano practice** travailler [1] son piano; 3 **to be out of practice** être rouillé; 4 **in practice** en pratique.

practise verb 1 travailler [1] (music, language, etc); **a week in Berlin to practise my German** une semaine à Berlin pour travailler mon allemand; 2 (in a sport) s'entraîner [1]; **the team practises on Wednesdays** l'équipe s'entraîne le mercredi.

praise verb **to praise somebody for something** féliciter [1] quelqu'un de quelque chose.

pram noun landau Masc.

prawn noun crevette Fem.

pray verb prier [1].

prayer noun prière Fem.

precaution noun précaution Fem.; **to take precautions** prendre ses précautions.

precinct noun **a shopping precinct** un quartier commerçant; **a pedestrian precinct** une zone piétonne.

precious adjective précieux (Fem. précieuse).

precise adjective précis.

precisely adverb précisément; **at eleven o'clock precisely** à onze heures précises.

preface noun préface Fem.

prefer verb préférer [24]; **I prefer coffee to tea** je préfère le café au thé.

pregnancy noun grossesse Fem.

pregnant adjective enceinte.

prejudice noun préjugé Masc.; **a prejudice** un préjugé; **to fight against racial prejudice** lutter contre les préjugés raciaux.

prejudiced adjective **to be prejudiced** avoir des préjugés.

preliminary adjective préliminaire.

première noun première Fem. (of a play or film).

prep noun devoirs Masc. plural; **my English prep** mes devoirs d'anglais.

preparation noun **1** préparation Fem.; **2 the preparations for** les préparatifs Masc. plural pour; **our preparations for Christmas** nos préparatifs pour Noël.

prepare verb préparer [1]; **to prepare somebody for** préparer quelqu'un à (a surprise or shock).

prepared adjective prêt; **I'm prepared to pay half** je suis prêt à en payer la moitié; **to be prepared for the worst** s'attendre [3] au pire.

preposition noun préposition Fem.

prep school noun école Fem. primaire privée.

prescribe verb prescrire [38].

prescription noun ordonnance Fem.; **on prescription** sur ordonnance.

presence noun présence Fem.; **in my presence** en ma présence.

presence of mind noun présence Fem. d'esprit.

present noun **1** (a gift) cadeau Masc. (plural cadeaux); **to give somebody a present** offrir un cadeau à quelqu'un; **2** (the time now) présent Masc.; **in the present (tense)** au présent; **that's all for the present** c'est tout pour le moment.

present adjective **1** (attending) présent; **is Tracy present?** est-ce que Tracy est présente?; **to be present at** assister [1] à; **fifty people were present at the funeral** cinquante personnes ont assisté à l'enterrement; **2** (existing now) actuel (Fem. actuelle); **the present situation** la situation actuelle; **3 at the present time** actuellement.

present verb **1** remettre [11] (a prize); **2** (introduce) présenter [1].

presenter noun (on TV) présentateur Masc., présentatrice Fem.

presently adverb (soon) bientôt.

president noun président Masc., présidente Fem.

press noun **the press** la presse.

press verb **1** (to push) appuyer [41]; **press here to open** appuyez ici pour ouvrir; **2** appuyer [41] sur (a button, switch, or pedal); **he pressed the button** il a appuyé sur le bouton.

press conference noun conférence Fem. de presse.

pressure noun pression Fem.

pressure gauge noun indicateur Masc. de pression.

pressure group noun groupe Masc. de pression.

pretend verb **to pretend to do** faire [10] semblant de faire; **he's**

a
b
c
d
e
f
g
h
i
j
k
l
m
n
o
p
q
r
s
t
u
v
w
x
y
z

pretending not to hear il fait semblant de ne pas entendre.

pretty *adjective* joli (*goes before the noun*); **a pretty dress** une jolie robe.

pretty *adverb* plutôt; **it was pretty silly** c'était plutôt bête.

prevent *verb* to prevent somebody from doing empêcher [1] quelqu'un de faire; **there's nothing to prevent you from leaving** rien ne vous empêche de partir.

previous *adjective* précédent.

previously *adverb* auparavant.

price *noun* prix *Masc.*; **the price per kilo** le prix du kilo; **CDs have gone up in price** les CD ont augmenté.

price list *noun* liste *Fem.* des prix.

price ticket *noun* étiquette *Fem.*

prick *verb* piquer [1]; **to prick your finger** se piquer le doigt.

pride *noun* fierté *Fem.*

priest *noun* prêtre *Masc.*

primary school *noun* école *Fem.* primaire.

primary (school) teacher *noun* instituteur *Masc.*, institutrice *Fem.*

prime minister *noun* Premier ministre *Masc.*

primrose *noun* primevère *Fem.*

prince *noun* prince *Masc.*; **Prince Charles** le prince Charles.

princess *noun* princesse *Fem.*; **Princess Anne** la princesse Anne.

principal *noun* (*of a college*) directeur *Masc.*, directrice *Fem.*

principal *adjective* (*main*) principal (*Masc. plural* principaux).

principle *noun* principe *Masc.*; **on principle** par principe; **that's true in principle** cela est vrai en principe.

print *noun* **1** (*letters*) caractères *Masc. plural*; **in small print** en petits caractères; **2** (*a photo*) tirage *Masc.*; **a colour print** un tirage en couleur.

printer *noun* imprimante *Fem.*

print-out *noun* copie *Fem.* papier.

prison *noun* prison *Fem.*; **in prison** en prison.

prisoner *noun* prisonnier *Masc.*, prisonnière *Fem.*

private *adjective* **1** privé; **a private school** une école privée; **'private property'** 'propriété privée'; **2** particulier (*Fem.* particulière) (*lesson*); **to have private lessons** prendre des cours particuliers.

privately *adverb* en privé.

prize *noun* prix *Masc.*; **to win a prize** gagner un prix.

prize-giving *noun* distribution *Fem.* des prix.

prizewinner *noun* gagnant *Masc.*, gagnante *Fem.*

probable *adjective* probable.

probably *adverb* probablement.

problem *noun* problème *Masc.*; **it's a serious problem** c'est un grave problème; **no problem!** pas de problème!

process *noun* **1** processus *Masc.*; **2** to be in the process of doing être en train de faire.

procession noun **1** (*in parade*) défilé Masc.; **2** (*at religious festival*) procession Fem.

produce noun (*food*) produits Masc. plural.

produce verb produire [26]; **I produced my passport** j'ai produit mon passeport; **it produces a lot of heat** ça produit beaucoup de chaleur.

producer noun (*of a film or programme*) metteur Masc. en scène.

product noun produit Masc.

production noun **1** (*of a film or opera*) production Fem.; **2** (*of a play*) mise Fem. en scène; **a new production of Hamlet** une nouvelle mise en scène de Hamlet; **3** (*by a factory*) production Fem.

profession noun profession Fem.

professional noun professionnel Masc., professionnelle Fem.; **he's a professional** c'est un professionnel.

professional adjective professionnel (Fem. professionnelle); **she's a professional singer** c'est une chanteuse professionnelle.

professor noun professeur Masc.

profile noun profil Masc.

profit noun bénéfice Masc.

profitable adjective rentable.

program noun **a computer program** un programme informatique.

programme noun **1** (*for a play or an event*) programme Masc.; **2** (*on TV or radio*) émission Fem.

programmer noun programmateur Masc., programmatrice Fem.

progress noun **1** progrès Masc.; **to make progress** faire des progrès; **2 to be in progress** être en cours.

project noun **1** (*at school*) dossier Masc.; **2** (*a plan*) projet Masc.; **a project to build a bridge** un projet pour construire un pont.

projector noun projecteur Masc.

promise noun promesse Fem.; **to make a promise** faire une promesse; **to break a promise** manquer à sa promesse; **it's a promise!** c'est promis!

promise verb **to promise to do** promettre [11] de faire; **I've promised to be home by ten** j'ai promis de rentrer avant dix heures.

promote verb **to be promoted** être [6] promu.

promotion noun promotion Fem.

prompt adjective rapide; **a prompt reply** une réponse rapide.

promptly adjective **1** (*at once*) immédiatement; **he promptly fell off again** il est retombé immédiatement; **2** (*quickly*) rapidement; **please reply promptly** répondez rapidement s'il vous plaît; **3 promptly at nine o'clock** à neuf heures précises.

pronoun noun pronom Masc.

pronounce verb prononcer [61]; **it's hard to pronounce** c'est difficile à prononcer.

pronunciation noun prononciation Fem.

proof noun preuve Fem.; **there's no proof that** ... rien ne prouve que ....

a
b
c
d
e
f
g
h
i
j
k
l
m
n
o
p
q
r
s
t
u
v
w
x
y
z

propaganda noun propagande Fem.

propeller noun hélice Fem.

proper adjective **1** (real, genuine) vrai; **a proper doctor** un vrai médecin; **I need a proper meal** j'ai besoin d'un vrai repas; **2** (correct) bon (Fem. bonne); **the proper answer** la bonne réponse; **the proper tool** le bon outil; **in its proper place** à sa place.

properly adverb comme il faut; **hold it properly** tiens-le comme il faut; **is it properly wrapped?** est-ce que c'est emballé comme il faut?

property noun (your belongings) affaires Fem. plural, propriété Fem.; **'private property'** 'propriété privée'.

proposal noun proposition Fem.

propose verb **1** (suggest) proposer [1]; **2** (marriage) **he proposed to her** il l'a demandée en mariage.

prostitute noun prostituée Fem.

protect verb protéger [15].

protection noun protection Fem.

protein noun protéine Fem.

protest noun protestation Fem.; **in spite of their protests** malgré leurs protestations.

protest verb **1** (to grumble) protester [1]; **he protested, but ...** il a protesté, mais ...; **2** (demonstrate) manifester [1].

Protestant noun, adjective protestant Masc., protestante Fem.

protester noun manifestant Masc., manifestante Fem.

protest march noun manifestation Fem.

proud adjective fier (Fem. fière).

prove verb prouver [1].

proverb noun proverbe Masc.

provide verb fournir [2].

provided conjunction à condition que; **provided you do it now** à condition que tu le fasses maintenant (note that a verb in the subjunctive is needed).

province noun province Fem.

prune noun pruneau Masc. (plural pruneaux).

PS (at end of letter) P.S.

psychiatrist noun psychiatre Masc. & Fem.; **he's a psychiatrist** il est psychiatre.

psychological adjective psychologique.

psychologist noun psychologue Masc. & Fem.; **she's a psychologist** ele est psychologue.

psychology noun psychologie Fem.

PTO TSVP (= tournez s'il vous plaît).

pub noun pub Masc.

public noun **the public** le public; **in public** en public.

public adjective **1** public (Fem. publique); **2 the public library** la bibliothèque municipale.

public address system noun sonorisation Fem.

public holiday noun jour Masc. férié; **January 1 is a public holiday** le premier janvier est férié.

publicity noun publicité Fem.

public school noun école Fem. privée.

public transport noun transports Masc. plural en commun.

publish verb publier [1].

publisher noun éditeur Masc.

pudding noun (dessert) dessert Masc.; **for pudding we've got strawberries** comme dessert nous avons des fraises.

puddle noun flaque Fem.

Puerto Rico noun Puerto Rico Fem.

Puerto Rican noun Puertoricain Masc., puertocain Fem., adjective puertoricain.

puff noun (of smoke) bouffée Fem.

puff pastry noun pâte Fem. feuilletée.

pull verb tirer [1]; **pull hard!** tire fort!; **to pull a rope** tirer sur une corde; **he pulled a letter out of his pocket** il a tiré une lettre de sa poche; ★ **you're pulling my leg!** tu me fais marcher!

● **to pull down** baisser [1] (a blind).

● **to pull in** (at the roadside) s'arrêter [1].

pullover noun pull-over Masc.

pulse noun pouls Masc.; **the doctor took my pulse** le médecin a pris mon pouls.

pump noun pompe Fem.; **a bicycle pump** une pompe à vélo.

pump verb pomper [1]; **they were pumping the water out of the cellar** ils pompaient l'eau de la cave.

● **to pump up** gonfler [1] (a tyre).

pumpkin noun citrouille Fem.

punch noun 1 (in boxing) coup Masc. de poing; 2 (drink) punch Masc.

punch verb 1 **to punch somebody** donner [1] un coup de poing à quelqu'un; **he punched me** il m'a donné un coup de poing; 2 composter [1] (a ticket).

punctual adjective ponctuel (Fem. ponctuelle).

punctuation noun ponctuation Fem.

punctuation mark noun signe Masc. de ponctuation.

puncture noun crevaison Fem.; **we had a puncture on the way** nous avons crevé en route.

punish verb punir [2].

punishment noun punition Fem.

pupil noun élève Masc. & Fem.

puppet noun marionnette Fem.

puppy noun chiot Masc.; **a labrador puppy** un chiot labrador.

pure adjective pur.

purple adjective violet (Fem. violette).

purpose noun 1 but Masc.; **what was the purpose of her call?** quel était le but de son appel?; 2 **on purpose** exprès; **she did it on purpose** elle l'a fait exprès; **he closed the door on purpose** il a fait exprès de fermer la porte.

purr verb ronronner [1].

purse noun porte-monnaie Masc. (plural **porte-monnaie**).

push noun **to give something a push** pousser [1] quelque chose.

push verb 1 pousser [1]; **he pushed me** il m'a poussé; 2 (to press) appuyer [41] sur (a bell or button);

a b c d e f g h i j k l m n o p q r s t u v w x y z

3 to push somebody to do pousser [1] quelqu'un à faire; **his teacher is pushing him to sit the exam** son prof le pousse à passer l'examen.

● **to push something away** repousser [1] quelque chose; **she pushed her plate away** elle a repoussé son assiette.

pushchair noun poussette Fem.

put verb **1** mettre [11]; **you can put the cream in the fridge** tu peux mettre la crème au frigo; **where did you put my bag?** où est-ce que tu as mis mon sac?; **put your suitcase here** mets ta valise ici; **2** (write) écrire [38]; **put your address here** écris ton adresse ici.

● **to put away** ranger [52]; **I'll put the shopping away** je vais ranger les courses.

● **to put back 1** remettre [11]; **I put it back in the drawer** je l'ai remis dans le tiroir; **2** (postpone) remettre [11]; **the meeting has been put back until Thursday** la réunion a été remise à jeudi.

● **to put down** poser [1]; **she put the vase down on the table** elle a posé le vase sur la table.

● **to put off 1** (postpone) remettre [11]; **he's put off my lesson till Thursday** il a remis ma leçon à jeudi; **2** (turn off) éteindre [60] (a light or TV); **don't forget to put off the lights** n'oublie pas d'éteindre la lumière; **3 to put somebody off something** dégoûter [1] quelqu'un de quelque chose; **it really put me off Chinese food!** ça m'a vraiment dégoûté de la nourriture chinoise!;

4 to be put off (doing something) se décourager [52]; **don't be put off!** ne te décourage pas!

● **to put on 1** mettre [11] (clothing, make-up, CD); **I'll just put my shoes on** je vais juste mettre mes chaussures; **il a mis Oasis** he's put on Oasis; **2** (switch on) allumer [1] (a light or heating); **could you put the lamp on?** est-ce que tu peux allumer la lampe?; **3** monter [1] (a play); **we're putting on a French play** nous sommes en train de monter une pièce française.

● **to put out 1** (put outside) sortir [72]; **have you put the rubbish out?** as-tu sorti les ordures?; **2** éteindre [60] (a fire, light, or cigarette); **I've put the lights out** j'ai éteint la lumière; **3 to put out your hand** tendre [3] la main.

● **to put through** passer [1]; **I'll put you through to the manager** je vous passe le responsable.

● **to put up 1** lever [50] (your hand); **I put up my hand** j'ai levé la main; **2** mettre [11] (picture); **I've put up some photos in my room** j'ai mis des photos dans ma chambre; **3** afficher [1] (a notice); **4** augmenter [1] (the price); **they've put up the price of the tickets** ils ont augmenté le prix des billets; **5** (for the night) héberger [52]; **can you put me up on Friday?** est-ce que tu peux m'héberger vendredi?

● **to put up with something** supporter [1]; **I don't know how she puts up with it** je ne sais pas comment elle le supporte.

puzzle noun (jigsaw) puzzle Masc.

puzzled adjective perplexe.

pyjamas *plural noun* pyjama *Masc. singular*; **a pair of pyjamas** un pyjama; **where are my pyjamas?** où est mon pyjama?

pylon *noun* pilône *Masc.*

Pyrenees *noun* les Pyrénées *Fem. plural*; **in the Pyrenees** dans les Pyrénées.

Qq

quail *noun* caille *Fem.*

qualification *noun* **1** diplôme *Masc.* (*certificate, exam, degree*); **2** qualifications qualifications *Fem. plural*; **vocational qualifications** les qualifications professionnelles.

qualified *adjective* **1** qualifié; **she's a qualified ski instructor** c'est une monitrice de ski qualifiée; **2** (*having a degree or a diploma*) diplômé; **a qualified architect** un architecte diplômé.

qualify *verb* **1** (*to be eligible*) avoir [5] droit à; **we don't qualify for a reduction** nous n'avons pas droit à une réduction; **2** (*in sport*) se qualifier [1].

quality *noun* qualité *Fem.*; **good quality vegetables** des légumes de bonne qualité.

quantity *noun* quantité *Fem.*

quarantine *noun* quarantaine *Fem.*

quarrel *noun* dispute *Fem.*; **to have a quarrel** se disputer [1].

quarrel *verb* se disputer [1]; **they're always quarrelling** ils sont tout le temps en train de se disputer.

quarry *noun* carrière *Fem.*

quarter *noun* **1** quart *Masc.*; **a quarter of the class** le quart de la classe; **three quarters of the class** les trois quarts de la classe; **2 a quarter past ten** dix heures et quart; **a quarter to ten** dix heures moins le quart; **a quarter of an hour** un quart d'heure; **three quarters of an hour** trois quarts d'heure; **an hour and a quarter** une heure et quart.

quarter-final *noun* quart *Masc.* de finale.

quartet *noun* quatuor *Masc.*; **a jazz quartet** un quatuor de jazz.

quay *noun* quai *Masc.*

queen *noun* reine *Fem.*; **Queen Elizabeth** la reine Elizabeth; **the Queen Mother** la reine mère.

query *noun* question *Fem.*; **are there any queries?** y a-t-il des questions?

question *noun* question *Fem.*; **to ask a question** poser une question; **I asked her a question** je lui ai posé une question; **it's a question of time** c'est une question de temps; **it's out of the question!** c'est hors de question!

question *verb* interroger [52].

question mark *noun* point *Masc.* d'interrogation.

questionnaire *noun* questionnaire *Masc.*; **to fill in a questionnaire** remplir un questionnaire.

a b c d e f g h i j k l m n o p q r s t u v w x y z

queue noun **1** (*of people*) queue Fem.; **to stand in a queue** faire la queue; **2** (*of cars*) file Fem.

queue verb faire [10] la queue; **we were queueing for check-in** nous faisions la queue pour l'enregistrement.

quick adjective **1** rapide; **a quick lunch** un déjeuner rapide; **it's quicker on the motorway** c'est plus rapide par l'autoroute; **to have a quick look at something** jeter un coup d'il rapide à quelque chose; **2 quick! there's the bus!** vite! voilà le bus!; **be quick!** dépêche-toi!

quickly adverb vite; **I'll just quickly phone my mother** je vais vite appeler ma mère.

quiet adjective **1** (*silent*) silencieux (Fem. silencieuse); **the children are very quiet** les enfants sont très silencieux [76]; **please keep quiet** taisez-vous, s'il vous plaît; **3** (*gentle*) doux (Fem. douce); **some quiet music** de la musique douce; **in a quiet voice** à voix basse; **4** (*peaceful*) tranquille; **a quiet street** une rue tranquille; **a quiet day at home** une journée tranquille à la maison.

quietly adverb **1** (*to move*) sans bruit; **he got up quietly** il s'est levé sans bruit; **2** (*speak*) doucement; **3** (*read or play*) en silence.

quilt noun couette Fem.

quite adverb **1** assez; **it's quite cold outside** il fait assez froid dehors; **that's quite a good idea** c'est une assez bonne idée; **he sings quite well** il chante assez bien; **quite often** assez souvent;

2 not quite pas tout à fait; **the meat's not quite cooked** la viande n'est pas tout à fait cuite; **3** quite a lot of pas mal de; **we've got quite a lot of friends here** nous avons pas mal d'amis ici; **quite a few people** pas mal de gens.

quiz noun quiz Masc.

quotation noun (*from a book*) citation Fem.

quotation marks plural noun guillemets Masc. plural; **in quotation marks** entre guillemets.

quote noun **1** (*from a book*) citation Fem.; **2** (*estimate*) devis Masc.; **3 in quotes** entre guillemets.

quote verb citer [1].

Rr

rabbi noun rabbin Masc.

rabbit noun lapin Masc.

rabbit hutch noun clapier Masc.

rabies noun rage Fem.

race noun **1** (*a sports event*) course Fem.; **a cycle race** une course cycliste; **to have a race** faire la course; **2** (*an ethnic group*) race Fem.

racer noun (*bike*) vélo Masc. de course.

racetrack noun **1** (*for horses*) champ Masc. de course; **2** (*for cars*) circuit Masc.; **3** (*for cycles*) piste Fem.

racial adjective racial (Masc. plural raciaux); **racial discrimination** la discrimination raciale.

racing noun courses Fem. plural.

racing car noun voiture Fem. de course.

racing driver noun pilote Masc. de course.

racism noun racisme Masc.

racist noun, adjective raciste Masc. & Fem.

rack noun (for luggage) porte-bagages Masc.

racket noun 1 (for tennis) raquette Fem.; **here's your tennis racket** voici ta raquette de tennis; 2 (noise) vacarme Fem.

radar noun radar Masc.

radiation noun radiation Fem.

radiator noun radiateur Masc.

radio noun radio Fem.; **to listen to the radio** écouter la radio; **to hear something on the radio** entendre quelque chose à la radio.

radioactive adjective radioactif (Fem. radioactive).

radio-controlled adjective téléguidé.

radio station noun station Fem. de radio.

radish noun radis Masc.

radius noun rayon Masc.

raffle noun tombola Fem.

raft noun radeau Masc.

rag noun chiffon Masc.

rage noun colère Fem.; **she's in a rage** elle est furieuse; ★ **it's all the rage** ça fait fureur.

raid noun 1 hold-up Masc.; 2 (by the police) rafle Fem.

rail noun 1 (the railway) **to go by rail** prendre le train; 2 (on a balcony or bridge) balustrade Fem.;

3 (on stairs) rampe Fem.; 4 (for a train) rail Masc.

railing(s) noun grille Fem.

rail strike noun grève Fem. des cheminots.

railway noun 1 (the system) chemin Masc. de fer; **the railways** les chemins de fer; 2 **a railway line** une ligne de chemin de fer (from one place to another); 3 **on the railway line** sur la voie ferrée (the rails).

railway carriage noun wagon Masc.

railway station noun gare Fem.; **opposite the railway station** en face de la gare.

rain noun pluie Fem.; **in the rain** sous la pluie.

rain verb pleuvoir [63]; **it's raining** il pleut; **it's going to rain** il va pleuvoir.

rainbow noun arc-en-ciel Masc. (plural arcs-en-ciel).

raincoat noun imperméable Masc.

raindrop noun goutte Fem. de pluie.

rainfall noun niveau Masc. de précipitations.

rainy adjective pluvieux (Fem. pluvieuse).

raise verb 1 (lift up) lever [50]; **she raised her head** elle a levé la tête; 2 (increase) augmenter [1] (a price or a salary); 3 **to raise money for something** collecter [1] des fonds pour quelque chose; 4 (to raise the alarm) donner [1] l'alarme; 5 (to raise somebody's spirits) remonter [1] le moral à quelqu'un.

raisin noun raisin Masc. sec.

rake noun rateau Masc. (plural rateaux).

rally noun 1 (a meeting) rassemblement Masc.; 2 (for sport) rallye Masc.; 3 (in tennis) échange Masc.

rambler noun randonneur Masc., randonneuse Fem.

rambling noun randonnée Fem.

ramp noun (for a wheelchair, for example) rampe Fem.

ranch noun ranch Masc.

range noun 1 (a choice) gamme Fem.; **we offer a range of sports** nous vous proposons une gamme de sports; **in a wide range of colours** dans un grand choix de coloris; **a top-of-the-range computer** un ordinateur haut de gamme; 2 (of mountains) chaîne Fem.

rap noun rap Masc. (music).

rape noun viol Masc.

rape verb violer [1].

rare adjective 1 rare; **a rare bird** un oiseau rare; 2 saignant (a steak); **medium-rare** à point.

rarely adverb rarement.

rash noun rougeurs Fem. plural; **I've got a rash on my arms** j'ai des rougeurs sur les bras.

rash adjective irréfléchi; **a rash decision** une décision irréfléchie.

raspberry noun framboise Fem.; **raspberry jam** la confiture de framboises; **a raspberry tart** une tarte aux framboises.

rat noun rat Masc.

rate noun 1 (a charge) tarif Masc.; **what are the rates for children?** quels sont les tarifs pour les enfants?; **reduced rates** les tarifs réduits; 2 (a level) taux Masc.; **a high cancellation rate** un taux élevé d'annulation; 3 **at any rate** en tout cas.

rather adverb 1 plutôt; **I'm rather busy** je suis plutôt occupé; 2 **rather than** plutôt que; **in summer rather than winter** en été plutôt qu'en hiver; 3 **I'd rather wait** je préfère attendre; **they'd rather come on Thursday** ils préfèrent venir jeudi; 4 **rather a lot of** pas mal de; **I've got rather a lot of shopping to do** j'ai pas mal de courses à faire.

rave noun rave Fem. (a party).

raw adjective cru.

ray noun rayon Masc.

razor noun rasoir Masc.

razor blade noun lame Fem. de rasoir.

RE noun éducation Fem. religieuse.

reach noun portée Fem.; **out of reach** hors de portée; **within reach** (of your hand) à portée de main; **within easy reach of the sea** à proximité de la mer.

reach verb 1 arriver [1] à; **when you reach the church** quand vous arrivez à l'église; **to reach a decision** arriver à une décision; 2 **to reach the final** arriver [1] à la finale.

react verb réagir [2].

reaction noun réaction Fem.

read verb lire [51]; **what are you reading at the moment?** qu'est-ce que tu lis en ce moment?; **I'm reading a detective novel** je lis un roman policier; **he read out the list** il a lu la liste à haute voix.

reading noun lecture Fem.; **I don't much like reading** je n'aime pas beaucoup la lecture; **some easy reading for the beach** de la lecture facile pour la plage.

ready adjective prêt; **supper's not ready yet** le dîner n'est pas encore prêt; **are you ready to leave?** est-ce que tu es prêt à partir?; **to get ready** se préparer [1]; **I'm getting ready to go out** je me prépare pour sortir; **I was getting ready for bed** je me préparais pour me coucher; **I'll get your room ready** je vais préparer ta chambre.

real adjective vrai; **it's a real diamond** c'est un vrai diamant; **he's a real bore** c'est un vrai casse-pieds; **is that his real name?** est-ce que c'est son vrai nom?; **her real father is dead** son vrai père est mort.

realistic adjective réaliste.

reality noun réalité Fem.

realize verb se rendre [3] compte; **I hadn't realized** je ne m'en étais pas rendu compte; **I didn't realize he was French** je ne me suis pas rendu compte qu'il était français; **do you realize what time it is?** est-ce que tu te rends compte de l'heure qu'il est?

really adverb vraiment; **not really** pas vraiment; **is it really midnight?** est-il vraiment minuit?; **the film was really good** le film était vraiment très bon; **really?** c'est vrai?

rear noun arrière Masc.

rear adjective arrière; **the rear door** la porte arrière.

reason noun raison Fem.; **the reason for the delay** la raison du retard; **the reason why I phoned** la raison pour laquelle j'ai appelé.

reasonable adjective raisonnable.

reassure verb rassurer [1].

reassuring adjective rassurant.

rebel noun rebelle Masc. & Fem.

rebellion noun rébellion Fem., révolte Fem.

rebuild verb reconstruire [26].

receipt noun reçu Masc.

receive verb recevoir [66].

receiver noun combiné Masc.; **to pick up the receiver** décrocher [1].

recent adjective récent.

recently adverb récemment.

reception noun 1 réception Fem.; **he's waiting at reception** il attend à la réception; **a big wedding reception** une grande réception de mariage; 2 **to get a good reception** avoir un bon accueil.

receptionist noun réceptionniste Masc. & Fem.

recipe noun recette Fem.; **can I have the recipe for your salad?** est-ce que je peux prendre la recette de ta salade?

reckon verb penser [1]; **I reckon it's a good idea** je pense que c'est une bonne idée.

recognize verb reconnaître [27].

recommend verb conseiller [1]; **can you recommend a dentist?** est-ce que vous pouvez me conseiller un dentiste?; **I recommend the fish soup** je vous conseille la soupe de poisson.

a
b
c
d
e
f
g
h
i
j
k
l
m
n
o
p
q
r
s
t
u
v
w
x
y
z

recommendation noun
recommandation Fem.

record noun 1 record Masc.; **it's a
world record** c'est le record
mondial; **record sales for the CD**
des ventes record pour le CD; **the
hottest summer on record** l'été le
plus chaud qu'on ait jamais
enregistré; 2 **to keep a record of
something** noter quelque chose;
3 (music) disque Masc.; **a Miles
Davis record** un disque de Miles
Davis; 4 (office files) dossier Masc.;
I'll just check your records je vais
juste vérifier votre dossier.

record verb (on tape or CD)
enregistrer [1]; **they're recording a
new album** ils sont en train
d'enregistrer un nouvel album.

recorder noun 1 flûte Fem. à bec;
to play the recorder jouer de la
flûte à bec; 2 **a cassette recorder**
un magnétophone à cassettes; **a
video recorder** un magnétoscope.

recording noun enregistrement
Masc.

record player noun tourne-
disque Masc.

recover verb se remettre [11];
she's recovered now elle s'est
maintenant remise.

recovery noun (from an illness)
rétablissement Masc.

recovery vehicle noun camion
Masc. de dépannage.

rectangle noun rectangle Masc.

rectangular adjective
rectangulaire.

recycle verb recycler [1].

red adjective 1 rouge; **a red shirt**
une chemise rouge; **a bright red**

car une voiture rouge vif; **to go red**
rougir [2]; 2 roux (Fem. rousse)
(hair); **to have red hair** avoir les
cheveux roux.

Red Cross noun **the Red Cross** la
Croix-Rouge.

redcurrant noun groseille Fem.;
redcurrant jelly la gelée de
groseilles.

redecorate verb refaire [10];
they've redecorated the kitchen
ils ont refait la cuisine.

redo verb refaire [10].

reduce verb réduire [68]; **they've
reduced the price** ils ont réduit le
prix; **to reduce speed** ralentir [2].

reduction noun réduction Fem.

redundant adjective **to be made
redundant** être licencié.

reel noun (of cotton) bobine Fem.

refer verb **refer to** parler [1] de;
she's referring to you elle parle de
vous.

referee noun (in sport) arbitre
Masc.

reference noun références Fem.
plural (for a job); **she gave me a
good reference** elle m'a fourni de
bonnes références.

reference book noun ouvrage
Masc. de référence.

refill noun recharge Fem.

reflect verb refléter [24].

reflection noun 1 (in a mirror)
image Fem.; 2 (thought) réflexion
Fem.; **on reflection** à la réflexion.

reflexive adjective **a reflexive
verb** un verbe réfléchi.

refreshing adjective
rafraîchissant.

refreshment noun
rafraîchissement Masc.

refrigerator noun réfrigérateur
Masc.

refuge noun refuge Masc.; **a
mountain refuge** un refuge (de
montagne); **to take refuge in** se
réfugier [1] dans.

refugee noun refugié Masc.,
refugiée Fem.

refund noun remboursement Masc.

refund verb rembourser [1].

refusal noun refus Masc.

refuse noun (rubbish) ordures
Fem. plural.

refuse verb refuser [1]; **I refused**
j'ai refusé; **he refuses to help** il
refuse de nous aider.

regards plural noun amitiés Fem.
plural; **'regards to your parents'**
'mes amitiés à vos parents'; **Nat
sends his regards** tu as le bonjour
de Nat.

reggae noun reggae Masc.

region noun région Fem.

regional adjective régional (Masc.
plural régionaux).

register noun (in school) cahier
Masc. des absences.

register verb s'inscrire [38].

registered letter noun lettre
Fem. recommandée.

registration number noun
numéro Masc. d'immatriculation
(of a vehicle).

regret verb regretter [1].

regular adjective régulier (Fem.
régulière); **regular visits** des
visites régulières.

regularly adverb régulièrement.

regulation noun règlement Masc.

rehearsal noun répétition Fem.

rehearse verb répéter [24].

reheat verb réchauffer [1].

reign noun règne Masc.

rein noun rêne Fem.

reject verb rejeter [48].

related adjective apparenté; **we're
not related** nous ne sommes pas
apparentés.

relation noun **my relations** ma
famille; **there were just relations
and close friends** il n'y avait que
la famille et des amis proches;
she's got relations in France elle a
de la famille en France.

relationship noun relations Fem.
plural; **we have a good relationship**
nous avons de bonnes relations.

relative noun membre Masc. de la
famille; **there were a few relatives
at the funeral** il y avait quelques
membres de la famille à
l'enterrement; **all my relatives**
toute ma famille.

relatively adverb relativement.

relax verb se détendre [3]; **I'm
going to relax and watch telly
tonight** je vais me détendre en
regardant la télé ce soir.

relaxation noun détente Fem.

relaxed adjective détendu.

relaxing adjective reposant.

relay race noun course Fem. de
relais.

release noun **1** nouveauté Fem.;
this week's new releases les
nouveautés de la semaine; **2** (of a
prisoner or hostage) libération Fem.

a
b
c
d
e
f
g
h
i
j
k
l
m
n
o
p
q
r
s
t
u
v
w
x
y
z

release verb **1** sortir [72] (a record or a video); **2** libérer [24] (a person).

relevant adjective pertinent.

reliable adjective fiable.

relief noun soulagement Masc.; **what a relief!** quel soulagement!

relieve verb soulager [52] (pain).

relieved adjective soulagé; **I was relieved to hear you'd arrived** j'ai été soulagé d'apprendre que tu étais arrivé.

religion noun religion Fem.

religious adjective **1** croyant (a person); **Jane's not religious** Jane n'est pas croyante; **2** religieux (Fem. religieuse) (art or music, for example).

reluctant adj réticent; **he's reluctant to go** il est peu disposé à y aller.

rely verb **to rely on somebody** compter [1] sur quelqu'un; **I'm relying on you for Saturday** je compte sur toi pour samedi.

remain verb rester [1].

remains plural noun restes Masc. plural; **the remains of the chicken** les restes du poulet; **the remains of a castle** les restes d'un château.

remark noun remarque Fem.; **to make remarks about** faire des remarques sur.

remarkable adjective remarquable.

remarkably adverb remarquablement.

remember verb **1** se souvenir [81]; **I don't remember** je ne me souviens plus; **2 to remember something** se souvenir [81] de quelque chose; **I can't remember the number** je ne me souviens pas du numéro; **3 to remember to do** ne pas oublier [1] de faire; **remember to shut the door** n'oublie pas de fermer la porte; **I remembered to bring the CDs** je n'ai pas oublié d'apporter les CD.

remind verb rappeler [18] **1 to remind somebody to do** rappeler à quelqu'un de faire; **remind your mother to pick me up** rappelle à ta mère de venir me chercher; **2** faire [10] penser; **it reminds me of Paris** ça me fait penser à Paris; **he reminds me of Frank** il me fait penser à Frank; **oh, that reminds me ...** tiens, j'y pense ....

remote adjective isolé.

remote control noun télécommande Fem.

remove verb enlever [50]; **he removed his jacket** il a enlevé sa veste; **the chairs had all been removed** quelqu'un avait enlevé toutes les chaises.

renew verb renouveler [18] (a passport or licence).

rent noun loyer Masc.

rent verb louer [1]; **Simon's rented a flat** Simon a loué un appartement.

rental noun location Fem.

reorganize verb réorganiser [1].

repair noun réparation Fem.

repair verb réparer [1]; **to get something repaired** faire [10] réparer quelque chose; **we've had the television repaired** nous avons fait réparer la télévision.

repay verb rembourser [1]; **he repaid me the money he owed me**

il m'a remboursé l'argent qu'il me devait.

repeat noun reprise Fem. (of a programme).

repeat verb répéter [24].

repeatedly adverb à plusieurs reprises.

repertoire noun répertoire Masc.

repetitive adjective répétitif (Fem. répétitive).

replace verb remplacer [61].

replacement noun 1 (person) remplaçant Masc., remplaçante Fem.; 2 (thing) can you find me a replacement? est-ce que vous pouvez le/la remplacer?

replay verb 1 (game) rejouer [1]; 2 (video) repasser [1].

reply noun réponse Fem.; I didn't get a reply to my letter je n'ai pas reçu de réponse à ma lettre; there's no reply ça ne répond pas (on the telephone).

reply verb répondre [3]; I still haven't replied to the letter je n'ai toujours pas répondu à la lettre.

report noun 1 (of an event) compte rendu Masc.; 2 (school report) bulletin Masc. scolaire.

report verb 1 signaler [1] (a problem or accident); we've reported the theft nous avons signalé le vol; 2 se présenter [1]; I had to report to reception je devais me présenter à la réception.

reporter noun journaliste Masc. & Fem.

represent verb représenter [1].

representative noun représentant Masc., représentante Fem..

reproach noun reproche Masc.

reproach verb reprocher [1].

reproduction noun reproduction Fem.

reptile noun reptile Masc.

republic noun république Fem.

reputation noun réputation Fem.; a good reputation une bonne réputation; she has a reputation for honesty elle a la réputation d'être honnête.

request noun demande Fem.; on request sur demande.

request verb demander [1].

rescue noun secours Masc.; to come to somebody's rescue venir au secours de quelqu'un.

rescue verb sauver [1]; they rescued the dog ils ont sauvé le chien.

rescue party noun équipe Fem. de secours.

rescue worker noun secouriste Masc. & Fem.

research noun recherche Fem.; for research into Aids pour la recherche sur le Sida; to do research faire des recherches.

research verb to research into faire [10] des recherches sur; a well-researched programme un programme bien documenté.

resemblance noun ressemblance Fem.

resemble verb ressembler [1] à; she resembles her aunt elle ressemble à sa tante.

reservation noun (a booking) réservation Fem.; to make a reservation faire une réservation.

a
b
c
d
e
f
g
h
i
j
k
l
m
n
o
p
q
r
s
t
u
v
w
x
y
z

reserve noun **1** réserve Fem.; **we have some in reserve** nous en avons en réserve; **2 a nature reserve** une réserve naturelle; **3** (for a match) remplaçant Masc., remplaçante Fem.

reserve verb réserver [1]; **this table is reserved** cette table est réservée.

reservoir noun réservoir Masc.

resident noun résident Masc., résidente Fem.

residential adjective résidentiel (Fem. résidentielle); **a residential area** un quartier résidentiel.

resign verb démissionner [1].

resignation noun (from a post) démission Fem.

resist verb résister [1] à (an offer or temptation); **I can't resist!** je ne peux pas résister!

resit verb repasser [1] (an exam).

resort noun **1** (for holidays) **a holiday resort** un lieu de villégiature; **a ski resort** une station de ski; **a seaside resort** une station balnéaire; **2 as a last resort** en dernier recours.

respect noun respect Masc.

respect verb respecter [1].

respectable adjective respectable.

respectful adjective respectueux (Fem. respectueuse).

responsibility noun responsabilité Fem.

responsible adjective **1** (to blame) responsable; **he's responsible for the delay** il est responsable du retard; **2** (in charge) responsable; **I'm responsible for booking the rooms** je suis responsable de la réservation des chambres; **3** (reliable) sérieux (Fem. sérieuse); **he's not very responsible** il n'est pas très sérieux.

rest noun **1 the rest** le reste; **the rest of the day** le reste du jour; **the rest of the bread** le reste du pain; **2** (the others) les autres; **the rest have gone home** les autres sont rentrés; **3** repos Masc., ; **ten days' complete rest** dix jours de repos total; **to have a rest** se reposer [1]; **4** (a short break) pause Fem.; **to stop for a rest** faire une pause.

rest (have a rest) se reposer [1].

restaurant noun restaurant Masc.

restful adjective reposant.

restless adjective nerveux (Fem. nerveuse).

restore verb restaurer [1]

restrain verb retenir [77].

restrict verb limiter [1].

restriction noun limitation Fem.

result noun **1** résultat Masc.; **the exam results** les résultats des examens; **2 as a result** par conséquent; **as a result we missed the ferry** par conséquent nous avons raté le ferry.

retire verb (from work) prendre [64] sa retraite; **she retires in June** elle prend sa retraite en juin; **for retired people** pour les retraités.

retirement noun retraite Fem.

return noun **1** retour Masc.; **the return journey** le voyage de retour; **by return of post** par retour de courrier; **2 in return** en échange; **in return for his help** en échange de son aide; ★ **many happy returns!** bon anniversaire!

return *verb* **1** (*come back*) revenir [81]; **he returned ten minutes later** il est revenu dix minutes plus tard; **2** (*get home*) rentrer [1]; **to return from holiday** rentrer de vacances; **I'll ask her to phone as soon as she returns** je lui demanderai de vous appeler dès qu'elle rentrera; **3** (*to give back*) rendre [3]; **Gemma's never returned the video** Gemma n'a jamais rendu le vidéo.

return fare *noun* prix *Masc.* d'un billet aller-retour.

return ticket *noun* billet *Masc.* aller-retour.

reunion *noun* réunion *Fem.*; **a class reunion** une réunion d'anciens élèves.

reveal *verb* révéler [24].

revenge *noun* vengeance *Fem.*; **to get one's revenge on someone** se venger [52] de quelqu'un.

reverse *noun* **1** (*of a coin*) revers *Masc.*; **2** (*of a page*) dos *Masc.*; **3** (*opposite*) **the reverse is true** le contraire est vrai; **4** (*gear*) marche *Fem.* arrière.

reverse *verb* **1** (*in a car*) faire [10] marche arrière; **he reversed the car out of the garage** il a sorti la voiture du garage en marche arrière; **2 to reverse the charges** faire [10] un appel en PCV.

review *noun* (*of a book, play, or film*) critique *Fem.*

review *verb* faire [10] la critique de (*a play or concert*); **the film was well reviewed** le film a eu une bonne critique.

revise *verb* réviser [1]; **Tessa's busy revising for her exams** Tessa est en train de réviser pour ses examens.

revision *noun* révision *Fem.*

revive *verb* ranimer [1].

revolting *adjective* infect; **the sausages are revolting** les saucisses sont infectes.

revolution *noun* révolution *Fem.*; **the Fench Revolution** la Révolution française.

revolving door *noun* porte *Fem.* à tambour.

reward *noun* récompense *Fem.*; **a £100 reward** cent livres de récompense.

reward *verb* récompenser [1].

rewarding *adjective* enrichissant.

rewind *verb* rembobiner [1] (*a cassette or video*).

rhinoceros *noun* rhinocéros *Masc.*

rhubarb *noun* rhubarbe *Fem.*

rhyme *noun* rime *Fem.*

rhythm *noun* rythme *Masc.*

rib *noun* côte *Fem.*

ribbon *noun* ruban *Masc.*

rice *noun* riz *Masc.*; **chicken and rice** du poulet au riz; **rice pudding** le riz au lait.

rich *adjective* riche; **we're not very rich** nous ne sommes pas très riches; **the rich and the poor** les riches et les pauvres.

rid *adjective* **to get rid of something** se débarrasser de quelque chose; **we got rid of the car** nous nous sommes débarrassés de la voiture.

a
b
c
d
e
f
g
h
i
j
k
l
m
n
o
p
q
r
s
t
u
v
w
x
y
z

a **riddle** noun devinette Fem.

ride noun tour Masc.; **to go for a ride (on a bike)** faire [10] un tour à vélo; **to go for a ride (on a horse)** faire une promenade à cheval.

d **ride** verb **1** **to learn to ride a bike** apprendre [64] à faire du vélo; **can you ride a bike?** sais-tu faire du vélo?; **2** **to learn to ride (a horse)** apprendre [64] à monter à cheval; **I've never ridden a horse** je ne suis jamais monté à cheval.

rider noun **1** (on a horse) cavalier Masc., cavalière Fem.; **2** (on a bike) cycliste Masc. & Fem.; **3** (on a motorbike) motocycliste Masc. & Fem.

ridiculous adjective ridicule.

riding noun équitation Fem.; **to go riding** faire [10] de l'équitation.

riding school noun école Fem. d'équitation.

rifle noun fusil Masc.

right noun **1** (not left) droite Fem.; **on the right** à droite; **on my right** à ma droite; **2** (to do something) droit Masc.; **the right to strike** le droit de grève; **you have no right to say that** tu n'as pas le droit de dire ça.

right adjective **1** (not left) droit; **my right hand** ma main droite; **2** (correct) bon (Fem. bonne); **the right answer** la bonne réponse; **the right telephone number** le bon numéro de téléphone; **the right amount of** la bonne quantité de; **is this the right address?** est-ce que c'est la bonne adresse?; **3** **to be right** (a person) avoir [5] raison; **you see, I was right** tu vois, j'avais raison; **4** **you were right to stay at home** tu as bien fait de rester chez

toi; **he was right not to say anything** il a bien fait de ne rien dire; **5** (moral) bien; **it's not right to talk like that** ce n'est pas bien de parler comme ça.

right adverb **1** (direction) à droite; **turn right at the lights** tournez à droite aux feux; **2** (correctly) comme il faut; **you're not doing it right** tu ne le fais pas comme il faut; **3** (completely) tout; **right at the bottom** tout au fond; **right at the beginning** tout au début; **right now** tout de suite; **right in the middle** en plein milieu; **4** (okay) bon; **right, let's go** bon, allons-y.

right-click noun clic Masc. sur le bouton droit de la souris.

right-hand adjective **on the right-hand side** à droite.

right-handed adjective droitier (Fem. droitière).

rind noun **1** (on fruit) peau Fem.; **2** (on cheese) croûte Fem.

ring noun **1** (on the phone) **to give somebody a ring** appeler [18] quelqu'un; **2** (for your finger) bague Fem.; **3** (circle) cercle Masc.; **4** **there was a ring at the door** on a sonné à la porte.

ring verb **1** (a bell or phone) sonner [1]; **the phone rang** le téléphone a sonné; **2** (phone) appeler [18]; **I'll ring you tomorrow** je t'appellerai demain; **could you ring for a taxi?** est-ce que tu peux appeler un taxi?

● **to ring back** rappeler [18]; **I'll ring you back later** je te rappellerai tout à l'heure.

● **to ring off** raccrocher [1].

ring road noun rocade Fem.

rinse verb rincer [61].

riot noun émeute Fem.

rioting noun émeutes Fem. plural.

rip verb déchirer [1].

ripe adjective mûr; **are the tomatoes ripe?** est-ce que les tomates sont mûres?

rip-off noun **it's a rip-off!** c'est de l'arnaque!

rise noun **1** hausse Fem.; **a rise in price** une hausse de prix; **2 a pay rise** une augmentation.

rise verb **1** (the sun) se lever [50]; **when the sun rose** quand le soleil s'est levé; **2** (prices) augmenter [1].

risk noun risque Masc.; **to take risks** prendre des risques.

risk verb risquer [1]; **he risks losing his job** il risque de perdre son emploi.

rival noun rival Masc. (plural rivaux), rivale Fem.

river noun **1** rivière Fem.; **we picnicked on the edge of a river** nous avons pique-niqué au bord d'une rivière; **2** fleuve Masc.; **the rivers of Europe** les fleuves de l'Europe ('fleuve' is only used for a river which flows directly into the sea like the Thames in Britain or the Seine in France).

Riviera noun **the French Riviera** la Côte d'Azur.

road noun **1** route Fem.; **the road to London** la route de Londres; **2** (in a town) rue Fem.; **the butcher's is on the other side of the road** la boucherie est de l'autre côté de la rue; **3 across the road** en face; **they live across the road from us** ils habitent en face de chez nous.

road accident noun accident Masc. de la route.

road map noun carte Fem. routière.

roadside noun **by the roadside** au bord de la route.

road sign noun panneau Masc. de signalisation (plural **panneaux de signalisation**).

roadworks plural noun travaux Masc. plural.

roast noun rôti Masc.

roast adjective rôti; **roast potatoes** les pommes de terre rôties; **roast beef** le rôti de bœuf.

rob verb **1** voler [1] (a person); **2** dévaliser [1] (a bank).

robber noun voleur Masc., voleuse Fem.

robbery noun vol Masc.; **a bank robbery** un hold-up.

robot noun robot Masc.

rock noun **1** (a big stone) rocher Masc.; **she was sitting on a rock** elle était assise sur un rocher; **2** (the material) roche Fem.; **3** (music) rock Masc.; **a rock band** un groupe de rock; **to dance rock and roll** danser le rock.

rock climbing noun escalade Fem.; **to go rock climbing** faire de l'escalade.

rocket noun fusée Fem.

rocking horse noun cheval Masc. à bascule.

rock star noun rock-star Fem.

rocky adjective rocailleux (Fem. rocailleuse).

rod noun **a fishing rod** une canne à pêche.

a b c d e f g h i j k l m n o p q r s t u v w x y z

a

b

c

d

e

f

g

h

i

j

k

l

m

n

o

p

q

r

s

t

u

v

w

x

y

z

role noun rôle Masc.; **to play the role of** jouer le rôle de.

roll noun **1** rouleau Masc. (*plural* **rouleaux**); **a roll of fabric** un rouleau de tissu; **a roll of sellotape™** un rouleau de scotch™; **a toilet roll** un rouleau de papier hygiénique; **2 a bread roll** un petit pain.

roll verb rouler [1].

● **to roll something up 1** rouler [1] (*a carpet*); **2** retrousser [1] (*sleeves*); **he rolled up his sleeves** il a retroussé ses manches

roller noun rouleau Masc. (*plural* **rouleaux**).

rollerblades plural noun rollers Masc. plural.

rollercoaster noun montagnes Fem. plural russes (*literally: Russian mountains*).

roller skates plural noun patins Masc. plural à roulettes.

Roman Catholic noun, adjective catholique Masc. & Fem.

romantic adjective romantique.

roof noun toit Masc.

roof rack noun galerie Fem.

rook noun **1** (*in chess*) tour Fem.; **2** (*bird*) freux Masc.

room noun **1** pièce Fem.; **she's in the other room** elle est dans l'autre pièce; **it's the biggest room in the house** c'est la pièce la plus grande de la maison; **a three-room flat** un appartement à trois pièces; **2** (*a bedroom*) chambre Fem.; **Freda's in her room** Freda est dans sa chambre; **I tidied my room last night** j'ai rangé ma chambre hier soir; **3** (*space*) place Fem.; **enough**

room for two assez de place pour deux; **very little room** très peu de place.

roommate noun camarade Masc. & Fem. de chambre.

root noun racine Fem.

rope noun corde Fem.

rose noun rose Fem.

rosebush noun rosier Masc.

rot verb pourrir [2].

rota noun tableau Masc. de service.

rotten adjective pourri.

rough adjective **1** (*scratchy*) rugueux (Fem. rugueuse); **2** (*vague*) approximatif (Fem. approximative); **a rough idea** une idée approximative; **3** (*stormy*) agité; **a rough sea** une mer agitée; **in rough weather** par gros temps; **4** (*difficult*) **to have a rough time** passer par une période difficile; **5 to sleep rough** dormir à la dure.

roughly adjective (*approximately*) **roughly ten per cent** à peu près dix pour cent; **it takes roughly three hours** ça prend à peu près trois heures.

round noun **1** (*in a tournament*) manche Fem.; **2** (*of cards*) partie Fem.; **3 a round of drinks** une tournée; **it's my round** c'est ma tournée.

round adjective rond; **a round table** une table ronde.

round preposition **1** autour de; **round the city** autour de la ville; **round my arm** autour de mon bras; **they were sitting round the table** ils étaient assis autour de la table; **2 to go round the shops** faire les magasins; **to go round a museum**

visiter un musée; **it's just round the corner** c'est tout près.

round *adverb* **1 to go round to somebody's house** aller chez quelqu'un; **we invited Sally round for lunch** nous avons invité Sally à déjeuner; **2 all the year round** toute l'année.

roundabout *noun* **1** (*for traffic*) rond-point *Masc.*; **2** (*in a fairground*) manège *Masc.*

route *noun* **1** (*that you plan*) itinéraire *Masc.*; **the best route is via Calais** le meilleur itinéraire est par Calais; **2 a bus route** un parcours de bus.

routine *noun* routine *Fem.*

row[1] *noun* **1** rang *Masc.*; **in the front row** au premier rang; **in the back row** au dernier rang; **2 a row** *Fem.*; **a row of books** une rangée de livres; **3 four times in a row** quatre fois de suite.

row[2] *verb* (*in a boat*) ramer [1]; **it's your turn to row** c'est à toi de ramer; **we rowed across the lake** nous avons traversé le lac à la rame.

row[3] *noun* **1** (*a quarrel*) dispute *Fem.*; **to have a row** se disputer; **they've had a row** ils se sont disputés; **I had a row with my parents** je me suis disputé avec mes parents; **2** (*noise*) vacarme *Masc.*; **they were making a terrible row!** ils faisaient un vacarme pas possible!

rowing *noun* aviron *Masc.*; **to go rowing** faire [10] de l'aviron.

rowing boat *noun* barque *Fem.*

royal *adjective* royal (*Masc. plural* royaux); **the royal family** la famille royale.

rub *verb* frotter [1]; **to rub your eyes** se frotter les yeux.

● **to rub something out** effacer [61] quelque chose.

rubber *noun* **1** (*an eraser*) gomme *Fem.*; **2** (*material*) caoutchouc *Masc.*; **rubber soles** des semelles en caoutchouc.

rubbish *noun* **1** (*for the bin*) ordures *Fem. plural*; **2** (*nonsense*) bêtises *Fem. plural*; **you're talking rubbish!** tu dis des bêtises!

rubbish *adjective* nul (*Fem.* nulle); **the film was rubbish** le film était nul; **they're a rubbish band** c'est un groupe nul.

rubbish bin *noun* poubelle *Fem.*

rucksack *noun* sac *Masc.* à dos.

rude *adjective* **1** impoli; **that's rude** c'est impoli; **2 a rude joke** une plaisanterie grossière; **a rude word** un gros mot.

rug *noun* **1** tapis *Masc.*; **2** (*a blanket*) couverture *Fem.*

rugby *noun* rugby *Masc.*; **to play rugby** jouer au rugby; **a rugby match** un match de rugby.

ruin *noun* ruine *Fem.*; **in ruins** en ruines.

ruin *verb* **1** abîmer [1]; **you'll ruin your jacket** tu vas abîmer ta veste; **2** gâcher [1] (*day, holiday*); **it ruined my evening** ça m'a gâché la soirée.

rule *noun* **1** règle *Fem.*; **the rules of the game** les règles du jeu; **2 the school rules** le règlement de l'école; **3 as a rule** en général.

ruler noun règle Fem.; **I've lost my ruler** j'ai perdu ma règle.

rum noun rhum Masc.

rumour noun rumeur Fem.

run noun 1 **to go for a run** courir [29]; 2 (in cricket) point Masc.; **to score fifteen runs** marquer quinze points; 3 **in the long run** à long terme.

run verb 1 courir [29]; **I ran ten kilometres** j'ai couru dix kilomètres; **he ran across the pitch** il a traversé le terrain en courant; **Kitty ran for the bus** Kitty a couru pour attraper le bus; 2 (organize) organiser [1]; **who's running this concert?** qui est-ce qui organise ce concert?; 3 diriger [52] (a business); **he ran the firm for forty years** il a dirigé l'entreprise pendant quarante ans; 4 (a train or bus) circuler [1]; **the buses don't run on Sundays** les bus ne circulent pas le dimanche; 5 **to run a bath** faire [10] couler un bain.

● **to run away** s'enfuir [44].

● **to run into** rentrer [1] dans; **the car ran into a lamppost** la voiture est rentrée dans un réverbère.

● **to run out of something: we've run out of bread** il ne reste plus de pain; **I'm running out of money** je n'ai presque plus d'argent.

● **to run somebody over** écraser [1] quelqu'un; **you'll get run over!** tu vas te faire écraser!

runner noun coureur Masc., coureuse Fem.

runner-up noun second Masc., seconde Fem.

running noun (for exercise) course Fem.

running adjective 1 **running water** l'eau courante; 2 **three days running** trois jours de suite; **six times running** six fois de suite.

runway noun piste Fem.

rush noun (a hurry) **to be in a rush** être pressé; **sorry, I'm in a rush** désolé, je suis pressé.

rush verb 1 (hurry) se dépêcher [1]; **I must rush!** il faut que je me dépêche!; 2 (run) se précipiter [1]; **she rushed into the street** elle s'est précipitée dans la rue; 3 **Louise was rushed to hospital** on a emmené Louise d'urgence à l'hôpital.

rush hour noun heures Fem. plural de pointe; **in the rush hour** aux heures de pointe.

Russia noun Russie Fem.; **in Russia** en Russie.

Russian noun 1 (a person) Russe Masc. & Fem.; 2 (the language) russe Masc.

Russian adjective russe.

rust noun rouille Fem.

rusty adjective rouillé.

rye noun seigle Masc.

Ss

Sabbath noun 1 (Jewish) sabbat Masc.; 2 (Christian) dimanche Masc.

sack noun 1 sac Masc.; 2 **to get the sack** être mis à la porte.

sack verb **to sack somebody** mettre [11] quelqu'un à la porte.

sacred adjective sacré.

sacrifice noun sacrifice Masc.

sad adjective triste.

saddle noun selle Fem.

saddlebag noun sacoche Fem.

sadly adverb **1** tristement; **she looked at me sadly** elle m'a regardé tristement; **2** (unfortunately) malheureusement.

safe adjective **1** (out of danger) hors de danger; **to feel safe** se sentir en sécurité; **2** (not dangerous) pas dangereux (Fem. pas dangereuse); **the path is safe** le sentier n'est pas dangereux; **it's not safe** c'est dangereux.

safety noun sécurité Fem.

safety belt noun ceinture Fem. de sécurité.

safety pin noun épingle Fem. de nourrice.

Sagittarius noun Sagittaire Masc.; **Kylie's Sagittarius** Kylie est Sagittaire.

sail noun voile Fem.

sailing noun voile Fem.; **to go sailing** faire [10] de la voile; **she does a lot of sailing** elle fait beaucoup de voile.

sailing boat noun voilier Masc.

sailor noun marin Masc.

saint noun saint Masc., sainte Fem.

sake noun **1 for your mother's sake** par égard pour ta mère; **2 for heaven's sake** nom de Dieu!

salad noun salade Fem.; **a tomato salad** une salade de tomates.

salad dressing noun vinaigrette Fem.

salami noun saucisson Masc.

salary noun salaire Masc.

sale noun **1** (selling) vente Fem.; **the sale of the house** la vente de la maison; **'for sale'** 'à vendre'; **2 the sales** les soldes Fem. plural; **I bought it in the sales** je l'ai acheté en solde.

sales assistant noun vendeur Masc., vendeuse Fem.

salesman noun représentant Masc.; **he's a salesman** il est représentant.

saleswoman noun représentante Fem.

saliva noun salive Fem.

salmon noun saumon Masc.

salt noun sel Masc.

salty adjective salé.

Salvation Army noun armée Fem. du Salut.

same adjective **1** même; **she said the same thing** elle a dit la même chose; **her birthday's the same day as mine** son anniversaire est le même jour que le mien; **at the same time** en même temps; **their car's the same as ours** ils ont la même voiture que nous; **2 the same** (after verb) pareil; **the two bikes are not the same** les deux vélos ne sont pas pareils; **it's not the same** ce n'est pas pareil.

sample noun échantillon Masc.; **a free sample** un échantillon gratuit.

sand noun sable Masc.

sandal noun sandale Fem.; **a pair of sandals** une paire de sandales.

a
b
c
d
e
f
g
h
i
j
k
l
m
n
o
p
q
r
s
t
u
v
w
x
y
z

sand castle noun château Masc. de sable (plural **châteaux de sable**).

sandpaper noun papier Masc. de verre.

sandwich noun sandwich Masc.; a **ham sandwich** un sandwich au jambon.

sanitary towel noun serviette Fem. hygiénique.

Santa Claus noun le père Noël.

sarcasm noun sarcasme Masc.

sarcastic adjective sarcastique.

sardine noun sardine Fem.

satchel noun cartable Masc.

SARS noun pneumopathie Fem. atypique.

satellite noun satellite Masc.

satellite dish noun antenne Fem. parabolique.

satellite television noun télévision Fem. par satellite.

satisfactory adjective satisfaisant.

satisfied adjective satisfait.

satisfy verb satisfaire [10].

satisfying adjective 1 (pleasing) satisfaisant; 2 a **satisfying meal** un repas consistant.

Saturday noun samedi Masc.; on **Saturday** samedi; I'm going out on **Saturday** je sors samedi; see you on **Saturday!** à samedi!; on **Saturdays** le samedi; the museum is closed on **Saturdays** le musée est fermé le samedi; every **Saturday** tous les samedis; last **Saturday** samedi dernier; next **Saturday** samedi prochain; to

have a **Saturday job** travailler le samedi.

sauce noun sauce Fem.

saucepan noun casserole Fem.

saucer noun soucoupe Fem.

sausage noun 1 saucisse Fem.; 2 (salami) saucisson Masc.

savage noun sauvage Masc. & Fem.

save verb 1 (rescue) sauver [1]; to **save somebody's life** sauver la vie à quelqu'un; the doctors saved his life les médecins lui ont sauvé la vie; 2 mettre [11] de côté (money, food); I've saved £60 j'ai mis soixante livres de côté; 3 (avoid spending) économiser [1]; I walk to school to save money je vais à l'école à pied pour économiser de l'argent; 4 to save time gagner [1] du temps; we'll take a taxi to save time on va prendre un taxi pour gagner du temps; 5 (on a computer) sauvegarder [1].

● to **save up** mettre [11] de l'argent de côté; I'm saving up to go to Spain je mets de l'argent de côté pour aller en Espagne.

savings plural noun économies Fem. plural; I've spent all my savings j'ai dépensé toutes mes économies.

savoury adjective salé; I prefer savoury things to sweet things j'aime mieux les choses salées que les choses sucrées.

saw noun scie Fem.

sawdust noun sciure Fem.

sax noun saxo Masc. (informal); to play the sax jouer du saxo.

saxophone noun saxophone Masc.; **to play the saxophone** jouer du saxophone.

say verb 1 dire [9]; **what did you say?** qu'est-ce que tu as dit?; **she says she's tired** elle dit qu'elle est fatiguée; **he said to wait here** il a dit d'attendre ici; **as they say** comme on dit; **that goes without saying** cela va sans dire; 2 **to say something again** répéter [24] quelque chose.

saying noun dicton Masc.; **as the saying goes** comme on dit.

scab noun croûte Fem.

scale noun 1 (of a map or model) échelle Fem.; **large-scale** à grande échelle; 2 (extent) ampleur Fem.; **the scale of the disaster** l'ampleur du désastre; 3 (in music) gamme Fem.; 4 (of a fish) écaille Fem.

scales noun 1 balance Fem. singular; **kitchen scales** une balance de cuisine; 2 **bathroom scales** un pèse-personne Masc. singular.

scallop noun coquille Fem. Saint-Jacques.

scalp noun cuir Masc. chevelu.

scandal noun 1 scandale Masc.; 2 (gossip) ragots Masc. plural.

Scandinavia noun Scandinavie Fem.

Scandinavian adjective scandinave.

scanner noun scanner Masc.

scar noun cicatrice Fem.

scarce adjective rare.

scarcely adverb à peine.

scare noun 1 panique Fem.; **it caused a scare** cela a provoqué une panique; 2 **a bomb scare** une alerte à la bombe.

scare verb **to scare somebody** faire [10] peur à quelqu'un; **you scared me!** tu m'as fait peur!

scarecrow noun épouvantail Masc.

scared adjective **to be scared** avoir [5] peur; **I'm scared!** j'ai peur; **to be scared of** avoir [5] peur de; **he's scared of dogs** il a peur des chiens; **I'm scared of falling** j'ai peur de tomber.

scarf noun 1 (silky) foulard Masc.; 2 (long, warm) écharpe Fem.

scary adjective effrayant.

scene noun 1 (of an incident or a crime) lieux Masc. plural; **to be on the scene** être sur les lieux; **the scene of the crime** le lieu du crime; 2 (world) monde Masc.; **on the music scene** dans le monde de la musique; 3 **scenes of violence** des incidents violents; 4 **to make a scene** faire une scène.

scenery noun 1 (landscape) paysage Masc.; 2 (theatrical) décors Masc. plural.

scent noun parfum Masc.

scented adjective parfumé.

schedule noun programme Masc.

scheduled flight noun vol Masc. régulier.

scheme noun projet Masc.

scholarship noun bourse Fem.

school noun école Fem.; **at school** à l'école; **to go to school** aller à l'école.

a
b
c
d
e
f
g
h
i
j
k
l
m
n
o
p
q
r
s
t
u
v
w
x
y
z

a **schoolbook** noun livre Masc. scolaire.

b **schoolboy** noun écolier Masc.

schoolchildren plural noun écoliers Masc. plural.

c **schoolfriend** noun camarade Masc. & Fem. de classe.

d **schoolgirl** noun écolière Fem.

e **science** noun science Fem.; **I like science** j'aime la science; **the science teacher** le prof des sciences.

f

g **science fiction** noun science-fiction Fem.

h **scientific** adjective scientifique.

i **scientist** noun scientifique Masc. & Fem.

j **scissors** plural noun ciseaux Masc. plural; **a pair of scissors** une paire de ciseaux.

k

l **scoff** verb (eat) bouffer [1] (informal).

m **scoop** noun 1 (utensil) cuillère Fem. à glace; 2 (content) boule Fem.; **how many scoops would you like?** vous voulez combien de boules?

n

o

p **scooter** noun 1 (motor scooter) scooter Masc.; 2 (for a child) trottinette Fem.

q

score noun score Masc.; **the score was three two** le score était trois à deux.

r

s **score** verb 1 marquer [1]; **Lenny scored a goal** Lenny a marqué un but; **I scored three points** j'ai marqué trois points; 2 (keep score) compter [1] les points.

t

u

v

w **Scorpio** noun Scorpion Masc.; **Jess is Scorpio** Jess est Scorpion.

x

y

z

Scot noun Écossais Masc., Écossaise Fem.; **the Scots** les Écossais Masc. plural.

Scotland noun Écosse Fem.; **in Scotland** en Écosse; **to Scotland** en Écosse; **Pauline's from Scotland** Pauline est écossaise.

Scots adjective écossais; **a Scots accent** un accent écossais.

Scotsman noun Écossais Masc.

Scotswoman noun Écossaise Fem.

Scottish adjective écossais; **a Scottish accent** un accent écossais.

scout noun scout Masc.

scrambled eggs noun œufs Masc. plural brouillés.

scrap noun **a scrap of paper** un bout de papier.

scrapbook noun album Masc.

scrape verb gratter [1].

scratch noun 1 (on your skin) égratignure Fem.; 2 (on a surface) rayure Fem.; ★ **to start from scratch** partir de zéro.

scratch verb (scratch yourself) se gratter [1]; **to scratch your head** se gratter la tête.

scream noun cri Masc.

scream verb crier [1].

screen noun écran Masc.; **on the screen** à l'écran.

screw noun vis Fem.

screw verb visser [1].

screwdriver noun tournevis Masc.

scribble verb griffonner [1].

scrub verb récurer [1] (a saucepan); **to scrub your nails** se brosser [1] les ongles.

scuba diving noun plongée Fem. sous-marine.

sculptor noun sculpteur Masc., sculpteuse Fem; **Rebecca's a sculptor** Rebecca est sculpteur.

sculpture noun sculpture Fem.

sea noun mer Fem.

seafood noun fruits Masc. plural de mer; **I love seafood** j'adore les fruits de mer.

seagull noun mouette Fem.

seal noun (animal) phoque Masc.

seal verb coller [1] (envelope).

seaman noun marin Masc.

search verb 1 fouiller [1]; **I've searched my desk but I can't find the letter** j'ai fouillé dans mon bureau mais je ne trouve pas la lettre; **the police searched the house/the room** la police a fouillé la maison/la chambre; 2 **to search for** chercher [1]; **I've been searching everywhere for the scissors** j'ai cherché les ciseaux partout.

search noun fouille Fem.

seashell noun coquillage Masc.

seasick adjective **to be seasick** avoir le mal de mer.

seaside noun **at the seaside** au bord de la mer.

season noun saison Fem.; **the rugby season** la saison de rugby; **strawberries are not in season at the moment** ce n'est pas la saison des fraises en ce moment; **off-season prices** des prix hors saison.

season ticket noun carte Fem. d'abonnement.

seat noun 1 siège Masc.; (in a car) **the front seat** le siège avant; **the back seat** le siège arrière; **take a seat** assieds-toi; 2 (in a cinema, theatre, etc) place Fem.; **to book a seat** réserver une place; **can you keep my seat?** est-ce que tu peux garder ma place?

seatbelt noun ceinture Fem. de sécurité.

seaweed noun algues Fem. plural.

second noun seconde Fem.; **can you wait a second?** est-ce que tu peux attendre une seconde?

second adjective 1 deuxième; **for the second time** pour la deuxième fois; 2 **the second of July** le deux juillet.

secondary school noun 1 collège Masc. (up to the end of the equivalent of Year 10); 2 lycée Masc. (for the equivalent of Years 11 to 13).

second class noun (category) deuxième classe Fem.; **a second class team** une équipe de niveau très moyen.

secondhand adjective, adverb d'occasion; **a secondhand bike** un vélo d'occasion; **I bought it secondhand** je l'ai acheté d'occasion.

secondly adverb deuxièmement.

secret noun secret Masc.; **to keep a secret** garder un secret; **in secret** en secret.

secret adjective secret (Fem. secrète); **a secret plan** un projet secret.

secretarial college noun école Fem. de secrétariat.

secretary noun secrétaire Masc. & Fem.; **she's a secretary** elle est secrétaire; **the secretary's office** le secrétariat.

secretly adverb secrètement.

sect noun secte Fem.

section noun section Fem.

security noun sécurité Fem.

security guard noun vigile Masc.; **he's a security guard** il est vigile.

see verb **1** voir [13]; **I saw Lindy yesterday** j'ai vu Lindy hier; **have you seen the film?** est-ce que tu as vu le film?; **I haven't seen her for ages** ça fait une éternité que je ne l'ai pas vue; **I'll see what I can do** je vais voir ce que je peux faire; **2** **to be able to see** voir [13]; **I can't see anything** je ne vois rien; **3** **see you!** salut!; **see you on Saturday!** à samedi!; **see you soon!** à bientôt!

● **to see to something** s'occuper [1] de quelque chose; **Jo's seeing to the drinks** Jo s'occupe des boissons.

seed noun graine Fem.; **to plant seeds** semer des graines.

seem verb **1** paraître [57]; **it seems odd to me** ça me paraît bizarre; **it seems he's left** il paraît qu'il est parti; **2** (look, appear to be) avoir [5] l'air; **he seems a bit shy** il a l'air un peu timide; **the museum seems to be closed** le musée a l'air d'être fermé.

seesaw noun tapecul Masc.

select verb sélectionner [1].

selection noun sélection Fem.

self-confidence noun confiance Fem. en soi; **she doesn't have much self-confidence** elle n'a pas beaucoup de confiance en elle.

self-confident adjective plein d'assurance; **he's very self-confident** il est très sûr de lui.

self-conscious adjective timide.

self-contained noun **a self-contained flat** un appartement indépendant.

self-employed noun **the self-employed** les travailleurs indépendants Masc. plural.

self-employed adjective **to be self-employed** travailler à son compte; **my parents are self-employed** mes parents travaillent à leur compte.

selfish adjective égoïste.

self-service adjective **a self-service restaurant** un self (informal).

sell verb vendre [3]; **to sell something to somebody** vendre quelque chose à quelqu'un; **I sold him my bike** je lui ai vendu mon vélo; **the house has been sold** la maison a été vendue; **the concert's sold out** il ne reste plus de billets pour le concert.

sell-by date noun date Fem. limite de vente.

seller noun vendeur Masc., vendeuse Fem.

Sellotape™ noun Scotch™ Masc.

Sellotape™ verb **to sellotape something** scotcher [1] quelque chose (informal).

semi noun maison Fem. jumelée (literally: a twinned house); **we live in a semi** nous habitons dans une maison jumelée.

semicircle noun demi-cercle Masc.

semicolon noun point-virgule Masc.

semi-detached house noun maison Fem. jumelée (literally: a twinned house); **we live in a semi-detached house** nous habitons dans une maison jumelée.

semi-final noun demi-finale Fem.

semi-skimmed milk noun lait Masc. demi-écrémé.

send verb envoyer [40]; **to send something to somebody** envoyer quelque chose à quelqu'un; **I sent her a present for her birthday** je lui ai envoyé un cadeau pour son anniversaire.

● **to send back: to send somebody back** renvoyer [40] quelqu'un; **to send something back** renvoyer [40] quelque chose.

sender noun expéditeur Masc., expéditrice Fem.

senior citizen noun personne Fem. du troisième âge.

sensation noun 1 (feeling) sensation Fem.; 2 (impact) sensation Fem.; **she caused a sensation** elle a fait sensation.

sensational adjective sensationnel (Fem. sensationnelle).

sense noun 1 sens Masc.; **common sense** le bon sens; **it doesn't make sense** ça n'a pas de sens; **it makes sense** ça paraît logique; **to have a sense of humour** avoir le sens de l'humour; **she has no sense of humour** elle n'a aucun sens de l'humour; 2 **the sense of smell** l'odorat Masc.; **the sense of touch** le toucher.

sensible adjective raisonnable; **she's very sensible** elle est très raisonnable; **it's a sensible decision** c'est une décision raisonnable.

sensitive adjective sensible; **for sensitive skin** pour peaux sensibles.

sentence noun 1 phrase Fem.; **écris une phrase en français write a sentence in French**; 2 **the death sentence** la peine de mort.

sentence verb condamner [1]; **to be sentenced to death** être condamné à mort.

sentimental adjective sentimental (Masc. plural sentimentaux).

separate adjective 1 à part; **in a separate pile** dans une pile à part; **on a separate sheet of paper** sur une feuille à part; 2 (different) autre; **that's a separate problem** c'est un autre problème; 3 **they have separate rooms** ils ont chacun leur chambre.

separate verb 1 séparer [1]; 2 (a couple) se séparer [1].

separately adverb séparément.

separation noun séparation Fem.

September noun septembre Masc.; **in September** en septembre.

sequel noun suite Fem.

sequence noun 1 série Fem.; **a sequence of events** une série

a
b
c
d
e
f
g
h
i
j
k
l
m
n
o
p
q
r
s
t
u
v
w
x
y
z

d'événements; **2 in sequence** dans l'ordre; **3** (*in a film*) séquence *Fem*.

sergeant *noun* **1** (*in the police*) brigadier *Masc*.; **2** (*in the army*) sergent *Masc*.

serial *noun* feuilleton *Masc*.

series *noun* série *Fem*.; **a television series** une série télévisée.

serious *adjective* **1** sérieux (*Fem*. sérieuse); **a serious discussion** une discussion sérieuse; **are you serious?** sérieusement?; **2** grave (*illness, injury, mistake, problem*); **we have a serious problem** nous avons un grave problème.

seriously *adverb* **1** sérieusement; **seriously, I have to go now** sérieusement je dois partir maintenant; **seriously?** vraiment?; **2 to take somebody seriously** prendre quelqu'un au sérieux; **3** gravement (*ill, injured*); **she is seriously ill** elle est gravement malade.

servant *noun* domestique *Masc*. & *Fem*.

serve *noun* (*in tennis*) service *Masc*.; **it's my serve** c'est à moi de servir.

serve *verb* **1** (*in tennis*) servir [71]; **2** servir; **can you serve the vegetables, please?** est-ce que tu peux servir les légumes, s'il te plaît?; **they served the fish with a lemon sauce** ils ont servi le poisson accompagné d'une sauce au citron; ★ **it serves him right** c'est bien fait pour lui.

service *noun* **1** (*in a restaurant, from a company, etc*) service *Masc*.; **the service is very slow** le service

est très lent; **service is included** le service est compris; **is there a maid service?** est-ce qu'il y a une femme de ménage?; **2 the emergency services** les services des urgences; **3** (*church service*) office *Masc*.; **4** (*of a car or machine*) révision *Fem*.

service *verb* réviser [1] (*a car or a machine*).

service area *noun* aire *Fem*. de services.

service charge *noun* service *Masc*.; **what is the service charge?** le service est de combien?; **there is no service charge** le service est compris.

service station *noun* station-service *Fem*. (*plural* stations-service*).

serviette *noun* serviette *Fem*.

session *noun* séance *Fem*.

set *noun* **1** (*for playing a game*) jeu *Masc*. (*plural* jeux); **a chess set** un jeu d'échecs; **2 a train set** un petit train; **3** (*in tennis*) set *Masc*.

set *adjective* fixe; **at a set time** à une heure fixe; **a set menu** un menu fixe.

set *verb* **1** fixer [1] (*date, time*); **2** établir [2] (*record*); **3 to set the table** mettre [11] la table; **to set an alarm clock** mettre [11] un réveil; **I've set my alarm for seven** j'ai mis mon réveil à sept heures; **4 to set a watch** régler [24] une montre; **5** (*sun*) se coucher [1].

● **to set off** partir [58]; **we're setting off at ten** nous allons partir à dix heures; **they set off for Paris yesterday** ils sont partis pour Paris hier.

● **to set off something 1** faire [10] partir (*firework*); **2** faire [10] exploser (*bomb*); **3** déclencher [1] (*alarm*).

● **to set out** partir [58]; **they set out for Paris yesterday** ils sont partis pour Paris hier.

settee *noun* canapé *Masc.*

settle *verb* régler [24] (*a bill or a problem*).

seven *number* sept; **Rosie's seven** Rosie a sept ans.

seventeen *number* dix-sept; **Jonny's seventeen** Jonny a dix-sept ans.

seventh *adjective* septième; **on the seventh floor** au septième étage; **the seventh of July** le sept juillet.

seventies *plural noun* **the seventies** les années soixante-dix; **in the seventies** aux années soixante-dix.

seventieth *adjective* soixante-dixième; **it's her seventieth birthday** elle fête ses soixante-dix ans.

seventy *number* soixante-dix; **my grandma's seventy** ma grand-mère a soixante-dix ans.

several *adjective, pronoun* plusieurs; **I've seen her several times** je l'ai vue plusieurs fois; **I've read several of her novels** j'ai lu plusieurs de ses romans; **he took several** il en a pris plusieurs.

severe *adjective* **1** (*person*) sévère; **2** (*weather*) rigoureux (*Fem.* rigoureuse); **3** (*injuries*) grave.

sew *verb* coudre [28].

sewer *noun* égout *Masc.*

sewing *noun* couture *Fem.*; **I like sewing** j'aime la couture.

sewing machine *noun* machine *Fem.* à coudre.

sex *noun* **1** (*gender*) sexe *Masc.*; **2** (*intercourse*) rapports *Masc. plural* sexuels; **to have sex with someone** coucher avec quelqu'un.

sex education *noun* éducation *Fem.* sexuelle.

sexism *noun* sexisme *Masc.*

sexist *adjective* sexiste; **sexist remarks** des propos sexistes.

sexual *adjective* sexuel (*Fem.* sexuelle).

sexual harassment *noun* harcèlement *Masc.* sexuel.

sexuality *noun* sexualité *Fem.*

sexy *adjective* sexy.

shabby *adjective* miteux (*Fem.* miteuse).

shade *noun* **1** (*of a colour*) ton *Masc.*; **a pretty shade of green** un joli vert; **2 in the shade** à l'ombre.

shadow *noun* ombre *Fem.*

shake *verb* **1** (*tremble*) trembler [1]; **my hands are shaking** j'ai les mains qui tremblent; **2 to shake something** secouer [1] quelque chose; **3 to shake hands with somebody** serrer [1] la main à quelqu'un; **she shook hands with me** elle m'a serré la main; **we shook hands** nous nous sommes serré la main; **4 to shake your head** (*meaning no*) faire [10] non de la tête.

shaken *adjective* bouleversé; **I was shaken by the news** j'ai été bouleversé par la nouvelle.

a
b
c
d
e
f
g
h
i
j
k
l
m
n
o
p
q
r
s
t
u
v
w
x
y
z

shall verb **shall I come with you?** tu veux que je t'accompagne?; **shall we stop now?** si on s'arrêtait maintenant?

shallow adjective peu profond; **the water's very shallow here** l'eau est très peu profonde ici.

shallow end noun partie Fem. la moins profonde de la piscine.

shambles noun pagaille Fem. (informal); **it was a total shambles!** ça a été la pagaille complète!

shame noun **1** honte Fem.; **shame on you!** tu devrais avoir honte!; **2 what a shame!** quel dommage!; **it's a shame she can't come** c'est dommage qu'elle ne puisse pas venir (note that 'c'est dommage que' is followed by a verb in the subjunctive).

shameful adjective honteux (Fem. honteuse).

shampoo noun shampooing Masc.; **I bought some shampoo** j'ai acheté du shampooing.

shamrock noun trèfle Masc.

shandy noun panaché Masc.; **a half of shandy** un demi panaché.

shape noun forme Fem.

share noun **1** part Fem.; **your share of the money** ta part de l'argent; **he paid his fair share** il a payé sa part; **2** (in a company) action Fem.

share verb partager [52]; **I'm sharing a room with Emma** je partage une chambre avec Emma.

● **to share out** partager [52], répartir [58].

shark noun requin Masc.

sharp adjective **1** (knife) bien aiguisé; **this knife isn't very sharp** ce couteau ne coupe pas très bien; **2 a sharp pencil** un crayon bien taillé; **3 a sharp bend** un virage brusque; **4** (clever) intelligent.

sharpen verb **1** (a pencil) tailler [1]; **2** (a knife) aiguiser [1].

sharpener noun taille-crayon Masc.

shave verb **1** (have a shave) se raser [1]; **he's just shaving** il est en train de se raser; **2 to shave your legs** se raser [1] les jambes; **to shave off your beard** se raser la barbe.

shaver noun **an electric shaver** un rasoir électrique.

shaving cream noun crème Fem. à raser.

shaving foam noun mousse Fem. à raser.

she pronoun elle; **she's in her room** elle est dans sa chambre; **she's a student** elle est étudiante; **she's a very good teacher** c'est un très bon prof; **here she is!** la voici!; **there she is!** la voilà!

shed noun remise Fem.

sheep noun mouton Masc.

sheepdog noun chien Masc. de berger (plural chiens de berger).

sheer adjective **1** pur; **it's sheer stupidity!** c'est de la pure bêtise!; **2** (tights) extra-fin.

sheet noun **1** (for a bed) drap Masc.; **2 a sheet of paper** une feuille de papier; **a blank sheet** une feuille blanche; **3** (of glass or metal) plaque; ★ **to be as white as a sheet** être blanc comme un linge;

she was as white as a sheet elle était blanche comme un linge.

shelf noun 1 (in the home) étagère Fem.; **a set of shelves** une étagère; 2 (in a shop, in a fridge) rayon Masc.

shell noun 1 (of an egg or a nut) coquille Fem.; 2 (seashell) coquillage Fem.; 3 (explosive) obus Masc.

shellfish noun fruits Masc. plural de mer.

shelter noun 1 abri Masc.; **in the shelter of** à l'abri de; **to take shelter from the rain** se mettre à l'abri de la pluie; 2 **a bus shelter** un abribus™.

shepherd noun berger Masc.

sheriff noun shérif Masc.

sherry noun sherry Masc.

Shetland Islands noun îles Fem. plural Shetland.

shield noun bouclier Masc.

shift noun service Masc.; **the night shift** le service de nuit; **to be on night shift** être de nuit.

shift verb **to shift something** déplacer [61] quelque chose; **can you help me shift this table?** est-ce que tu peux m'aider à déplacer cette table?

shifty adjective louche; **he looks a bit shifty** il a l'air un peu louche; **a shifty-looking guy** un type un peu louche.

shin noun tibia Masc.

shine verb briller [1].

shiny adjective brillant.

ship noun 1 bateau Masc.; 2 **a passenger ship** un paquebot; 3 (large naval vessel) navire Masc.

shipbuilding noun construction Fem. navale.

shipyard noun chantier Masc. naval.

shirt noun 1 (man's) chemise Fem.; 2 (woman's) chemisier Masc.

shiver verb frissonner [1].

shock noun 1 choc Masc.; **it was a shock** ça a été un choc; **it gave me a shock** j'ai eu un choc; 2 **an electric shock** une décharge; **to get an electric shock** prendre une décharge.

shock verb choquer [1].

shocked adjective choqué.

shocking adjective choquant.

shoe noun chaussure Fem.; **a pair of shoes** une paire de chaussures.

shoelace noun lacet Masc.

shoe polish noun cirage Masc.

shoe shop noun magasin Masc. de chaussures.

shoot verb 1 (fire) tirer [1]; **to shoot at somebody** tirer sur quelqu'un; **she shot him in the leg** elle lui a tiré une balle dans la jambe; **he was shot in the arm** il a reçu une balle dans le bras; 2 (kill) abattre [21]; **he was shot by terrorists** il a été abattu par des terroristes; 3 (execute) fusiller [1]; 4 (in football, hockey) shooter [1]; 5 **to shoot a film** tourner [1] un film.

shooting noun tir Masc.

shop noun magasin Masc.; **a shoe shop** un magasin de chaussures; **to go round the shops** faire les magasins.

a b c d e f g h i j k l m n o p q r s t u v w x y z

a

shop assistant noun vendeur Masc., vendeuse Fem.; **Brad's a shop assistant** Brad est vendeur.

b

c **shopkeeper** noun commerçant Masc., commerçante Fem.

d **shoplifter** noun voleur Masc. à l'étalage, voleuse Fem. à l'étalage.

e **shoplifting** noun vol Masc. à l'étalage.

f

g **shopping** noun courses Fem. plural; **can you put the shopping away?** est-ce que tu peux ranger les courses?; **I've got a lot of shopping to do** j'ai beaucoup de courses à faire; **to go shopping** (for food) faire des courses; (for fun, to buy clothes or presents) faire du shopping.

h

i

j

k

l **shopping bag** noun sac Masc. à provisions.

m **shopping centre** noun centre Masc. commercial.

n **shopping trolley** noun 1 (in a supermarket) chariot Masc.; 2 (personal) caddie™ Masc.

o

p **shop window** noun vitrine Fem.

q **shore** noun côte Fem.

r

s **short** adjective 1 court; **a short dress** une robe courte; **she has short hair** elle a les cheveux courts; **2 a short break** une petite pause; **to go for a short walk** faire une petite promenade; **it's a short walk from the station** c'est à quelques minutes à pied de la gare; **3 to be short of something** ne pas avoir beaucoup de quelque chose; **we're a bit short of money at the moment** nous n'avons pas beaucoup d'argent en ce moment;

t

u

v

w

x

y

z

we're getting short of time il ne nous reste pas beaucoup de temps.

shortage noun pénurie Fem.

shortbread noun sablé Masc.

shortcrust pastry noun pâte Fem. brisée.

short cut noun raccourci Masc.; **we took a short cut** nous avons pris un raccourci.

shorten verb 1 (clothes) raccourcir [2]; 2 (a stay, journey) écourter [1].

shortly adverb bientôt.

shorts plural noun short Masc. singular; **a pair of shorts** un short; **my red shorts** mon short rouge.

short-sighted adjective myope; **I'm short-sighted** je suis myope.

short story noun nouvelle Fem.

shot noun 1 (from a gun) coup Masc. de feu (plural coups de feu); 2 (a photo) photo Fem.; **I took several shots of the garden** j'ai pris plusieurs photos du jardin.

shotgun noun fusil Masc. de chasse (plural fusils de chasse).

should verb 1 ('should' meaning 'ought to' is translated by the conditional tense of 'devoir' [8]; **you should ask Simon** tu devrais demander à Simon; **the potatoes should be cooked now** les pommes de terre devraient être cuites maintenant; 2 ('should have' is translated by the past conditional tense of 'devoir') **you should have told me** tu aurais dû me le dire; **I shouldn't have stayed** je n'aurais pas dû rester; 3 ('should' meaning 'would' is translated by the conditional tense of the verb) **I should forget it if I were you** à ta place je l'oublierais; **4 I should think** à mon avis; **I should think he's forgotten** à mon avis, il a oublié.

shoulder noun épaule Fem.

shoulder bag noun sac Masc. à bandoulière.

shout noun cri Masc.

shout verb crier [1]; **stop shouting!** arrêtez de crier!; **they shouted at us to come back** ils nous ont crié de revenir.

shovel noun pelle Fem.

show noun **1** (on stage) spectacle Masc.; **we went to see a show** nous sommes allés voir un spectacle; **2** (on TV) émission; **he has a TV show** il a une émission à la télé; **3** (exhibition) salon; **the motor show** le salon des automobiles.

show verb **1** montrer [1]; **to show something to somebody** montrer quelque chose à quelqu'un; **I'll show you my photos** je te montrerai mes photos; **to show somebody how to do** montrer à quelqu'un comment on fait; **he showed me how to make pancakes** il m'a montré comment on fait les crêpes; **2 it shows!** ça se voit!

● **to show off** frimer [1] (informal).

shower noun **1** (in a bathroom) douche Fem.; **to have a shower** prendre une douche; **2** (of rain) averse Fem.

show-jumping noun saut Masc. d'obstacles.

show-off noun frimeur Masc., frimeuse Fem. (informal).

shriek verb hurler [1].

shrimp noun crevette Fem.

shrine noun autel Masc.

shrink verb rétrécir [2].

Shrove Tuesday noun mardi Masc. gras.

shrug verb **to shrug your shoulders** hausser [1] les épaules.

shuffle verb **to shuffle the cards** battre [21] les cartes.

shut adjective fermé; **the shops are shut** les magasins sont fermés.

shut verb fermer [1]; **can you shut the door please?** est-ce que tu peux fermer la porte, s'il te plaît?; **the shops shut at six** les magasins ferment à six heures.

● **to shut up** (be quiet) se taire [76]; **shut up!** tais-toi!

shutter noun volet Masc.

shuttle noun navette Fem.; **there's a shuttle service from the airport** il y a une navette de l'aéroport.

shuttlecock noun volant Masc.

shy adjective timide.

shyness noun timidité Fem.

Sicily noun Sicile Fem.; **to Sicily** en Sicile; **in Sicily** en Sicile.

sick adjective **1** (ill) malade; **2 to be sick** (vomit) vomir [2]; **I was sick several times** j'ai vomi plusieurs fois; **to feel sick** avoir [5] mal au cœur; **3 a sick joke** une plaisanterie malsaine; **4 to be sick of something** en avoir assez de quelque chose; **I'm sick of staying at home every night** j'en ai assez de rester à la maison tous les soirs.

sickness noun maladie Fem.

side noun 1 côté Masc.; **on the
other side of the street** de l'autre
côté de la rue; **on the wrong side**
du mauvais côté; **I'm on your side**
(I agree with you) je suis de ton
côté; 2 (edge) bord Masc.; **at the
side of the road** au bord de la
route; **by the side of the pool** au
bord de la piscine; 3 (team) équipe;
she plays on our side elle joue
dans notre équipe; 4 **to take sides**
prendre parti; 5 **side by side** côte à
côte.

sideboard noun buffet Masc.

sideburns noun pattes Fem. plural.

side-effect noun effet Masc.
secondaire.

side street noun petite rue Fem.

siege noun siège Masc.

sieve noun passoire Fem.

sigh noun soupir Masc.

sigh verb pousser [1] un soupir.

sight noun 1 spectacle Masc.; **it was
a marvellous sight** c'était un
spectacle merveilleux; 2 **at the
sight of** à la vue de; 3 (eyesight) vue
Fem.; **to have poor sight** avoir une
mauvaise vue; **to know somebody
by sight** connaître quelqu'un de
vue; **out of sight** caché; 4 **to see
the sights** visiter les attractions
touristiques.

sightseeing noun tourisme Masc.;
to do some sightseeing faire du
tourisme.

sign noun 1 (notice) panneau Masc.
(plural panneaux); **there's a sign
on the door** il y a un panneau sur
la porte; 2 (trace, indication) signe
Masc.; 3 (of the Zodiac) signe Masc.;
what sign are you? tu es de quel
signe?

sign verb 1 signer [1]; **to sign a
cheque** signer un chèque; 2 (using
sign language) communiquer [1] en
langage par signes.

● **to sign on** (as unemployed)
s'inscrire [38] au chômage.

signal noun signal Masc. (plural
signaux).

signature noun signature Fem.

significance noun importance
Fem.

significant adjective important.

sign language noun langage
Masc. par signes.

signpost noun poteau Masc.
indicateur (plural poteaux
indicateurs).

silence noun silence Masc.

silent adjective silencieux (Fem.
silencieuse).

silicon chip noun puce Fem.
électronique.

silk noun soie Fem.

silk adjective en soie; **a silk shirt**
une chemise en soie.

silky adjective soyeux (Fem.
soyeuse).

silly adjective idiot; **it was a really
silly thing to do** c'était vraiment
idiot.

silver noun argent Masc.

silver adjective **a silver spoon** une
cuillère en argent; **a silver medal**
une médaille d'argent.

SIM card noun carte Fem. SIM.

similar adjective semblable.

similarity noun ressemblance
Fem.

simmer verb to simmer something faire [10] mijoter quelque chose.

simple adjective facile.

simplify verb simplifier [1].

simply adverb simplement.

sin noun péché Masc.

since preposition, adverb, conjunction **1** depuis (notice that French uses the present tense where English uses 'have done' or 'have been doing') **I have been in Paris since Saturday** je suis à Paris depuis samedi; **I've been learning French since last year** j'apprends le français depuis l'année dernière; **2** depuis que (the same thing happens with tenses here as above) **since I have known him** depuis que je le connais; **since I've been learning French** depuis que j'apprends le français; **3 I haven't seen her since** je ne l'ai pas revue depuis; **I haven't seen her since Monday** je ne l'ai pas revue depuis lundi; **since when?** depuis quand?; **4** (because) puisque; **since it was raining, the match was cancelled** puisqu'il pleuvait le match a été annulé.

sincere adjective sincère.

sincerely adverb sincèrement (in a business letter) Veuillez agréer Madame (or Monsieur) l'expression de mes sentiments distingués; (to somebody you know) Cordialement (in French there are very formal and rigid formulae for signing letters).

sing verb chanter [1].

singer noun chanteur Masc., chanteuse Fem.

singing noun **1** chant Masc.; a **singing lesson** une leçon de chant; **2 I like singing** j'aime chanter.

single noun aller Masc. simple; a **single to Lyons, please** un aller simple pour Lyon, s'il vous plaît.

single adjective **1** (not married) célibataire; **2 a single room** une chambre pour une personne; **a single bed** un lit pour une personne; **3 not a single** pas un seul, pas une seule; **I haven't had a single reply** je n'ai pas reçu une seule réponse.

single parent noun **she's a single parent** elle élève ses enfants toute seule; **a single-parent family** une famille monoparentale.

singles plural noun (in tennis) simple Masc. singular; **the women's singles** le simple dames; **the men's singles** le simple messieurs.

singular noun singulier Masc.; **in the singular** au singulier.

sink noun évier Masc.

sink verb couler [1].

sir noun monsieur Masc.; **yes, sir** oui, Monsieur.

siren noun sirène Fem.

sister noun sœur Fem.; **my sister's ten** ma sœur a dix ans.

sister-in-law noun belle-sœur Fem. (plural belles-sœurs).

sit verb **1** s'asseoir [20]; **you can sit on the sofa** tu peux t'asseoir sur le canapé; **I can sit on the floor** je peux m'asseoir par terre; **2 to be sitting** être [6] assis; **Leila was sitting on the sofa** Leila était

a
b
c
d
e
f
g
h
i
j
k
l
m
n
o
p
q
r
s
t
u
v
w
x
y
z

assise sur le canapé; **3 to sit an exam** passer [1] un examen; **she's sitting her driving test on Thursday** elle passe son permis jeudi.

● **to sit down** s'asseoir [20]; **he sat down on a chair** il s'est assis sur une chaise; **do sit down** asseyez-vous.

sitcom noun comédie Fem. de situation (plural **comédies de situation**).

site noun **1 a building site** un chantier; **2 a camping site** un camping; **3 an archaeological site** un site archéologique.

sitting room noun salon Masc.

situated adjective **to be situated** être situé; **the house is situated in a small village** la maison est située dans un petit village.

situation noun situation Fem.

six number six; **Harry's six** Harry a six ans.

sixteen number seize; **Alice is sixteen** Alice a seize ans.

sixth adjective sixième; **on the sixth floor** au sixième étage; **the sixth of July** le six juillet.

sixty number soixante; **she's sixty** elle a soixante ans.

size noun **1** grandeur Fem.; **it depends on the size of the house** ça dépend de la grandeur de la maison; **2** (precise measurements) dimensions Fem. plural; **what size is the window?** quelles sont les dimensions de la fenêtre?; **3** (in clothes) taille Fem.; **what size do you take?** quelle taille faites-vous?; **4** (of shoes) pointure; **I take**

a size thirty-eight je fais du trente-huit.

skate noun **1 an ice skate** un patin à glace; **2 a roller skate** un patin à roulettes.

skate verb **1** (ice-skate) faire [10] du patin à glace; **2** (roller-skate) faire [10] du patin à roulettes.

skateboard noun skateboard Masc.

skateboarding noun skateboard Masc.; **to do** (or **go**) **skateboarding** faire du skateboard.

skater noun patineur Masc., patineuse Fem.

skating noun **1** (ice) patin Masc. à glace; **to go skating** faire du patin à glace; **2** roller-skating le patin à roulettes; **to go roller-skating** faire du patin à roulettes.

skating rink noun patinoire Fem.

skeleton noun squelette Masc.

sketch noun **1** (drawing) croquis Masc.; (comedy routine) sketch Masc.

ski noun ski Masc.

ski verb faire [10] du ski; **he can ski** il sait faire du ski.

ski boot noun chaussure Fem. de ski.

skid verb déraper [1]; **the car skidded** la voiture a dérapé.

skier noun skieur Masc., skieuse Fem.

skiing noun ski Masc.; **to go skiing** faire du ski.

ski lift noun remonte-pente Masc.

skill noun compétence Fem.

skimmed milk noun lait Masc. écrémé.

skin noun peau Fem. (plural peaux).

skinhead noun skinhead Masc. & Fem.

skinny adjective maigre.

skip noun (for rubbish) benne Fem.

skip verb 1 sauter [1] (a meal, part of a book); **I skipped a few chapters** j'ai sauté quelques chapitres; **2 to skip a lesson** sécher un cours (informal).

ski pants noun fuseau Masc. singular; **I bought some ski pants** j'ai acheté un fuseau.

skipping rope noun corde Fem. à sauter.

skirt noun jupe Fem.; **a long skirt** une jupe longue; **a straight skirt** une jupe droite; **a mini-skirt** une mini-jupe.

ski suit noun combinaison Fem. de ski.

skittles plural noun quilles Fem. plural; **to play skittles** jouer aux quilles.

skull noun crâne Masc.

sky noun ciel Masc.

skyscraper noun gratte-ciel Masc. (plural gratte-ciel).

slam verb claquer [1]; **she slammed the door** elle a claqué la porte.

slang noun argot Masc.

slap noun claque Fem.

slap verb **to slap somebody** donner [1] une claque à quelqu'un.

slate noun ardoise Fem.

slave noun esclave Masc. & Fem.

sledge noun luge Fem.

sledging noun **to go sledging** faire [10] de la luge.

sleep noun sommeil Masc.; **I had a good sleep** j'ai bien dormi; **to go to sleep** s'endormir [37].

sleep verb dormir [37]; **she's sleeping** elle dort.

sleeping bag noun sac Masc. de couchage.

sleeping pill noun somnifère Masc.

sleepy adjective **to be sleepy** avoir [5] sommeil; **I feel sleepy** j'ai sommeil; **he was getting sleepy** il commençait à avoir sommeil.

sleet noun neige Fem. fondue.

sleeve noun manche Fem.; **a long-sleeved jumper** un pull à manches longues; **a short-sleeved shirt** une chemise à manches courtes; **to roll up your sleeves** retrousser ses manches.

slice noun tranche Fem.; **a slice of ham** une tranche de jambon.

slice verb **to slice something** couper [1] quelque chose en tranches.

slide noun 1 (photo) diapositive Fem.; 2 (hairslide) barrette Fem.; 3 (for sliding down) toboggan Masc.

slight adjective léger (Fem. légère); **there is a slight problem** il y a un léger problème.

slightly adverb légèrement.

slim adjective mince.

slim verb **I'm slimming** je fais un régime.

sling noun écharpe Fem.; **to have your arm in a sling** avoir le bras en écharpe.

a b c d e f g h i j k l m n o p q r s t u v w x y z

slip 558 ENGLISH-FRENCH

slip noun 1 (*mistake*) erreur Fem.; 2 (*petticoat*) (*from waist*) jupon Masc. (*full-length*) combinaison Fem.

slip verb 1 (*slide*) glisser [1]; 2 it had slipped my mind j'avais oublié.

slipper noun pantoufle Fem.

slippery adjective glissant.

slope noun pente Fem.

slot noun fente Fem.

slot machine noun 1 (*games machine*) machine Fem. à sous; 2 (*vending machine*) distributeur Masc. automatique.

slow adjective 1 lent; the service is a bit slow le service est une peu lent; 2 my watch is slow ma montre retarde.

● to slow down ralentir [2].

slowly adverb 1 lentement; he got up slowly il s'est levé lentement; 2 (*speak, drive*) doucement; can you speak more slowly, please? est-ce que vous pouvez parler plus doucement, s'il vous plaît?

slug noun limace Fem.

slum noun quartier Masc. démuni.

slush noun neige Fem. fondue.

sly adjective (*person*) rusé; ★ on the sly en douce.

smack noun claque Fem.

smack verb to smack somebody donner [1] une claque à quelqu'un.

small adjective petit (*goes before the noun*); a small dog un petit chien.

smart adjective 1 (*well-dressed, posh*) chic; a smart restaurant un restaurant chic; 2 (*clever*) intelligent.

smash noun a car smash un accident de voiture.

smash verb casser [1]; they smashed a window ils ont cassé une vitre.

smashing adjective formidable.

smell noun odeur Fem.; a nasty smell une mauvaise odeur; there's a smell of burning ça sent le brûlé.

smell verb 1 sentir [58]; I can't smell anything je ne sens rien; I can smell lavender ça sent la lavande; 2 (*smell bad*) sentir [58] mauvais; the drains smell les égouts sentent mauvais.

smelly adjective qui sent mauvais; her smelly dog son chien qui sent mauvais.

smile noun sourire Masc.

smile verb sourire [68].

smoke noun fumée Fem.

smoke verb fumer [1]; she doesn't smoke elle ne fume pas; he smokes a pipe il fume la pipe.

smoked adjective fumé; smoked salmon du saumon fumé.

smoker noun fumeur Masc., fumeuse Fem.

smoking noun 'no smoking' 'défense de fumer'; to give up smoking arrêter de fumer.

smooth adjective 1 lisse; a smooth surface une surface lisse; 2 (*person*) mielleux (Fem. mielleuse).

smug adjective suffisant.

smuggle verb to smuggle something faire [10] passer quelque chose en contrebande.

smuggler noun 1 contrebandier Masc., contrebandière Fem.; 2 a drugs smuggler un passeur de drogue.

smuggling noun **1** contrebande Fem.; **2** (of drugs or arms) trafic Masc.

snack noun casse-croûte Masc.

snack bar noun sandwicherie Fem., snack-bar Masc.

snail noun escargot Masc.

snake noun serpent Masc.

snap noun (card game) bataille Fem.

snap verb **1** (break) casser [1]; **2 to snap your fingers** faire [10] claquer ses doigts.

snapshot noun photo Fem.

snarl verb gronder [1].

snatch verb arracher [1]; **to snatch something from somebody** arracher quelque chose à quelqu'un; **he snatched my book** il m'a arraché mon livre; **she had her bag snatched** on lui a arraché son sac.

sneak verb **to sneak in** entrer [1] furtivement; **to sneak out** sortir [72] furtivement; **he sneaked up on me** il s'est approché de moi sans faire de bruit.

sneeze verb éternuer [1].

sniff verb renifler [1].

snob noun snob Masc. & Fem.

snobbery noun snobisme Masc.

snooker noun snooker Masc.; **to play snooker** jouer au snooker.

snooze noun somme Masc.; **to have a snooze** faire un petit somme.

snore verb ronfler [1].

snow noun neige Fem.

snow verb neiger [52]; **it's snowing** il neige; **it's going to snow** il va neiger.

snowball noun boule Fem. de neige (plural boules de neige).

snowdrift noun congère Fem.

snowman noun bonhomme Masc. de neige (plural bonhommes de neige).

snowy adjective enneigé; **it was very snowy** il y avait beaucoup de neige.

so conjunction, adverb **1** tellement; **he's so lazy** il est tellement paresseux; **the coffee's so hot I can't drink it** le café est tellement chaud que je n'arrive pas à le boire; **2 not so** moins; **our house is a bit like yours, but not so big** notre maison est un peu comme la vôtre, mais moins grande; **3 so much** tellement; **I hate it so much!** je le déteste tellement!; **4 so much, so many** tellement de; **I have so much work to do** j'ai tellement de travail à faire; **we've got so many problems** nous avons tellement de problèmes; **5** (therefore) donc; **he got up late, so he missed his train** il s'est levé tard, donc il a raté son train; **6** (starting a sentence) alors; **so what's your name?** alors, tu t'appelles comment?; **so what shall we do?** alors, qu'est-ce qu'on fait?; **so what?** et alors?; **7 so do I, so did I** moi aussi; **'I live in Leeds' – 'so do I'** 'j'habite à Leeds' – 'moi aussi'; **'I hated the film' – 'so did I'** 'j'ai détesté le film' – 'moi aussi'; **so am I** moi aussi; **so do we** nous aussi; **8 I think so** je crois; **I hope so** j'espère.

soak verb tremper [1].

soaked adjective trempé; ★ **to be soaked to the skin** être trempé

a
b
c
d
e
f
g
h
i
j
k
l
m
n
o
p
q
r
s
t
u
v
w
x
y
z

a jusqu'aux os (*literally: to be soaked to the bones*).

b **soaking** *adjective* trempé; **soaking wet** trempé.

c **soap** *noun* 1 savon *Masc.*; **a cake of soap** un savon; 2 (*soap opera: on TV*) feuilleton *Masc.*

d **soap powder** *noun* lessive *Fem.*

e **sober** *adjective* **to be sober** ne pas avoir bu; **he's sober** il n'a pas bu; **are you sure she's sober?** tu es sûr qu'elle n'a pas bu?

f **soccer** *noun* football *Masc.*; **to play soccer** jouer au football.

g **social** *adjective* social (*Masc. plural* sociaux).

h **socialism** *noun* socialisme *Masc.*

i **socialist** *noun, adjective* socialiste *Masc. & Fem.*

j **social security** *noun* 1 aide *Fem.* sociale; **to be on social security** recevoir de l'aide sociale; 2 **the social security** (*the system*) sécurité sociale *Fem.*

k **social worker** *noun* travailleur *Masc.* social (*plural* **travailleurs sociaux**), travailleuse *Fem.* sociale; **she's a social worker** elle est travailleuse sociale.

l **society** *noun* société *Fem.*

m **sociology** *noun* sociologie *Fem.*

n **sock** *noun* chaussette *Fem.*; **a pair of socks** une paire de chaussettes.

o **socket** *noun* (*power point*) prise *Fem.* de courant (*plural* **prises de courant**).

p **sofa** *noun* canapé *Masc.*

q **sofa bed** *noun* canapé-lit *Masc.*

r **soft** *adjective* doux (*Fem.* douce);
★ **to have a soft spot for**

somebody avoir un faible pour quelqu'un.

soft drink *noun* boisson *Fem.* non alcoolisée.

soft toy *noun* peluche *Fem.*

software *noun* logiciel *Masc.*

soil *noun* terre *Fem.*

solar energy *noun* énergie *Fem.* solaire.

soldier *noun* soldat *Masc.*

solicitor *noun* 1 (*dealing with property or documents*) notaire *Masc.*; **she's a solicitor** elle est notaire; 2 (*dealing with lawsuits*) avocat *Masc.*, avocate *Fem.*; **she's a solicitor** elle est avocate.

solid *adjective* 1 massif (*Fem.* massive); **a table made of solid pine** une table en pin massif; **a solid gold ring** une bague en or massif; **solid silver** argent massif; 2 (*not flimsy*) solide; **a solid structure** une structure solide.

solo *noun* solo *Masc.*; **a guitar solo** un solo de guitare.

solo *adjective, adverb* en solo; **a solo album** un album en solo; **to play solo** jouer en solo.

soloist *noun* soliste *Masc. & Fem.*

solution *noun* solution *Fem.*

solve *verb* résoudre [67].

some *adjective, adverb* 1 (*followed by a singular noun*), du (*with a masculine noun*), de la (*with a feminine noun*), de l' (*with a noun beginning with a vowel or silent 'h'*); **would you like some butter?** voulez-vous du beurre?; **may I have some salad?** puis-je avoir de la salade?; **can you lend me some money?** est-ce que tu peux me prêter de l'argent?; 2 (followed by a plural noun) des; **I've bought some apples** j'ai acheté des pommes; 3 (referring to something that has been mentioned) en; **'would you like butter?' – 'thanks, I've got some'** 'veux-tu du beurre?' – 'merci, j'en ai'; **he's eaten some of it** il en a mangé un peu; 4 **some people think he's wrong** il y a des gens qui pensent qu'il a tort; 5 **some day** un de ces jours.

somebody, someone pronoun quelqu'un; **there's somebody in the garden** il y a quelqu'un dans le jardin.

somehow adverb 1 d'une manière ou d'une autre; **I've got to finish this essay somehow** je dois finir cette rédaction d'une manière ou d'une autre; 2 **I somehow think they won't come** quelque chose me dit qu'ils ne viendront pas.

somersault noun 1 (child's) galipette Fem.; 2 (gymnast's) roulade Fem.; 3 (diver's) saut Masc. périlleux.

something pronoun quelque chose; **I've got something to tell you** j'ai quelque chose à te dire; **something pretty** quelque chose de joli; **something interesting** quelque chose d'intéressant; **there's something wrong** il y a quelque chose qui ne va pas; **their house is really something!** leur maison c'est vraiment quelque chose!; **a guy called Colin something or other** un type qui s'appelle Colin quelque chose.

sometime adverb un de ces jours; **give me a ring sometime** appelle-

moi un de ces jours; **I'll ring you sometime next week** je t'appellerai dans le courant de la semaine prochaine.

sometimes adverb quelquefois; **I sometimes take the train** quelquefois je prends le train.

somewhere adverb quelque part; **I've put my bag down somewhere** j'ai posé mon sac quelque part; **I've met you somewhere before** je vous ai déjà vu quelque part.

son noun fils Masc.

song noun chanson Fem.

son-in-law noun gendre Masc.

soon adverb 1 bientôt; **it will soon be the holidays** c'est bientôt les vacances; **see you soon!** à bientôt; 2 **as soon as** dès que; **as soon as she arrives** dès qu'elle arrivera; **as soon as possible** dès que possible; 3 **it's too soon** c'est trop tôt.

sooner adverb 1 plus tôt; **we should have started sooner** nous aurions dû commencer plus tôt; 2 **I'd sooner wait** je préfère attendre; ★ **sooner or later** tôt ou tard.

soprano noun soprano Masc. & Fem.

sore noun plaie Fem.

sore adjective **to have a sore leg** avoir mal à la jambe; **to have a sore throat** avoir mal à la gorge; **my arm's sore** j'ai mal au bras; ★ **it's a sore point** c'est un sujet délicat.

sorry adjective 1 désolé; **I'm really sorry** je suis vraiment désolé; **sorry to disturb you** je suis désolé de vous déranger; **I'm sorry I**

a b c d e f g h i j k l m n o p q r s t u v w x y z

forgot your birthday je suis désolé d'avoir oublié ton anniversaire; **2 sorry!** excusez-moi!; **3 sorry?** comment?; **4 to feel sorry for somebody** plaindre [31] quelqu'un.

sort noun sorte Fem.; **what sort of music do you like?** tu aimes quelle sorte de musique?; **all sorts of** toutes sortes de; **for all sorts of reasons** pour toutes sortes de raisons.

● **to sort something out 1** mettre [11] de l'ordre dans (room, desk, papers, possessions); **I must sort out my room tonight** je dois mettre de l'ordre dans ma chambre ce soir; **2** s'occuper [1] de (problem, arrangement); **Liz is sorting it out** Liz s'en occupe.

so-so adjective moyen (Fem. moyenne); **'how was the film?' – 'so-so'** 'c'était comment le film?' – 'moyen'.

soul noun **1** âme Fem.; **2** (music) soul Masc.

sound noun **1** (noise) bruit ; **the sound of voices** le bruit des voix; **2** (volume) volume; **to turn down the sound** baisser le volume.

sound verb **it sounds easy** ça a l'air facile; **it sounds as if she's happy** elle a l'air d'être heureuse.

sound asleep adjective profondément endormi.

sound effect noun effet Masc. sonore.

soundtrack noun bande Fem. sonore.

soup noun soupe Fem.; **mushroom soup** la soupe aux champignons.

soup plate noun assiette Fem. creuse la soupe.

soup spoon noun cuillère Fem. à soupe.

sour adjective **1** (taste) aigre; **2 the milk has gone sour** le lait a tourné.

south noun sud Masc.; **in the south** au sud.

south adjective, adverb sud (never agrees); **the south side** le côté sud; **a south wind** un vent du sud; **south of Paris** au sud de Paris.

South Africa noun Afrique Fem. du Sud.

South America noun Amérique Fem. du Sud.

South American noun Sud-Américain Masc., Sud-Américaine Fem.

South American adjective sud-américain.

southeast noun sud-est Masc.

southeast adjective **in southeast England** au sud-est de l'Angleterre.

South Pole noun pôle Masc. Sud.

southwest noun sud-ouest Masc.

southwest adjective **in southwest England** au sud-ouest de l'Angleterre.

souvenir noun souvenir Masc.

soya noun soja Masc.

soy sauce noun sauce Fem. de soja.

space noun **1** (room) place Fem.; **is there enough space?** est-ce qu'il y a de la place?; **there's enough space for two** il y a de la place pour deux; **2** (gap) espace Masc.; **leave a space** laissez un espace; **3** (outer *space*) espace Masc.; **in space** dans l'espace.

spacecraft noun engin Masc. spatial.

spade noun **1** pelle Fem.; **2** (*in cards*) pique Masc.; **the queen of spades** la reine de pique.

spaghetti noun spaghetti Masc. plural.

Spain noun Espagne Fem.; **in Spain** en Espagne; **to Spain** en Espagne.

Spaniard noun Espagnol Masc., Espagnole Fem.

spaniel noun épagneul Masc.

Spanish noun **1** (*language*) espagnol Masc.; **I'm learning Spanish** j'apprends l'espagnol; **2 the Spanish** (*people*) les Espagnols Masc. plural.

Spanish adjective espagnol; **Pedro is Spanish** Pedro est espagnol.

spank verb **to spank somebody** donner [1] une fessée à quelqu'un.

spanner noun clé Fem. anglaise.

spare adjective (*part, battery*) de rechange; **we have a spare ticket** nous avons un billet de trop.

spare verb **I can't spare the time** je n'ai pas le temps; **can you spare a moment?** est-ce que tu as un instant?

spare part noun pièce Fem. de rechange.

spare room noun chambre Fem. d'amis.

spare time noun temps Masc. libre; **in my spare time** dans mon temps libre.

spare wheel noun roue Fem. de secours.

sparkling adjective **sparkling (mineral) water** l'eau (minérale) pétillante; **sparkling wine** le vin mousseux.

sparrow noun moineau Masc. (*plural* moineaux).

speak verb **1** parler [1]; **do you speak French?** est-ce que vous parlez français?; **spoken French** le français parlé; **2 to speak to somebody** parler [1] à quelqu'un; **she's speaking to Mike** elle parle à Mike; **I've never spoken to her** je ne lui ai jamais parlé; **I'll speak to him about it** je vais lui en parler; **3 who's speaking?** (*on the phone*) c'est qui à l'appareil?

speaker noun **1** (*on a music system*) enceinte Fem.; **2** (*at a public lecture*) conférencier Masc., conférencière Fem.; **3** (*of a language*) **a French speaker** un/ une francophone; **an English speaker** un/une anglophone.

spear noun lance Fem.

special adjective spécial (Masc. plural spéciaux).

specialist noun spécialiste Masc. & Fem.

specialize verb **to specialize in** être [6] spécialisé dans; **we specialize in French cars** nous sommes spécialisés dans les voitures françaises.

specially adverb **1** spécialement; **not specially** pas spécialement; **the poems have been specially chosen for small children** les poèmes ont été spécialement choisis pour les petits enfants; **2** (*specifically*) exprès; **I came**

a b c d e f g h i j k l m n o p q r s t u v w x y z

a
b
c
d
e
f
g
h
i
j
k
l
m
n
o
p
q
r
s
t
u
v
w
x
y
z

specially in order to see you je suis venu exprès pour te voir; **I made this cake specially for you** j'ai fait ce gâteau exprès pour toi.

species noun espèce Fem.

specific adjective précis.

spectacles noun lunettes Fem. plural.

spectacular adjective spectaculaire.

spectator noun spectateur Masc., spectatrice Fem.

speech noun discours Masc.; **to make a speech** faire un discours.

speechless adjective muet (Fem. muette); **to be speechless with rage** rester muet de colère; **I was speechless** j'étais stupéfait.

speed noun vitesse Fem.; **at top speed** à toute vitesse; **what speed was he doing?** il roulait à quelle vitesse?; **a twelve-speed bike** un vélo à douze vitesses.

● **to speed up** accélérer [24].

speeding noun excès Masc. de vitesse; **he was fined for speeding** il a reçu une contravention pour excès de vitesse.

speed limit noun limitation Fem. de vitesse.

spell noun (of time) période Fem.; **a cold spell** une période de temps froid; **sunny spells** des éclaircies Fem. plural.

spell verb 1 (in writing) écrire [38]; **how do you spell it?** ça s'écrit comment?; **how do you spell your surname?** ça s'écrit comment, ton nom de famille?; 2 (out loud) épeler [18].

spell checker noun correcteur Masc. orthographique.

spelling noun orthographe Fem.; **a spelling mistake** une faute d'orthographe.

spend verb 1 dépenser [1] (money); **I've spent all my money** j'ai dépensé tout mon argent; 2 passer [1] (time); **we spent three days in Paris** nous avons passé trois jours à Paris; **she spends her time writing letters** elle passe son temps à écrire des lettres.

spice noun épice Fem.

spicy adjective épicé; **he doesn't like spicy food** il n'aime pas les choses épicées.

spider noun araignée Fem.

spill verb renverser [1]; **I've spilled my wine on the carpet** j'ai renversé mon vin sur la moquette.

spinach noun épinards Masc. plural; **do you like spinach?** est-ce que tu aimes les épinards?

spine noun colonne Fem. vertébrale.

spiral noun spirale Fem.

spiral staircase noun escalier Masc. en colimaçon.

spire noun flèche Fem.

spirit noun 1 (energy) énergie Fem.; 2 **to get into the spirit of the occasion** se mettre dans l'ambiance.

spirits noun 1 (alcohol) alcools Masc. plural forts; 2 **to be in good spirits** être de bonne humeur.

spit verb cracher [1]; **to spit something out** cracher quelque chose.

spite *noun* **1 in spite of** malgré; **we decided to go in spite of the rain** nous avons décidé d'y aller malgré la pluie; **2** (*nastiness*) méchanceté *Fem.*; **to do something out of spite** faire quelque chose par méchanceté.

spiteful *adjective* méchant.

splash *noun* **1** (*noise*) plouf *Masc.*; **2 a splash of colour** une touche de couleur.

splash *verb* éclabousser [1].

splendid *adjective* splendide.

splinter *noun* écharde *Fem.*

split *verb* **1** (*with an axe or a knife*) fendre [3]; **to split a piece of wood** fendre un morceau de bois; **2** (*come apart*) se fendre [3]; **the lining has split** la doublure s'est fendue; **3** (*divide up*) partager [52]; **they split the money between them** ils ont partagé l'argent entre eux.

● **to split up 1** (*a couple or group*) se séparer [1]; **2 she's split up with her boyfriend** elle a rompu avec son copain.

spoil *verb* **1** gâcher [1]; **it completely spoiled the evening** ça a complètement gâché la soirée; **to spoil the surprise** gâcher la surprise; **2** gâter [1] (*a child*).

spoiled *adjective* gâté; **a spoiled child** un enfant gâté.

spoilsport *noun* trouble-fête *Masc. & Fem.*

spoke *noun* (*of a wheel*) rayon *Masc.*

spokesman *noun* porte-parole *Masc.* (*plural* **porte-parole**).

spokeswoman *noun* porte-parole *Masc.* (*plural* **porte-parole**).

sponge *noun* éponge *Fem.*

sponge bag *noun* trousse *Fem.* de toilette.

sponge cake *noun* génoise *Fem.*

sponsor *noun* sponsor *Masc.*

sponsor *verb* sponsoriser [1].

spontaneous *adjective* spontané.

spooky *adjective* **1** (*atmosphere*) sinistre; **2 a spooky story** une histoire qui fait froid dans le dos.

spoon *noun* cuillère *Fem.*; **a soup spoon** une cuillère à soupe; **a teaspoon** une petite cuillère.

spoonful *noun* cuillère *Fem.*

sport *noun* sport *Masc.*; **to be good at sport** être bon en sport; **my favourite sport** mon sport préféré.

sports bag *noun* sac *Masc.* de sport.

sports car *noun* voiture *Fem.* de sport.

sports centre *noun* centre *Masc.* sportif.

sports club *noun* club *Masc.* sportif.

sportsman *noun* sportif *Masc.*

sportswear *noun* vêtements *Masc. plural* de sport.

sportswoman *noun* sportive *Fem.*

sporty *adjective* sportif (*Fem.* sportive); **she's very sporty** elle est très sportive.

spot *noun* **1** (*in fabric*) pois *Masc.*; **a red tie with black spots** une cravate rouge aux pois noirs; **2** (*on your skin*) bouton; **I've got spots** j'ai des boutons; **to be covered in spots** être couvert de boutons; **3** (*stain*) tache *Fem.*; **you've got a spot on your tie** tu as une tache sur ta cravate; **4** (*spotlight*)

spot projecteur *Masc.*; (*in the home*) spot *Masc.*; **5 on the spot** (*immediately*) sur-le-champ; **we'll do it for you on the spot** nous le ferons sur-le-champ; **6** (*at hand*) sur place; **they have experts on the spot** ils ont des experts sur place.

spot *verb* repérer [24]; **I spotted her in the crowd** je l'ai repérée dans la foule.

spotless *adjective* impeccable.

spotlight *noun* **1** projecteur *Masc.*; **2** (*in the home*) spot *Masc.*

spotty *adjective* (*pimply*) boutonneux (*Fem.* boutonneuse).

spouse *noun* époux *Masc.*, épouse *Fem.*

sprain *noun* entorse *Fem.*

sprain *verb* **to sprain your ankle** se faire [10] une entorse à la cheville.

spray *noun* (*spray can*) bombe *Fem.*

spray *verb* vaporiser [1] (*liquid*).

spread *noun* pâte *Fem.* à tartiner; **cheese spread** le fromage à tartiner.

spread *verb* **1** (*news or a disease*) se propager [52]; **2** étaler [1] (*butter, jam, cement, glue, etc.*).

spreadsheet *noun* (*on a computer*) tableur *Masc.*

spring *noun* **1** (*the season*) printemps *Masc.*; **in the spring** au printemps; **spring flowers** les fleurs du printemps; **2** (*made of metal*) ressort *Masc.*; **3** (*providing water*) source *Fem.*

spring-cleaning *noun* grand nettoyage *Masc.* de printemps.

springtime *noun* printemps *Masc.*; **in springtime** au printemps.

spring water *noun* eau *Fem.* de source.

sprint *noun* sprint *Masc.*

sprint *verb* courir [2] à toute vitesse.

sprinter *noun* sprinteur *Masc.*, sprinteuse *Fem.*

sprout *noun* (*Brussels sprout*) chou *Masc.* de Bruxelles (*plural* **choux de Bruxelles**).

spy *noun* espion *Masc.*, espionne *Fem.*

spy *verb* **to spy on somebody** espionner [1] quelqu'un.

spying *noun* espionnage *Masc.*

squabble *verb* se disputer [1].

square *noun* **1** (*shape*) carré *Masc.*; **2** (*in a town or village*) place *Fem.*; **the village square** la place du village; ★ **to go back to square one** retourner à la case départ.

square *adjective* carré; **a square box** une boîte carrée; **three square metres** trois mètres carrés; **the room is four metres square** la pièce fait quatre mètres carrés.

squash *noun* **1** (*drink*) sirop *Masc.*; **orange squash** le sirop d'orange; **2** (*sport*) squash *Masc.*; **to play squash** jouer au squash.

squeak *verb* **1** (*door, hinge*) grincer [61]; **2** (*person, animal*) pousser [1] un petit cri.

squeeze *verb* **1** serrer [1] (*somebody's arm, hand, etc*); **2** presser [1] (*toothpaste*).

squid *noun* calmar *Masc.*

squirrel *noun* écureuil *Masc.*

stab *verb* poignarder [1].

stable *noun* écurie *Fem.*

stable *adjective* stable.

stack noun **1** (pile) pile Fem.; **2** stacks of plein de; **she's got stacks of CDs** elle a plein de CD.

stadium noun stade Masc.

staff noun **1** (of a company) personnel Masc.; **2** (in a school) professeurs Masc. plural.

stage noun **1** (for a performance) scène Fem.; **on stage** sur scène; **2** (phase) stade Masc.; **at this stage of the project** à ce stade du projet; **at this stage it's hard to know** pour l'instant il est difficile de savoir.

staggered adjective (amazed) stupéfié.

stain noun tache Fem.

stain verb tacher [1].

stainless steel noun inox Masc.; **a stainless steel sink** un évier en inox.

stair noun **1** (step) marche Fem.; **2** stairs escalier Masc.; **I met her on the stairs** je l'ai croisée dans l'escalier.

staircase noun escalier Masc.

stale adjective (bread) rassis.

stalemate noun (in chess) pat Masc.

stall noun **1** (at a market or fair) stand Masc.; **2** the stalls (in a theatre) l'orchestre Masc. singular.

stammer noun to have a stammer bégayer [59].

stammer verb bégayer [59].

stamp noun timbre Masc.

stamp verb **1** affranchir [2] (a letter); **2** to stamp your foot taper [1] du pied.

stamp album noun album Masc. de timbres.

stamp collection noun collection Fem. de timbres.

stand verb **1** être [6] debout; **several people were standing** plusieurs personnes étaient debout; **2** (when you say somebody is standing somewhere 'standing' is not usually translated)** we were standing outside the cinema nous étions devant le cinéma; **I'm standing here waiting for you** je suis là en train de t'attendre; **3** (bear) supporter [1]; **I can't stand her** je ne la supporte pas; **I can't stand waiting** je ne supporte pas d'attendre.

● **to stand for something** (be short for) être [6] l'abréviation de; **'UN' stands for 'United Nations'** 'UN' est l'abréviation de 'United Nations'.

● **stand up** se lever [50]; **everybody stood up** tout le monde s'est levé.

standard noun niveau Masc.; **her work is of a high standard** son travail est d'un bon niveau; **the standard of living** le niveau de vie.

standard adjective standard; **the standard price** le prix standard.

Standard grades noun plural
You can explain Standard grades as follows: Ce sont des examens que les lycéens écossais passent à l'âge d'environ 16 ans dans six ou sept matières. La meilleure note que l'on peut obtenir est 1 et la note la plus basse est 7. Une fois qu'ils ont obtenu leurs Standard grades, de nombreux étudiants se préparent pour les Highers; SEE Highers.

stands noun (in a stadium) tribune Fem. singular.

staple noun agrafe Fem.

staple verb agrafer [1]; **to staple the pages together** agrafer les feuilles.

stapler noun agrafeuse Fem.

star noun 1 (in the sky) étoile Fem.; 2 (person) vedette; **he's a film star** c'est une vedette de cinéma.

star verb **to star in a film** être [6] la vedette d'un film.

stare verb regarder [1] fixement; **he was staring at me** il me regardait fixement; **what are you staring at?** qu'est-ce que tu regardes?

star sign noun signe Masc. astrologique; **what star sign are you?** de quel signe êtes-vous?

start noun 1 début Masc.; **at the start** au début; **at the start of the book** au début du livre; **from the start** dès le début; **we knew from the start that it was dangerous** nous savions dès le début que c'était dangereux; 2 **to make a start on something** commencer à faire quelque chose; **I've made a start on my homework** j'ai commencé à faire mes devoirs; 3 (of a race) départ Masc.

start verb 1 commencer [61]; **the film starts at eight** le film commence à huit heures; **I've started the book** j'ai commencé le livre; 2 **to start doing** commencer [61] à faire; **I've started learning Spanish** j'ai commencé à apprendre l'espagnol; 3 **to start a business** créer [32] une entreprise; 4 **to start a car** faire [10] démarrer une voiture; **she started the car** elle a fait démarrer la voiture; **the**

car wouldn't start la voiture n'a pas voulu démarrer.

starter noun (in a meal) entrée Fem.; **what would you like as a starter?** qu'est-ce que vous voulez comme entrée?

starve verb mourir [54] de faim; **I'm starving!** je meurs de faim!

state noun 1 état Masc.; **the house is in a very bad state** la maison est en très mauvais état; 2 (administrative) état Masc.; **the state** l'État; 3 **the States** les États-Unis Masc. plural; **they live in the States** ils habitent aux États-Unis.

state verb 1 déclarer [1] (intention, opinion); 2 indiquer [1] (address, income, occupation, reason, etc.).

stately home noun château Masc. (plural châteaux).

statement noun déclaration Fem.

station noun gare Fem.; **the railway station** la gare; **the bus station** la gare routière; **the police station** le commissariat; **a radio station** une station de radio.

stationary adjective à l'arrêt.

stationer's noun papeterie Fem.

stationery noun papeterie Fem.

statistics noun 1 (subject) statistique Fem.; 2 **the statistics** (figures) les statistiques.

statue noun statue Fem.

status noun position Fem.

stay noun séjour Masc.; **our stay in Paris** notre séjour à Paris; **enjoy your stay!** bon séjour!

stay verb 1 rester [1]; **I'll stay here** je reste ici; **how long are you staying?** vous restez combien de temps?; 2 (with time) **we're going**

to stay in Berlin for three days nous allons passer trois jours à Berlin; 3 (at somebody's house) to stay with somebody aller [7] chez quelqu'un; I'm going to stay with my sister this weekend je vais chez ma sœur ce weekend; 4 (be temporarily lodged) loger [52]; where are you staying? où est-ce que vous logez?

● to stay in rester [1] à la maison; I'm staying in tonight je reste à la maison ce soir.

steady adjective 1 stable; a steady job un emploi stable; 2 régulier (Fem. régulière); a steady increase une augmentation régulière; 3 (hand, voice) ferme; 4 to hold something steady bien tenir quelque chose.

steak noun steack Masc.; steak and chips un steack frites.

steal verb voler [1].

steam noun vapeur Fem.

steam engine noun locomotive Fem. à vapeur.

steam iron noun fer Masc. à vapeur.

steel noun acier Masc.

steep adjective raide; a steep slope une pente raide.

steeple noun 1 (spire) flèche Fem.; 2 (bell tower) clocher Masc.

steering wheel noun volant Masc.

step noun 1 pas Masc.; to take a step forwards faire un pas en avant; to take a step backwards faire un pas en arrière; 2 (stair) marche Fem.; 'mind the step' 'attention à la marche'.

● to step back faire [10] un pas en arrière.

● to step forward faire [10] un pas en avant.

● to step into entrer [1] dans (a lift).

stepbrother noun demi-frère Masc. (plural demi-frères).

stepdaughter noun belle-fille Fem. (plural belles-filles).

stepfather noun beau-père Masc.

stepladder noun escabeau Masc. (plural escabeaux).

stepmother noun belle-mère Fem.

stepsister noun demi-sœur Fem. (plural demi-sœurs).

stepson noun beau-fils Masc. (plural beaux-fils).

stereo noun chaîne Fem. stéréo (plural chaînes stéréo).

sterling noun sterling Masc.; in sterling en livres sterling.

stew noun ragoût Masc.

steward noun steward Masc.

stewardess noun hôtesse Fem.

stick noun 1 bâton Masc.; 2 a walking stick une canne; 3 a hockey stick une crosse de hockey.

stick verb 1 (with glue) coller [1]; 2 (put) mettre [11]; stick them on my desk mets-les sur mon bureau.

sticker noun autocollant Masc.

sticky adjective 1 poisseux (Fem. poisseuse); my hands are sticky j'ai les mains poisseuses; 2 adhésif (Fem. adhésive); sticky paper le papier adhésif.

sticky tape noun Scotch™ Masc.

stiff adjective 1 to feel stiff avoir [5] des courbatures; to have stiff legs

a b c d e f g h i j k l m n o p q r s t u v w x y z

avoir des courbatures dans les jambes; **2 to be bored stiff** s'ennuyer [41] à mourir; **to be scared stiff** être [6] mort de peur.

still *adjective* **1 sit still!** tiens-toi tranquille!; **keep still!** ne bouge pas!; **2 still mineral water** l'eau minérale non-gazeuse.

still *adverb* **1** toujours; **do you still live in London?** est-ce que tu habites toujours à Londres?; **I've still not finished** je n'ai toujours pas fini; **he's still working** il est toujours en train de travailler; **2** encore; **there's still a lot of beer left** il reste encore beaucoup de bière; **3 better still** encore mieux.

sting *noun* piqûre Fem.; **a wasp sting** une piqûre de guêpe.

sting *verb* piquer [1]; **I was stung by a bee** je me suis fait piquer par une abeille.

stink *noun* odeur Fem.; **what a stink!** ça pue!

stink *verb* puer [1]; **it stinks of cigarette smoke in here** ça pue la cigarette ici.

stir *verb* remuer [1].

stitch *noun* **1** (in sewing) point Masc.; **2** (in knitting) maille Fem.; **3** (surgical) point Masc. de suture (*plural* **points de suture**).

stock *noun* **1** (in a shop) stock Masc.; **to have something in stock** avoir quelque chose en stock; **2** (supply) réserve; **I always have a stock of pencils** j'ai toujours une réserve de crayons; **3** (for cooking) bouillon; **chicken stock** le bouillon de poulet.

stock *verb* (in a shop) vendre [3]; **they don't stock dictionaries** ils ne vendent pas les dictionnaires.

● **to stock up on something** s'approvisionner [1] en quelque chose.

stock cube *noun* bouillon-cube Masc.

stock exchange *noun* Bourse Fem. (des valeurs).

stocking *noun* bas Masc.

stomach *noun* estomac Masc.

stomachache *noun* **to have stomachache** avoir mal au ventre.

stone *noun* **1** pierre Fem.; **a stone wall** un mur en pierre; **2** (pebble) caillou Masc.; **3** (in fruit) noyau Masc. (*plural* **noyaux**).

stool *noun* tabouret Masc.

stop *noun* arrêt Masc.; **the bus stop** l'arrêt de bus.

stop *verb* **1** s'arrêter [1]; **he stopped in front of the shop** il s'est arrêté devant le magasin; **the music stopped** la musique s'est arrêtée; **does the train stop in Dijon?** est-ce que le train s'arrête à Dijon?; **2 to stop somebody/something** arrêter [1] quelque chose/quelqu'un; **she stopped me in the street** elle m'a arrêté dans la rue; **3 to stop doing** arrêter [1] de faire; **he's stopped smoking** il a arrêté de fumer; **she never stops asking questions** elle n'arrête pas de poser des questions; **4 to stop somebody doing** empêcher [1] quelqu'un de faire; **there's nothing to stop you going on your own** rien ne t'empêche d'y aller tout seul.

stopwatch noun chronomètre Masc.

store noun (shop) magasin Masc.

store verb 1 garder [1]; 2 (on a computer) mémoriser [1].

storey noun étage Masc.; **a three-storey house** une maison à trois étages.

stork noun cigogne Fem.

storm noun 1 (wind) tempête Fem.; **a snowstorm** une tempête de neige; **a rainstorm** une tempête de pluie; 2 (thunderstorm) orage Masc.

stormy adjective orageux (Fem. orageuse).

story noun histoire Fem.; **to tell a story** raconter une histoire.

stove noun (cooker) cuisinière Fem.

straight adjective 1 droit; **a straight line** une ligne droite; 2 **to have straight hair** avoir les cheveux raides.

straight adverb 1 (in direction) droit; **go straight ahead** continuez tout droit; 2 (in time) directement; **he went straight to the doctor's** il est allé directement chez le médecin; 3 **straight away** tout de suite.

straightforward adjective simple.

strain noun stress Masc.; **the strain of the last few weeks** le stress de ces dernières semaines; **to be a strain** être stressant.

strain verb 1 se faire [10] mal à (part of the body); **he's strained his back** il s'est fait mal au dos; 2 (a muscle) se froisser [1]; 3 (vegetables, rice) égoutter [1].

strange adjective bizarre; **a strange situation** une situation bizarre.

stranger noun inconnu Masc., inconnue Fem.

strangle verb étrangler [1].

strap noun 1 (on case, bag, camera) courroie Fem.; 2 (on a garment) bretelle Fem.; 3 (of a watch) bracelet Masc.; **a watchstrap** un bracelet de montre; 4 (on a shoe) lanière Fem.

strapless adjective sans bretelles.

straw noun paille Fem. (both the material and for drinking with); **a straw hat** un chapeau de paille.

strawberry noun fraise Fem.; **strawberry jam** la confiture de fraises; **a strawberry yoghurt** un yaourt à la fraise.

stray adjective **a stray dog** un chien perdu.

stream noun (small river) ruisseau Masc. (plural ruisseaux).

street noun rue Fem.; **I met Simon in the street** j'ai croisé Simon dans la rue.

streetlamp noun réverbère Masc.

street map noun plan Masc. de la ville.

streetwise adjective dégourdi.

strength noun force Fem.

stress noun stress Masc.

stress verb (emphasize) souligner [1]; **to stress the importance of something** souligner l'importance de quelque chose.

stretch verb 1 (garment) se déformer [1]; **this jumper has**

a b c d e f g h i j k l m n o p q r s t u v w x y z

stretched ce pull s'est déformé; **2** (shoes) s'élargir [2].

stretcher noun brancard Masc.

stretchy adjective élastique.

strict adjective strict.

strike noun grève Fem.; **to go on strike** faire grève; **to be on strike** être en grève.

strike verb **1** (hit) frapper [1]; **2** (clock) sonner [1]; **the clock struck six** l'horloge a sonné six heures; **3** (go on strike) faire [10] grève.

striker noun **1** (in football) buteur Masc.; **2** (person on strike) gréviste Masc. & Fem.

striking adjective frappant; **a striking resemblance** une ressemblance frappante.

string noun **1** (for tying) ficelle Fem.; **2** (for a musical instrument) corde Fem.

strip noun bande Fem.

strip verb (undress) se déshabiller [1].

strip cartoon noun bande Fem. dessinée.

stripe noun rayure Fem.

striped adjective rayé.

stroke noun **1** (style of swimming) nage Fem.; **2** (medical) attaque Fem.; **to have a stroke** avoir une attaque; ★ **a stroke of luck** un coup de chance.

stroke verb caresser [1].

stroll noun **to go for a stroll** faire une petite promenade.

stroll verb se promener [50].

strong adjective **1** (person, drink) fort; **2** (feeling) puissant; **3** (material) solide.

strongly adverb **1** (believe) fermement; **2** (support) fortement; **3** (advise, oppose) vivement.

struggle noun **1** lutte Fem.; **the struggle for independence** la lutte pour l'indépendance; **a power struggle** une lutte pour le pouvoir; **2** it's been a struggle ça a été très dur.

struggle verb **1** (to obtain something) se battre [21]; **they have struggled to survive** ils se sont battus pour survivre; **2** (physically, in order to escape or reach something) se débattre [21]; **3** (have difficulty in doing) avoir [5] du mal à faire; **I'm struggling to finish my homework** j'ai du mal à finir mes devoirs.

stub noun **a cigarette stub** un mégot.

● **to stub out** écraser [1] (a cigarette).

stubborn adjective têtu.

stuck adjective **1** (jammed) coincé; **the drawer's stuck** le tiroir est coincé; **2** (person) **to get stuck** rester coincé (in a lift, traffic jam, or place).

stud noun **1** (on a belt or jacket) clou Masc.; **2** (on a boot) clou Masc.; **3** (earring) boucle Fem. d'oreille.

student noun étudiant Masc., étudiante Fem.

studio noun **1** (film, TV) studio Masc.; **2** (artist's) atelier Masc.

studio flat noun studio Masc.

study verb **1** réviser [1]; **he's busy studying for his exams** il est en train de réviser pour ses examens; **2** faire [10] des études de (a subject);

she's studying medicine elle fait des études de médecine.

stuff noun 1 (things) trucs Masc. plural (informal); **we can put all that stuff in the attic** on peut mettre tous ces trucs au grenier; 2 (personal belongings) affaires Fem. plural; **you can leave your stuff at my house** tu peux laisser tes affaires chez moi; 3 (substance) truc Masc. (informal); **some antiseptic stuff** un truc antiseptique.

stuff verb 1 (shove) fourrer [1] (informal); **she stuffed some things into a suitcase** elle a fourré quelques affaires dans une valise; 2 farcir [2] (chicken, turkey, vegetables); **stuffed aubergines** des aubergines farcies.

stuffing noun (for cooking) farce Fem.

stuffy adjective (airless) étouffant.

stumble verb (trip) trébucher [1].

stunned adjective (amazed) stupéfait.

stunning adjective sensationnel (Fem. sensationnelle).

stunt noun (in a film) cascade Fem.

stuntman noun cascadeur Masc.

stuntwoman noun cascadeuse Fem.

stupid adjective bête; **that was really stupid** c'était vraiment bête; **to do something stupid** faire une bêtise.

stutter noun **to have a stutter** bégayer [59].

stutter verb bégayer [59].

style noun 1 style Masc.; **a style of living** un style de vie; **he has his** own style il a son propre style; 2 (fashion) mode Fem.; **it's the latest style** c'est la dernière mode.

subject noun 1 sujet Masc.; **the subject of my talk** le sujet de mon exposé; 2 (at school) matière Fem.; **my favourite subject is biology** ma matière préférée c'est la biologie.

submarine noun sous-marin Masc. (plural **sous-marins**).

subscription noun abonnement Masc.; **to take out a subscription to** s'abonner à.

subsidy noun subvention Fem.

substance noun substance Fem.

substitute noun (person) remplaçant Masc., remplaçante Fem.

substitute verb substituer [1].

subtitled adjective (film) sous-titré.

subtitles plural noun sous-titres Masc. plural.

subtle adjective subtil.

subtract verb soustraire [78].

suburb noun banlieue Fem.; **a suburb of Edinburgh** une banlieue d'Édimbourg; **in the suburbs of London** dans la banlieue de Londres.

suburban adjective de banlieue.

subway noun (underpass) passage Masc. souterrain.

succeed verb réussir [2]; **to succeed in doing** réussir à faire; **we've succeeded in contacting her** nous avons réussi à la contacter.

a
b
c
d
e
f
g
h
i
j
k
l
m
n
o
p
q
r
s
t
u
v
w
x
y
z

success noun succès Masc.; **a great success** un grand succès.

successful adjective **1** réussi; **he's a successful writer** c'est un écrivain à succès; **2 to be successful in doing** réussir à faire.

successfully adverb avec succès.

such adverb **1** tellement; **they're such nice people!** ils sont tellement gentils!; **I've had such a busy day!** j'ai eu une journée tellement chargée!; **it's such a long way** c'est tellement loin; **it's such a pity** c'est tellement dommage; **2 such a lot of** tellement de; **I've got such a lot of things to tell you!** j'ai tellement de choses à te dire!; **3 such as** comme; **in big cities such as Glasgow** dans les grandes villes comme Glasgow; **4 there's no such thing** ça n'existe pas.

suck verb sucer [61].

sudden adjective soudain; ★ **all of a sudden** tout d'un coup.

suddenly adverb **1** tout d'un coup; **he suddenly started to laugh** tout d'un coup il s'est mis à rire; **suddenly the light went out** tout d'un coup la lumière s'est éteinte; **2 to die suddenly** mourir subitement.

suede noun daim Masc.; **a suede jacket** une veste en daim.

suffer verb souffrir [73].

sufficiently adverb suffisamment.

sugar noun sucre Masc.; **would you like sugar?** est-ce que tu veux du sucre?; **brown sugar** le sucre roux.

suggest verb suggérer [24]; **he suggested I should speak to you abou it** il m'a suggéré de vous en parler.

suggestion noun suggestion Fem.; **to make a suggestion** faire une suggestion.

suicide noun suicide Masc.; **to commit suicide** se suicider.

suit noun **1** (man's) costume Masc.; **2** (woman's) tailleur Masc.

suitable adjective **1** (clothing) approprié; **I don't have any suitable shoes** je n'ai pas de chaussures appropriées; **2** convenable; **a suitable hotel** un hôtel convenable; **3 to be suitable for** convenir à.

suitcase noun valise Fem.

sulk verb bouder [1].

sum noun **1** somme Fem.; **a sum of money** une somme d'argent; **a large sum** une grosse somme; **2** (calculation) calcul Masc.

● **to sum up** résumer [1].

summarize verb résumer [1].

summary noun résumé Masc.

summer noun été Masc.; **in summer** en été; **summer clothes** les vêtements d'été; **the summer holidays** les grandes vacances.

summertime noun été Masc.; **in summertime** en été.

summit noun sommet Masc.

sun noun soleil Masc.; **in the sun** au soleil.

sunbathe verb se bronzer [1].

sunblock noun crème Fem. écran total.

sunburn noun coup Masc. de soleil.

a
b
c
d
e
f
g
h
i
j
k
l
m
n
o
p
q
r
s
t
u
v
w
x
y
z

sunburned adjective **1** (tanned) bronzé; **2 to get sunburned** (burned) attraper un coup de soleil.

Sunday noun dimanche Masc.; **on Sunday** dimanche; **I'm going out on Sunday** je sors dimanche; **see you on Sunday!** à dimanche!; **on Sundays** le dimanche; **the museum is closed on Sundays** le musée est fermé le dimanche; **every Sunday** tous les dimanches; **last Sunday** dimanche dernier; **next Sunday** dimanche prochain.

sunflower noun tournesol Masc.; **sunflower oil** l'huile Fem. de tournesol.

sunglasses plural noun lunettes Fem. plural de soleil.

sunlight noun soleil Masc.

sunny adjective **1 it's a sunny day** il fait du soleil; **it's going to be sunny** il va faire du soleil; **2** (place) ensoleillé; **in a sunny corner of the garden** dans un coin ensoleillé du jardin.

sunrise noun lever Masc. du soleil.

sunroof noun toit Masc. ouvrant.

sunset noun coucher Masc. du soleil.

sunshine noun soleil Masc.

sunstroke noun insolation Fem.; **to get sunstroke** attraper une insolation.

suntan noun bronzage Masc.; **to get a suntan** bronzer.

suntan lotion noun lotion Fem. solaire.

suntan oil noun huile Fem. solaire.

super adjective formidable; **we had a super time!** c'était formidable!

supermarket noun supermarché Masc.

supernatural adjective surnaturel (Fem. surnaturelle).

superstitious adjective superstitieux (Fem. superstitieuse).

supervise verb surveiller [1].

supervisor noun **1** (in a shop) responsable Masc. & Fem.; **2** (in a factory) contremaître Masc.

supper noun dîner Masc.; **I had supper at Sandy's** j'ai dîné chez Sandy.

supplement noun supplément Masc.

supplies plural noun (of food) provisions Fem. plural.

supply noun **1** (stock) réserves Fem. plural; **2 to be in short supply** être difficile à trouver.

supply verb fournir [2]; **the school supplies the paper** c'est l'école qui fournit le papier; **to supply somebody with something** fournir quelque chose à quelqu'un.

supply teacher noun suppléant Masc., suppléante Fem.

support noun soutien Masc.; **he has a lot of support** il a beaucoup de soutien.

support verb **1** (back up) soutenir [77]; **her teachers have really supported her** ses professeurs l'ont vraiment soutenue; **2** être [6] supporter de (a team); **Graeme supports Liverpool** Graeme est supporter de Liverpool; **3** (financially) **to support a family** subvenir [81] aux besoins d'une famille.

a **supporter** noun supporter Masc.; a
  Manchester United supporter un
  supporter de Manchester United.

b **suppose** verb **I suppose she's**
  forgotten elle a sans doute oublié.

c

d **supposed** adjective **to be**
  supposed to do être censé faire;
  you're supposed to wear a helmet
e on est censé porter un casque; **he**
  was supposed to be here at six il
f devait être là à six heures.

g **sure** adjective sûr; **are you sure?** tu
  es sûr?; **are you sure you've had**
h **enough to eat?** tu es sûr que tu as
  assez mangé?; **are you sure you**
i **saw her?** tu es sûr de l'avoir vue?;
  'can you shut the door?' – 'sure!'
j 'peux-tu fermer la porte?' – 'bien
  sûr!'

k
l **surely** adverb quand même; **surely**
  she couldn't have forgotten! elle
m ne peut pas avoir oublié quand
  même!

n **surf** noun écume Fem.

o **surf** verb **to surf the Net/Web**
  surfer [1] Internet/le web.

p **surface** noun surface Fem.

q **surfboard** noun planche Fem. de
  surf (plural planches de surf).

r
s **surfer** noun **1** (on the sea) surfeur
  Masc., surfeuse Fem.; **2** (on the Net)
t cybernaute Masc. & Fem.,
  internaute Masc. & Fem.

u **surfing** noun surf Masc.; **to go**
  surfing faire du surf.

v
w **surgeon** noun chirurgien Masc.;
  she's a surgeon elle est
x chirurgien.

y **surgery** noun **1** (procedure)
  chirurgie Fem.; **to have surgery** se
z faire opérer; **laser surgery** la

chirurgie au laser; **2** (doctor's)
cabinet Masc. médical; **the**
dentist's surgery le cabinet
dentaire.

surname noun nom Masc. de
famille (plural noms de famille).

surprise noun surprise Fem.; **what**
a surprise! quelle surprise!

surprised adjective étonné; **I was**
surprised to see her j'ai été étonné
de la voir.

surprising adjective étonnant.

surrender verb **1** (soldiers) se
rendre [3]; **2** (country) capituler [1];
3 livrer [1] (a town, castle).

surrender noun (by sportsman)
abandon Masc.; (by army)
capitulation Fem.

surround verb **1** encercler [1]; **2 to**
be surrounded by être [6] entouré
de; **she's surrounded by friends**
elle est entourée d'amis.

survey noun enquête Fem.

survive verb survivre [82].

survivor noun survivant Masc.,
survivante Fem.

suspect noun suspect Masc.,
suspecte Fem.

suspect adjective douteux (Fem.
douteuse).

suspect verb soupçonner [1].

suspend verb **1** (hang) suspendre
[3]; **2 to be suspended** (from
school) être [6] exclu.

suspense noun suspense Masc.

suspicious adjective **1** méfiant; **to**
be suspicious of se méfier de; **2 a**
suspicious parcel un paquet
suspect; **3 a suspicious-looking**
individual un individu louche.

swallow noun (bird) hirondelle Fem.

swallow verb avaler.

swan noun cygne Masc.

swap verb 1 échanger [52]; **do you want to swap?** tu veux qu'on échange?; **he's swapped his bike for a computer** il a échangé son vélo contre un ordinateur; **2 to swap seats with somebody** changer [52] de place avec quelqu'un.

swear verb (use bad language) utiliser [1] des gros mots; **he swears a lot** il utilise beaucoup de gros mots.

swearword noun gros mot Masc.

sweat noun transpiration Fem.

sweat verb transpirer [1].

sweater noun pull Masc.

sweatshirt noun sweatshirt Masc.

swede noun (vegetable) rutabaga Masc.

Swede noun Suédois Masc., Suédoise Fem.

Sweden noun Suède Fem.; **in Sweden** en Suède; **to Sweden** en Suède.

Swedish noun (language) suédois Masc.

Swedish adjective suédois.

sweep verb balayer [59].

sweet noun 1 bonbon Masc.; **I bought her some sweets** je lui ai acheté des bonbons; **2** (dessert) dessert Masc.

sweet adjective 1 (food) sucré; **I try not to eat sweet things** j'essaie d'éviter les choses sucrées; **2** (kind) gentil (Fem. gentille); **she's a really sweet person** elle est vraiment

gentille; **it was really sweet of him** c'était vraiment gentil de sa part; **3** (cute) mignon (Fem. mignonne); **he looks really sweet in that hat!** il est mignon avec ce chapeau!

sweetcorn noun maïs Masc.

swell verb (part of the body) enfler [1].

swelling noun enflure Fem.; **he has a swelling on his knee** il a le genou enflé.

swerve verb faire [10] un écart; **the car swerved to avoid the dog** la voiture a fait un écart pour éviter le chien.

swim noun to go for a swim aller [7] se baigner.

swim verb nager [52]; **can he swim?** est-ce qu'il sait nager?; **to swim across a lake** traverser [1] un lac à la nage.

swimmer noun nageur Masc., nageuse Fem.; **she's a strong swimmer** c'est une bonne nageuse.

swimming noun natation Fem.; **to go swimming** faire de la natation.

swimming cap noun bonnet Masc. de bain.

swimming costume noun maillot Masc. de bain.

swimming pool noun piscine Fem.

swimming trunks noun maillot Masc. de bain.

swimsuit noun maillot Masc. de bain.

swindle noun escroquerie Fem.; **what a swindle!** quelle escroquerie!

swing noun balançoire Fem.

a b c d e f g h i j k l m n o p q r s t u v w x y z

Swiss noun (person) Suisse Masc. & Fem.; **the Swiss** les Suisses Masc. plural.

Swiss adjective suisse.

switch noun 1 (button type: electrical) bouton Masc.; 2 (up-down type) interrupteur Masc.

switch verb (change) changer [52] de; **to switch places** changer de place.

● **to switch something off** éteindre [60] quelque chose.

● **to switch something on** allumer [1] quelque chose.

Switzerland noun Suisse Fem.; **in Switzerland** en Suisse; **to Switzerland** en Suisse.

swollen adjective enflé.

swop verb SEE **swap**.

sword noun épée Fem.

swordfish noun espadon Masc.

sycamore noun sycomore Masc.

syllabus noun programme Masc.; **to be on the syllabus** être au programme.

symbol noun symbole Masc.

symbolic adjective symbolique.

sympathetic adjective compréhensif (Fem. compréhensive).

sympathize verb **to sympathize with somebody** comprendre [64] quelqu'un; **I sympathize with her** je la comprends.

sympathy noun compassion Fem.

symphony noun symphonie Fem.

symphony orchestra noun orchestre Masc. symphonique.

symptom noun symptôme Masc.

synagogue noun synagogue Fem.

synthesizer noun synthétiseur Masc.

synthetic adjective synthétique.

syringe noun seringue Fem.

system noun système Masc.

Tt

table noun table Fem.; **on the table** sur la table; **to lay the table** mettre la table; **to clear the table** débarrasser la table.

tablecloth noun nappe Fem.

table football noun baby-foot Masc.

tablemat noun 1 (for individual plates) set Masc. de table; 2 (for dish) dessous-de-plat Masc.

tablespoon noun grande cuillère Fem.; (in recipes) **a tablespoon of flour** une cuillère à soupe de farine.

tablet noun comprimé Masc.

table tennis noun ping-pong™ Masc.; **to play table tennis** jouer au ping-pong.

tabloid noun quotidien Masc. populaire.

tackle noun 1 (in football) tacle Masc.; 2 (in rugby) plaquage Masc.

tackle verb 1 (in football or hockey) tacler [1]; 2 s'attaquer [1] à (a job or problem).

tact noun tact Masc.

tactful adjective plein de tact; **that wasn't very tactful** ça a manqué un peu de tact.

tactic noun tactique Fem.

tadpole noun têtard Masc.

tail noun **1** queue Fem.; **2** 'heads or tails?' – 'tails' 'pile ou face?' – 'pile'.

tailor noun tailleur Masc.

take verb **1** prendre [64]; he took a chocolate il a pris un chocolat; take my hand prends ma main; I took the bus j'ai pris le bus; to take a holiday prendre des vacances; do you take sugar? est-ce que vous prenez du sucre?; who's taken my keys? qui a pris mes clefs?; it takes two hours ça prend deux heures; he took the news badly il a mal pris la nouvelle; **2** (to accompany) emmener [50] (a person); I'm taking Jake to the doctor's j'emmène Jake chez le médecin; I must take the car to the garage je dois emmener la voiture au garage; **3** (carry away) emporter [1]; she's taken some work to do at home elle a emporté du travail pour faire chez elle; **4** to take something up(stairs) monter [1] quelque chose; could you take these towels up? est-ce que tu peux monter ces serviettes?; **5** to take something down(stairs) descendre [3] quelque chose; Cheryl's taken the cups down Cheryl a descendu les tasses; **6** accepter [1] (a credit card or a cheque); do you take cheques? est-ce que vous acceptez les chèques?; **7** passer [1] (an exam); she's taking her driving test tomorrow elle passe son permis demain; **8** it takes a lot of courage il faut beaucoup de courage; **9** what size do you take? quelle taille faites-vous?

● to take something apart démonter [1] quelque chose.

● to take something back rapporter [1] quelque chose.

● to take off **1** (a plane) décoller [1]; **2** enlever [50] (clothes or shoes); he took off his shirt il a enlevé sa chemise; **3** déduire [26] (money); he took five pounds off the price il a déduit cinq livres du prix

● to take out **1** (from a bag or pocket) sortir [72]; Eric took out his wallet Eric a sorti son porte-feuille; **2** he's taking me out to lunch il m'emmène déjeuner; she took me out to the theatre elle m'a emmenée au théâtre

takeaway noun **1** (a meal) repas Masc. à emporter; an Indian takeaway un repas indien à emporter; **2** (where you buy it) restaurant Masc. qui fait des plats à emporter.

take-off noun décollage Masc. (of a plane).

tale noun histoire Fem.

talent noun talent Masc.; to have a talent for something être doué pour quelque chose.

talented adjective doué; he's really talented il est vraiment doué.

talk noun **1** (a chat) conversation Fem.; I had a talk with Roy about it j'ai eu une conversation avec Roy à ce sujet; **2** exposé Masc.; she's giving a talk on Hungary elle fait un exposé sur la Hongrie.

talk verb **1** parler [1]; I was talking to Jeevan about football je parlais du foot avec Jeevan; what's he talking about? de quoi parle-t-il?

a
b
c
d
e
f
g
h
i
j
k
l
m
n
o
p
q
r
s
t
u
v
w
x
y
z

talkative

parlera plus tard; **2** *(to gossip)*
bavarder [1]; **they're always
talking** ils n'arrêtent pas de
bavarder.

talkative *adjective* bavard; **he's
not exactly talkative!** on ne
pourrait pas dire qu'il est bavard!

tall *adjective* **1** grand; **she's very
tall** elle est très grande; **I'm 1.7
metres tall** je mesure un mètre
soixante-dix; **2** haut *(a building or
tree)*.

tambourine *noun* tambourin
Masc.

tame *adjective* apprivoisé *(an
animal)*.

tampon *noun* tampon *Masc.*

tan *noun* bronzage *Masc.*; **to get a
tan** bronzer.

tan *verb* bronzer [1]; **I tan easily** je
bronze facilement.

tangerine *noun* mandarine *Fem.*

tank *noun* **1** *(for petrol or water)*
réservoir *Masc.*; **2 a fish tank** un
aquarium; **3** *(military)* char *Masc.*

tanker *noun* **1** *(ship)* navire-
citerne *Masc.*; **2** *(on road)* camion-
citerne *Masc.*

tanned *adjective* bronzé.

tap *noun* **1** robinet *Masc.*; **to turn
on the tap** ouvrir le robinet; **to
turn off the tap** fermer le robinet;
the hot tap le robinet d'eau
chaude; **2** *(a pat)* petite tape *Fem.*

tap *verb* taper [1].

tap-dancing *noun* claquettes *Fem.
plural*; **to do tap-dancing** faire des
claquettes.

tape *noun* **1** cassette *Fem.*; **my tape
of the Stones** ma cassette des

Stones; **I've got it on tape** je l'ai en
cassette; **2 sticky tape** scotch™.

tape *verb* enregistrer [1]; **I want to
tape the film** je veux enregistrer le
film.

tape measure *noun* mètre *Masc.*
à ruban.

tape recorder *noun*
magnétophone *Masc.*

tapestry *noun* tapisserie *Fem.*

tar *noun* goudron *Masc.*

target *noun* cible *Fem.*

tart *noun* tarte *Fem.*; **a raspberry
tart** une tarte aux framboises.

tartan *adjective* écossais; **a tartan
skirt** une jupe écossaise.

task *noun* tâche *Fem.*

taste *noun* goût *Masc.*; **the taste of
onions** le goût des oignons; **in bad
taste** de mauvais goût.

taste *verb* **1** goûter [1]; **do you
want to taste?** tu veux goûter?; **the
soup tastes horrible** la soupe a un
goût infect; **2 to taste of** avoir [5]
un goût de; **it tastes of
strawberries** ça a un goût de
fraises.

tasty *adjective* savoureux *(Fem.
savoureuse)*.

tattoo *noun* tatouage *Masc.*; **he's
got a tattoo on his arm** il a un
tatouage sur le bras.

Taurus *noun* Taureau *Masc.*;
Josephine's Taurus Josephine est
Taureau.

tax *noun* **1** impôts *Masc. plural*; **2** *(on
goods)* taxe *Fem.*

taxi *noun* taxi *Masc.*; **by taxi** en taxi;
to take a taxi prendre un taxi.

Stones; **I've got it on tape** je l'ai en
cassette; **2 sticky tape** scotch™.

tape *verb* enregistrer [1]; **I want to
tape the film** je veux enregistrer le
film.

taxi driver noun chauffeur Masc. de taxi.

taxi rank noun station Fem. de taxis.

TB noun tuberculose Fem.

tea noun **1** thé Masc.; **a cup of tea** une tasse de thé; **to have tea** prendre le thé; **2** (evening meal) dîner Masc.

teabag noun sachet Masc. de thé.

teach verb **1** apprendre [64]; **she's teaching me Italian** elle m'apprend l'italien; **that'll teach you!** ça t'apprendra!; **2** enseigner [1]; **her mum teaches maths** sa mère enseigne les maths; **3 to teach yourself something** apprendre [64] quelque chose tout seul; **Anne taught herself Italian** Anne a appris l'italien toute seule.

teacher noun **1** (in a secondary school) professeur Masc.; **my mother's a teacher** ma mère est professeur; **our biology teacher** notre professeur de biologie; **2** (in primary school) instituteur Masc., institutrice Fem.; **she's a primary school teacher** elle est institutrice.

teaching noun enseignement Masc.

team noun équipe Fem.; **a football team** une équipe de foot; **our team won** notre équipe a gagné.

teapot noun théière Fem.

tear¹ noun (a rip) accroc Masc.; **I've got a tear in my jeans** j'ai un accroc dans mon jean.

tear verb **1** déchirer [1]; **you've torn your shirt** tu as déchiré ta chemise; **she tore up my letter** elle

a déchiré ma lettre; **2** se déchirer [1]; **be careful, it tears easily** attention, ça se déchire facilement.

● **to tear off, to tear open 1** (carefully) détacher [1]; **2** (violently) arracher [1].

tear² noun (when you cry) larme Fem.; **to be in tears** être en larmes; **to burst into tears** fondre en larmes.

tease verb **1** taquiner [1] (a person); **2** tourmenter [1] (an animal).

teaspoon noun petite cuillère Fem.; (in recipes) **a teaspoonful of ...** une cuillère à café de ....

teatime noun l'heure Fem. du dîner (evening meal).

tea towel noun torchon Masc.

technical adjective technique.

technical college noun lycée Masc. technique.

technician noun technicien Masc., technicienne Fem.

technique noun technique Fem.

techno noun techno Fem. (music).

technological adjective technologique.

technology noun technologie Fem.; **information technology** l'informatique Fem.

teddy bear noun nounours Masc.

teenage adjective **1** adolescent (Fem. adolescente); **they have a teenage son** ils ont un fils adolescent; **2** (films, magazines, etc.) pour les jeunes; **a teenage magazine** un magazine pour les jeunes.

a b c d e f g h i j k l m n o p q r s t u v w x y z

teenager noun **1** jeune Masc. & Fem.; **a group of teenagers** une bande de jeunes; **2** (more precisely) adolescent Masc., adolescente Fem.; **when I was a teenager** quand j'étais adolescent.

teens plural noun adolescence Fem.; **he's in his teens** c'est un adolescent.

tee-shirt noun tee-shirt Masc.

telegraph pole noun poteau Masc. télégraphique.

telephone noun téléphone Masc.; **on the telephone** au téléphone.

telephone verb appeler [18]; **I'll telephone the bank** je vais appeler la banque.

telephone box noun cabine Fem. téléphonique.

telephone call noun coup Masc. de téléphone.

telephone card noun carte Fem. de téléphone.

telephone directory noun annuaire Masc.

telephone number noun numéro Masc. de téléphone.

telescope noun télescope Masc.

televise verb téléviser [1]; **they're televising the match** on va téléviser le match.

television noun télévision Fem.; **she was watching television** elle regardait la télévision; **I saw it on television** je l'ai vu à la télévision.

television programme noun émission Fem. de télévision.

tell verb **1 to tell somebody something** dire [9] quelque chose à quelqu'un; **that's what she told me** c'est ce qu'elle m'a dit; **I told**

him **it was silly** je lui ai dit que c'était idiot; **have you told Sara?** est-ce que tu l'as dit à Sara?; **2 to tell somebody to do** dire [9] à quelqu'un de faire; **he told me to do it myself** il m'a dit de le faire moi-même; **she told me not to wait** elle m'a dit de ne pas attendre; **3** (explain) **can you tell me how to do it?** est-ce que vous pouvez m'expliquer comment on le fait?; **4** raconter [1] (a story); **tell me about your holiday** raconte-moi tes vacances; **5** (to see) voir [13]; **you can tell it's old** on voit bien que c'est ancien; **you can tell she's cross** on voit bien qu'elle est fâchée; **I can't tell them apart** je n'arrive pas à les distinguer.

telly noun télé Fem.; **to watch telly** regarder la télé; **I saw her on telly** je l'ai vue à la télé.

temp noun intérimaire Masc. & Fem.

temper noun **to be in a temper** être en colère; **to lose your temper** se mettre en colère.

temperature noun **1** température Fem.; **the oven temperature** la température du four; **2 to have a temperature** avoir de la fièvre.

temple noun temple Masc.

temporary adjective temporaire.

temptation noun tentation Fem.

tempted adjective tenté; **I'm really tempted to go** je suis vraiment tenté d'y aller.

tempting adjective tentant.

ten number dix Masc.; **Harry's ten** Harry a dix ans.

tend verb to tend to do avoir [5] tendance à faire; **he tends to talk a lot** il a tendance à beaucoup parler.

tendency noun tendance Fem.; **to have a tendency to** avoir [5] tendance à.

tender adjective tendre.

tennis noun tennis Masc.; **to play tennis** jouer au tennis.

tennis ball noun balle Fem. de tennis.

tennis court noun tennis Masc.

tennis player noun joueur de tennis Masc., joueuse de tennis Fem.

tennis racket noun raquette Fem. de tennis.

tenor noun ténor Masc.

tenpin bowling noun bowling Masc.; **to go tenpin bowling** jouer au bowling.

tense noun **the present tense** le présent; **in the future tense** au futur.

tense adjective tendu.

tent noun tente Fem.

tenth number dixième Masc.; **on the tenth floor** au dixième étage; **the tenth of April** le dix avril.

term noun 1 (in school) trimestre Masc.; 2 **to be on good terms with somebody** être en bons termes avec quelqu'un.

terminal noun 1 (at an airport) aérogare Fem.; **terminal two** l'aérogare numéro deux; 2 **a ferry terminal** une gare maritime; 3 (a computer terminal) terminal Masc. (plural **terminaux**).

terrace noun 1 (of a house or hotel) terrasse Fem.; 2 **the terraces** (at a stadium) les gradins Masc. plural.

terrible adjective épouvantable; **the weather was terrible** il a fait un temps épouvantable.

terribly adverb 1 (very) très; **not terribly clean** pas très propre; 2 (badly) affreusement mal; **I played terribly** j'ai joué affreusement mal.

terrific adjective 1 **at a terrific speed** à une vitesse folle; **a terrific amount** une quantité énorme; 2 **terrific!** formidable!

terrified adjective terrifié.

terrify verb terrifier [1].

territory noun territoire Masc.

terrorism noun terrorisme Masc.

terrorist noun terroriste Masc. & Fem.

test noun 1 (in school) contrôle Masc.; **we've got a maths test tomorrow** nous avons un contrôle de maths demain; 2 (of your skills or patience) test Masc.; 3 (medical) analyse Fem.; **a blood test** une analyse de sang; 4 **a driving test** un examen de permis de conduire; **she's doing her driving test on Friday** elle passe son permis vendredi; **he passed his driving test** il a eu son permis.

test verb 1 (in school) contrôler [1]; 2 **to test something out** essayer [59] quelque chose.

test tube noun éprouvette Fem.

text noun texte Masc.

text verb **to text someone** envoyer [40] un texto à quelqu'un; **I'll text**

textbook noun manuel Masc.

text message noun texto™ Masc.

Thames noun the Thames la Tamise.

than preposition, conjunction 1 que; their new album's better than the last one leur nouveau CD est meilleur que le dernier; they have more money than we do ils ont plus d'argent que nous; 2 (for quantities) de; more than forty plus de quarante; more than thirty years plus de trente ans.

thank verb remercier [1].

thanks plural noun 1 merci; no thanks non merci; thanks a lot merci beaucoup; thanks for your letter merci pour ta lettre; 2 with thanks for avec mes remerciements pour; 3 thanks to grâce à; it was thanks to Micky c'était grâce à Micky.

thank adverb merci; thank you very much for the cheque merci beaucoup pour le chèque; no thank you non merci; a thank-you letter une lettre de remerciements.

that adjective 1 ce (Fem. cette) (but 'ce' becomes 'cet' before a masculine noun beginning with a vowel or a silent 'h') that dog ce chien; that man cet homme; that blue car cette voiture bleue; 2 that one celui-là Masc., celle-là Fem.; 'which cake would you like?' – 'that one, please' 'tu veux quel gâteau?' – 'celui-là, s'il te plaît'; I like all the dresses but I'm going to buy that one j'aime toutes les robes mais je vais acheter celle-là.

that adverb 1 it's not that silly ce n'est pas si idiot que ça; their house isn't that big leur maison n'est pas si grande que ça; 2 it was that high c'était haut comme ça.

that pronoun 1 (before verb 'être') ce, c' (before a vowel); that's not true ce n'est pas vrai; that's not what you told me ce n'est pas ce que tu m'as dit; what's that? qu'est-ce que c'est?; that smells good ça sent bon; who's that? c'est qui?; where's that? c'est où?; is that Mandy? c'est Mandy?; 2 ça; did you see that? tu as vu ça?; that's my bedroom ça c'est ma chambre; 3 qui; the book that's on the table le livre qui est sur la table; 4 que, qu' (before a vowel or a silent 'h'); the book that I lent you le livre que je t'ai prêté.

that conjunction que, qu' (before a vowel or a silent 'h'); I knew that he was wrong je savais qu'il avait tort.

thaw noun fonte Fem. des neiges.

the definite article 1 (before a noun which is masculine in French) le, l' (before a vowel or silent 'h') the cat le chat; the tree l'arbre; 2 (before a noun which is feminine in French) la, l' (before a vowel or silent 'h') the table la table; the orange l'orange; 3 les (before all plural nouns); the windows les fenêtres.

theatre noun théâtre Masc.; to go to the theatre aller au théâtre.

theft noun vol Masc.

their adjective leur (plural leurs); their flat leur appartement; their mother leur mère; their presents leurs cadeaux.

theirs *pronoun* **1** le leur (*when standing for a masculine noun*); **our garden's smaller than theirs** notre jardin est plus petit que le leur; **2** la leur (*when standing for a feminine noun*); **your house is bigger than theirs** votre maison est plus grande que la leur; **3** les leurs (*when standing for a plural noun*); **our children are older than theirs** nos enfants sont plus âgés que les leurs; **4** à eux, à elles; **the yellow car's theirs** la voiture jaune est à eux; **it's theirs** c'est à eux.

them *pronoun* **1** les; **I know them** je les connais; **I don't know them** je ne les connais pas; **listen to them!** écoute-les!; **I saw them last week** je les ai vus la semaine dernière; **2** (*to them*) leur; **I gave them my address** je leur ai donné mon adresse; **3** (*after a preposition*) eux (*Fem.* elles); **I'll go with them** j'irai avec eux; (*if they are all female*) j'irai avec elles; **without them** sans eux, sans elles; (*in comparisons*) **she's older than them** elle est plus âgée qu'eux; (*if all female*) elle est plus âgée qu'elles.

theme *noun* thème *Fem.*

theme park *noun* parc *Masc.* de loisirs.

themselves *pronoun* **1** se; **they've helped themselves** ils se sont servis; **2** (*for emphasis*) eux-mêmes *Masc.*, elles-mêmes *Fem.*; **the boys can do it themselves** les garçons peuvent le faire eux-mêmes; **the girls will tell you themselves** les filles vous le diront elles-mêmes.

then *adverb* **1** (*next*) ensuite; **I wash up and then I make the bed** je fais la vaisselle et ensuite je fais le lit; **I went to the post office and then the bank** je suis allé à la poste et ensuite à la banque; **2** (*at that time*) à l'époque; **we were living in York then** nous habitions à York à l'époque; **3** (*in that case*) alors; **then why worry?** alors pourquoi s'inquiéter?; **that's all right then** ça va alors; **4 by then** déjà; **by then it was too late** il était déjà trop tard.

theory *noun* théorie *Fem.*; **in theory** en théorie.

there *adverb* **1** là; **put it there** mets-le là; **stand there** mettez-vous là; **they're in there** ils sont là; **2 over there** là-bas; **she's over there talking to Mark** elle est là-bas en train de discuter avec Mark; **down there** là-bas; **3 up there** là-haut; **look up there!** regarde là-haut!; **4** y (*when the place 'there' stands for has already been mentioned*); **I've seen photos of Oxford but I've never been there** j'ai vu des photos d'Oxford mais je n'y suis jamais allé; **yes, I'm going there on Tuesday** oui, j'y vais mardi; **5 there is** il y a; **there's a cat in the garden** il y a un chat dans le jardin; **there was no bread** il n'y avait pas de pain; **yes, there's enough** oui, il y en a assez; **6 there are** il y a; **there are plenty of seats** il y a beaucoup de places; **7 there they are!** les voilà!; **there she is!** la voilà!; **there's the bus coming!** voilà le bus qui arrive!

therefore *adverb* donc.

thermometer noun thermomètre Masc.

these adjective ces; **these books** ces livres.

they pronoun **1** ils (when standing for a masculine noun); **'where are the knives?' – 'they're in the drawer'** 'où sont les couteaux?'– 'ils sont dans le tiroir'; **2** elles (when standing for a feminine noun); **I bought some apples but they're not very nice** j'ai acheté des pommes mais elles ne sont pas très bonnes.

thick adjective épais (Fem. épaisse); **a thick layer of butter** une couche épaisse de beurre.

thickness noun épaisseur Fem.

thief noun voleur Masc., voleuse Fem.

thigh noun cuisse Fem.

thin adjective **1** mince (a slice or a person); **2** (too thin, skinny) maigre; **she's got terribly thin** elle a beaucoup maigri.

thing noun **1** (an object) chose Fem.; **shops full of pretty things** des magasins remplis de jolies choses; **she told me some surprising things** elle m'a raconté des choses étonnantes; **2** (a whatsit) truc Masc. (informal); **tu peux utiliser ce truc-là pour l'ouvrir** you can use that thing to open it; **that thing next to the hammer** ce truc à côté du marteau; **3 things** (belongings) affaires Fem. plural; **you can put your things in my room** tu peux mettre tes affaires dans ma chambre; **4 the best thing to do is** ... ce qu'il faut faire, c'est ...; **the**

thing is, I've lost her address ce qu'il y a, c'est que j'ai perdu son adresse; **how are things with you?** comment ça va?

think verb **1** (believe) croire [33]; **do you think they'll come?** tu crois qu'ils vont venir?; **no, I don't think so** non, je ne crois pas; **I think he's already left** je crois qu'il est déjà parti; **2** penser [1]; **I'm thinking about you** je pense à toi; **Tony thinks it's silly** Tony pense que c'est bête; **what do you think of my new jacket?** qu'est-ce que tu penses de ma nouvelle veste?; **what do you think of that?** qu'en penses-tu?; **3** (to think carefully) réfléchir [2]; **he thought for a moment** il a réfléchi un instant; **I've thought it over carefully** j'y ai bien réfléchi; **4** (imagine) imaginer [1]; **just think! we'll soon be in Spain!** imagine! on va bientôt être en Espagne!; **I never thought it would be like this!** je n'avais jamais imaginé que ce serait comme ça.

third noun tiers Masc.; **a third of the population** un tiers de la population.

third adjective troisième **1**; **on the third floor** au troisième étage; **the third of March** le trois mars.

thirdly adverb troisièmement.

Third World noun tiers-monde Masc.

thirst noun soif Fem.

thirsty adjective **to be thirsty** avoir [5] soif; **I'm thirsty** j'ai soif; **we were all thirsty** nous avions tous soif.

thirteen number treize Masc.; **Ahmed's thirteen** Ahmed a treize ans.

thirty number trente Masc.

this adjective 1 ce (before a masculine noun), cet (before a masculine noun beginning with a vowel or a silent 'h'), cette (before a feminine noun); **this paintbrush** ce pinceau; **this tree** cet arbre; **this cup** cette tasse; **this morning** ce matin; **this evening** ce soir; **this afternoon** cet après-midi; **2 this one** celui-ci Masc., celle-ci Fem.; **if you need a pen you can use this one** si tu as besoin d'un stylo tu peux utiliser celui-ci; **if you want a lamp you can borrow this one** si tu veux une lampe tu peux emprunter celle-ci.

this pronoun 1 ça; **can you hold this for a moment?** est-ce que tu peux prendre ça un instant?; **2 what's this?** qu'est-ce que c'est?; **this is Tracy speaking** (on the phone) c'est Tracy à l'appareil; **3** (in introductions) **this is my sister Carla** je te présente ma sœur Carla.

thistle noun chardon Masc.

thorn noun épine Fem.

thorough adjective 1 (search) minutieux (Fem. minutieuse); **2** (person) consciencieux (Fem. consciencieuse).

those adjective ces; **those books** ces livres.

those pronoun ceux-là Masc., celles-là Fem.; **if you want some knives you can take those** si tu veux des couteaux tu peux prendre ceux-là; **if you want some plates**

you can take those si tu veux des assiettes tu peux prendre celles-là.

though conjunction, adverb 1 bien que (followed by a verb in the subjunctive); **though it's cold** bien qu'il fasse froid; **though he's older than she is** bien qu'il soit plus âgé qu'elle; **2 it was a good idea, though** et pourtant, c'était une bonne idée.

thought noun pensée Fem.

thoughtful adjective 1 (considerate) gentil (Fem. gentille); **it was really thoughtful of you** c'était vraiment gentil de ta part; **2** (deep in thought) pensif (Fem. pensive).

thoughtless adjective irréfléchi.

thousand number 1 mille Masc.; **a thousand** mille; **three thousand** trois mille; **2 thousands of** des milliers de; **there were thousands of tourists in Venice** il y avait des milliers de touristes à Venise.

thread noun fil Masc.

thread verb enfiler [1] (a needle).

threat noun menace Fem.

threaten verb menacer [61]; **to threaten to do** menacer de faire.

three number trois Masc.; **Oskar's three** Oskar a trois ans.

three-quarters noun trois-quarts Masc. plural; **three-quarters full** plein aux trois-quarts.

thrilled adjective ravi; **I was thrilled to hear from you** j'ai été ravi d'avoir de tes nouvelles.

thriller noun thriller Masc.

thrilling adjective palpitant.

throat noun gorge Fem.; **to have a sore throat** avoir mal à la gorge.

a
b
c
d
e
f
g
h
i
j
k
l
m
n
o
p
q
r
s
t
u
v
w
x
y
z

through preposition **1** (across) à travers; **through the forest** à travers la forêt; **the water went right through** l'eau est passée à travers; **the police let us through** la police nous a laissés passer; **2** (via) par; **the train went through Leeds** le train est passé par Leeds; **through the window** par la fenêtre; **I know them through my cousins** je les connais par mes cousins; **3 to go through something** traverser quelque chose; **we went through the park** nous avons traversé le parc; **4 right through the day** toute la journée.

through adjective direct (a train or flight).

throughout preposition **throughout the match** pendant tout le match; **throughout the world** partout dans le monde.

throw verb **1** jeter [48]; **I threw the letter into the bin** j'ai jeté la lettre dans la poubelle; **he threw the book on the floor** il a jeté le livre par terre; **2** (taking aim) lancer [61]; **throw me the ball!** lance-moi le ballon!; **we were throwing snowballs** on lançait des boules de neige.

● **to throw something away** jeter [48] quelque chose; **I've thrown away the old newspapers** j'ai jeté les vieux journaux.

● **to throw somebody out** expulser [1] quelqu'un.

● **to throw something out** jeter [48] quelque chose (rubbish).

● **to throw up** vomir [2].

thumb noun pouce Masc.

thump verb taper [1].

thunder noun tonnerre Masc.; **a peal of thunder** un roulement de tonnerre.

thunderstorm noun orage Masc.

thundery adjective orageux (Fem. orageuse).

Thursday noun jeudi Masc.; **on Thursday** jeudi; **I'm going out on Thursday** je sors jeudi; **see you on Thursday!** à jeudi!; **on Thursdays** le jeudi; **the museum is closed on Thursdays** le musée est fermé le jeudi; **every Thursday** tous les jeudis; **last Thursday** jeudi dernier; **next Thursday** jeudi prochain.

thyme noun thym Masc.

tick verb **1** (tick-tock) faire [10] tic-tac; **2** (on paper) cocher [1]; **tick the box** cochez la case.

ticket noun **1** billet Masc. (for a plane, a train, an exhibition, a theatre or cinema) **two tickets for the concert** deux billets pour le concert; **2** (for the underground, the bus, or left luggage) ticket Masc.; **a bus ticket** un ticket de bus; **3 a parking ticket** un PV (informal).

ticket inspector noun contrôleur Masc.

ticket office noun (at a station) guichet Masc.

tickle verb chatouiller [1].

tide noun marée Fem.; **at high tide** à marée haute; **the tide is out** c'est la marée basse.

tidy adjective **1** bien rangé (a room); **2** soigné (homework); **3** ordonné (a person).

tidy verb ranger [52]; **I'll tidy (up) the kitchen** je rangerai la cuisine.

tie *noun* **1** cravate *Fem.*; **a red tie** une cravate rouge; **2** (*in a match*) match *Masc.* nul.

tie *verb* **1** nouer [1]; **to tie your shoelaces** nouer ses lacets; **2 to tie a knot in something** faire [10] un nœud à quelque chose; **3** (*in a match*) **we tied two all** nous avons fait match nul, deux partout.

tiger *noun* tigre *Masc.*

tight *adjective* **1** juste; **the skirt's a bit tight** la jupe est un peu juste; **these shoes are too tight** ces chaussures me serrent; **2** (*close-fitting*) moulant; **she was wearing a tight dress** elle portait une robe moulante.

tighten *verb* serrer [1].

tightly *adverb* fermement.

tights *plural noun* collant *Masc. singular*; **a pair of purple tights** un collant violet.

tile *noun* **1** (*on a floor or wall*) carreau *Masc.* (*plural* **carreaux**); **2** (*on a roof*) tuile *Fem.*

till¹ *preposition, conjunction* **1** jusqu'à; **they're here till Sunday** ils sont là jusqu'à dimanche; **till then** jusque là; **till now** jusqu'à présent; **2 not till** (pas avant); **she won't be back till ten** elle ne sera pas rentrée avant dix heures; **we won't know till Monday** nous ne le saurons pas avant lundi.

till² *noun* caisse *Fem.*; **pay at the till** payez à la caisse.

time *noun* **1** (*on the clock*) heure *Fem.*; **what time is it?** quelle heure est-il?; **it's time for lunch** c'est l'heure du déjeuner; **on time** à l'heure; **ten o'clock French time**

dix heures heure française; **2** (*an amount of time*) temps *Masc.*; **we've got lots of time** nous avons beaucoup de temps; **there's not much time left** il ne reste plus beaucoup de temps; **for a long time** longtemps; **from time to time** de temps en temps; **3** (*moment*) moment *Masc.*; **is this a good time to phone?** est-ce que c'est le bon moment pour vous appeler?; **at times** par moments; **for the time being** pour le moment; **any time now** d'un moment à l'autre; **4** (*in a series*) fois *Fem.*; **six times** six fois; **the first time** la première fois; **the first time I saw you** la première fois que je t'ai vu; **three times a year** trois fois par an; **three times two is six** trois fois deux égalent six; **5 to have a good time** bien s'amuser [1]; **we had a really good time** nous nous sommes très bien amusés; **have a good time!** amusez-vous bien!

time off *noun* **1** (*free time*) temps *Masc.* libre; **2** (*leave*) congé *Masc.*

timetable *noun* **1** (*in school*) emploi *Masc.* du temps; **2** (*for trains or buses*) horaire *Masc.*; **the bus timetable** l'horaire des bus.

tin *noun* boîte *Fem.*; **a tin of tomatoes** une boîte de tomates.

tin-foil *noun* papier *Masc.* aluminium.

tinned *adjective* en conserve; **tinned peas** des petits pois en conserve.

tin opener *noun* ouvre-boîte *Masc.*

tinted *adjective* teinté.

tiny *adjective* minuscule.

tip noun 1 (the end) bout Masc.; **the tip of my finger** le bout de mon doigt; 2 (money) pourboire Masc.; 3 (a useful hint) tuyau Masc. (plural **tuyaux**) (informal).

tip verb 1 (to give money to) donner [1] un pourboire à; **we tipped the waiter** nous avons donné un pourboire au garçon; 2 verser [1] (liquid).

tiptoe noun on **tiptoe** sur la pointe des pieds.

tired adjective 1 fatigué; **I'm tired** je suis fatigué; **you look tired** tu as l'air fatigué; 2 **to be tired of** en avoir assez de; **I'm tired of London** j'en ai assez de Londres; **I'm tired of watching TV** j'en ai assez de regarder la télé.

tiring adjective fatigant.

tissue noun (a paper hanky) kleenex™ Masc.; **do you have a tissue?** est-ce que tu as un kleenex?

tissue paper noun papier Masc. de soie.

title noun titre Masc.

to preposition 1 (to a place or person) à (note that 'à + le' becomes 'au' and 'à + les' becomes 'aux') **to go to London** aller à Londres; **give the book to Leila** donne le livre à Leila; **I'm going to school** je vais à l'école; **she's gone to the office** elle est partie au bureau; **a letter to parents** une lettre aux parents; **from Monday to Friday** du lundi au vendredi; 2 (with names of countries) en (BUT) **they're going to Spain** ils vont en Espagne; (BUT) **they're going to Japan** ils vont au Japon ('en' with feminine countries, 'au'

with most masculine countries); 3 à; **I have nothing to do** je n'ai rien à faire; **I had a lot of homework to do** j'avais beaucoup de devoirs à faire; **we're ready to go** nous sommes prêts à partir; **it's easy to do** c'est facile à faire; 4 (to somebody's house, shop, surgery) chez; **I went round to Paul's house** je suis allé chez Paul; **we're going to the Browns' for supper** on va dîner chez les Brown; **I'm going to the dentist's tomorrow** je vais chez le dentiste demain; **she's gone to the hairdresser's** elle est allée chez le coiffeur; 5 (talking about the time) **it's ten to nine** il est neuf heures moins dix; **it's twenty to** il est moins vingt; 6 (in order to) pour; **he gave me some money to buy a sandwich** il m'a donné de l'argent pour acheter un sandwich.

toad noun crapaud Masc.

toadstool noun champignon Masc.; **a poisonous toadstool** un champignon vénéneux.

toast noun 1 pain Masc. grillé; **two slices of toast** deux tranches de pain grillé; 2 (to your health) toast Masc.; **to drink a toast to the future** lever un verre à l'avenir.

toaster noun grille-pain Masc.

tobacco noun tabac Masc.

tobacconist's noun bureau Masc. de tabac.

today noun aujourd'hui Masc.; **today's her birthday** c'est son anniversaire aujourd'hui.

toe noun doigt Masc. de pied; **my big toe** mon gros orteil.

toenail noun ongle Masc. de pied.

toffee noun caramel Masc.

together adverb 1 ensemble; **Kate and Lenny arrived together** Kate et Lenny sont arrivés ensemble; 2 (at the same time) en même temps; **they all left together** ils sont tous partis en même temps.

toilet noun toilettes Fem. plural; **where's the toilet?** où sont les toilettes?; **she's gone to the toilet** elle est allé aux toilettes.

toilet paper noun papier Masc. hygiénique.

toilet roll noun rouleau Masc. de papier hygiénique.

token noun 1 (for a machine or game) jeton Masc.; 2 **a record token** un chèque-cadeaux Masc. pour disque.

tolerant adjective tolérant.

toll noun 1 péage Masc; 2 (number of dead) nombre Masc.; **the death toll is now 25** le nombre de victimes s'élève maintenant à 25.

tomato noun tomate Fem.; **a tomato salad** une salade de tomates; **tomato sauce** la sauce tomate.

tomorrow adverb demain; **I'll do it tomorrow** je le ferai demain; **tomorrow afternoon** demain après-midi; **tomorrow morning** demain matin; **tomorrow night** demain soir; **the day after tomorrow** après-demain.

ton noun tonne Fem.; **she gets tons of letters** elle reçoit des tonnes de lettres.

tone noun 1 (on an answerphone) tonalité Fem.; **speak after the tone** parlez après la tonalité; 2 (of a voice or a letter) ton Masc.

tongue noun langue Fem.; **to stick your tongue out** tirer la langue; ★ **it's on the tip of my tongue** je l'ai sur le bout de la langue.

tonic noun Schweppes™ Masc.; **a gin and tonic** un gin tonic.

tonight adverb 1 (this evening) ce soir; **I'm going out with my mates tonight** je sors avec les copains ce soir; 2 (after bedtime) cette nuit.

tonsillitis noun angine Fem.

too adverb 1 trop; **it's too expensive** c'est trop cher; **too often** trop souvent; 2 **too much, too many** trop; **it takes too much time** ça prend trop de temps; **there are too many accidents** il y a trop d'accidents; **he eats too much** il mange trop; 3 (as well) aussi; **Karen's coming too** Karen vient aussi; **me too!** moi aussi!

tool noun outil Masc.

tool box noun boîte Fem. à outils.

tool kit noun trousse Fem. à outils.

tooth noun dent Fem.; **to brush your teeth** se brosser les dents.

toothache noun mal Masc. de dents; **to have toothache** avoir mal aux dents.

toothbrush noun brosse Fem. à dents.

toothpaste noun dentifrice Masc.

top noun 1 haut Masc. (of a page, a ladder, or stairs) or stairs; **at the top of the stairs** en haut de l'escalier; 2 (of a container or box) dessus Masc.; **it's on top of the chest-of-drawers** c'est sur la commode; 3 (of a mountain) sommet Masc.; 4 (a lid)

a
b
c
d
e
f
g
h
i
j
k
l
m
n
o
p
q
r
s
t
u
v
w
x
y
z

top (of a pen) capuchon Masc.; (of a bottle) capsule Fem.; **5** (to wear) haut Masc.; **6 to be at the top of the list** être en tête de la liste.

top adjective **1** (a step or floor) dernier (Fem. dernière); **it's on the top floor** c'est au dernier étage; **2** de haut (a bunk), **3** du haut (a shelf); **4 in the top left-hand corner** en haut à gauche; ★ **and on top of all that** et par-dessus le marché; ★ **it was a bit over the top** c'était un peu exagéré.

topic noun sujet Masc.

topping noun garniture Fem.; **which topping would you like on your pizza?** vous voulez une pizza à quoi?

torch noun lampe Fem. de poche.

torn adjective déchiré.

tornado noun tornade Fem.

tortoise noun tortue Fem.

torture noun torture Fem.

torture verb torturer [1].

Tory noun conservateur Masc., conservatrice Fem.

total noun total Masc.

total adjective total (Masc. plural totaux).

totally adverb complètement.

touch noun **1** (contact) to get in touch with somebody prendre contact avec quelqu'un; **to stay in touch with somebody** rester en contact avec quelqu'un; **2 we've lost touch** on s'est perdu de vue; **I've lost touch with her recently** je l'ai perdue de vue récemment; **3** (a little bit) petit peu Masc.; **a touch of vanilla** un petit peu de vanille; **it was a touch**

embarrassing c'était un petit peu gênant.

touch verb toucher [1].

touched adjective touché.

touching adjective touchant.

tough adjective **1** dur; **the meat's a bit tough** la viande est un peu dure; **it's a tough area** c'est un quartier dur; **things are a bit tough at the moment** la vie est un peu dure en ce moment; **a tough guy** un dur; **2** robuste; **you need to be tough to survive** il faut être robuste pour survivre!; **a tough fabric** un tissu robuste; **3** (tough luck) tant pis; **tough, you're too late** tant pis pour toi, tu arrives trop tard.

tour noun **1** visite Fem.; **we did the tour of the castle** nous avons fait la visite du château; **a tour of the city** une visite de la ville; **2 a package tour** un voyage organisé; **3** (by a band or theatre group) tournée Fem.; **to go on tour** partir en tournée.

tour verb (performer) être [6] en tournée; **they're touring the States** ils sont en tournée aux États-Unis.

tourism noun tourisme Masc.

tourist noun touriste Masc. & Fem.

tourist information office noun syndicat Masc. d'initiative.

tournament noun tournoi Masc.; **a tennis tournament** un tournoi de tennis.

tow verb **to be towed away** (by the police) être [6] emmené à la fourrière; (by a breakdown truck) être [6] remorqué.

towards *preposition* en direction de; **she went off towards the lake** elle est partie en direction du lac.

towel *noun* serviette *Fem.*

tower *noun* tour *Fem.*; **the Eiffel Tower** la tour Eiffel.

tower block *noun* tour *Fem.*

town *noun* ville *Fem.*; **to go into town** aller en ville.

town centre *noun* centre-ville *Masc.*

town hall *noun* mairie *Fem.*

toxic *adjective* toxique.

toy *noun* jouet *Masc.*; **a toy car** une petite voiture.

toyshop *noun* magasin *Masc.* de jouets.

trace *noun* trace *Fem.*; **there was no trace of it** il n'en restait aucune trace.

trace *verb* retrouver [1].

tracing paper *noun* papier *Masc.* calque.

track *noun* **1** (*for sport*) piste *Fem.*; **a track event** une épreuve de vitesse; **a racing track** (*for cars*) un circuit; **2** (*a path*) chemin *Masc.*; **3** (*song*) chanson; **this is my favourite track** c'est ma chanson préférée.

track suit *noun* survêtement *Masc.*

tractor *noun* tracteur *Masc.*

trade *noun* (*a profession*) métier *Masc.*

trademark *noun* marque *Fem.*; **registered trademark** marque déposée.

trade union *noun* syndicat *Masc.*

tradition *noun* tradition *Fem.*

traditional *adjective* traditionnel (*Fem.* traditionnelle).

traffic *noun* circulation *Fem.*

traffic island *noun* refuge *Masc.*

traffic jam *noun* embouteillage *Masc.*

traffic lights *plural noun* feux *Masc.* plural.

traffic warden *noun* contractuel *Masc.*, contractuelle *Fem.*

tragedy *noun* tragédie *Fem.*

tragic *adjective* tragique.

trail *noun* (*a path*) sentier *Masc.*; **a nature trail** un sentier écologique.

trailer *noun* remorque *Fem.*

train *noun* train *Masc.*; **he's coming by train** il prend le train; **I met her on the train** je l'ai rencontrée dans le train; **the train to York** le train pour York.

train *verb* **1** former [1] (*a student*); **2 to train to be something** suivre [75] une formation de quelque chose; **he's training to be a nurse** il suit une formation d'infirmier; **3** (*in sport*) s'entraîner [1]; **the team trains on Saturdays** l'équipe s'entraîne le samedi.

trainee *noun* stagiaire *Masc.* & *Fem.*

trainer *noun* **1** (*of an athlete or a horse*) entraîneur *Masc.*, entraîneuse *Fem.*; **2** (*shoe*) basket *Masc.*; **my new trainers** mes nouveaux baskets.

training *noun* **1** (*for a career*) formation *Fem.*; **2** (*for sport*) entraînement *Masc.*

train ticket *noun* billet *Masc.* de train.

train timetable noun horaire Masc. des trains.

tram noun tramway Masc.

tramp noun clochard Masc., clocharde Fem.

trampoline noun trampoline Masc.

transfer noun 1 (of money) virement Masc.; 2 (of employee, footballer) transfert Masc.; 3 (sticker) décalcomanie Fem.

transform verb transformer [1].

transistor noun transistor Masc.

translate verb traduire [26]; **to translate something into French** traduire quelque chose en français.

translation noun traduction Fem.

translator noun traducteur Masc., traductrice Fem.; **I'd like to be a translator** j'aimerais être traducteur.

transparent adjective transparent.

transplant noun 1 (operation) transplantation Fem.; 2 (organ) transplant Masc.

transport noun transport Masc.; **air transport** le transport aérien; **public transport** les transports en commun.

trap noun piège Masc.

travel noun voyages Masc. plural; **foreign travel** les voyages à l'étranger; **a travel brochure** une brochure de voyages.

travel verb voyager [52].

travel agency noun agence Fem. de voyages.

travel agent noun agent Masc. de voyages.

traveller's cheque noun chèque-voyage Masc. (plural chèques-voyage).

traveller noun 1 voyageur Masc., voyageuse Fem.; 2 (gypsy) nomade Masc. & Fem.

travelling noun voyages Masc. plural; **I like travelling** j'aime partir en voyage.

travel-sick noun **to be or get travel-sick** souffrir [73] du mal de voyage.

tray noun plateau Masc. (plural plateaux).

tread verb **to tread on something** marcher [1] sur quelque chose.

treasure noun trésor Masc.

treat noun 1 **I took them to the circus as a treat** je les ai emmenés au cirque pour leur faire plaisir; 2 (food) gâterie Fem.; **it's a little treat** c'est une petite gâterie.

treat verb 1 traiter [1]; **he treats his dog well** il traite bien son chien; **the doctor who treated you** le médecin qui vous a traité; 2 **to treat somebody to something** offrir [56] quelque chose à quelqu'un; **I'll treat you to a drink** je vous offre à boire; **I treated myself to a new dress** je me suis offert une nouvelle robe.

treatment noun traitement Masc.

treaty noun traité Masc.

tree noun arbre Masc.

tree trunk noun tronc Masc. d'arbre.

tremble verb trembler [1].

tremendous adjective fantastique; **a tremendous**

victory/defeat une victoire/défaite écrasante.

trend noun **1** (a fashion) mode Fem.; **2** (a tendency) tendance Fem.

trendy adjective branché.

trial noun (legal) procès Masc..

triangle noun triangle Masc.

tribe noun tribu Fem.

tribute noun hommage Masc.; **many tributes were paid to the Pope** de nombreuses personnes ont rendu hommage au Pape.

trick noun **1** (by a conjuror, or as a joke) tour Masc.; **to play a trick on somebody** jouer un tour à quelqu'un; **2** (a knack) astuce Fem.; **it doesn't work, there must be a trick to it** ça ne marche pas, il doit y avoir une astuce.

trick verb rouler [1]; **he tricked me!** il m'a roulé!

tricky adjective délicat; **it's a tricky situation** c'est une situation délicate.

tricycle noun tricycle Masc.

trim verb couper [1] (hair or fabric).

Trinidad noun (île de) la Trinité. **Trinidadian** noun Trinidadien Masc., Trinidadienne Fem.

Trinidadian adjective trinidadien (Fem. trinidadienne).

trip noun voyage Masc.; **a trip to Florida** un voyage en Floride; **he's on a business trip** il est en voyage d'affaires; **a day trip to France** une excursion d'une journée en France.

trip verb (to stumble) trébucher [1]; **Nicky tripped over a stone** Nicky a trébuché sur un gros caillou.

triple verb tripler [1]; **the price has tripled** le prix a triplé.

triumph noun triomphe Masc.

trolley noun chariot Masc.

trombone noun trombone Masc.; **to play the trombone** jouer du trombone.

troops plural noun troupes Fem. plural.

trophy noun trophée Masc.

tropical adjective tropical (Masc. plural tropicaux).

trot verb trotter [1].

trouble noun **1** problèmes Masc. plural; **we've had trouble with the car** nous avons eu des problèmes avec la voiture; **the trouble is, I've forgotten the number** le problème, c'est que j'ai oublié le numéro; **2** (personal problems) ennuis Masc. plural; **Steph's in trouble** Steph a des ennuis; **what's the trouble?** qu'est-ce qui ne va pas?; **3** (difficulty) **to have trouble doing** avoir du mal à faire; **I had trouble finding a seat** j'ai eu du mal à trouver une place; **it's not worth the trouble** cela ne vaut pas la peine; **it's no trouble!** ça ne me dérange pas!

trousers plural noun pantalon Masc. singular; **my old trousers** mon vieux pantalon; **a new pair of trousers** un pantalon neuf.

trout noun truite Fem.

truant noun **to play truant** faire [10] l'école buissonnière; **she's playing truant** elle fait l'école buissonnière.

truck noun camion Masc.

a
b
c
d
e
f
g
h
i
j
k
l
m
n
o
p
q
r
s
t
u
v
w
x
y
z

true *adjective* vrai; **a true story** une histoire vraie; **is that true?** c'est vrai?; **it's true she's absent-minded** c'est vrai qu'elle est distraite.

truly *adverb* vraiment.

trump *noun* atout *Masc.*; **spades are trumps** atout pique.

trumpet *noun* trompette *Fem.*; **to play the trumpet** jouer de la trompette.

trunk *noun* **1** (*of a tree*) tronc *Masc.*; **2** (*of an elephant*) trompe *Fem.*; **3** (*a suitcase*) malle *Fem.*

trunks *plural noun* **swimming trunks** maillot *Masc.* de bain.

trust *noun* confiance *Fem.*

trust *verb* **I trust her** je lui fais confiance.

truth *noun* vérité *Fem.*; **to tell the truth, I'd completely forgotten** à vrai dire, j'avais complètement oublié.

try *noun* essai *Masc.*; **it's my first try** c'est mon premier essai; **to have a try** essayer [59]; **you should give it a try** tu devrais l'essayer.

try *verb* essayer [59]; **to try to do** essayer de faire; **I'm trying to open the door** j'essaie d'ouvrir la porte; **to try hard to do** faire [10] de gros efforts pour faire.

● **to try something on** essayer [59] quelque chose (*a garment*).

T-shirt *noun* tee-shirt *Masc.*

tub *noun* **1** (*food container*) pot *Masc.*; **2** (*bath*) baignoire *Fem.*

tube *noun* tube *Masc.*

tuberculosis *noun* tuberculose *Fem.*

Tuesday *noun* mardi *Masc.*; **on Tuesday** mardi; **I'm going out on Tuesday** je sors mardi; **see you on Tuesday!** à mardi!; **on Tuesdays** le mardi; **the museum is closed on Tuesdays** le musée est fermé le mardi; **every Tuesday** tous les mardis; **last Tuesday** mardi dernier; **next Tuesday** mardi prochain.

tug *verb* tirer [1].

tuition *noun* cours *Masc. plural*; **piano tuition** des cours de piano; **private tuition** des cours particuliers.

tulip *noun* tulipe *Fem.*

tumble-drier *noun* sèche-linge *Masc.*

tumbler *noun* verre *Masc.* droit.

tummy *noun* estomac *Masc.*

tuna *noun* thon *Masc.*

tune *noun* air *Masc.*

Tunisia *noun* Tunisie *Fem.*; **in Tunisia** en Tunisie.

tunnel *noun* tunnel *Masc.*; **the Channel Tunnel** le tunnel sous la Manche.

turban *noun* turban *Masc.*

turf *noun* gazon *Masc.*

turkey *noun* dinde *Fem.*

Turkey *noun* Turquie *Fem.*; **in Turkey** en Turquie; **to Turkey** en Turquie.

Turkish *noun* turc *Masc.* (*language*).

Turkish *adjective* turc (*Fem.* turque).

turn *noun* **1** (*in a game*) tour *Masc.*; **it's your turn** c'est ton tour; **whose turn is it?** c'est à qui le tour?; **it's Jane's turn to play** c'est à Jane de jouer; **to take turns driving** conduire à tour de rôle; **2** (*in a road*) virage *Masc.*

turn *verb* **1** tourner [1]; **turn your chair round** tourne ta chaise; **turn left at the next set of lights** tournez à gauche aux prochains feux; **2** (*become*) devenir [81]; **she turned red** elle est devenue rouge.

● **to turn back** faire [10] demi-tour; **we turned back** nous avons fait demi-tour.

● **to turn off 1** (*from a road*) tourner [1]; **2** (*switch off*) éteindre [60] (*a light, an oven, a TV or radio*); fermer [1] (*a tap*); couper [1] (*gas or electricity*).

● **to turn on** allumer [1] (*the oven, TV, radio, or a light*); ouvrir [30] (*a tap*).

● **to turn out 1 to turn out well** bien se terminer [1]; **the holiday turned out badly** les vacances se sont mal terminées; **it all turned out alright in the end** finalement tout s'est arrangé; **2 it turned out that I was wrong** il s'est avéré que j'avais tort.

● **to turn over 1** (*roll over*) se retourner [1]; **2** tourner [1] (*a page*).

● **to turn up 1** (*to arrive*) arriver [1]; **they turned up an hour later** ils sont arrivés une heure plus tard; **2** augmenter [1] (*the gas or the heating*); **3** (*make louder*) **can you turn up the volume?** est-ce que tu peux monter le son?

turning *noun* virage *Masc.*; **take the third turning on the right** prenez la troisième rue à gauche.

turnip *noun* navet *Masc.*

turquoise *adjective* turquoise.

turtle *noun* tortue *Fem.* marine.

turtle dove *noun* tourterelle *Fem.*

TV *noun* télé *Fem.*; **I saw her on TV** je l'ai vue à la télé.

tweezers *noun* pince *Fem. singular* à épiler.

twelfth *number* douzième; **on the twelfth floor** au douzième étage; **the twelfth of May** le douze mai.

twelve *number* **1** douze *Masc.*; **Tara's twelve** Tara a douze ans; **2 at twelve o'clock** (*midday*) à midi; (*midnight*) à minuit.

twenty *number* vingt *Masc.*; **Marie's twenty** Marie a vingt ans; **twenty-one** vingt-et-un; **twenty-five** vingt-cinq.

twice *adverb* deux fois; **I've asked him twice** je lui ai demandé deux fois; **twice as much** deux fois plus.

twig *noun* brindille *Fem.*

twilight *noun* crépuscule *Masc.*

twin *noun* jumeau *Masc.* (*plural* jumeaux), jumelle *Fem.*; **Helen and Tim are twins** Helen et Tim sont jumeaux; **her twin sister** sa sœur jumelle.

twin *verb* **Oxford is twinned with Grenoble** Oxford est jumelée avec Grenoble.

twist *verb* tordre [3].

two *number* deux *Masc.*; **Ben's two** Ben a deux ans; **two by two** deux par deux.

type *noun* type *Masc.*; **what type of computer is it?** c'est quel type d'ordinateur?

type *verb* (*on a typewriter*) taper [1]; **I'm learning to type** j'apprends à taper à la machine; **I was busy**

a b c d e f g h i j k l m n o p q r s t u v w x y z

a
b
c
d
e
f
g
h
i
j
k
l
m
n
o
p
q
r
s
t
u
v
w
x
y
z

typing some letters j'étais en train de taper des lettres.

typewriter noun machine Fem. à écrire.

typical adjective typique.

typing noun dactylographie Fem.; **her typing is awful** elle tape très , mal.

tyre noun pneu Masc.

Uu

UFO noun ovni Masc.

ugly adjective laid.

UK noun (short for United Kingdom) Royaume-Uni Masc.

ulcer noun ulcère Masc.

Ulster noun Irlande Fem. du Nord.

umbrella noun parapluie Masc.

umpire noun arbitre Masc.

UN noun O.N.U. Fem. (short for Organisation des Nations Unies).

unable adjective **to be unable to do** ne pas pouvoir faire; **he's unable to come** il ne peut pas venir.

unanimous adjective unanime.

unattractive adjective peu attrayant (person, place).

unavoidable adjective inévitable.

unbearable adjective insupportable.

unbelievable adjective incroyable.

uncertain adjective incertain; **I'm uncertain whether they're coming** je ne suis pas sûr qu'ils viennent.

unchanged adjective inchangé.

uncivilized adjective barbare.

uncle noun oncle Masc.; **my Uncle Julian** mon oncle Julian.

uncomfortable adjective
1 inconfortable (shoes or a chair);
2 pénible (a journey or a situation).

uncommon adjective rare.

unconscious adjective (out cold) sans connaissance; **Tessa's still unconscious** Tessa est toujours sans connaissance.

under preposition 1 (underneath) sous; **under the bed** sous le lit; **perhaps it's under there** peut-être là-dessous; 2 (less than) moins de; **under £20** moins de vingt livres; **children under five** les enfants de moins de cinq ans.

under-age noun **to be under-age** être mineur (Fem. mineure).

underclothes plural noun sous-vêtements Masc. plural.

undercooked adjective pas assez cuit.

underestimate verb sous-estimer [1].

underground noun (a railway) métro Masc.; **I saw her on the underground** je l'ai vue dans le métro; **shall we go by underground?** on prend le métro?

underground adjective souterrain; **an underground carpark** un parking souterrain.

underline verb souligner [1].

underneath preposition sous; **it's underneath these papers** c'est sous ces papiers.

underneath adverb dessous; **look underneath** cherche dessous.

underpants *plural noun* slip
Masc. singular; **my underpants** mon
slip.

underpass *noun* **1** (*pedestrian*)
passage Masc. souterrain; **2** (*for
traffic*) passage Masc. inférieur.

understand *verb* comprendre
[64]; **I don't understand** je ne
comprends pas; **I couldn't
understand what he was saying**
je n'ai pas compris ce qu'il disait.

understandable *adjective* that's
understandable ça se comprend.

understanding *noun*
compréhension Fem.

understanding *adjective*
compréhensif (Fem.
compréhensive); **he was very
understanding** il a été très
compréhensif.

underwear *noun* sous-vêtements
Masc. plural.

undo *verb* **1** défaire [10] (*a button or
a lock*); **2** ouvrir [30] (*a parcel*).

undone *adjective* to come undone
se défaire [10].

undress *verb* to get undressed
se déshabiller [1]; **I got undressed**
je me suis déshabillé.

unemployed *noun* the
unemployed les chômeurs; **work
for the unemployed** du travail
pour les chômeurs.

unemployed *adjective* au
chômage; **she's unemployed** elle
est au chômage.

unemployment *noun* chômage
Masc.

uneven *adjective* irrégulier (Fem.
irrégulière).

unexpected *adjective* imprévu.

unexpectedly *adverb* (*to happen,
arrive*) à l'improviste.

unfair *adjective* injuste; **it's unfair
to young people** c'est injuste pour
les jeunes.

unfashionable *adjective* démodé.

unfasten *verb* défaire [10].

unfit *adjective* I'm terribly unfit
je ne suis pas du tout en forme.

unfold *verb* déplier [1].

unforgettable *adjective*
inoubliable.

unfortunate *adjective*
regrettable.

unfortunately *adverb*
malheureusement.

unfriendly *adjective* pas très
sympathique.

unfurnished *adjective* non
meublé.

ungrateful *adjective* ingrat.

unhappy *adjective* malheureux
(Fem. malheureuse).

unhealthy *adjective* **1** maladif
(Fem. maladive) (*a person*);
2 malsain (*food*).

unhurt *adjective* indemne.

uniform *noun* uniforme Masc.;
in school uniform en uniforme
scolaire.

uninhabited *adjective* inhabité.

union *noun* (*a trade union*)
syndicat Masc.

Union Jack *noun* the Union Jack
le drapeau du Royaume-Uni.

unique *adjective* unique.

unit *noun* **1** (*for measuring, for
example*) unité Fem.; **2** (*in a kitchen*)
élément Masc.; **3** (*a hospital
department*) service Masc.

United Kingdom noun
Royaume-Uni Masc.

United Nations noun O.N.U
(Organisation des Nations Unies).

United States (of America)
plural noun États-Unis Masc. plural;
in the United States aux États-Unis; **to the United States** aux
États-Unis.

universe noun univers Masc.

university noun université Fem.;
to go to university aller à
l'université.

unjust adjective injuste.

unkind adjective pas gentil (Fem.
pas gentille).

unknown adjective inconnu.

unleaded petrol noun essence
Fem. sans plomb.

unless conjunction **unless he
does it** à moins qu'il ne le fasse;
unless you tell her à moins que tu
ne le lui dises (note that 'à moins
que' is followed by a subjunctive).

unlike adjective 1 **unlike me, she
hates dogs** contrairement à moi,
elle déteste les chiens; 2 **it's unlike
her to be late** ce n'est pas son
genre d'être en retard.

unlikely adjective peu probable;
it's unlikely c'est peu probable.

unlimited adjective illimité.

unload verb décharger [52].

unlock verb ouvrir [30]; **the car's
unlocked** la voiture est ouverte.

unlucky adjective 1 **to be unlucky**
(a person) ne pas avoir de chance; **I
was unlucky, it was shut** je n'ai
pas eu de chance, c'était fermé;

2 **thirteen is an unlucky number**
le treize porte malheur.

unmarried adjective célibataire.

unnatural adjective anormal
(Masc. plural anormaux).

unnecessary adjective inutile;
it's unnecessary to book il est
inutile de réserver.

unpack verb défaire [10]; **I
unpacked my rucksack** j'ai défait
mon sac à dos; **I'll just unpack and
then come down** je vais juste
défaire ma valise et puis je
descendrai.

unpaid adjective 1 impayé (a bill);
2 non rémunéré (work).

unpleasant adjective
désagréable.

unplug verb débrancher [1].

unpopular adjective impopulaire.

unrealistic adjective peu réaliste.

unreasonable adjective pas
raisonnable; **he's being really
unreasonable** il n'est vraiment pas
raisonnable.

unrecognizable adjective
méconnaissable.

unreliable adjective peu fiable
(information or equipment); **he's
unreliable** on ne peut pas compter
sur lui.

unroll verb dérouler [1].

unsafe adjective dangereux (Fem.
dangereuse) (wiring, for instance).

unsatisfactory adjective
insatisfaisant.

unscrew verb dévisser [1].

unshaven adjective pas rasé.

unsuccessful adjective **to be
unsuccessful** ne pas réussir; **I**

tried, but I was unsuccessful j'ai essayé mais je n'ai pas réussi; an unsuccessful attempt un essai vain.

unsuitable adjective inapproprié.

untidy adjective en désordre; the house is always untidy la maison est toujours en désordre [10].

untie verb défaire [10].

until preposition 1 jusqu'à; until Monday jusqu'à lundi; until the tenth jusqu'au dix; until now jusqu'à présent; until then jusque-là; 2 not until pas avant; not until September pas avant septembre; it won't be finished until Friday ce ne sera pas fini avant vendredi.

unusual adjective peu commun; an unusual beetle un scarabée peu commun; storms are unusual in June c'est rare d'avoir des orages au mois de juin.

unwilling adjective to be unwilling to do ne pas vouloir faire; he's unwilling to wait il ne veut pas attendre.

unwrap verb déballer [1].

up preposition, adverb 1 (out of bed) to be up être levé; Liz isn't up yet Liz n'est pas encore levée; to get up se lever [50]; we got up at six nous nous sommes levés à six heures; I was up late last night je me suis couché tard hier soir; 2 (higher up) en haut; hands up! haut les mains!; up on the roof en haut sur le toit; up here ici; up there là-haut; we went up the road nous avons remonté la rue; it's just up the road c'est tout près; up in Glasgow à Glasgow; 3 (wrong) what's up?

qu'est-ce qui se passe?; what's up with him? qu'est-ce qu'il a?; 4 up to jusqu'à; up to here jusqu'ici; up to fifty people jusqu'à cinquante personnes; she came up to me elle s'est approchée de moi; 5 what's she up to? qu'est-ce qu'elle fait?; it's up to you (to decide) c'est à toi de décider; ★ time's up! c'est l'heure!

update noun mise Fem. à jour; here's an update on the delays voici une mise à jour des retards.

update verb 1 (revise) mettre [11] à jour (timetables or information); 2 moderniser [1] (styles or furnishings).

upheaval noun bouleversement Masc.

uphill adverb en montée.

upright adjective droit; put it upright mets-le droit; to stand upright se tenir droit.

upset noun a stomach upset une indigestion.

upset adjective contrarié; he's upset il est contrarié.

upset verb to upset somebody contrarier [1] quelqu'un.

upside down adjective à l'envers.

upstairs adverb en haut; Mum's upstairs maman est en haut; to go upstairs monter [1].

up-to-date adjective 1 (in fashion) moderne; 2 (information) à jour.

upwards adjective vers le haut.

urgent adjective urgent.

urgently adverb d'urgence; she wants to see you urgently elle veut vous voir d'urgence.

US noun U.S.A. Masc. plural.

us *pronoun* nous; **she knows us** elle nous connaît; **they saw us** ils nous ont vus; **he gave us a cheque** il nous a donné un chèque; **with us** avec nous.

USA *noun* U.S.A. *Masc. plural.*

use *noun* 1 emploi *Masc.*; **the instructions for use** le mode d'emploi; **2 it's no use** ça ne sert à rien; **it's no use phoning** ça ne sert à rien de téléphoner.

use *verb* utiliser [1]; **we used the dictionary** nous avons utilisé le dictionnaire; **to use something to do** se servir [71] de quelque chose pour faire; **I used a knife to open the parcel** je me suis servi d'un couteau pour ouvrir le paquet.

● **to use up 1** consommer [1] *(food or petrol)*; **2** dépenser [1] *(money)*.

used *adjective* **1 to be used to something** être [6] habitué à quelque chose; **I'm not used to cats** je ne suis pas habitué aux chats; **I'm not used to it!** je n'ai pas l'habitude; **2 to be used to doing something** avoir [5] l'habitude de faire quelque chose; **I'm not used to eating in restaurants** je n'ai pas l'habitude de manger au restaurant; **3 to get used to something** s'habituer à; **I've got used to living here** je me suis habitué à habiter ici; **you'll get used to it!** tu t'y habitueras!

used *verb* **they used to live in the country** ils habitaient à la campagne avant; **she used to smoke** elle fumait avant.

useful *adjective* utile.

useless *adjective* nul *(Fem. nulle)*; **this knife's useless** ce couteau est nul; **you're completely useless!** tu es complètement nul!

user *noun* utilisateur *Masc.*, utilisatrice *Fem.*

user-friendly *adjective* convivial *(Masc. plural* conviviaux).

usual *adjective* habituel *(Fem. habituelle)*; **it's the usual problem** c'est le problème habituel; **as usual** comme d'habitude; **it's colder than usual** il fait plus froid que d'habitude.

usually *adjective* d'habitude; **I usually leave at eight** d'habitude je pars à huit heures.

utensil *noun* ustensile *Masc.*

Vv

vacancy *noun* 1 *(in a hotel)* 'vacancies' 'chambres libres'; 'no vacancies' 'complet'; **2 a job vacancy** un poste vacant.

vacant *adjective* libre.

vaccinate *verb* vacciner [1].

vaccination *noun* vaccination *Fem.*

vacuum *noun* vide *Masc.*

vacuum *verb* passer [1] l'aspirateur; **I'm going to vacuum my room** je vais passer l'aspirateur dans ma chambre.

vacuum cleaner *noun* aspirateur *Masc.*

vagina *noun* vagin *Masc.*

vague *adjective* vague.

vaguely adverb vaguement.

vain adjective vaniteux (Fem. vaniteuse); **in vain** en vain.

Valentine's Day noun la Saint-Valentin.

valentine card noun carte Fem. pour la Saint-Valentin.

valid adjective valable.

valley noun vallée Fem.

valuable adjective **1** de valeur; **to be valuable** avoir de la valeur; **that watch is very valuable** cette montre a une grande valeur; **2** (appreciated) précieux (Fem. précieuse); **he gave us some valuable information** il nous a donné des renseignements précieux.

value noun valeur Fem.

value verb apprécier [1] (somebody's help, opinion, or friendship).

van noun (small) fourgon Masc., (large) camionnette Fem.

vandal noun vandale Masc. & Fem.

vandalism noun vandalisme Masc.

vandalize verb vandaliser [1].

vanilla noun vanille Fem.; **a vanilla ice cream** une glace à la vanille.

vanish verb disparaître [27].

variety noun variété Fem.

various adjective plusieurs; **there are various ways of doing it** il y a plusieurs façons de le faire.

vary verb varier [1]; **it varies a lot** ça varie beaucoup.

vase noun vase Masc.

VAT noun TVA Fem.

VCR noun magnétoscope Masc.

VDU noun console Fem.

veal noun veau Masc.

vegan noun végétalien Masc., végétalienne Fem.

vegetable noun légume Masc.

vegetarian noun, adjective végétarien Masc., végétarienne Fem.; **he's vegetarian** il est végétarien.

vehicle noun véhicule Masc.

vein noun veine Fem.

velvet noun velours Masc.

vending machine noun distributeur Masc. automatique.

ventilation noun aération Fem.

verb noun verbe Masc.

verdict noun verdict Masc.

verge noun **1** (the roadside) accotement Masc.; **2 to be on the verge of doing** être [6] sur le point de faire; **I was on the verge of leaving** j'étais sur le point de partir.

version noun version Fem.

versus preposition contre; **Bath versus Chelsea** Bath contre Chelsea.

vertical adjective vertical (Masc. plural verticaux).

vertigo noun vertige Masc.

very adverb **it's very difficult** c'est très difficile; **very well** très bien; **very much** beaucoup.

very adjective **1 the very person I need!** exactement la personne qu'il me faut!; **the very thing he was looking for** exactement ce qu'il cherchait; **2 in the very middle** en plein milieu; **at the very end** tout à la fin; **at the very front** tout devant.

vest noun maillot Masc. de corps.

a
b
c
d
e
f
g
h
i
j
k
l
m
n
o
p
q
r
s
t
u
v
w
x
y
z

vet noun vétérinaire Masc. & Fem.; **she's a vet** elle est vétérinaire.

via preposition **to go via** passer par; **we're going via Dover** nous allons passer par Douvres; **we'll go via the bank** on va passer par la banque.

vicar noun pasteur Masc.

vicious adjective **1** méchant (a dog); **2** brutal (Masc. plural brutaux) (an attack).

victim noun victime Fem.

victory noun victoire Fem.

video noun **1** (film) vidéo Fem.; **to watch a video** regarder une vidéo; **I've got it on video** je l'ai en vidéo; **2** (cassette) cassette Fem. vidéo; **I bought a video** j'ai acheté une cassette vidéo; **3** (video recorder) magnétoscope Masc.

video verb enregistrer [1]; **I'll video it for you** je te l'enregistrerai.

video cassette noun cassette Fem. vidéo.

video game noun jeu Masc. vidéo (plural jeux vidéo).

video recorder noun magnétoscope Masc.

video shop noun vidéoclub Masc.

view noun **1** vue Fem.; **a room with a view of the lake** une chambre avec vue sur le lac; **2** (opinion) avis Masc.; **in my view** à mon avis; **a point of view** un point de vue.

viewer noun (on TV) téléspectateur Masc., téléspectatrice Fem.

viewpoint noun point Masc. de vue.

vigorous adjective vigoureux (Fem. vigoureuse).

vile adjective abominable.

villa noun villa Fem.

village noun village Masc.

villager noun villageois Masc., villageoise Fem.

vine noun vigne Fem.

vinegar noun vinaigre Masc.

vineyard noun vignoble Masc.

violence noun violence Fem.

violent adjective violent.

violin noun violon Masc.; **to play the violin** jouer du violon.

violinist noun violoniste Masc. & Fem.

virgin noun vierge Fem.

Virgo noun Vierge Fem.; **Robert's Virgo** Robert est Vierge.

virtual reality noun réalité Fem. virtuelle.

virus noun **1** (in medicine) virus Masc.; **2** (in computing) virus Masc.; **anti-virus software** un logiciel antivirus.

visa noun visa Masc.

visible adjective visible.

visit noun **1** (stay) séjour Masc.; **my last visit to France** mon dernier séjour en France; **2** visite Fem. (to a house, museum).

visit verb **1** visiter [1] (museum, castle, town); **2** aller [7] voir (a person); **we visited Auntie Pat at Christmas** nous sommes allés voir tante Pat à Noël.

visitor noun **1** invité Masc., invitée Fem.; **we've got visitors tonight** on a des invités ce soir; **2** (a tourist) visiteur Masc., visiteuse Fem.

visual adjective visuel (Fem. visuelle).

vital *adjective* indispensable; **it's vital to book** il est indispensable de réserver.

vitamin *noun* vitamine *Fem.*

vivid *adjective* **1** (*colour*) vif (*Fem.* vive); **2 to have a vivid imagination** exagérer.

vocabulary *noun* vocabulaire *Masc.*

vocational *adjective* professionnel (*Fem.* professionnelle).

vodka *noun* vodka *Masc.*

voice *noun* voix *Fem.*

volcano *noun* volcan *Masc.*

volleyball *noun* volley-ball *Masc.*; **to play volleyball** jouer au volley-ball.

volume *noun* volume *Masc.*; **could you turn down the volume?** est-ce que tu peux baisser le volume?

voluntary *adjective* **1** (*not compulsory*) volontaire; **2 to do voluntary work** travailler bénévolement.

volunteer *noun* **1** (*for a job*) volontaire *Masc. & Fem.*; **2** (*in charity work*) bénévole *Masc. & Fem.*

vomit *verb* vomir [2].

vote *noun* vote *Masc.*; **she got 20 votes** elle a obtenu 20 votes.

vote *verb* voter [1]; **she always votes Green** elle vote toujours pour les Verts.

voucher *noun* bon *Masc.*

vowel *noun* voyelle *Fem.*

voyage *noun* voyage *Masc.*

vulgar *adjective* vulgaire.

Ww

waffle *noun* (*to eat*) gaufre *Fem.*

wage(s) *noun* salaire *Masc.*

wagon *noun* **1** (*for transport*) chariot *Masc.*; **2** (*on railway*) wagon *Masc.* de marchandises.

waist *noun* taille *Fem.*

waistcoat *noun* gilet *Masc.*

waist measurement *noun* tour *Masc.* de taille.

wait *noun* attente *Fem.*; **an hour's wait** une heure d'attente.

wait *verb* **1** attendre [3]; **they're waiting in the car** ils attendent dans la voiture; **she kept me waiting** elle m'a fait attendre; **2 to wait for** attendre [3]; **wait for me!** attends-moi!; **wait for the signal** attendez le signal; **3 I can't wait to open it!** j'ai hâte de l'ouvrir!

waiter *noun* serveur *Masc.*

waiting list *noun* liste *Fem.* d'attente.

waiting room *noun* salle *Fem.* d'attente.

waitress *noun* serveuse *Fem.*

wake *verb* **1** réveiller [1] (*somebody else*); **Jess woke me at six** Jess m'a réveillé à six heures; **2** se réveiller [1]; **I woke (up) at six** je me suis réveillé à six heures; **wake up!** réveille-toi!

Wales *noun* pays *Masc.* de Galles; **in Wales** au pays de Galles; **to Wales** au pays de Galles.

walk *noun* promenade *Fem.* (*a little stroll*) tour *Masc.*; **to go for a walk** faire une promenade; **we went for a walk in the woods** nous avons

a b c d e f g h i j k l m n o p q r s t u v w x y z

fait une promenade dans la forêt;
we'll go for a little walk round the village on va faire un petit tour au village; **to take the dog for a walk** promener [50] le chien; **it's about five minutes' walk from here** c'est à environ cinq minutes à pied d'ici.

walk *verb* **1** marcher [1]; **I like walking on sand** j'aime marcher sur le sable; **2** (*walk around*) se promener [50]; **we walked around the old town** nous nous sommes promenés dans la vieille ville; **3** (*go*) aller [7]; **I'll walk to the bus stop with you** j'irai avec toi jusqu'à l'arrêt de bus; **it's not far, we can walk** ce n'est pas loin, on peut y aller à pied.

walkie-talkie *noun* talkie-talkie *Masc.* (*plural* talkies-walkies).

walking *noun* (*hiking*) randonnée *Fem.*; **we're going walking in Scotland** nous allons faire de la randonnée en Écosse.

walking distance *noun* **it's within walking distance of the sea** c'est à quelques minutes à pied de la mer.

walking stick *noun* canne *Fem.*

walkman™ *noun* walkman™ *Masc.*

wall *noun* **1** (*of a house*) mur *Masc.*; **2** (*of a city*) muraille *Fem.*; **the southern wall was destroyed** la muraille sud a été détruite; **the city walls** les fortifications de la ville.

wallet *noun* portefeuille *Masc.*

wallpaper *noun* papier *Masc.* peint.

walnut *noun* noix *Fem.* (*plural* noix).

wander *verb* **to wander around town** se balader [1] en ville; **to wander off** s'éloigner [1].

want *noun* **all our wants** tous nos besoins.

want *verb* vouloir [14]; **do you want some coffee?** tu veux du café?; **what do you want to do?** qu'est-ce que tu veux faire?; **I don't want to bother him** je ne veux pas le déranger.

war *noun* guerre *Fem.*

ward *noun* salle *Fem.* (*in a hospital*).

wardrobe *noun* **1** (*cupboard*) armoire *Fem.*; **2** (*clothes*) garde-robe *Fem.*

warehouse *noun* entrepôt *Masc.*

warm *adjective* **1** chaud; **a warm drink** une boisson chaude; **it's warm today** il fait chaud aujourd'hui; **I am warm** j'ai chaud; **are you warm enough?** as-tu assez chaud?; **I'll keep your dinner warm** je tiendrai ton dîner au chaud; **2** (*friendly*) chaleureux (*Fem.* chaleureuse); **a warm welcome** un accueil chaleureux.

warm *verb* chauffer [1]; **warm the plates** chauffez les assiettes.

● **to warm up 1** (*the weather*) s'adoucir [2]; **2** (*an athlete*) s'échauffer [1]; **3** (*to heat up*) réchauffer [1] (*food*); **I'll warm up some soup for you** je vous réchaufferai de la soupe.

warmth *noun* chaleur *Fem.*

warn *verb* prévenir [81]; **I warn you, it's expensive** je vous préviens que c'est cher; **to warn**

somebody to do conseiller [1] à quelqu'un de faire; **he warned me to lock the car** il m'a conseillé de fermer la voiture.

warning noun avertissement Masc.

wart noun verrue Fem.

wash noun **to give something a wash** laver [1] quelque chose; **to have a wash** se laver.

wash verb laver [1]; **I've washed your jeans** j'ai lavé ton jean; **to wash your hands** se laver les mains; **I washed my hands** je me suis lavé les mains; **to wash your hair** se laver les cheveux; **to get washed** se laver; **to wash the dishes** faire [10] la vaisselle.

● **to wash up** faire [10] la vaisselle.

washbasin noun lavabo Masc.

washing noun **1** (dirty) linge Masc. sale; **2** (clean) linge Masc.

washing machine noun machine Fem. à laver.

washing powder noun lessive Fem.

washing-up noun vaisselle Fem.; **to do the washing-up** faire la vaisselle.

washing-up liquid noun liquide Masc. à vaisselle.

wasp noun guêpe Fem.

waste noun **1** (of food, money, paper) gaspillage Masc.; **2** (of time) perte Fem.; **it's a waste of time** c'est une perte de temps.

waste verb **1** gaspiller [1] (food, money, paper); **2** perdre [3] (time); **you're wasting your time** tu perds ton temps.

waste-bin noun poubelle Fem.

wastepaper-basket noun corbeille Fem. à papier.

watch noun montre Fem.; **my watch is fast** ma montre avance; **my watch is slow** ma montre retarde.

watch verb **1** (to look at) regarder [1]; **I was watching TV** je regardais la télé; **2** (keep a check on) surveiller [1]; **watch the time** surveille l'heure; **3** (to be careful) faire [10] attention; **watch you don't spill it** fais attention de ne pas le renverser; **watch out for black ice** faites attention au verglas; **watch out!** attention!

water noun eau Fem.

water verb arroser [1]; **to water the plants** arroser les plantes.

watercolours noun peinture Fem. pour aquarelle.

waterfall noun cascade Fem.

watering can noun arrosoir Masc.

water melon noun pastèque Fem.

waterproof adjective imperméable.

water-skiing noun ski Masc. nautique; **to go water-skiing** faire du ski nautique.

water sports plural noun sports Masc. plural nautiques.

wave noun **1** (in the sea) vague Fem.; **2** (with your hand) signe Masc.; **she gave him a wave from the bus** elle lui a fait signe du bus.

wave verb **1** (with your hand) saluer [1] de la main; **2** (flap) agiter [1] (your ticket or the newspaper, for example).

wax noun cire Fem.

a b c d e f g h i j k l m n o p q r s t u v w x y z

way noun 1 (*a route or road*) chemin *Masc.*; **the way to town** le chemin pour aller en ville; **we asked the way to the station** nous avons demandé le chemin pour aller à la gare; **on the way back** sur le chemin de retour; **on the way** en route; **'way in'** 'entrée'; **'way out'** 'sortie'; 2 (*direction*) direction *Fem.*; **which way did he go?** en quelle direction est-il parti?; **come this way** venez par ici; **to be in the way** gêner le passage; 3 (*side*) sens *Masc.*; **the right way up** à l'endroit; **the wrong way round** à l'envers; 4 (*distance*) **it's a long way** c'est loin; **Terry went all the way to York** Terry est allé jusqu'à York; 5 (*manner*) façon *Fem.*; **a way of talking** une façon de parler; **he does it his way** il le fait à sa façon; **either way, she's wrong** de toute façon elle a tort; **do it this way** faisle comme ceci; 6 **no way!** pas question!; 7 **by the way** à propos.

way in noun entrée *Fem.*

way out noun sortie *Fem.*

we pronoun nous; (*informally*) on; **we live in Carlisle** nous habitons Carlisle; **we're going to the cinema tonight** on va au cinéma ce soir.

weak adjective 1 (*feeble*) faible; **her voice was weak** sa voix était faible; 2 léger (*Fem.* légère) (*coffee or tea*).

wealth noun fortune *Fem.*; **the wealth of the nation** la richesse de la nation.

wealthy adjective riche.

weapon noun arme *Fem.*

wear noun children's wear vêtements *Masc. plural* pour enfants; **sports wear** vêtements de sport.

wear verb porter [1]; **Tamsin's wearing her trainers** Tamsin porte ses baskets; **she often wears red** elle est souvent en rouge; **to wear make-up** se maquiller [1].

weather noun temps *Masc.*; **what's the weather like?** quel temps fait-il?; **in fine weather** quand il fait beau; **the weather was cold** il faisait froid; **the weather here is terrible** il fait un temps affreux ici.

weather forecast noun météo *Fem.*; **the weather forecast says it will rain** selon la météo il va pleuvoir.

web noun 1 (*spider's*) toile *Fem.*; 2 (*Internet*) the Web le web *Masc.*, la Toile *Fem.*

web site noun site *Masc.* internet.

wedding noun mariage *Masc.*

Wednesday noun mercredi *Masc.*; **on Wednesday** mercredi; **I'm going out on Wednesday** je sors mercredi; **see you on Wednesday!** à mercredi!; **on Wednesdays** le mercredi; **the museum is closed on Wednesdays** le musée est fermé le mercredi; **every Wednesday** tous les mercredis; **last Wednesday** mercredi dernier; **next Wednesday** mercredi prochain.

weed noun mauvaise herbe *Fem.*

week noun semaine *Fem.*; **last week** la semaine dernière; **next week** la semaine prochaine; **this week** cette semaine; **for weeks**

pendant des semaines; **a week today** aujourd'hui en huit.

weekday noun **on weekdays** en semaine.

weekend noun week-end Masc.; **last weekend** le weekend dernier; **next weekend** le weekend prochain; **they're coming for the weekend** ils vont passer le weekend chez nous; **I'll do it at the weekend** je le ferai pendant le week-end; **have a nice weekend!** bon weekend!

weekly adverb une fois par semaine; **I see her weekly** je la vois toutes les semaines.

weekly adjective hebdomadaire; **a weekly magazine** un magazine hebdomadaire.

weigh verb peser [50]; **to weigh something** peser quelque chose; **how much do you weigh?** combien pèses-tu?; **I weigh 50 kilos** je pèse cinquante kilos; **to weigh yourself** se peser.

weight noun poids Masc.; **to put on weight** prendre du poids; **to lose weight** perdre du poids.

weightlifting noun haltérophilie Fem.

weird adjective bizarre.

welcome noun accueil Masc.; **they gave us a warm welcome** ils nous ont fait un accueil chaleureux; **welcome to Oxford!** bienvenue à Oxford!.

welcome adjective bienvenu; **you're welcome any time** vous êtes toujours les bienvenus; **'thank you!' – 'you're welcome!'** 'merci!' – 'de rien!'

welcome verb accueillir [35].

well[1] noun puits Masc.

well[2] adverb 1 **to feel well** se sentir bien; **I'm very well, thank you** ça va très bien, merci; 2 bien; **Terry played well** Terry a bien joué; **the operation went well** l'opération s'est bien passée; **well done!** bravo!; 3 **as well** aussi; **Kevin's coming as well** Kevin vient aussi; 4 alors; **well then, what's the problem?** alors, quel est le problème?; **5 very well then, you can go** très bien, tu peux y aller.

well-behaved adjective sage.

well-done adjective bien cuit (a steak).

wellington (boot) noun botte Fem. en caoutchouc.

well-known adjective célèbre.

well-off adjective aisé.

Welsh noun 1 **the Welsh** (people) les Gallois Masc. plural; 2 (language) gallois Masc.

Welsh adjective gallois.

Welshman noun Gallois Masc.

Welshwoman noun Galloise Fem.

west noun ouest Masc.; **in the west** à l'ouest.

west adjective, adverb ouest (never agrees); **the west side** le côté ouest; **a west wind** un vent d'ouest; **west of Paris** à l'ouest de Paris.

western noun (a film) western Masc.

West Indian noun Antillais Masc., Antillaise Fem.

West Indian adjective antillais.

a b c d e f g h i j k l m n o p q r s t u v w x y z

West Indies plural noun Antilles Fem. plural; **in the West Indies** aux Antilles.

wet adjective **1** (damp) mouillé; **the grass is wet** l'herbe est mouillée; **we got wet** nous nous sommes fait mouiller; **2 a wet day** un jour de pluie.

whale noun baleine Fem.

what pronoun, adjective **1** qu'est-ce que (in questions as the object of a verb); **what did you say?** qu'est-ce que tu as dit?; **what's she doing?** qu'est-ce qu'elle fait?; **what did you buy?** qu'est-ce que tu as acheté?; **what is it?** qu'est-ce que c'est?; **what's the matter?** qu'est-ce qu'il y a?; **2** qu'est-ce qui (in questions as the subject of the verb); **what's happening?** qu'est-ce qui se passe?; **3** ce que (relative pronoun as the object of a verb); **tell me what you bought** dis-moi ce que tu as acheté; **4** ce qui (relative pronoun as the subject of a verb); **she told me what had happened** elle m'a dit ce qui s'était passé; **5** quel Masc., quelle Fem.; **what's your address?** quelle est ton adresse?; **what country is it in?** c'est dans quel pays?; **what colour is it?** c'est de quelle couleur?; **what make is it?** c'est quelle marque?; **6 what's her name?** elle s'appelle comment?; **what?** comment?

wheat noun blé Masc.

wheel noun roue Fem.; **the spare wheel** la roue de rechange; **the steering wheel** le volant.

wheelbarrow noun brouette Fem.

wheelchair noun fauteuil Masc. roulant.

when adverb, conjunction quand; **when is she arriving?** quand est-ce qu'elle arrive?; **when's your birthday?** c'est quand, ton anniversaire?; **it was raining when I went out** il pleuvait quand je suis sorti.

where adverb, conjunction où; **where are the plates?** où sont les assiettes?; **where do you live?** tu habites où?; **where are you going?** où vas-tu?; **I don't know where they live** je ne sais pas où ils habitent.

whether si; **I don't know whether he's back or not** je ne sais pas s'il est rentré ou non.

which adjective quel (Fem. quelle); **which CD did you buy?** quel CD as-tu acheté?

which pronoun **1** (which one) lequel Masc., laquelle Fem.; **'I saw your brother' – 'which one?'** j'ai vu ton frère – lequel?'; **'I saw your sister' – 'which one?'** j'ai vu ta sœur' – 'laquelle?'; **which of these jackets is yours?** laquelle de ces vestes est à toi?; **2** (relative pronoun) qui (as the subject of the verb); **the lamp which is on the table** la lampe qui est sur la table; **3** (relative pronoun) que (as object of the verb); **the book which you borrowed from me** le livre que tu m'as emprunté.

while noun for a while pendant quelque temps; **she worked here for a while** elle a travaillé ici pendant quelque temps; **after a while** au bout d'un moment.

while conjunction pendant que; **you can make some tea while I'm**

finishing my homework tu peux faire du thé pendant que je finirai mes devoirs.

whip noun (for a horse) cravache Fem.

whip verb fouetter [1]; **whipped cream** la crème fouettée.

whirlpool noun tourbillon Masc.

whiskers plural noun moustaches Fem. plural.

whisky noun whisky Masc.

whisper noun chuchotement Masc.; **to speak in a whisper** chuchoter [1].

whisper verb chuchoter [1].

whistle noun sifflet Masc.

whistle verb siffler [1].

white noun blanc Masc.; **an egg white** un blanc d'œuf.

white adjective blanc (Fem. blanche); **a white shirt** une chemise blanche.

white coffee noun café Masc. au lait.

Whitsun noun Pentecôte Fem.

who pronoun 1 (in questions) qui; **who wants some chocolate?** qui veut du chocolat?; 2 (relative pronoun) qui (as subject of the verb); **my friend who lives in Paris** mon ami qui habite à Paris; 3 (relative pronoun) que (as object of the verb); **the friends who we invited** les amis que nous avons invités.

whole noun **the whole of the class** la classe tout entière; **on the whole** dans l'ensemble.

whole adjective tout; **the whole family** toute la famille; **the whole morning** toute la matinée; **the**

whole time tout le temps; **the whole world** le monde entier.

wholemeal adjective complet (Fem. complète); **wholemeal bread** le pain complet.

whom pronoun 1 que; **the person whom I saw** la personne que j'ai vue; 2 (after a preposition) qui; **the person to whom I wrote** la personne à qui j'ai écrit.

whose pronoun, adjective 1 à qui; **whose is this jacket?** à qui est cette veste?; **whose shoes are these?** à qui sont ces chaussures?; **whose is it?** à qui c'est?; **I know whose it is** je sais à qui c'est; 2 dont; **the man whose car has been stolen** le monsieur dont la voiture a été volée.

why adverb pourquoi; **why did she phone?** pourquoi a-t-elle appelé?; **nobody knows why he did it** personne ne sait pourquoi il l'a fait.

wicked adjective 1 (bad) méchant; 2 (brilliant) génial (Masc. plural géniaux).

wide adjective 1 large; **the Thames is very wide here** la Tamise est très large ici; **a piece of paper 20 cm wide** une feuille de papier de vingt centimètres de large; 2 **a wide range** une vaste gamme.

wide adverb **the door was wide open** la porte était grande ouverte.

wide awake adjective complètement éveillé.

widen verb élargir [2].

widow noun veuve Fem.

widower noun veuf Masc.

a b c d e f g h i j k l m n o p q r s t u v w x y z

width noun largeur Fem.

wife noun femme Fem.

wig noun perruque Fem.

wild adjective **1** sauvage (an animal or plant); **wild birds** les oiseaux sauvages; **2** (crazy) fou (Fem. folle) (idea, party, person); **3 to be wild about something** être un/une fana de quelque chose.

wild life noun **a programme on wild life in Africa** un programme sur la nature en Afrique.

wild life park noun réserve Fem. naturelle.

will verb **1** (if you are unsure of the future tense of a French verb, you can check in the verb tables in the centre of the dictionary) **I'll see you soon** je te reverrai bientôt; **he'll be pleased to see you** il sera content de te voir; **it won't rain** il ne pleuvra pas; **there won't be a problem** il n'y aura pas de problème; **2** aller [7] (can be used for the immediate future); **I'll phone them at once** je vais les appeler tout de suite; **3** (in offers and requests) **will you have a drink?** est-ce que vous prenez quelque chose à boire?; **will you help me?** est-ce que tu peux m'aider?; **'will you write to me?'** - 'of course I will!' 'est-ce que tu m'écriras?' - 'bien sûr que oui!'; **4 he won't open the door** il ne veut pas ouvrir la porte; **the car won't start** la voiture ne veut pas démarrer; **the drawer won't open** je n'arrive pas à ouvrir le tiroir.

willing adjective **to be willing to do** être prêt à faire; **I'm willing to**

pay half je suis prêt à payer la moitié.

willingly adverb volontiers.

willow noun saule Fem.; **a weeping willow** un saule pleureur.

win noun victoire Fem.; **our win over Everton** notre victoire sur Everton.

win verb gagner [1]; **we won!** nous avons gagné!; **Rovers won by two goals** Rovers ont gagné de deux buts.

wind¹ noun vent Masc.; **the North wind** le vent du nord.

wind² verb **1** enrouler [1] (a wire or a rope, for example); **2** remonter [1] (a clock).

wind farm noun ferme Fem. d'éoliennes.

wind instrument noun instrument Masc. à vent.

window noun **1** (in a building) fenêtre Fem.; **to look out of the window** regarder par la fenêtre; **2** (in a car, bus, train) vitre Fem.

windscreen noun pare-brise Masc. (plural **pare-brise**).

windscreen wipers plural noun essuie-glace Masc.

windsurfing noun planche Fem. à voile; **to go windsurfing** faire [10] de la planche à voile.

windy adjective **1** venteux (Fem. venteuse) (a place); **2 it's windy today** il fait du vent aujourd'hui.

wine noun vin Masc.; **a glass of white wine** un verre de vin blanc.

wing noun **1** aile Fem.; **2** (in sport) ailier Masc.

wink *verb* to wink at somebody faire [10] un clin d'œil à quelqu'un.

winner *noun* gagnant *Masc.*, gagnante *Fem.*

winning *adjective* gagnant.

winnings *plural noun* gains *Masc. plural.*

winter *noun* hiver *Masc.*; in winter en hiver.

wipe *verb* essuyer [41]; I'll just wipe the table je vais juste essuyer la table; to wipe your nose se moucher [1].

● to wipe up (*dishes*) essuyer [41] la vaisselle.

wire *noun* fil *Masc.*; an electric wire un fil électrique.

wire netting *noun* grillage *Masc.*

wise *adjective* sage.

wish *noun* 1 vœu *Masc.* (*plural* vœux); make a wish! fais un vœu!; 2 (*a desire*) désir *Masc.*; 3 best wishes on your birthday meilleurs vœux pour ton anniversaire.

wish *verb* 1 I wish he were here si seulement il était ici; 2 I wished him happy birthday je lui ai souhaité un bon anniversaire.

wit *noun* esprit *Masc.*

witch *noun* sorcière *Fem.*

with *preposition* 1 avec; with James avec James; with me avec moi; with pleasure avec plaisir; beat the eggs with a fork battez les œufs avec une fourchette; he took his umbrella with him il a pris son parapluie; 2 (*at the house of*) chez; we're staying the night with Frank on va passer la nuit chez Frank; 3 (*in descriptions*) a girl with red hair une fille aux cheveux roux; the boy with the broken arm le garçon au bras cassé; 4 de; filled with water rempli d'eau; covered with mud couvert de boue; red with rage rouge de colère.

without *preposition* sans; without you sans toi; without sugar sans sucre; without a sweater sans pull; without looking sans regarder.

witness *noun* témoin *Masc.*

witty *adjective* spirituel (*Fem.* spirituelle).

wizard *noun* magicien *Masc.*

wolf *noun* loup *Masc.*

woman *noun* femme *Fem.*; a woman friend une amie; a woman doctor une femme médecin.

wonder *noun* 1 merveille *Fem.*; 2 it's no wonder you're tired ce n'est pas étonnant si tu es fatigué.

wonder *verb* se demander [1]; I wonder why je me demande pourquoi; I wonder where Jake is je me demande où est Jake.

wonderful *adjective* merveilleux (*Fem.* merveilleuse).

wood *noun* bois *Masc.*; the lamp is made of wood la lampe est en bois.

wooden *adjective* en bois.

woodwork *noun* menuiserie *Fem.*

wool *noun* laine *Fem.*

woollen *adjective* en laine.

word *noun* 1 mot *Masc.*; a long word un mot long; what's the French word for 'window'? comment dit-on 'window' en français?; in other words autrement dit; to have a word with somebody parler avec quelqu'un;

a
b
c
d
e
f
g
h
i
j
k
l
m
n
o
p
q
r
s
t
u
v
w
x
y
z

2 (*promise*) **to give somebody your word** donner sa parole à quelqu'un; **he broke his word** il n'a pas tenu parole; **3 the words of a song** les paroles d'une chanson.

word processing *noun* traitement *Masc.* de texte.

word processor *noun* machine *Fem.* à traitement de texte.

work *noun* travail *Masc.* (*plural* **travaux**); **Mum's at work** maman est au travail; **I've got some work to do** j'ai du travail à faire; **he's out of work** il est sans emploi; **Ben's off work** (*sick*) Ben est en arrêt de travail; (*on holiday*) Ben est en congé.

work *verb* **1** travailler [1]; **she works in an office** elle travaille dans un bureau; **Dad works at home** papa travaille à domicile; **Ruth works in advertising** Ruth travaille dans la publicité; **he works nights** il travaille de nuit; **2** (*to operate*) se servir [71] de; **can you work the video?** sais-tu te servir du magnétoscope?; **3** (*function*) marcher [1]; **the dishwasher's not working** le lave-vaisselle est en panne; **that worked really well!** ça a bien marché!

• **to work out 1** (*understand*) comprendre [64]; **I can't work out why** je ne comprends pas pourquoi; **2** (*exercise*) s'entraîner [1]; **3** (*to go well*) (*a plan*) marcher [1]; **4** (*calculate*) calculer [1]; **I'll work out how much it would cost** je vais calculer combien ç coûterait

worked up *adjective* **to get worked up** s'énerver [1].

worker *noun* (*in a factory*) ouvrier *Masc.*, ouvrière *Fem.*

worker *noun* ouvrier *Masc.*, ouvrière *Fem.*

work experience *noun* stage *Masc.*; **to do work experience** faire un stage; **to be on work experience** être en stage.

working-class *adjective* ouvrier (*Fem.* ouvrière); **a working-class background** un milieu ouvrier.

work of art *noun* œuvre *Fem.* d'art.

workshop *noun* atelier *Masc.*

workstation *noun* (*computer*) poste *Masc.* de travail (*plural* postes de travail).

world *noun* monde *Masc.*; **the best in the world** le meilleur du monde; **the Western world** les pays occidentaux.

World Cup *noun* **the World Cup** la Coupe du Monde.

world war *noun* guerre *Fem.* mondiale; **the Second World War** la Seconde Guerre mondiale.

worm *noun* ver *Masc.*

worn out *adjective* **1** (*a person*) épuisé; **2** (*clothes or shoes*) complètement usé.

worried *adjective* inquiet (*Fem.* inquiète); **they're worried** ils s'inquiètent; **to be worried about** s'inquiéter pour; **we're worried about Susan** nous nous inquiétons pour Susan.

worry *noun* soucis *Masc. plural.*

worry *verb* s'inquiéter [24]; **don't worry!** ne t'inquiète pas!; **there's nothing to worry about** il n'y a pas de quoi s'inquiéter.

worrying *adjective* inquiétant.

worse *adjective* pire; **it was even worse than the last time** c'était encore pire que la dernière fois; **to get worse** empirer [1]; **the weather's getting worse** le temps empire; **things are getting worse and worse** ça va de pire en pire.

worst *adjective* **the worst** le plus mauvais; **it was the worst day of my life** ça a été la journée la plus mauvaise de ma vie; **if the worst comes to the worst** au pire.

worth *adjective* **to be worth** valoir [80]; **how much is it worth?** ça vaut combien?; **to be worth doing** valoir la peine de faire; **it's worth trying** ça vaut la peine d'essayer; **it's not worth it** ça ne vaut pas la peine.

would *verb* **1 would you like something to eat?** voulez-vous quelque chose à manger?; **2 he wouldn't answer** il n'a pas voulu répondre; **the car wouldn't start** la voiture n'a pas voulu démarrer; **3 I would like an omelette** je voudrais une omelette; **I'd like to go to the cinema** j'aimerais aller au cinéma; **that would be a good idea** ce serait une bonne idée; **if we asked her she would help us** elle nous aiderait, si nous le lui demandions.

wound *noun* blessure *Fem.*

wound *verb* blesser [1].

wrap *verb* emballer [1]; **I'm going to wrap (up) my presents** je vais emballer mes cadeaux; **could you wrap it for me please?** voulez-vous me faire un paquet cadeau, s'il vous plaît?

wrapping paper *noun* papier *Masc.* cadeau.

wreck *noun* **1** (*of a crashed car or plane*) épave *Fem.*; **2 I feel a wreck!** je suis une loque!

wreck *verb* **1** détruire [26]; **2** gâcher [1] (*plans, occasion*); **it completely wrecked my evening!** ça m'a complètement gâché la soirée!

wrestler *noun* catcheur *Masc.*, catcheuse *Fem.*

wrestling *noun* catch *Masc.*

wrinkle *noun* ride *Fem.*

wrinkled *adjective* ridé.

wrist *noun* poignet *Masc.*

write *verb* écrire [38] (*a letter or a story*); **I'll write her a letter** je lui écrirai une lettre; **to write to somebody** écrire à quelqu'un; **I wrote to Jean yesterday** j'ai écrit à Jean hier.

● **to write down** noter [1]; **I wrote down her name** j'ai noté son nom.

writer *noun* écrivain *Masc.*

writing *noun* écriture *Fem.*

wrong *adjective* **1** (*not correct*) mauvais; **the wrong answer** la mauvaise réponse; **it's the wrong address** ce n'est pas la bonne adresse; **I've brought the wrong file** je n'ai pas apporté le bon classeur; **you've got the wrong number** vous vous êtes trompé de numéro; **2 to be wrong** (*mistaken*) se tromper; **I was wrong** je me suis trompé; **I was wrong when I said it was finished** je me suis trompé en disant que c'était fini; **3 what's wrong?** qu'est-ce qu'il y a?; **4** (*false*) faux (*Fem.* fausse); **the**

a b c d e f g h i j k l m n o p q r s t u v w x y z

information was wrong les renseignements étaient faux.

Xx

xerox™ *noun* photocopie *Fem.*

xerox™ *verb* photocopier [1].

Xmas *noun* Christmas.

X-ray *noun* radio *Fem.*; **I saw the X-rays** j'ai vu les radios.

X-ray *verb* faire [10] une radio de; **they X-rayed her ankle** ils ont fait une radio de sa cheville.

Yy

yacht *noun* **1** (*sailing boat*) voilier *Masc.*; **2** (*large luxury boat*) yacht *Masc.*

yawn *verb* bâiller [1].

year *noun* **1** an *Masc.*; (*the whole period*) année *Fem.*; **six years ago** il y a six ans; **the whole year** toute l'année; **they lived in Moscow for years** ils ont habité Moscou pendant des années; **2** (*for someone's age*) an *Masc.*; **he's seventeen years old** il a dix-sept ans; **a two-year-old child** un enfant de deux ans; **3** (*in secondary schools in France the years go from 'sixième', the equivalent of Year 7, to 'terminale', the equivalent of Year 13*); **I'm in Year 10** je suis en troisième; **I'm in Year 11** je suis en seconde.

yearly *adjective* annuel (*Fem.* annuelle); **a yearly event** un événement annuel.

yearly *adverb* tous les ans; **he goes to Normandy yearly** il va en Normandie tous les ans.

yell *verb* hurler [1].

yellow *adjective* jaune.

yes *adverb* **1** oui; **yes, I know** oui, je sais; **'is Tom in his room?' – 'yes, he is'** 'est-ce que Tom est dans sa chambre?' – 'oui'; **2** (*answering a negative*) si; **'you don't want to go, do you?' – 'yes, I do!'** 'tu ne veux pas y aller, n'est-ce pas?' – 'mais si!'; **'you haven't finished, have you?' – 'yes, I have'** 'tu n'as pas fini?' – 'si si'.

yesterday *adverb* hier; **I saw her yesterday** je l'ai vue hier; **yesterday afternoon** hier après-midi; **yesterday morning** hier matin; **the day before yesterday** avant-hier.

yet *adverb* not yet pas encore; **it's not ready yet** ce n'est pas encore prêt.

yoga *noun* yoga *Masc.*

yoghurt *noun* yaourt *Masc.*; **a banana yoghurt** un yaourt à la banane.

yolk *noun* jaune *Masc.* d'œuf (*plural* jaunes d'œuf).

you *pronoun* **1** tu (*'tu' is the familiar way of talking to family members, close friends, and people of your own age; 'vous' is more polite*); **do you want to go to the cinema tonight?** tu veux aller au cinéma ce soir?; **2** te (*the object form of 'tu'*); **I'll lend**

you my bike je te prêterai mon vélo; **I'll invite you** je t'inviterai; **I'll write to you** je t'écrirai; **3** toi *(after prepositions and in comparisons)*; **I'll go with you** j'irai avec toi; **he's older than you** il est plus âgé que toi; **4** *(more polite or to several people)* vous; **can you tell me where the station is, please?** est-ce que vous pouvez m'indiquer la gare, s'il vous plaît?; **I'll invite you all!** je vous inviterai tous!

young *adjective* jeune; **he's younger than me** il est plus jeune que moi; **Tessa's two years younger than me** Tessa a deux ans de moins que moi; **young people** les jeunes.

your *adjective* **1** ton *Masc.*, ta *Fem.* *(plural* tes*) (this is the familiar way of talking to family members, close friends, and people of your own age; 'vous' is more polite)* **I met your Dad** j'ai rencontré ton père; **I like your skirt!** j'aime bien ta jupe!; **you've forgotten your CDs** tu as oublié tes CD; **2** *(more polite or to several people)* votre *(plural* vos*);* **thank you for your hospitality** merci pour votre hospitalité; **you can all bring your friends** vous pouvez tous amener vos amis.

yours *pronoun* **1** le tien *Masc.*, la tienne *Fem.* *(plural* les tiens *Masc.*, les tiennes *Fem.*) *(this is the familiar way of talking to somebody of your own age or belonging to your family; otherwise you should use 'vôtre')* **my brother's younger than yours** mon frère est plus jeune que le tien; **2** *(formally or to several people)* le vôtre *Masc.*, la

vôtre *Fem. (plural* les vôtres *);* **my children are younger than yours** mes enfants sont plus jeunes que les vôtres; **3** à toi, à vous *(polite form);* **is this pen yours?** est-ce que ce stylo est à toi?

yourself *pronoun* **1** *(informal)* te; *(formal)* vous; **you'll hurt yourself** tu vas te faire mal; **2** *(for emphasis)* toi-même; *(formal)* vous-même; **did you do it yourself?** est-ce que tu l'as fait toi-même?; **3 all by yourself** tout seul *(Fem.* toute seule).

yourselves *pronoun* **1** vous; **help yourselves** servez-vous; **2** *(for emphasis)* vous-mêmes; **did you do it yourselves?** est-ce que vous l'avez fait vous-mêmes?

youth *noun* **1** *(stage in life)* jeunesse *Fem.;* **2** *(young people)* les jeunes *Masc. plural;* **today's youth** les jeunes d'aujourd'hui; **3** *(young male)* jeune *Masc.*

youth hostel *noun* auberge *Fem.* de jeunesse *(plural* auberges *Fem.* de jeunesse).

Yugoslavia *noun* Yougoslavie *Fem.;* **the former Yugoslavia** l'ex-Yougoslavie.

Zz

zany *adjective* loufoque.

zebra *noun* zèbre *Masc.*

zebra crossing *noun* passage *Masc.* pour piétons.

zero *noun* zéro *Masc.*

zigzag *verb* zigzaguer [1].

a   **zip** *noun* fermeture *Fem.* éclair™.

b   **zodiac** *noun* zodiaque *Masc.*; **the**
c   **signs of the zodiac** les signes du
         zodiaque.

c   **zone** *noun* zone *Fem.*

d   **zoo** *noun* zoo *Masc.*

e   **zoom lens** *noun* zoom *Masc.*

f

g

h

i

j

k

l

m

n

o

p

q

r

s

t

u

v

w

x

y

z

FRENCH LIFE AND CULTURE

At school 621

At home 622

Shopping, food, and eating out . . . 624

On holiday in France 626

Places of interest 628

At school

le bac	the exam taken by students who have stayed at school to the age of 18, *bac* is short for *baccalauréat*
le collège	state school for students aged 11-15 years old
le lycée	state school for 15-18 year olds
la journée scolaire	the school day: the length of the day varies, but can be from 8.30 a.m. to 5 p.m.
la rentrée	the return to school in September

Did you know... ?
that students in state schools do not wear uniforms?

Je vais à l'école à pied.	I walk to school.
Je suis en sixième.	I'm in Year 7.
Il y a 25 élèves dans ma classe.	There are 25 students in my class.
Les cours commencent à neuf heures.	Lessons start at 9 o'clock.
À midi, je mange à la cantine.	At lunchtime, I eat in the canteen.
On a beaucoup de devoirs.	We have a lot of homework.
Entrez!	Come in!
Sortez vos cahiers.	Take out your exercise books.
Ouvrez vos livres, page 23.	Open your books at p23.
Travaillez avec une partenaire.	Work in pairs.
Écoutez et répétez.	Listen and repeat.

Il me faut...
I need...

mon cahier.	my exercise book.	*ma trousse.*	my pencil case.
		ma règle.	my ruler
mon crayon.	my pencil.		

Ma matière préférée, c'est...
My favourite subject is...

l'éducation civique.	Citizenship/PSHE.
l'EPS.	PE.

At home

Dans ma famille, nous sommes cinq.	There are five of us in my family.
J'ai...	I've got...
un frère / une sœur.	a brother / a sister.
un demi-frère / une demi-sœur.	a half-brother / a half-sister.
un jumeau / une jumelle.	a twin brother / a twin sister.
Je suis fils / fille unique.	I'm an only child.

J'habite...	I live...		
(dans) une maison.	in a house.	*(dans) un appartement.*	in a flat.
en Angleterre.	in England.	*(à) Londres.*	in London.

Il y a...	There is...		
une cuisine.	a kitchen.	*une salle de bains.*	a bathroom.
trois chambres.	three bedrooms.	*des toilettes / des W.C.*	a toilet.
une salle de séjour.	a living room.	*un jardin.*	a garden

Mon passe-temps préféré, c'est...	My favourite hobby is...		
faire du vélo.	cycling.	*regarder la télévision.*	watching TV.
faire du VTT.	mountain biking.	*sortir avec des copains.*	going out with friends.
faire du roller.	roller-blading.	*jouer au foot / volley.*	playing football / volleyball.
lire.	reading.	*faire du skateboard.*	skateboarding.
écouter de la musique.	listening to music.		

Je vais regarder...
I'm going to watch...

la télé.	TV.	*une émission sportive.*	a sports programme.
un jeu.	a game show.	*ma série préférée.*	my favourite series.

J'ai...
I have...

un (lecteur) e-Reader	an e-Reader
un iPod®	an iPod®
une console de jeux	a games console
une télévision (grand écran)	a (wide screen) TV
un (téléphone) portable	a (mobile) phone
un portable	a laptop
une webcam	a webcam
un appareil photo numérique	a digital camera
un ordinateur	a computer

Sur mon ordinateur...
On my computer...

je fais me devoirs.	I do my homework.
je télécharge de la musique.	I download music.
je cherche quelque chose sur Internet / un site web.	I look something up on the Internet / a website.
j'envoie des mails.	I send emails.
je twitte.	I tweet.
je vais sur les réseaux sociaux.	I go on social network sites.
je vais sur les chats.	I visit chatrooms.

Did you know... ?

- that in email addresses (*les adresses électroniques*), @ is called *arobase* and dot is called *point*?
- that many French Internet sites (*les sites Internet français*) end with *.fr* ?

Shopping, food, and eating out

Je fais des courses...
I go shopping (for food)...

à la pâtisserie.	at the cake shop.	*à la charcuterie.*	at the delicatessen.
à l'épicerie.	at the grocer's.	*au marché.*	at the market.
à la boulangerie.	at the baker's.	*au supermarché.*	at the supermarket.
à la boucherie.	at the butcher's.	*sur Internet.*	on the Internet.

C'est combien? How much is it?

Je voudrais...
I'd like...

un pain.	a loaf of bread.	*un kilo de pommes.*	a kilo of apples.
quatre petits pains.	four rolls.		

Did you know... ?

• that shops are often closed (*fermés*) at lunchtime, but are open (*ouverts*) late into the evening?

Food

les baguettes	French bread, slices of baguette spread with butter are called *tartines*
la crème Chantilly	fresh cream whipped with sugar and vanilla
les chips	crisps, chips (French fries) are called *frites*
les crêpes	pancakes, a *crêperie* serves both sweet and savoury pancakes
les escargots	snails, they are considered a treat, not everyday food!
le fromage	cheese, the French are famous for their cheeses
les glaces	ice creams, flavours include *cassis* (blackcurrant), *pistache* (pistachio), *noisette* (hazelnut), *citron vert* (lime)
la ratatouille	a spicy vegetable dish made with tomatoes, onions, garlic, courgettes, and often aubergine

Meals (*les repas*)

le petit déjeuner	breakfast	le goûter	afternoon snack
le déjeuner	lunch	le dîner	dinner

> **Did you know... ?**
> • that, at breakfast, many French people drink from a bowl (*un bol*) rather than a cup?

Vous désirez?
What would you like?

Je voudrais...
I'd like...

un jus d'orange.	an orange juice.
un thé.	a cup of tea.
un café.	a coffee.
le plat du jour.	the meal of the day.

Vous avez des glaces à la vanille? Have you got any vanilla ice cream?

Comme plat principal, je voudrais...
For my main course I'd like...

le coq au vin.	chicken in wine sauce.
un hamburger.	a burger.
avec...	with...
des frites.	chips.
une salade.	salad.

Comme dessert, je voudrais...
For dessert I'd like...

la mousse au chocolat.	chocolate mousse.
une glace à la fraise.	strawberry ice cream.

Comme boisson, je vais prendre...
To drink I'll have...

de l'eau minérale.	mineral water.
un coca.	a Coke®.

J'ai faim.	I'm hungry.
J'ai soif.	I'm thirsty.
C'est délicieux!	It's delicious!
L'addition, s'il vous plaît.	The bill, please.
J'ai une allergie / Je suis allergique à la / au /aux	I'm allergic to...

On holiday in France

L'été dernier, je suis allé(e) en France.	Last summer, I went to France.
L'été prochain, je vais aller à Paris.	Next summer, I'll be going to Paris.

Je suis resté(e)...	I stayed...
à l'hôtel.	in a hotel.
dans un gîte rural.	in a holiday home in the country.
dans un terrain de camping.	on a campsite.

On a voyagé...	We travelled...		
en avion.	by plane.	en car.	by coach.
en voiture.	by car.	en train.	by train.
en bateau.	by boat / ship.	à vélo.	by bike.

un bal public	Many events end with a *bal public*: dancing for all in the town or village square.
les boules	(also called *la pétanque*) the game of bowls
la carte d'identité	Identity card. Many French people use their *carte d'identité* instead of a passport to travel within the EU. (European Union)
les départements	France is divided into 95 *départements*. Each has a number e.g. central Paris is 75. This number is used in postcodes and on car number plates.
une fête	a party. In summer, many towns and villages have *fêtes*, with music, stalls, dancing, etc.
l'Hôtel de Ville	the town hall
le Stade de France	a very large stadium in Paris

le Tour de France   a famous cycle race which takes place every summer. It is divided into sections called *étapes*. The previous day's winner wears a special yellow jersey (*le maillot jaune*).

Did you know... ?

- that you often have to validate your train / bus ticket by putting it into a machine at the train station or on the bus? The machine will punch (*composter*) your ticket.
- that some main railway lines operate high-speed trains called *le TGV®* (*train à grande vitesse*)?
- that the Channel Tunnel is known as *le tunnel sous la Manche*? (*La Manche*—'the sleeve'—is the French name for the Channel.)
- that the Paris underground is called *le métro*?
- that most French motorways (*autoroutes*) charge a toll (*péage*)?
- that French motorways have service stations (*aires de services*) and rest areas (*aires de repos*)?

Places of interest

L'Arc de Triomphe   a grand arch in Paris, at the end of the Champs-Élysées

la Bretagne   Brittany: a popular tourist area in northwestern France, with a rocky coast and sandy beaches

les Champs-Élysées   the grandest street in Paris, lined with luxury shops, cafes, and hotels

la Côte d'Azur   the French Riviera: the most fashionable stretch of the French Mediterranean coast, including St Tropez, Cannes, Nice, and Monte Carlo

Disneyland Paris®   This is one of two well-known theme parks (parcs d'attractions) near Paris. The other one is le Parc Astérix.

Le musée du Louvre   the most famous museum in Paris

le Midi   the south of France

le Mont Blanc   This is western Europe's highest mountain. Mont Blanc is in the Alps.

le Mont Saint-Michel   a tiny island off the northwestern coast of France, joined to the mainland by a causeway

la tour Eiffel   The Eiffel Tower was built in 1889, 100 years after the French Revolution.

Versailles   a magnificent royal palace built in the town of Versailles, near Paris